PUBLICATIONS OF THE NEW CHAUCER SOCIETY

THE NEW CHAUCER SOCIETY

Studies in the Age of Chaucer, the yearbook of The New Chaucer Society, is published annually. Each issue contains substantial articles on all aspects of Chaucer and his age, book reviews, and an annotated Chaucer bibliography. Manuscripts should follow the *Chicago Manual of Style*, 14th edition. Unsolicited reviews are not accepted. Authors receive free twenty offprints of articles and ten of reviews. All correspondence regarding manuscript submissions should be directed to the Editor, David Matthews, School of Arts, Histories and Cultures, University of Manchester, Oxford Road Manchester, M13 9PL, United Kingdom. Subscriptions to The New Chaucer Society and information about the Society's activities should be directed to David Lawton, Department of English, Washington University, CB 1122, One Brookings Drive, St. Louis, MO 63130. Back issues of the journal may be ordered from The University of Notre Dame Press, Chicago Distribution Center, 11030 South Langley Avenue, Chicago, IL 60628; phone: 800-621-2736; fax: 800-621-8476, from outside the United States: phone: 773-702-7000; fax: 773-702-7212.

Studies in the Age of Chaucer

In memoriam
Derek Brewer
1923–2008

Studies in the Age of Chaucer

Volume 30
2008

EDITOR

DAVID MATTHEWS

PUBLISHED ANNUALLY BY THE NEW CHAUCER SOCIETY

WASHINGTON UNIVERSITY IN ST. LOUIS

Copyright © 2008 by The New Chaucer Society, Washington University. First edition. Published by the University of Notre Dame Press for The New Chaucer Society.

ISBN 0-933784-32-5
ISSN 0190-2407

CONTENTS

CONTENTS

Studies in the Age of Chaucer

Manuscript Studies, Literary Value, and the Object of Chaucer Studies

Robert J. Meyer-Lee
Indiana University, South Bend

> The poetry that modern editorial practice assigns to Chaucer may be charming, astute, and, simply, beautiful, but the stable Chaucer whose agency determines this achievement—the Chaucer who serves as a canonical center against whom the marginal voices of vernacular culture have been defined—is more the creation of a Shakespearian-focused textual criticism than a historical medieval reality.
>
> —Tim William Machan[1]

> Few would deny that Chaucer's work has distinctive value.
>
> —Peggy Knapp[2]

THE ORIGIN OF THIS ESSAY lies in a bad-faith pedagogical practice for which I am perhaps seeking to do some penance. When I teach the *Canterbury Tales,* on the first day of the course, despite attempts to forestall the impulse, I inevitably cast the work as a wonderfully complex linked set of short stories, wholly conceived as such in all its details—a much more capacious and generically adventurous version of, say, *Dubliners.* Of course, such a characterization of the *Tales* is an utter fiction, a fact that, on that same first day, I make no attempt to conceal from the students. And yet—in the same way that, although Milton continuously reminds his readers that Satan is, well, Satan, we nonetheless remain fascinated by the character—no matter how much I empha-

For their helpful feedback on this article, I owe thanks to Matthew Giancarlo, Ashby Kinch, Frank Grady, and the anonymous readers of *SAC*. None should be blamed for its opinions, however.

[1] Tim William Machan, "'I endowed thy purposes': Shakespeare, Editing, and Middle English Literature," *Text* 13 (2000): 9–25 (quotation on p. 23).

[2] Peggy A. Knapp, "Aesthetic Attention and the Chaucerian Text," *ChauR* 39 (2005): 241–58 (quotation on p. 241).

size the unfinished state, manuscript messiness, and variety of objectionable motives behind the canonization of the *Tales,* somehow the work always ends up a Work (by the capitalization of which I mean, here and throughout, a putatively unified aesthetic object abstracted from any of its material witnesses). What sparked this essay is the reflection that my repeated falling into this temptation may not merely be a personal weakness but rather a symptom of a more significant critical conundrum, the result of a conflict between trends in the scholarship on premodern texts and inherited approaches to the criticism and pedagogy of Chaucer's works.

The principal trend in scholarship to which I refer is that which is evident in the Machan quotation above: extending well beyond Chaucer studies, it consists of the now-familiar amalgamation of late twentieth-century critiques of authorship, authority, and canonicity; historicism and the consequent emphasis on material culture in interpretive studies; and the self-consciousness about the theory and practice of textual criticism that has arisen, in Middle English studies, in the wake of the Athlone *Piers Plowman* editions and from the prompting of textual critics of other periods and traditions, such as Jerome J. McGann and Bernard Cerquiglini. For convenience, I will call this amalgamation "manuscript studies," recognizing that not all the scholars working under this label would want themselves associated with all (or perhaps any) of the elements of this definition.[3]

The conflict to which I refer is evident in Machan's opposing of the "beautiful" canonical Chaucer enshrined in the products of "modern editorial practice" with the Chaucer of "historical medieval reality." This conflict, in one sense, is hardly new. As David Matthews has shown, the beautiful, canonical Chaucer had a centuries-long history (in contrast with the rest of Middle English literature) until colliding with historicism in the form of nineteenth-century philology—in this instance, a productive, mutually beneficial collision, which inaugurated, under the auspices of the first Chaucer Society, modern Chaucer studies.[4] As Ethan Knapp suggests, in his recent review of Chaucer criticism, Chaucer's

---

[3] Machan, for example—at least in " 'I endowed' "—seeks to disassociate his position from "relativism, post-modernism, and other perceived threats to the integrity of the subject, whether that of the author, the critic, or the society" (25), even though his historicism is plainly the product of the age in which these threats became literary-critical commonplaces.

[4] See David Matthews, *The Making of Middle English, 1765–1910* (Minneapolis: University of Minnesota Press, 1999), pp. 162–86.

subsequent eligibility for admission into the university in the late nineteenth century rested on his dual status as a poet "gifted with visionary insight and universal applicability" (that is, as a proleptic Romantic canonical poet) and as an "object of analysis for philology and *Textkritik*" (that is, as an object of rigorous, scientific historicism).[5] To an extent complementary, these two apprehensions of Chaucer nevertheless possess antithetical principles, and the tension between them has been felt in various ways throughout the history of Chaucer studies, sometimes in the form of oppositional schools (as in New Criticism versus Exegetics), and sometimes in the work of individual scholars (as in the disjunction between the philological and literary critical work of such Chaucerians as George Lyman Kittredge and John Livingston Lowes).[6]

Although, as Knapp suggests, the critical movements of the last thirty-some years have so shifted the terms of this conflict that we may in some respects have moved beyond it, the rise of manuscript studies has revived it powerfully in at least one specific fashion. As Machan's remarks indicate, a manuscript-informed historicist skepticism has put into question that which has served as both the long-standing product and object of Chaucer studies, the critical edition. The editorial tradition that marked the first phase of modern Chaucer studies—and that persists into the present in the form of *The Riverside Chaucer*—has sought, as Stephanie Trigg puts it, to produce critical editions answerable both to "generalist" and "specialist" readers of Chaucer. Trigg characterizes these audiences as, at present, those without and within medieval studies, respectively, but the division also aligns with the Romantic/philological split lying at the origin of modern Chaucer studies.[7] In simplistic terms, the *Riverside,* like all the products of this editorial tradition, seeks to answer to this split by being at once an object of artistic excellence and an object of historical authenticity. But as the notions of authorship and canonicity underwriting the former object have given way, and commitment to the latter object has, in various forms, come to dominate interpretive criticism, the fusion of aims represented by the *River-*

---

[5] Ethan Knapp, "Chaucer Criticism and Its Legacies," in *The Yale Companion to Chaucer,* ed. Seth Lerer (New Haven: Yale University Press, 2006), pp. 324–56 (322).

[6] For these oppositions—in addition to Ethan Knapp, "Chaucer Criticism"—see the influential account of the history of Chaucer studies in Lee Patterson, *Negotiating the Past: The Historical Understanding of Medieval Literature* (Madison: University of Wisconsin Press, 1987), pp. 3–39.

[7] See Stephanie Trigg, *Congenial Souls: Reading Chaucer from Medieval to Postmodern* (Minneapolis: University of Minnesota Press, 2002), pp. 10–14.

side has come to be seen in many quarters as an ill-founded, misleading anachronism.

As early as 1985 (while the *Riverside* was still being compiled), in an article published in a collection edited by McGann, Derek Pearsall suggested as much in his characteristically witty fashion, comparing the "the sterile operating theater (or terminal intensive care unit) of the modern critical edition" to listening to "medieval music played on modern instruments." Nonetheless, he maintained a commitment to the critical edition as a "practical necessity for the needs of readers and students"; conceding the rift between generalist and specialist readers later described by Trigg, he suggested that different objects be constituted for each of these audiences.[8] More recently, Theresa Tinkle, focusing specifically on the importance of manuscript *mise-en-page,* has offered a similar account of the liabilities of the critical edition: "Modern editors adopt a page layout that insists on Chaucer's alienation from medieval annotations and, accordingly, from scholasticism, medieval Catholicism, and Latinity. The page layout pronounces medieval readers and ways of reading at best irrelevant, at worst stodgily wrongheaded. The uncomplicated page also asserts that the text is immediately accessible, that every reader is sufficient to it. Chaucer's medieval alterity becomes invisible."[9] Tinkle's comments, with their implication that accessibility to Chaucer's work should give way to his "medieval alterity," typifies many of the statements on the topic from the time of Pearsall's article to the present.[10] As Trigg remarks, today's "professional Chaucerians . . . seem

[8] Derek Pearsall, "Editing Medieval Texts: Some Developments and Some Problems," in *Textual Criticism and Literary Interpretation,* ed. Jerome J. McGann (Chicago: University of Chicago Press, 1985), pp. 92–106 (105, 106). This suggestion reflects Pearsall's well-known, if sometimes inscrutably harmonized, commitments both to artistic excellence and historical authenticity. With his remarkably multifaceted career, Pearsall is perhaps better able than anyone else to negotiate the potential conflicts between these commitments.

[9] Theresa Tinkle, "The Wife of Bath's Textual/Sexual Lives," in *The Iconic Page in Manuscript, Print, and Digital Culture,* ed. George Bornstein and Theresa Tinkle (Ann Arbor: University of Michigan Press, 1998), pp. 55–88 (74). Tinkle traces this treatment of Chaucer all the way back to William Thynne's 1532 *Workes of Geffray Chaucer.*

[10] For two of many possible examples of such statements, see the pair of consecutive articles, Murray McGillivray, "Towards a Post-Critical Edition: Theory, Hypertext, and the Presentation of Middle English Works," *Text* 7 (1994): 175–99, and Daniel W. Mosser, "Reading and Editing the *Canterbury Tales:* Past, Present, and Future (?)," *Text* 7 (1994): 201–32. Helen Cooper, "Averting Chaucer's Prophecies: Miswriting, Mismetering, and Misunderstanding," in *A Guide to Editing Middle English,* ed. Vincent P. McCarren and Douglas Moffat (Ann Arbor: University of Michigan Press, 1998), pp. 79–93, offers a similar but more balanced conclusion: "Editions of Chaucer . . . are not

willing to make it more difficult to read Chaucer,"[11] and they do so, as in Tinkle's privileging of "medieval readers and ways of reading," in the name of historical authenticity unmoored from debunked Romantic notions of authorship and canon.

Tinkle's exceptional study—which, through close examination of text, gloss, and *mise-en-page* of the versions of the Wife of Bath's Prologue in different manuscripts, limns the different ways that early readers, editors, and scribes apprehended the Wife of Bath—represents one possible avenue for the literary critical response to the de-authorization of the critical edition. This response involves the elevation of the medieval manuscript to the status of central object of inquiry, not just for those who have been traditionally concerned with manuscripts (e.g., textual critics, paleographers) but also for many who fill the departmental ranks of medieval literary hermeneuts.[12] In studies such as Tinkle's, investigators put aside that which used to be the end of the labor devoted to manuscripts, the critical edition, in favor of the means to this end—or, more specifically, the material conditions of the production and dissemination of late medieval books, the state of those books, and their reception and use by various audiences. This is the sort of work (whether or not Tinkle intends the association) that Stephen Nichols affirms in the introduction to the 1990 "New Philology" issue of *Speculum,* a mode of investigation he describes as an examination of the "manuscript matrix" rather than merely the texts represented in editions, "and of both language and manuscript [in interaction] with the social context and networks they inscribe."[13] Tinkle's article exemplifies

---

safe as a basis for certain kinds of critical work, and it may be impossible to tell when one crosses the boundary into danger" (86).

[11] Trigg, *Congenial Souls,* p. 14.

[12] For a wonderfully personalized account of this shift, among those working on manuscripts, see Derek Pearsall, "The Value/s of Manuscript Study: A Personal Retrospect," *Journal of the Early Book Society* 3 (2000): 167–81.

[13] Stephen G. Nichols, "Introduction: Philology in a Manuscript Culture," *Speculum* 65 (1990): 1–10 (9). Cf. John Dagenais, "That Bothersome Residue: Toward a Theory of the Physical Text," in *Vox intexta: Orality and Textuality in the Middle Ages,* ed. A. N. Doane and Carol Braun Pasternack (Madison: University of Wisconsin Press, 1991), pp. 246–59: "What I would propose as the first level is a simple shift in the unit we study from 'text' to . . . the individual, unique, concrete manuscript codex" (252). Although New Philology, as a label, has not achieved widespread currency, and the special issue of *Speculum* represented an observation of an ongoing and diverse shift in scholarship rather than a point of origin, Nichols's articulation of this shift remains influential. See, for example, Siân Echard and Stephen Partridge, "Introduction: Varieties of Editing: History, Theory, and Technology," in *The Book Unbound: Editing and Reading Medieval Manuscripts and Texts,* ed. Siân Echard and Stephen Partridge (Toronto:

its undoubted productivity, as do other recent interpretative engagements with Chaucer's "manuscript matrix," such as Maidie Hilmo's study of the pilgrim portraits in the Ellesmere manuscript.[14]

Given the demonstrative productivity of manuscript studies—along with its confluence of the old and the new, the empirical and the theoretical, and strands of several different widely adopted critical movements—one would expect a pronounced influence on Chaucer studies. In particular, one might surmise that the neglect, in published readings of Chaucer's poetry, of its critique of the critical edition would characterize these readings as old-fashioned: conservative, naïve, ahistorical, presentist attempts to cover up the conflicts, fix *variance,* reprivilege the canon, and just generally bring back the good old days. Yet, in fact, by far the majority of readings of Chaucer—even the most avant-garde, such as Aranye Fradenburg's *Sacrifice Your Love*—generally restrict themselves to the *Riverside.*[15] A manuscript studies approach to Chaucer like Tinkle's or Hilmo's remains the exception to the rule and does not appear to be gaining much ground on the much more typical interpretive approach, which, as inclusive as it may be of a variety of intertexts, for

---

University of Toronto Press, 2004), pp. xi–xxi. Matthews, too, explicitly registers his sympathy with these ideas, although in *The Making of Middle English* he adapts them "in a way that does not privilege manuscript culture over copy technology" (xxi). Most recently, Carol Symes, "Manuscript Matrix, Modern Canon," in *Oxford Twenty-First Century Approaches to Literature: Middle English,* ed. Paul Strohm (Oxford: Oxford University Press, 2007), pp. 7–22, in reproaching a Bloomian approach to literary criticism, offers more or less the same argument as Nichols and Dagenais.

[14] Maidie Hilmo, "Framing the Canterbury Pilgrims for the Aristocratic Readers of the Ellesmere Manuscript," in *The Medieval Professional Reader at Work: Evidence from Manuscripts of Chaucer, Langland, Kempe, and Gower,* ed. Kathryn Kerby-Fulton and Hilmo (Victoria, B.C.: University of Victoria, 2001), pp. 14–55, which also appears as the final chapter in Maidie Hilmo, *Medieval Images, Icons, and Illustrated English Literary Texts: From Ruthwell Cross to the Ellesmere Chaucer* (Aldershot: Ashgate, 2004), pp. 160–99. For other examples (and by no means the only ones) of interpretive work on Chaucer that follows a manuscript studies approach, see the essays collected in *Reading from the Margins: Textual Studies, Chaucer, and Medieval Literature,* ed. Seth Lerer (San Marino, Calif.: Huntington Library Press, 1996); Thomas A. Prendergast and Barbara Kline, eds., *Rewriting Chaucer: Culture, Authority, and the Idea of the Authentic Text, 1400–1602* (Columbus: Ohio State University Press, 1999); and the studies described as such cited below.

[15] L. O. Aranye Fradenburg, *Sacrifice Your Love: Psychoanalysis, Historicism, Chaucer* (Minneapolis: University of Minnesota Press, 2002). One need only browse through the last several volumes of *SAC* and *The Chaucer Review* to confirm this point. Anecdotally, I can report that, for a project involving the *Merchant's* and *Franklin's Tales,* I asked my two research assistants, whom I assigned to read several decades of criticism on the tales, to keep track of how many studies make use of manuscripts in more than a cursory manner. After six weeks, the count was one.

Chaucer generally does not look beyond the text of a critical edition and, less frequently, that edition's textual apparatus. Although Fradenburg, for example, is certainly more than willing to complicate our reading of Chaucer (as well as of Chaucer studies), she and most other Chaucer interpreters show little interest in locating that complexity in the material object of study. In comparison, outside of Chaucer studies the influence of manuscript studies is stronger. Recent books, such as Katherine Kerby-Fulton and Denise L. Despres's *Iconography and the Professional Reader* and Andrew Taylor's *Textual Situations,* testify to its vitality.[16] Indeed, Taylor, wondering about this apparent discrepancy, especially in comparison with the literary criticism on texts in the romance vernaculars, issued a call for papers for the 2008 New Chaucer Society (NCS) conference in which he posed the question of whether "Middle English manuscript studies and Middle English literary criticism constitute distinct academic cultures."[17] Perhaps manuscript studies has provoked simply the most recent evolution of the mixed motivations behind the foundation of Chaucer studies, in which Chaucer's texts as objects of literary value sit uncomfortably next to his texts as objects of historical inquiry.

The distinction between the "academic cultures" of manuscript studies and literary criticism, insofar as it exists, surely does not derive from mutual ignorance, since studies that call attention to this distinction—such as Trigg's and, more particularly, those of Ralph Hanna cited below—have been widely read in the field. Inasmuch as the literary critic accepts, then, the critique, marshaled by manuscript studies, of the aims, methods, and ideologies of the Chaucer edition, that critic's continued use of such an edition may involve (as I suggested in my opening) a degree of bad faith. This situation can lead to some awkward moments, not just for the critic but also, perhaps more important, for the teacher of Chaucer in the undergraduate classroom. As students file in on that first day—students who are unlikely to know much if anything about the late Middle Ages, much less about late medieval literary culture—does one begin by debunking the (expensive) editions of Chau-

---

[16] Kathryn Kerby-Fulton and Denise L. Despres, *Iconography and the Professional Reader: The Politics of Book Production in the Douce Piers Plowman* (Minneapolis: University of Minnesota Press, 1999); Andrew Taylor, *Textual Situations: Three Medieval Manuscripts and Their Readers* (Philadelphia: University of Pennsylvania Press, 2002).

[17] Andrew Taylor, "Session 3 (Papers): 'In Praise of the Middle English Variant,'" *The New Chaucer Society Newsletter* 29 (2007): 2.

cer that they have just purchased? In an institutional economy in which study of the Middle Ages has been marginalized and, at some institutions, faces the loss of faculty positions, how much ought a teacher emphasize that the *Canterbury Tales,* already in forbidding Middle English, is, as a Work, merely a modern editor's fiction?[18] If the solution to this awkwardness is the development of better teaching materials (and, in turn, better materials upon which to practice criticism), then the question arises about the constitution of these materials—the question, that is, of what should replace the Chaucer edition as the basic object of teaching and criticism.

In an article assessing the implications of the *Canterbury Tales* Project, Charlotte Morse suggests, with only partial enthusiasm, "Perhaps we will eventually prefer an electronic text for teaching students struggling with Middle English, a text with hypertext glosses and notes, whose parts we could reorder at will, whose text we could modify, leaving in or out, for example . . . the Man of Law's Endlink."[19] In the early 1990s, when the rise of manuscript studies coincided with the excitement over the then-nascent revolution in the electronic accessibility and representation of information, similar suggestions appeared with relatively more degrees of enthusiasm. For Murray McGillivray, for example, a hypertext edition could be "an editorial vehicle that responds to the real nature of medieval textuality by presenting medieval works in their original state, as series of varying manuscript texts."[20] Yet, despite the

---

[18] Revealingly, among recent discussions of Chaucer pedagogy, the most common matter of concern is not how best to respect late medieval manuscript culture or the fragmented, uncertain state of the surviving evidence (a topic that typically appears only briefly), but rather whether or not to teach Chaucer in modern English translation. See, for example, the essays collected by Christine Rose for the "Teaching Chaucer in the Nineties" symposium published in *Exemplaria* 8 (1996) and those in Gail Ashton and Louise Sylvester, eds., *Teaching Chaucer* (Basingstoke: Palgrave Macmillan, 2007). Obviously, if one decides to teach Chaucer in translation, one is unlikely to devote much class time to the manuscript variation hidden by the editions upon which those translations are based.

[19] Charlotte C. Morse, "What the *Clerk's Tale* Suggests about Manly and Rickert's Edition—and the *Canterbury Tales* Project," in *Middle English Poetry: Texts and Traditions: Essays in Honour of Derek Pearsall,* ed. A. J. Minnis (Woodbridge: York Medieval Press, 2001), pp. 41–56 (42). Morse sees this idea as a technologically more sophisticated version of the proposal of Derek Pearsall, *The Canterbury Tales* (London: Routledge, 1985), for an edition of the *Tales* packaged as a partially bound book containing "a set of fragments in folders, with the incomplete information as to their nature and placement fully displayed" (23). For an overview of the *Canterbury Tales* Project, see its website, http://www.canterburytalesproject.org, and Peter Robinson, "The History, Discoveries, and Aims of the Canterbury Tales Project," *ChauR* 38 (2003): 126–39.

[20] McGillivray, "Towards a Post-Critical," 192. See also Mosser, "Reading," and Tim William Machan, "Chaucer's Poetry, Versioning, and Hypertext," *PQ* 73 (1994): 299–

subsequent electronic publications of the *Canterbury Tales* Project and the widespread use of the Web as a pedagogical resource, the printed critical edition remains the basic object of criticism and teaching, a fact that is evident in Ethan Knapp's still-hopeful nod toward the future possibilities of an electronic edition in his 2006 review of Chaucer criticism.[21] This persistence, I argue, does not merely reflect the predictable lag between the promise and practicability of new technology, nor does it only derive from legitimate uncertainty about whether an electronic edition truly would respond to the "real nature of medieval textuality" better than a printed critical edition. Rather, it represents, more profoundly, a resistance to an edition of Chaucer, and especially of the *Canterbury Tales,* that would announce in its very structure its own impossibility—an edition that admits, in its material realization, that there really is no *Canterbury Tales,* conceived of as a Work, but instead only eighty-some manuscripts dressed up to look like one.

This resistance, in its most reflective form, is not stubbornly traditionalist but speculatively interrogative: it asks why the "real nature of medieval textuality" ought necessarily to be the most appropriate object of study. It wonders if the best material realization of an object of study is necessarily the one that is, in theory, the most historically authentic. And, relatedly, it asks on what basis ought we to allocate more scholarly and interpretative attention to some objects of study over others. Manuscript studies has shaken loose these and other foundational questions from their formerly secure institutional underpinnings. In what follows, while I initiate an exploration of these questions, I devote most attention to the question that they collectively imply: that of the place and function of *literary value* in the field of Chaucer studies. I argue that, inasmuch as a conception of literary value remains integral to scholarly and pedagogical practice, even if it often goes unacknowledged, it continues to possess a claim on the nature of the material realizations of the objects of study and pedagogy. Further, I argue that this claim is neither fully avoidable, nor theoretically indefensible, nor wholly undesirable.

To make this case, I have much to define, especially the term "literary value." But before venturing toward this end, I should make plain that, in broaching this topic, I am not in any fashion seeking a return, with some Ghost of Criticism Past, to the days when Great Works could

---

316, who, after painting a picture of an ideal hypertext edition of the *Canterbury Tales,* offers a more sober assessment of the potential for one.

[21] Ethan Knapp, "Chaucer Criticism," 355 n. 73.

simply be studied and taught as Great Works. Rather, I am claiming that the considerable achievements of manuscript studies over the last twenty years or so have released some ghosts that have not really left us: in particular, the ghosts that had informed some central New Critical presuppositions. In this essay, I aim not to reanimate these ghosts but rather to confront the implications of the continued influence of one in particular, the ghost of judgment.

New Critical Revenant

It is no coincidence that the rise of manuscript studies coincided with the demise of New Criticism as the dominant ideology and set of practices governing literary studies and pedagogy. Although manuscript studies cannot claim much credit for this demise, several of its practitioners make plain that New Critical hegemony was a hostile environment, one premised on an *a priori* hierarchical disjunction between manuscript studies—in its earlier, edition-oriented formation—and literary criticism. As Machan describes it:

Within this interpretative framework [of New Criticism], the labors of textual critics of any historical period could only be pedestrian: they provided the texts necessary for serious and sensitive scholars to do serious and sensitive work. The transcendent verbal icon by nature simply is, and so any inquiries about its origin or development are non-questions; indeed, when the New Critics themselves glanced at textual criticism, the attention they manifested was often in essence indifference or ignorance.[22]

Although Machan offers here, for polemical purposes, something of a caricature of New Criticism, he fairly calls attention to New Criticism's notorious emphasis on the autonomy of the literary object and its consequent de-emphasis of that object's historically contingent material origins. Even when formalists and textual scholars were, so to speak, on the same side (and in this regard names such as George Kane and E. T. Donaldson are inevitable), their assumptions regarding the critical utility of such basic categories as intention made the perspectives of the two roles rather different, and hence registered a division of hierarchy be-

[22] Tim William Machan, "Middle English Text Production and Modern Textual Criticism," in *Crux and Controversy in Middle English Textual Criticism,* ed. A. J. Minnis and Charlotte Brewer (Cambridge: D. S. Brewer, 1992), pp. 1–18 (8).

tween their labors. As Machan notes, to create the "medieval verbal icon" out of the surviving manuscript evidence, editors relied on "the supposition that an author's final intentions and an authoritative text lay in the distant but recoverable textual past."[23] The edition was thus an edifice constructed out of authorial intention, and yet, when that edition subsequently became an object of critical explication, considerations of intention became categorically suspect, if not simply relegated to the realm of fallacy.

In practice, New Criticism—especially as applied to Chaucer—was rarely so categorical, but it nonetheless did maintain the inherited conception of manuscripts as, to put it figuratively, shadows on a cave wall cast by the light of genius shining on a Work. Only with the loosening of New Criticism's grip on the academy—first by poststructuralism and then by historicism and cultural studies—has it been possible to undo this conception. At present, what has been accomplished within some quarters of manuscript studies is akin to Marx's standing of Hegel on his head: the materiality and multiplicity of manuscript matrices have become the real, and the edition a sort of false consciousness. This demystification has been largely salutary, and, again, I have no wish to turn the clock back in this regard. Nonetheless, while few, if any, still claim the identity of New Critic, formalism more generally maintains an influence on Chaucer criticism. In part, this influence consists of the continued, if obscured, legacy of such powerful critics as Donaldson and Charles Muscatine, whose shaping of Chaucer studies, particularly in contestation with D. W. Robertson and the Exegetical school, has been well documented by Lee Patterson.[24] In part, too, this influence is simply that which has been carried forward within some versions of historicist criticism; as Alan Liu and others have argued, the historicism practiced under the label "cultural poetics," for example, represents not so much a correction to formalism as a projection of it into the space of history and culture.[25]

In addition, formalism retains its dominance in the normative practices of close reading that prevail in the classroom and, as Seth Lerer has pointed out, in the criticism of certain types of Middle English texts,

---

[23] Machan, "Middle English Text Production," p. 10.

[24] See Patterson, *Negotiating the Past*, pp. 3–39. For a recent assessment of Donaldson's influence in particular, see *ChauR* 41 (2007), a special issue devoted to his legacy.

[25] Alan Liu, "The Power of Formalism: The New Historicism," *ELH* 56 (1989): 721–71.

such as the lyric. Indeed, Lerer, while expressing dissatisfaction with New Critical readings of Middle English lyrics that still possess currency (and have hence led to the genre's marginalization in the current critical climate), concludes his essay by calling for a renewed attention to form as a locus of historical contingency.[26] With this conclusion he takes a position that has to date gathered more momentum among critics of later periods of literature. Many of these critics—sometimes labeled "new formalists"—maintain that inattention to the specific nature of literary forms, deriving from the historicist denial of the autonomous art object, has in fact circumscribed the analytical reach of historicism.[27] Several signs suggest that this revitalized concern with form, while very diverse in its emphases, is making significant inroads into Chaucer studies. In addition to the three sessions devoted to close reading at the 2006 NCS conference (New York, July 27–31), one may cite, for example, recent articles by Maura Nolan and Peggy Knapp (the first sentence of which, affirming the ubiquitous certainty of Chaucer's value, follows the quotation from Machan in my epigraph) that reconsider the critical and pedagogical importance of the category of the aesthetic.[28]

The distinct historicity of form, as well as its relation to the historicity of other elements of the text and contexts of a work of literature, is surely worth the renewed attention that it is receiving. And yet, while formalism and manuscript studies are by no means mutually exclusive, formalist analysis still often tends to put demands on its object of study (though not as many or as rigidly as did New Criticism) that manuscript studies would resist. For example, a formalist reading of the Wife of

[26] Seth Lerer, "The Endurance of Formalism in Middle English Studies," *Literature Compass* 1 (2003): 1–15. For an example of how New Critical readings of a (supposed) Middle English lyric can be overturned by manuscript studies, see Siegfried Wenzel, "Poets, Preachers, and the Plight of Literary Critics," *Speculum* 60 (1985): 343–63.

[27] See, for example, Ellen Rooney, "Form and Contentment," *MLQ* 61 (2000): 17–40; and Stephen Cohen, "Between Form and Culture: New Historicism and the Promise of a Historical Formalism," in *Renaissance Literature and Its Formal Engagements,* ed. Mark David Rasmussen (New York: Palgrave, 2002), pp. 17–41; as well as the other essays collected in these volumes (Rooney's article appears in a special *MLQ* issue devoted to formalism). For an overview of the so-called new formalism as a movement, see Marjorie Levinson, "What Is New Formalism," *PMLA* 122 (2007): 558–69, the longer version of which Levinson has made available at http://sitemaker.umich.edu/pmla_article/home.

[28] See Maura Nolan, "Beauty," in *Oxford Twenty-First Century Approaches,* ed. Strohm, pp. 207–21, and Peggy Knapp, "Aesthetic Attention," as well as the other articles in the special issue of *ChauR,* devoted to "Chaucer and Aesthetics," in which the latter appears. The three NCS sessions were "Historicism as Close Reading," "The Value of Close Reading: Theory," and "The Value of Close Reading: Practice."

Bath might closely examine her speech habits for evidence of her attitudes toward sexuality, but, as Tinkle's article shows, variation in the wording of the Wife's speeches on this topic between the Ellesmere and Hengwrt manuscripts makes a determination of these attitudes for *the* Wife of Bath (as distinct from either the Ellesmere or Hengwrt Wife) problematic.[29] Without the mooring of a critical edition and its restriction of variation to a carefully circumscribed apparatus, any instance of formalist analysis may potentially transmogrify into either an epiphenomenon of an editorial debate (such as that of the relative authority of Ellesmere and Hengwrt) or, as in Tinkle's study, analysis of something other than the meaning of a literary text (for example, of that text's reception, rewriting, or misunderstanding by a professional reader). And when one extends the scope of formalist analysis beyond lexical detail to structure, the situation becomes proportionally more tenuous, especially in regard to the *Canterbury Tales,* with its manuscripts' radical variation in tale order and links. To be sure, these manuscripts, especially the earliest ones, share a great deal more than, say, the manuscripts of the notoriously variant popular romances, and editors have resolved differences in accidentals and wording, in many cases, with a high degree of certainty.[30] Moreover, countless formal characteristics, such as Chaucer's use of rime royal for particular tales, are universally attested. Nonetheless, despite the hopes some may hold for the *Canterbury Tales* Project or, many generations ago, the monumental efforts of J. M. Manly and Edith Rickert to construct a definitive edition from all available witnesses, a single form for the *Tales* will necessarily remain an editorial fiction, and hence the ground of formalist treatments of its text always, to greater and lesser degrees, shaky.[31]

In response to this situation, a manuscript-alert, historically robust formalism might consist of context-saturated studies of the literary

[29] See Tinkle, "The Wife," p. 64.

[30] For *variance* and the popular romance, see, among other studies, Jennifer Fellows, "Author, Author, Author . . . : An Apology for Parallel Texts," in *A Guide to Editing Middle English,* ed. McCarren and Moffat, pp. 15–24.

[31] For one explanation why the *Tales* cannot be reduced to a single form, see Derek Pearsall, "Authorial Revision in Some Late-Medieval English Texts," in *Crux and Controversy,* ed. Minnis and Brewer, pp. 39–48; for another, see Stephen Knight, "Textual Variants: Textual Variance," *Southern Review* 16 (1983): 44–54, an early, wide-ranging account of the difficulties and history of Chaucer editing that anticipates many of the topics later taken up by others. For Manly and Rickert's project, see John M. Manly and Edith Rickert, *The Text of the Canterbury Tales: Studied on the Basis of all Known Manuscripts,* 8 vols. (Chicago: University of Chicago Press, 1940).

forms evident in individual or particular sets of manuscripts (that is more or less what Tinkle achieves in her article). But this sort of project, in making the manuscript the central object of study, returns us to the basic questions this essay seeks to explore, which may now be rephrased as, what rationale remains for *not* giving the manuscript this place of honor? For Ralph Hanna, one of the most prominent practitioners of manuscript studies (in several of its variations), the production of critical editions is still necessary, but only so that the distinct features of individual manuscripts may thereby be cast into relief. In *Pursuing History,* he argues that the notion of a stable, authorial text that transcends any of its manuscript witnesses—a postulate that had undergirded the autonomous New Critical verbal icon, the putative unity of which depended upon lexical and structural constancy—still possesses heuristic power, in that it provides access to precisely those materials that the New Critical verbal icon hid: "History is not to be found initially in 'the genuinely authorial' but only through what is 'inauthentic,' 'not genuine.' And erroneous readings only reveal themselves to editorial judgment, to a knowledge of how textual transmission occurs within a manuscript culture. Hence, identifying possibly authorial (or at least archetypal, O^1) readings remains important as allowing a more pervasive historicization, that of medieval literary communities."[32] The authorial text—paradoxically, a prerequisite for New Criticism, despite its purporting to care little about authorial intention—remains for Hanna necessary, but primarily for its position within a negative dialectic that yields the "more pervasive historicization" evident in the departures from this text.

Hanna's argument is a powerful one, but it also exacerbates the awkwardness of the current situation, as it calls for considerable energy to be devoted to producing editions in whose critical priority (and even authority) we ought no longer to believe.[33] Hanna calls for a continua-

[32] Ralph Hanna, *Pursuing History: Middle English Manuscripts and Their Texts* (Stanford: Stanford University Press, 1996), p. 11. Tinkle's article provides a good example of how such "erroneous readings" can become fruitful objects of study.

[33] I do not mean to imply that Hanna's views in this regard stand for the consensus of practitioners of manuscript studies or, more narrowly, textual critics. In fact, how much and what kind of a role the project of discerning the authorial text still possesses are matters of some debate—see, for example, the essays collected in McCarren and Moffat, eds., *A Guide to Editing Middle English,* especially those in the first section, "Author, Scribe, and Editor."

tion of traditional author-centered editorial activity, but only so that we may use the traditional result of this activity—the supposed canonical text—to unearth a more important object, the "Middle English literary communities the record of whose existence Chaucerian canonical hegemony had by and large suppressed."[34] In effect, Hanna calls for the production of two distinct but interdependent material realizations of objects of study—the critical edition and the collection of "erroneous readings" that carry the history of "medieval literary communities"—and then asks us to prioritize the latter over the former. And yet, in his own account of the origin and outcome of his career-long pursuit of just this choice, he offers a sort of parable about literary value that may help explain why this choice, in practice, is so difficult (and perhaps impossible) to carry through fully.

This account requires some close attention, as, for the purposes of this present essay, it serves a paradigm for the persistence of literary value even among those scholars who have most consciously devoted their work elsewhere. As Hanna describes, his first exposure to Chaucer occurred at the age of twelve, when his father, reprimanding him for his use of questionable language, made an offhand comment about Chaucer's use of such language. In response, Hanna developed what may be described as, for lack of a more sophisticated term, a passion: "But I'd also discovered a poet apparently salty enough for twelve-year-old tastes (and within a week acquired a used Vintage Chaucer at a Guadalupe Street bookstore) and discovered that 'in form of speche is change.' I was hooked irrevocably, however I tried to wriggle away."[35] Hanna's experience is, precociously, that of so many undergraduates in their first encounter with Chaucer: initially attracted by the poet's salacious reputation, they soon are drawn by other aspects of his writing, and, in some cases, become "hooked irrevocably." And, like many of those who become so hooked that they pursue postgraduate study, Hanna later experienced a demystification of his former passion. As with his initial encounter, this experience was a precocious one, although in this instance (with its anticanonical sensibility) it was so in respect to the history of Chaucer criticism:

I began to realize that what I felt alienated me from Chaucer was, not knowability, but overfamiliarity—not Chaucer's ease, but what modern literary study

[34] Hanna, *Pursuing History,* p. 7.
[35] Ibid., p. 1.

had made of Chaucer . . . the Chaucer we read had come to be conceived of as the ultimate New Critical poetic text. . . . In this critical context, the notion that Chaucer or his readers had a history and were embroiled in one was largely suppressed. Whatever the effect of such repression upon "the father," the effect on study of his contemporaries and successors was even more dispiriting. Informatively, the literary canons that privileged Chaucer's Art directed attention from these figures as of interest only "historically"—but then failed to outline what such a history would be.[36]

Hanna discovered that the object of his initial attraction was a New Critical object, and, as he learned about all that New Criticism had "largely suppressed," he began a search for an alternative object. This object became the local histories of medieval literary communities, as they have been transmitted by the specificities of individual manuscripts: "I began to wonder whether some aggressive use of the primary evidence for the existence of such {noncanonical} literary figures—the manuscripts themselves—might undo what Chaucer studies had done only too well, return these figures to a historical context and direct research toward a local knowledge that would uncover that context, whatever it was."[37]

No one would dispute that Hanna, in his many publications, has made a remarkable contribution to the "local knowledge" of the "historical context" of the production and dissemination of Middle English literary texts. And yet this very book, which states so clearly in these introductory remarks its anticanonical intentions, makes a major contribution to Chaucer studies:[38] half of its sixteen chapters take some aspect of one or more of Chaucer's texts as their basic topic, and Chaucer features significantly in several others. Conscious of this potential contradiction, Hanna seeks to explain it as follows:

The center of the volume in the main takes up Chaucerian problems. This block of six essays consists of studies I should have preferred not to have undertaken, deviations from the major areas of my concern. (All, in fact, began as accidents.) However, writing about the text of Chaucer, the poet's ipsissima verba, may be construed as an inevitability: just as Shakespeare's text has always triggered

---

[36] Ibid., pp. 2–3.

[37] Ibid., p. 3

[38] Or, to be more precise, the book represents the major contribution to Chaucer studies that Hanna, at this juncture in his career, had already made, since only two of the sixteen chapters are entirely new.

the most exciting advances in general bibliographic studies, so the canonically central medieval poet demands the attention of anyone involved with Middle English textual dissemination.[39]

As Hanna describes, the return to a canonical author is "an inevitability," indeed, one that supersedes the will of the critic. In pursuing what he calls the "precanonical" history of medieval literary communities in the evidence provided by manuscripts, Hanna is led repeatedly back to the manuscripts of "the canonically central medieval poet." The reason for this recursion (other than the "accidents" that initiated each study) seems to lie in the fact that, because so much attention has already been bestowed on the study of Chaucer manuscripts, as in the case of the folios and quartos of Shakespeare, they have become the principal vehicles for reflections on the complexities in the relations between surviving documents and the myriad histories to which they attest. Because Chaucer's canonicity has garnered his texts so much scholarly attention, even studies with noncanonical intentions are drawn into the orbit of that canonicity. As a result, *Pursuing History,* however much it seeks to circumvent Chaucer's value, makes Chaucer's texts one of its principal objects, thereby contributing, against its intentions, to Chaucer's prominence within Middle English studies.[40]

This parable, as I have characterized it, thus tells the story of a boy drawn to a literary work by values that seem intrinsic to it (for example, its saltiness). Later, as a young man, he realizes that, whatever qualities the work in fact possesses, its character has been constructed for him by an interpretative heritage (New Criticism) that suppresses the real (local histories). He therefore puts aside intrinsic literary value as an object and sets off in pursuit of the real. As an older man, however, he discovers that, in this very pursuit, he has returned to the scene of the value that he earlier put aside, albeit in a different interpretative fashion. This parable, when extrapolated from the career of one particular scholar, may well tell the story of the rise of manuscript studies more generally: at both the beginning and on the horizon of this trend (as well as at beginnings and ends of many individual projects) stands literary value,

---

[39] Ibid., pp. 14–15.
[40] In this light, one might understand Hanna's most recent book, *London Literature, 1300–1380* (Cambridge: Cambridge University Press, 2005), as a less diverted culmination of his project, in that it steadfastly focuses on "local knowledge" of the literary communities extant in London before Chaucer's major productions.

even though practitioners do not usually consider such value integral and sometimes—as with Hanna in the introduction to *Pursuing History*—depict it as hostile. More particularly, the parable tells the story of the uneasy relation between Middle English manuscript studies and Chaucer's literary value, in which the former both draws on and resists the energies of the latter.

The New Critical ghost that has not left Chaucer studies—and with which the rise of manuscript studies necessitates confrontation—is then the ghost of judgment, the assessment of the relative value of a literary work.[41] Of course, judgment, as a task of criticism, was hardly invented by New Critics. Going back at least as far as Aristotle and Plato, the critical imperative of evaluation was, as mentioned above, particularly integral to the constitution of modern Chaucer studies in the nineteenth century. It was the long history of affirmative judgment of Chaucer's poetry that formed the somewhat uncomfortable companion to scientific philology in the academic establishment of Chaucer studies. Moreover, I do not mean to overemphasize the influence of New Criticism on Chaucer studies; in comparison with, say, the early modern lyric, Chaucer's works (especially the long narratives) were less amenable to the approach, and many scholars, for a variety of reasons (Robertsonianism being one of them), were unwilling to accept it. Inasmuch as I address the judgment of Chaucer's texts per se, then, my topic necessarily has origins further back than the shifts in critical approaches over the last half century. Nonetheless, these shifts are enormously revealing, both because the influence of New Criticism on Chaucer studies—albeit not comprehensive—is unquestionable (as, for example, Hanna's and Machan's negative reactions to it attest) and because judgment was, in comparison to other approaches, so central to New Criticism.

New Criticism's ghost of judgment, however, has been easy to ignore for at least two principal reasons. First, it is such an obvious target for both poststructuralist and historicist (and, for that matter, any of the post–New Critical) approaches to literature. Evaluative terms such as "great," "better," and "more valuable" have been justifiably considered cheap ideological Trojan horses, and the most cursory survey of literary

---

[41] Notice of this ghost is also a consequence of the resurgence of interest in form and aesthetics, as Jeff Dolven, "Shakespeare and the New Aestheticism," *Literary Imagination* 5 (2003): 95–109, has suggested in respect to Shakespeare studies. In Chaucer studies, however, the so-called new aestheticism is itself a response to manuscript studies, as well as, more obviously, historicism more generally.

history proves characterizations of worth to be among the most evanescent of literary pronouncements. One may thus decisively discredit judgment categorically, without a deeper examination of whether one has in fact thereby evaded it. Second, New Critics themselves expressed varying degrees of ambivalence toward judgment; not wishing their method to appear impressionistic like that of so many of their predecessors outside the academy, they typically framed their arguments in terms of explication or understanding rather than evaluation.[42] The critique of New Criticism marshaled by manuscript studies has consequently focused on the former's principles of explication, especially its anti-historicism, anti-intentionalism, and requirement of a singular, fixed text—that is, all that Machan places together under the label "transcendent verbal icon."

Yet, for New Critics, understanding always implied judgment, since explication was a process of disclosing how all the elements of a poem either succeed at contributing to a whole or fail to do so. As W. K. Wimsatt put it, "Our main critical problem is always how to push understanding and value as far as possible in union, or how to make our understanding evaluative."[43] Indeed, in Wimsatt's and Monroe C. Beardsley's famous polemic against the "intentional fallacy," it is the fundamental category of judgment that makes intention (as well as history) relatively unimportant in critical practice: "How is he [the critic] to find out what the poet tried to do? If the poet succeeded in doing it, then the poem itself shows what he was trying to do. . . . Judging a poem is like judging a pudding or a machine. One demands that it work. It is only because an artifact works that we infer the intention of an artificer."[44] For Wimsatt and Beardsley, and New Criticism generally, the determination of the relative success of a poem—that is, its aesthetic merit—is identical to the process of understanding it. A poem becomes less successful to the extent that appeals to intention or historical context, deemed external, are required for this understanding.

[42] See Gerald Graff, *Professing Literature: An Institutional History* (Chicago: University of Chicago Press, 1987), esp. pp. 121–61.

[43] W. K. Wimsatt with Monroe C. Beardsley, *The Verbal Icon: Studies in the Meaning of Poetry* (Lexington: University of Kentucky Press, 1954), p. 251. Cf. René Wellek and Austin Warren, *Theory of Literature* (New York: Harcourt, Brace and Company, 1949): "an essay which appears to be purely exegetical must, by its very existence, offer some minimal judgment of worth. . . . To spend time and attention on a poet or poem is already a judgment of value" (262).

[44] Wimsatt and Beardsley, *The Verbal Icon,* p. 4.

Hence, given judgment's foundational role, a critique of New Criticism that does not fully account for literary value leaves itself open to be haunted by what it has supposedly left behind.

In the field of English literature generally, and especially in the products of its institutionalization, the ghost of judgment is not hard to find. In addition to the type of vexing presence evident in Hanna's *Pursuing History*, it makes, pervasively, more straightforward appearances. For example, for all the changes to the *Norton Anthology* over the last few editions to bring it in line with changing notions of literary history—the greater variety of texts, the retuned historical introductions to periods, the tables of texts juxtaposed with contexts, the groups of texts centered on historical and cultural issues such as "women in power"—the headnotes to authors are so consistently laudatory of aesthetic prowess that most undergraduates must come away with a powerful sense of judgment's role in the discipline. (For just one example, chosen more or less at random, see the headnote to Andrew Marvell, which proclaims that his "finest poems are second to none in this or any other period.")[45] Similarly, one also expends little effort in finding offhand remarks of judgment in Middle English criticism. In addition to the opening sentence of Peggy Knapp's article cited in my epigraph, an example especially resonant for my purposes (although with Langland standing in for Chaucer as the self-evident instance of literary value) appears in Kerby-Fulton's response to what she perceives as Hanna's charge, in his negative review of *Iconography and the Professional Reader,* that she and Despres undervalued *Piers Plowman:* "The particular approach under disapproval here is our reception history. Contrary to what Hanna implies, it is an approach, we feel, that pays Langland the profoundest authorial compliment: we *know* he's a great poet, and we do not feel we have to prove that in every sentence we write. (Previous generations did carry this burden, and established his poetic reputation brilliantly.)"[46] For Kerby-Fulton, the value of Langland's poem is irrelevant to her project, not

---

[45] *The Norton Anthology of English Literature,* 7th ed., ed. M. H. Abrams and Stephen Greenblatt (New York: W. W. Norton, 2000), 1:1684. This quotation is from the opening sentence of the headnote, which, with its unmistakable suggestion of an aesthetic value unbound to a historical moment, first appeared in the edition cited and has been retained in the most recent (eighth) edition.

[46] Kathryn Kerby-Fulton with Denise Despres, "Fabricating Failure: The Professional Reader as Textual Terrorist," *YLS* 13 (1999): 193–206 (194), emphasis in the original. Hanna's review directly precedes the response in the same volume—Ralph Hanna, *"Piers Plowman* and the Radically Chic," *YLS* 13 (1999): 179–92.

because such evaluative terms as "great poet" are ideologically freighted or mere historical contingencies, but rather because this value has been so well established it need no longer be of concern. Moreover, she positions her and Despres's critical project neither in opposition, nor even as an alternative, to the activity of judgment. Instead, she suggests that manuscript-based reception study, while not directly evaluative, is in its very existence affirmative of the worth of Langland's poem—since, presumably, only a "great poet" justifies such extensive critical attention to a single manuscript. Inasmuch as *Iconography and the Professional Reader* succeeds, then, it testifies not only to the historical interest in the Douce *Piers Plowman* but also to the continuing value of the Work, *Piers Plowman*. As in the parable of Hanna's *Pursuing History,* once again a manuscript-oriented study begins with value (the already-established "poetic reputation" of Langland) and ends with value (the "profoundest authorial compliment" the study represents).[47]

The Object of Value

If the ghost of judgment—whether in the form of Langland, Chaucer, or some other signifier of literary excellence—thus continues to haunt late medieval English literary studies, then we must ask what the nature of this ghost is and what the consequences of its haunting are. For New Critics, that one piece of language could possess more "greatness" or aesthetic value than another was the preexisting condition that made literary criticism, as a definably distinct intellectual activity, both possible and necessary. Without the assumption that texts possessed relative greatness, the task of criticism (conceived of as, most fundamentally, judgment) was meaningless; hence, the object of study that both justified the discipline and was its product was the *notional object of literary value.* What was held to constitute this value was theorized in different ways by different groups of formalists (and thus tended to distinguish one from another, for example, the New Critics from the Chicago School). For present purposes, I will put aside such theorization, even though, as I suggest in my conclusion, it remains an essential activity.

[47] One may also consider in this regard that, while the study of Middle English documents by literary scholars has expanded aggressively into the arena of the nonliterary, the most celebrated work of this sort in recent years—Linne Mooney's use of documentary records to identify Adam Pinkhurst as the scribe of Hengwrt and Ellesmere—is plainly invested in the value we continue to ascribe to the *Canterbury Tales:* see Linne R. Mooney, "Chaucer's Scribe," *Speculum* 81 (2006): 97–138.

Inasmuch as a definition of "literary value" requires a definition of "literary," it raises the questions of the nature of the literary per se and whether and how texts may possess relative amounts of it—questions that, as is well known, go back as far as the oldest surviving writings about literature, and that have received an intimidating array of answers. At this point, I wish to emphasize only the *structural role* that literary value plays in the field of Chaucer studies as a *concept* (hence my label "notional object"), conceiving of it first as a placeholder in a institutionalized system of scholarship and teaching, prior to whatever content this placeholder may contain.

Literary value, despite some attempts to demonstrate otherwise, was not available to formalist investigators in a tangible sense but was extant, rather, as a collective surmise: if a group of investigators—under the ineluctable influence of a long tradition of judgment both within and without the academy—assumes that some texts are somehow better than others, then the selection, production, and elucidation of these texts become justifiable scholarly and pedagogical activities. For New Critics, the structural position held by literary value could thus function institutionally as centripetal mission, the notional center around which the discipline was organized. And, for individual acts of critical practice, literary value could function as both anchor point (what one looks for in a text) and outcome (what one finds or does not find). The notional center hence enabled the myriad activities of literary studies and was at the same time (that is, dialectically) confirmed and defined by them: the presumed existence of this quality necessarily preceded the act of formalist criticism, and the evidence for its presence, or lack thereof, was that act's product.[48]

New Critics acknowledged other relevant and related objects of study but considered them adjuncts to the object of value and named as "fallacies" those critical practices that sought to put one of these lesser objects into the central role held by the object of value. For example, for Wimsatt and Beardsley, as is evident in the first axiom that they propose in their essay on the intentional fallacy, a poem is unarguably, from one perspective, an object of intention: "A poem does not come into exis-

---

[48] That this sort of critical activity thus possessed a marked logical circularity—as its conclusions ("the poem succeeds") are more or less restatements of its assumptions ("the poem is an object of value")—has been argued well and often. For a trenchant, early articulation of this point, see Stanley E. Fish, "Interpreting the *Variorum*," *Critical Inquiry* 2 (1976): 465–85.

tence by accident. The words of a poem . . . come out of a head, not out of a hat." But, as their next assertion makes plain, a critic errs when making this object the focus of investigation: "Yet to insist on the designing intellect as a *cause* of a poem is not to grant the design or intention as a *standard* by which the critic is to judge the worth of the poet's performance."[49] The authors' two emphases in this statement mark two different objects of study, and, for Wimsatt and Beardsley, the second object—the object of "worth" or value—is the logical *a priori* that, for poetry, would lend any interest at all to the first, the object of intention.

As I have suggested, such a hierarchy was also, until the rise of manuscript studies, largely assumed among the scholars who concerned themselves with Chaucer's manuscripts and whose primary aim was the production of editions of Works. Although the more immediate object of study in this field was the object of intention—that is, authorial readings—practitioners readily acknowledged the subordination of this object to the object of value. The search for authorial readings among the manuscripts of the *Canterbury Tales,* for example, proceeded on the assumption that the *Tales,* as a singular literary Work in the very process of being constituted by the editor, *a priori* possessed value, which thereby justified the effort. Putatively cordoned off from consideration until the scientific work of the editor was complete, this *a priori* object of value in fact not only initiated the effort but also, as many have shown (and as most editors would admit), was a determining factor in the minutest editorial decisions, regardless of editorial method—for example, recension, best-text, or eclectic.[50] Editors conceived of the

---

[49] Wimsatt and Beardsley, *The Verbal Icon,* p. 4.

[50] For Middle English studies, the editor/critics Donaldson and Kane have been especially vocal in their insistence on the role of subjective judgment in all methods of editorial work. For Donaldson's views on this topic, see "The Psychology of Editors of Middle English Texts," in E. Talbot Donaldson, *Speaking of Chaucer* (London: Athlone Press, 1970), pp. 102–18. Among Kane's many statements of his views, see the brief summary (in respect of *Piers Plowman*) in George Kane, "The Text," in *A Companion to "Piers Plowman,"* ed. John A. Alford (Berkeley and Los Angeles: University of California Press, 1988), pp. 175–200 (194–98). For a consideration of the affiliations between New Criticism and Kane's and Donaldson's editing practices, see "The Logic of Textual Criticism and the Way of Genius: The Kane-Donaldson *Piers Plowman* in Historical Perspective," in Patterson, *Negotiating the Past,* pp. 77–113. For this view in respect to English literature more generally, see G. Thomas Tanselle, *Textual Criticism and Scholarly Editing* (Charlottesville: University Press of Virginia, 1990), who argues the point throughout this collection of essays—e.g., "In scholarly editing the role of literary judgment is vital to all decisions—those concerning accidentals as well as those concerning substantives" (329–30).

completed effort—the edition—as an imperfect reification of the notional object of value, the material substitute upon which critical judgment of value may be exercised, a substitute assumed stable until
subsequent editors constituted new, presumably less imperfect reifications.

Given this history, the persistence of these considerations of value
subsequent to the rise of manuscript studies (even among those scholars
whose work exemplifies this trend) raises the question of how much the
New Critical hierarchy of objects has changed. Manuscript studies, as
evident in Hanna's emphasis on "Middle English literary communities,"
has in many instances appeared to subordinate the object of value to, if
not wholly replace it with, the object of cultural significance (or, less
neutrally, the object of ideology). This object, which often goes under
the name "material culture," is also more or less the one that interpretive historicism has sought to put at its center of inquiry. As Catherine
Gallagher and Stephen Greenblatt suggest, while historicism has by no
means rejected the object of value, it has—under the influence of cultural anthropologists such as Clifford Geertz—subordinated it to the
more general "cultural text," demoting it to the status of just one historical integer among others. This move "vastly expands the range of objects available to be read and interpreted" and thus in turn entails, to
some degree, an attitude "skeptical, wary, demystifying, critical, and
even adversarial" toward the object of value that no longer holds center
stage.[51] It is the move that David Wallace, in his general preface to *The
Cambridge History of Medieval Literature,* describes as especially well suited
to the study of the late medieval literatures produced in Britain (and
which that volume of literary history hence seeks to epitomize), and the
one that Charlotte Morse understands as (among other things) transforming the largely formalist-inspired notion of "Ricardian poetry" into
the project of "Ricardian studies."[52] And, to many of those who remain
committed to the central position of literary value—even such manu-
script-savvy and historically informed critics like Pearsall and John Bur
row—it is a move that therefore threatens the discipline by its failure to

[51] Catherine Gallagher and Stephen Greenblatt, *Practicing New Historicism* (Chicago:
University of Chicago Press, 2000), p. 9.

[52] David Wallace, ed., *The Cambridge History of Medieval English Literature* (Cambridge:
Cambridge University Press, 1999), pp. xi–xxiii; Charlotte C. Morse, "From 'Ricardian
Poetry' to Ricardian Studies," in *Essays on Ricardian Literature: In Honour of J. A. Burrow,*
ed. A. J. Minnis, Charlotte C. Morse, and Thorlac Turville-Petre (Oxford: Clarendon
Press, 1997), pp. 316–44.

distinguish works of lesser and "greater intrinsic literary significance" and its tendency to push literature "aside in the quest for socio-political significance."[53]

Manuscript studies is, as I have suggested, not reducible to historicism and in many ways arose independently of it—as evident, for example, in the fact that a scholar such as Pearsall can be so active in the former even while taking an adversarial stance toward elements of the latter. Nonetheless, historicism's apparent shift in the object of study provides crucial legitimation to the elevation of the manuscript from means to end; as a key element of the "cultural text," the individual manuscript, at least for Middle English investigators, becomes the most important of the vastly expanded "range of objects to be read and interpreted." Dovetailing with initiatives in the theory of textual criticism (in particular, the demotion of the authorial text), this historicist interest in the individual manuscript creates the common ground between literary critic and manuscript scholar that is so visible in such studies as Tinkle's or, in a somewhat different vein, Seth Lerer's *Chaucer and His Readers*.[54] In the latter, Lerer constructs, from a codicological study of fifteenth-century manuscripts and early printed books, an understanding of how, and to what end, the authority of Chaucer was constituted vis-à-vis the particular time, place, and constituency of the producers and audiences of those documents. The cultural significance of such manuscripts—to a much greater extent than the timeless literary value

[53] Derek Pearsall, "Medieval Literature and Historical Enquiry," *MLR* 99 (2004): xxxi–xlii (xl, xxxvii). In the first quotation, Pearsall refers specifically to James Simpson, *The Oxford English Literary History, Vol. 2, 1350–1547: Reform and Cultural Revolution* (Oxford: Oxford University Press, 2002), and, in the second, to Lee Patterson, *Chaucer and the Subject of History* (Madison: University of Wisconsin Press, 1991). In this article, Pearsall follows, with some qualifications, the disciplinary diagnosis of J. A. Burrow, "Should We Leave Medieval Literature to the Medievalists?" *EIC* 53 (2003): 278–83, but adduces different causes. As many readers will recognize, in citing the sentiments of these two articles, I broach the hoary theoretical and institutional debate between literary and cultural studies, one recently given new animus with the advent of new formalism. And, in many ways, my argument in this essay rests on the ambiguous position of manuscript studies within this debate, with Chaucer studies standing for literary studies and medieval studies standing for cultural studies. Inasmuch as it is possible, I hope to skirt the margins of this debate rather than plunge into it, as I do not find it fruitful, although my conclusions regarding Chaucer editions necessarily bear on it.

[54] Seth Lerer, *Chaucer and His Readers: Imagining the Author in Late-Medieval England* (Princeton: Princeton University Press, 1993). Prendergast formulates this common ground explicitly in his introduction to the manuscript studies anthology *Rewriting Chaucer*. See also the introductory statement of aims in Echard and Partridge, eds., *The Book Unbound*.

of Chaucer's Works—appears to serve as the *a priori* notional object of study that, dialectically, both enables the investigation and is that investigation's product. Indeed, from the perspective of this and similar studies—or from a metacritical perspective such as Trigg's—the object of literary value might well seem an ideological screen to be overcome, the false transmutation of historically contingent, material conditions into a historically transcendent virtue, one that blinds us both to history and to the ideological uses to which literature is put. In short, the object of value may seem everything that the many exposers of the conservative ideologies of New Criticism have accused it of being.[55]

From this perspective, if the Chaucer editions produced under traditional editorial paradigms are reifications of the notional object of value, then the subordination of this object would seem to necessitate a corresponding subordination of its reifications to more suitable ones—and, indeed, it is precisely the persistence of the traditional reifications that prompts the complaint by Machan quoted in my epigraph. In their place should be, say, reifications of cultural significance (that is, of the complexity of cultural influence and transmission, properly historicized), such as might be achieved by a representation of various interlaced manuscript matrices, in which manuscript reproductions are linked rhizomically to each other and hypertextually embedded in myriad informing contexts—perhaps one of the dynamically reconfigurable electronic editions mentioned above. For both scholarship and pedagogy, this replacement material realization of the object of study would correspond to the shift in the central self-justifying task of the field from judgment to, say, something like Hanna's discernment of "medieval literary communities."

We have already seen, however, that this shift away from judgment has not been decisive, and further consideration of Hanna's remark about how "Shakespeare's text has always triggered the most exciting advances in general bibliographic studies" suggests the source of the resistance to editions of Chaucer not constructed as objects of value. Hanna's remark reminds us that the presumed value of Shakespeare's Works remains firmly in place despite the considerable attention given to the textual indeterminacy of these Works and their lack of authorial imprimatur; indeed, as the remark further implies, this very attention

[55] See, for example, Terry Eagleton, *Literary Theory: An Introduction,* 2nd ed. (Minneapolis: University of Minnesota Press, 1996), pp. 15–46.

has more likely perpetuated this value than diminished it. (In Machan's view, the literary value attributed to Shakespeare's Works has not only determined the entire history of Shakespeare editing but also that of Anglo-American textual criticism generally, so that Chaucer's texts have been edited to accord with the model of value set by the Bard's plays.)[56] Similarly, within the realm of interpretive historicism, the immense amount of attention given to the culture of early modern England over the last quarter century or so has done nothing to displace the centrality of the Bard in either early modern criticism or in British literature curricula. (In this regard, one may observe that many—perhaps most— historicist studies, such as Gallagher and Greenblatt's, do not hesitate to include valorizations of such traditional objects of value as Shakespeare's texts, although such valorizations tend to be of the incidental nature discussed above.) Although Chaucer has never possessed literary capital on the scale of Shakespeare, even within the boundaries of Middle English studies, his Works nonetheless continue to play an analogous role in the disciplinary economy. As much as, say, the topics of Lollardy, Lancastrian politics, and women's literary activities have turned critical energies in other, often explicitly noncanonical, directions, Chaucer's Works still retain their prominence in the field (if having received, in recent years, a challenge in this regard from *Piers Plowman*). As Nicholas Watson observes, in his response to the 2006 NCS conference (and despite what he considers, on the one hand, to be the field's broadening concerns and, on the other, the potential negative consequences of its continued dependence on Chaucer),

It's obvious that, for many here [at the conference], Chaucer remains simply the most interesting and demanding of all the writers in our field to study and to think with; and that even for those of us whose most passionate attachments are elsewhere [as in Watson's case], Chaucer is still the place where many of our new intellectual perspectives come from or find their ultimate test (the question "does it work for Chaucer?" can still make or break in this business), as well as being the bedrock of our medieval teaching.[57]

One wonders, from such comments as these, how subordinated the object of value actually is; one begins to suspect that, though ostensibly

---

[56] This is the argument of Machan, " 'I endowed.' "
[57] Nicholas Watson, "Response to the New Chaucer Society Conference, New York, July 27–31, 2006," *The New Chaucer Society Newsletter* 28 (2006): 1–5 (2).

secondary to cultural significance, it still possesses a determining, if sub-terranean, influence over the latter. For if cultural significance were in-deed the determining object, then one would expect, for example, that the *Middle English Prose Brut,* with its 181 surviving manuscripts—or even the *Prick of Conscience,* with 117—would be receiving as much at-tention as the surviving manuscripts of the *Canterbury Tales,* if not more. Surely these collections of manuscripts were as least as culturally sig-nificant and ideologically powerful in late medieval England as the manuscripts of the *Tales.* To this observation, an obvious rejoinder is that the *Tales,* unlike the *Brut* or the *Prick of Conscience,* has *continued* to possess cultural significance. Yet this argument effectively extends the object of cultural significance through the full history of Chaucer reception and thereby dilutes historical specificity from that object, reducing it to the generality that Chaucer has been significant for particular constituencies in particular times and places. And this generality is simply another way of saying that Chaucer's texts have been regularly construed, by various constituencies for various reasons, as possessing more value than other texts. In effect, the object of cultural significance, at least when posited within the ambit of "studies in the age of Chaucer," becomes merely a *displaced object of value,* which, though obscured, thereby retains its role as the disciplinary center of gravity. What changes through this dis-placement, however, is the perception of this object's ownership and the perceived need to assign it stable content: by naming the object cultural significance, we are able define it as someone else's object of value rather than ours, and we may thereby allow the content of that object to be whatever these others need or desire it to be at their particular historical moments.

Hence, even when projects do not concern Chaucer directly (or an-other established object of value, such as *Piers Plowman*) and avoid even such aesthetically neutral evaluative terms as "significance" in favor of a notional object of historical authenticity, they may still depend on a displaced object of value, at some level of indirection. For example, Hanna has declared that "the ultimate goal of manuscript studies should be the composition of cultural histories. . . . At every step, one strives to integrate minutiae toward a holistic analysis which reaches beyond books, indeed literature, to society and history."[58] In this formu-

---

[58] Ralph Hanna, "Analytical Survey 4: Middle English Manuscripts and the Study of Literature," *NML* 4 (2001): 243–64 (255–56).

lation, "cultural histories," rather than any special significance within them, are the stated object. Yet, as much twentieth-century historiography has taught us, simply to notice something in the past is already to conceive of its value for, and bearing on, the present. A study of, say, the manuscripts of Wycliffite sermons, then, is also an argument for why these manuscripts matter to us. If this study appears in *Studies in the Age of Chaucer,* then implicitly this argument must be, in part, that these manuscripts convey a significant aspect of the culture that also included Chaucer, and hence they may (among other functions, of course) help explicate Chaucer's texts. And the only reason that Chaucer's texts require such explication is because they have already been conceived as an object of value.

To be sure, I do not mean to imply that the entire world of late medieval English studies revolves around a Chaucerian star. Moreover, as I have mentioned, I realize that the position of the object of value vis-à-vis manuscript studies depends at some level on the ambiguous and contested institutional and theoretical distinctions between Chaucer studies and medieval studies (distinctions further blurred by the bridge term, "studies in the age of Chaucer")—or those between their more general (and more contested) formations as literary and cultural studies. Indeed, for the latter's advocates, one of the benefits of the interdisciplinary nature of cultural studies is that it tolerates multiple, competing objects of study (which, of course, is one of its liabilities to its detractors). But the corollary to this point is that, inasmuch as Chaucer studies remains part of literary studies (and as long as the term "literary" remains in any way meaningful), the institutionalization of the latter carries with it an inherited commitment to value that we may put at arm's length but that we cannot finally evade.

Reifying the *Canterbury Tales*

If we cannot then escape the historically sedimented investments of the institutions in which we first learned about Chaucer, and in which we now teach and produce criticism, one might argue that we should at least seek exactly this arm's length distance—the critical distance that levels of indirection from the object of value may achieve. And, certainly, the substitution of cultural significance, or simply cultural history, for the object of value serves this function in the work of many, if not most, current Chaucerians. Yet this critical distance, from another perspective, remains an attempt at evasion. If, as I have argued, the object of cultural significance in Chaucer studies ultimately translates into the object of value as perceived by historically distant others, and if this object's cultural significance extends, *mutatis mutandis,* to the present and thus includes us, then we have performed a sort of conceptual sleight of hand. The attribution of the object of value to historically distant others enables our own inherited commitments to that object to remain in some inchoate state—to varying degrees offhand, intuitive, impressionistic, and unexamined, if not simply submerged and unacknowledged—even while they continue to structure the field.[59] Moreover, by conceiving of the content of the other's object of value as historically contingent, we exempt ourselves from the responsibility of defining the content of the object of value to which we remain committed—on the argument that to do so would merely reflect our own historical conditioning. Again, as a tactic of critical distance, these evasions have use, but they nonetheless remain evasions, and hence the decisions that we might make on the basis of them bear reexamination.

One of these potential decisions returns us to the question of whether the best material realization of an object of study is necessarily the most historically authentic—by which I mean, at this point, whether a reification of the notional object of historical authenticity is necessarily the most desirable material object upon which to practice criticism and pedagogy. This question, as I have indicated, has become newly pertinent because the rise of manuscript studies has, for quite justifiable reasons, begun to drive a wedge between this notional object and the one of value. As long as the aim of the various tasks involving manuscripts remained the production of a Work (in the form of an edition), the objects of intention, cultural significance, and historical authenticity were subordinate to the object of value and hence not thoroughly distinguished from it. But as the quotation from Machan in my epigraph indicates, reifications of value, inasmuch as they are historically vitiated, are now precisely what manuscript studies would subordinate, if not reject altogether. As Machan puts it elsewhere, "All of the modern edi-

---

[59] In this regard, it is to Pearsall's credit that, in his defense of Chaucer's literary value in "Medieval Literature," he concludes his essay with what one rarely encounters in current Chaucer criticism: an explicit attempt to define poetic literary value and to demonstrate its presence in Chaucer's verse (but see also the essays pertaining to Chaucer's aesthetics cited above). That this demonstration should seem so much like a formalist exercise is striking.

tions of Chaucer's complete works contain carefully presented, artistically pleasing poetry, but none of them offer genuine examples of works produced within the discourse of Middle English manuscripts, since the Chaucer they imply can only be a projection of postmedieval thinking."[60] Even if we grant the categories Machan wields here (and I am fully willing to do so), we nonetheless remain confronted with the question of whether to choose for critical and pedagogical practice "modern editions" with their "artistically pleasing poetry" or something that better reifies "genuine examples of works produced within the discourse of Middle English manuscripts"—perhaps, say, the electronic edition described by Morse.

Given the predominance of historicism in Chaucer studies, the choice might seem to fall unhesitatingly to the latter—if not yet to an electronic edition, to some more adequate printed representation. Yet, if the notional object of value remains, as I have argued, the central structuring force in the field, why should not we choose instead the reification that best represents this object? What necessary logic justifies the choice (to consider an extreme dichotomy of options) of an electronic, rhizomic, dynamically reconfigurable, variant-comprehensive, hypertext edition of the *Canterbury Tales* over, say, the Donaldson edition, if (and this "if" is crucial) the latter represents more effectively the object of value and thus more effectively serves the field's actual organization? Upon reflection, one has little basis on which to claim the former as a more legitimate material literary object than the latter. Both are historical composites produced by multiple agents, in essence collaborative projects involving numerous individuals, most unknown to one another, pursued over the course of hundreds of years. Both lift material from one, uncertain aesthetic context and place it in another, better known but radically different one. Both may be the objects of rigorous and illuminating interpretative practice, although in both cases the interpreter must take care to respect the multiple intentions and contexts informing the work.

As is well known, Donaldson produced his edition under the New Critical assumption that complex artistic unity is what makes a literary Work valuable, and he manipulated the surviving material record of the *Tales* to create a Work possessing ample amounts of this quality (most

---

[60] Tim William Machan, *Textual Criticism and Middle English Texts* (Charlottesville: University Press of Virginia, 1994), p. 181.

strikingly, perhaps, by having the "Wif of Bathe" disrupt the Host's plan in the Man of Law's Endlink, revealingly defending his decision by simply remarking, "this gives coherence to the chosen order").[61] This quality is, without question, "postmedieval" (to use Machan's phrasing), but this fact alone does not make his version *a priori* any less legitimate as a material literary object. His version, rather, is simply one produced over time by diverse agents with different motivations. The same description applies in fact to the very earliest witnesses to the *Tales,* such as the Hengwrt and Ellesmere manuscripts (and especially the latter). Although the temporal distances among the several agents responsible for these manuscripts are, obviously, much smaller than those of any printed edition, these agents plainly still possessed diverse motivations, as Haimo's and Tinkle's studies amply demonstrate. In Tinkle's apt phrasing, the pages of any manuscript reflect a "hybrid, cumulative authorship."[62] Hence, even what is arguably the most historically authentic version of the *Tales,* the Hengwrt, is already a historical composite—as indeed is any material literary object in any era. What necessary reason dictates that a less radically composite work (the Hengwrt) be chosen over one that is more so (the Donaldson edition) if—and again this "if" is crucial—the latter better represents the object of value?[63]

The proposed electronic *Canterbury Tales* would also, obviously, be a historical composite, one even more radical than the Donaldson edition, although, in contrast, it possesses the (equally postmedieval) motivation to represent the "discourse of Middle English manuscripts" with as much authenticity as possible. If one chooses this version of the *Tales* solely because its constitution possesses this motivation, despite finding more literary value in the Donaldson version, then, in effect, one self-contradictorily chooses to diminish the "greatness" of the *Tales* even while that very quality (whatever it may consist of) remains the reason

---

[61] *Chaucer's Poetry: An Anthology for the Modern Reader,* ed. E. T. Donaldson, 2nd ed. (New York: HarperCollins, 1975), p 1074.

[62] Tinkle, "The Wife," p. 76.

[63] One may similarly ask, given that changes in technology throughout the history of literary production and reception have engendered a broad diversity of experiences of what is nominally the same literary object, on what necessary basis do we decide which of these experiences is most worthy of critical attention? In raising such questions—and, more generally, in my willingness to see the printed edition and the manuscript as equally legitimate, if vastly different, material literary objects—I echo arguments made to somewhat different ends by Michelle R. Warren, "Post-Philology," in *Postcolonial Moves: Medieval Through Modern,* ed. Patricia Clare Ingham and Michelle R. Warren (New York: Palgrave Macmillan, 2003), pp. 19–45.

why any critical energy is expended upon it. This potential self-contradiction is the essence of the resistance to manuscript studies. Because Chaucer studies is still organized around the notional object of value, its practitioners will continue to resist changes in the reifications of this object that seem to diminish value, even while those same practitioners are ideologically and practically committed to historical authenticity.

An imagined scenario may make my point plainer. Suppose tomorrow someone unearthed incontrovertible evidence that corroborated the speculation David Lawton made years ago, that Thomas Hoccleve authored some of the linking passages in the *Canterbury Tales*.[64] Say (to make the scenario more extreme) this individual discovered a manuscript—in the attic of an obscure descendant of Adam Pinkhurst—that contained *all* the linking passages, as well their most important revisions, and that concluded with an envoy to Pinkhurst in which Hoccleve pseudo-humbly proclaims his inadequacy to complete the work of his recently deceased master; and all this appears in Hoccleve's holograph, dated November 1400. Obviously, scholarly understanding of a number of things would change rather dramatically, but how should this discovery affect the manner in which editions of the *Canterbury Tales* appear? Should the linking passages be bracketed, supplied but not lineated, relegated to endnotes, or just dropped altogether? In my view, editors should use the new evidence to maximize aesthetic power—to produce, say, an edition with the tales and links more seamlessly and confidently integrated than previously, despite the fact that this edition would correspond to no actual manuscript. To choose one of the other options would be, as in the example of the Donaldson edition, to choose the object of historical authenticity over that of value, thereby diminishing the very quality that continues to sustain critical interest in the *Tales*. Figuratively speaking, it would be to settle begrudgingly for the undressed salad, even while one longingly looks over at a neighbor's pizza—and my argument is that most Chaucerians, no matter how nutritionally informed, still want the pizza.[65]

[64] See David Lawton, *Chaucer's Narrators* (Cambridge: D. S. Brewer, 1985), pp. 127–29.

[65] I offer this far-fetched example of Hoccleve's co-authorship, rather than one of the many actual debates about how the *Tales* ought to be represented, to avoid digression into textual controversies. But readers may easily see how the debate about, say, the status of the penitential treatise and so-called *Retractions* that stand at the end of the *Tales* (whether, that is, they belong in the *Tales* at all) depends not just on textual questions but also on both the inertia of the literary value attributed to the current constitution of the *Tales* and the likelihood that a new constitution (ending with the Parson's Prologue) would possess more. For the argument that the *Parson's Tale* and

Clearly, the key conditional assumption in both of these examples is that one version of the *Tales* better reifies the object of value than another (or, for that matter, that one likes pizza better than an undressed salad). In these examples I have assumed a specific content for the object of value, one rather tendentiously calibrated to my opening admission of teaching the *Tales* as a linked set of short stories. This assumption is mostly heuristic, inasmuch as my aim has been to call attention to the persistence of the structuring power of literary value in Chaucer studies rather than to define the nature of this value. Given this structuring power, however, the obvious implication is that, as a conscientiously reflexive postmodern literary critic, one ought to make such assumptions explicit, interrogate their ideologies, investigate their theoretical bases, and, I would add, continue to embrace them to the extent that, after this process, one still believes in them.

Although I cannot pursue this task here, I offer, by way of conclusion, two considerations (which in various ways have hovered over this essay throughout) to take into account in its undertaking. First, literary value in general and that of Chaucer in particular neither originated in, nor is decisively controlled by, the academy. Rather, literary value was one of the enabling conditions of the initial academic institutionalization of Chaucer studies, and its sustained presence outside the academy is, in part, what continues to legitimize, shape, and perpetuate the field. In this regard, Hanna's youthful extracurricular encounter with Chaucer may stand as a representative illustration of how broadly disseminated and influential extra-institutional literary value continues to be. Also revealing in this regard is Hanna's comparison of Shakespeare's and Chaucer's roles in their respective bibliographic studies. Shakespeare scholarship has been from the start, and continues to be, pendant on the immense value perceived, outside the academy, to reside in the Bard's plays. Hence institutions such as Indiana University may choose, as Patrick Brantlinger has described, to suspend Shakespeare requirements not so much as an attempt to shift the object of study from value to culture (as Brantlinger himself might wish) but simply because

---

Retractions are a scribal appendage, see Charles A. Owen Jr., "The *Canterbury Tales:* Beginnings (3) and Endings (2 + 1)," *Chaucer Yearbook* 1 (1992): 189–211, and, more extensively, Míceál F. Vaughan, "Creating Comfortable Boundaries: Scribes, Editors, and the Invention of the *Parson's Tale*," in *Rewriting Chaucer*, ed. Prendergast and Kline, pp. 45–90.

students will take Shakespeare regardless of requirements.[66] This consideration suggests that, no matter how we within the academy choose to define the content of literary value, we would do well to take into account, in some fashion, the definitions current outside the academy. It also confirms the suspicion that, if literary value not only organizes the field of Chaucer studies from within but also sustains it from without, then, even while manuscript studies continues to reap its impressive scholarly harvest, we will be best served if we retain a material object of study that, at the very least, does not obscure this value. If, in the future, Chaucer studies becomes fully submerged within medieval cultural studies, then this concern with value may no longer apply. But I do not foresee this submersion occurring until Chaucer no longer possesses literary value outside the academy, at which point it will occur by default.

The second consideration is that the specific content of the object of value is always multiple and unstable, for individual readers as well as among different readers. Attempts to define this content are, as I have suggested, an essential component of reflexive criticism but are also thus necessarily partial, in both senses of that term. When, therefore, Fradenburg, in the final pages of *Sacrifice Your Love,* critiques both John Guillory's adaptation of Pierre Bourdieu's theory of cultural capital and the principles of New Philology as articulated by Stephen Nichols, she does so to promote one content of literary value—"enjoyment" in the psychoanalytic sense—over others (or, in the case of New Philology, over a different object of study).[67] The supposed agon between psychoanalysis and historicism (which Fradenburg seeks to dispose of as a false dichotomy) may thus be understood as a debate about the content of literary value and how much any individual ascription of content should determine our critical practice. Similarly, the conflict still perceived in some quarters between historically rigorous and supposedly anachronistic the-

---

[66] See Patrick Brantlinger, *Who Killed Shakespeare? What's Happened to English since the Radical Sixties* (New York: Routledge, 2001), pp. 13–30. For a general consideration of how literary canonicity is not nearly as much a function of the academy as academics tend to believe, see E. Dean Kolbas, *Critical Theory and the Literary Canon* (Boulder: Westview Press, 2001).

[67] Fradenburg, *Sacrifice Your Love,* pp. 243–52. Knight is similarly forthcoming about his rather different sense of the literary value of Chaucer's texts when he frankly admits, in his work as editor, "when faced by equally possible variants I will print the one which has the maximum possible historical tension, the reading which loads the text most strongly with ideology" ("Textual Variants," p. 49).

oretical approaches to Chaucer dissipates when one understands the latter as performing a necessary definition and interrogation of literary value. Hence, whether one theorizes the content of the object of value as *jouissance,* cultural capital, commodity fetish, resistance, alterity, hybridity, misprision, defamiliarization, aesthetic unity, the sublime, beauty, truth, or *sentence* fused with *solas* (to name just a few of the many possibilities), axiological theorization, no matter how putatively anachronistic, is a mark of literary critical integrity.

Having developed and defended an axiology of the *Canterbury Tales,* does one then construct an edition of the *Tales* that best corresponds to one's personal axiology and use this version in one's criticism and teaching? Although this conclusion is ridiculous (equivalent, analogously, to mistaking license for liberty, as Milton defined the terms), it is not in fact far from the position taken by eminent textual critic G. Thomas Tanselle many decades ago in his account of the editor's aims and responsibilities—a position that amounts to a more radical version of Pearsall's proposal for different editions for different audiences:

A person of taste and sensitivity, choosing among variant readings on the basis of his own preference and making additional emendations of his own, can be expected to produce a text that is aesthetically satisfying and effective. Whether or not it is what the author wrote is another matter; but editing which does not have as its goal the recovery of the author's words is not necessarily illegitimate—it is creative, rather than scholarly, but not therefore unthinkable. . . . [I]t is . . . obvious that an editor could conceivably produce a version of a work aesthetically superior to the original. In such a case the editor would in effect become a collaborator of the author, in the way that publishers' editors or literary executors sometimes are. So long as one is concerned only with individual aesthetic objects, there can be no objection to the procedure; but if one is interested in the work as part of an author's total career, one must insist on having the words which that author actually wrote.[68]

In effect, Tanselle divides the universe of editions into two—the "creative" ones that correspond to literary value (in his terms, aesthetic superiority) and the "scholarly" ones that correspond to historical authenticity (which he equates with "the recovery of the author's words")—and willingly grants legitimacy to the former. But, as Chaucer editors have known all along and as manuscript studies has repeat-

[68] Tanselle, *Textual Criticism,* p. 329.

edly taught us, all existing print editions (not to mention the manuscript witnesses themselves) are to some degree creative. They all are the product of one or more individuals of (ideally) "taste and sensitivity," who have manipulated the evidence according to preconceived notions of aesthetic superiority—precisely because such notions are irrecoverably entangled with those individuals' perceptions of what "the author's words" might have been. But the solution to this situation is not, therefore, wholly to abandon creative or value-based editions. To do so would be to sever the field from the axiological energies that in fact sustain it. Neither, however, is the solution to hold all creative editions equally worthy objects of study simply because no edition may escape being to some degree creative. Such would be to mistake solipsism for subjectivity. Instead, the solution is to continue to create and use value-potent editions that nonetheless recognize, in some fashion, both in themselves and in the criticism that uses them, the constraints of the latest historical and textual findings. One of the tasks of Chaucer criticism is not just to make its own and its chosen edition's axiology explicit but also to shift the axiological grounds in such a way as to keep the creative and the scholarly in conversation.

Perhaps, as Chaucer studies continues to evolve, these grounds may shift enough to make the question of what best reifies the object of study once again moot (or, alternatively, Chaucer studies, as such, will vanish as the energies that supply it dissipate). In the meantime, Chaucer critics may view the options already extant or proposed—options varying from a New Critical collection of lightly annotated short stories, to a critical edition presenting a text and variants, to a hypertext representation of manuscript matrix and cultural nexus—as vehicles for articulating their axiologies. And I may well continue to teach the *Tales* as I do currently, at times pretending a critical edition is a collection of short stories and, at other times, encouraging discussion of how both that literary idea and the edition itself are critical fictions. But I will do so with considerably less guilt.

Hybrid Discourse in the *General Prologue* Portraits

Thomas J. Farrell
Stetson University

T HE TWO CHAPTERS DEVOTED to the *General Prologue* in *Sources and Analogues of the Canterbury Tales* substantiate recent interest in the framing of the *Canterbury Tales* and a more long-standing concern for the sources of its portraits' details.[1] But Chaucer's experiment with the structure of discourse in the *Prologue,* especially in the series of portraits at its center, receives scant attention in that reference work, as indeed in the sixty years of scholarship that it summarizes. Nor do earlier summaries of scholarship suggest models of portraiture that adequately account for the strikingly "new art" in the *Prologue*'s narration, the hybridization of different discursive registers within the narrative.[2]

Portions of this article were presented at the 38th and 39th International Congresses on Medieval Studies at Western Michigan University in 2003 and 2004. Revision of that work was supported by the Stetson University Professional Development Program, and greatly assisted by the substantial suggestions made by Lorraine K. Stock and Peter G. Beidler, who read an earlier complete draft. I was also helped by the generous advice provided by Miriam Fuller, Alan Baragona, and two anonymous readers for *Studies in the Age of Chaucer.*

[1] Robert R. Raymo, "The General Prologue," in *Sources and Analogues of the Canterbury Tales,* ed. Robert M. Correale and Mary Hamel, 2 vols. (Woodbridge, Suffolk: D. S. Brewer, 2002–5), 1:1–85, discusses the portraits individually, but not the construction of the whole. Helen Cooper also discusses the Prologue in her chapter "The Frame," 1:1–22. Although both of them rightly address current interest in the *Decameron* as a source for the *Prologue,* Boccaccio provides no models for the kind of narrative description we find in the *Tales.* As Thomas G. Bergin notes, "Individual characterization is sketchy and to an English-speaking reader who approaches the *{Decameron}* looking for something like the *Canterbury Tales,* may be a little disconcerting." *Boccaccio* (New York: Viking, 1981), p. 292.

[2] Charles A. Owen Jr., "Development of the Art of Portraiture in Chaucer's *General Prologue,*" *LeedsSE* 14 (1983): 116–33, referred to the "whole new art" (p. 116) of the Prologue's portraits, an art built in part from "the indirections, the many different ways we receive information," including "the voice of the pilgrim" (p. 126); but the novelty he identified has remained substantially unexplored.

While Robert A. Pratt and Karl Young noted in 1941 that the thirty-one highly generic descriptions in Benoît de Sainte-Maure's *Roman de Troie,* produced more or less mechanically from a standardized menu of physical or moral traits, are "comparable" to those in the *Prologue,* they add that "one could hardly suggest, however, that [Benoît] served as a model" for the *Prologue:*[3]

> Achillès fù de grant beauté
> Gros ot le piz, espès e lé,
> E les membres granz e pleniers,
> Les ieuz el chief hardiz e fiers;
> Crespes cheveus ot e aubornes.
> Ne fu mie pensis ne mornes:
> La chiere aveit liee e joiose
> E vers son enemi irose.[4]

Narratologists employ various taxonomies in describing this technique but agree about its orientation to entirely external and objectified information; subjectivity is not the point.[5] Anyone who knew the *Roman de Troie* could readily understand Derek Pearsall's warning that the *General Prologue*'s series of portraits might similarly constitute "a recipe for certain disaster, for repetitive schematisation and yawning monotony, something that a deranged *rhétoriqueur* might have dreamed up."[6]

[3] "The Literary Framework of the Canterbury Tales," in *Sources and Analogues of Chaucer's Canterbury Tales,* ed. W. F. Bryan and Germaine Dempster (1941; rpt. Atlantic Highlands, N.J.: Humanities Press, 1958), p. 5.

[4] *Le Roman de Troie par Benoit de Sainte-Maure,* ed. Léopold Constans (Paris: Firmin Didot, 1906), vol. 1, pp. 267–68, lines 5157–64. "Achilles was very handsome. He was big-chested, broad and imposing. His limbs were large and powerful. The eyes in his head were keen and bold. He had curly auburn hair. He was not at all given to brooding or sorrow: his face was cheerful and happy; but he was wrathful towards his foe." The series of portraits in Benoît stretches through lines 5093–582, about two hundred fewer lines than Chaucer devotes to the pilgrims. Benoît is drawing on the possibly even less engaging antecedent in *Daretis Phrygii de Excidio Troiae Historia,* ed. Ferdinand Meister (Wiesbaden: Teubner, 1873), p. 16.

[5] Gérard Genette, *Narrative Discourse: An Essay in Method,* trans. Jane E. Lewin (Ithaca: Cornell University Press, 1980), p. 248, names such narration "extradiegetic heterodiegetic"; for Dorrit Cohn, "The Encirclement of Narrative: On Franz Stanzel's *Theorie des Erzählens,*" *Poetics Today* 2 (1981): 157–82, it is "authorial third-person." Cohn's article builds on the simpler model discussed in her *Transparent Minds: Narrative Modes for Presenting Consciousness in Fiction* (Princeton: Princeton University Press, 1978), p. 179. See also Genette's *Narrative Discourse Revisited,* trans. Jane E. Lewin (Ithaca: Cornell University Press, 1988), p. 121, which cites Cohn's article.

[6] *The Canterbury Tales* (London: G. Allen and Unwin, 1985), p. 56.

The Riverside Chaucer adduces further parallels, like the sculptures out-side the Garden of Love in Guillaume de Lorris's *Roman de la Rose*.[7] But Guillaume, though a better poet than Benoît, also avoids what Chaucer provides (as critics have long recognized) with some consistency: the depiction of a character's self-understanding.[8] Guillaume's Vielleice does not tell us what Age thinks about being old. In contrast, another, more recently proposed antecedent to the *Prologue,* the Confession of the Folk from the A-text of *Piers Plowman,* does allow its personifications ample scope for expressing their subjectivity:[9]

> "I haue [ben] coueit[ous]," quaþ [þat caitif], "I [bi]knowe [hit] h[e]re,
> For sum tyme I seruide symme at þe nok
> And was his prentis ypliȝt his profit to loke.
> Ferst I lernide to leiȝe a lef oþer tweiȝe;
> Wykkidly to weiȝe was my ferste lessoun."

Langland's use of Coveitise's directly quoted discourse is extended fur-ther in the B-text, which develops a dialogue between Coveitise and Repentaunce.

> "Repentedestow euere," quod Repentaunce, "or restitucion madest?"
> "ȝis: ones I was yherberwed," quod he, "wiþ an heep of chapmen;
> I roos whan þei were areste and riflede hire males."
> "That was no restitucion," quod Repentaunce, "but a robberis þefte;
> Thow haddest be bettre worþi ben hanged þerfore."
> "I wende riflynge were restitucion for I lerned neuere rede on boke,
> And I kan no frenssh in feiþ but of þe ferþest ende of Northfolk."[10]

---

[7] *The Riverside Chaucer,* gen. ed. Larry D. Benson (Boston: Houghton Mifflin, 1987), p. 798, which cites earlier work tracing this and other influences. I consistently cite this edition of Chaucer's works.

[8] Jerome Mandel, "Other Voices in the 'Canterbury Tales,'" *Criticism* 19 (1977): 338–49, identifies passages in which "Chaucer reveals an attitude not his own in words that are not his own" (p. 341); he does not use the term "free indirect discourse" but is clearly enough interested in something like that phenomenon. While Mandel's early recognition that characters' voices can appear in narrative in different forms and for different purposes is significant, the fact that he finds only three such passages testifies to the limited value of searching for FID in the Prologue.

[9] Helen Cooper, "Langland's and Chaucer's Prologues," *YLS* 1 (1987): 71–81, argues that *Piers* A influenced the shape and content of the *General Prologue.* Her argument focuses on the Prologue to *Piers,* but she also notes that "[T]he third analysis of society in the A text is done on the basis not of profession but of sin, in the confession passus, and this too provides some analogues to the General Prologue" (p. 76).

[10] The first passage quotes George Kane, ed., *Piers Plowman: The A Version: Will's Visions of Piers Plowman and Do-well,* rev. ed. (London: Athlone Press, 1988), Passus V.114–18; the second passage quotes George Kane and E. Talbot Donaldson, eds.,

By allowing Coveitise to speak for himself, Langland points his joke a great deal more sharply, and it is not entirely surprising that his reference to provincial French will find its echo in Chaucer's *Prologue*. Such a dramatized self-presentation, also deeply imbibed in Jean de Meun's continuation of *Le Roman de la Rose,* obviously influenced several of the *Tales* and their prologues in rather straightforward and well-documented ways.[11] But the technique characteristic of the *General Prologue* is far more indirect: the longest explicit quotation from a pilgrim is the Summoner's "Purs is the ercedekenes helle" (I. 658). The *Prologue* chooses very consistently to present a single narrative discourse that blends those pilgrims' voices, and other forms of discourse, into a distinctively hybridized narration.

Because of my primary interest in that process of hybridization, I am not in this essay much concerned with the vexed issue of the pilgrim persona in the *Prologue,* that is, with "a fictional individual to whom the first-person pronouns of the narratorial discourse consistently refer."[12] Despite the familiarity of the cheerful and slightly dim-witted pilgrim character, such a narrator need not be imagined as always present and is demonstrably not present in many parts of the portraits.[13] The critical literature has long recognized two strands in the *Prologue*'s narration, whether the difference is imagined cognitively (as in E. Talbot Donaldson's poet/pilgrim distinction), or temporally (as in present-tense recorder of a past-tense interlocutor with the pilgrims crucial for both David Lawton and H. Marshall Leicester Jr.), or vocationally (as in Barbara Nolan's distinction between clerkly and pilgrim voices).[14] The con-

---

Piers Plowman: The B Version: Will's Vision of Piers Plowman, Do-Well, Do-Better, and Do-Best (London: Athlone Press, 1975), Passus V.230–36.

[11] The debt of the Pardoner's Prologue to Faux Semblant (*Sources and Analogues,* ed. Correale and Hamel, 1:269–77) and of the Wife of Bath's Prologue to La Vieille 2:353–55 and 366–79) indicates clearly enough Chaucer's interest in Jean's technique.

[12] A. C. Spearing, *Textual Subjectivity: The Representation of Subjectivity in Medieval Narratives and Lyrics* (New York: Oxford University Press, 2005), p. 120. Spearing wishes to moderate and reduce invocations of such narrators in medieval texts. He extends the argument of David Lawton, who notes (to different ends) that "a voice of narration is not a narrator-*persona*: it is the index, and prime mover, of a performance." *Chaucer's Narrators* (Cambridge: D. S. Brewer, 1985), p. 101.

[13] This very old argument, traceable back to Bertrand H. Bronson, *In Search of Chaucer* (Toronto: University of Toronto Press, 1960), pp. 3–33, has recently been reinforced in Spearing, "Textual Performance: Chaucerian Prologues and the French *Dit,*" in *Text and Voice: The Rhetoric of Authority in the Middle Ages,* ed. Marianne Børch (Odense: University Press of Southern Denmark, 2004), pp. 21–45.

[14] I cite especially influential discussions of the Prologue's "narrator" from the huge literature: E. Talbot Donaldson, "Chaucer the Pilgrim," 1954; rpt. in *Speaking of Chaucer*

tinuing widespread narratological reliance on Gérard Genette's definition of the narrator as the one "who speaks," emphasizing the narrator's voice and thus (implicitly) the narrator as a character, tends to elide that distinction.[15] To avoid confusion on that account, I follow other theorists who have found a different term for texts that, like the *Prologue*, sometimes present themselves as voiced and sometimes as written, that sometimes come to us personalized and sometimes not. Mieke Bal defines the *narrative agent* as whatever subjectivity "expresses itself in the language that constitutes the text," whether it takes the form of an "external narrator" or a "character-bound" one. Along the same lines, F. K. Stanzel subsumes both "personalized" and "unpersonalized" narrators under the term "narrative agent."[16] Since the central issue through most of this essay is the incorporation by the narrative agent—pilgrim-Chaucer or not—of other forms of discourse, the more general term is appropriate to my argument. In its latter stages, however, I want to consider moments at which identifiable motives shape the process of hybridization. To highlight the ways that such motives personalize the narration, I will at that point have recourse to the more familiar term

---

(New York: W. W. Norton, 1970): 1–12; Lawton, *Chaucer's Narrators*, pp. 99–105; H. Marshall Leicester Jr., "The Art of Impersonation: A General Prologue to the *Canterbury Tales*," *PMLA* 95 (1980): 213–24; Barbara Nolan, "'A Poet Ther Was': Chaucer's Voices in the General Prologue to the *Canterbury Tales*," *PMLA* 101 (1986): 154–69. See also Thomas J. Garbáty, "The Degradation of Chaucer's 'Geffrey,'" *PMLA* 89 (1974): 97–104. Leicester, pp. 217–18, particularly emphasizes the concept of "voice" made an issue by Spearing (see note 36 below).

Spearing's critique of automatic invocations of "the narrator" frequently proceeds by delineating the different kinds of subjectivity encoded within texts: the juxtaposed presence of a seriously textual subjectivity and a comic parody of that poet (often inflected as if for oral performance) is consistent with Spearing's distinction between the subjectivities of a writer of poems and a minstrel performer of them in *Havelok* (*Textual Subjectivity*, pp. 48–67); see also his discussion of Robert Mannyng (pp. 15–17).

[15] Genette, *Narrative Discourse*, p. 186. Jonathan Culler, *Literary Theory: A Very Short Introduction* (New York: Oxford University Press, 1997), pp. 86–90, builds much of his synthetic discussion of narration on the foundation of Genette's two basic questions, *Who speaks?* and *Who sees?* F. K. Stanzel, *A Theory of Narrative*, trans. Charlotte Goedsche (Cambridge: Cambridge University Press, 1984), notes: "The unreliability of the first-person narrator is not, however, based on his personal qualities as a fictional figure, e.g., character, sincerity, love of truth, and so on, but on the ontological basis of the position of the first-person narrator in the world of the narrative" (p. 89).

[16] Mieke Bal, *Narratology: Introduction to the Theory of Narrative*, 2nd ed. (Toronto: University of Toronto Press, 1997), pp. 16–22. Stanzel, *Theory of Narrative*, p. 48. Neither usage is entirely unproblematic: Bal oddly uses "narrator" interchangeably with "narrative agent," while Stanzel includes a third category, called reflectors, in his narrative agent; Genette, *Narrative Discourse Revisited*, pp. 114–22, records various objections to that tripartite system.

narrator, by which I always mean a "personalized" or "character-bound" mode of narration.

In the *Prologue,* then, the narrative agent describes the pilgrims largely by combining within what is formally his own narration other strands of discourse (in principle unlimited and in fact very large in number), of which I am particularly concerned with two: the voices of the pilgrims and the common opinions of his society as expressed in widely practiced and frequently anonymous textual genres, especially estates satire.[17] The tremendous influence of Jill Mann's demonstration that Chaucer used estates material pervasively has lent perhaps too much authority to her frequently reiterated claim, based on the fairly simple narratology available to her in 1973, that Chaucer's merely partial incorporation of material from such texts effectively disabled the sort of moral criticism that estates satire existed to articulate. More recently circulated narratological principles make it easier to recognize that Chaucer made complex use of estates commentary, just as he did with the language of the pilgrims, within a single narrative and for his own purposes.

Most obviously, one might turn to discourse theorists for such analysis. Over the last thirty-five years, however, two tendencies have turned that field in directions likely to prove less useful for medievalists. First, theorists have attended overwhelmingly to narrative strategies for incorporating characters' mental lives, a form of hybridization that is generally agreed to have begun in the nineteenth century and that dominates the modernist novels most often mined for examples.[18] As a result, the incorporation of external textual discourses within narrative has largely been ignored, and—this is the second tendency—an extraordinary amount of energy has gone into the definition of the phenomenon now usually called free indirect discourse (FID), which is, predictably, the modernists' favorite technique for recording their characters' mental lives.[19] Analysts of older discourses will quickly recognize that both the

---

[17] The classic treatment, about which I will have much more comment, is Jill Mann, *Chaucer and Medieval Estates Satire: The Literature of Social Classes and the "General Prologue" to the "Canterbury Tales"* (Cambridge: Cambridge University Press, 1973).

[18] Cohn, *Transparent Minds,* signals her interest in mental phenomena clearly enough in her title. Monika Fludernik, *The Fictions of Language and the Languages of Fiction* (London: Routledge, 1993), demonstrates that "early free indirect discourse examples . . . are almost without exception examples of *speech* representation" (p. 96).

[19] FID occurs when the pronouns, temporal adverbs, and other deictic signals of a character's speech have been reoriented away from an original speaker to match those of the narrative agent. My discussion is largely based on Fludernik, *Fictions of Language,*

definition and the practice of FID have changed over even the last two hundred years.[20] As a result, while Chaucer does occasionally use FID as it is now defined, his practice differs significantly in two ways: he employs what its later history allows us to see as a very narrow subset of FID, and, perhaps in compensation, he employs a wide range of related techniques of hybridization not susceptible to analysis as FID.

Discourse theorists have begun to notice these problems. In her detailed study of FID and other "languages of fiction," Monika Fludernik emphasizes that FID frequently records not the precise language assigned to a character, but a summary of many speeches, a distinctly shaded interpretation of speech, a précis of a more complex speech-act, the sort of speech that might be imputed to a character (rather than an actual speech-act), or the kind of thing that people generally say in a given situation. In these ways it resembles, as Fludernik notes, both direct (quoted) discourse and indirect discourse.[21] The category of "what people usually think" might well enable the analysis of textual discourse within FID structures, but such discussion has remained embryonic. Moreover, Fludernik's recognition of the similarities between FID and other strategies for incorporating a variety of discursive forms leads her to doubt "whether the *form* of free indirect discourse is all that important or whether the attempt to distinguish it from other forms of speech and

---

who cites this example from D. H. Lawrence's *The Rainbow:* "He stayed the afternoon with the girl, and wanted to stay the night. She, however, told him that this was impossible: her own man would be back by dark, and she must be with him." The two clauses after the colon represent the girl's speech, *My own man will be back by dark and I must be with him* (I adopt the asterisk from historical linguistics to indicate a reconstructed utterance, one not recorded in any text but usefully posited to explain the form that does occur in the text).

[20] Richardson, for example, sometimes printed FID within quotation marks (a practice that continued in Austen and later writers). In the second letter of *Clarissa* we read the eponymous heroine's recapitulation of a conversation with her older sibling: "My sister made me a visit there the day after Mr Lovelace had been introduced, and seemed highly pleased with the gentleman. . . . 'So handsome a man!—O her beloved Clary!' (for then she was ready to love me dearly, from the overflowings of her good humor on his account!) 'He was but too handsome a man for *her!*'" (*Clarissa, or the History of a Young Lady*, ed. Angus Ross [Harmondsworth: Penguin, 1985], p. 42). In "Austen, Joyce, O'Brian, and Chaucer's Squire: Bakhtin and Medieval Narratology" (forthcoming in *MedPers* 23 [2008]), I argue in more detail the insufficiency of FID for medieval texts and discuss hybridization in the portrait of the Squire.

[21] Fludernik discusses these topics, summarized to suit my own purposes, in *Fictions of Language*, pp. 398–432. See also Genette's related concept of "pseudo-iteration" in *Narrative Discourse*, pp. 121–23.

thought representation" has been worth the effort scholars have given it.[22]

In contrast, scholars building on the work of Mikhail Bakhtin have been articulating and developing insights about hybridized texts for several years. Bakhtin himself described "pseudo-objective" discourse, a category in which the author's objective narrative suddenly exhibits the "subjective belief system of his characters, or of general opinion" and that, although broader than FID, like it assumes grammatically predictable forms.[23] Gary Saul Morson and Caryl Emerson have extended that principle by describing what they call the "pseudo subjective" statement, a concept readily applied to the description of Criseyde standing in the Trojan temple.

> she let falle
> Hire look a lite aside in swich manere,
> Ascaunces, "What, may I nat stonden here?"[24]

Although it is not difficult to find in the critical literature analysis of Criseyde's "speech" in this scene, the adverb "ascaunces" emphasizes that she remains silent; her words are a narratorial invention, translating her body language into English.[25] That makes it a "pseudo subjective" statement, one describing an attitude perfectly appropriate to a character in language suitable to that character, but never actually spoken because the character knows better (as Criseyde certainly does) than to utter such words aloud: a pseudo-subjective statement thus constructs an indirect diegetic commentary on the character.[26] While Fludernik simply notes that discourse can be used in this way, Bakhtin's approach

---

[22] Fludernik, *Fictions of Language*, p. 79. Genette, *Narrative Discourse*, pp. 171–73, divides narrative discourse into "narratized," "transposed," and "reported" categories, combining ID and FID under "transposed." He does not grant what most readers would, the frequently greater fidelity of FID than ID to the supposed original discourse.

[23] "Discourse in the Novel," in *The Dialogic Imagination*, ed. Michael Holquist, trans. Caryl Emerson and Michael Holquist (Austin: University of Texas Press, 1981), pp. 259–422 (305).

[24] *Troilus and Criseyde* I.290–92.

[25] T. E. Hill, *"She, This in Black": Vision, Truth, and Will in Geoffrey Chaucer's "Troilus and Criseyde"* (New York: Routledge, 2006), pp. 60–61, seems to criticize her word choice.

[26] *Mikhail Bakhtin: Creation of a Prosaics* (Stanford: Stanford University Press, 1990), pp. 335–36. I will discuss Chaucer's use of the technique in the portrait of the Friar, below.

has much more substantially proven its value in analyzing such passages.

Just as Bakhtinian analysis avoids the overemphasis of voice in FID, it also usefully emphasizes the workings of less familiar forms of hybridization. When Helen Phillips recognizes FID in Chaucerian narrative, she confidently explains how it enables a satirical strategy: "The Friar's portrait shows Chaucer's language offering the reader opportunities for moral judgment, without explicit condemnation from the narrative voice. . . . the Free Indirect Discourse . . . captures the Friar's own topsy-turvy values in the disdain for sick lepers."[27] But her response to a different technique of hybridization in the portrait of the Guildsmen differs significantly:

> Wel semed ech of hem a fair burgeys
> To sitten in a yeldehalle on a deys.
> Everich, for the wisdom that he kan,
> Was shaply for to been an alderman.
> For catel hadde they ynogh and rente,
> And eek hir wyves wolde it wel assente.
>
> (369–74)

This time, her reaction is much more tentative: "As often with Chaucer's satire or social comment, we do not know from whose point of view these rich men seem to have the wisdom to be civic leaders." She has some suspicion that "it is the guildsmen's own viewpoint that is being represented and mocked," but only when she is able to adduce some historical evidence will she conclude that this portrait also satirizes the Guildsmen.[28] In other words, because the Guildsmen's portrait does not use the more familiar technique of FID, her recognition and acceptance of a satirical narrative position is more hesitant, and perhaps less complete, than in the case of the Friar. But rather than obscuring the satire, the choice not to employ FID in this passage might be seen as creating interesting repercussions not possible in FID. There is no question that it contains the requisite "discourse of alterity" which signals

[27] Helen Phillips, *An Introduction to the Canterbury Tales: Reading, Fiction, Context* (New York: St Martin's Press, 2000), pp. 41–42.

[28] Phillips, *Introduction to the Canterbury Tales*, p. 33, citing Brian W. Gastle, "Chaucer's 'Shaply' Guildsmen and Mercantile Pretensions," *NM* 99 (1998): 211–16.

some form of hybrid discourse;[29] all readers learn something of the Guildsmen's desires in these lines. But whereas FID (as practiced by Chaucer) would necessarily signal something the Guildsmen *said,* the less determinately hybridized technique used in this portrait usefully requires us to consider whether it represents the Guildsmen's words, their thoughts, or their inarticulate (even subconscious) longings. And the discourse also suggests the desires of the Guildsmen's wives for civic prominence, present in a way no analysis of the "speaker" of those words—and therefore no model of FID—can account for.[30] The wives are not on the pilgrimage, so their ideas cannot be presented directly: but we sense their assent (or is it incitement?) to the social and political advancement of their husbands despite our inability to know whether it was reported by the Guildsmen themselves, or intuited—or invented—by the narrative agent. That kind of meaning is not FID, but, understood as hybrid discourse, it gives pungent narrative pleasure.

Bakhtin developed his ideas about hybrid discourse and the related concept of the character zone in "Discourse in the Novel." Although completed in 1935, that essay (like his succeeding discussions of novelistic discourse) remained unpublished until 1975 and existed only in Russian until 1981;[31] consequently it had no influence on the major developments in discourse theory as it stands today. Yet his work is unquestionably relevant to those theorists even while it stands outside their usual concerns. Fludernik, who published her major study in 1993, never makes Bakhtin's ideas central to her argument, but she stops several times to note how his concepts are "very enlightening" despite a tendency among linguists to apply them too simplistically.[32] For all of

[29] Monika Fludernik argues that FID is defined first by a reader's recognition of a "discourse of alterity" like the one that Phillips's comment evidences, and then by "alignment of 'personal' referential expressions to the deictic center of the reporting discourse" and the absence of a verb plus complement structure. "The Linguistic Illusion of Alterity: The Free Indirect as a Paradigm of Discourse Representation," *Diacritics* 25 (1995): 89–115 (95).

[30] Alfred David, *The Strumpet Muse: Art and Morals in Chaucer's Poetry* (Bloomington: Indiana University Press, 1976), also notices this intrusion: "The Gildsmen's wives take an interest in their husbands' careers for excellent reasons" (p. 65). Lawton, *Chaucer's Narrators,* has also found that classification as FID can unhelpfully obscure "kinship with other narratorial comments" (p. 4).

[31] Katerina Clark and Michael Holquist, *Mikhail Bakhtin* (Cambridge, Mass.: Harvard University Press, 1984), pp. 354–56, provide a good bibliography of Bakhtin's work; it lists "Slovo v romane" as being written in 1934–35 but first published in the collection *Voprosy literatury i èstetiki* from 1975, the year of Bakhtin's death.

[32] *Fictions of Language,* pp. 324–25. Bakhtinians have also been slow in responding to discourse theory: Charles Lock argues that FID was essentially moribund by 1929, thus ignoring the debate ignited by Banfield in 1982, and asserts that " 'dialogic' is Bakhtin's

those reasons, we need to consider Bakhtin's definition of hybrid discourse: "[A] hybrid construction is an utterance that belongs, by its grammatical (syntactic) and compositional markers, to a single speaker, but that actually contains mixed within it two utterances, two speech manners, two styles, two 'languages,' two semantic and axiological belief systems."[33] He establishes the basic function of the technique by analyzing this passage from the opening of Book II, chapter 24 of Dickens's *Little Dorrit:* "That illustrious man and great national ornament, Mr. Merdle, continued his shining course. It began to be widely understood that one who had done society the admirable service *of making so much money out of it,* could not be suffered to remain a commoner" (Bakhtin's italics).[34] No FID occurs in this example; instead, a constructed discourse—the "hypocritically ceremonial common opinion about Merdle"—is suddenly disrupted by an entirely unmarked shift to the register and opinion of the narrative agent.[35] Even without formal designation of a new speaker, that language obviously clashes with the sense of the original and, with its increased specificity and directness, radically shifts the style. The passage provides a subtle, complex satire: hardly deigning to impugn Merdle, whose values are so obviously at odds with those of the agent that saying so would be otiose, the satire

word and radically altered concept for what had been termed by Vološinov quasi-direct speech" (p. 85); he thus ignores the more specific and relevant terms from "Discourse in the Novel": double-voiced and hybrid discourse. "Double Voicing, Sharing Words: Bakhtin's Dialogism and the History of Free Indirect Discourse," in *The Novelness of Bakhtin: Perspectives and Possibilities,* ed. Jørgen Bruhn and Jan Lundquist (Copenhagen: Museum Tusculanum Press, 2001), pp. 71–87 (85).

[33] "Discourse in the Novel," p. 304. The discussion of hybrid constructions is central to this essay, occupying pp. 301–20; Bakhtin's examples of hybrid discourse range chronologically from Rabelais to Dickens and include Pushkin, like Chaucer a writer of verse narrative.

[34] "Discourse in the Novel," p. 306. I have used the text of Dickens in the form presented by Bakhtin. My analysis extends Bakhtin's comments on the passage.

[35] Ibid., p. 306. Bal, *Narratology,* pp. 31–34, identifies a special category ("Non-Narrative Comments") for what she calls "argumentative" statements within a narrative, emphasizing the ideological work they perform (32). Her dubious attitude toward such work is a recent phenomenon; such statements appear frequently in epic as a generically overt and appropriate invocation of social norms, as in "þæt wæs gōd cyning!" (*Beowulf* 11b). It is no surprise, then, that theorists of genre, especially those grounded in epic, respond more generously and effectively to the expression of widely shared social attitudes: see Georg Lukács, *Theory of the Novel,* trans. Anna Bostock (Cambridge, Mass.: MIT Press, 1971), p. 66; Walter Benjamin, "The Storyteller," in *Illuminations,* trans. Harry Zahn (New York: Schocken Books, 1969), p. 87; and Bakhtin, "Epic and Novel," in *The Dialogic Imagination,* p. 35. As Bakhtin's examples help to show, much of what Spearing demonstrates in medieval narrative is much more widely true.

reaches out to those obsequious strata of society whose language has blinded them to Merdle's selfishness. The relevance of such analysis to the *General Prologue* is striking: sudden shifts in the way we imagine the narrating voice, complex ironies and satires whose main target is not overtly castigated at all and which allow for criticism of various parties to the flaws under discussion—all of these are also part of Chaucer's new art. Recognizing how much "the ceremonial language of official pronouncements" has contributed to the mocked opinion about Merdle, moreover, Bakhtin suggests how the analysis of hybrid discourse can readily account for such social and textual influences in the *Prologue*.[36]

In addition, hybrid discourse is interested in the gradual instantiation or partial presence of a hybridized discourse within the narrative. Bakhtin's central insight—"The word in language is half someone else's"— highlights an awareness that all language is borrowed; all language is shared.[37] His principle of the "character zone," which might more generally be called the "discourse zone," helps to explain how that borrowing and sharing works, presenting partial expressions of the "specific points of view on the world" articulated by different characters or different social groups.[38] Bakhtin defines a character zone as a "sphere of influence on the authorial context surrounding [a character], a sphere

[36] "Discourse in the Novel," p. 306. Spearing, *Textual Subjectivity,* p. 10 n. 9, argues that Bakhtinian approaches have encouraged an obsession with voice rather than writing in our reading of medieval texts that "has been almost entirely harmful." Here I argue that the problem is neither specific to nor ineradicable from Bakhtinian approaches, but I concur that many extant Bakhtinian readings use his terms, including voice, in too freely metaphoric a manner. Fludernik, *Fictions of Language,* seems to agree, arguing that "stylistic interaction between the narrative and the reported discourse can no longer be discussed without reference to Bakhtin's dialogic principle, a concept that has suffered much critical sleight of hand" (p. 7). Lawton, *Chaucer's Narrators,* sees that Bakhtin could contribute to "a modern reading of Chaucer's narratorial voices" (p. 2); for Lawton, however, Bakhtin's key term is *heteroglossia,* problematically used by Bakhtin to describe both an irreducible fact of language and two different narrative techniques developed along with the novel. I have addressed Bakhtin's multiplicity of terms in "Bakhtin, Liminality, and Medieval Literature," in *Bakhtin and Medieval Voices,* ed. Thomas J. Farrell (Gainesville: University Press of Florida, 1996), pp. 2–4.

[37] "Discourse in the Novel," p. 293.

[38] Ibid., p. 291. For Bakhtin, language always carries values and ideology: In *Problems of Dostoevsky's Poetics,* ed. and trans. Caryl Emerson (Minneapolis: University of Minnesota Press, 1984), p. 88, he argues that "human thought becomes genuine thought, that is, an idea, only under conditions of living contact with another and alien thought, a thought embodied in someone else's voice, that is, in someone else's consciousness expressed in discourse." See also the discussion in Jørgen Bruhn and Jan Lundquist, "Introduction: A Novelness of Bakhtin?" in *The Novelness of Bakhtin,* ed. Bruhn and Lundquist, pp. 11–50, esp. p. 34.

that extends—and often quite far—beyond the boundaries of the direct discourse allotted to him."[39] To the extent that that influence is present, the narrative will be nudged away from the values concomitant with its usual linguistic register: wholly, or not at all, or anywhere in between. Since (as in FID) neither formal or any other markers distinguish hybridized narration, we cannot identify exactly where one ends and another begins without analysis. As Morson and Emerson explain, "In essence, 'quotation marks' are a matter of degree"—a truth even more potent in medieval texts that had not yet begun to use modern punctuation practices.[40] And, crucially, those different discourse zones do not all possess equal importance:

> The language of the prose writer deploys itself according to degrees of greater or lesser proximity to the author and to his ultimate semantic instantiation: certain aspects of language directly and unmediatedly express (as in poetry) the semantic and expressive intentions of the author, others refract these intentions; the writer of prose does not meld completely with any of these words, but rather accents each of them in a particular way—humorously, ironically, parodically and so forth; yet another group may stand even further from the author's ultimate semantic instantiation, still more thoroughly refracting his intentions; and there are, finally, those words that are completely denied any authorial intentions: the author does not express *himself* in them (as the author of the word)—rather, he *exhibits* them as a unique speech-thing, they function for him as something completely reified.[41]

Bakhtin would argue that, in the full novelistic tradition which is his principal concern, the point of hybrid discourse is usually comic deflation of language that pretends to self-sufficiency.[42] But even in prenovelistic texts, hybrid discourse typically effects a kind of deflation quite unlike the denunciations typical of medieval genres that rely on direct criticism, like estates satire. First, although such indirect attacks eliminate a certain characteristic vitriol, criticism is by no means ne-

[39] "Discourse in the Novel," p. 320.
[40] *Mikhail Bakhtin,* p. 326. On the ambiguity in medieval manuscripts between different forms of discourse, see Howell Chickering, "Unpunctuating Chaucer," *ChauR* 25 (1990): 96–109, esp. 97–99.
[41] "Discourse in the Novel," p. 299. Bakhtin's word "prose" here is a synonym for what he elsewhere and more accurately calls "novelistic discourse," a concept not dependent on formatting on the page.
[42] See the key insight in "From the Prehistory of Novelistic Discourse," in *The Dialogic Imagination,* p. 49, that "novelistic discourse is always criticizing itself."

gated. Second, since the narrator's whole performance will articulate a system of values constantly available for the reader's comparison, some figures may (like Merdle) be spared any explicit condemnation without suggesting in any way that their behavior is acceptable.[43] Third, passages employing hybrid discourse are likely to identify multiple targets who must share in the criticism offered: the reader is implicitly invited to consider how various, perhaps unsuspected entities may have contributed to society's sorry state, and is given a fair amount of latitude to distribute blame among them.

The effects of hybrid discourse understood in these terms are quite clear: "Thus a prose writer can distance himself from the language of his own work, while at the same time distancing himself, in varying degrees, from the different layers and aspects of his work. He can make use of language without wholly giving himself up to it, he may treat it as semi-alien or completely alien to himself, while compelling language ultimately to serve all his own intentions."[44] Language used in that manner, while borrowed from and shared with its original speaker or generic form, no longer belongs to its original context: once hybridized, its primary meaning becomes its meaning within the writer's intention.[45] Hybrid discourse—a strategy for refracting the intentionality of an extant discourse to a different, authorial intention—thus leads us away from a conundrum created by our most sophisticated scholars and theorists, who have asserted repeatedly—but without noticeable effect on the reading habits of most Chaucerians—that the presence of the Monk's voice, or the absence of an explicit narrative condemnation of the Physician's behavior, radically reduces or eliminates the possibility

---

[43] Chaucerians have long recognized how "the narrator's whole performance will articulate a system of values." A good recent example may be found in Alcuin Blamires, "Chaucer the Reactionary: Ideology and the General Prologue to the *Canterbury Tales, RES* 51 (2000): 523–39.

[44] "Discourse in the Novel," p. 299. Many critics, invoking Bakhtin and specifically the concept of *dialogue* primarily as manifestations of poststructuralist thought working against discursive authority, minimize this strain in Bakhtin's analysis. Yet a recognition that authors privilege language they more fully agree with must be the starting point for any ideological analysis of texts. Bakhtin's treatment of Dickens demonstrates that a satirical purpose requires either the direct presentation of authorial ideas or an authorially approved narrative subjectivity.

[45] Fludernik, *Fictions of Language,* explicitly endorses the Bakhtinian notion that premodern fiction "juxtaposed a univocal author's voice (which united in itself the positions of authorial omniscience, omnipresence, and reliable evaluation of the story world) with the characters' utterances as 'reported' direct speech, subordinating the alterity of figural language to its own mastery of and by the narrative discourse" (331).

of moral judgment of such characters.[46] Our most learned models for reading the *Prologue* are willing to suggest that when the narrator tells us that he approved the Monk's opinions, those opinions acquire a certain irreducible validity, because "the speaker's amused enjoyment of the Monk's forthright humanity is too patent to let us see him as just a moralist."[47] Or they tell us that if Chaucer does not itemize "the high cost of the drugs, or their ineffectiveness," then "the patient's benefit is not in question" and we have "no *evidence* that the doctor is a grasping charlatan" and must not imagine that the portrait satirizes him.[48] I will argue on the contrary that, because they are part of a recognizable narratological strategy, the ideas borrowed from the pilgrims' voices and the estates tradition must be evaluated within that strategy. A pilgrim's self-understanding is not a sufficient basis for judgment; nor does an incomplete evocation of estates commentary create an insufficient basis for judgment. Instead, I will suggest, the narrative strategy in which a character's idiosyncratic values or society's typical judgments are presented will usually provide a reliable guide to the significance that those discourses possess within the portrait. And the exceptions, discussed separately, will be cases in which the narrative agent's strategy becomes, for one reason or another, incoherent.

The Role of Character Voices

To address the most important issues in the analysis of the *Prologue*'s language, it will be convenient to discuss separately the hybridization of

[46] On February 8, 2005, I asked the online Chaucer discussion group (Chaucer@lists erv.uic.edu) how critically the *Prologue* treats the Monk; proposed answers ranged from "Not at all" to "Utterly." The admittedly self-selecting respondents confirmed the results of less formal questions asked at conferences over several years: something like 80 percent read the portrait as either entirely or heavily critical of the Monk.

[47] Leicester, "Art of Impersonation," p. 220. Maria K. Greenwood, "What He Heard and What He Saw: Past Tenses and Characterization in Chaucer's 'General Prologue,'" *L'articulation Langue—Littérature dans les Textes Médiévaux Anglais* (Nancy: AMAES, 1999), pp. 161–62, claims: "A Monk ther **was**, a fair for the maistrie, / An outridere, that **lovede** venerie" (her emphasis) uses two distinct versions of the simple past tense that allow us to recognize "Free Indirect Speech" in the second clause and that the Monk and the Friar "create an atmosphere of jolly fellowship by their frank worldliness." While the second claim illustrates my argument that acceptance of and attention to a pilgrim's voice has encouraged (excessive) tolerance, the first claim is very dubious on several grounds.

[48] Mann, *Chaucer and Medieval Estates Satire,* pp. 96, 98. I will discuss below the difficulty of quoting Mann in a way that is entirely fair to her argument and her genuine recognition of criticism of the pilgrims. The point I wish to isolate is her inappropriate insistence that prosecutorial incompetence by the narrator requires that we acquit the Physician on charges of colluding with the pharmacist to bilk his patients.

character voices and of textual materials, choosing exemplary portraits in which each of those strategies is dominant. My selections are heuristic rather than absolute of course, useful ways of organizing my analysis rather than distinct categories of portraits that appear in the *Prologue*. My discussions of them will inevitably overlap to some degree, but they allow for recognition of the *Prologue*'s strategies in distinctive terms.

As the first obvious example of incorporating a pilgrim's voice, as a particularly pointed one, and as a regular touchstone in critical discussion, the portrait of the Monk is a good place to begin:

> The reule of Seint Maure or of Seint Beneit—
> By cause that it was old and somdel streit
> This ilke Monk leet olde thynges pace,
> And heeld after the newe world the space.
> He yaf nat of that text a pulled hen,
> That seith that hunters ben nat hooly men,
> Ne that a monk, whan he is recchelees,
> Is likned til a fissh that is waterlees—
> This is to seyn, a monk out of his cloystre.
> But thilke text heeld he nat worth an oystre;
> And I seyde his opinion was good.
>
> (173–83)

The anacoluthon in lines 173–75 signals, at least in retrospect, a transition from the narrative description of the Monk out riding to the Monk's own analysis of his vocation. The shifting tenses and illocutionary verbs may lead us to suspect the presence of FID, but it is the unmistakable response to another speaker in line 183 that ultimately forces our recognition that we have been reading the Monk's opinion rather than any sort of narrative judgment. The claim that the Monk's just-cited opinion is "good" has energized many interpretive discussions of the narrator, from the critic who finds that line 183 "certainly means that [Chaucer] thinks it was bad," to the one who believes that "it discloses traditional ideology as made anachronistic by the practices and new language of thriving Christian institutions in 'the newe world.'"[49]

---

[49] I have quoted from, respectively, John V. Fleming, "Gospel Asceticism: Some Chaucerian Images of Perfection," in *Chaucer and Scriptural Tradition,* ed. David Lyle Jeffrey ([Ottawa]: University of Ottawa Press, 1984), pp. 190–91, and David Aers, *Chaucer* (Atlantic Highlands, N.J.: Humanities Press International, 1986), p. 18.

The disconnect between such irreconcilable opinions suggests that "I seyde his opinion was good" is less important as a verdict on the Monk than as a clear delineation for readers that the narrative agent has ceded control of the discourse to the Monk's character zone, and that we must therefore begin (or already have begun) to read the text differently. The next few lines, perhaps (to anticipate a point I will argue more fully in a moment) developing into FID, further encourage that tendency:

> What sholde he studie and make hymselven wood,
> Upon a book in cloystre alwey to poure,
> Or swynken with his handes, and laboure,
> As Austyn bit? How shal the world be served?
> Lat Austyn have his swynk to hym reserved!
>
> (184–88)

The injunction about Augustine provides no more certain information about the opinion of the narrative agent than "I seyde his opinion was good" did; it, too, most urgently invites readers' analysis of the Monk's ideas. And when the Monk's thoroughly hybrid discourse is recognized, it becomes susceptible to a direct, holistic evaluation within the *Prologue*'s discourse. Regardless of the relevance of old principles to the monasticism of the fourteenth century, his argument implodes. Whether or not serving the world had become a legitimate goal, his evident unwillingness either to study or to labor constitutes his calculation of how the world can serve him.

Having recognized the Monk's voice and the narrative treatment of it, we are more prepared for the Friar's portrait, which, while it signals the presence of the pilgrim's own words more clearly than any other, also embodies the fullest and subtlest range of strategies for incorporating the pilgrim's voice in the narrator's description:

> For he hadde power of confessioun,
> As seyde hymself, moore than a curat,
> For of his ordre he was licenciat.
>
> (218–20)

Critics have been quick to reconstruct from this free indirect discourse the hypothetical quotation lying behind it, *viz.* the Friar's comment to Geoffrey that **I have more power of confession than a curate, since I am licensed* *by my order*. But other hybrid forms in this portrait have not been treated as fully. David Burnley is one of a few scholars reading a later tense shift as another signal of the Friar's proper voice:[50]

> For unto swich a worthy man as he
> Acorded nat, as by his facultee,
> To have with sike lazars aqueyntaunce.
> It is nat honest, it may nat avaunce,
> For to deelen with no swich poraille.
>
> (243–47)

The present tense of "is" and "may" (246), alongside the ring of self-justification in "honest" and "avaunce," the dismissive "poraille," and the greater rhetorical relevance of the last two lines to the Friar (the narrative agent has little reason to make such a comment) contribute to our sense that we are overhearing the Friar's self-understanding in these lines. But the specifically hybrid nature of these constructions and the difficulty of analyzing them as FID can be glimpsed by asking how much of the preceding sentence is the Friar's.[51] Specifically, how about the phrase "as by his facultee," which occurs before the tense shift and has long been a bit of a puzzle to editors and scholars? It is credible either as something the Friar might have said himself or as exactly the sort of corroborative detail that the narrative agent might borrow from familiar textual discourse about friars. Moreover, the different available senses of the word "facultee" encourage quite different responses. If it is taken to mean "a field of knowledge or experience," the passage is hybridized by the Friar's voice: his experience (he explains) has taught him the inappropriateness of associating with sick lepers. In that case, the narrative agent's other uses of hybrid discourse encourage us to read the whole passage from 243–47 as a bitingly ironic indictment of him. But if we read "facultee" in a different sense, as a "power [or] ability," then perhaps the narrative agent places the Friar above the lepers in order to

---

[50] *A Guide to Chaucer's Language* (Norman: University of Oklahoma Press, 1983), p. 50. See Fludernik, *Fictions of Language,* p. 194 and note 55 below. Simon Horobin, *Chaucer's Language* (New York: Palgrave Macmillan, 2007), does not address such structures.

[51] Owen, "Development of the Art," p. 124, also addresses this question, but not in detail.

explain the unsuitability of his involvement with them.[52] That reading more or less creates the pilgrim persona in the passage—"worthy" is a frequently cited marker of that character's vocabulary—and the satire is somewhat muted. Thus, the genuine ambiguity of "facultee" is an effective strategy for creating a hybrid discourse that blurs our understanding of who is speaking. Both of those readings seem viable to me, although I suspect that the more carefully we consider the passage, the more of the Friar's voice we are likely to hear. But in that process, the possibility of exaggeration—of believing all of these ideas to be the Friar's beyond what we can effectively demonstrate—always remains. (I will return to a narrative willingness to have us overevaluate in my discussion of the Prioress, below.)

If passages like the one about his "facultee" urge caution in recognizing the Friar's discourse, others demonstrate that the Friar's subjectivity may be detected even when there are no overt signs that he is speaking or has spoken:

> In love-dayes ther koude he muchel help,
> For ther he was nat lyk a cloysterer
> With a thredbare cope, as is a povre scoler,
> But he was lyk a maister or a pope.
> Of double worstede was his semycope,
> That rounded as a belle out of the presse.
>
> (258–63)

There are no obvious markers of indirect or free indirect discourse; nor is there unusual vocabulary, most easily explained as part of the Friar's personal idiom or professional expertise, that signaled hybrid discourse in "It is nat honest." No one has suggested an original **I am like a master or a pope* comment from the Friar. But there is also no obvious reason for the narrative agent to concern himself with the Friar's participation in "love-dayes"; that extrajudicial system of conflict resolution in the later fourteenth-century forms no part of typical commentary on friars.[53] As a result, the remarkable series of five comparisons for the

---

[52] See *Middle English Dictionary,* "faculte" n. 2a and 1, respectively. The word can also mean "possessions" (n. 3), a sense that may seem more appropriate in the mouth of the pilgrim persona, but that nevertheless inescapably condemns a character sworn to poverty.

[53] John Webster Spargo, "Chaucer's Love-Days," *Speculum* 15 (1940): 36–56, and Josephine Waters Bennett, "The Mediaeval Loveday," *Speculum* 33 (1958): 351–70, cite negative and positive (respectively) connotations of the love day. Mann, p. 42, discusses the line entirely in terms of the Friar's possible sexual adventures.

Friar and his garment—rounded like a bell, it makes him look like a master or a pope, but unlike a cloisterer or a poor scholar—again suggests the possible presence of the Friar's character zone. As presented, the rhetoric is suspiciously awkward for the narrative agent, who has little reason to provide both positive and negative counterexamples to the Friar's dress. But, unlike the narrator, the Friar has good reasons for making, if only mentally, these comparisons. It is well within the Friar's purpose to cement his importance by contrasting his sumptuous clothing with that of "a cloysterer / With a thredbare cope." Unfortunately for him, that purpose is frustrated when the comparison reminds attentive readers and (above all) the Friar himself that both our overall impression of the Monk in the present company and the one detail of his clothing we are given—"his sleves purfiled" (193)—indicates that he is also rather splendidly dressed.[54] The Friar's first attempt to point out his superiority therefore points to an absence, and so he points again, more successfully, to "a povre scholer." Within some thirty lines readers will recognize that the Clerk provides the best possible example of inferiority to the Friar—at least in the Friar's terms—since "Ful thredbare was his overeste courtepy" (290). The more we are willing to hear this passage as hybrid discourse—as a representation not of the Friar's voice, but of his subjectivity—the more sense this part of the portrait will make.

Most complex of all, however, is a passage that we encounter immediately after learning about the Friar's self-proclaimedly superlative power as a confessor:

> Ful swetely herde he confessioun,
> And plesaunt was his absolucioun
> He was an esy man to yeve penaunce,
> Ther as he wiste to have a good pitaunce.
> For unto a povre ordre for to yive
> Is signe that a man is wel yshryve;
> For if he yaf, he dorste make avaunt,
> He wiste that a man was repentaunt.
>
> (221–28)

---

[54] Laura F. Hodges, "A Reconsideration of the Monk's Costume," *ChauR* 26 (1991): 133–46, incorporated as pp. 112–32 of her *Chaucer and Clothing: Clerical and Academic Costume in the General Prologue to the Canterbury Tales,* Chaucer Studies 34 (Woodbridge, Suffolk: D. S. Brewer, 2005).

Spearing argues that the sentence in lines 227–28 is (using Banfield's term) "unspeakable," and therefore that it can only be a representation of the Friar's speech or thought: *I dare say that a man who makes a donation is repentant.*[55] This is a live possibility, but others also exist. It is certainly the Friar who dares, but who *tells* us that he dares? Perhaps the Friar, but the narrative agent also might so label the Friar's simpler statement that *I know that a man is repentant if he gives.*

That ambivalence prepares us for other difficulties in this passage. Although the couplet form combines with the markers of hybrid discourse to suggest the presence in 227–28 of the Friar's own words in some form, we are forced by the logical connections between them and the comments that surround them to recognize that those words are in fact part of a larger speech act whose boundaries are much less clear. The Friar's words, we will find, insinuate themselves gradually into and remove themselves gradually from the narrator's own language. To be more precise, the Friar's comments about those who give act as a gloss on, an expansion or explanation of, the preceding two lines, which are also, to some (perhaps lesser) extent, his words: *A gift to an order sworn to poverty is a sign of a good confession*—and therefore, *A man who does give must be repentant.* The first two lines articulate a principle that underlies the conclusion the Friar draws explicitly in 227–28. Two grammatical facts support this reading: the first "he" in line 227 arises from the antecedent "a man" in line 226, and the preterite form "yaf" in line 227 makes sense only as a reification of the hypothetical infinitive "to yive" of line 225.

The grammatical siphon, however, does not stop there. If we attribute the idea that *A gift to an order sworn to poverty is a sign of a good confession* to the Friar because we know that he made the following comment, which exists to explain that first one, then we must also find some means of explaining the causal "For" that begins line 225: the statement about signs of a good confession is itself concatenated onto the earlier

---

[55] "Textual Performance," pp. 35–36; see Ann Banfield, *Unspeakable Sentences: Narration and Representation in the Language of Fiction* (Boston: Routledge and Kegan Paul, 1982). Spearing (p. 36) accepts the proposition that "the Friar's own views, and probably . . . his very words" are present in lines 225–28 (i.e., somewhat more of the passage than I am confident about). On the basis of verb tenses, Fludernik, *Fictions of Language,* p. 194, considers the whole passage from lines 225–32 and 243–47 to be either FID or possibly, in line 246, direct quotation. She does not consider the plausibility of the Friar articulating such ideas in either passage. Mandel, "Other Voices," pp. 342–43, attributes lines 225–32 to the Friar.

articulation of the Friar's ready willingness to give penance to a deep pocket. Rhetorically this hypothesis works fine: the ideas in these three couplets are quite coherent:

1. he was a lenient confessor when he expected a donation—
2. because a donation to the friars is a sign of a good confession—
3. because, since he did give, that man must have been repentant.

But while I have shown that (3) must represent something close to the Friar's words, and while it is certainly a useful hypothesis that (2) is at least a paraphrase of something he said, it is more than a bit of a stretch to imagine the Friar articulating anything that could readily be turned into (1): he is very unlikely to blurt out that *I am a lenient confessor when I can see a big contribution in the offing.* The Friar is, after all, not the Pardoner: such brazenness is not his style. Or, as Morson and Emerson explain the effect of pseudo-subjective discourse, "The author discovers that hypocrisy for him."[56] That is, the discussion of the Friar's willingness to give penance belongs to the same rhetorical register as the preceding couplet, in which references to his "swetely herde" confession and "plesaunt" absolution may be understood as the narrative agent's determination to invoke fourteenth-century stereotypes holding that friars were notable for an "eagerness to make money from hearing confessions."[57] The process of incorporating the Friar's voice proves so unobtrusive as to remain almost unmarked until an explicit statement— "he dorste make avaunt"—forces us to recognize its presence, developed imperceptibly from the narrative agent's analysis through words that become first some form of paraphrase and ultimately a close representation of the Friar's words.

And the same thing happens on the other side of the originally marked lines.

> For if he yaf, he dorste make avaunt,
> He wiste that a man was repentaunt;
> For many a man so hard is of his herte,
> He may nat wepe, althogh hym soore smerte.

[56] See note 26 above. Chaucer dis-covers the Friar's hypocritical understanding of Penance by connecting his words and practices in ways that he would not do himself.
[57] Mann, *Chaucer and Medieval Estates Satire,* pp. 47–48, lists several examples of this topos.

>   Therfore in stede of wepynge and preyeres
>   Men moote yeve silver to the povre freres.
>   (227–32)

How much of that passage may we attribute to the Friar? The first two lines are, as we have seen, inescapably his in some terms. And we meet at the beginning of the last two couplets more direct logical connectors—"For . . . Therfore"—implying that what follows depends on what we have just read, and therefore implying some sort of connectedness with what we know that the Friar has said.[58] But the echo of biblical injunctions against hardening one's heart reveals the author here again gradually "dis-covering" the Friar's hypocrisy, firmly connecting what he actually said to the anticlimactic identification of "silver" as the appropriate substitute for weeping and prayers that concludes the passage.[59]

Hybrid discourse, then, marks the portrait of the Friar in several ways. Sometimes we hear the Friar's voice; at other times, only his character zone is invoked. As a result, the description of the Friar consistently blends what the character actually said with a narrative determination to ravel those ideas out to their logical conclusions. We read what the Friar said, and the conclusions deduced from or imputed to those beliefs, in a grammatical construction that identifies both of those discursive polarities clearly enough, but takes great pains to blur the boundary lines between them. As a result, the Friar's voice is made to contribute to a narrative statement about the Friar's excesses.

My interpretation of the Monk and Friar is not new, but its reliance on an analysis of the pilgrims' voices in the portraits to develop that satirical conclusion varies somewhat from prominent extant treatments of voice like Leicester's. He attends primarily to the Monk, agreeing "with most critics" that the Monk "is being half-quoted, that we hear his style, for example, in the turn of a phrase like 'nat worth an oystre!' " and that the Monk is satirized and criticized. But his emphasis falls elsewhere: "A sense of the positive claims made by the pilgrim's vitality, his "manliness," is also registered by the portrait. . . . The tensions among

---

[58] Spearing, *Textual Subjectivity,* notes of *The Man of Law's Tale* that the connective *For* "does not indicate mere sequence but purports to offer an explanation, and this constitutes yet another blurring of the distinction between story and storyteller" (pp. 129–30).

[59] Mann, *Chaucer and Medieval Estates Satire,* p. 49. See Psalm 95.8–9: "hodie si vocem eius audieritis nolite indurare corda vestra / Sicut in irritatione secundum diem tentationis in deserto ubi temptaverunt me patres vestri."

social, moral, and existential worlds are embodied in a single voice here, and they are embodied precisely *as tensions,* not as a resolution or a synthesis, for we cannot tell exactly what the speaker thinks either of the Monk or of conventional morality."[60] It is with the proposition that the presence of a single voice reduces all included ideas to dialectic tensions that I take issue: in hybrid discourse, such tensions are neither wholly equivocal nor necessarily irresolvable.[61] In a separate article, Leicester expresses a similar agnosticism about the Friar: "We can suspect all kinds of typical Mendicant vices, but we cannot prove them."[62] Perhaps not, but Chaucer's strategies are intended as poetic, not legal ones. The narrative agent, subtly hybridizing the Friar's words into a damning context, consistently undercuts any excuses for his behavior:

> And over al, ther as profit sholde arise,
> Curteis he was and lowely of servyse.
>
> (249–50)

[60] Leicester, "Art of Impersonation," p. 220.

[61] Mann, *Chaucer and Medieval Estates Satire,* also argues that the "method" of the Prologue "is not additive, but dialectic" (p. 190). But a Bakhtinian approach must disagree about the fundamental nature of the text. Matthew Roberts explains why readings based on dialogue are incompatible with those based on dialectic. "Poetics Hermeneutics Dialogics: Bakhtin and Paul de Man," in *Rethinking Bakhtin: Extensions and Challenges,* ed. Gary Saul Morson and Caryl Emerson (Evanston: Northwestern University Press, 1989), pp. 115–34 (responding to Paul de Man, "Dialogue and Dialogism," reprinted in the same volume, pp. 105–14). See also Morson and Emerson, *Mikhail Bakhtin,* p. 325.

A parallel issue arises in discourse theory: In *Unspeakable Sentences,* Ann Banfield sparked a sharp debate by insisting that the phenomenon she calls Represented Speech and Thought (somewhat narrower than FID) contains only one voice; passages from Bakhtin like the one I cite in note 44 above could be adduced in support of this idea. Brian McHale, "Unspeakable Sentences, Unnatural Acts: Linguistics and Poetics Revisited," *Poetics Today* 4 (1983): 17–45, rebuts this claim, arguing for the simultaneous presence of multiple voices in a text (pp. 35–37); he might use the passage cited in note 33 above to buttress that argument. The nondialectical nature of dialogism appears in the recognition that Bakhtin sees both one voice and two voices in hybrid discourse, and that the autonomy of a character's voice within the narration is often inversely proportional to the value allowed it.

[62] H. Marshall Leicester Jr., "'No Vileyns Word': Social Context and Performance in Chaucer's *Friar's Tale,*" *ChauR* 17 (1982): 21–39 (21). Leicester further approves Mann's verdict that "it is the constant use of ambivalent words which make it hard to subject the Friar to moral analysis." Mann's discussion of the Friar (*Chaucer and Medieval Estates Satire,* p. 49) provides a useful reminder that *Le Roman de la Rose*'s portrait of Faus Semblant lurks not far beneath the surface of this portrait. The presence of that indisputably satiric text, more relevant to the next section of my essay, also contributes to the strongly condemnatory tone of the portrait; Malcolm Andrew, *The Variorum Edition of the Works of Geoffrey Chaucer, Volume II, Part One B, The General Prologue: Explanatory Notes* (Norman: University of Oklahoma Press, 1993), pp. 217–21, records a consistent

Anyone who sees that profit is not the proper end of courtesy or humility gets the point: the Friar is in no way an admirable or even likable character, and Leicester (like everyone else) recognizes his deficiencies clearly.[63] To say so much is to acknowledge that, in the end, the Friar's self-analysis does not articulate meaningfully separate criteria for evaluation; within hybrid discourse, separate criteria are always inherently unequal. The narrative strategy reinserts the Friar into a social order that radically devalues his protestations.

Hybridizing Textual Discourse

Because the medieval textual discourses employed in the *Prologue* are diverse, and because the pilgrims stand in strikingly different relationships to the comments made about them by such texts, the uses to which those discourses are put vary significantly.[64] In this discussion, however, I will concentrate on the *Prologue*'s incorporation of estates satire, which appears more consistently than any other textual tradition, and which has, in the wake of Mann's famous argument about "Chaucer's *consistent removal of the possibility of moral judgement*" from the *Prologue*, influenced ensuing commentary most strongly.[65]

Mann's thesis is a good deal more subtle than that one comment might suggest: she achieves nuance by consistently shading such forthright claims with contrastive or less emphatic statements elsewhere. As a result, it can be difficult to quote her position with complete fairness. My primary concern is with the ensuing critical climate, one that postulates that the *Prologue* "is, as Jill Mann demonstrated conclusively a few years ago, an estates satire," but one that, repeatedly neglecting significant parts of its generic mission, becomes unable to articulate effective satire.[66] One cannot argue with Mann's evidence about Chaucer's debt

---

critical emphasis on the Friar's hypocrisy. Throughout this article, I am greatly indebted to Andrew's extraordinarily complete and judicious discussions.

[63] "It is clear that by the fourteenth century many friars enjoyed, and society sanctioned, the worldly eminence their profession gave them without paying much attention to its ostensible spiritual justification" (Leicester, " 'No Vileyns Word,' " p. 29). Again, "It is one thing to understand the Friar, it is another to like him" (p. 37).

[64] Ann W. Astell, "The *Translatio* of Chaucer's Pardoner," *Exemplaria* 4 (1992): 411–28, has demonstrated the dependence of the Old Man in *The Pardoner's Tale* on literary representations of Avarice. See esp. pp. 416–19.

[65] Mann, *Chaucer and Medieval Estates Satire*, p. 197.

[66] I quote H. Marshall Leicester Jr., "Structure as Deconstruction: 'Chaucer and Estates Satire' in the General Prologue, or Reading Chaucer as a Prologue to the History of Disenchantment," *Exemplaria* 2 (1990): 241–61 (246). Cooper, "Langland's and Chaucer's Prologues," p. 71, also considers Chaucer's Prologue to be "based on estates satire," and so discusses what is included in the portraits more than how it is included.

to the tradition—I will cite it at several points—but I want to argue that Chaucer's experiments with the use of borrowed language have reconfigured the possibility of moral judgment, not removed it. In the first two, relatively simple portraits discussed below, estates material appears not on its own terms but as part of a sophisticated and variable strategy of hybridization that rewards close examination. The social attitudes invoked in them do not "remove" moral judgment but reflect it in a variety of ways and in conjunction with a variety of alternative scales of evaluation.

The Parson is frequently read as an ideal figure constructed by the superimposition of a large red universal "Not" symbol on top of a straightforward list of pastoral abuses borrowed directly from the estates tradition. Significant articles have been written about that portrait's reliance on binary structures like the repeated "not / but" rhetoric it employs.[67] As a result, the Parson emerges as a paragon, along with his brother the Plowman by now the sole surviving members of the class of "ideal" pilgrims for some readers. The current consensus also reads the Parson as shaped by estates material, whose negative verdict on the clergy is consistently and unambiguously denied in the portrait. I find the portrait similarly unambiguous but less univocal: the usual concerns of estates discourse only become crucial relatively late in the portrait, and they are not the only constituent of the portrait's structure: the Parson's own voice certainly echoes as well. My interest continues to lie in the ways that the narrative agent employs various "discourses of alterity" to find, develop, and articulate his responses to and verdicts on the pilgrims he creates.

The third line of the portrait, "But riche he was of hooly thoght and werk" (479) delineates for the first time the Parson's combination of the mental and physical aspects of his vocation. Returns of that motif will demarcate three distinct sections or movements in the portrait. In the first movement, the priest is praised with a list of straightforward, positive terms dependent on generations of Christian moralizing about the qualities that a priest should have: "good . . . povre . . . lerned . . . Benygne . . . wonder diligent . . . pacient" (477–84). This language belongs to a very broadly understood Christian tradition rather than any narrow subset of it like medieval estates satire; the same list could be

---

[67] Eamon Grennan, "'Dual Characterization': A Note on Chaucer's Use of 'But' in the Portrait of the Parson," *ChauR* 16 (1982): 195–200.

used to praise a twenty-first-century cleric. In this first movement, the narrative agent gives priority to the Parson's preaching—"Cristes gospel trewely wolde [he] preche; / His parisshens devoutly wolde he teche" (481–82). Only afterward does he mention the Parson's holy works, like his unwillingness to extort payment of tithes through excommunication (486).

Those works are adduced in a structure that defines the Parson as good simply because he does not act badly: "he ne lefte nat . . . to visite / The ferreste in his parisshe" (492–94). The simultaneous appearance of an emphasis on work and the use of such negative and binary character-ization is significant, because both are typical of the Parson's character zone, which, first appearing here, will in a few lines dominate the second movement of the portrait. That second section begins with a signifi-cantly reversed articulation of the motif: "first he wroghte, and after-ward he taughte" (497). Although "the gospel" (498; see Matthew 5:19) is identified as the ultimate source of the *wroghte/taughte* complex, the narrator owes his awareness of that connection to the Parson's words.[68]

> Out of the gospel he tho wordes caughte,
> And this figure he added eek therto,
> That if gold ruste, what shal iren do?
> (498–500)

The dualistic rhetoric, further evidenced in the shame attributed to "A shiten shepherde and a clene sheep" (504), therefore derives from the Parson's voice.[69] Beginning with the invocation of the priest's "noble example" (496), the eleven lines of the second movement provide what amounts to self-characterization, employing a binary style that always emphasizes the Parson's deeds and minimizes attention to his previously emphasized preaching. Indeed, his point is that behavior is paramount because the people will inevitably attend to what a priest does rather

---

[68] Charles A. Owen Jr. argues that "the aphoristic pungency of the Parson's speech is in fact repeatedly imitated in the portrait by the strong consonance of the words wroghte and taughte." This is misleading: the *Prologue*'s past tense is due (as it would be in FID) to the hybridized status of the discourse. The Parson's words would have been *First I werche and afterward I teche,* in which consonance is much less striking. " 'Thy Drasty Ryming,' " *SP* 63 (1966): 533–64 (560).

[69] On the presence of the Parson's voice in these lines, see also Owen, *Pilgrimage and Storytelling in the Canterbury Tales: The Dialectic of Ernest and Game* (Norman: University of Oklahoma Press, 1977), pp. 74–77.

than what he says. These lines touch on preaching only to the extent that their language ultimately belongs to the Parson: he preaches that behavior is much more important than preaching.

At line 507, the narrative agent again emerges from the Parson's voice and finally—this is the third movement—addresses much more specifically the issues defined by estates satire. At the same time, the technique of negative characterization becomes much more intense: the narrator now lists ten denials that this Parson acts in the bad ways that other fourteenth-century priests are widely thought to act. Although such negative characterization is used first in the portrait of the Knight—"He nevere yet no vileynye ne sayde" (70)—the extent of its use to characterize the Parson is unparalleled, and it goes a long way to explain the unusual length of this portrait. Here, as it always does, the technique signals approval of the pilgrim: at the extreme it gives us the "negative superlative" of "A bettre preest I trowe that nowher noon ys" (524).[70] Since the estates tradition makes its emphatically positive assertions to criticize the typical behavior of estate members, simple negation of those assertions tends to idealize the portrait, that is to render it simultaneously enthusiastic in tone and rather general in character: the Parson chose not to abandon his parish for more lucrative practice in London, he was not a mercenary, he was not spiteful to sinners, and so on.[71]

As a result, we garner little new information in the portrait's final section. Having already been told (in a widely praised early detail) that the Parson visited his flock incessantly, "Upon his feet, and in his hand a staf" (495), we cannot be surprised that he has not taken up a sinecure in a London chantry (509–10). What is new is the mimicry by the narrative agent of the Parson's rhetorical strategy and emphasis on deeds. In that rhetoric of redoubled contrast, the adversative conjunction necessarily has an important role; even so, its final appearance retains the power to surprise:

[70] Owen, "Development of the Art," pp. 127–29, discusses both the negative superlative and characterization through negation in the portraits of the Knight and Parson.

[71] In very different ways, both Grennan, "'Dual Characterization,'" and Ronald A. Sarno, S.J., "Chaucer and the Satirical Tradition," *Classical Folia* 21 (1967): 41–61, explore the dichotomies of good priest / bad priest constructed by the negative characterization as a technique of strengthening the narrator's specifically moral and satirical point.

He waited after no pompe and reverence,
Ne maked him a spiced conscience,
But Cristes loore and his apostles twelve
He taughte; but first he folwed it hymselve.

(525–28)

The Parson avoids, we are told, the ill habits attributed to too many of his contemporaries by estates satire: he was a teacher of Christ's lore. But the more striking adversative of the final line disjoins that praiseworthy behavior—the basis of the narrator's initial praise—from an even better behavior, one whose value the narrator would seem to have learned from the Parson's emphasis on deeds as they are reflected in section 2.[72]

The fact that the portrait develops an increasingly strong emphasis on the practice of the tenets of Christianity, on what the Parson does rather than what he is (section 1) or says (section 2), is not often emphasized; the way in which the Parson has shaped that development has not been emphasized at all.[73] This portrait adopts the language of estates satire with full approval, but only after it has learned from the Parson's own discourse how to sharpen the previously rather bland praise—"A good man . . . of religioun" (477)—into a much more pointed commentary. Estates satire becomes a useful way of developing an originally rather banal set of ideas, instigated by the more specific emphasis provided by the Parson himself. Although there is nothing surprising about the narrative use of estates material here, the point of the portrait does not depend in any way on how much or how little of it is employed, on any oddities or omissions of common traits: the narrative agent has used "the kind of thing that people generally say" about parish priests not as an independently valid external standard of judg-

---

[72] Grennan, "'Dual Characterization,'" comments: "Critical perceptions of the Narrator either as naïve simpleton or holy fool are, therefore, inadequate in face of what his creator allows us to see of him here" (p. 199).

[73] Katherine Little, "Chaucer's Parson and the Specter of Wycliffism," *SAC* 23 (2001): 225–53, effectively discusses the Parson's preaching in the context of an emerging late fourteenth-century orthodoxy and the desire for a reformed priesthood; she does not address the importance attributed to works in the portrait. Larry Scanlon, *Narrative, Authority, and Power: The Medieval Exemplum and the Chaucerian Tradition* (Cambridge: Cambridge University Press, 1994), pp. 7–11, has a complementary discussion of the role of exemplarity in the portrait of the Parson. See also Owen, "Development of the Art," p. 127.

ment, but as evidence supporting his own already formed impression of the pilgrim.[74]

The Clerk has been described as a slightly less perfect version of the Parson, the two of them forming in the first estate the equivalent of the pairing of Knight and Squire from the second.[75] The structure of the *Prologue* does not connect the two clerics, however, and the two portraits are constructed very differently. The opening gambit, that the Clerk is still at Oxford even though many years have passed since he first began his studies in the trivium, does not carry the narrative agent very far.[76] He then seizes on more promising material: a description of the pilgrim's poverty that plugs directly into widespread stereotypes of the poor student:

> As leene was his hors as is a rake,
> And he nas nat right fat, I undertake,
> But looked holwe, and therto sobrely.
> Ful thredbare was his overeste courtepy,
> For he hadde geten hym yet no benefice,
> Ne was so worldly for to have office.
>
> (287–92)

Mann traces responses to the estates tradition at half a dozen points in the Clerk's portrait, but it is more apparent in these lines than anywhere

[74]Little's emphasis on the relatively slippery definition of orthodoxy at this point is useful; it is in effect reinforced by the conclusion drawn by Douglas J. Wurtele, "The Anti-Lollardry of Chaucer's Parson," *Mediaevalia* 11 (1989 [for 1985]): 151–68, who demonstrates that the criticisms articulated in the portrait, while consistent with complaints made by the Lollards, also echo similar complaints made by churchmen whose orthodoxy was never in question. The agent pointedly declines to hybridize the kinds of statements—"*He never asked the flock to believe in an accident without subject*" (on one side) or "*He never impugned the sacraments administered by other priests*" (on the other)—that would have clarified the Parson's position in Wycliffite controversies. To anticipate my argument about the narrator's dependence on Chaucer's ideology, those would seem to be questions Chaucer wished not to raise. This provides at least one kind of answer to what David Aers calls an "open question" about the Parson's orthodoxy at the end of "Chaucer's *Tale of Melibee:* Whose Virtues?" in *Medieval Literature and Historical Inquiry: Essays in Honor of Derek Pearsall,* ed. David Aers (Cambridge: D. S. Brewer, 2000), pp. 69–81 (81).

[75]Loretta Valtz Mannucci, *Fourteenth-Century England and the Canterbury Tales* (Milan: Coopli, 1975), notes as I have the importance of thought and work in the portrait of the Parson, "distinguishing him from the Clerk, who had not works" (p. 149).

[76]Andrew's summary of commentary in the "Explanatory Notes" to the *Variorum General Prologue* clarifies the inconclusive significance of what we are told about the Clerk's studies: "The additional implications which have been discerned here are conspicuously varied" (pp. 272–73).

else, largely because they employ more fully than the rest the strategy of negation so perfectly developed in the Parson's portrait.

For Mann, the mention of the Clerk's unbeneficed status is an important hesitation in the narrator's largely positive response: while it might reflect (on one hand) the Clerk's commendable unwillingness to go grubbing, or even bribing his way into a sinecure, it might (on the other) signal a rather orgulous unwillingness to take on the inevitably limiting responsibilities of parish work, the kind of work so admired in the Parson.[77] Mann moves quickly to disarm her opening assertion that the Clerk provides "an ideal representative of the life of study" by analyzing the ways the portrait limits its approbation of that life by emphasizing "the professional nature of the Clerk's studies" and his failure to "look beyond their immediate object to their ultimate goal."[78] In her reading, positive and negative reactions remain in balance or in tension.

As we encounter it, however, the narrative structure of the portrait develops a clear and approbative momentum. The points about which the narrator is most hesitant come first, and they pretty quickly become recognizable as a familiar, middle-class suspicion of intellectual pursuits. Old John the Carpenter responds to Oxford intellectuals more emphatically—"He saugh nat that" (I.3461)—but in much the same vein. The narrative agent directs our attention first to the Clerk's poverty, and estates texts quickly supply the details of thinness in both the Clerk's body and his clothing that support that verdict. Poverty results from the lack of a job. The hesitation over the cause of the Clerk's unemployment is real, but the narrative agent never engages concerns about whether the Clerk is too young to become a parson, does not really want to become a parson, or has been passed over by a system unresponsive to intellectual merit.[79] The narrative conclusion that the Clerk refuses to be "worldly" comprehends all of those possibilities and relies on that word's long and straightforward history before Chaucer's use of it here. To be worldly was to be "related to secular human activities or concerns, . . . not belonging or pertaining to the religious life, . . . [or] caught up

---

[77] Mann, *Chaucer and Medieval Estates Satire,* pp. 82–84.
[78] Ibid., pp. 74 and 84, respectively.
[79] D. W. Robertson, Jr. ed., *The Literature of Medieval England* (New York: McGraw-Hill, 1970), glosses that "the Clerk had not obtained a parish, placed it in the hands of a vicar, and used the income to study" (p. 486); see Nicholas Orme, "Chaucer and Education," *ChauR* 16 (1981): 38–59 (51).

in or given over to secular human activities."[80] How unworldly is the Clerk? The agent uses a simple but frequently misread stratagem for suggesting the magnitude of that trait:

> For hym was levere have at his beddes heed
> Twenty bookes, clad in blak or reed,
> Of Aristotle and his philosophie
> Than robes riche, or fithele, or gay sautrie.
>
> (293–96)

Despite the generations of critics who have ingeniously explained how such a poor scholar could own a library worth fifty or a hundred times his income—perhaps "twenty" is rounded up from a lower number? or the Clerk saved by copying them himself? or rich friends presented them as gifts? or he bought them used?—the comment indicates nothing more literal than surprise that the Clerk, in the odd way of scholars, might actually think that twenty dry-as-dust volumes really were preferable to better clothes or some lively musical entertainment.[81] If later comments about the gravity of the Clerk's conversation are accurate, he will surely not have been boasting about his library. The comment works much less problematically as a narrative agent's reflection of perennial attitudes toward scholars, extensively paralleled in the estates

---

[80] *Middle English Dictionary, worldli* adj., definitions 3 a, b, and c (respectively). The passage about the Clerk is cited as the first example of 3c, but the other, closely related senses have all been in use since Old English, as has sense 4: "Reflecting or embodying the temptations, pleasures, allure, etc. of this world, profane."

[81] Robinson, in both his editions of *The Works of Geoffrey Chaucer* (1933, 1957), hints that "*Twenty* is here of course a round number" (2nd ed., p. 658); Beverly Boyd, *Chaucer and the Medieval Book* (San Marino, Calif.: Huntington Library, 1973), argues that the Clerk could have copied from university-owned fascicles of books (pp. 90–92); Muriel Bowden, *A Commentary on the General Prologue to the Canterbury Tales* (New York: Macmillan, 1949), suggests "[t]hat the Clerk also accepts monetary gifts from his friends is perhaps because of his expensive taste for books," and that he "would probably buy second-hand books at reduced prices, as many students do today" (pp. 156, 159); Martin Stevens, "The Ellesmere Miniatures as Illustrations of Chaucer's *Canterbury Tales,*" *Studies in Iconography* 7–8 (1981–82): 113–34, argues that the Ellesmere miniature of the Clerk, with books in each hand, implies that "he rides nowhere without a part of his treasured library" (p. 115); Anne Middleton, "Chaucer's 'Newe Men' and the Good of Literature in the *Canterbury Tales,*" in *Literature and Society,* ed. Edward W. Said (Baltimore: Johns Hopkins University Press, 1980), pp. 15–56, sounds a more reasonable note: "Not even the 'twenty bokes' we always attribute to him in memory necessarily belong to him, according to the grammar of the sentence" (p. 45); in the *Riverside,* Warren Ginsberg agrees that "the Clerk . . . does not have twenty books" (p. 811).

tradition.[82] It characterizes the Clerk as someone who *would* make such choices, not someone who has made them. We do not know how many books the Clerk owned, or the names of their authors, or the colors of their bindings: we do learn the more general point established by this familiar and obviously hyperbolic reaffirmation of the pilgrim's unworldliness.

Both the opening emphasis on poverty and the succeeding portrayal of unworldliness lead to a climax in the very small joke about the failure of the Clerk's learning to put any money in his pocket. Once the joke is made, however, the rest of the portrait, although it still relies heavily on the estates tradition, changes course radically. In the Parson's portrait, a reduplicated "but" clarified the narrator's emphasis; in the Clerk's, the same strategy significantly redirects the tenor of his ultimate evaluation:

> But al be that he was a philosophre,
> Yet hadde he but litel gold in cofre;
> But al that he myghte of his freendes hente,
> On bookes and on lernynge he it spente,
> And bisily gan for the soules preye
> Of hem that yaf hym wherwith to scoleye.
>
> (297–302)

Donaldson believes that "the logic [of 'But' in 299] is far from clear, and I suspect that its chief function is to express the narrator's difficulty in coming to terms with the Clerk's budgetary peculiarity."[83] The logic is, I have suggested, rhetorical, but Donaldson has nailed the function. The difficulty is overcome not by any actual "coming to terms," but by a simple abandonment of easy scorn for such idiosyncrasy in favor of a more sober validation of a different, more crucial set of traits: the Clerk's devotion (whose usual absence the estates tradition laments), the pithi-

---

[82] Estates texts typically praise bookishness in clerks, and even name Aristotle as an appropriate author (Mann, *Chaucer and Medieval Estates Satire,* pp. 74–75). Moreover, the unworldly bookishness usually associated with Chaucerian narrators would presumably generate a certain degree of sympathy for the clerk. Hence my emphasis on perennial attitudes, perhaps with a distinctly Chaucerian nudge about precisely which books the Clerk enjoys.

[83] E. Talbot Donaldson, "Adventures with the Adversative Conjunction in the General Prologue to the *Canterbury Tales,* or What's Before the But?" in *"So meny people, longages, and tonges": Philological Essays in Scots and Medieval English presented to Angus McIntosh,* ed. Michael Benskin and M. L. Samuels (Edinburgh: privately printed, 1981), pp. 355–66 (362) .

ness of his expression (whose usual absence the estates tradition laments), the moral tone of his discourse (whose usual absence the estates tradition laments), and his cheerful participation in the activities of a scholar.[84] Perhaps the ghost of the Clerk's own voice is invoked in those descriptions of his speech; if so, the Clerk has, in a fashion analogous to the action of the Parson's portrait, gently pushed the tenor of the portrait in an appropriate direction. But the rhetorical strategy in this portrait distinguishes it from that of the Parson, even though both use estates material to fashion a positive characterization. The Parson rather famously lacks a physical description, and the narrative brings his inner being into consistently clearer focus. With the Clerk, the narrative agent false-starts by beginning with external appearances, but he soon dodges past that pointless emphasis to present a more significant and positive evaluation of his character. In each case, estates material appears only when it is useful to the narrator's judgment, and always in the service of that judgment.

In concluding my discussion of character voices, I sought to frame my argument as a confirmation of part of Leicester's response to the Friar and as a correction to the hyperbole that his theoretical model sometimes led him into. Similarly, Mann, even while noting that a scholarly life was "even more likely in medieval than in modern times to be associated with an 'ivory tower,'" concludes that "such an impression does not affect our admiration for the way in which the Clerk performs the role of the ideal scholar."[85] The narrative agent floats *topoi* contrary to that evaluation, and those ideas continue to enhance the complexity of the portrait, but they are finally subordinated to a positive judgment.

In Mann's argument, estates material is almost always a moderating influence: its presence encourages her to find the Clerk less admirable and the Friar less culpable than most other readers do. This tendency is attributable to both her careful comparison of typical estates texts to the *Prologue* and to a less defensible assumption that all discourses discernible in the text must carry equal authority, that is, that any attribution of greater authority to one discourse by a reader can only be arbitrary. My assumption, following Bakhtin, is that hybridization creates an array of discourses in hierarchical form. Therefore, the *Prologue*

---

[84] Mann, *Chaucer and Medieval Estates Satire*, pp. 75–79.
[85] Ibid., p. 74.

never presents estates material for its own sake: it never becomes an estates satire. Rather, the narrative agent frequently finds estates material a useful tool, deployed as a means of invoking readerly responses consonant with his rhetorical goals.[86] Although Chaucer recognizes that reality does not always conform to estates stereotypes (notably in the case of the Parson), he never challenges the fundamental accuracy of the tradition. So his occasional omissions of material common in fourteenth-century critiques of an estate do not indicate a new, more generous kind of estates satire, but the subordination of estates and other discourses to the narrative agent's goals. Those goals, whether praise, blame, or a combination of the two, always take priority over the material they employ. His strategy is more to hint than to accuse, but, as John Gardner has noted, "a comic writer's hints have special force."[87]

The portrait of the Sergeant at Law, adjacent to that of the Clerk, differs from the others less in its use of estates discourse than in the clarity and coherence of such narrative goals. The narrative agent never defines for the Sergeant the clear purpose that was consistently present in the portrait of the Parson and that developed during that of the Clerk. Partly for that reason, the Sergeant provides one of Mann's strongest arguments for the effects of omission of the victim, and (consequently) the elusiveness if not illusoriness of satire against him. She quotes Gower railing in *Vox clamantis* against a lawyer who "enjoys the delights acquired from the poor man's property, but counts the losses of the other as nothing" because, Gower explains, the lawyer's mind does not attend to the victims of his efforts. Mann then demonstrates how Chaucer's technique, by attending solely to the Sergeant's mind, erases our awareness of the victims of his behavior from the portrait, precisely because the Sergeant's consciousness does not reach so far.[88]

Beyond Mann's argument, there is also a body of legal literature whose tendency is pretty strongly approbative of the Sergeant, at least *as* a Sergeant at Law: according to Isobel McKenna, he is "an honour-

---

[86] J. Stephen Russell, *Chaucer and the Trivium: The Mindsong of the Canterbury Tales* (Gainesville: University Press of Florida, 1998), argues that readings of the assembled details of each portrait "are *sense-makings,* unilateral attempts to connect details of the portraits to preconceived notions or ethical judgments about the characters" (p. 64).

[87] John Gardner, *The Poetry of Chaucer* (Carbondale: Southern Illinois University Press, 1977), p. 233. Gardner's comment is made about the portrait of the Squire.

[88] Mann, *Chaucer and Medieval Estates Satire,* p. 90, quoting *Vox clamantis* VI.347–50. She discusses the Sergeant in a chapter on omission of the victim (pp. 86–105), along with the Doctor of Physic, the Merchant, and the Guildsmen.

able leader in his field, a model of excellence for his profession."[89] A
similar judgment that the Sergeant is "professionally correct" also appears in Laura F. Hodges's recent analysis of his costume, which, albeit
more cautiously, confirms his characterization as a successful and powerful lawyer.[90] The significance of this evidence cannot be wished away:
the claims for the Sergeant's professional skill, the echoes of his pride in
his own accomplishments, and the substantial place that he has achieved
in society must remain a significant element in his portrait. In all these
ways, the Sergeant presents a significant challenge to any attempt to
read the portrait as purely ironic, just as (and for much the same reasons
as) he would have presented a challenge to anyone opposing him in
court.

Hints of the Sergeant's character zone in the portrait are mostly restricted to individual legal terms. Words like *patente* and *pleyn commissi-
oun* (315), *fee symple* (319), and *termes* (323) testify to significant legal
experience and expertise and justify the claim that "his wordes weren so
wise" (313). Yet the narrative agent keeps a greater distance from the
Sergeant's voice than he did in the portraits of the Monk, Friar, Parson,
or even Clerk. Thus a curious pattern emerges, one that will persist
throughout the portrait: the agent is simultaneously impressed and un-
impressed by the Sergeant, and the conflict between those two attitudes
is expressed to a degree unmatched in any other portrait:

> Discreet he was and of greet reverence—
> He semed swich, his wordes weren so wise.
>
> (312–13)

The anticlimactic withdrawal of apparent praise effected by the narrative emphasis on surface has been a favorite locus of commentary by
those wishing to read the portrait ironically, and that attitude appears
as persistently as the strategies for reading it more favorably that I have
discussed above:[91]

---

[89] "The Making of a Fourteenth Century Sergeant of the Law," *Revue de l'Université
d'Ottawa* 45 (1975): 244–62 (262). McKenna's article, appearing just two years after
Mann's book, does not cite it; nevertheless, their common emphasis on evaluation of
the Sergeant in strictly professional terms is striking.

[90] Laura F. Hodges, *Chaucer and Costume: The Secular Pilgrims in the General Prologue*
(Cambridge: D. S. Brewer, 2000), pp. 101–25.

[91] Joseph E. Grennan, "Chaucer's Man of Law and the Constancy of Justice," *JEGP*
84 (1985): 498–514.

> Nowher so bisy a man as he ther nas,
> And yet he semed bisier than he was.
>   (321–22)

Such commentary must affect our response to the Sergeant, but it also shifts our sense of the narrative agent. By suggesting that the information he presents to us cannot be taken at face value, he undercuts his own authority, forfeits the invisibility usually associated with the role of agent, and becomes a "narrator," although this narrator is clearly not the dim-witted and gregarious "pilgrim-Chaucer": the comments that question the Sergeant's status have the appearance of perspicuity, and this narrator operates largely by creating significant and meaningful silences. But the presenter of the Sergeant's portrait has, deliberately or not, become at least potentially fallible, like the more recent novelistic narrators who have influenced our expectations, a subjectivity whose values cannot be taken as absolutely valid.[92] That narrator tells us how the Sergeant frequented the "Parvys," how rapidly he has acquired wealth and land, what he seemed like, and how he wore a simple coat and an opulent belt. And that narrator declines to tell us about the clients the Sergeant went to the Parvys to meet, or about how he accumulated that wealth, or about his values or ideology; that narrator (as Hodges notes) makes no mention about what most distinguished a Sergeant, the coif or "howve" that was seen as analogous to a knight's helmet and that Sergeants were always required to wear, even in the presence of the king.[93] Since that final omission—the literally missing mark of honor—strongly suggests significance in the earlier absences, we can reasonably wonder about the Sergeant's clients and his treatment of them. Mann reads the omissions as evidence that the case repeatedly made against the Sergeant must be rejected as "not proved"; but we have seen other, clearly satirical portraits that were not concerned to prove their subjects' vices. Hodges takes the opposite tack, arguing in effect that the Sergeant's innocence is also "not proved," since the professional acumen demonstrated by his formal humility and rich accou-

---

[92] Spearing, *Textual Subjectivity*, pp. 17–31.

[93] Hodges, *Chaucer and Costume*, pp. 107–11. V. A. Kolve, *Chaucer and the Imagery of Narrative: The First Five Canterbury Tales* (Stanford: Stanford University Press, 1984), notes that the Ellesmere portrait of the Sergeant does include the *howve* (p. 290). The Sergeant is not among the ten illustrations discussed by Stevens, "The Ellesmere Miniatures," who notes in passing the depiction of the "medlee cote" but does not discuss the presence of the *howve* in the portrait (p. 116).

terments cannot make up for the absent coif with its implication that the personal honor expected in a Sergeant is also missing;[94] but we have not before seen the narrative agent reduced to such a tepid hint of blame for a pilgrim of whom he disapproves. It is true that the Sergeant is a complex case; but the narrative agent creates a significant part of the complexity by his refusal or inability to define the significance of the details he presents, to clarify the point of this portrait. It is not a matter of equivocation; the problem with the Sergeant is finally a narrative silence about who he is: "Of his array I telle no lenger tale" (330)—and not just of his array.[95]

Unless we consider the narrative intent in this portrait, then, we are at Dulcarnon. The kinds of flaws that drive the satire of the Monk, Friar, Physician, and Summoner are, as it were, inventoried, but satire of the Sergeant is never orchestrated as cogently as in those portraits. Since the agent who sometimes asserts that society's criticisms of its members do not apply to a specified individual still never denies their general validity, his willingness to raise questions about the Sergeant by invoking the stereotypes of the acquisitive lawyer who gives little thought to his clients must be meaningful; but his inability or unwillingness to make those objections plain also matters.[96] The oddity of this portrait is further evidenced by the presence of that open sore, the apparent reference to a real Sergeant at Law with whom the fourteenth-century Londoner named Geoffrey Chaucer had a minor legal entanglement:

> Therto he koude endite, and make a thyng,
> Ther koude no wight pynche at his writyng.
> (325–26)

Although the basic thrust of John M. Manly's old thesis that the portraits consistently describe Chaucer's fellow citizens has long since been discarded, at this one point it is still readily invoked, for the simple reason that no better explanation of these lines has ever presented itself: the political alignment of Thomas Pynchbeck, Sergeant at Law, appar-

---

[94] Hodges, *Chaucer and Costume,* p. 125.

[95] Hodges emphasizes the reticence of the portrait's concluding line, "I telle no longer tale" (ibid., p. 125). So does Leicester, "Structure as Deconstruction," although he mistakenly considers the "medlee cote" as "off-duty dress" (p. 249). See also Richard Firth Green, "Chaucer's Man of Law and Collusive Recovery," *N&Q* 238 (1993): 303–5.

[96] Kolve, *Chaucer and the Imagery of Narrative,* pp. 290–91.

ently differed from Chaucer's, and he signed a writ for the poet's arrest in 1388.[97] But what a small-minded, halfhearted thrust those lines make! Unlike the Sergeant's, the agent's own writing already appears pinched by the Sergeant's power.

In fact, that explanation goes a long way to sorting out the apparent contradictions of this portrait. In other portraits that invoke a comparable sense of the pilgrim's importance, like the Knight's, the narrative agent clearly endorses that prominence as evidence of worthiness. Here the awe is granted more grudgingly, and is consistently qualified or circumscribed once it is invoked.[98] Unlike the Friar, the Sergeant will not provide the hybridized evidence to convict himself, and the narrative agent declines to treat the Sergeant as he has treated the Monk, the Friar, the Merchant, that is, to satirize the Sergeant openly. As Chaucer may have had reason to know, the Sergeant (unlike the Summoner) is both a dangerous man and a dangerous target of criticism. The narrator's reticence is ample testimony to the difficulty of criticizing such people, however dubious their achievements.[99]

In these ways, the portrait of the Sergeant differs from the others I have examined in structure and therefore in effect. Again the narrative agent ventriloquizes many discourses to make a singularly complex statement about a pilgrim: typical estates comments on the pilgrim's profession articulate—faintly—criticisms of lawyers that were in the air; the Sergeant's words are invoked, albeit at some distance, and only to suggest his legal learning; the rhetoric of costume offers both explicitly complimentary and implicitly critical testimony; and the voice of experience, *viz.,* of Chaucer's experience, emerges for a moment of confirma-

---

[97] John Matthews Manly, *Some New Light on Chaucer* (New York: Henry Holt, 1926), pp. 131–57, esp. 150–57; see also Martin M. Crow and Clair C. Olson, eds., *Chaucer Life-Records* (Oxford: Clarendon Press, 1966), p. 386. Manly's interpretation is still cited by the *Riverside Chaucer,* p. 811, and has been repeatedly reinforced: Derek Brewer, *An Introduction to Chaucer* (London: Longman, 1984), p. 174, discusses the Sergeant among other evidence that the "portraits were certainly based on people in real life," and Kolve, *Chaucer and the Imagery of Narrative,* also affirming the reference to a historical figure, further argues the smallness of the personal thrust of the joke and the difficulty of a purely critical reading of the portrait, although to ends different from mine (p. 291).

[98] Yet the awe is real: whether the elaborate introduction to Fragment II indicates that the Man of Law was originally the first tale-teller or simply arises out of a need to introduce him appropriately, he cannot be imagined as in any way a negligible figure.

[99] Mann, *Chaucer and Medieval Estates Satire,* makes something of the same argument—that social considerations interfere with criticisms that could be made—about the Friar (p. 54). But the evidence of the Friar's social position is, as I have shown, almost entirely presented as the Friar's opinion; the Sergeant is a very different case.

tion that the Sergeant is, like anyone so powerful, dangerous. What is different is the narrator's unwillingness in this portrait to take ownership of the praise or criticism implicit in many of those other voices, either to assimilate them fully to, or to distance them ironically from, his own discourse: the agent here is not, in the Bakhtinian phrase I quoted above, "compelling language ultimately to serve all his own intentions." As a result, the "apocryphal" voices noticed by Lawton, the fallen language discerned by Nolan, the tensions descried by Leicester, are more apparent here than anywhere else in the *Prologue*.[100] Criticism of the Sergeant is all around us, but because the narrator never combines it with his own voice, it must remain tentative, unanchored.

The Narrative Agenda

The *Prologue* frequently entertains different judgments about the pilgrims, but most often sorts through those differing opinions to a central or final emphasis, albeit one that is often complex. The rare moments of genuine ambivalence most often arise, as in the portrait of the Sergeant, not from the presence or absence of specific details of estates material, or of a pilgrim's voice, but from a failure by the narrative agent to present such material within a coherent plan, with what can reasonably be called a narrative agenda. "Agendas" have bad connotations nowadays, but it is useful to remember that a narrative agent necessarily has a narrative agenda. Most often, of course, it remains invisible by being unexceptionable: there is nothing noteworthy in the agent's determination to criticize corrupt or hypocritical churchmen, or to praise the humble industriousness of good ones.

But who sets the agenda? Since Michel Foucault described the "author function," or perhaps even since Wayne Booth invented the "implied author," narratologists have been wary of invoking the author directly. Bal's attitude is typical: "It hardly needs mentioning that this [narrative] agent is not the (biographical) author of the narrative," and of course the notion that ideas presented narratorially in the text cannot

---

[100] Lawton, *Chaucer's Narrators,* pp. 99–100 (see pp. 13–14); Nolan, "'A Poet Ther Was,'" pp. 159–61; Leicester, "Art of Impersonation," pp. 218–19. In Bakhtin's terms, the strands of heteroglossia in this portrait are not brought into meaningful interaction with one another; they remain un-dialogized.

always be attributed to the author is quite sound.[101] But since *cannot always be attributed* is not equivalent to Bal's implicit *must never be attributed,* we might consider the terminology of Stanzel and Cohn (who preserve echoes of Bakhtin and countless earlier writers). Their use of the adjective "authorial" to classify unpersonalized narrative relies on a principle that has never been rigorously refuted: the narrative agenda is created by the author, who then designs a narrative agent suitable for its implementation.[102] Given that the *Parliament of Fowls* is an occasional poem, it makes perfect sense to ask when a court official named Geoffrey Chaucer might have thought such a poem appropriate: he was the author who decided to commemorate some occasion with it.[103] For those reasons, there is an inescapable sense in which the narrative agent is always a subset of the poet; the language of the Chaucerian agent necessarily depends in some terms on the language of Chaucer. Because of certain opinions held and choices made by Chaucer, as well as the accidents of his birth, the narrative agent of the *Prologue* writes in English, and in a specific London dialect that distinguishes him from the agents of other important poets who lived nearby. Moreover, the books that the agent makes use of as discourses of alterity in his text are all books

[101] Michel Foucault, "What is an Author?" in *Language, Counter-Memory, Practice: Selected Essays and Interviews,* ed. Donald F. Bouchard, trans. Donald F. Bouchard and Sherry Simon (Ithaca: Cornell University Press, 1977), pp. 113–38; Wayne C. Booth, *The Rhetoric of Fiction* (Chicago: University of Chicago Press, 1961), p. 74–77, discusses the implied author. Bal, *Narratology,* argues that the implied author is "the result of the investigation of the meaning of a text, and not the source of that meaning" (p. 18), but Booth himself emphasizes that the term "is capable of calling attention to [the text] as the product of a choosing, evaluating person rather than as a self-existing thing" (p. 74).

[102] Stanzel, *Theory of Narrative,* pp. 89–91; Cohn, "The Encirclement of Narrative," pp. 157–82. Later, in *The Distinction of Fiction* (Baltimore: Johns Hopkins University Press, 1999), pp. 125–31, Cohn notices that the separation of author and narrator has proceeded on an ad hoc basis and argues that it is a distinguishing element of fictional texts. But while the belief that the two can be forced apart is self-fulfilling, it is not therefore correct. In what sense does the peroration on the death of Jo in chapter 47 of *Bleak House*—"Dead, your Majesty. Dead, my lords and gentlemen. Dead, Right Reverends and Wrong Reverends of every order. . . . And dying thus around us every day"—not articulate Dickens's agenda? Or consider the first line of Yeats's "To Be Carved on a Stone at Thoor Ballylee" (which is, significantly, carved on a stone at Yeats's home at Thoor Ballylee): "I, the poet, William Yeats." Speaker, poet, author: how can we tell the dancer from the dance? Spearing, *Textual Subjectivity,* pp. 121–23, also notes the author's construction of the poetry in *The Man of Law's Tale.*

[103] Larry D. Benson, "The Occasion of *The Parliament of Fowls,*" in *The Wisdom of Poetry: Essays in Early English Literature in Honor of Morton W. Bloomfield,* ed. Larry D. Benson and Siegfried Wenzel (Kalamazoo: Western Michigan University, 1982), pp. 123–44.

read by Geoffrey Chaucer, and the verse forms he employs mirror in unsurprising ways those in the books Geoffrey Chaucer's service to various courts had given him the chance to read. None of the attitudes expressed directly by the agent would have been unacceptable in the mouth of Geoffrey Chaucer. The agent's language is—presumably; the point is not susceptible of proof—not identical to the language of Chaucer, but the agent does not formulate any ideas that lie outside Chaucer's linguistic competence. Conversely, the limits of Geoffrey Chaucer's imagination will occasionally be reflected in the narrative voice, and his narrative agenda will begin to seem less legitimate than it was in the case of the Friar or Parson when readers begin to object to Chaucer's narrative goals.[104]

A sense of Chaucer's limited (and limiting) attitudes toward women has suggested to readers like Helen Phillips that the portrait of the Prioress expresses an illegitimate agenda: "Is there something sexist, a hatchet job, in the way he first devises an unmarried woman with some independent authority, analogous to a headmistress or college principal, and then undermines her dignity, implying that her air of having a position in life is false and what she really—naturally—wants is to attract men?"[105] "Yes," answers Phillips: in her reading, Chaucer's gender politics construct the faults we see in the Prioress. The issue of "attracting men" invokes the portrait's courtly values, a topic I too want to discuss. But before I do, let me note that two other similar volumes, also written by eminent Chaucerians, locate blame at both of the other positions on the rhetorical triangle of Author, Subject, Reader. Helen Cooper blames the Prioress herself: "the balance and substance of the portrait are clearly amiss for a nun, with their concentration on her imitation of 'cheere of court,' her table manners, her pet dogs, and the attractiveness of her appearance."[106] Derek Pearsall, meanwhile, censures the overcens-

---

[104] Although not often explicitly defended, this principle underlies a wide range of important critical commentary, beginning with the Retractions and more recently evidenced in the famous comment by Donaldson, "Chaucer the Pilgrim," that "the fact that [Chaucer the pilgrim, Chaucer the poet, and Chaucer the civil-servant] are three separate entities does not, naturally, exclude the probability—or rather the certainty—that they bore a close resemblance to one another, and that, indeed, they frequently got together in the same body" (p. 1). The crucial opposing point, clearly articulated in Stephanie Trigg, *Congenial Souls: Reading Chaucer from Medieval to Postmodern* (Minneapolis: University of Minnesota Press, 2002), is to avoid using a misplaced reverence for a Chaucer whose congeniality is constructed by his canonicity to reinforce the ideology discerned in the text.

[105] Phillips, *Introduction to the Canterbury Tales,* p. 39.

[106] Cooper, *The Canterbury Tales,* p. 38.

orious reader. Having dismissed somewhat desperate efforts to fault her habit of swearing by a saint, he goes on: "There are many other details in the description of the Prioress that have provoked a raising of the eyebrows, but where the fuller effect is to oblige the reader to identify himself as a harsh and unjust moralist or at best as embarrassingly unsubtle."[107] These three authorities will provide useful touchstones of the critical climate for my own discussion, as I consider five or six different moments in the portrait that have generated direct criticism of the Prioress. In some of those moments she has been ably defended by critics like Pearsall; in others the kind of satire discerned by Cooper is still widely recognized. But I am less concerned with whether we should censure the Prioress than with why we want to, and in particular how narratorial strategies, strategies whose source must be Geoffrey Chaucer, encourage us to think of her in satirical terms. Phillips's comment about narration introduces a discussion ultimately headed elsewhere; I want to pursue the possibility that a Chaucerian narrative agenda loads the dice against the Prioress and therefore propels (or even *com*pels) criticism of her.

This is a tricky position to inhabit: it will occasionally require me to advance arguments for positions I do not hold, in order to test the limits of the traditional positions I have already outlined and to unravel the implications of some unusual features of the portrait. Nor do I want to rely entirely on a sense that the Prioress is for Chaucer an intractably feminine "Other." Although that may be true, it does not get at the peculiarities I want to discuss.[108] The Prioress is not the only pilgrim whose otherness makes the narrative agent palpably uncomfortable, but even the Pardoner is treated more comprehensibly, one might say more rationally than the Prioress. After mention of his duet with the Summoner, he receives an extended physical description:

> This Pardoner hadde heer as yelow as wex,
> But smothe it heeng as dooth a strike of flex;
> By ounces henge his lokkes that he hadde,

---

[107] Pearsall, *The Canterbury Tales*, pp. 68–69.

[108] Strikingly, touchstone feminist readings of the *Canterbury Tales* have little to say about the Prioress: Carolyn Dinshaw, *Chaucer's Sexual Poetics* (Madison: University of Wisconsin Press, 1989), Jill Mann, *Geoffrey Chaucer* (New York: Harvester Wheatsheaf, 1991) (in the "Feminist Readings" series), and Elaine Tuttle Hansen, *Chaucer and the Fictions of Gender* (Berkeley and Los Angeles: University of California Press, 1992) all ignore her character.

> And therwith he his shuldres overspradde;
> But thynne it lay, by colpons oon and oon.
> But hood, for jolitee, wered he noon,
> For it was trussed up in his walet.
> Hym thoughte he rood al of the newe jet;
> Dischevelee, save his cappe, he rood al bare.
> Swiche glarynge eyen hadde he as an hare.
>
> (675–84)

This description both generates and partially explains a growing dis-comfort in the face of the Pardoner's ambiguous sexuality and gender:

> A vernycle hadde he sowed upon his cappe;
> His walet, biforn hym in his lappe,
> Bretful of pardoun, comen from Rome al hoot.
> A voys he hadde as smal as hath a goot.
> No berd hadde he, ne nevere sholde have;
> As smothe it was as it were late shave.
>
> (685–90)

We see the Pardoner much more fully than we see most of the other pilgrims—certainly more than the Friar, the Parson, the Clerk, or the Sergeant—and the unusual length of description occurs because of the intellectual flailing (note the three occurrences of "But") that finally leads to a desperate stab at analysis: "I trowe he were a geldyng or a mare" (691).[109] The narrator never achieves much insight, but at least his placement of evidence before his conclusion is methodologically sound.

The Prioress too comes under close observation, but the narrative proceeds very differently in her case. As I will show, the narrative agent invokes several textual traditions of dubious relevance. In addition, he repeatedly postpones telling us facts about the Prioress until an implica-tion that structures our interpretation of those facts has been estab-lished. Both habits encourage us to form impressions, or even firm conclusions about the Prioress, before we have an adequate basis upon which to entertain them. A familiar critical *topos*—that the Prioress is

---

[109] Robert S. Sturges, *Chaucer's Pardoner and Gender Theory: Bodies of Discourse* (New York: St. Martin's Press, 2000), esp. pp. 21–33, explores the narrator's inability to make the Pardoner conform to the ideas he brings to the act of narration.

not *as bad* as we think, or that the portrait's satire is not *as sharp*—responds at some level to an awareness that the conclusions drawn in the portrait are not fully supported by its details. Considering the elements of the portrait in reverse order will highlight those two oddities.

The incorporation of written discourses is nowhere more obvious than in the Prioress's brooch, inscribed "amor vincit omnia" (162). Those words originally come, in a slightly different order, from Virgil's Tenth *Eclogue,* where they provide a highly indirect and wry observation about the losing battle that humans frequently wage against their sexuality.[110] Lowes's famous comment about the Prioress and her motto—"I think she thought she meant love celestial"—perhaps leans a bit heavily on this distant Virgilian context:[111] medieval readers would have been more aware that the phrase, now arranged in the Prioress's order, had been marshaled into the enormously prolonged and complex efforts to make classical literature serve the Church, in which context it really did speak of celestial love. Some readers may even have seen analogues to the Prioress's brooch: a thirteenth-century ring, now in the Victoria and Albert Museum, contains the inscription "Ave Maria . . . Amor Vinci[t] O[m]nia."[112] But Chaucer probably knew the phrase best (and in the *Prologue*'s word order) from *Le Roman de la Rose,* a more satirical or cynical version of the Virgilian original.[113] Focused as we have been since Lowes on defining exactly what kind of *Amor* the bracelet names—which discourse, if any, emerges from the clashing repetitions of the

[110] Virgil, *Eclogue* X, 69. The addressee of the tenth *Eclogue,* Gallus, was an important military leader in the Civil Wars. Andrew, *Variorum General Prologue,* Commentary, p. 167, cites Leigh Hunt's mistaken attribution of the phrase to Ovid.

[111] John Livingston Lowes, *Convention and Revolt in Poetry* (Boston: Houghton Mifflin, 1919), p. 66. See also the discussion in Cooper, *The Canterbury Tales:* "'Amor vincit omnia,' reads the Prioress's brooch, and it would be a foolhardy critic who could say definitively what the words refer to, or what the pilgrim Chaucer who records them thinks they mean, or what the poet Chaucer wants us to think the Prioress thinks they mean" (p. 29).

[112] Hodges's *Chaucer and Clothing,* pp. 103–8, discusses the ring as evidence of the appropriately religious function of the brooch and its motto—including its appearance in Latin rather than a vernacular language—to balance the perhaps overly secular readings now common. To invoke one more strand of language in the passage, John Block Friedman, "The Prioress's Beads 'Of Small Coral,'" *MÆ* 39 (1970): 301–5, notes that coral was believed to act as a defense against demons.

[113] *Le Roman de la Rose,* ed. Félix Lecoy (Paris: Champion, 1982), vol. 3, lines 21,299–303, reinforces the military context already invoked in Virgil's language: Venus's flaming brand has already scattered the defenders of the castle and made possible the liberation of Bel Acueill, whose permission to pluck the rose is being sought before Cortaisie speaks the words "Amors vaint tout . . . et nous la devons recevoir," citing Virgil as source.

phrase—we may overemphasize the Prioress's ignorance about the meaning of her brooch, thereby suggesting a bit smugly that we know exactly what it means. We might rather recognize a hopelessly vain belief that she—or we—can control its inevitably multifaceted meaning.

More unanchored meaning appears quite clearly in the discussion of her famous countenance:

> But sikerly she hadde a fair forheed;
> It was almoost a spanne brood, I trowe;
> For, hardily, she was nat undergrowe.
>
> (154–56)

The standard understanding of these lines has been that the Prioress has a forehead some eight or nine inches wide. The dominant view appears to be that Madame Eglentyne was obese, but readers have also taken the phrase "nat undergrowe" to mean that the Prioress is extremely tall, or—among some male readers—that she has strikingly large breasts.[114] This is the kind of reading that almost makes Pearsall's argument for him: quite clearly, readers have imagined "nat undergrowe" in terms that suit their own not-very-subtle fancies, despite the absence of decisive textual evidence. The simple multiplicity of ways that "nat undergrowe" can be understood should weaken our certainty that any one of them must be right. Moreover, there is good evidence, never challenged, that the phrase "a spanne brood" must mean "three to four inches high."[115] These lines forge an impression that what is in fact a fairly ordinary forehead is a synecdoche for a body that is—must be—*somehow* extravagant. The narrative prods our imaginations about the parameters

---

[114] Cooper, *The Canterbury Tales,* argues that "'Nat undergrowe' cannot, in this context, mean 'well-proportioned'. . . . The Prioress is a *large* woman" (p. 38). Obesity in the Prioress has been in question since the 1930s: for a recent argument, see Chauncey Wood, "Chaucer's Use of Signs in His Portrait of the Prioress," in *Signs and Symbols in Chaucer's Poetry,* ed. John P. Hermann and John J. Burke (University: University of Alabama Press, 1981), pp. 81–101, esp. 95–97. Among those reading "nat undergrowe" as indicating a sexually desirable shapeliness are James Winny, ed., *The General Prologue to the Canterbury Tales* (Cambridge: Cambridge University Press, 1965), p. 89; E. T. Donaldson, ed., *Chaucer's Poetry: An Anthology for the Modern Reader,* 2nd ed. (New York: Ronald Press, 1975), p. 1044; Bowden, *A Commentary on the General Prologue,* p. 95; and Friedman, "The Prioress's Beads," p. 301.

[115] I quote from the never-rebutted article by Stephen Knight, "'Almoost a spanne brood,'" *Neophil* 52 (1968): 178–80 (see 179), which I have endorsed in "The Prioress's Fair Forehead," *ChauR* 42 (2007): 101–11.

of Eglentyne's body—and so traps us into thinking of her primarily *as* a (female) body.

A similar narrative two-step characterizes the description of the Prioress's "conscience," which certainly augments an impulse to find her culpable:

> Of smale houndes hadde she that she fedde
> With rosted flessh, or milk and wastel-breed.
> But soore wepte she if oon of hem were deed,
> Or if men smoot it with a yerde smerte.
>
> (146–49)

The indulgence of her dogs is one of the Prioress's most evident weaknesses, and not even Pearsall defends it. But looking back a few lines, we can see that the narrative has again set us up to read the Prioress's canine sympathies in the harshest possible light:

> But for to speken of hire conscience,
> She was so charitable and so pitous
> She wolde wepe, if that she saugh a mous
> Kaught in a trappe, if it were deed or bledde.
>
> (142–45)

We are the more ready to see her misplaced priorities with the dogs because we have already seen her tears spent on animals universally regarded as pests. But like the comment about the Clerk's books, this one is essentially rhetorical; it presents not a fact but an image of the Prioress's pity chosen to communicate a judgment about her sentiment. Not incidentally, that simile is the most effective setup possible for the agent's comments about her hounds, about whose treatment he professes more certain knowledge.

The hypothetical nature of the narrative comments on mice does not make indulging the dogs any less culpable; I just want to correct a surprisingly strong tendency to read the hypothetical image as reported fact. We have been told that "it is the suffering of a mouse which calls forth her sympathy," that "she wept when she saw a dead mouse and coddled her little dogs," that she "weeps out of charity and pity when she sees mice caught in traps," and that she reserved her sympathy for "a trapped mouse or a chastised pet" as if the two statements existed in parallel.[116] Once again, the rhetoric whets our appetite for additional, more factual details to support the censorious attitude already evoked. Readers indulge in the cheap moralization chastised by Pearsall because the narrative amply encourages us to do so. Here perhaps more clearly than anywhere else, all three of the critics whom I cited earlier are correct. The Prioress is clearly at fault for keeping those well-fed dogs, *and* readers have been excessively censorious in generalizing that *culpa* into a lifestyle of indulging animals, *and* the narrative agent's hatchet has been at work clearing a broad path for such readers.

That pattern of putting the conclusion before the evidence matters in surprising ways to the narrator's early summary of the Prioress's character:

> sikerly she was of greet desport,
> And ful plesaunt, and amyable of port,
> And peyned hire to countrefete cheere
> Of court, and to been estatlich of manere,
> And to ben holden digne of reverence.
>
> (137–41)

As Phillips notes, we see in these lines "someone who has mastered the difficult social skills required of a woman in a position of authority, as a prioress was."[117] We also see undeniably that her mastery is skewed by the narrator's emphasis on the struggle with which it has been attained: the verbs "peyned," "countrefete," and "been holden" all suggest an unseemly class striving in the Prioress: "A Prioress who counterfeits courtly behavior becomes a counterfeit nun."[118] But let me explore for a moment how the counterargument—one of those arguments I do not actually want to make—would go. The *MED* cites this passage in its definitions of both "peynen" and "countrefeten," but in both cases em-

---

[116] Respectively: Bowden, *A Commentary on the General Prologue,* p. 99 (a reading called "highly influential" in Andrew's *Variorum* commentary); John Fisher, "Embarrassment of Riches," *College Language Association Journal* 7 (1963): 1–12 (2–3); Larry Sklute, *Virtue of Necessity: Inconclusiveness and Narrative Form in Chaucer's Poetry* (Columbus: Ohio State University Press, 1984), p. 105; Phyllis Hodgson, ed., *Chaucer: General Prologue, The Canterbury Tales* (London: Athlone Press, 1969), p. 81. More subtly, Donaldson suggests that the Prioress's conscience "proves no more substantial than the little mouse caught in a trap that so arouses the Prioress' charity, pity, and tears" ("Adventures with the Adversative Conjunction," p. 361).

[117] Phillips, *Introduction to the Canterbury Tales,* p. 39.

[118] Wood, "Chaucer's Use of Signs," p. 92.

ploys it to illustrate a lesser degree of criticism: it suggests reading *peyned* to mean that the Prioress exerted herself, but without overreaching; *contrefete* is taken to mean the simple following of a pattern of behavior rather than passing one's self off as something false. Of course, the *MED*'s entries no more exonerate the Prioress than the fact that the Clerk praises Grisilde by calling her "So benigne and so digne of reverence" (IV.411): the difference between being worthy of respect and striving to achieve that sort of reputation will not, and should not, long escape the reader. The Prioress is praised with a series of damns that become much less faint with repetition. By itself, any one of those terms might escape commentary: it is the narrative agent's choice to iterate those verbs that generates our ability, our willingness—perhaps our need?—to read the kind of positive social skills delineated by Phillips as a sign of the Prioress's bad behavior.

The manner in which those skills are undercut raises a further complication: the Prioress's effort "to countrefete cheere / Of court" sums up not her exercise of authority in the convent but her table manners, and anyone who has completed a first class in Chaucer knows that her table manners are borrowed from the monologue of La Vieille in the *Roman de la Rose*.[119] This passage, with its brilliant hybridization of Jean de Meun's language with his own, has always flown under the critical radar, despite the fact that such language is so foreign to the presumable concerns of a Prioress. Nothing quite so drastic is found anywhere else in the *Prologue*. Most readers, falling for this narratorial ploy, have blamed the Prioress for, to cite an extreme example, "studying, with the aid of the *Roman de la Rose,* how to play the courtly lady."[120] If the Prioress were, like the Friar, being hoist by the petard of her own words anticipating or confirming what the narrator "knows" about prioresses (or women generally), the hybrid structure would presumably work in just that way. But here we all too often condemn the Prioress for paying more attention to the cleanness of her lips than her soul, not because *she* has identified table etiquette as the center of her spiritual life, but because the narrative agent describes her in terms borrowed from Geoffrey Chaucer's favorite poem. For generations, readers have understood the Prioress's values, or rather foibles, in the completely external terms defined by the Chaucerian narrator's invocation of Jean de Meun.

[119] *Sources and Analogues,* ed. Correale and Hamel, 1:15–18.
[120] Hope Phyllis Weissman, "Antifeminism and Chaucer's Characterization of Women," in *Geoffrey Chaucer: A Collection of Original Articles,* ed. George D. Economou (New York: McGraw-Hill, 1976), 93–110 (104).

And it's not just that the Prioress does not get the joke: she *cannot* get the joke. After all, "Frenssh of Parys was to hire unknowe" (126). Since, as Pearsall quite rightly notes, "It would of course be more of a moral criticism of the Prioress if she had worked hard to cultivate Parisian French, as a way of keeping up with the *haute monde*" (69), the point of this detail is initially obscure.[121] But anyone ignorant of "Frenssh of Parys" must also remain ignorant of the advice on table manners offered by Jean de Meun in his portion of the *Roman de la Rose*. Since Jean's poem is written in Parisian French, no one who had read it could be said to lack knowledge of that language.[122] When we learn that "Frenssh of Parys was to hire unknowe," we also learn—again well before we know why it should be important—that the Prioress has not, cannot have read, the *Roman*. That pointed assurance constitutes one of the narrative agent's nastier moves—a legerdemain nastier still for being uncommented on so long. It supports a Chaucerian agenda having nothing to do with articulating the Prioress's concerns. Instead, the poet has provided for the narrative agent a satiric voice-over, with Woody Allen's *What's Up, Tiger Lily?* as analogue.[123]

One further anomaly about the portrait of the Prioress points explicitly toward an argument I actually do want to make. The first-person singular pronoun "I" appears in the portrait section of the *Prologue* fifteen times; of these, twelve exemplify what has been called "epistemological I" by introducing a clause indicating the parameters of the narrative's knowledge: "I gesse," "I trowe," "I saugh," "I undertake," "I woot," and so on.[124] Only one portrait—that of the Prioress—contains more than one occurrence of epistemological I. More pointedly, the epistemological use of "I" reaches a self-reflective peak here: "Ful fetys was hir cloke, as I was war" (157). The narrator's awareness of his awareness of the Prioress retrospectively warns us that we should have been more aware of his awareness of her; more specifically, we should

---

[121] Pearsall, *Canterbury Tales,* p. 69

[122] Jean was associated with the University of Paris through much of his life and wrote his portion of the *Roman* "selonc le langage de France" (line 10,613), which is the Parisian dialect of the Île de France.

[123] Donald Howard, *The Idea of the Canterbury Tales* (Berkeley and Los Angeles: University of California Press, 1976), notes a similar connivance in the Pardoner's Prologue, by which that unsavory character creates an alliance with his audience (including us) and against the fools who are taken in by his chicanery (p. 350).

[124] Lawton, *Chaucer's Narrators,* also calls such pronouns "epistemological," but he does not discuss line I.157 (p. 100).

all along have been considering how the narrative agenda skews our perceptions of the Prioress. When we do, we will quickly note the scant reliance in this part of his narration on the two sources that contribute so much to his other portraits. This pilgrim's voice barely registers: we hear the oath she swore but not what her oath affirmed. And estates discourse, while it does contribute to the passage on the dogs, for example, still plays a much smaller role than other textual voices like the *Roman de la Rose* and the attenuated citation of Virgil on the brooch, both of which import highly gendered attitudes into the portrait.

Because the narrative agent so substantially limits what we know about the Prioress, we never do know as much about her as we think. What Donaldson has well expressed—"many of our sympathetic responses to her are actually responses to the narrator's manipulation of her and of us"—is also true of our unsympathetic responses.[125] The bits that we do know have fostered the basic critical approaches to her character, which therefore have a degree of validity. But the gaps in our knowledge created by the narrative obtrusions reveal a hermeneutic circle. The portrait does satirize the Prioress's behavior: Cooper. But contradictory premises in that satire have implicated readers in its terms, leaving us too eager to display moral superiority: Pearsall, *contra* Cooper. And many of those contradictions are best understood as the products of a Chaucerian agenda unwilling to countenance an independently successful woman: Phillips, *contra* Pearsall. That's who the Prioress might be—if it were not for those moral failings: Cooper, *contra* Phillips. In other portraits, I have argued that an insufficient attention to the narrator's persistent hybridization has often led us to read carefully orchestrated complexity as irresolvable ambiguity. The same hybrid technique, however, employed with less relevant textual material, does render the Prioress truly unknowable rather than merely ambiguous.[126]

---

[125] "Cressid False, Criseyde Untrue: An Ambiguity Revisited," in *Poetic Traditions of the English Renaissance,* ed. Maynard Mack and George de Forest Lord (New Haven: Yale University Press, 1982): 67–83 (69). Like many of his critics, Donaldson links the narratorial treatment of Criseyde and the Prioress: see "Four Women of Style," in *Speaking of Chaucer,* pp. 46–64, at 59. Robert Hanning, "The Theme of Art and Life in Chaucer's Poetry," in *Geoffrey Chaucer: A Collection of Original Articles,* ed. Economou, pp. 15–36, concludes that "our attempt to find the real woman behind the [courtly] mask" cannot succeed (p. 32).

[126] Among other characters manipulated by their narrators, perhaps Vladimir Nabokov's *Lolita* is most suggestive: "Lolita" is the fictitious persona (the character's given name is Dolores) structured by and giving structure to the understanding of the novel's narrator.

Many readers, acknowledging her flaws and shortcomings as a nun, take the Prioress to be a woman who is temperamentally unsuited to a cloistered and meditative life.[127] Her faults become the perhaps inevitable result of a class system that encouraged convent life for women regardless of a religious vocation. The portrait of the Prioress (read that way) becomes much like the rest of the portraits (read that way): it criticizes the pilgrim's flaws even while finding something human in her that Chaucer—or is it the foolish persona?—can approve. But this portrait shows very little evidence of that typically genial persona. A genuine narratorial intolerance of the Prioress resonates much more strongly than any meaningful approbation of her, and that intolerance is built deeply into the structure of the portrait. There is no statement here, as there will be for the Monk, that the narrator thought *her* opinions good; we rather strikingly do not hear the Prioress's opinions. And so we have concluded, perhaps—but not surely—correctly, that she has no opinions worth our attention. The vacuum thus created fills itself with a narrative manipulation of our response to both her strengths and weaknesses of character. As a result, judgment depends more on the reader's tendencies to indulgence or censoriousness than on the Prioress's own accomplishments and failings. The author's decision to hybridize texts more relevant to the gender politics of his own agenda than to her life makes it impossible to consider her with the seriousness that would make genuine evaluation possible.

Conclusion

A. C. Spearing has warned us about the dangers of reading Chaucer anachronistically:

In the *Canterbury Tales,* Chaucer really was beginning a movement that would culminate in the nineteenth-century dramatic monologue and the twentieth-century fallible narrator, but he was *only* beginning it. The culmination of that movement as a comprehensive system was far out of sight in Chaucer's time, and must have been beyond what Chaucer could have imagined, and probably

---

[127] Famously, Donaldson, *Chaucer's Poetry* argues that "she is a complex of qualities that make a most attractive woman but do not make a woman into a nun" (p. 1044). George J. Englehardt asserts that "the Prioress has been thrust upon her convent . . . by the wealth or influence of her family." "The Ecclesiastical Pilgrims of the *Canterbury Tales:* A Study in Ethology," *Mediaeval Studies* 37 (1975): 287–315 (291). Sklute, *Virtue of Necessity,* suggests that the Prioress is "deficient both as a nun and as a courtly lady" (p. 106).

beyond what he would have wished for. We need to resist reading back into Chaucer's own work the full development, so familiar to us, that he couldn't have envisioned, and the systematic practice that he never aimed at.[128]

In one sense, my approach differs from Spearing's: his italicized *"only"* (like the suggestion that Chaucer would have found, say, *The Sound and the Fury* an unnerving read) emphasizes the ways in which Chaucer remains outside the tradition of novelistic narration as we know it, while I begin from an interest in the possibility that "Chaucer really was beginning" to blaze that trail by experimenting with a hybridized discourse very uncharacteristic of his own age but which has since become naturalized for readers by the practice of countless novelists.

In another sense, however, my argument complements Spearing's in suggesting that we should not expect the same kind of sophistication from Chaucer as from those later writers. Chaucer's experiments with hybrid discourse are interesting partly because the norms developed by writers in a realistic or modernistic mode—like the codified principles of free indirect discourse—did not exist for him. Indeed, codification, what Spearing calls "systematic practice," seems very much the wrong kind of interest for Chaucer studies. Even a quick perusal of *Sources and Analogues* teaches us both how varied the influences to which our author was sensitive were and how little constraint he generally felt in making use of those influences.

Little evidence suggests that "perfection," in either the etymological or common meaning of that noun, worried Chaucer greatly. The Chaucerian canon contains many unfinished poems, and Spearing has more recently argued that even great and polished poems like the *Troilus* are better understood as experiments than as perfectly accomplished examples of a later kind of art.[129] If "it is obvious that [Chaucer's] satiric manner required a sophistication not usually possessed in the Middle Ages," then it is also true that his was an idiosyncratic sophistication, one that later writers did not share.[130] An innovator as consistent and effective as Chaucer was cannot be unsophisticated (any more than a

---

[128] Spearing, "Textual Performance," p. 23. Owen, "Development of the Art," concurs that Chaucer "could have had, I think, only a partial vision of what his efforts were leading up to" (p. 117).

[129] Spearing, *Textual Subjectivity,* pp. 74–75.

[130] Rosemary Woolf, "Chaucer as Satirist" (1959), rpt. in *Art and Doctrine: Essays on Medieval Literature,* ed. Heather O'Donoghue (London: Hambledon Press, 1986), pp. 77–84, discussing the *General Prologue* on p. 83.

Collector of Customs can be naive), but it is folly to expect him to be sophisticated in the ways we most readily expect.

The pervasive, determined combination of a wide range of discourses within the narrative constitutes Chaucer's principal innovation in the *Prologue,* the source of its distinctive sophistication (the etymological sense of that word is also at work). The overall success of that experiment has long been apparent, and our sense of its most striking examples—the Monk and Friar, for example—has very consistently depended on a sure if somewhat inarticulate recognition of the poet's ability to choreograph that variety of discourses into a satirical effect. The Clerk, Guildsmen, and Parson (and many others) are limned using much the same strategy, even if to a less spectacular, and frequently less satirical, end. We should note that the Prioress, too, demonstrates brilliance of technique, even if the ultimate effect in that portrait—the first first-estate pilgrim to be described becomes perhaps the least consequential member of the company—has led many readers to disapprove of this portrait, however great its technical mastery. In rejecting on ideological grounds what the poet has done, those readers exhibit a frequently invoked and wholly valid critical response. What matters is that we distinguish principled objection to what the poet has successfully carried out from the judgment that the poet has failed, or not done his task well, or has actually been trying to do something else: we need to be honest about our responses, and need to be clear which one we are making.[131] And finally, we cannot be surprised that Chaucer's experiments do occasionally fail. That an uncoordinated narrative agenda leaves the Sergeant (and perhaps others) an ambiguous figure ought not to startle readers of Chaucer; nor would I suggest that the incompleteness, the imperfection of that portrait, wholly negates what it accomplishes. At least it avoids that potential for "certain disaster" inherent in the *Prologue*'s plan, a disaster averted (as Pearsall continues) by consistently varying the technique from portrait to portrait.[132] Malcolm Andrew comes to a parallel conclusion, noting how methods of elucidation helpful at one point in the *Prologue* often prove to be inappropriate or unhelpful when applied more generally: "If we acknowledge that Chaucer's technique is not only subtle and elusive but also complex and vari-

---

[131] Spearing, *Textual Subjectivity,* frequently disparages critical readings in which he perceives the rejection of the content of a poem disguised as an attempt to unmask or ironize a fallible narrative persona: pp. 98–99, 113–16, 148–49, 202–5.

[132] Pearsall, *The Canterbury Tales,* pp. 57–60.

ous, then we may be able to proceed to the recognition that each of these approaches is valid—though not absolutely or exclusively so."[133] Andrew cites Manly and D. W. Robertson Jr. as exemplifying the partially but not "absolutely" valid approaches of "contextualizing" and "moral commentary," respectively; contrarily, he cites Mann as exemplary in avoiding the fault of an "exclusive" approach.[134] In my reading, Mann's unstated assumption (picked up and stated, as I have noted, by other critics) that the *Prologue* can be read as an estates satire is another form of such contextualization, and the contention of various critics that any invocation of voice entails equivocation becomes as categorical as an insistence that all medieval texts promote *caritas.* Seduced by their historical and theoretical contexts into occasional but influential overstatement about the ambiguity created by complexity of discourse in the *Prologue,* some of our best scholars privilege what Andrew calls "a literal interpretation often based on tenuous reasoning while simultaneously demoting (implicitly or explicitly) what would otherwise be seen as clear (if by its very nature, unspecific) symbolic or 'poetic' meaning."[135]

The example of Dante (for all his poetic difference from Chaucer) suggests how we might extend Andrew's insight. The cantos of the *Comedy* are famously unique, each deliberately developed with imagistic and stylistic techniques that distinguish it from its neighbors: the Dantean narrative agent has defined a distinctive technique for each unit. So too the *General Prologue* portraits draw on various sources of information about the pilgrims, and develop those sources in different directions, also under the influence of distinctive narrative purposes. Dantists habitually read the cantos in isolation, as texts with distinctive rules and procedures. I have similarly urged that we must recognize the idiosyncratic design of each portrait to read it effectively. We can benefit from thinking of the portraits as such meaningfully juxtaposed but essentially distinct units even more fully than we already do.

[133] Malcolm Andrew, "Context and Judgment in the *General Prologue*," *ChauR* 23 (1989): 316–37 (331–32).

[134] Ibid., pp. 321–28.

[135] Ibid., p. 324. The ability of scholars to trace in the *Prologue* resemblances to other expressions of medieval culture also encourages my sense that we are mistaken to read it as an estates satire. See, e.g., John Ganim, "The Literary Uses of the New History," in *The Idea of Medieval Literature: New Essays on Chaucer and Medieval Culture in Honor of Donald R. Howard,* ed. James M. Dean and Christian K. Zacher (Newark: University of Delaware Press, 1992), 209–26, who usefully asks "What happens if we think of the form of the General Prologue as akin to the ridings, processions, and entries that march through late medieval and early modern cities with so much regularity?" (p. 222).

"Fer in the north; I kan nat telle where":

Dialect, Regionalism, and Philologism

Robert Epstein
Fairfield University

W HEN J. R. R. TOLKIEN, in his famous analysis of the use of dialect in *The Reeve's Tale,* termed Chaucer a "philologist," he was affording him his highest compliment. What Tolkien meant, primarily, was that the distinctive speech Chaucer gave to the Cambridge clerks John and Aleyn was a precisely accurate rendering of a particular dialect of far northern England. But it is clear that identifying "Chaucer as a philologist" meant more than this to Tolkien. It meant that Chaucer was not merely interested in using linguistic differences for the sake of humor or characterization, but that he was interested in language in itself: "For Chaucer was interested in 'language,' and in the forms of his own tongue."[1] It meant, even more importantly, that Chaucer was *disinterested.* Tolkien's effort was to show that Chaucer did not "just pander to popular linguistic prejudices," but rather that he possessed that combination of expertise and dispassionate objectivity that sets the true scholar apart from the mass of humanity: "Chaucer deliberately relies on the easy laughter that is roused by 'dialect' in the ignorant or the unphilological. But he gives not mere popular ideas of dialect: he gives the genuine thing."[2] Thus, for Tolkien, "philology," with its objective observation, systematic analysis, and precise recording, is the opposite of "ignorance." In fact, it is literally a higher calling. "Many may laugh," he wrote, "but few can analyse or record."[3]

Much of the analysis of the use of dialect in *The Reeve's Tale* has similarly focused on its relative accuracy in depicting a dialect of northern

---

[1] J. R. R. Tolkien, "Chaucer as a Philologist: *The Reeve's Tale,*" *Transactions of the Philological Society* (1934): 1–70 (quotations on p. 1).

[2] Ibid., p. 3.

[3] Ibid., p. 4.

English, and much of it has echoed Tolkien's impression of Chaucer's dialectologically disinterested and unbiased observation and representation, his impartial and objective interest in the speech habits of others. Nor is it my intention to challenge this. But from the perspective of more recent sociolinguistic theory, particularly that of Pierre Bourdieu, the ostensible objectivity of Chaucer's social-scientific stance, what we might term his "philologism," can be seen to grant him specific social advantages. Postmodern and postcolonial criticism has exposed the unseen workings of power by which certain individuals benefit from subject positions that may otherwise seem, even to themselves, neutral and objective. So it is with Chaucer; the "philological" inclination he shows in *The Reeve's Tale* is informed by and contributes to a broader tendency to use generalizations of linguistic difference to construct hierarchized Northern and Southern regional identities within England, often much earlier than has previously been acknowledged. Only in this light can subsequent uses of dialect in English literature, notably in the Wakefield *Second Shepherds' Play,* be properly understood.

Chaucer's Southern Accent

The dialect writing in *The Reeve's Tale,* apparently the first instance of what would become a great English tradition, has always been of interest to historians of English, but those who have studied it most extensively have paradoxically insisted on its limited sociolinguistic significance. There are two main reasons for this, one internal and the other external. The external reason is that the late fourteenth century seems, to many historians of the language, too early to imagine the use of specific English dialects as markers of social status. Such hierarchization could only come with the establishment of a national standard, with greater conformity to the standard granting greater linguistic authority and greater variance marking social marginalization.[4] This standardization would be perfected with the elaboration of prescriptive grammatical systems based on neoclassical models in the seventeenth and eighteenth centuries, and although its roots can be traced to politi-

---

[4] On the process of linguistic standardization, see Einar Haugen, *The Ecology of Language,* ed. Anwar S. Dil (Stanford: Stanford University Press, 1972); James Milroy and Lesley Milroy, *Authority in Language: Investigating Language Prescription and Standardisation* (London: Routledge, 1985).

cal and cultural centralization in the sixteenth century or to the advent of print or even to the rise of several regular forms of written English, including Chancery Standard, in the mid-fifteenth century, most scholars doubt that any regularization of the language in the medieval periods meets the requirements of true standardization.[5] Standardization consists not merely of a trend toward linguistic conformity but also of sociolinguistic phenomena involving the assertion and recognition of linguistic authority. Due to the variety of written as well as spoken English and the persistent cultural authority of languages other than English, primarily French, few linguistic historians recognize the emergence of standard English before the end of the Middle English period. Tim William Machan notes that Chancery, "lacking broad acceptance and still restricted in its domains . . . , was sustained neither by formal, published codification nor by cultivation in education, and a truly standardized written variety of English did not exist until the eighteenth century."[6]

For Tolkien, therefore, the use of dialect in *The Reeve's Tale* is "a linguistic joke" inspired by "private philological interest," a joke so private that even Chaucer's contemporaries did not get it.[7] In the clerks' speech, Tolkien concludes, Chaucer renders the dialect of a specific place in far northern England—"the land beyond the Tees," but still in Northumbria, not Scotland—and does so with such accuracy that his fifteenth-century copyists are not able to recognize or to maintain the distinctions.[8]

Norman Blake has shown that John and Aleyn's dialect is less specific than Tolkien believed, and also that the fifteenth-century scribes of the *Canterbury Tales* often understood quite well the linguistic distinctions Chaucer was drawing between his characters and on occasion aug-

[5] See Arthur O. Sandved, "Prolegomena to a Renewed Study of the Rise of Standard English," in *So meny people longages and tonges: Philological Essays in Scots and Mediaeval English presented to Angus McIntosh,* ed. Michael Benskin and M. L. Samuels (Edinburgh: M. Benskin and M. L. Samuels, 1981), pp. 31–42, 383–84; M. L. Samuels, "Spelling and Dialect in the Late and Post-Middle English Periods," in Benskin and Samuels, *So meny people longages and tonges,* pp. 43–54, 384–85; J. D. Burnley, "Sources of Standardisation in Later Middle English," in *Standardizing English: Essays in the History of Language Change,* ed. Joseph B. Trahern Jr. (Knoxville: University of Tennessee Press, 1989); Simon Horobin, *The Language of the Chaucer Tradition* (Cambridge: D. S. Brewer, 2003), pp. 13–15.
[6] Tim William Machan, *English in the Middle Ages* (Oxford: Oxford University Press, 2003), p. 97.
[7] Tolkien, "Chaucer as a Philologist," pp. 2, 3.
[8] Ibid., p. 58.

mented them.[9] But Blake also maintains that the absence of a formal standard for English, at least before the rise of Chancery English, meant "the absence of regional dialect registers in medieval English literature."[10] The dialect writing in *The Reeve's Tale,* therefore, is merely an attempt to paint some local color for the sake of genre, and even this conception of dialect differences is essentially foreign to fourteenth-century England: "To Chaucer it probably appeared that *fabliaux* ought to include some provincial speech, but this was an attitude which was imported from abroad rather than one which arose from the state of the language and the reactions of indigenous speakers to it."[11]

Machan has recently tried to contextualize Middle English dialectology within a broader analysis of the "ecology" of medieval English, but this leads him, like Blake, to doubt the sociolinguistic relevance of the few instances of Middle English dialect writing. Differences among the innumerable variants of spoken Middle English, Machan finds, were dwarfed by the greater question of the place of English among other, competing languages, primarily French: "Indeed, both the diglossia of medieval England and the relative rigidity of the estates worked against the sociolinguistic utility—even viability—of mapping any social rank onto any variety of English."[12] While Machan is able to identify, starting in the fourteenth century, examples of dialect *awareness,* such observations of synchronic variations within Middle English do not amount to evaluations of the status, authority, or appropriateness of different dialects or regionalist generalizations about the characters of their speakers. To Machan, status distinctions among different dialects were unavailable to Middle English speakers:

[W]ithout widespread, institutionalized access to powerful domains such as education, government, and business and without the codification of printed

---

[9] "All we can say definitively is that Chaucer gives a portrayal of northern language which is so generalized that it cannot be localized with accuracy, though it may be located north of the Ribble-Humber line. At the same time it is clear that many scribes knew more about the northern dialects than Chaucer included in the speech of the undergraduates and so modified their speech accordingly." N. F. Blake, *Non-Standard Language in English Literature* (London: André Deutsch, 1981), p. 33.

[10] N. F. Blake, *The English Language in Medieval Literature* (London: Methuen, 1979), p. 46. Blake does concede, however, on the evidence of Higden's *Polychronicon* and Trevisa's translation, that by the late fourteenth century, "Dialect prejudice was beginning to emerge and language was now available as a marker of social class and of humour" (*Non-Standard Language,* p. 27).

[11] Ibid., p. 45.

[12] Machan, *English in the Middle Ages,* p. 95.

grammar books and dictionaries—the very factors that established a tenacious connection between language and class in the early modern era—English remained without a standard variety, spoken or written, throughout the entire medieval period. Lacking these institutional supports and a standard variety, in turn, speakers of Middle English had neither the means to represent social stratification in language nor a sociolinguistic context in which such a representation could have been easily conceived.[13]

In the few recognized instances of Middle English dialect writing, therefore, the authors cannot be using dialect differences to indicate class differences or generalized regional character. "Aleyn and John in Chaucer's *Reeve's Tale* and Mak in the *Second Shepherds' Play*," Machan writes, "clearly speak northern and southern English, respectively, utilizing a collection of primarily lexical, phonological, and morphological forms predominant in works known to have been produced in specific regions of England. But within the ecology of Middle English their language was not Northern or Southern."[14] This may be a rather surprising assertion with regard to the Wakefield Master, since Mak explicitly imitates the "sothren tothe" while assuming a Southern identity and making claims of class privilege, but with regard to Chaucer it seems widely accepted. Jeremy Smith, who has done much to reveal the regularization of written English in the fifteenth century and explain the enormous changes in spoken English at the end of the Middle Ages, shies away from claims to the sociolinguistic significance of dialect awareness in Chaucer's time. "Contemporary references to accent tend to focus on the oddity of outsiders—such as the young students in *The Reeve's Tale,* or Trevisa's notorious addition to his translation of Higden's *Polychronicon*—rather than on socially marked usages," Smith writes.[15]

[13] Ibid., pp. 100–101.
[14] Ibid., p. 104.
[15] Jeremy J. Smith, "John Gower and London English," in *A Companion to Gower,* ed. Siân Echard (Cambridge: D. S. Brewer, 2004), pp. 61–72 (quotation on p. 66). On the standardization of English, see also Jeremy Smith, "The Use of English: Language Contact, Dialect Variation, and Written Standardisation During the Middle English Period," in *English in Its Social Context: Essays in Historical Sociolinguistics,* ed. Tim William Machan and Charles T. Scott (New York: Oxford University Press, 1992), pp. 47–68, and "Standard Language in Early Middle English?" in *Placing Middle English in Context,* ed. Irma Taavitsainen et al. (Berlin: Mouton de Gruyter, 2000), pp. 125–39; as well as John Hurt Fisher, "Chancery and the Emergence of Standard Written English in the Fifteenth Century," *Speculum* 52 (1977): 870–99; Sandved, "Prolegomena to a Renewed Study," pp. 31–42, 383–84; Horobin, *Language of the Chaucer Tradition;* J. D. Burnley, "Sources of Standardisation in Later Middle English," in *Standardizing English: Essays in the History of Language Change in Honor of John Hurt Fisher,* ed. Joseph B. Trahern Jr. (Knoxville: University of Tennessee Press, 1989), pp. 23–41.

As Smith's remarks suggest, it is not merely *a priori* assumptions about the chronology of English standardization that lead scholars to downplay the social significance of the use of dialect in *The Reeve's Tale;* it is also the ambiguities of the relative status of the characters and their speech in the tale itself. Though Blake and Machan insist that readers are anachronistically imposing their own prejudices on the fourteenth-century text if they imagine that it opposes a Northern variant to a Southern standard, they nonetheless acknowledge that there is potential comedy whenever someone else's manner of speech is represented. And Tolkien, while asserting Chaucer's objective expertise, grants that the tale indulges popular impressions of the comic nature of Northern speech. In at least one instance, there is internal evidence that Chaucer does intend the clerks' speech to seem not just different but comically so. It comes when John explains to Symkyn why he and Aleyn, rather than their manciple, have brought the corn:

> "Symond," quod John, "by God, nede has na peer.
> Hym boes serve hymself that has na swayn,
> Or elles he is a fool, as clerkes sayn.
> Oure manciple, I hope he wil be deed,
> Swa werkes ay the wanges in his heed;
> And forthy as I come, and eek Alayn,
> To grynde oure corn and carie it ham agayn;
> I pray yow spede us heythen that ye may."
>   (I.4026–33)[16]

All of the most distinctive features of John and Aleyn's dialect are on display in this passage: the phonological (*na* for *no, swa* for *so*); the inflexional (*werkes* in the third-person present indicative, instead of *werketh*); and the lexical (*heythen* for *hennes*.)[17] But one particular lexical feature stands out: the use of the word "hope" to mean "anticipate" or "fear." Chaucer deliberately employs this regional idiom, recognizably foreign to his prime readership, in such a way as to make it seem ridiculous: "Oure manciple, I hope he wil be deed."[18] Here is evidence, then,

[16] Citations of the *Canterbury Tales* are from *The Riverside Chaucer*, gen. ed. Larry D. Benson, 3rd. ed. (Boston: Houghton Mifflin, 1987).
[17] See J. A. Burrow and Thorlac Turville-Petre, *A Book of Middle English*, 2nd. ed. (Oxford: Blackwell, 1992), p. 6.
[18] See David Burnley, "Lexis and Semantics," *The Cambridge History of the English Language, Volume II, 1066–1476*, ed. Norman Blake (Cambridge: Cambridge University Press, 1992), p. 411.

that however accurately he portrays the regional dialect of the clerks, Chaucer is inviting laughter at their unfamiliar speech and encouraging the reader to assume that they are comically rustic rubes.

Indeed, this is the role that John and Aleyn seem to play in the first part of the tale. In the preceding *Miller's Tale,* Nicholas declares that "A clerk hadde litherly biset his whyle, / But if he koude a carpenter bigyle" (I.3299–3300), and John the carpenter obligingly proves himself a gullible yokel. John and Aleyn are equally confident that they can outwit the local miller, but they are immediately and easily bested by Symkyn, who needs only to set their horse loose to foil their hopes of exposing his deceit. Any reader who has assumed that their outlandish accents mark them as rubes has been given evidence to justify the assumption. In fact, even modern critics sometimes suggest that John and Aleyn's dialect is innately comical, indicative of the clerks' incompetence and evidence of the "lowness" of the tale and its teller.[19]

But the social status of Chaucer's clerks, relative to that of the miller, is quite ambiguous. It is they, after all, who are receiving the Cambridge education. Even after sending them chasing after their borrowed horse while he steals their corn, so that when they return bedraggled from the field they must beg hospitality from their abuser and even offer to pay for it, Symkyn mocks them not for their rusticity but for the abstraction and sophistry of their philosophical training:

> Myn hous is streit, but ye han lerned art;
> Ye konne by argumentes make a place
> A myle brood of twenty foot of space.
> Lat se now if this place may suffise,
> Or make it rowm with speche, as is youre gise.
>   (I.4122–26)[20]

---

[19] Thus, in one of the best-known articles on the tale, Robert Worth Frank Jr. asserts, "Part of the fun is the fact that the characters and their actions are, as Professor Higgins said of Eliza Doolittle, 'so deliciously low.'" ("The *Reeve's Tale* and the Comedy of Limitation," in *Directions in Literary Criticism: Contemporary Approaches to Literature,* ed. Stanley Weintraub and Philip Young (University Park: Pennsylvania State University Press, 1973), pp. 53–69 (quotation on p. 57).) Frank's citation of the greatest linguist in English dramatic history is revealing of his philological perspective. If he and Chaucer, and we as readers, are likened to Professor Higgins, then John and Aleyn are Elizas: "The use of dialect is a brilliant device. . . . Its primary effect is to label them as 'outlanders,' if not precisely 'low,' certainly comic to Chaucer's London audience and disarmingly 'sely' to Simkin and possibly 'low' in his eyes as well" (58).

[20] See Blake, *Non-Standard Language,* pp. 28–29.

John and Aleyn's subsequent conversations are marked by just such academic reasoning, unnecessarily complex and hermetically theoretical; Aleyn, quite unlike the ostensibly bookish Nicholas, is revealed as the kind of intellectual who feels compelled to cite a legal principle in order to justify to himself his own fornication: "For, John, ther is a lawe that says thus: / That gif a man in a point be agreved, / That in another he sal be releved" (I.4180–82). And in the end, the clerks return to their college with their grain restored and their libidos slaked, while the miller is injured both in his body and, more dearly, in his preciously guarded lineage.

Whatever the initial impression of their speech, therefore, the tale would seem ultimately to leave the two dialects it dramatizes on equal footing. Chaucer invites social prejudices based on linguistic differences only to challenge and undermine them. What is Chaucer's use of dialect in the tale, then, but *philological,* as Tolkien originally suggested? Is it not an objective observation and transcription of linguistic variety, interested in speech but uninterested in the relative status of its different registers, and in fact sedulous to dramatize their equal standing?

Following Tolkien, many critics have seen the tale as embodying Chaucer's, or the Reeve's, linguistic capacity, its facility in representing "foreign" speech forms. Robert Worth Frank Jr. calls the tale a "glorious glossary."[21] C. David Benson, defining the tale's essential features within the "drama of style" of the greater work, points to the dialect of the clerks as evidence of the "*Reeve*-poet's particular skill with language."[22] Benson's view is supported by Christopher Cannon's lexical analysis of the *Canterbury Tales.*[23] And it is extended even further, into the realm of Middle English linguistic ecology, by Machan. Noting as others have that in a few instances the Reeve himself seems to use linguistic forms typical of his native Norfolk, Machan argues ingeniously for the Reeve as a philologist: the dialect writing in the tale is a feature of "Oswald's linguistic strategies," and evince a character with "a high degree of metalinguistic awareness," which would be appropriate, Machan claims, to a man of the Reeve's station in late fourteenth-century Norfolk.[24]

---

[21] Frank, "The *Reeve's Tale* and the Comedy of Limitation," p. 63.

[22] C. David Benson, *Chaucer's Drama of Style: Poetic Variety and Contrast in the "Canterbury Tales"* (Chapel Hill: University of North Carolina Press, 1986), p. 99.

[23] Christopher Cannon, *The Making of Chaucer's English: A Study of Words* (Cambridge: Cambridge University Press, 1998), p. 127.

[24] Machan, *English in the Middle Ages,* pp. 121–30 (122, 124).

But the significance of Chaucer's use of dialect writing cannot be limited to the single tale in which it occurs or to its fictional teller. Cannon argues that Chaucer's poetry makes implicit claims for its own stylistic superiority: "By presenting traditional forms as alternatives and grading them, Chaucer presents *his* English as the salvific form that can extract the good from the bad and become the best." Chaucer's performances of "linguistic capacity" are exhibitions of his linguistic *capaciousness*—ostensible proof, that is, that his English comprehends and supersedes all other variants.[25] Cannon's focus is on lexicography and style, but I believe *The Reeve's Tale* bears out his argument in the realm of dialect.

If such a critique of linguistic self-promotion seems to imply self-interested calculation on Chaucer's part, then it is all the more important to take note of those sociolinguistic models that reveal the potential symbolic profit available even to unintentional participants in a privileged subject position. We can depersonalize this claim to linguistic preeminence, showing it to be an unconscious participation in broad cultural assumptions about region, status, and dialect, and in the case of *The Reeve's Tale,* we can specifically locate the mechanism in the privileged subject position of the "philological" observer.

The Strategy of Condescension

Pierre Bourdieu understands the world of language by way of the same model he constructs for the social universe as a whole, as an arena of constant competition among individual agents for profit in an endless series of overlapping fields. Agents unconsciously internalize and reduplicate social conventions that can work against their own interests in the competition for symbolic and material profit; they can also profit from privileged subject positions of which they are not consciously aware.

The arena of verbal exchange, therefore, is a marketplace, and every transaction produces a profit: "The construction of a linguistic market creates the conditions for an objective competition in and through which the legitimate competence can function as linguistic capital, producing a *profit of distinction* on the occasion of each social exchange."[26] The key

[25] Cannon, *Making of Chaucer's English,* pp. 137, 150.
[26] Pierre Bourdieu, *Language and Symbolic Power,* ed. John B. Thompson, trans. Gino Raymond and Matthew Adamson (Cambridge, Mass.: Harvard University Press, 1991), p. 55. All emphases are Bourdieu's.

for Bourdieu is that in the social context of language there is always a dominant competence. In any linguistic environment there are innumerable modes and registers, and any given individual is capable of employing a variety of forms with some competency, but all of the participants must be aware of the dominant competence and of its superior social status. "The dominant competence," Bourdieu writes, "functions as linguistic capital, only in so far as certain conditions (the unification of the market and the unequal distribution of the chances of access to the means of places of expression) are continuously fulfilled, so that the groups which possess that competence are able to impose it as the only legitimate one in the formal markets (the fashionable, educational, political and administrative markets) and in most of the linguistic interactions in which they are involved."[27] Each verbal exchange reveals some participant's greater access to the dominant competence. Though each participant has a sense of what abilities and strategies produce symbolic profit—a feel for the game, as Bourdieu figures it—this understanding is largely unconsciously habituated, and a speaker may therefore accrue profit despite his or her conscious or stated intentions.

One of Bourdieu's prime examples of such an unintentional route to sociolinguistic profit is a phenomenon he calls "the strategy of condescension," which, he says,

consists in deriving *profit* from the objective relation of power between the languages that confront one another in practice . . . in the very act of symbolically negating that relation, namely, the hierarchy of the languages and those who speak them. Such a strategy is possible whenever the objective disparity between persons present (that is, between their social properties) is sufficiently known and recognized by everyone (particularly those involved in the interaction, as agents or spectators) so that the symbolic negation of the hierarchy (by using the "common touch," for instance) enables the speaker to combine the profits linked to the undiminished hierarchy with those derived from the directly symbolic negation of the hierarchy—not the least of which is the strengthening of the hierarchy implied by the recognition accorded to the way of using the hierarchical relation.[28]

Bourdieu illustrates this concept (which, one must admit, is in desperate need of illustration) with an anecdote about the mayor of Pau, a town

[27] Ibid., 56–57.
[28] Ibid., p. 68.

in the Pyrenean province of Béarn (and, although he does not identify it as such, Bourdieu's home province.) In Béarn, as in much of provincial France through the mid-twentieth century, large portions of the population spoke primarily local dialect rather than standard French. Bourdieu notes a report in a French-language newspaper of a ceremony in honor of a Béarnais poet at which the mayor spoke partly in the Béarnais dialect, a gesture that, according to the printed account, "greatly moved" the audience.[29] It may seem to us, as it apparently did to the mayor's contemporary audience, that by speaking in dialect in this public and official context he has struck a blow for the legitimacy of Béarnais as against the hegemony of standard French. Bourdieu points out, however, "In order for an audience of people whose mother tongue is Béarnais to perceive as a 'thoughtful gesture' the fact that a Béarnais mayor should speak to them in Béarnais, they must tacitly recognize the unwritten law which prescribes French as the only acceptable language for formal speeches in formal situations."[30] The mayor's capacity to offer an apparent challenge to this law derives from the same linguistic authority that undergirds the status of standard French itself. He has advanced degrees and other trappings of cultural status that evince his fluency in French and demonstrate his qualification for public office. The same Béarnais words that the mayor speaks would have no cultural value coming from the mouth of a local speaker who did not have the mayor's *bona fides* vouching for his access to the dominant competence. So the mayor gains a profit of distinction from his use of the subordinate language that simultaneously depends on and denies its subordinate status.

For the mayor of Pau and his listeners in twentieth-century France, the unassailable authority of Paris French is universally recognized, maintained by a vast and intricate network of cultural privilege, and institutionalized throughout the systems of education, governmental bureaucracy, and public media. The absence, or at least the paucity, of such formal and institutional linguistic authority in medieval England has led language historians to deny the cultural supremacy of London dialect over other forms in Chaucer's time. But as important as institutional structures, in Bourdieu's model, are the individual "players of the game" themselves, who construct power paradigms through their ac-

---

[29] Ibid. See also John Thompson's "Editor's Introduction," pp. 18–19.
[30] Bourdieu, *Language and Symbolic Power*, p. 68.

tions, as well as internalizing received distinctions. Chaucer is one such player, and the *Canterbury Tales* participates in the construction of a linguistic hierarchy. For all of the "variety" that has been recognized as the hallmark of Chaucerian style virtually from the beginning, the dialect of the work—of the authorial voice of the pilgrimage frame, of all the pilgrims, of all the characters within the various tales—is of a piece. The speech of the merchant of Seynt-Denys in *The Shipman's Tale* is seasoned with fragments of French ("*Quy la?*" [VII.214]) for local color, and the Miller, in his Prologue and his Tale, employs in many ways registers distinct from those of the Knight or the Parson, but all of them use the same English, Chaucer's own Southern dialect. So do all the characters in *The Summoner's Tale,* though it is set in Yorkshire. The single exception, the variant dialect of John and Aleyn in *The Reeve's Tale,* proves the rule.[31]

For while the conflict between the miller's speech and the clerks' speech in *The Reeve's Tale* leaves neither victorious, the greater drama plays out between the clerks' speech and Chaucer's. If the work as a whole were a collection of voices speaking in a variety of dialects, they could reasonably be recognized as having equal standing. But in fact Chaucer's unique use of a variant dialect is subsumed into the dialect of the greater work. There may be little external to the work to grant that dialect superior status, but the *Canterbury Tales* itself works to make it the standard, and therefore to cast variants as exceptional. The work itself, furthermore, as a compendium of fictional and poetic styles, genres, and modes, helps to establish the Chaucerian dialect's standing as a literary language. The one-time appearance of a variant dialect in the *Canterbury Tales* does not elevate Northern dialect to the status of a literary language. On the contrary, it serves to demonstrate that only the London dialect is the proper form for artistic expression, all other dialects becoming variations from the norm.

Crucially, the Chaucerian dialect functions as a dominant competence in that it is not universally accessible.[32] The characters in *The Reeve's Tale*

---

[31] The other possible exception is Oswald the Reeve himself, who seems to speak partially in Norfolk dialect, about which more below.

[32] Given Bourdieu's insistence that all the members of a language group must recognize the symbolic value of competencies that gain profit for a minority, it is important to address whether Chaucer's uses of divergent dialect were recognizable to his contemporaries. Tolkien calls Chaucer's dialect-writing a "philological joke" that was lost on his fifteenth-century scribes, and it is commonly observed that the Paris manuscript, copied in the North Midlands circa 1430, gives the work as a whole Northern linguistic features, thereby erasing the distinction between the speech of the clerks and that of the miller. But Simon Horobin has recently demonstrated that most of the fifteenth-

speak their different dialects to each other without any suggestion of status, or any problems of comprehension, which is fortunate, since each can presumably speak only in his or her own dialect; John and Aleyn must be able to speak Latin, but in English they can speak only their native tongue. Chaucer, on the other hand, has access to all of these competencies. Bourdieu stresses that there is no profit to speaking an unauthorized language unless the audience is aware that the speaker is not doing so out of *necessity*.[33] Just as the mayor of Pau in speaking in Béarnais gains a symbolic profit that is not available to most of his Béarnais-speaking audience, Chaucer profits from his use of Northern dialect when John and Aleyn do not. Chaucer is master of his own language in all of its registers, including its most elevated forms of poetic style, and he can also perform the speech of others. There is an inherent symbolic profit in this performative capacity, to be able, like Shakespeare's Prince Hal, "to drink with any tinker in his own language."[34] But in Chaucer's case it is elevated to the "strategy of condescension" when he gains further profit in the very act of denying the existence of the linguistic privileges even as he benefits from them. Even as *The Reeve's Tale* negates any presumed hierarchies among the dialects it represents, the *Canterbury Tales* demonstrates that Chaucer's literary language is capacious enough to include all other forms of the language, which now must be perceived as variant and non-normative.

It is clear enough that Chaucer's modern readers understand the dialect differences in the tale to conform to Bourdieu's concept of relative competence within the authorized language. The evidence is in the critical responses to *The Reeve's Tale*. Robert Worth Frank Jr., in one of the best-known essays on the tale, comments that "Simkin speaks English competent enough to play with sophistical argument; it is the clerks who speak a tongue uncouth and not quite acceptable."[35] Simon Horobin, in the latest and most sophisticated philological analysis of the tale, writes, "Chaucer's representation of dialect was no doubt further constrained by the nature of his Southern, courtly audience, who would

---

century manuscripts do in fact retain the Northern quality of the clerks' speech as distinct from the dialect of the miller and of Chaucer. See "J.R.R. Tolkien as a Philologist: A Reconsideration of the Northernisms in Chaucer's *Reeve's Tale*," *ES* 82 (2001): 97–105.

[33] Bourdieu, *Language and Symbolic Power*, p. 69.

[34] William Shakespeare, *Henry IV, Part 1*, 2.4.18–19. *The Riverside Shakespeare*, ed. G. Blakemore Evans (Boston: Houghton Mifflin, 1974).

[35] Frank, "The *Reeve's Tale* and the Comedy of Limitation," 62.

perhaps have had difficulties comprehending the more extreme provincialisms of Northern speech."[36] This is surely true—but it further demonstrates that one of the effects of dialect writing in *The Reeve's Tale* is to mark the clerks' dialect as "extremely provincial," and thereby to grant Chaucer's speech cultural centrality.

Ultimately, it is, I think, quite accurate to call Chaucer a "philologist" in *The Reeve's Tale,* but not in the purely laudatory sense that Tolkien bestows the epithet. We should not speak of Chaucer's "philology," that is, without addressing his "philologism." The idea and the term "philologism" can be traced to the early twentieth-century writings of V. N. Vološinov. To Vološinov, "philologism," which is the linguistic impulse itself, is an "abstract objectivism" that constructs the object of linguistic study as dead, static, and alien.[37] Inherent in Vološinov's analysis is a critique of the unconscious biases fostered by the training and expertise of the social scientist.[38] Similar concepts inform Michelle Warren's recent coinage of the term "post-philology," which she formulates as an analogue of "postmodernism" and "postcolonialism," and as a reaction, primarily, to the nationalist origins of modern philology. Post-philology would "address the complex relationships among political, linguistic, and literary histories."[39] Philology is of course integral to the Orientalist project as Edward Said defines it; the central chapters of *Orientalism* focus on the professionalization of Semitic linguistics and the scientific classification of Near Eastern languages.[40] The "philologism" of *The Reeve's Tale* derives from the impartiality and objectivity of its observation of foreign speech, which grant Chaucer the authority to represent it, to improvise within it, and to incorporate it as a foreign variant within his own language—which in turn takes on the status of the dominant competence.

[36] "Tolkien as a Philologist," p. 104.

[37] V. N. Vološinov, "Language, Speech, and Utterance," *Marxism and the Philosophy of Language,* trans. Ladislav Matejka and I. R. Titunik (Cambridge, Mass.: Harvard University Press, 1986), pp. 65–82 (67, 73). Vološinov may or may not have been a pseudonym of Mikhail Bakhtin; see Matejka and Titunik, "Translators' Preface, 1986," pp. vii–xii.

[38] See Pierre Bourdieu, "The Economics of Linguistic Exchange," *Social Science Information* 16 (1977): 645–68 (quotation on 663 n. 1).

[39] Michelle R. Warren, "Post-Philology," in *Postcolonial Moves: Medieval through Modern,* ed. Patricia Clare Ingham and Michelle R. Warren (New York: Palgrave Macmillan, 2003), pp. 19–45 (quotation on p. 31).

[40] Edward W. Said, *Orientalism* (New York: Vintage Books, 1979). See particularly pp. 123–66.

Vološinov claims to be describing a transhistorical phenomenon: "Philologism is the inevitable distinguishing mark of the whole of European linguistics as determined by the historical vicissitudes of its birth and development. However far back we may go in tracing the history of linguistic categories and methods, we find philologists everywhere. Not just the Alexandrians, but the ancient Romans were philologists, as were the Greeks. . . . Also, the ancient Hindus were philologists."[41] Vološinov does not mention, and might not recognize, medieval philologists, but surely they existed and belong in the list. When Tolkien, therefore, remarks on Chaucer's resemblance to a philologist, he is accurately detecting Chaucer's "philologism." Chaucer's representation of multiple linguistic competencies, despite its apparent impartiality and empirical accuracy, nonetheless—perhaps unintentionally—grants Chaucer a privileged subject position and in fact inscribes the hierarchies of linguistic distinction that it seems to deny.

Northernisms and Northernism

It is important to remember that the "strategy of condescension" does not depend for its effect on the conscious intention of the agent. It grows out of one's habituated "sense of the game," which leads one to seek social advantages that one may not consciously aspire to—that one may think, in fact, one is resisting or denying. Similarly, "philologism" refers to the symbolic profit the linguist accrues in the process of exercising what he imagines to be his objective and impartial expertise. In his most philological moments, therefore, Chaucer's literary practice is informed by and contributes to subtle but widespread and deeply ingrained linguistic assumptions and performances. He neither invents this mode of Middle English philological representation nor practices it alone.

While rejecting the stratification of Middle English dialects by relative social status, at least before the second half of the fifteenth century, scholars recognize numerous instances of dialect *awareness,* when speakers or writers betray a consciousness of distinctions between different types of English.[42] The best known is William Caxton's prologue to the *Eneydos,* in which he illustrates the challenge of writing and compiling

---

[41] Vološinov, "Language, Speech, and Utterance," p. 71.
[42] See Machan, *English in the Middle Ages,* pp. 86–96.

vernacular books for a contemporary English audience with an anecdote
of a merchant trying to buy eggs:

For we englysshe men / ben borne vnder the domynacyon of the mone. whiche
is neuer stedfaste / but euer wauerynge / wexynge one season / and waneth ꝫ
dyscreaseth another season / And that comyn englysshe that is spoken in one
shyre varyeth from a nother. In so moche that in my dayes happened that
certayn marchauntes were in a shippe in tamyse for to haue sayled ouer the see
into ʒelande / and for lacke of wynde thei taryed atte forlond. and wente to
lande for to refreshe them And one of theym named sheffelde a mercer cam in
to an hows and axed for mete. and specyally he axyd after eggys And the good
wyf answerde. that she coude speke no frenshe. And the marchaunt was angry.
for he also coude speke no frenshe. but wold haue hadde egges / and she vnders-
tode hym not / And thenne at laste a nother sayd that he wolde haue eyren /
then the good wyf sayd that she vnderstod hym wel / Loo what sholde a man
in thyse dayes now wryte. egges or eyren / certaynly it is harde to playse euery
man / by cause of dyuersite ꝫ chaunge of langage.[43]

Caxton means this story to demonstrate the irreducible multiplicity of
contemporary English. It is clear, also, that he takes all of the forms of
the language to be of equal standing; the lack of a formal standard, in
fact, is the root of his complaint: "what sholde a man in thyse dayes
now wryte?" And it hardly seems likely that even Caxton intended this
winning anecdote to be taken as historical fact, given its lack of detail,
its vague invocation of circumstance ("in my dayes happened that certayn marchauntes"), and its perfect punchline, in which the wife accuses
the merchant of speaking French, the English speaker's omnipresent
embodiment of linguistic otherness. There is also the fact that of innumerable variations among the different Middle English dialects, this
story hinges on a simple lexical difference: "egges," a form common in
the north, as opposed to "eyren," more common in the south. As soon as
another merchant substitutes the southern form, the linguistic confusion
disappears and the wife "vnderstod hym wel." It is telling, therefore,
that the anecdote provides only two specific details: the Thameside setting, locating the wife's speech, and the merchant's surname: "sheffelde." He is, apparently, a Yorkshireman. Caxton evokes this anecdote
in order to illustrate the multiplicity of contemporary dialects, but it

---

[43] *The Prologues and Epilogues of William Caxton,* ed. W. J. B. Crotch, EETS, o.s. 176
(London: Oxford University Press, 1956 [1928]), p. 108.

actually dramatizes a dichotomy, and this dichotomy is imagined as an opposition of the North and the South.

A similar tendency can be found in many of the instances of dialect awareness in Middle English. The most notorious example is in Trevisa's translation of Higden's *Polychronicon:*

men of þe est wiþ men of the west, as hyt were vnder þe same party of heuene, acordeþ more in sounynge of speche þan men of þe norþ wiþ men of þe souþ. Þerfore hyt ys þat Mercii, þat buþ men of myddel Engelond, as hyt were parteners of þe endes, vnderstondeþ betre þe syde longages, norþeron and souþeron, þan norþeron and souþeron vnderstondeþ eyþer oþer

Al þe longage of þe norþhumbres, and specialych at ȝork, ys so scharp slytting and frotyng and vnschape þat we souþeron men may þat longage vnneþe vnderstonde. Y trowe þat þat ys bycause þat a buþ nyȝ to straunge men and aliens þat spekeþ straungelych and also bycause þat þe kynges of engelond woneþ alwey fer fram þat contray.[44]

As Ronald Waldron explains, the first of these two paragraphs is Higden's interpolation, while the second follows quite closely his source in William of Malmesbury, and Trevisa translates both faithfully. Waldron suggests, therefore, that while William clearly thinks of himself as southern, Higden, a Cheshire native, imagines himself a man of "myddel Engelond," and Trevisa's sympathies are unclear.[45] Still, William's perspective is duly transmitted from the twelfth century to the fifteenth and from Latin into English, and with it his "philologism": linguistic observation, with its pretenses of objectivity and expertise (explaining phonological difference by proximity to foreign speakers), leads to chauvinistic dismissal of the tongue more foreign to the observer and more remote from the seat of cultural power and authority—here, the English kings. The result is that, though the speakers at the two linguistic poles are presumably mutually unintelligible, it is the northern speech that is characterized as "so scharp and slyttyng and frotyng and vnschape."

[44] *Polychronicon Ranulphi Higden Monachi Cestrensis together with the English Translations of John Trevisa and an Unknown Writer of the Fifteenth Century,* ed. Churchill Babington and J. R. Lumby, RS 41, 9 vols. (London: Longman, 1865–86), 2:163.

[45] Ronald Waldron, "Dialect Aspects of Manuscripts of Trevisa's Translation of the *Polychronicon,*" in *Regionalism in Late Medieval Manuscripts and Texts,* ed. Felicity Riddy (Cambridge: D. S. Brewer, 1991), pp. 67–87 (68–69). See also Machan, *English in the Middle Ages,* pp. 95–96.

In reality, Middle English speech was multifarious, and English people were aware of local variation. They were not, however, always as ready as Higden was to conceive of themselves as occupying individual points in a linguistic continuum. Richard Beadle has shown, for instance, that "the East Anglian counties, and more particularly Norfolk, were perceived to be linguistically, and . . . somewhat culturally distinct from early times."[46] Among Beadle's evidence are examples of scribal translation of source texts into their own dialect. In one instance, Thomas Bareyle, a Norfolk scribe, adds this colophon to a copy of Richard Rolle's *Form of Living:* "Here endith the informacion of Richard the Ermyte þat he wrote to an Ankyr, translate oute of Northowrn tunge into Sutherne that it schulde the betir be understondyn of men that be of the Selbe countre."[47] East Anglia, the region of which Norfolk forms the northern portion, is in relation to the greater geography of England neither northern nor southern but, precisely, eastern. Norwich is as remote from London as it is from Hampole. If, as Beadle persuasively demonstrates, spoken and written Norfolk English was manifestly distinct from other dialects throughout the Middle English period, then why would Bareyle characterize his Norfolk translation of Rolle's Yorkshire text as "translate oute of Northowrn tunge into Sutherne"?

It seems that many Middle English speakers habitually conceived their language differences along a North-South axis, turning observed pluralities into generalized dualities. Inevitably, these dualities cast one element as normative and dominant and the other as variant and subordinate. Indeed, the inherent hierarchy of the binary can be seen as the motivation for its construction rather than an incidental result. As much as writers from Malmesbury to Caxton emphasize the incomprehensibility of Northern speech to Southern ears, it may be that North-South differences are emphasized less because they inhibit communication than because the northernmost forms are *sufficiently* different to *justify* a dichotomy. This may explain why John and Aleyn's speech is the only sustained use of dialect-writing in the *Canterbury Tales.* I say sustained because there is at least one other example, in the speech of the Reeve himself, as in the first line that he speaks in his Prologue: "So theek . . .

[46] Richard Beadle, "Prolegomena to a Literary Geography of Later Medieval Norfolk," in Riddy, ed., *Regionalism in Late Medieval Manuscripts and Texts,* pp. 89–108 (92).

[47] Hope Emily Allen, ed., *English Writings of Richard Rolle, Hermit of Hampole* (Oxford: Oxford University Press, 1931; reprint Gloucester: Alan Sutton, 1988), p. 84. See also Beadle, "Prolegomena," p. 93; Machan, *English in the Middle Ages,* p. 87.

ful wel koude I thee quite" (I.3864). "Theek"—"may I thrive"—is an East Midlands form, appropriate to the Reeve, who, we are told in the General Prologue, is from Baldeswelle in Norfolk. Oswald is a linguistic kinsman of Thomas Bareyle. However, as Douglas Gray notes, Chaucer "does not consistently represent the speech of the Reeve in his own person; only a few indications of pronunciation (e.g., *lemes, abegge*) suggest East Anglia."[48] Why is Chaucer's depiction of Oswald's Norfolk dialect so much less thorough than his representation of the "Northern" dialect of John and Aleyn? And why does he attempt this kind of linguistic characterization nowhere else?[49] Whatever the reasons, Chaucer's handling of the Reeve's and the clerks' dialects in *The Reeve's Prologue and Tale* is revealing. Of the two variant dialects, the more northerly is the one that is at greater variance with the standard dialect of the work as a whole. This one is more recognizable to readers and, apparently, easier for the author to imitate consistently. Chaucer's abbreviated attempt to depict Oswald's dialect therefore points to the significance of the clerks' speech: unlike Norfolk speech or any other contemporary dialect, it is different enough from Chaucer's own speech to be sustainably mimicable. The differentness of their speech must therefore stand for all linguistic difference within Middle English. The tale does not merely dramatize objectively real linguistic differences. It uses the most extreme linguistic variations available in order to maintain distinctions. It is telling, therefore, that Chaucer locates John and Aleyn's home in the unidentifiable town of "Strother," saying only that it is "Fer in the north; I kan nat telle where" (I.4015). He tells us nothing more because nothing else matters. The clerks, and their speech, are simply "Northern," and in being Northern they are remote, foreign, unknown, and vague. A master of language like Chaucer, however—a *"grant trans-*

---

[48] From the explanatory notes to *The Reeve's Tale* in the *Riverside Chaucer,* pp. 848–49. See also Norman Davis, review of J. A.W. Bennett, *Chaucer at Oxford and Cambridge, RES* 27 (1976): 336–37. Simon Horobin, however, finds greater evidence for Chaucer's depiction of Norfolk dialect in the Reeve's speech, conceding nonetheless that his "depiction of Northern speech was much more thorough." "Chaucer's Norfolk Reeve," *Neophil* 86 (2002): 609–12 (611). See also Juliette Dor, "Chaucer and Dialectology," *Studia Anglica Posnaniensia* 20 (1987): 59–68.

[49] One might wonder if Chaucer at some point intended that each of his pilgrims would speak in a geographically distinct manner. If so, then perhaps he was unable to accomplish such a diversely polyvocal representation; perhaps he was not enough of a "philologist" to make the *Canterbury Tales* into a kind of *Linguistic Atlas of Late Mediaeval English.* But outside of *The Reeve's Prologue and Tale,* there is no evidence for any such project.

lateur," as Deschamps famously dubbed him—can control the foreign tongue and present it in a tamed and generalized form for the delectation and edification of the Southern reader.

Chaucer's interest in Northern dialect, then, particularly in its seeming accuracy and objectivity, constitutes a kind of "Northernism," and Chaucer's role resembles Said's description of the Orientalist: "The Orientalist can imitate the Orient without the opposite being true. What he says about the Orient is therefore to be understood as description obtained in a one-way exchange: as *they* spoke and behaved, *he* observed and wrote down. His power was to have existed among them as a native speaker, as it were, and also as a secret writer. And what he wrote was intended as useful knowledge, not for them, but for Europe and its various disseminative institutions."[50] Philology is, in this conception, instrumental to Orientalism; it serves to help the West dominate the East by defining it. But "philologism" can be said always to possess these qualities. The pretenses of social-scientific objectivity inherent in philology construct the linguistic object of study as a mute, static, and inert other, and correlatively establish a privileged subject position for the speaker. What Said attributes to the Orientalist, therefore, also applies to Chaucer. He can imitate his Northern clerks, though they would not be able to imitate him. His record of their speech seems accurate and therefore based on personal observation, implying a familiarity with his subjects, but it is a unidirectional familiarity that amounts to a position of power. And the power resides ultimately in the fact that, whatever the familiarity between the representatives of different linguistic competencies, only one of them will carry away from the encounter the opportunity to represent the other. This representation is objective, accurate, for the purpose of "useful knowledge"—but the knowledge is useful to groups already in socially superior positions, whose authority is further legitimated by their access to philological knowledge.

Debates over the "accuracy" of Chaucer's depiction of John and Aleyn's dialect obscure the fact that this supposed dialect was never spoken. It is, rather, a generalized representation of an imagined dialect. This "dialect" was not spoken by any actual individuals in any real place at any specific time.[51] Nor was the precise representation of actual

[50] Said, *Orientalism,* p. 160.

[51] Machan (*English in the Middle Ages,* p. 117) relates this representation of speech to the kind of "colourless regional language" described by M. L. Samuels in "Spelling and Dialect in the Late and Post-Middle English Periods," *So meny people longages and tonges,* pp. 43–54.

speech Chaucer's intention, as he declares when he states that Strother is "Fer in the north; I kan nat telle where." He does not know where Strother is, and he does not care, except insofar as it is "Northern." He is not trying to delineate a specific local dialect; rather, he is using differences to make generalizations. Such generalizations are most readily constructed as North-South binaries. The greatest philological power, however, derives from the pretense that these generalizations are neutral, making both writer and reader complicit in the power of social-scientific authority and expertise to make generalizations and to benefit from them.

To some extent this "Northernism" is perpetuated when modern philology asserts that the dialect introduced into *The Reeve's Tale* is characterized by "Northernisms." To call a linguistic feature a "Northernism" is itself a regionalist generalization. It takes particular linguistic features as givens of a geographical area when in fact defining a dialect always entails combining a set of generalizations that in effect generate a region. It is itself a philologistic reification of a social construct. This is the essence of "philologism." As Vološinov says, "The *isolated, finished, monologic utterance,* divorced from its verbal and actual context and standing open not to any possible sort of active response but to passive understanding on the part of the philologist—that is the ultimate 'donnée' and the starting point of linguistic thought."[52]

Chaucer is generating a regional identity through an accretion of linguistic generalizations. In fact, he is creating two regional identities, constructing "Southernness" through its contrast with "Northernness." It is not only in *The Reeve's Tale* that Chaucer engages in this kind of regionalist generalization. In his Prologue, the Parson protests to the Host, "But trusteth wel, I am a Southren man; / I kan nat geeste 'rum, ram, ruf,' by lettre" (X.43–44). The Parson apparently has not read Ralph Hanna's pugnacious essay in the *Cambridge History of Medieval English Literature,* disproving that alliterative poetry was an exclusively regional phenomenon, providing evidence instead of the production of alliterative verse throughout England, including in London. Hanna concludes, "Alliterative poetry, although it had a vital circulation in Chaucerian surroundings, does remain Chaucer's Other. But this Otherness essentially occupies a space of consciousness, not of geography."[53] The

---

[52] Vološinov, "Language, Speech, and Utterance," p. 73 (italics in original).

[53] Ralph Hanna, "Alliterative Poetry," *The Cambridge History of Medieval English Literature,* ed. David Wallace (Cambridge: Cambridge University Press, 1999), pp. 488–512 (511). Machan denies that the Parson can be making a regionalist distinction in these lines, claiming that "the plentiful existence of alliterative poetry in fifteenth-century southern manuscripts argues strongly against just such putative chauvinism" (*English in*

Canterbury Tales contributes to the creation of a geography of conscious-ness, a map of regionalist generalizations overlaid on the physical land-scape of late-medieval England. Chaucer participates in the construction of "Northernness" as a state of physical, linguistic, economic, social, political, and geographical otherness within the English language and the English nation.[54]

---

the Middle Ages, p. 95). But of course the point is that Chaucer makes such a claim when it is not empirically true. I believe that other poets may also use alliteration in verse as a marker of regional affiliation and social status. John Lydgate's "Mumming at Hertford," introduced by John Shirley as "a disguysing of þe rude vpplandisshe people compley-nyng on hir wyves, with þe boystous aunswere of hir wyves" (*The Minor Poems of John Lydgate, Part II: Secular Poems,* ed. Henry Noble MacCracken, EETS, o.s. 192 [1934; repr. London: Oxford University Press, 1961], p. 675), presents a host of rude mechani-cals, all abused husbands and domineering wives. These couples are depicted in lan-guage that is evocatively, and comically, alliterative, as in the presentation of Thom the Tinker's wife:

> Hir name was cleped Tybot Tapister.
> To brawle and broyle she nad no maner fer,
> To thakke his pilche, stoundemel nowe and þanne,
> Thikker þane Thome koude clowten any panne.
> (121–24)

The clashing consonants of the alliteration are meant to evoke Tyb's bruising abuse of Thom and to echo Thom's beating of his tins, but in addition Lydgate almost seems to be mimicking the verse style associated—in the imagination of the southern elite at least—with the rural north. Conversely, Lydgate shows that although he is a "southren man" like Chaucer's Parson, he *can* "geeste 'rum, ram, ruf' by lettre." In this context, the rustic couples are associated with language that is clearly, as Shirley says, "rude" and "upplandisshe"—unlearned, rustic, provincial, common, and not ours. The language is also exceptionally rich in entertaining and extravagant colloquialisms. Norman Blake remarks, "The absence of regional dialect registers in medieval English literature is echoed by the absence of argot, slang, archaisms or class dialects as markers of character or indices of atmosphere in descriptions" (*The English Language in Medieval Literature,* 46). And Machan asserts, "Nothing in the record of Old or Middle English, moreover, implies the kind of correlation between regional variety and social stratification present in the geographic and linguistic implications of Latin *rusticus,* which from the republic period signifies both a rural dweller and someone who is coarse, awkward, clownish, or linguistically backward" (*English in the Middle Ages,* 94–95). I would suggest that Lyd-gate's "Mumming at Hertford" does use slang as a class marker in a literary context, and that "upplandishe," as used by Shirley, is a close corollary to *rusticus.*

[54] Wendy Scase has hypothesized that John and Aleyn's use of dialect is "theatrical," a *performance* that "announces that they are not from the area, and therefore cannot yet know of Symkyn's reputation for dishonesty." "Tolkien, Philology, and the Reeve's Tale: Towards the Cultural Move in Middle English Studies," *SAC* 24 (2002): 325–34 (333). It is an intriguing notion, though the clerks persist in their dialect even when Symkyn and his family are sound asleep and snoring loudly around them. But if it is true, then the clerks are also participating in a regionalist linguistic hierarchy, in which Northern-ness is a performance of rusticity, provinciality, and *naïveté* and Southernness, by con-trast, is a normative national identity, which can be performed, as Chaucer performs it, for cultural profit.

The Wakefield Master as a Philologist

It is in a "Northern" text, however, that we encounter the first instance of English dialect-writing that indisputably dramatizes gradations of social status. "We have to wait until the Wakefield *Second Shepherds' Play*, usually dated to the first half of the fifteenth century," writes Jeremy Smith, "before there is fairly clear indication that southern speech has a higher social status than that of the north."[55]

In delineating that status hierarchy, the Wakefield play proudly asserts the positive value of déclassé Northernness. The play performs a linguistic burlesque intended to affirm community by defining outsiders, and it therefore employs strategies of mimicry that generally imply a degree of social superiority and control. But the *Second Shepherds' Play* also reveals that its author or authors, as well as its assumed audience, share with Southern authors assumptions about the relationship between Northern and Southern speech. It thus unintentionally perpetuates status distinctions that it claims to critique and reject.

After they have made their initial complaints against lords, wives, and the weather, the shepherds of the Wakefield play are joined by the nefarious Mak. In a vain attempt to hide his identity as a sheep-stealer, Mak pretends to be a southern gentleman by adopting a southern dialect:

> What! ich be a yoman,
> I tell you, of the king,
> The self and the some,
> Sond from a greatt lording,
> And sich.
>
> (291–95)[56]

Mak's southern speech is not merely a regional disguise; he is trying to avail himself of the symbolic capital that accrues to the London dialect. It is above all a class marker, connoting links to the landholding class, the aristocracy, the higher clergy, and even the monarchy.[57] Mak there-

---

[55] Smith, "Gower and London English," p. 66.

[56] Martin Stevens and A. C. Cawley, eds., *The Towneley Plays*, vol. 1 (Oxford: Oxford University Press, 1994), EETS, supp. series, p. 13.

[57] See Blake, *The English Language in Medieval Literature*, p. 45. Of Mak's attempted impersonation Blake says, "There is little doubt that his use of the southern dialect is an indication of the growing prestige of the standard London speech, an influence which can be traced in other fifteenth-century records. Its occurrence shows how the development of the standard would foster an attitude of elitism among those who spoke it so that they would look down on those who failed to conform" (46).

fore demands from the shepherds the respect due his station, and his speech becomes self-consciously elevated:

> Fy on you! Goyth hence
> Out of my presence!
> I must haue reverence.
> Why, who be ich?
>
> (204–7)

It is tempting—indeed, it is the intended effect of this vignette—to see Mak's assumed accent as marking him as a corrupt outsider for varying from the "natural" speech of the shepherds and presumably of the audience.[58] We would then take the south Yorkshire dialect of the manuscript as a whole as a "natural" marker of the play's community. In doing so, however, we may overlook the fact that the pageant stages this linguistic opposition in order to create an idea of communal identity. Bourdieu shows that the idea of a region is formed in the same way as the idea of a nation, and that all dialects, including regional forms as opposed to authorized national languages, are boundary-defining performances. "Nobody would want to claim today that there exist criteria capable of founding 'natural' classifications on 'natural' regions, separated by 'natural' frontiers," Bourdieu says. "Regionalist discourse is a *performative discourse* which aims to impose as legitimate a new definition of the frontiers and to get people to know and recognize the *region* that is thus delimited in opposition to the dominant definition, and which is misrecognized as such and thus recognized as legitimate, and which does not acknowledge that new region."[59]

Of course, the most obvious feature of Mak's imitation of southern speech is its inconsistency. Like a Hollywood star affecting a Southern U.S. accent, Mak gets it right only about half the time; he keeps forgetting to say "ich" for "I," for instance. But this partial competence, apart from being comical, is sociolinguistically appropriate. Bourdieu notes that "the social mechanisms of cultural transmission tend to reproduce the structural disparity between the very unequal *knowledge* of the legitimate language and the much more uniform *recognition* of this lan-

---

[58] See, for instance, Lynn Forest-Hill, *Trangressive Language in Medieval English Drama: Signs of Challenge and Change* (Aldershot: Ashgate, 2000), p. 67.

[59] Bourdieu, *Language and Symbolic Power*, pp. 222–23.

guage."[60] The social effects of dialects in a stratified linguistic system require all the parties to recognize the social distinction, the symbolic capital, represented by speech patterns that can be successfully employed only by an elite few. Therefore, when Mak says with mock indignation, "Why, who be ich?" the shepherds have a ready reply. They know who Mak is, and they also know who he is pretending to be. They all recognize the elevated vocabulary and the assumptions of class privilege in Mak's southern speech as easily as they spot its variant pronouns and declensions. Far from being cowed, however, they immediately reject Mak's speech as foreign, pretentious, and self-righteous:

> *1 Pastor.* Why make ye it so qwaynt?
> Mak, ye do wrang.
> *2 Pastor.* Bot, Mak, lyst ye saynt?
> I trow that ye lang.
> *3 Pastor.* I trow the shrew can paynt,
> The dewyll myght hym hang!
> *Mak.* Ich shall make complaynt,
> And make you all to thwang
> At a worde,
> And tell euyn how ye doth.
> *1 Pastor.* Bot, Mak, is that sothe?
> Now take outt that Sothren tothe,
> And sett in a torde!
> (300–312)

No, the shepherds are not fooled and are justifiably mistrustful of Mak. They reject Mak's speech and indignantly reassert their own discourse. In keeping with the egalitarian tone of the play, and of the manuscript as a whole, the shepherds proudly assert the self-worth of the local speakers. Here we see the Wakefield Master as a sociolinguist, showing forth objectively recognized differences of regional dialects and dramatizing their social operation in claiming status and privilege.

At the same time, however, the shepherds' response to Mak's pretensions reveals something further. With its vulgarity and its threat of violence, it exemplifies what Bourdieu characterizes as the typical regionalist, lower-class, and particularly masculine response to speech perceived as elevated. Bourdieu notes that "in the case of the lower

---

[60] Ibid., p. 62.

classes, articulatory style is quite clearly part of a relation to the body that is dominated by the refusal of 'airs and graces' (i.e., the refusal of stylization and the imposition of form) and by the valorization of virility—one aspect of a more general disposition to appreciate what is 'natural.'"[61] Not only do the shepherds reject Mak's speech, but also they use their own language to assert as positive values those qualities—rusticity, lack of education and sophistication, physical labor—that signify their lack of material and symbolic capital.[62] Nowhere is this clearer than when the first shepherd puts an end to Mak's masquerade by ordering him to "take outt that Sothren tothe, / And sett in a torde!" The shepherd's vulgarism seems innocuous enough, but we should remember that for Bourdieu speech is a key element of the *habitus,* the nexus of instituted and learned social tendencies that shape not only behavior but the body itself; "articulatory style," therefore, is part of *"an overall way of using the mouth."* Bourdieu relates this to the dual conceptions of the mouth in French as *la bouche* ("more closed, pinched, i.e. tense and censored, and therefore feminine") and *la gueule* ("unashamedly wide open . . . i.e. relaxed and free, and therefore masculine").[63] La gueule, Bourdieu says,

designates a capacity for verbal violence, identified with the sheer strength of the voice. . . . It also designates a capacity for the physical violence to which it alludes, especially in insults (*casser la gueule, mon poing sur la gueule, ferme ta gueule*—'smash your face in,' 'a punch in the mouth,' 'shut your face') which, through the *gueule,* regarded as both the 'seat' of personal identity . . . and as its main means of expression . . . aims at the very essence of the interlocutor's social identity and self-image.[64]

The first shepherd's impulsive reaction to Mak's assumed dialect, the urge to take out the Southern "tothe" and put in a turd, is a Middle

---

[61] Ibid., p. 86.

[62] Mak is using dialect to demand subservience. Bourdieu goes on to say that popular speech like slang "constitutes *one* of the exemplary, and one might say ideal, expressions . . . of the vision, developed essentially to combat feminine (or effeminate) 'weakness' and 'submissiveness', through which the men most deprived of economic and cultural capital grasp their virile identity and perceive a social world conceived of purely in terms of toughness" (96). Bourdieu is here extending into sociolinguistics the sociology of Paul Willis, whom he credits. See also the useful explanation by John B. Thompson, "Editor's Introduction," *Language and Symbolic Power,* p. 22.

[63] *Language and Symbolic Power,* p. 86.

[64] Ibid., p. 87.

English example of the same phenomenon: the threat of physical violence directed toward the mouth that embodies the greater status of authorized speech. It is through the rejection of speech that carries the greatest cultural authority and status that individuals of lower status most comprehensively signal their acceptance of a language system's inherent hierarchies. The first shepherd's reply to Mak, the threat of responding to elevated talk by replacing the tooth with excrement, exemplifies what Bourdieu elsewhere calls an "opposition of distinction":

censorship turned into second nature, and the *outspokenness* which flouts the taboos of ordinary language—the rules of grammar and politeness—and hierarchical barriers . . . and which is defined by "the relaxation of articulatory tension" . . . and of all the censorships which propriety imposes, and particularly on the tabooed parts of the body, the belly, the arse, and the genitals and, perhaps above all, on the relation to the social world which the tabooed parts make it possible to express, through the reversal of hierarchies . . . or the demeaning of what is exalted (grub, guts, shit).[65]

In this brief episode, the Wakefield pageant introduces an imitation of another speech into its own South Yorkshire dialect and allows their idioms to play off one another. The one is presented as elevated, artificial, foreign, fey, and connected to wealth and power, the other as native, honest, bluff, colloquial, virile, and rooted in the work and world of common men. The effect of this interplay is important for this very communal mode of theater. It serves to define the community of the drama in terms of region and class. It is a community of northern, rural, common layfolk, and it is defined by a common dialect. This speech unifies not only the characters in the play but also the audience with them. Mak, by trying to talk like a Southern gentleman, helps to initiate a discourse of South Yorkshire regionalism. Yet in Bourdieu's conception of the sociological function of unauthorized dialects, there is an underlying irony to the defiant tone of the episode. In rejecting Mak's "Sothren tothe," the shepherds, and the drama they inhabit, are actually affirming their recognition and even acceptance of the relationship between Northern and Southern dialects and the gradations of status that they symbolize. The *Second Shepherds' Play* does not perform the authorization of the audience's language, but rather it valorizes their linguistic marginalization.

[65] Bourdieu, "The Economics of Linguistic Exchange," p. 663.

It is conceivable that a work like the Wakefield pageant could perform the opposite function, and serve to establish Yorkshire dialect as an authorized language with claims to equal status as the London dialect. Doing so, however, would require more than just asserting the value of provincial speech. As Bourdieu says of the mayor of Pau, "If Béarnais (or, elsewhere, Creole) is one day spoken on formal occasions, this will be by virtue of its takeover by speakers of the dominant language, who have enough claims to linguistic legitimacy (at least in the eyes of their interlocutors) to avoid being suspected of resorting to the stigmatized language *faute de mieux.*"[66] To truly challenge the dominant status of the competing dialect, the Wakefield dramatists would have to use social mechanisms that grant authority and status to define their tongue as dominant rather than as provincial.

What would such a valorization look like? It might take the form of the most time-honored strategy, the attempt to demonstrate the flexibility, gravitas, and cultural centrality of a language by showing that it can bear the weight of nationalist epic. It might, then, look something like this:

> Our antecessowris that we suld of reide
> And hald in mynde thar nobille worthi deid,
> We lat ourslide throw verray sleuthfulness,
> And castis us evir till uthir besynes.
> Till honour ennymyis is our haile entent:
> It has beyne seyne in thir tymys bywent.
> Our ald ennemys cummyn of Saxonys blud,
> That nevyr yeit to Scotland wald do gud
> Bot evir on fors and contrar haile thar will,
> Quhow gret kyndnes that has beyne kyth thaim till.[67]

These are the opening lines of the *Wallace.* Hary writes "hald" for *hold,* "haile" for *whole,* "ald" for *old.* He uses "I" as the first-person pronoun and forms the third-person present indicative with "-es". When John and Aleyn use such forms, they are labeled "Northernisms." When a Wakefield shepherd says "I," he recognizes it as the personal pronoun of a provincial rustic. Scotland is even more northerly than Strother

---

[66] Bourdieu, *Language and Symbolic Power,* p. 69.

[67] *The Wallace: Selections,* ed. Anne McKim (Kalamazoo: Medieval Institute Publications, 2003).

(wherever that might be), but Hary claims to speak for a nation, not a region, and makes no apologies for his dialect as he seeks to distinguish his race from the "ald ennemys . . . of Saxonys blud."

The status of native language and literature in late medieval Scotland is an extremely complex topic and not one I hope to explicate here. Gavin Douglas, in the prologue to his translation of the *Aeneid,* seems to echo Trevisa when he complains of writing "With bad harsk spech and lewit barbour tong."[68] But Douglas seems intent on redeeming his language through the *translatio imperii* implicit in his classical transla-tion, which, he says, is "Written in the langage of Scottis natioun."[69] Just as complex as Scottish linguistic insecurities is the literary and cul-tural relationship of Scotland and England in the fifteenth and sixteenth centuries. But a writer like Douglas seems at least implicitly aware that the status of a variant dialect can be lifted only by making it standard rather than variant.[70] The Wakefield shepherds do not even imagine this as a goal for their Northern tooth.

In medieval England, Chaucer and his predecessors as well as his suc-cessors, North and South, were engaged, consciously or not, in a process of dialectical and regional stratification, creating "Southernness" and "Northernness," linguistically, geographically, and socially. The *Second Shepherds' Play,* which appears to be the initial instance of the use of

[68] *The Poetical Works of Gavin Douglas, Bishop of Dunkeld, with Memoir, Notes, and Glos-sary,* ed. John Small, 4 vols. (Edinburgh: W. Paterson, 1874), vol. 2, p. 3, line 21. One might wonder, when Douglas refers to his "lewit barbour tong," whether he is thinking not only of the seeming barbarity of a language being turned for the first time to classical epic but also of the language of John Barbour, author of the *Bruce,* the original Scottish epic.

[69] Vol. 2, p. 6, line 21.

[70] Douglas is as determined as Hary is to distinguish the Scottish from the English, and he does so purely in the arena of language. He devotes much of his first prologue to an attack on Caxton and his *Eneydos*—in the preface to which Caxton had extempo-rized on the unbridgeable differences between northern and southern English:

> . . . Wilʒame Caxtoun, of Inglis natioun,
> In proys hes prent ane buke of Inglis gros,
> Clepend it Virgill in Eneados,
> Quhilk that he says of Franch he did translait,
> It has na thing ado tharwith, God wait,
> Ne na mair lyke than the devill and Sanct Austyne . . .
> (p. 7, line 26–p. 8, line 1)

For Douglas, Caxton's inferior translation and his debased scholarship and particularly his "Inglis gros" elevate Douglas's own work and justify the cultural autonomy of Scot-land and of "Scottis."

dialect with social consciousness, is in fact a reaction to a tradition by then already long-standing and becoming ever more entrenched—and even that reaction, in seeking to speak for those dispossessed by the privileges of the dominant competence, ends up reinscribing its assumptions.

Violence, Law, and Ciceronian Ethics in Chaucer's *Tale of Melibee*

Patricia DeMarco
Ohio Wesleyan University

Not only the suggestion that different societies have had widely different moral beliefs, but also the more radical suggestion that the conceptual schemes embodied in their moralities have differed widely, would appear as a banal truism to any anthropologist. . . . But the notion of a single, unvarying conceptual structure for morality dies hard; and from the eighteenth century to this day, the English utilitarians and idealists, logical empiricists and analytical philosophers, have all been willing to discuss moral philosophy on the assumption that there was something to be called "*the* moral consciousness" or, in a later idiom, "*the* language of morals." The questions "*Whose* moral consciousness?" or "*Which* language?" have rarely, if ever, been raised.
—Alasdair MacIntyre, *Against the Self-Images of the Age,* p. 136

WHETHER IDENTIFIED as an exercise in parody, a self-consuming artifact generated by Chaucerian irony, or recognized as a serious work, "a sound, if somewhat dull work of moral instruction,"[1] Chaucer's *Tale of Melibee* has rarely generated sustained critical examination of its moral philosophy. Perhaps the very clarity of Chaucer's vernacular prose tale—its use of doublets to translate its key conceptual terms, its carefully adumbrated structure, its explicit marking of transitions between topics, and its very indebtedness to pedagogically oriented *florilegia*—has masked the need for anything more than a replication of Prudence's method: the piling up of citations to exhibit the tale's *sentence.* In Chaucer's *Melibee,* quotations speak for themselves.[2] Or so the quotidian nature of the proverbial utterance has often suggested.

---

[1] C. David Benson, "Their Telling Difference: Chaucer the Pilgrim and His Two Contrasting Tales," *ChauR* 18 (1983): 61–76 (quotation on p. 70).
[2] Although a widely shared assumption, the argument has been made explicitly by Edward E. Foster, "Has Anyone Here Read *Melibee?*" *ChauR* 34 (2000): 398–409.

But perhaps this transparency is an illusion, a consequence of assuming that "a single unvarying conceptual structure," something we could identify as "*the* moral consciousness" of the age, informs Prudence's pragmatic didacticism. As Alasdair MacIntyre has observed of the post-enlightenment disciplines of political science and philosophy, such assumptions die hard—and one suspects his corrective may carry even greater force when applied not to the moral philosophy of Kierkegaard or Kant but to that of the Christian Middle Ages. Such a presupposition may well lie behind the tendency to treat the content of Chaucer's *Tale of Melibee* in the broadest of summary form or to abridge it radically when assigning the tale to students (assuming it is assigned at all).[3] It may also help to account for a pattern in *Melibee* criticism, a tendency persistent since at least the 1970s, to locate the importance of the *Tale* in relation to something *other* than its content, most frequently its meta-critical force. We have thus learned much about how *Melibee* might be appreciated as an exercise in stylistic variation or contrasting artistic modes,[4] a self-authorizing model of rhetorical eloquence,[5] or a critical

[3] Compare the disdain heaped on Prudence's "pedestrian orthodoxy" to the high regard accorded Chaucer's "more serious philosophical" investigations. See for instance, the detailed treatment given by Alastair J. Minnis to the metaphysical complexities of Theseus' pagan views on necessity and fame in *The Knight's Tale* in *Chaucer and Pagan Antiquity* (Totowa, N.J.: Rowman and Littlefield, 1982). And for a recent reexamination of Chaucer's dream visions in relation to contemporary issues in speculative philosophy, see Kathryn Lynch, *Chaucer's Philosophical Visions* (Cambridge: D. S. Brewer, 2000). As Matthew Giancarlo has recently observed, criticism on *Troilus and Criseyde* is practically coterminous with studies on the "topics of fate and free will—or of determinism, predestination, and freedom, necessity and chance, causality and destiny" ("The Structure of Fate and the Devising of History in Chaucer's *Troilus and Criseyde*," *SAC* 26 [2004]: 227–66 [p. 227]). Our tendency to assume that "serious philosophical" inquiry excludes the realm of ethics operates as an obstacle here to the appreciation of the *Melibee*. Scholars working in the field of theology have been more apt to recognize the philosophical rigor of medieval ethics. See, most notably, Richard Newhauser's endeavor to contextualize *The Parson's Tale* in relation to the theology of penance in *Sources and Analogues of "The Canterbury Tales,"* gen. ed. Robert M. Correale and Mary Hamel, vol. 1 (Cambridge: D. S. Brewer, 2002), pp. 529–41, and his *Treatise on Vices and Virtues in the Latin and the Vernacular* (Turnhout: Brepols, 1993).

[4] See C. David Benson's influential argument that "the real drama in the *Thopas-Melibee* section is the artistic opposition of these two tales": "Their Telling Difference," p. 65. Alan Gaylord's argument that the subject of the *Thopas-Melibee* pairing is "tale-telling itself" is another example of this critical pattern: "*Sentence and Solaas* in Fragment VII of the *Canterbury Tales:* Harry Bailly as Horseback Editor," *PMLA* 82 (1967): 226–35; cited by Benson, p. 75.

[5] See David Wallace's reading, in which he argues that the *Tale of Melibee* registers Chaucer's interest in the capacity of rhetorical performance to check the violence of men within the household. As for the ethical content of Prudence's counsel, it tends to be subordinated to the efficacious functioning of rhetoric. Thus, for instance, Wallace argues that "it is important to grasp that Prudence's excursus on 'richesse' is not meant

meditation on the "problem of self-representation."[6] We have gleaned much less understanding, however, of what, following MacIntyre, we might describe as the "conceptual schemes" embodied in the *moralité* of the *Melibee*.[7] Indeed, for most scholars, Prudence's insights are so obvious and immediately available that little explication is deemed necessary.

What is at stake in challenging such assumptions? In one of the few studies to provide a detailed assessment of the moral discourses of *Melibee*, David Aers has quite pointedly challenged the usual presupposition that Prudence's pragmatism (and by extension Chaucer's own moral thinking) is consonant with orthodox Christian morality.[8] Examining Prudence's arguments that Melibee must eschew vengeance and seek reconciliation with his attackers, Aers notes that the tale lacks reference to the major sacraments of the Church, most conspicuously to the sacra-

---

to be read as *doctrine*, but as one element of a rhetorical strategy whose aim is the prevention of war." *Chaucerian Polity: Absolutist Lineages and Associational Forms in England and Italy* (Stanford: Stanford University Press, 1997), p. 242. Similarly, he glosses Prudence's rewriting of the seventh Beatitude: "This last proposition is perhaps the most audacious example of Prudence's willingness to use any material that lies to hand (including the seventh Beatitude) to further the immediate needs of her argument" (p. 242). This sort of framing is what seems to lead David Aers to call into question the ethics of such a pragmatism.

[6] Lee Patterson, "'What Man Artow?' Authorial Self-Definition in *The Tale of Sir Thopas* and *The Tale of Melibee*," *SAC* 11 (1989): 117–75 (p. 138). Patterson sees the "pragmatic didacticism" of the *Tale* not as something worthy of analysis, but as an experiment in style designed by Chaucer to comment on the limited traditions available to poets of his anomalous social positioning. Just as "the adoption of a minstrel identity" in *Thopas* registers Chaucer's frustration with the constraints of courtly making, so "the pragmatic didacticism of *Melibee*" dramatizes Chaucer's anxiety that, lacking the capacity to emulate the illustrious *poete*, the vernacular English poet will be stuck "dutifully" penning "pedestrian orthodoxy" (p. 154).

[7] Notable exceptions include James Flynn's defense of the coherence of Prudence's counsel against readings of the tale as ironic and self-contradictory in "The Art of Telling and the Prudence of Interpreting the *Tale of Melibee* and Its Context," *Medieval Perspectives* 7 (1992): 53–63. See also the treatment of Melibee as illustrating the characteristically Senecan vice of those enraged by passion or ire, and lacking self-control by J. D. Burnley, *Chaucer's Language and the Philosophers' Tradition* (Cambridge: D. S. Brewer, 1979). Although providing a rich and nuanced reading of the moral complexities of a wide range of *Canterbury Tales*, Alcuin Blamires's *Chaucer, Ethics, and Gender* (New York: Oxford University Press, 2006) offers surprisingly little comment on *Melibee's* ethical discourse.

[8] For one such reading, see Ann Dobyns, "Chaucer and the Rhetoric of Justice," *Disputatio* 4 (1999): 75–89; Dobyns claims that Chaucer's intention in *The Tale of Melibee* and throughout the *Canterbury Tales* is to bring about the reform of a corrupt legal system, through "the application of Thomistic precept" (p. 83), thus "bring[ing] legal practice into alignment with the principles of natural law" (p. 75) as it reflects divine law.

ment of penance, a reference that might well be expected "in a work of Catholic Christianity devoted to the virtues that enable reconciliation and peace."[9] Similarly, he observes that Chaucer's tale fails to invoke any of the theological virtues or the concept of grace, and provides only the briefest of references to Christ's incarnation and resurrection (and this in the service of defending women's agency as advisers). All the while Prudence declines to offer "any conceivable Christian theology of forgiveness." Thus Aers concludes that either the tale is more sympathetic to a heterodox, possibly Wycliffite, criticism of the "traditional Catholic understanding of the virtues" than critics have recognized (p. 80), or Chaucer has some other interest in having Prudence advance a "thoroughly secular pragmatism." Whatever those interests may be, Aers emphatically glosses Prudence's pragmatism as one that works to allow "murderous feelings" and revengeful "dispositions" to be rationalized in the service of aristocratic self-interest.[10]

In this essay, I will offer a more positive reading of the *Melibee*'s secular pragmatism. I will suggest that the *Melibee* mines the resources of classical ethics and Roman juridical thought in such a way as to offer a means of satisfying the practical ends of social existence, especially the drive to satisfy honor, that is both pragmatic and ethically rigorous. While the secular pragmatism informing *The Tale of Melibee* could be seen as incompatible with orthodox Christianity—and Aers is certainly right to point to areas of significant conflict—the tale's situationist ethics was also one capable of being assimilated to the demands of Christian morality. Such an accommodation seems to have attracted Chaucer, for even as he dramatizes the potential conflicts between these ethical discourses, he seeks to make creative use of those tensions.[11]

My central assertion—that the conceptual structure to which the

---

[9] David Aers, "Chaucer's *Tale of Melibee:* Whose Virtues?" in *Medieval Literature and Historical Inquiry: Essays in Honour of Derek Pearsall,* ed. David Aers (Cambridge: D. S. Brewer, 2000), pp. 69–82 (73).

[10] Ibid., pp. 75, 80, 76, 77.

[11] Alcuin Blamires dexterously situates Chaucer in relation to Stoic, and especially Senecan, ethics in a way that has much informed my own treatment here in *Chaucer, Ethics, and Gender.* Blamires unfolds Chaucer's "creative adoptions of ethical ideas" revealing his penchant for exposing the "moral grey areas" made visible through the awkward fit of ancient ethics and Christian morality (p. 19). He observes that whereas most of Chaucer's contemporaries acknowledge classical ethics merely as "a useful corroboration of Christian morals" (p. 15), Chaucer directs his readers' attentions to "the ragged seams, and . . . overlaps where the nap of each cloth [Stoic ethics and Christian morality] does not run quite in the same direction" (p. 19).

Melibee is indebted is fundamentally a secular one—warrants some further preliminary remark. On the one hand, it rests far afield from the usual assumption that *Melibee*'s prudential dictums represent commonplace Christian sentiments of the most unobjectionable and indeed prosaic sort. On the other hand, it is consonant with a wave of recent criticism arguing for a renewed consideration of Chaucer as a philosophical poet, as someone whose most searching literary endeavors were not wholly bound within a conventional understanding of courtly poetics or within a conventional understanding of Christian moral teaching.[12] Some of this criticism is indebted to fifteenth-century reception of Chaucer, highlighting the moral seriousness in which his readers of that moment were interested; other criticism is motivated by a desire to diversify the sorts of philosophical languages that we might see deployed in Chaucer as a corrective to some of the monotonies of midcentury Robertsonian exegesis.[13] Despite the rich diversity of this recent work, however, most of these efforts are guided by a tacit assumption that ethics in the late medieval period was, by and large, coequal with the resources of theology.[14] This assumption is not entirely inappropriate, especially if we examine the paradigmatic representatives of ethical conduct in Chaucer's *Canterbury Tales*. But the assumption begins to falter once we recognize the gender specificity of Chaucer's ethical inquiries and the distinctiveness of *Melibee* in this regard.

[12] See Mark Miller, *Philosophical Chaucer: Love, Sex, and Agency in the Canterbury Tales* (Cambridge: Cambridge University Press, 2004).

[13] For a discussion of fourteenth- and fifteenth-century portraits and an assessment of the impact of late medieval scholastic philosophy on Chaucer's literary corpus, see Kathryn L. Lynch's bibliographic survey in *Chaucer's Philosophical Visions*. Her defense of Chaucer's philosophical disposition and knowledge is complemented by Ann Astell's survey of the shaping influence of didascalic literature on Chaucer's structuring of the *Canterbury Tales* in *Chaucer and the Universe of Learning* (Ithaca: Cornell University Press, 1996). For apt cautions against overestimating Chaucer's formal education and for methodological suggestions on how claims for Chaucer's philosophical knowledge ought to be substantiated, see Minnis, *Chaucer and Pagan Antiquity*, pp. 7–30.

[14] I have found it useful here to consider Larry Scanlon's suggestion that we see Chaucer affirming "the authority of the lay within the general system of Christian belief" and the "radical otherness of moral authority." See *Narrative, Authority, and Power: The Medieval Exemplum and the Chaucerian Tradition* (Cambridge: Cambridge University Press, 1994), pp. 219, 221. Thus we might look in the *Melibee* for an effort not to harmonize Roman ethics with Christian theology per se, but for the appropriation of Roman ethics as regards a general system of Christian belief, one not exhausted by the discourses of theology. Scanlon argues that the historical distinction between clerical and lay better situates Chaucer than the more modern opposition between medieval and humanist. Such a distinction helpfully situates Prudence as a (nonclerical) figure of moral authority.

Gender and Virtue in the *Canterbury Tales*

Before turning to the secular discourses informing Chaucer's *Tale of Melibee,* I will consider briefly how gender shapes Chaucer's inquiry in respect to the larger narrative to which the *Melibee* tale belongs.[15] While many have observed that those *Canterbury Tales* that highlight Christian agency in the world characteristically center on female characters, few have noted that those concerned with men's achievement of virtue are nearly all set in the pagan past. As an emerging consensus of recent scholarship has begun to establish, Christian virtue is strongly marked as feminine virtue. Elizabeth Robertson points out: "Every religious tale has a woman at its center as the protagonist or teller."[16] And in these tales, the most highly lauded and frequently illustrated virtues—humility, constancy and patience, faithful obedience, and suffraunce—are coded, both directly and indirectly, as feminine virtues (as evident in the demeanor and behavior of Chaucer's "holy women": Cecilia, Custance, Griselda, and the heroine of *The Prioress's Tale,* the Virgin Mary).[17] So strong is the gendering of Christian virtue in *The Tale of Melibee* that characters within the narrative mark the association explicitly. As Janet Cowgill notes, Melibee's enemies assume that he will seek vengeance, but "they identify as womanly the more forgiving attitude of Prudence: 'And therefore noble lady, we biseke to youre wommanly pitee.' "[18] The

[15] See Blamires's own powerful reassessment in *Chaucer, Ethics, and Gender,* esp. pp. 1–19.

[16] Elizabeth Robertson, "Aspects of Female Piety in the *Prioress's Tale,*" in *Chaucer's Religious Tales,* ed. C. David Benson and Elizabeth Robertson (Rochester: Boydell and Brewer, 1990), pp. 145–60 (146).

[17] For a discussion of the way Chaucer uses four female protagonists (as each illustrates a cardinal virtue) to explore the tensions between moral philosophy and literature, see Denise Baker, "Chaucer and Moral Philosophy: The Virtuous Women of the *Canterbury Tales,*" *MÆ* 60 (1991): 241–56. I've learned much from her astute reading of the Ciceronian inflection in Prudence's character.

[18] Janet Cowgill, "Patterns of Feminine and Masculine Persuasion in the *Melibee* and the *Parson's Tale,*" in *Chaucer's Religious Tales,* p. 175. The strong sense that compassion and forgiveness, as well as patient *suffraunce,* are marked as feminine has even suggested to several critics that when male characters adopt them they appear "feminized." David Wallace remarks, for instance, that "when a man needs to cultivate *mansuetude* and its associated virtues, then he is best advised to mirror himself in a woman" (*Chaucerian Polity,* p. 239). For discussion of other feminized male characters in the *Canterbury Tales,* see Jill Mann, *Geoffrey Chaucer* (Atlantic Highlands, N.J.: Humanities Press International, 1991), pp. 165–182; J. A. Burrow, *Ricardian Poetry: Chaucer, Gower, Langland, and the "Gawain" Poet* (London: Routledge and Kegan Paul, 1971), pp. 93–129; both cited and discussed by Monica MacAlpine, "Criseyde's Prudence," *SAC* 25 (2003): 199–244 (201). Also relevant here is Elaine Tuttle Hansen, *Chaucer and the Fictions of Gender*

strong association of Christian virtue with female characters dovetails smoothly with what C. David Benson has termed Chaucer's "Christian feminism." In the *Canterbury Tales,* he wryly observes, Christian women "do more than equal men, they surpass them."[19] Cowgill concludes similarly that "the feminine team is consistent in its personal virtues, in the effectiveness of its discourse, and in the devotion to the moral development of others."[20]

While Chaucer's virtuous women operate within conceptual schemes shaped by Christian theology and illustrate the ideals of Christian ecclesiology in their worldly interactions, their Christian male counterparts are typically corrupt or morally suspect (as with the ecclesiastical figures of the Friar, Pardoner, Monk, and Summoner).[21] By contrast, Chaucer's lay characters inhabit almost exclusively a pagan world, a world in which they struggle, often admirably, to make virtue of necessity. Chaucer may have expected readers of these pagan tales (*The Knight's Tale, Franklin's Tale, Wife of Bath's Tale, Physician's Tale,* and *Manciple's Tale*) to supply a Christian perspective unavailable to his pagan protagonists, but his decision to use these pagan settings as a forum for some of his most sustained ethical inquiries deserves greater attention.[22]

Chaucer's apportioning of his male and female characters helps us to attend to the remarkable fact that the *Melibee* is the only narrative tale that uses a Christian setting to thematize masculine virtue.[23] And what

---

(Berkeley and Los Angeles: University of California Press, 1992). For a challenge to this emerging consensus, see Blamires, who introduces a reading of the highest of ethical ideals and practice in *Chaucer, Ethics, and Gender* as those developed within the bounds of *amicitia,* thus reserving the exercise of the "highest public virtues" to men (p. 28). I have found his reading most insightful. I would merely add that we are in the realm here not of Christian virtue or ecclesiological models, but of ancient ethics.

[19] And conversely, Benson suggests, "Christian feminism so dominates Chaucer's religious tales that men are viewed with approval *only* when they begin to act like women— the message, of course, of the long prose *Melibee*." C. David Benson, "Introduction," *Chaucer's Religious Tales,* p. 6.

[20] Cowgill, "Patterns of Feminine and Masculine Persuasion," pp. 182–83.

[21] I exclude as a group the male characters of Chaucer's fabliaux, for, as has often been recognized, they exist outside an ethical framework of judgment, the genre suspending the kind of ethical inquiry or focus on virtue characteristic of both Chaucer's religious tales and those tales set in the pagan past. For an insightful discussion of the fabliaux in this regard, see chapter 5, "The *Miller's Tale* and the Politics of Laughter," in Lee Patterson, *Chaucer and the Subject of History* (Madison: University of Wisconsin Press, 1991), pp. 244–79, and R. Howard Bloch, *The Scandal of the Fabliaux* (Chicago: University of Chicago Press, 1986).

[22] The classic study is that of Minnis, *Chaucer and Pagan Antiquity.*

[23] I hope that it will not be considered special pleading to exempt *The Parson's Tale.* It is not a narrative per se, and the Parson is not, as Melibee is, a protagonist or narrative

The Tale of Melibee does with its unique context is striking. *Melibee* offers little by way of the Church's teaching on the virtues, and even less of theological precept on the sacraments.[24] There is, however, one section in the *Tale* in which Prudence engages substantially with Christian ethics, and in this section Melibee rejects Christian virtue as incompatible with the identity and interests of a man of honor like himself. Once Prudence has offered Melibee guidance on attaining good counsel and demonstrated that he lacks the legal grounds to avenge himself against his enemies, Prudence recommends a virtuous course of action for him: "enclyne and bowe youre herte to take the pacience of our Lord Jhesu Crist, as seith Seint Peter in his Epistles./ 'Jhesu Crist,' he seith, 'hath suffred for us and yeven ensample to every man to folwer and sewe hym,/ for he dide nevere synne, ne nevere cam ther a vileyns word out of his mouth./ Whan men cursed hym, he cursed hem noght, and whan men beten hym, he manaced hem noght'" (VII.1501–4).[25] Here Prudence appeals to those most feminized of Christ's virtues: deference ("enclyne and bowe youre herte"), pacience, and suffraunce ("hath suffred"). Moreover, she ties these virtues to the latent pacifism of the Gospels, advising Melibee not merely to have pity and forgive his enemies, but to suffer their violent attacks passively. Melibee's rejection of Prudence's teaching is, as Lee Patterson has described it, "devastating," but not because he has misapprehended her teaching or regressed to some state of "primitive emotionalism."[26] Rather, it is devastating because he apprehends perfectly well her Christian message and rejects it.[27] Melibee responds: "Certes . . . I graunte yow, dame Prudence, that pacience is a greet virtu of perfeccioun; / but every man may nat have the perfeccioun that ye seken; / ne I nam nat of the nombre of right

---

agent of ethical action in the world; thus I would argue that its transcendent focus leaves *Melibee* unique. The only other male character who might fit the bill is not human at all, but rather a chicken. I refer of course to Chaunticleer in Chaucer's beast fable, *The Nun's Priest's Tale*.

[24] See Aers, "Chaucer's *Tale of Melibee*."

[25] All citations of *The Tale of Melibee* are from Larry Benson, gen. ed., *The Riverside Chaucer*, 3d ed. (Boston: Houghton Mifflin, 1987), with fragment and line numbers in parentheses.

[26] "'What Man Artow?'" p. 157. The second phrase is that of Wallace, *Chaucerian Polity*, p. 240.

[27] For an alternate (and acute) account of the "deep male anxieties about the meek, silent Christ," see Daniel Rubey, "The Five Wounds of Melibee's Daughter: Transforming Masculinities," in *Masculinities in Chaucer: Approaches to Maleness in the "Canterbury Tales" and "Troilus and Criseyde*," ed. Peter G. Beidler (Cambridge: D. S. Brewer, 1998), pp. 157–71 (171).

parfite men for myn herte may nevere been in pees unto the tyme it be venged" (VII.1518–21). For Melibee it is all well and good to expect Jesus, his saints, Prudence (and, we may assume, other women) to embrace patient suffering as an ecclesiological model, but for a man of honor, whose good name is predicated on a manly disposition, such a vision of Christian virtue is deemed untenable.

Melibee cannot see a way to embrace peace and forgiveness without sacrificing his masculine identity as an honor man. Thus, when Prudence advises him to reconcile with his enemies, he accuses her of not caring about his "honour, ne my worshipe" (VII.1681). Incredulously, he asks how she can expect him to "go and meke me, and obeye me to hem, and crie them mercy? / For sothe, that were nat my worshipe" (VII.1684–85). Melibee's careful marking of the subordination demanded of him and his sensitivity to the public shame he will incur are shot through with the anxiety of embracing non-normative gendered behavior. In this regard, the tale dramatizes tensions between culturally dominant modes of masculine behavior and affect and Christian ethics, tensions that Chaucer's other tales, set in a pagan past or focused tightly on virtuous women, are able to avoid.

While *Melibee*'s Christian setting allows the tale to stage the clash between the secular dictates of honor and Christian models of virtuous conduct, the honor mentality also defines the parameters by which most of Chaucer's pagan male characters understand the ethical dilemmas before them and decide on a course of action. Palamon and Arcite renounce their sworn fellowship and take up arms against each other in *The Knight's Tale*—their private quarrel marked, as Melibee's also is, as an illegitimate act of private violence. In *The Franklin's Tale,* honor is both provocation and palliative, as Arveragus insists that his wife, Dorigen, uphold her *trouthe* but keep their submission to Aurelius's amorous demands secret to guard Arveragus's public honor. The ideals of gentility are accorded almost magical powers to thwart the violent imposition of Aurelius's desires, much as the Old Wife's appeal to the ideals of a "gentil herte" transform the rapist knight in *The Wife of Bath's Tale.* Less optimistically, in *The Manciple's Tale* it is Phebus Apollo's wounded honor that provokes the unleashing of deadly fury upon his reportedly adulterous wife, killing her and depriving the one who has shamed him of speech. Similarly in *The Physician's Tale,* a man's desire to protect his honor serves to direct deadly violence against a woman, as Virginius slays his daughter to preserve her sexual purity from the grasping Clau-

133

dius and ensure that Virginius is not publicly dishonored. As this summary is meant to highlight, protecting one's good name is a paramount concern for Chaucer's (pagan) male protagonists, and as readers of the tales we are invited to consider critically, but never dismissively, how they come to understand their situations as ethical dilemmas and determine the virtuous course of action, all the while preserving their status as honor men.

Finally we may observe how frequently the main action in the antique tales concerns the sexual possession of a woman (Emily, Dorigen, Phebus's wife, Virginia, the raped girl/the Old Wife) as one man's honor is threatened (Theseus's, Arveragus's, Virginius's, Arthur's) by another man (Palamon and Arcite, Aurelius, Claudius, the unnamed adulterer, and the unnamed rapist) and his desire for the female character. Characteristically in these poems, violence is attenuated, rendered figurative or literary as it is assimilated to the conventions of courtly love poetry, whether by positive appeal to the ideals of *fin amor* (*Knight's Tale, Franklin's Tale*) or by perversion and violation of its ideals (*Manciple's Tale, Physician's Tale, Wife of Bath's Tale*). In the *Melibee,* however, the literary pattern of masculine honor and female violation is made literal appropriately enough given the tale's prose form, as a physical assault on the household of Melibee: on the wife, Prudence, and daughter, Sophie, and on the domicile itself. Once again *Melibee* emerges from a patterned constellation of thematic attributes as unique in some crucial feature.

Recognizing the distinctiveness of the *Melibee* in this regard helps us to attend to the particular nature of the violence that drives the tale, and it requires that we recognize a field of ethical inquiry in the *Melibee* that is both more diverse than that of other *Canterbury Tales* as well as more secular. To appreciate this diverse array of secular discourses, we will need to examine two contexts for the *Melibee.* The first is the tale's legal context. Here the most important juridical models were derived from Justinian's civil law writings, and they were particularly important in answering a perennial provocation in ethics: the violence of the honor man. Since ethical language always takes shape in the workings of given institutional practices—and for Chaucer and his peers, one of the most important of these seems to have been the law—if we are to appreciate the ethical language of the *Melibee,* we will need to look at the way the tale mines the resources of (both continental and English) legal precept and practice. Second—and most important for appreciating the distinctiveness of the ethical discourse Chaucer deploys in *The Tale of Melibee*—

will be the conceptual structure of Ciceronian ethics. Some of the richest studies of Chaucer's moral thinking have focused on the Christian assimilation of ancient Stoic thought, clarifying Chaucer's complex negotiation of the tensions between Stoicism and late medieval Christian discourses.[28] These studies have, however, often overlooked the divergence of Ciceronian and Senecan ethics. While overlapping in some significant ways with Stoic thought, for whom Seneca was a central figure throughout the Middle Ages, Ciceronian ethics are characterized by several crucial, distinctive features, and these seem to have garnered widespread interest among civic laymen involved in the day-to-day workings of law and governance. In concluding this essay, I will return to the crisis scene in which Melibee rejects Christian *suffraunce,* and suggest a way to understand Prudence's effort to dissolve the tensions between Christian ideals of virtuous conduct and the secular dictates of honor.

Melibee's Sources: The Juridical Context

The nature of the violence visited upon the women of the *Melibee* is a very different sort from that we have traced in Chaucer's pagan tales. Three old adversaries of the young and rich Melibee break into his home while he is away, beat his wife, Prudence, and wound his daughter, Sophie.[29] Melibee returns home and, enraged by the assault, calls together a motley crew of neighbors and associates to advise him on a course of action. Arguments for and against "meeting violence with violence" are leveled, and largely because Melibee has indicated his desire to avenge himself on his adversaries, the majority counsel war. Following the council, Prudence offers a critical assessment of his proposed

---

[28] The foundational study is Burnley's *Chaucer's Language and the Philosophers' Tradition.* Blamires's *Chaucer, Ethics, and Gender* offers both a nuanced account of the function of Stoic concepts in Chaucer's corpus generally and a set of detailed readings of the way in which certain ethical postures and dilemmas are gendered. On the recourse to Seneca as a moral philosopher by Christian writers, see Leighton D. Reynolds, *The Medieval Tradition of Seneca's Letters* (London: Oxford University Press, 1965).

[29] For a discussion of the particular crimes committed here, see Kathleen Kennedy, "Maintaining Love through Accord in the *Tale of Melibee,*" *ChauR* 39 (2004): 165–76. Kennedy accounts for Chaucer's decision to supply a name for the daughter, "Sophie," as consistent with the requirement "under English law [that] the victim of a felony had to be named in the indictment," and she argues that the detailed account of her wounds alerts the audience to the "felonious nature of the 'outrages' perpetuated on Melibee's household" (p. 168). While I find this legal dimension consistent with my diagnosis of the tale's literalization of violence against its female characters, I would not want to deny that the naming of Sophie has additional allegorical resonance.

retribution, and after a lengthy and contentious exchange Melibee agrees to abandon his plans for war. Prudence then meets privately with Melibee's enemies in order to stage a later public reconciliation between them and her husband. The text concludes with a final disagreement between husband and wife, as Melibee announces his intent to impose harsh penalties on his adversaries. Prudence denies his right to impose punishment and convinces him to forgive his enemies.

For most of the tale's critical history, scholars have assumed that the violence at issue in the *Melibee* amounts to public warfare, and many have attempted to discern Chaucer's attitude toward it, with positions ranging from Robert Yeager's attribution to Chaucer of a critical, even pacifist stance against warfare and chivalric militarism to David Aers's assessment of the tale as an exercise in the legitimation of the aristocrat's preferred route to wealth and fame.[30] These are obviously very different assessments of Chaucer's attitude toward war and peace, but they share one common assumption: that if *Melibee* advances an ascertainable position on violence—if it is meant, that is, as a guide to contemporary morality—that position concerns England's foreign policy, variously centered on the Hundred Years' War with France, England's policy in Scotland, its negotiations with Flanders, or the campaigns of Gaunt in Castile.[31]

As a corollary, Chaucer's attitude toward warfare is largely assumed to be a universal, ethical stance; and a framework of interpretation is imposed on the *Melibee* that admits no distinction between the legal and philosophical parameters relevant to just public warfare and those

[30] R. F. Yeager, "*Pax Poetica:* On the Pacifism of Chaucer and Gower," *SAC* 9 (1987): 97–121.

[31] See, respectively, Gardiner Stillwell, "The Political Meaning of Chaucer's *Tale of Melibee,*" *Speculum* 19 (1944): 433–44; V. J. Scattergood, "Chaucer and the French War: *Sir Thopas* and *Melibee,*" in *Court and Poet: Selected Proceedings of the Third Congress of the International Courtly Literature Society,* ed. Glyn S. Burgess (Liverpool: Francis Cairns, 1981), pp. 287–96; and J. Leslie Hotson, "The Tale of Melibeus and John of Gaunt," *SP* 18 (1921): 429–52. In more recent scholarship situating the work in relation to the political turmoil of the Ricardian court in the 1380s and conflict over England's military policy, two treatments are especially important: Lynn Staley Johnson, "Inverse Counsel: Contexts for the *Melibee,*" *SP* 87 (1990): 137–55; and Judith Ferster, *Fictions of Advice: The Literature and Politics of Counsel in Late Medieval England* (Philadelphia: University of Pennsylvania Press, 1996), esp. pp. 89–107. The benefit of such readings is that they account for those passages in the tale addressing the evils attendant upon all forms of warfare, and can speak to the reader's sense that the tale has a deep investment in peace. But with such a broad moral compass, critics may overlook the tale's central intention: to discriminate between forms of violence, both legally and ethically.

relevant to private warfare. As we shall see, however, both the tale itself and Chaucer's handling of the material he inherited—what he adds to his source texts, what he omits in his translation, and what persists as the thematic heart of the tale—suggest that he was interested in this tale precisely because it bracketed the question of the public war (conducted by the sovereign prince) to focus on the issue of private warfare (undertaken by individuals acting outside the law and without juridical authority).[32] By taking seriously the emphasis on the problem of private violence in the *Melibee* and its sources, we can better understand how Chaucer used the tale to confront the centrality of vengeance to aristocratic masculinity, exploring the possibilities for overcoming one of the primary obstacles to peace in the localities: namely, the honor man's fear that to restrict private violence was to undermine the very foundations of that identity as it was performatively reiterated through both legal and extralegal means.

A concern to delimit the sphere in which individuals might legitimately level private warfare runs throughout the original Latin dialogue of Prudence and Melibee, Albertano of Brescia's *Liber consolationis et consilii* (c. 1246), a text that Chaucer translated via a French intermediary.[33]

---

[32] Wallace's important work on the *Melibee* as a meditation on rhetoric's capacity to assuage "the imminent threat of masculine anger" as it erupts within the domestic space (*Chaucerian Polity*, p. 233) acknowledges the distinction between public and private violence, as do two recent essays situating the narrative in relation to insular criminal law and the civil law tradition: see, respectively, Kennedy, "Maintaining Love," pp. 165–76, and Dobyns, "Chaucer and the Rhetoric of Justice." The tale continues to be read within the *Fürstenspiegel* tradition as advice to Richard II on matters of statecraft, including (the extremely controversial) war with France. See, for instance, Lynn Staley, *Languages of Power in the Age of Richard II* (University Park: Pennsylvania State University Press, 2005). Without denying the *Melibee* tale a range of possible contemporary resonances, I would observe that there is an immediate resonance to *Melibee's* treatment of violence in the localities—the issue was perennially raised in parliament, a subject of regular complaint among chroniclers, and a frequent preoccupation of landowners as witnessed by extant legal records. Violence in the localities might be seen as a matter for political commentary in the late 1390s, as Andrew Galloway so astutely observes. See his essay, "The Literature of 1388 and the Politics of Pity in Gower's *Confessio Amantis*," in *The Letter of the Law: Legal Practice and Literary Production in Medieval England*, ed. Emily Steiner and Candace Barrington (Ithaca: Cornell University Press, 2002), pp. 67–104, esp. pp. 81–82.

[33] Albertano's corpus, including the two companion texts to the *Liber consolationis et consilii* (c. 1246) and his lay sermons, achieved wide circulation; his biographer estimates that there may be more than five hundred manuscripts of Albertano's writings extant in Latin and various vernaculars, situating Albertano as "among the most popular medieval authors." James Powell, *Albertano of Brescia: The Pursuit of Happiness in the Early Thirteenth Century* (Philadelphia: University of Pennsylvania Press, 1992), 14 n. 22. For a recent overview of translations, see Angus Graham, "Albertano of Brescia: A Prelimi-

The treatise's Brescian milieu helps to contextualize Albertano's interest in legal resources for addressing the problem of private violence. As Albertano's most recent biographer, James Powell, has emphasized, thirteenth-century Brescia was a city torn apart by warring factions, and Albertano looked to his own professional class of lawyers, judges, and *podestà* for civic solutions to the endemic state of feud in Italian city-states such as his own Brescia.[34] The resources available to Albertano to tackle such an ambitious project have been a subject of some controversy among scholars, with biographers such as Powell stressing the influence of lay confraternities and Senecan writings on Albertano's ideals of individual moral reform and communal rule, and critics such as David Wallace emphasizing a broader tradition from which rhetoric emerged as a tool to be deployed by "go-betweens" seeking to stem the violence of powerful men within the household.[35] Given Albertano's rich and complex intellectual background, all these emphases deserve attention, but the one I would like to stress here is his legal learning. Albertano was a man of law, and his crowning achievement, *Liber consolationis et consilii,* is a treatise deeply marked by his juridical vocation.[36] Albertano was

---

nary Census of Vernacular Manuscripts," *Studi Medievali* 41 (2000): 891–924. For a discussion of Albertano's influence on Chaucer and the question of the mediation of Renaud of Louens's translation, see William Askins, "The Tale of Melibee," in *Sources and Analogues of the Canterbury Tales,* gen. ed. Robert M. Correale and Mary Hamel (Cambridge: D. S. Brewer, 2002), pp. 321–28. For discussion of the English manuscript tradition, see Wallace, *Chaucerian Polity,* esp. pp. 214, 229–31, and (in the endnotes) pp. 451–52.

[34] David Wallace has suggested that Chaucer's Italian diplomatic trips may have given him an understanding of the "ideological warfare [that] raged continuously" between Trecento Florence and Lombardy. See *Chaucerian Polity,* p. 1.

[35] On the way Albertano's experience of lay confraternities and his knowledge of Senecan moral philosophy may have shaped his reception of religious ideals of a voluntary accepted rule, see Powell, *Albertano of Brescia,* pp. 90–104. Wallace emphasizes Albertano's connection to—and later identification with—the fraternal orders through the many sermons he wrote and preached to the friars of the area and the association of his confraternity of fellow Brescian men of law to the Franciscans. See *Chaucerian Polity,* pp. 217–21. This is a guise Wallace links to the importance of rhetoric as a tool for stemming violence, one that both friars and wives were expected to deploy as "go-betweens."

[36] A point Powell denies in his effort to redirect attention to the influence of fraternal orders that, in his thesis, most shaped Albertano's civic ethics. Wallace follows Powell to clear a space for a discussion of the significance of a rhetorical tradition: "[Albertano] never gets bogged down in the minutiae of legal learning, nor does he attempt to construct a legal basis for his arguments" (p. 218). Subsequent argument will challenge this view, but here let me make a small, pedestrian point about the amount of space devoted to legal minutiae by invoking chapter 49 of Albertano's treatise, which categorizes in great detail different types of war, calling upon the Romanists' and the Decretalists' formulations; the chapter also defines the various legitimizing *causa belli* of a just

active from 1226 to 1251 as judge and *causidicus*—or legal counselor—for the Italian city of Brescia, and he was an active member of that city's confraternity of men-at-law.[37] Not surprisingly, *Liber consolationis et consilii* draws heavily from the civil law tradition. In his treatise we find, for instance, citations of all three parts of Justinian's *Corpus juris civilis* as well as evidence of firsthand knowledge of the Glossator's commentaries on Justinian's corpus and references to the thinking of a range of Decretists and Decretalists who commented upon Gratian's *Decretum* and Gregory's *Decretales*.[38] As even this brief survey suggests, Albertano's education and experience had given him access to a wide diversity of legal traditions.[39] As conversant with Augustine's theology of the just war as with the Romanists' unfolding of Justinian's civil law treatment of private violence, Albertano was well situated both to deploy their common insights and to take advantage of their diverse juridical solutions to complex problems of social disorder. In his influence on Chaucer and his version of the Melibee tale, it is Albertano's synthesis of theological and civil law treatments of two juridical categories, "authority" and "intention," that is most consequential. By contrast, we will find Chaucer exploiting subtle but significant points of distinction in his source texts, in his own handling of the legal complexities surrounding the legitimizing circumstances of war and self-defense.

---

war in a manner neither ignorant of civil law writings nor slavishly dependent on the opinions contained there—all presented with technical linguistic precision. See *Albertani Brixiensis: Liber Consolationis et Consilii ex quo Hausta est Fabula de Melibeo et Prudentia*, ed. Thor Sundby (London: Williams and Norgate, 1873). Unless otherwise noted, all references to Albertano of Brescia's original tale of Melibee are taken from this edition, which is also available at the Web site, http:// freespace.virgin.net/angus.graham/ Albertano.htm.

[37] See Powell's discussion of his offices and roles in *Albertano of Brescia*, pp. 1–11.

[38] Albertano's knowledge may have been gained through study in the Arts curriculum, in pursuit of the baccalaureate (which included study of Justinian's *Digest* and Gratian's *Decretum*), or as part of his work for an advanced degree in civil law. Or he may have accumulated such knowledge through some combination of learning and the experience of nearly thirty years of highly public legal service.

[39] Powell seeks to distinguish Albertano as an urban professional from university-trained legists and theologians. He thus argues against evidence for Albertano's formal legal education (evidence accepted by most Italian biographers of Albertano) even as he acknowledges that Albertano "must be judged an expert in both legal and practical matters" (p. 2). Similarly, he denies that Albertano was "interested in building a legal foundation to support his views . . . on the reform of society" (p. 48), even as he ties the fact that the *Liber* "cites legal sources from both Roman and canon law with greater frequency . . . than in any of his previous writings" to the text's concern to stem the endemic state of feud in Brescia by challenging the legitimacy of vendetta (pp. 76–77).

In all versions of the Melibee tale—Albertano's original Latin treatise, Renaud de Louens's revised French version, and Chaucer's translation— Prudence relies heavily on civil laws governing war in order to convince Melibee that he may not legitimately respond to the attack on his household with violence. According to the tenets of just-war theory, as they were established by Augustine and further developed in relation to Roman law by the Glossators, Gratian, and the Decretists, "no hostile act was licit or illicit by itself, but according to the authority on which it was committed."[40] For Augustine the ultimate authority for warfare—what Prudence terms "the final cause" of warfare—is God himself. Augustine argued that war had to be understood within the larger purposes of divine providence.[41] Whether a given war was divinely authorized or undertaken without the sanction of divine will, it functioned to execute divine justice. The violence inflicted upon an enemy, for instance, could function to punish sinful behavior, while the suffering of the just during war could work to test the patience of the faithful.[42]

At the level of individual ethics, the just war was distinguished from simple violence through the examination of intent. For Augustine, warfare was only just when it was conducted with a motive and a disposition consistent with this higher purpose.[43] Consequently, Augustine denied the right of private persons to exercise violence (in war or in self-defense) on their own authority and accorded the status of justness only to those wars initiated and conducted by the sovereign who, Augustine argued, was most capable of undertaking violent action with a just and charitable disposition.[44] Thus the theology of the just war gave birth to a po-

[40] Frederick H. Russell, *The Just War in the Middle Ages* (Cambridge: Cambridge University Press, 1975), p. 307.

[41] See Augustine, *Concerning the City of God against the Pagans,* trans. Henry Bettenson (Harmondsworth: Penguin Books, 1972), 4:34; and "Reply to Faustus the Manichaean," trans. R. Stothert, in *The Writings Against the Manichaeans and Against the Donatists, A Select Library of the Nicene and Post-Nicene Fathers,* first series, vol. 4, ed. Philip Schaff (1887; Grand Rapids: Eerdmans, 1996), 22:75.301. This is an admittedly selective overview; for a fuller account, see both Russell, *The Just War,* esp. chap. 3, and Jonathan Barnes, "The Just War," in *The Cambridge History of Later Medieval Philosophy,* ed. Norman Kretzmann et al. (Cambridge: Cambridge University Press, 1982), pp. 771–84.

[42] *City of God,* 19:7; and "Reply to Faustus," 22:75.301.

[43] "Reply to Faustus," 22:74.164 and 22:79.303–04.

[44] On the distinction between war conducted with charity and with hatred, see ibid., 22:74.301. On the illegitimacy of private acts of violence, see *De libero arbitrio,* in *Saint Augustine: The Teacher, The Free Choice of the Will, Grace and Free Will,* The Fathers of the Church, A New Translation, vol. 59, trans. Robert P. Russell (Washington, D.C.: Catholic University of America Press, 1968), 1.5.12. For the amplification of *auctoritas* as a crite-

tent and extremely influential conceptual division between the just, public warfare of the ruler and the unjust, private violence of the individual.

In the case of *The Tale of Melibee,* we can see that Prudence is concerned to counter Melibee's misrecognition of his own authority as a private person. In response to Melibee's declaration that he will avenge himself on his adversaries, Prudence observes that "rightfully mowe ye take no vengeance, as of youre propre auctoritee" (VII.1385). Moreover, she explains, "by right and resoun, ther may no man taken vengeance on no wight but the juge that hath the jurisdiccioun of it" (VII.1379). Prudence's distinction here between legitimate and illegitimate authority follows the basic lines of Augustinian just-war theory, but her location of legitimate authority in the person of a judge is, by way of contrast, a distinctive Romanist strategy. Glossators such as Azo, Odofredus, and Accursius—who was a contemporary of Albertano writing in Italy—declared that "vengeance" or "punishment" (*ultio*) for a violent attack could licitly be sought only in a court of law or by the authority of a judge.[45]

The most intriguing evidence we have for Chaucer's interest in Albertano's text as a work about private warfare is an omission following Melibee's rebuttal of Prudence's argument that only judges have the authority to exercise vengeance.[46] In opposition to Prudence, Melibee insists that were individuals "nevere [to] take vengeance . . . that were harm; / for by the vengeance-takyng been the wikked men disseevered fro the goode men" (VII.1429–31). We have already gestured toward a

---

rion, Russell points to the Decretist Huguccio's treatment in his *Summa,* commenting on 23 q.2 of Gratian's *Decretum;* see also 14 q.4 c.12, v. *ubi est ius belli; The Just War,* p. 89. For Huguccio's decisive influence here, see Wolfgang Müller, *Huguccio: The Life, Works, and Thought of a Twelfth-Century Jurist* (Washington, D.C.: Catholic University of America Press, 1994). For the representation of *auctoritas,* see Azo's commentary on the *Codex Iustinianus* 11.47 (hereafter *Cod.*) in *Summa Codicis;* see as well Accursius's treatment in *Glossa Ordinaria,* I, v. *movendorum* and Odofredus's in *Lectura Codicis;* all are cited fully by Russell, pp. 43–44.

[45] Azo, *Summa Codicis,* to *Cod.* 8.4 and *Lectura in Codicem,* to *Cod.* 8.4.6, v. *rescripto;* cited by Russell, *The Just War,* pp. 43–44. Odofredus, *Lectura Codicis,* to *Cod.* 9.12.7 and to *Cod.* 9.39; Russell, p. 44. Among the Decretists, Rufinus, Huguccio, and the *Summa Parisiensis* cast those who avenge their own injuries without judicial authority as sinful; Russell, p. 97.

[46] For evidence that Chaucer did actively shape the narrative he inherited rather than merely offer a slavish translation, see Askins's detailed discussion of Chaucer's translation practice: William Askins, "The Tale of Melibee," in *Sources and Analogues of the Canterbury Tales,* gen. ed. Correale and Hamel, pp. 321–28.

version of this argument in Augustine's understanding of war's function in instituting divine justice. Melibee's citation of this line of thinking is a crucial moment in the text, and its Augustinian inflection ought to function as a powerful bar to continuing to read Melibee's arguments as simply ignorant.[47] At precisely this point, however, Chaucer departs from his source texts. In Renaud de Louens's French text—believed by many scholars to be Chaucer's primary and perhaps sole source[48]— Prudence had *conceded* Melibee's general assessment of vengeance as a useful tool for the punishment of evildoers. She opens with this remark: "'Certes,' dist elle, 'je vous ottroye que de venge vient moult de biens" ("Certainly I grant you that from vengeance comes many goods").[49] So too in Albertano's original, she concedes, "Quae dixisti vera sunt" ("These things you have said are true").[50] Having acknowledged Melibee's defense of vengeance's punitive function, Prudence then offers (in both the Latin and the French source traditions) a carefully argued *distinctio* between the legitimate and illegitimate agents of such vengeance. In his *Tale of Melibee,* however, Chaucer omits Prudence's concession that vengeance is a good, and in his translation Prudence's counterargument *begins* with the distinction: "Right as a singuler persone synneth in takynge vengeance of another man, / right so synneth the juge if he do no vengeance of hem that it han disserved" (VII.1434–35). Prudence then reiterates her argument that Melibee lacks the proper authority to exercise vengeance: "If ye wol thanne take vengeance of youre enemys,

[47] Such readings typically accompany arguments that Chaucer intended his tale to be a self-deconstructing or parodic work. See, for instance, Daniel Kempton, "Chaucer's *Tale of Melibee:* 'A Litel Thyng in Prose,'" *Genre* 21 (1988): 263–78. A notable effort to challenge such "ironic" readings is Flynn's "The Art of Telling," which underscores the significance of Prudence and Melibee's different understandings of vengeance.

[48] While Chaucer most likely worked with Renaud de Louens's French adaptation of Albertano's text, *Livre de Melibée et de Dame Prudence,* J. D. Burnley has reassessed positively the evidence for Chaucer's engagement with the Latin original as well; see his "Curial Prose Style in England," *Speculum* 61 (1986): 593–614.

[49] This and subsequent citations of Chaucer's source texts are from William Askins, ed., "The Tale of Melibee," in *Sources and Analogues of the Canterbury Tales,* gen. ed. Correale and Hamel, pp. 331–408. The line cited here is from 39.1, p. 379 and reflects the attestation of the French manuscript deemed closest to Chaucer's source text by Askins, Severs, and previous editors of Chaucer (Bibliothèque Nationale MS fr. 578). Curiously the *Riverside* cites a different variant, one that adds a phrase "molt de maulx" ("many evils") to the passage. Thus, in the *Riverside,* Prudence is cited as conceding that "many evils and many goods" come from vengeance (See VII.1434, as supplied by the editors). This seems unwarranted to me as an emendation, and it obscures the nature of Prudence's concession in the French source text most likely to have been used by Chaucer.

[50] *Albertani Brixiensis: Liber Consolationis et Consilii,* 39, pp. 86–87.

ye shul retourne or have youre recours to the juge that hath the jurisdic-
cion upon hem, / and he shal punysse hem *as the lawe asketh and re-
quireth*" (VII.1442–43, Chaucer's addition emphasized). The *Riverside*
text leaves Chaucer's addition unnoted, while it obscures his omission
by supplying it from the intermediary French text of Renaud. As the
editors themselves note, however, there is absolutely no English manuscript evidence for the inclusion of this passage (which is why Manly
and Rickert had omitted the passage in their edition).[51] The Riverside
editors explain their choice to include the passage by observing that
Prudence's remarks seem necessary to the sense, and they postulate—as
did J. Burke Severs in his edition of the source—that Chaucer's French
source text must have omitted the passage. This is possible, of course,
but one might hesitate, for the passage is included in all but a single
extant French manuscript.[52]

I think we are justified, then, in asking why Chaucer might have
omitted the passage,[53] and I would suggest that the most likely reason
for the omission is that it clarifies Prudence's argument: her overarching
strategy is to insist that private persons lack the authority to engage in

[51] John M. Manly and Edith Rickert, *The Text of the "Canterbury Tales,"* vol. 4, pt. 2
(Chicago: University of Chicago Press, 1940), p. 188, note to 2623–24*.

[52] The passage is omitted only in the fifteenth-century text, Paris, Bibliothèque Nationale, MS fr. 1165. In his edition of Chaucer's source texts in *Sources and Analogues,* gen.
ed. Correale and Hamel, William Askins suggests that the line could have been lost as
a result of eye skip; see p. 379, note to 39.1. In the earlier edition of Renaud de Louens's
tale in *Sources and Analogues of Chaucer's "Canterbury Tales,"* ed. W. F. Bryan and Germaine Dempster (New York: Humanities Press, 1958), Severs hypothesized that the
passage had been omitted in Chaucer's French source text, and that Chaucer was merely
following his source text, even though Severs realized that BN MS fr. 1165 (the only
extant text omitting the passage) did not correspond to Chaucer's text as well as BN
MS fr. 578, which is the text Severs used as his base edition of Renaud's text. See Severs,
"The Tale of Melibeus," *Sources and Analogues,* ed. Bryan and Dempster, p. 593, note to
677–80; and see his discussion of Chaucer's omissions, pp. 564–65.

[53] Arguing, as I have, that Chaucer chose to omit the line does of course entail accept-
ing a blemished text. Without the passage, the switch in speakers (from Melibee to
Prudence) is left unmarked, and the reader is faced with inconsecutive passages. While
there can be little question that the omission disrupts the linear unfolding of the narrative, this is true regardless of whether one postulates that Chaucer's omission resulted
from following his source text or from a conscious decision to omit Prudence's problematic concession. Both interpretations leave us wondering why Chaucer did not smooth
out the material, as he does at other moments. Finally, while the unsatisfactory transition in speakers might lead one to embrace Askins's suggestion that the omission was
the result of eye skip (e.g., Chaucer would not have intentionally left inconsecutive
passages), the extant manuscripts—again, all but one omit the line—do not exactly
offer support for the supposition. Morever, a careful examination of how both Renaud
and Chaucer introduce occasional syntactical and semantic infelicities in their reworking
of Albertano's text shows that errors can of course possess authorial status.

private warfare; Chaucer may well have felt that her concession that "vengeance on evildoers is a good thing" was too much of a concession. If this is true, it suggests that Chaucer was being more Augustinian—or rather more a Romanist—than Augustine himself at this moment, refusing to allow the doctrine that "war punishes sinners" to be conflated with a justification of warfare.[54]

Melibee's second major strategy in the *Tale* also gains new significance when considered within a juridical context. And rather than read his argument, as has so often been done, as one in which we see a dim-witted Melibee fumbling his way toward an obvious truth about the illegitimacy of vengeance, I want again to suggest that Melibee's thinking is part of a staged recapitulation of a familiar debate in the history of juridical controversy over the status of private violence. In this instance, the tale isolates arguments surrounding the individual's right to deploy violence in self-defense. Melibee first approaches this issue by citing the "vileynye" of his adversaries. Given their "wikked wyl" and their rash heedlessness in attacking him, Melibee argues, he should be permitted to respond in kind: "And therfore me thynketh men oghten nat repreve me, though I putte me in peril for to venge me, / and though I do a greet excesse; that is to seyn, that I venge oon outrage by another" (VII.1524–25). Underlying Melibee's argument is a sophisticated premise, one given its sharpest articulation earlier in the narrative, as Melibee glossed the counsel he had received from the physicians. The physicians had advised him to undertake war, reasoning, as Melibee explains, that "right as they [my adversaries] han doon me a contrarie, right so sholde I doon hem another. / For as right as they han venged hem on me and doon me wrong, right so shal I venge me upon hem and doon hem wrong; and thanne have I cured oon contrarie by another" (VII.1277–79). As James Flynn and Judith Ferster have shown, the disagreement here stems from a conflict over the meaning of the concept of "contraries," such that where Melibee understands a *contrarie* as a "hostile act" that justifies responding to his adversaries' attack with vio-

---

[54] There is no necessary inconsistency between Albertano's own desire to delimit the sphere of private violence and Prudence's concessionary passage in the original thirteenth-century context. Arguably, much broader concessions were made by authorities such as Gratian, and by the Glossators as well as the Decretists. By the time Renaud and Chaucer were writing, however, the distinction between licit war and illicit vengeance had achieved much greater legal clarity, an effect of the expansion of royal jurisdiction over acts of violent self-help in both England and France (especially as compared to the Italian communes).

lence, Prudence glosses it as "one of a pair of opposed or contrasting qualities," and thus counsels that "wikkednesse shal be warisshed by goodnesse, discord by accord, werre by pees" (VII.1289).[55]

But more is at issue here than a scholastic dissection of the common proverb *"contrariis medici curant contraria,"*[56] for the argument that Melibee presents—"right asketh a man to defenden violence by violence and fightyng by fightyng" (VII.1533)—restates a troublesome maxim in the civil law tradition—"vim . . . vi defendere omnes leges omniaque iura permittunt," a maxim that established that all were permitted by the right of law to defend themselves.[57] This provision has a long history in efforts to delegitimize private violence. First of all, as Gratian himself had stated, natural law gave individuals the right to defend themselves against force, while the *ius gentium* conferred the right to repel injuries. Although Gratian was centrally concerned to restrict the execution of justice to public officials, and although he censured the vendetta in no uncertain terms, he nevertheless failed, as F. H. Russell has observed, to establish a clear basis upon which to distinguish the defense against violent force permitted to individuals and the repulsion of injuries restricted to superior authority.[58] An even greater difficulty was posed by feudal custom, one with which the Glossators as well as the Decretists and Decretalists wrestled as they sought to make sense of feudal *guerra* in relation to Roman law. As they commented on the *Libri feudorum,* for instance, the Glossators struggled with major incompatibilities between an ancient civil law tradition in which the authority to declare war was vested exclusively in the emperor and a contemporary reality in which political authority was fragmented, and kings, counts, and even lords assumed the right to defend their landed interests with retinues of armed men. The nature of feudal obligations complicated further efforts to distinguish vengeance (*ultio*) from either simple self-defense, on the one hand, or licit public warfare, on the other. Since vassals were expected to aid their lords militarily, they were often drawn into private

[55] Flynn, "The Art of Telling," p. 59; Ferster, *Fictions of Advice,* pp. 92–96 passim.

[56] "Doctors cure opposing things with opposing things." The ambiguity of the word "contrarium" permits vying interpretations. The physicians counsel war as the *contrary* or *antagonistic* response to his enemies' attack; Prudence insists that the correct interpretation of contrary as "opposite" reveals that the proper remedy for vengeance is peace.

[57] *The Digest of Justinian,* vol. 1, ed. Theodor Mommsen and trans. Alan Watson (Philadelphia: University of Pennsylvania Press, 1985), 9.2.45.4, p. 291.

[58] For a discussion of the dilemma Gratian faced, see Russell, *The Just War,* pp. 97, 131.

wars of vengeance. By acknowledging the vassal's obligation to assist his lord, commentators strained even the best efforts to delimit private violence.[59] Given these points of difficulty, one can see why Melibee might insist that "right asketh a man to defenden violence by violence and fightyng by fightyng" (VII.1533) even as Prudence avers, "ye knowen wel that ye maken no defense as now for to deffende yow, but to venge yow'" (VII.1537).[60]

In their effort to distinguish simple self-defense, the Glossators asserted that the act of "meeting violence with violence" in an act of self-defense was licit only when undertaken "incontinenti" and not "ex intervallo"—that is, when engaged in immediately and not when subject to delay.[61] They insisted further that self-defense must be exercised "cum moderamine"—that is, the amount of violence exercised needed to be proportionate to that received and must be only what was necessary to escape an attack.[62] These criteria—neither of which is in any way relevant to the public, defensive war of the sovereign—are exactly those by which Prudence denies Melibee's right to wage war on his enemies.[63]

[59] On the Romanists' efforts to define legitimate authority in relation to decentralized feudal lordship, see Russell, *The Just War,* pp. 43–46. For a comparison of the Decretalist Hostiensis's handling of a vassal's obligation to that of Innocent IV, see ibid., pp. 148–55.

[60] Prudence articulates Justinian's central caveat that individuals may defend themselves only insofar as is necessary for self-defense and not for revenge. The critical passage reads: "illum enim solum qui uim infert ferire conceditur et hoc, si tuendi dumtaxat, non etiam ulciscendi causa factum sit." *Digest of Justinian,* 9.2.45.4, p. 291.

[61] See Azo, *Summa Codicis,* to *Cod.* 8.4; cited by Russell, *The Just War,* p. 43. For Accursius, see *Glossa Ordinaria* to *Inst.* 4.15.6, v. *is ab eo,* and his commentary on *Dig.* 43.16.3.9, v. *continenti.* The Decretists reiterate the Glossators' conditions: see Rufinus's commentary on *Decretum* I. C.7 in *Die Summa Decretorum des Magister Rufinus,* ed. H. Singer (Paderborn, 1902), p. 9; cited by Russell, pp. 97–98. For a representative treatment by the Decretalists, see Hostiensis on *Decretales Gregorii* IX I.34 in *Summa Aurea;* cited by Russell, pp. 132–33.

[62] The Glossators were not the first to make these distinctions, but they gave the criteria new prominence within a more systematic treatment of the nature of self-defense and war. Compare, for instance, the passing reference to the need for moderation in Justinian's *Codex* 8.4.1 to the later commentaries on that very passage by the Glossators, Azo, Odofredus, and Accursius, cited extensively by Russell, *The Just War,* pp. 42–45. For Justinian, see *Corpus Iuris Civilis, Volumen Secundum: Codex Iustinianus,* ed. Paulus Krueger (Dublin: Weidmann, 1967), 8.4.1, p. 332. For Azo, see *Summa Codicis,* to *Cod.* 8.4; for Accursius, *Glossa Ordinaria,* to *Cod* 3.27.1, v. *ultionem,* and to *Cod.* 8.4.1, v. *moderatione.* The Decretists and Decretalists tend to reiterate the need for moderation without significant innovation. Raymond of Pennaforte, however, defines moderate force more narrowly, and calls for a much harsher penalty of excommunication for those willfully violating the standards. See *Summa de Casibus,* 2.5.12.18; cited by Russell, p. 132.

[63] While the content of VII.1534–36 shows an unmistakable citation of civil law definitions of legitimate self-defense as *incontinenti* and *cum moderamine,* Chaucer's source

Answering violence with violence is only legitimate, she argues, "whan the defense is doon withouten intervalle or without tariyng or delay, / for to deffenden hym and nat for to vengen him. And it behoveth a man putte swich attemperance in his defense that men have no cause ne matiere to repreven hym that deffendeth hym of excesse and outrage" (VII.1534–36). Prudence is a shrewd glossator and a conservative one as well. For while civil law commentators such as Azo had conceded that an "immediate" act of self-defense could extend, in certain circumstances, so as to justify a year's span of violent deeds, Prudence defines a much narrower field of permissible activity.[64]

One might well wonder whether this intricate legal machinery would have been an immediate part of Chaucer's interest in this narrative. It is worth emphasizing that Chaucer need not have had firsthand knowledge of civil law writings in order to recognize Prudence's juridical arguments or find them relevant. Thanks to Anthony Musson's work on the dissemination of legal knowledge among various social groups in late medieval England, we are well situated to appreciate the intimate knowledge of criminal and civil law that would have been possessed by those of Chaucer's background and education.[65] His experiences as juror, witness, and defendant gave him firsthand knowledge of court proce-

---

texts also marked these distinctions linguistically throughout the narrative: in his Latin text, Albertano often uses "incontinenti" to describe Melibee's proposed war, and the single adjectival form survives in Renaud's text where Melibee is said to desire "faire guerre incontinent" (Askins, *Sources and Analogues,* gen. ed. Correale and Hamel, 2.21, p. 335). For the corresponding example of Albertano's usage, see Sundby. There seems to be no single Middle English word that could have captured the legal sense of the Latin legal term; in any case, we find Chaucer rendering his source at these moments with simple noun phrases such as "the werre" (VII.1009).

[64] In commenting on *Cod.* 8.4, Azo concedes that self-defense need not be limited to the same day as an attack, so long as the individual's defense is continuous and without other intervening activity; see *Summa Codicis,* cited by Russell, *The Just War,* p. 43. Prudence's more narrowly defined field of legitimate conduct bears closer resemblance to Raymond of Pennaforte's treatment in *Summa de Casibus,* 2.5.12.18, pp. 185b–186b. D. R. Johnson argues for Chaucer's direct use of Raymond as a source in *The Parson's Tale:* See "'Homicide' in *The Parson's Tale,"* PMLA 57 (1942): 51–56.

[65] Anthony Musson, *Medieval Law in Context: The Growth of Legal Consciousness from Magna Carta to the Peasants' Revolt* (Manchester: Manchester University Press, 2001), pp. 103–19 and 120–24. See also C. J. Neville, "Common Knowledge of the Common Law in Later Medieval England," *Canadian Journal of History* 29 (1994): 461–79 (468). For a detailed examination of Chaucer's legal knowledge (and its inflection on the very structure of the *Canterbury Tales,* see Mary Flowers Braswell, *Chaucer's "Legal Fiction": Reading the Records* (Madison, N.J.: Fairleigh Dickinson University Press, 2001). On Chaucer's social circle and the education one might assume belonged to him by virtue of his "Oxford ties and Inns of Court connections," see Ann Astell's reassessment in *Chaucer and the Universe of Learning,* pp. 4–7.

dure and jurisdictions,[66] while his responsibilities as Controller of the Wool Customs and Member of Parliament[67] both required and provided avenues for specialized legal knowledge about contracts, inquests, and certain rules of law. Most significantly, Chaucer served as a Justice of the Peace for his town in Kent from 1385 to 1389, and in 1387 he served as Justice *ad inquirendum* in the Court of King's Bench. In these capacities, Chaucer was engaged with the examination of crimes ranging from theft and fraudulent practices in the selling of goods to violent acts of trespass and felony, including homicide.[68] Chaucer's duties as Justice of the Peace would have given him knowledge of property rights, laws of debt and covenant, assize laws governing trials, laws governing jurisdictions, and statutory laws.[69]

More specifically, as a member of the Peace Commissions, Chaucer would certainly have been familiar with English law on homicide.[70] Any reader of Bracton's discussion of homicide would have found terms used by the Glossators and the Decretists also present in his writings.[71] Most

[66] On the "substantive" knowledge of legal principle and procedures of jurors in fourteenth-century England more generally, see Musson, *Medieval Law in Context*, pp. 103, 112–19, 194. Jurors would have had access to sheriffs and coroner's rolls, had knowledge of case compilations, and would have been able to remedy any deficiencies in legal knowledge through consultation with legal handbooks, a common informal practice for those called upon to act in minor legal capacities. See pp. 38–42 and 68–69, and on those handbooks and treatises aimed at a more general audience, see pp. 122–24.

[67] As a Member of Parliament (for Kent) in 1386, Chaucer would have witnessed not only the approval of new regulations, but he would have also been privy to the complaints brought to parliament that year from across the shires, complaints that centered on corrupt judicial practices. On the legal knowledge and experience of MPs, see Musson, *Medieval Law in Context*, esp. pp. 194–96.

[68] The duties of commissions varied over time. See Musson, *Public Order and Law Enforcement: The Local Administration of Criminal Justice, 1294–1350* (Woodbridge: Boydell, 1996), pp. 229–34 and for a more in-depth treatment of the period of Chaucer's service, see Simon Walker, "Yorkshire Justices of the Peace, 1389–1413," *EHR* 427 (April 1993): 281–313 and Rosamond Sillem, "Commissions of the Peace, 1380–1485," *Bulletin of the Institute of Historical Research* 10 (1932): 81–104, esp. 94–5. For a fuller discussion of the substantive legal background Chaucer would have obtained in his various official capacities and a judicious appraisal of the extent to which specific legal experiences are recoverable, see Braswell, *Chaucer's "Legal Fiction,"* esp. pp. 13–30. See also Joseph Allen Hornsby's helpful chapter, "Chaucer's Legal Background," in his *Chaucer and the Law* (Norman, Okla.: Pilgrim Books, 1988), pp. 7–30.

[69] Chaucer's engagement with the law was apparently extensive enough that late in life he was asked to serve for an acquaintance as one of "attornatos meos": Braswell, *Chaucer's "Legal Fiction,"* p. 27.

[70] Neville observes that familiarity with the law on felonies would have been widespread in late medieval England; see "Common Knowledge of the Common Law," p. 468.

[71] We can trace the influence of the civil law tradition on *De legibus* by those passages Bracton takes directly—and verbatim—from the Glossator Azo's commentary in *Summa Codicis* as well as from Justinian's *Corpus* itself. For an assessment of Bracton's knowledge

relevant here is Bracton's distinction among four types of corporeal homicide. He contrasts the homicide committed licitly "in the administration of justice, as when a judge or officer kills one lawfully found guilty," to the homicide committed "by intention," as when an individual who "in anger or hatred or for the sake of gain, deliberately and in premeditated assault, has killed another wickedly and feloniously and in breach of the king's peace."[72] Bracton also addresses the question of self-defense, defining this type of homicide as licit only when it is "unavoidable" and when one "kills without premeditated hatred but with sorrow of heart, in order to save himself and his family, since he could not otherwise escape."[73] Used as measures of Melibee's desired recourse to violence, these categories render his proposed "self-defense" legally indefensible.[74]

---

of and reliance on various Continental legists, see Thorne's introduction to his edition and translation of George E. Woodbine's Latin text, *Bracton: On the Laws and Customs of England,* trans. Samuel E. Thorne, 4 vols. (Cambridge, Mass.: Belknap Press of Harvard University Press, 1968).

[72] Ibid., 2:340: "Iustitia, ut cum iudex vel minister reum iuste damnatum occidit." Bracton explains the justification as one derived both from the judge's authority and from his right disposition, what he calls his "love of justice" ("ex amore iustitiae"). On intentional homicide, see 2:341: "Voluntate, ut si quis ex certa scientia et in assultu praemeditato, ira vel odio vel causa lucri, nequiter et in felonia et contra pacem domini regis aliquem interfecerit." All references here and subsequently are taken from Woodbine's Latin edition, *De legibus et consuetudinibus angliae,* 4 vols. (New Haven: Yale University Press; London: Oxford University Press, 1915–42), which Thorne reproduces in his facing-page translation. In *Chaucer and the Law,* Hornsby discusses Bracton's categorization, compares it to the discussion of bodily homicide in *The Parson's Tale,* and notes that despite the Parson's omission of intentional homicide, his account is "an accurate, though uneven, account of both the canon law and the common law on the subject" (p. 111). Hornsby also notes *Melibee*'s citation of the civil law condition dictating moderate force, but he does not recognize the connection with Romanist thinking. Instead he suggests that Chaucer was following the canonist Raymond of Pennaforte's treatment in his penitential treatise. If this is the case, then Chaucer might have perceived how Albertano's treatise diverged from canonist treatments of the just war.

[73] *Bracton,* 2:340: "Si autem inevitabilis, quia occidit hominem sine odii meditatione in moto dolore animi, se et sua liberando cum aliter evadere non posset." Anthony Musson's research suggests that jurors would be familiar with the specific distinctions pertaining to homicide invoked here. Musson cites records of questions put to jurors by justices, wherein jurors were asked to consider whether a homicide was "premeditated" and whether in cases of claimed self defense the individual had "been tirelessly pursued while trying to escape"; similarly, jurors were asked to determine whether "any force used was commensurate with the attack" (*Medieval Law in Context,* p. 114).

[74] Ambiguities in the status of certain forms of violent self-help did of course exist. In *A Crisis of Truth: Literature and Law in Ricardian England* (Philadelphia: University of Pennsylvania Press, 1999), Richard Firth Green makes a compelling case for the persistence of residual folk ideals of violent self-help, suggesting that English understandings of legitimate self-defense were not necessarily consistent with the civil law tradition before the fourteenth century, especially as regards the violent punishment of crimes *in situ*. Green cites *The Mirror of Justice,* remarking, "It used to be 'that one could throw an arsonist on the fire and burn him if one caught him freshly in the act' [freschement

Perhaps the best evidence we have of Chaucer's interest in the Melibee narrative as a work that challenges the status of private violence are the additions he makes in translating his source text(s). Chaucer seems to have been interested in heightening the issue of Melibee's disposition or *intentio,* for in translating his French intermediary—a text to which he generally sticks quite closely—he frequently adds material to indicate that Melibee's disposition is improperly marked by anger and the desire for vengeance. Chaucer adds, for instance, descriptions of Melibee's "wilde hert" (VII.1325) and his "hastif wilfulnesse" (VII.1363) where neither his French nor Latin source texts emphasizes Melibee's emotional state. Elsewhere he heightens an emphasis in his source by providing a more expansive translation. Where Renaud's text narrates how Melibee "estoit moult courrociez,"[75] for example, Chaucer offers the intensified description: "in herte he baar a crueel ire" (VII.1008). Similarly, where in the French, Prudence asks Melibee to examine how many advisers "se consentent a ton conseil et a ta voulenté," in Chaucer's text she asks how many "consenten to thy conseil in thy wilfulnesse to doon hastif vengeance" (VII.1361).[76] Chaucer also emphasizes the link between Melibee's psychological disposition and his poor rational judgment: Melibee fails to discriminate or "to make division" (VII.1255), he throws the wisdom of the authorities "in an hochepot" (a legal term for the act of treating all claimants as equal [VII.1257]),[77] and as a consequence he advances proposals that are "agayn resoun and out of mesure" (VII.1848).[78] Just as Bracton in defining one type of

---

el fet]" (p. 87), and observes that "as late as 1300 private suitors . . . in cases of manifest theft were held to be entitled to execute the hand-having thief, providing always that they were themselves the owners or custodians of the goods concerned, a confession had been extracted from the offender, and there were reliable witnesses to the deed" (p. 88).

[75] *Sources and Analogues,* gen. ed. Correale and Hamel, 2.21, p. 335. Measures of intensity are of course extremely subjective, and most readers have—to this point—not credited Chaucer's additions with significance. One notable exception is Lynn Staley, who, in her recent book, *Languages of Power in the Age of Richard II,* has argued for the significance of Chaucer's additional emphasis on forgiveness in the final paragraphs of *Melibee.* For Staley, these function to counsel Richard II "in the ways of mercy" (p. 190) in the context of his conflict with the Appellants. William Askins argues, by contrast, that Chaucer's practice of deleting source material throughout the tale suggests an effort to preclude any interpretation of the Melibee narrative as political commentary on the Ricardian court.

[76] *Sources and Analogues,* gen. ed. Correale and Hamel, 35.11, p. 373.

[77] See *OED* s.v. hotchpot 3; discussed in the explanatory notes to *The Riverside Chaucer,* p. 926.

[78] As Burnley points out, Chaucer also emphasizes the corrective force of reason and the importance of acting with one's passions subdued with a series of phrases stressing

bodily homicide—that done "by intention, as where one in anger or hatred or for the sake of gain, deliberately and in premeditated assault, has killed another wickedly and feloniously"—draws on the resources of both canon and civil law in order to cast vengeance as both an immoral and an illegal act, so here Chaucer's additions to *The Tale of Melibee* serve to represent Melibee's disordered emotional state as both an expression of a defective will and the sign of a criminal intent.

Thus far we have seen how three legal categories—authority, circumstance, and intention—are invoked by Prudence to make an argument about the agents, forums, and circumstances of violence as well as the psychological disposition deemed necessary and proper to its legitimate exercise in the forms of war, self-defense, and judicial punishment. Insofar as this legal machinery functions ethically—that is, to the degree that legal dicta work to advance some particular set of ideals over and against some others (privileging this ideal of justice, rendering some other vision of the good incomprehensible)—the law functions as a productive field of power, even as its most visible modes remain those of prohibition and punishment. In the second half of this essay I aim to explore the tale's more positive mode of ethical thinking,[79] revealing how the *Melibee* advances an understanding of the nature of the good toward which individuals should be drawn. By investigating the way the explicitly philosophical discourse of the tale functions—drawing individuals like Melibee to seek certain licit pleasures and rewards, to find a sense of self-worth in the pursuit of certain socially valued activities—I hope to offer a satisfying account of two troublesome aspects of the tale: its ostensibly incoherent, tangential discussion of the "profitability" of Melibee's proposed violence, and the seemingly unprincipled, pragmatist nature of Prudence's arguments for a nonviolent resolution, for peace and forgiveness.

The Profitable and the Good: Prudence's Ciceronian Ethics

Let us begin to unpack these difficulties by retracing the emergence of crisis in the tale, turning to the scene in which Melibee declares the

---

the importance of "temperance" and discretion and invoking classical ideals of the mean (both in the *Melibee* and in other tales such as *The Knight's Tale* where the problem of vengeance is at issue). See *Chaucer's Language and the Philosophers' Tradition*, pp. 119, 121, and 125–26.

[79] By using the word "positive," I mean to indicate a statement that goes beyond either prohibition or critique to assert the parameters for ethical conduct.

Christian virtues of forgiveness and peace to be incompatible with his desire for honor. The scene comes to its dramatic apex as Prudence invokes the example of Christ and the saints suffering violent attacks against their person with "pacient suffraunce," and enjoins Melibee to recall Christ's passion: "Whan men cursed hym, he cursed hem noght, and whan men betten hym, he manaced hem noght" (VII.1504). Melibee concedes that "patience is greet vertu of perfeccioun," but with the brash confidence of the Wife of Bath demurs, "Every man may nat have the perfeccioun that ye seken; / ne I nam nat of the nombre of right parfite men, / for myn herte may nevere been in pees unto the tyme it be venged" (VII.1518–20). In the *Melibee,* the first and final obstacle to peace is Melibee's sense that only vengeance can satisfy the demands of honor.

Prudence's strategy of dealing with the problem is a complex one, but most critics are agreed that in its essential nature hers is a pragmatic solution; she deftly argues that Melibee lacks the resources and the help of associates and kin and points out that his enemies are greater in number, supporters, and might. All in all, she argues, there is no profit in war for Melibee. Combined with her seemingly inexplicable digression on the best way to gather riches and win friends and influence, the pragmatist turn in Prudence's argument can easily seem self-serving and, as Judith Ferster has argued, utterly devoid of principle.[80] One might be inclined then to agree with Aers that once Prudence abandons Christian ethics, the tale is left with a vacuous, even a vicious, secular pragmatism.[81]

Pragmatism need not, however, be opposed to serious ethical argumentation, although it certainly entails valuing an aspect of moral discourse that is often devalued, namely, the operation of practical reason. The French sociologist Pierre Bourdieu offers a trenchant assessment of just such a devaluation and provides us, in his attempt to define what distinguishes practical reason, with a way to approach the figure of Prudence in classical and Christian thought. Bourdieu contrasts the operation of practical reason—one that acknowledges the contingency of human existence, its definite social and economic conditions, its orientation toward practical ends, and the actualization of particular wishes or desires—with the operation of what he calls *skholè,* a form of thought

---

[80] *Fictions of Advice,* p. 96.
[81] "Chaucer's *Tale of Melibee,*" p. 75.

that seeks to distill truth through the application of pure reason, divorced from urgency, freed from any reference to situation or the social conditions of existence, separated from the claims of practical necessity.[82] Bourdieu not only usefully casts a skeptical light onto academic claims to a transcendent, epistemological position, he also helpfully diagnoses the tendency to privilege pure reason within classificatory systems organizing knowledge into divisions (or *scientia*).[83]

Within the philosophical sources informing *The Tale of Melibee*, the figure of prudence stands for something very close to Bourdieu's practical reason. In *De officiis*, one of the major source texts for the Melibee narrative, Cicero defines prudence as "practical knowledge of the things to be sought and to be avoided."[84] Cicero accords prudence a privileged role in the ethical life, as it is this faculty that allows humans to determine the social good and to orient their action toward its accomplishment. Cicero explains:

If wisdom is the most important of the virtues, as it certainly is, it necessarily follows that appropriate action, which is connected with the social obligation, is the most important duty. And service is better than theoretical knowledge, for the study and knowledge of the universe would be lame and defective were no practical results (*actio*) to follow. Such results, moreover, are best seen in the

---

[82] "The Scholastic Point of View," in *Practical Reason: On the Theory of Action*, trans. Randal Johnson et al. (Stanford: Stanford University Press, 1998), pp. 127–40.

[83] On the dramatic transformations of such hierarchical systems for classifying types of knowledge in the twelfth and thirteenth centuries as they form a pre-history to later vernacular writers' new vision of the status and function of rhetoric, see Rita Copeland's erudite overview in "Lydgate, Hawes, and the Science of Rhetoric in the Late Middle Ages," in *John Lydgate: Poetry, Culture, and Lancastrian England,* ed. Larry Scanlon and James Simpson (Notre Dame: University of Notre Dame Press, 2006).

[84] Cicero, *De officiis,* trans. Walter Miller, Loeb Classical Library (1913; Cambridge, Mass.: Harvard University Press, 1997), bk. 1, sec. 153: "rerum expetendarum fugiendarumque scientia." All subsequent citations are to this edition with book and section number indicated. One of the most typical forums in which medieval writers encountered such works of moral philosophy is through digests. A full digest of *De officiis* is given by Vincent of Beauvais in his *Speculum historiale,* to which I have compared passages cited here. For detailed discussion of the transmission of Cicero's text, see N. E. Nelson, "Cicero's *De Officiis* in Christian Thought: 300–1300," *Essays and Studies in English and Comparative Literature* 10 (1933): 59–160; see also Michael Winterbottom's survey of the English manuscript tradition in "The Transmission of Cicero's *De Officiis,*" *Classical Quarterly,* n.s. 43 (1993): 215–42; and Andrew Dyck's introductory remarks in *A Commentary on Cicero, De Officiis* (Ann Arbor: University of Michigan Press, 1996). On Beauvais as a major transmission route, see *Vincent of Beauvais and Alexander the Great: Studies on the "Speculum Maius" and Its Translations into Medieval Vernaculars,* ed. W. J. Aerts, E. R. Smiths, and J. B. Voorbij (Groningen: Egbert Forsten, 1986).

safeguarding of human interests. It is essential, then, to human society; and it should, therefore, be ranked above speculative knowledge.[85]

Even as Cicero recognizes an established field of relative value—where *prudentia* operates subordinate to the "most important of the virtues," *sapientia*—he refuses to accept such a hierarchical classification of value. Indeed, he challenges such a hierarchy by arguing for the superiority of a practical reason oriented toward the accomplishment of human interests over a more theoretical form devoted to the apprehension of truth.[86]

As Cicero's foremost modern commentator, Andrew Dyck, has argued, it would be a mistake to understand Cicero's sense of "human interest" as a self-serving pragmatism divorced from ethics. Indeed Dyck explains, "Cicero's major contribution to Roman political thought is his radical identification of *honestum* and *utile*," a semantically diffuse concept that incorporates the idea of what is expedient or profitable and what is beneficial to the human community.[87] In *De officiis*, Cicero insists that there was, properly speaking, no such thing as an expedient course of action that was immoral. Distinguishing himself from the Academician and the Epicurean philosophies,[88] Cicero argued that the profitable course of action was also *honestum*, the morally right course of action. For Cicero, the identity of *honestum* and *utilitas* was inherent in the laws of nature, which "forbid us to increase our means, wealth and resources

---

[85] *De officiis*, bk. I, sec. 153: "ea si maxima est, ut est certe, necesse est, quod a communitate ducatur officium, id esse maximum. Etenim cognitio contemplatioque naturae manca quodam modo atque inchoata sit, si nulla actio rerum consequatur. Ea autem actio in hominem commodis tuendis maxime cernitur; pertinet igitur ad societatem generis humani; ergo haec cognitioni anteponenda est."

[86] See also *De officiis*, bk. I, sec. 155: "Quibus rebus intellegitur studiis officiisque scientiae praeponenda esse officia iustitiae, quae pertinent ad hominum utilitatem, qua nihil homini esse debet antiquius" [From all this we conclude that the duties prescribed by justice must be given precedence over the pursuit of knowledge and the duties imposed by it; for the former concern the welfare of our fellow-men; and nothing ought to be more sacred in men's eyes than that."]

[87] *A Commentary on Cicero, De Officiis*, p. 33

[88] *De officiis*, bk. III, sec. 20: "quamquam et a veteribus Academicis et a Peripateticis vestris . . . quae honesta sunt, anteponuntur iis, quae videntur utilia, tamen splendidius haec ab eis disseruntur, quibus, quicquid honestum est, idem utile videtur nec utile quicquam, quod non honestum, quam ab iis, quibus et honestum aliquid non utile et utile non honestum" ["the older Academicians and your Peripatetics . . . give what is morally right the preference over what seems expedient; and yet the discussion of these problems, if conducted by those who consider whatever is morally right also expedient and nothing expedient that is not at the same time morally right, will be more illuminating than if conducted by those who think that something not expedient may be morally right and that something not morally right may be expedient"].

by despoiling others" (bk. III, sec. 22). Any act that harms one's fellow human threatens the bonds of social life, and thus cannot properly be said to benefit a member of that society. Understood in the "technical and true sense of the word," *honestum,* then, is always at one with *utilitas,* and anyone—for instance—who would claim that a course of action would be profitable although it would injure a neighbor would be guilty, at best, of a gross error in understanding the nature of *utilitas,* and, at worst, of bad faith, of seeking disingenuously to justify immoral behavior. Central to the argument of *De officiis,* then, is both a negative principle—the stricture that "one may do no harm"—and a positive duty to seek "the interest . . . of the whole body politic," understood to be identical with the true interest of the individual.[89]

For Cicero, the pursuit of material well-being was consistent with the *officium* of the virtuous citizen. Through industry, skill, and talent, humans pursue the daily business of living, and in acts of "giving and receiving"—the deeds of liberality and hospitality as well as those of the marketplace—members of the community supply one another's needs, thus "cement[ing] human society more closely together, man to man."[90] Of course, Cicero also recognized that the pursuit of material wealth in his own Roman society often failed to meet the rigorous ethical standard of conduct set out in *De officiis.* Even as he defends the identity of *honestum* and *utilitas,* he acknowledges that "we are so disposed that each to gain some personal profit will defraud or injure his neighbor."[91] He thus counsels that profit may only legitimately be sought in such a way that the "bonds of union between citizens should not be impaired."[92] And he warns against avoiding a virtuous course of action because of its costs, for "he is mistaken in thinking that any ills affecting either his person or his property are more serious than those affecting his soul."[93] Such ills, however great the loss or trouble to the individual, must be willingly borne to secure justice. Only thus can the "bonds of society" be preserved.

In *The Tale of Melibee,* Prudence sees no inherent contradiction between the dictates of justice, morality, and that which is profitable or expedient. She also recognizes, however, as Cicero himself had, that one

[89] Ibid., bk. III, sec. 26.
[90] Ibid., bk. I, sec. 22.
[91] Ibid., bk. III, sec. 21.
[92] Ibid., bk. III, sec. 23.
[93] Ibid., bk. III, sec. 26.

of the primary obstacles to justice was avarice. This is why, I believe, in the middle of discussion about whether Melibee may legitimately wreak vengeance on his enemies, Prudence turns to consideration of his desires for wealth, status, and honor. Following Cicero's understanding of the social benefits that follow the pursuit of material well-being, she explains that "by richesses ther comen manye goodes" (VII.1562), and she then turns to explain the appropriate means by which this end may be secured: "richesses been goode to hem that geten hem wel and to hem that wel usen tho richesses" (VII.1574), continuing for just under a hundred lines to set out the proper method of gathering riches, gaining one's neighbor's respect, and securing the possession of "worshippe." Melibee may legitimately seek what is profitable. The burden of Prudence's lecture, nevertheless, is to insist that the profitable course may not be pursued outside a consideration of *honestum*. She expresses the general principle of the *De officiis* thus: "We may do no thyng but oonly swich thyng as we may doon rightfully" (VII.1383). And she cites Cicero's golden rule: "For the lawe seith that 'ther maketh no man himselven riche, if he do harme to another wight'" (VII.1583). Cicero's guiding stricture receives further emphasis with an addition by Chaucer that serves to highlight this principle's derivation from natural law: "This is to seyn, that nature deffended and forbedeth by right that no man make hymself riche unto the harm of another persone" (VII.1584). Prudence's discussion may at first seem to digress, having left the central issue of vengeance far behind, but the tale's structure is actually quite coherent: vengeance is frequently fueled by avarice, and as the narrative moves from abstract principle to particular case, Prudence's discourse on riches has provided a means to challenge the expediency of private vengeance, enabling a diagnosis of one of the foremost obstacles to peace in the localities. More broadly, her intervention speaks to the very core of ethics, to what L. O. Aranye Fradenburg has powerfully framed as "the problem our desire poses for the suffering of the other."[94]

Given these concerns, to cast Prudence's arguments as *merely* pragmatic, in the sense of being divorced from an ethical system, would be to miss the ambition of *The Tale of Melibee*. Even when Prudence turns to Melibee's individual situation and assesses his material wealth as inadequate to the sustenance of a protracted feud, she is still speaking within

[94] *Sacrifice Your Love: Psychoanalysis, Historicism, Chaucer* (Minneapolis: University of Minnesota Press, 2002), p. 3.

the philosophical parameters of Ciceronian *utilitas.* Thus she argues that Melibee has misapprehended the truly profitable course: riches never suffice to maintain wars ("'I conseille yow that ye begynne no werre in trust of youre richesses for they ne suffisen noght werres to mayntene'" [VII.1650]). The truly expedient course is for Melibee to reconcile with his enemies, for "by concord and pees the smal richesses wexen grete" (VII.1675). Prudence's estimate of the profitability of peace attends—and thus ought not to be divorced from—her estimate of its status as the morally correct course of action.

Finally, in terms of thinking about the synthesis of ancient ethics with Christian theology, we can look to the continuation of Prudence's diagnosis where she identifies peace as the good toward which Melibee ought to strive: "And ye knowen wel that oon of the gretteste and moost sovereyn thyng that is in this world is unytee and pees. / And therfore seyde oure Lord Jhesu Crist to his apostles in this wise: / 'Wel happy and blessed been they that loven and purchacen pees, for they been called children of God'" (VII.1678–80). This is no superficial invocation of Christ. In her nature as *prudentia,* the practical intellect, Prudence has helped Melibee to recognize the particular good (*bonum apprehensum*) of peace, and she now demonstrates its connection to the final good, establishing the necessary conditions for Melibee's own will to incline and move toward the morally right action.[95] Philosophically, Prudence's method is wholly consistent with the dominant medieval understanding of prudence—one erected on the foundation of ancient philosophy—as the process of practical reasoning or deliberation that acts to identify the good that ought to be pursued in action.

Nevertheless, for many modern readers of *The Tale of Melibee,* Prudence seems to have conceded so much latitude to the pursuit of profit that her advice has often been cast as anachronistic (the spirit of her lecture has even been compared to the ethos described by Weber in

---

[95] On the character of practical reason in the intellectual tradition stretching from Aristotle to Aquinas, see Daniel Westberg, *Right Practical Reason: Aristotle, Action, and Prudence in Aquinas* (Oxford: Clarendon Press, 1994). For a discussion of Prudence's role within traditional scholastic thought, as it assumes not only the kind of social function found in ancient philosophy but also a spiritual purpose in guiding individuals to salvation (the final end), see Burnley, *Chaucer's Language and the Philosophers' Tradition,* pp. 46–56, and Flynn, "Art of Telling." Ann Astell brings a sensitivity to both spiritual and social function in discussing Chaucer's concern for the *utilitas* of his own poetry. See "On the Usefulness and Use Value of Books: A Medieval and Modern Inquiry," in *Medieval Rhetoric: A Casebook,* ed. Scott D. Troyan (New York: Routledge, 2004), pp. 41–62.

Protestant Ethics), and has been derided as a secular pragmatism that could only be in fundamental conflict with the Gospels and Christian teaching in the Middle Ages. To show that this is an unnecessary opposition—and one that, as I have asserted at the opening of this essay, tends to be predicated on the assumption of a monovocal and static "Christian morality," which is, in turn, assumed to be self-evidently opposed to the pursuit of material well-being—I wish to turn to the treatment of profit-oriented activity in scholastic thought.[96] Although Cicero's ethics did not receive the kind of systematic attention given to Book V of Aristotle's *Ethics* by scholastic commentaries, his effort to speak ethically about the pursuit of *utilitas* bears enough similarity to Aristotle's that it is worth considering how Christian writers, working from both within the commentary tradition and outside it, developed ancient ideals of profit-seeking. I will then turn back to Cicero and the reception of his ethical treatment of *utilitas* in the works of lay Christian writers that circulated more widely in late medieval society. These final two explorations will help us return to the *Melibee* prepared to situate its interest in the secular resources of legal and philosophical thought inherited from the classical past.

The scholastic reception of Aristotelian ethics in the late thirteenth and fourteenth centuries was central to the emergence of profound changes in the theoretical models and conceptual apparatus used by Christian writers to analyze economic exchange.[97] These developments

---

[96] An alternate route might approximate that taken by Burnley. To build a portrait of contemporary usage in Chaucer's day, Burnley cites the near-contemporary text, *The Folower of the Donet,* by the bishop of Chichester, Reginald Pecock. He accords Prudence both the characteristically Christian role of leading humans toward individual salvation and the civic role (still characteristic of that attributed by Christian writers) of leading humans in matters of daily governance. According to Pecock, Prudence is: "kunnyng to knowe how we schule bere vs to plese oure maystris, oure lordis, oure fadris, how to chastise oure children and seruantis, how to lyue pesabli with oure neiȝboris, *how to spende þat we falle not into pouerte,* and so forþ" (cited by Burnley, *Chaucer's Language and the Philosophers' Tradition,* p. 53; my emphasis).

[97] On Aristotle's influence on the economic views of scholastic thinkers and commentators on the *Ethics,* see Odd Langholm, *Wealth and Money in the Aristotelian Tradition* (Bergen: Universitetsforlaget, 1983). See also John Noonan, *The Scholastic Analysis of the Just Price: Romanists, Canonists, and Theologians in the Twelfth and Thirteenth Centuries,* Transactions of the American Philosophical Society, 49.4 (Philadelphia: American Philosophical Society, 1959). For an account emphasizing monetization itself as the force driving changes in scholarly views, see Joel Kaye, *Economy and Nature in the Fourteenth Century: Money, Market Exchange, and the Emergence of Scientific Thought,* Cambridge Studies in Medieval Life and Thought, 4th ser. (Cambridge: Cambridge University Press, 1998).

ushered in challenges to more traditional understandings of market-determined behavior and had an impact on the valuation of particular occupations and economic acts. More broadly, they helped to shape a new understanding of the relationship of profitable activity (understood initially in the narrow economic sense of activity that generates profit)[98] to the social good of the community, as well as to a significant expansion, at the level of personal ethics, of the limits within which virtue was understood to be compatible with the calculation of profit and the pursuit of material self-interest.

This is a complex process of development to which I cannot do justice here, but the most crucial features for our purposes may be culled from a single strand of inquiry. To extract this strand, we can begin with the core of Aristotle's analysis of economic exchange as a process of geometrical equalization wherein equality emerged from the (proportional) relations of the opposing needs and benefits of buyers and sellers. In Aristotle's model, value (price) emerged from the contingent circumstances of exchange.[99] Both the association of price with a continuum of value and the recognition of the marketplace's dynamic process of exchange equalization led scholastic commentators on Aristotle eventually to challenge his model's determination of value in reference to individuals (for example, where price is set through the free bargaining of producers, buyers, sellers) and to develop—what at some level was implicit in Aristotle's very conceptualization of market relations in geometrical terms—a model of the marketplace as entirely self-ordering, functioning through a suprapersonal process whereby value was understood to be the product of common estimation and, thus, based on aggregate

---

[98] As Kaye shows, the early focus on economic activity oriented toward financial profit gave way in the fourteenth century to a concern with a broader array of "profitable ends," including that of honor (ibid., p. 143). While Kaye defines honor within the context of the quantification of subjective qualities, the status of honor as "symbolic capital" clarifies its inclusion by later scholastic writers. Sharp distinctions between the tangible good of money and intangible qualities such as honor may reflect a more modern predilection; earlier writers such as Augustine made no such distinction in their treatment of the drive for status and that for riches. The development of a highly monetized society in the late Middle Ages, and the concomitant preoccupation with the status of money aside, late medieval writers would easily assimilate tangible and intangible forms of profit. Indeed Duns Scotus did exactly that.

[99] Rather than being located in the objects of exchange themselves (as in earlier and traditional accounts where value would be deemed to have a fixed essence). Evidence for these developments is laid out in a masterly fashion by Kaye in "The Aristotelian Model of Money and Economic Exchange," chap. 2 of *Economy and Nature in the Fourteenth Century*, pp. 37–55.

estimations and needs.[100] In terms of ethical determinations of licitness, the crucial point in these developments was the assertion that the "just price" of a given good or service equaled the "common estimation of value in the marketplace," one that could be determined independently of individual judgment or intention.[101]

Given this point's significance, we should not be surprised to find some resistance toward it in the works of early scholastic commentators. While Albertus Magnus deemed *"aestimatio communis"* a superior method of value determination (in keeping with the treatment of the Romanists as they glossed civil law texts that assumed the licitness of bargaining), Aquinas seems to have resisted the general trend to equate just price with market price, a resistance Joel Kaye sees as emerging from Aquinas's desire to insist that the justness of profit-oriented activity could be determined only in reference to the individual intent of participants.[102] As Kaye outlines so convincingly, Aquinas sought to maintain the centrality of individual rational choice, privileging the act of consciously ordered transactions (acts, that is, oriented toward the achievement of equality and the satisfaction of divine law) over the Aristotelian-derived model of geometric equalization, which posited that the marketplace functioned autonomously to equalize exchange and thus functioned normatively to produce equality without injustice.

Despite its cogency as a response to the profound theological and metaphysical challenges posed by these new models of economic exchange, Aquinas's insistence on individual intentionality and responsibility did not win acceptance among subsequent writers.[103] Throughout

[100] Ibid., p. 153.

[101] Ibid., p. 93. Scott Meikle challenges such an equation, arguing that it does not accurately represent Aristotle's view of fair exchange. See *Aristotle's Economic Thought* (Oxford: Clarendon Press, 1995), esp. 39–41. But Kaye's defense renders such an objection inconsequential: "What is important for this study, however, is not what Aristotle might have intended, but how scholastic thinkers understood him" (43 n. 22).

[102] On the reception of Albertus and Aquinas, see Kaye, *Economy and Nature in the Fourteenth Century*, pp. 95–99; on the Romanists, see pp. 92–93.

[103] Kaye offers a full account of how the traditional theological focus on individual responsibility and equality was supplanted, and here I will merely point to his argument for the decisive role played by a new appreciation for the way in which market activity served the common good. Outside the commentary tradition, the late thirteenth-century Franciscans, Peter John Olivi and Duns Scotus were key in developing the idea that market exchange was crucial to the *civitas*, serving the interests of the common good rather than being opposed to it, as had traditionally been asserted (ibid., pp. 125–27); similarly among fourteenth-century scholastic commentators such as Jean Buridan and Nichole Oresme, emphasis was placed now on the way in which money as a medium of exchange served properly as an instrument of the common good. Here we see an emphasis on the social benefit of the marketplace emerging alongside an

the fourteenth-century, scholastic commentators granted the marketplace extensive powers to set the just price through the process of exchange equalization, according an ever-diminished role to the conscious
ordering of economic transactions by individuals toward the achievement of equality. Indeed fourteenth-century thinkers had begun to perceive even acts of willed inequality (when an individual sought an unjust
profit) as a sufficient basis for just exchange, as willed inequality was
transformed by the marketplace into the equalization of utility of need
and desire among individuals engaged in price negotiation and agreement.[104]

In this regard, Cicero's ethics provided the kind of corrective Aquinas
himself sought: for Ciceronian ethics established (albeit without the
kind of systematic, proto-scientific model of geometric equalization provided by Aristotle) a sphere of legitimate profit-seeking, one that was
understood to encompass both the more narrow economic activity of
seeking profit and the broader activity of acting according to one's self-
interest. It also furnished a rigorous ethical system according to which
individuals were obliged to apprehend and pursue the course of action
that would be both profitable and just.

To return to *The Tale of Melibee,* we can now better appreciate the
Ciceronian inflection of Prudence's treatment of riches. Hers is a pragmatic, situationist ethic, one that is sensitive to the material needs and
desires of human existence and attuned to the monetized, commercial
nature of fourteenth-century England, but it is also one that seeks to
install a more rigorous, personal ethics than that which had been advanced in the universities and, earlier still, in the Roman civil law tradition.

We might well wonder whether the kind of reception afforded Aristotelian ethics can provide a model for the reception of Ciceronian ethics
in more widely circulating and broadly popular works. Similarly, we
might ask whether the highly systematic writings of scholastic philosophers can provide a measure of Albertano's and Chaucer's understanding of Ciceronian ethics. While gauging the place of Cicero's ethics in
the late Middle Ages lies beyond the scope of any single essay, it is
worth noting that *De officiis* received a broad and generally positive re-

---

understanding of the "quest for personal advantage [as] the natural condition of just
exchange" in the marketplace (p. 132).

[104] On the importance here of Geraldus Odonis and Jean Buridan, see ibid., pp.
131–32.

ception from writers ranging from Geraldus Cambrensis and Vincent of Beauvais to John of Salisbury and Brunetto Latini.[105] A brief look at the treatment of Cicero's *De officiis* in the *Livre dou tresor* of Brunetto Latini will provide a useful measure of the kind of reception Cicero's treatment of *honestum* and *utilitas* might receive at the hands of a Christian layman in the late Middle Ages, and it will provide us with a useful measure of the degree to which *The Tale of Melibee* might have been perceived as inconsistent with Christian thinking in more popular, didactic literature.

Brunetto Latini's *Li livres dou tresor* is an especially noteworthy treatment of Cicero's argument for the identity of moral virtue and expediency. Like his near contemporary, Albertano of Brescia, Brunetto was an urban professional embroiled in the politics of the Italian city-states of the thirteenth century. Exiled from his native Florence for opposing Manfred, he wrote his *Tresor* in Paris in the French vernacular, and upon returning to Florence subsequent to Manfred's death he took up an advisory role to the local *podestà* much as Albertano did in Brescia.[106] Seeking in ancient philosophy practical guidance for civic life, Brunetto and Albertano both turned to Cicero's *De officiis*. Although scholars have long recognized Brunetto's debt to Cicero's rhetorical writings in part III of the *Tresor,* they have not always recognized the extent to which "Les enseignemens de moralité," the second major section of the *Tresor,* is indebted to Cicero's *De officiis*.[107] In part, this influence is cloaked by the mediating source: the material from *De officiis* is derived from an intermediary, the *Moralium dogma philosophorum*.[108] It is also obscured by Brunetto's style of presentation: throughout the section on ethics, Brunetto cites a range of classical sources (including Seneca, Horace,

[105] Nelson offers an assessment of the extensive influence of the *De officiis* on thirteenth-century scholastic thought and on these particular writers in "Cicero's *De Officiis* in Christian Thought," pp. 59–160.

[106] For biographical details, see the introduction to *Brunetto Latini: "The Book of the Treasure" ("Li Livres dou Tresor"),* trans. Paul Barrette and Spurgeon Baldwin, Garland Library of Medieval Literature, vol. 90, ser. B (New York: Garland, 1993).

[107] On Brunetto's sources, see the introductory discussion of *Li Livres dou Trésor,* ed. Francis J. Carmody, University of California Publications in Modern Philology, 22 (Berkeley and Los Angeles: University of California Press, 1948). See also the brief discussion by Barrette and Baldwin, *Brunetto Latini.*

[108] On the *Moralium*'s extensive reliance on Cicero, see the introductory remarks in *Das Moralium Dogma Philosophorum des Guillaume de Conches: Lateinisch, Altfranzösisch und Mittelniederfränkisch,* ed. John Holmberg (Cambridge: W. Heffer & Sons, 1929), pp. 32–33. See also Nelson, "Cicero's *De Officiis* in Christian Thought," pp. 98–99 and 148–52, who offers a detailed case for Brunetto's liberal usage of Cicero's ideas, mediated by the *Moralium.*

Cicero, and Aristotle), providing commentary in his own voice. When treating the question of expediency and justice, however, Brunetto frequently offers commentary in his own voice that actually ventriloquizes Cicero's own expansive explanations of his ethical principles and his defense of them against competing doctrines.

The centrality of Ciceronian ethics to Brunetto's *Tresor* is best illustrated in a chapter entitled "De la querele qui est honeste et profitable." Brunetto begins by citing Cicero's doctrine of the identity of moral virtue and expediency:

dit Tulles que ces iij choses, bien, honeste et profit, sont si entremellé, que tout ce qui est bien est teni profitable, et tout ce qui est honeste est tenu bien. Tien donc à certes et ne doute pas que honeste est si profitable que nule chose n'est profitable se ele n'est honeste.

[Cicero says that these three things, good and honesty and profit, are so intermingled that all that is good is considered to be profitable, and all that is honest is held to be good, and from this it follows that all honest things are profitable. Consider therefore as certain, and have no doubts, that honesty is so profitable that nothing can be profitable if it is not honest.][109]

Having reiterated Cicero's case for the identity of *honestum* and *utilitas*, Brunetto engages his reader in applying Cicero's ethical standard to a particular case. Ostensibly the example is Brunetto's own, but it derives in fact from *De officiis*: "If someone asked me if some wise man is dying of hunger, should he not take the food of another who is worthless, I say no, because life is not more worthwhile to me than my will, through which I refrain from doing harm to another for my profit." Having offered this analysis, Brunetto turns from Cicero's golden rule, "one may do no harm," to a discussion of the proper understanding of *utilitas*:

[109] Brunetto Latini, *The Book of the Treasure,* bk. II, chap. 122, pp. 268–69. The English translation is based on one of the few extant thirteenth-century French manuscripts of Brunetto's text, the Escorial Library manuscript, one that had not been available to either of the French text's two previous editors, Carmody and Chabaille, and one that supplies major sections of text missing in all manuscripts of the second redaction (the version prepared by Brunetto following the end of his exile in France and his return to his native Florence). This fact and the close consultation with both French editions make the Garland edition invaluable. The French text I have cited here is from Chabaille's edition of the first redaction, *Li Livres Dou Tresor par Brunetto Latini,* Collection de documents inédits sur l'histoire de France 1, ser. Histoire litteraire, ed. P. Chabaille (Paris: Impériale, 1863), bk. II, chap. civ. All subsequent English translations of Brunetto Latini's text will be drawn from book II, chap. 122 in Barrette and Baldwin's Garland edition.

"Cicero says: nothing which is corrupted by vices can be profitable." Brunetto adds reassuringly, again in his own voice, that the truly virtuous course of action will turn out to "have a profit" even when "we did not hope for it."[110] Thus Brunetto carves out a space for the legitimate pursuit of wealth and advantage.

Compared to the treatment of expediency in the *Melibee,* however, Brunetto's work provides a much more skeptical reception to Cicero's treatment of *utilitas* in *De officiis.* As we have seen, Cicero himself commented on the tendency of his fellow Romans to pursue profit to the detriment of the community. Brunetto fixates on these possibilities for immoral action, and his treatment of the corrupting drive for riches and advantage comes very near to positing sin as the inevitable result of engagement with the material world, reiterating the older, more conservative position of Augustine. When, after invoking Boethius to castigate material goods as unstable, perishable, and foreign to our very being, Brunetto embraces the Senecan solution, his Stoic response comes as little surprise: "Desire and direct your thoughts to this: that you be satisfied with yourself and what comes from inside; for when a man pursues external things, he is immediately subjected to fortune."[111] The most secure state is that which does not attach its well-being to the goods of this world. But insofar as we are necessarily bound to satisfy our material needs while in this world, our best course is to embrace "happy poverty," for the individual who is poor but desires little will always be satisfied.[112]

Set alongside Prudence's assessment of poverty as "the mooder of ruyne," the source of "manye harmes and yveles" (VII.1562, 1564), Brunetto's asceticism strikes a dramatic point of contrast to Prudence's worldly pragmatism. Moreover, Brunetto's treatment of riches implies a far dimmer view of the capacity of human reason and will, of the ability of humans to exercise prudence and attain a just but profitable existence. In *Tresor,* avarice overrides the human inclination to good, destroying charity, corrupting justice, and provoking men to a violent and disordered existence. Such a portrait of human society reveals the optimism in Prudence's assessment of human nature. Prudence counsels the pursuit of the Peripatetic mean confidently: be neither too hasty nor too slow in seeking material goods, be neither too spendthrift nor too

[110] *Brunetto Latini,* trans. Barrette and Baldwin, pp. 269, 270.
[111] Ibid., p. 272.
[112] Ibid., p. 265.

miserly, apply a due measure of industry to avoid the evils of hunger and the temptations of idleness. Prudence's lecture assumes the capacity of humans to achieve the mean, and, as we see in her comments to Melibee's adversaries, she concludes that Melibee has succeeded in attaining the proper relation to riches himself: avarice does not afflict him.

Conclusion

Such an optimistic assessment of the capacity of humans to maintain a rational, just, and moral relation to profit directs our attention all the more forcefully to the drive for honor that threatens to prove a devastating obstacle to peace. While Melibee's concern for his honor is expressed throughout the narrative, it receives its most dramatic articulation in the section leading up to Prudence's negotiation with his enemies. When Prudence suggests that Melibee make peace with his adversaries, he stridently objects: "'A,' quod Melibee, 'now se I wel that ye loven nat myn honour ne my worshipe. / Ye knowen wel that myne adversaries han bigonnen this debaat and bryge by hire outrage, / and ye se wel that they ne requeren ne preyen me nat of pees, ne they asken nat to be reconsiled./ Wol ye thanne that I go and meke me, and obeye me to hem, and crie hem mercy? / For sothe, that were nat my worshipe" (VII.1681–85).

The moment at which *The Tale of Melibee* draws the problem of shame into central focus is significant. Up to this point, Prudence's deliberative function has determined the manner in which Melibee's chosen course of action was submitted to scrutiny. Melibee's decision to wreak vengeance on his neighbors was examined in relation to general principles (do no harm, pursue the expedient and morally right course), and Prudence used the particulars of Melibee's case to demonstrate that the violence he had proposed would violate these principles; similarly her careful adumbration of the distinction between legitimate just warfare, the violence licitly wielded through the institutions and persons of law, and the private vengeance Melibee seeks is structured by a process of reasoning that assesses the application of rules to particular cases.[113] Having helped Melibee to recognize that vengeance cannot be "a good"

---

[113] Kimberly Keller argues convincingly that the structure of Prudence's arguments builds on the structure of a scholastic arts lecture. See "Prudence's Pedagogy of the Oppressed," *NM* 94 (1997): 415–26. On the understanding of Prudence's role in the process of reasoning more generally, see Westberg, *Right Practical Reason*.

because its fails to satisfy these principles, Prudence then turns to the question of the end that he may justly and profitably seek. Melibee himself signals the shift in focus as he concedes to Prudence that he may not legitimately wage war on his adversaries, and asks what course of action he ought to take. At this point in the narrative, Prudence exercises another aspect of her faculty as *prudentia,* acting to identify reconciliation as the appropriate course of action, the proper means that will achieve the end of peace.

When Melibee protests that reconciliation with his enemies—although clearly a rational means to the end of peace—threatens his own honor, he expresses his concern that the proposed means threatens to destroy his reputation; how can this remedy be *utile* when it clearly contravenes his own interest? Having already suffered the attack on his household and the wounding of his daughter, and having thus also incurred an injury to his honor, Melibee can only conceive of reconciliation as a humiliation that will further injure his good name. And, indeed, well he might, for Prudence has already acknowledged the propriety of Melibee's concern. Like riches, honor is a legitimate good, as Prudence makes clear when she advises Melibee to guard well his good name by pursuing the virtuous course of action. Philosophically, we find here that the obtuseness with which Melibee so often has been charged by critics dissolves into a far more complex portrait: Melibee is indeed still struggling to ascertain the proper action (and also problematically subject to the eruption of anger), but the objection to reconciling with his enemies that he delivers is far more rationally coherent within the narrative's assumed legal and philosophical framework than is typically recognized.[114]

A local man of substance, if not of noble blood, Melibee seeks to redress the outrage he has suffered, and Prudence's appeal to her husband's desire to resuscitate his good name finds a solution to the problem of shame much like that of the old hag in *The Wife of Bath's Tale,* whose speech on the nature of *gentilesse* effects a dramatic transformation

---

[114] One also suspects that Chaucer's audience would have been sympathetic to Melibee's concern with his honor. As John Beckerman has demonstrated, the "need to satisfy affronted honor is still apparent in [English] plaints of trespass of the thirteenth century," and he suggests that the concern with insults to personal honor is evident in village ordinances from the county of Durham dating from as late as 1379: "Adding Insult to *Iniuria:* Affronts to Honor and the Origins of Trespass," in *On the Laws and Customs of England: Essays in Honor of Samuel E. Thorne,* ed. Morris S. Arnold et al. (Chapel Hill: University of North Carolina Press, 1981), pp. 159–81 (173–74).

in her husband. In *The Tale of Melibee,* Prudence attempts to convince Melibee that true gentility expresses itself not through vengeance but through mercy: "'Tullius seith, 'There is no thyng so comendable in a greet lord / as whan he is debonaire and meeke, and appeseth him lightly.' / And I prey yow that ye wole forbere now to do vengeance, / in swich a manere that youre goode name may be kept and conserved, / and that men mowe have cause and mateere to preyse yow of pitee and of mercy" (VII.1860–63). Much as Theseus in *The Knight's Tale* performatively reiterates his noble stature in acts of pity, renouncing his right to visit death on Palamon and Arcite for breaching the peace, so too may Melibee accrue symbolic capital through an act of mercy. Honor need not find its only satisfaction in the exercise of violence, but it may also be performed in an act of renouncing violence.[115] Prudence thus makes a compelling and ethically rigorous case that *honestum* and *utilitas* lie in Melibee's peaceful reconciliation with his enemies.

Prudence's effort to align gentility and peace is characteristic not only of Chaucer's thematic treatment of "pitee" throughout various Canterbury Tales, but it also finds an analogue in the writings of Chaucer's contemporary, John Gower. Like Chaucer, Gower develops this association in response to the perceived problem of the deployment of violence in the localities, and in both *The Tale of Melibee* and *Confessio Amantis* the primary conceptual resources derive from Cicero's treatment of justice in *De officiis* mediated by the work of Albertano of Brescia.[116] In Book 3 of *Confessio Amantis,* Amans asks his confessor whether a man may ever slay another without sin. Making one of only two uses of Albertano of Brescia's *Liber consolationis* in the *Confessio Amantis,* Gower distinguishes between the illegitimate violence of the private person and the violence legitimately wielded by the law. The Confessor affirms to Amans that judges are not only permitted but duty-bound by their office to wield violence:

---

[115] Compare Larry Scanlon's reading in *Narrative, Authority, and Power* of the way in which Melibee's decision to relinquish vengeance is predicated on his acquisition of a form of regal status "just as clearly characterized by the sovereignty to which he has submitted" (p. 213). Scanlon thus (quite brilliantly) reads the tale's conclusion as offering a paradoxical means of resolution to Melibee's crisis of identity, as his very renunciation of the power offered by his enemies serves to guarantee him a position of power superior to both his enemies and the law.

[116] For the identification of Gower's use of Albertano of Brescia's *Liber,* see Conrad Mainzer, "Albertano of Brescia's *Liber Consolationis et Consilii* as a Source-Book of Gower's *Confessio Amantis,*" *MÆ* 47 (1978): 88–90.

> My Sone, in sondri wise ye.
> What man that is of traiterie,
> Of moerdre or ellis robberie
> Atteint, the jugge schal nat lette,
> Bot he schal slen of pure dette,
> And doth gret Senne, if that he wonde.[117]

The Confessor's account of the legitimacy of law's violence finds its analogue in Prudence's argument that "right so synneth the juge if he do no vengeance of hem that it han disserved" (VII.1436), and her assessment that those who "so muchel suffre of the shrewes and mysdoeres" threaten the social order and destroy justice (VII.1474).

While Prudence concedes that vengeance belongs to the law, and pity is inappropriate as a judicial response to those who have deserved punishment, she insists that mercy, and not vengeance, is the appropriate response of a private person, and an admirable one for a man of Melibee's stature. Here too we find an analogue in *Confessio Amantis,* when Gower's Confessor in Book VII, once again drawing upon Albertano of Brescia's tale of Melibee, argues for the virtue of pity:

> Thapostle James in this wise
> Seith, what man scholde do juise,
> And hath not pite forth with al,
> The doom of him which demeth al
> He may himself fulsore drede,
> That him schal lakke upon the nede
> To fynde pite, whan he wolde.
>   (VII.3149–55)

The Confessor's remarks mirror Prudence's own final defense of the reconciliation that she has directed Melibee to pursue: "Lat mercy been in youre herte to th'effect and entente that God Almighty have mercy on yow in his laste juggement. / For Seint Jame seith in his Epistle: 'Juggement withouten mercy shal be doon to hym that hath no mercy of another wight'" (VII.1867–70). This final strategy of course brings the narrative to its resolution, as Melibee relinquishes his case for vengeance and embraces peace and the forgiveness of his enemies.

---

[117] *Confessio Amantis,* III.2210–15, in G. C. Macaulay, ed., *The Complete Works of John Gower,* vols. 2–3 (Oxford: Clarendon Press, 1901).

Those who have questioned Chaucer's orthodoxy in reference to this conclusion to *The Tale of Melibee* may still wish to assert that the absence of a penitential framework in the *Melibee* (structurally integral to *Confessio Amantis*) is sufficient evidence to suggest Chaucer's willingness to abandon "a specifically Christian ethical model," but the burden will now be to demonstrate that a characteristic strategy within civil and canon law, scholastic philosophy, and Ciceronian ethics of attempting to differentiate the legitimacy of violence enacted through institutions of law (punishment) and state (war) and the illegitimacy of private violence wielded by the individual does not represent an ethical achievement consonant with Christian theology.

As important an achievement is the recasting by Chaucer and Gower of gentility as a solution to the problem of local violence and feud. Like Prudence, Gower's Confessor appreciates the appeal of pity as a marker of true nobility: "And to Pite forto be servant, / Of al the worldes remenant / He is worthi to ben a lord" (VII.3139–41). The man of honor can feel no differently about wounded honor than he does, but such writers as Albertano, Chaucer, and Gower, drawing on the resources of Romanist legal thinking and Ciceronian ethics, each betray an optimism that the drive to preserve honor can be reoriented, turned into a habitus conducive of a virtuous and profitable life, productive of harmonious communal relationships, and Christian salvation.

Venus and Christ in Chaucer's *Complaint of Mars:* The Fairfax 16 Frontispiece

Jessica Brantley
Yale University

O XFORD, BODLEIAN LIBRARY MS Fairfax 16 contains one of the most accomplished illuminations to be associated with any of Chaucer's works. The full-page illustration preceding the *Complaint of Mars* (fol. 14v; fig. 1) rivals in skill even the much-discussed *Troilus* frontispiece (Corpus Christi College, Cambridge MS 61, fol. 1v), but Chaucer criticism has generally ignored the Fairfax picture.[1] This is so in part, of course, because the *Complaint of Mars* has held less intrinsic interest than *Troilus and Criseyde,* even though the two poems are so similar in theme that the *Complaint* has been called a "miniature *Troilus.*"[2] It is also— perhaps more—because the Fairfax image has been deemed unreadable in terms of the poem it accompanies. It has seemed all too clear, as Julia Boffey explains it, that the image derives from artistic precedents completely unconnected with Chaucer's work, and that it exists only because "a convenient iconographic tradition associated with the story

---

[1] For discussion of the *Troilus* frontispiece, see, for example, Derek Pearsall, "The Troilus Frontispiece and Chaucer's Audience," *YES* 7 (1977): 68–74; Elizabeth Salter, "The 'Troilus Frontispiece,'" in *Troilus and Criseyde: A Facsimile of Corpus Christi College Cambridge MS 61, ca. 1399–1413* (Cambridge: D. S. Brewer, 1978), pp. 15–23; and Laura Kendrick, *Chaucerian Play: Comedy and Control in "The Canterbury Tales"* (Berkeley and Los Angeles: University of California Press, 1988), pp. 163–74. The other Chaucerian illustrations that have occasioned much commentary are of course the Ellesmere pilgrim-portraits. See *The Canterbury Tales: The New Ellesmere Chaucer Facsimile,* ed. Daniel Woodward and Martin Stevens (Tokyo: Yushodo; San Marino, Calif.: Huntington Library Press, 1995), and its companion volume, *The Ellesmere Chaucer: Essays in Interpretation,* ed. Martin Stevens and Daniel Woodward (Tokyo: Yushodo; San Marino, Calif.: Huntington Library Press, 1995), especially Richard K. Emmerson, "Text and Image in the Ellesmere Portraits of the Tale-Tellers," pp. 143–70.

[2] John Norton-Smith, *Geoffrey Chaucer* (London: Routledge and Kegan Paul, 1974), p. 28. The comparison is commonly made: see, for example, Lee Patterson, *Chaucer and the Subject of History* (Madison: University of Wisconsin Press, 1991), p. 62.

Fig. 1. Mars. Oxford, Bodleian MS Fairfax 16, fol. 14v. Bodleian Library, University of Oxford.

of Mars and Venus was already available."[3] In a similar dismissal, Theresa Tinkle observes that the frontispiece "carries to Chaucer's poem little meaning but takes its meaning from that poem."[4] What we might wish to think an idiosyncratic visual reaction to Chaucer's rather unusual text appears from this perspective to be a thoroughly conventional medieval picture of Mars, Venus, and Jupiter.

But precisely for this reason, the Fairfax illumination poses in an acute form the question that is unfortunately central to the study of decoration in Chaucerian manuscripts: What can be learned from even the most perfunctory conjunction of image and text? Illustration of vernacular literature is so rare and so limited in late medieval England that many readers have echoed John Fleming's lament: "If we wish to visualize Chaucer with Gothic eyes we must turn to the painted pages of Boccaccio and Jean de Meun."[5] The overlooked Fairfax miniature demonstrates, on the contrary, that the native artistic tradition can on occasion offer significant visual context to readers of Middle English poetry. Moreover, although the picture is undoubtedly conventional, the interplay of its conventions brings meaning to its textual environment that—even if it was not planned for—enriches our experience of Chaucer's *Complaint*. Using techniques of deliberate borrowing between devotional and courtly art—techniques that Barbara Newman has recently termed "crossover"—the *Complaint of Mars* and the Fairfax frontispiece explore in parallel the relation of Christian ideas to classical ones.[6] The Fairfax artist adopts images central to the sacred tradition as symbols of

[3] *Manuscripts of English Courtly Love Lyrics in the Later Middle Ages,* Manuscript Studies 1 (Woodbridge: D. S. Brewer, 1985), p. 37. Norton-Smith also puts it baldly: "The iconographic 'traditions' had nothing to do with Chaucer's original literary aims" (*Geoffrey Chaucer,* 26 n. 12); see also his later opinion that "care has been taken to match text and picture," in *Bodleian Library MS Fairfax 16* (London: Scolar Press, 1979), p. xii.

[4] *Medieval Venuses and Cupids: Sexuality, Hermeneutics, and English Poetry* (Stanford: Stanford University Press, 1996), p. 92.

[5] "Chaucer and the Visual Arts of His Time," in *New Perspectives in Chaucer Criticism,* ed. Donald M. Rose, ed. (Norman, Okla.: Pilgrim Books, 1981), pp. 121–36 (127). For other perspectives on Chaucer and the arts, see also H. A. Kelly, "Chaucer's Arts and Our Arts," in *New Perspectives in Chaucer Criticism,* pp. 107–20; V. A. Kolve, "Chaucer and the Visual Arts," in *Geoffrey Chaucer: Writers and Their Background,* ed. D. S. Brewer (London: Bell, 1974), pp. 290–320; and Kolve, *Chaucer and the Imagery of Narrative* (Stanford: Stanford University Press, 1984).

[6] Newman defines crossover as "the intentional borrowing and adaptation of courtly themes in devotional art and vice versa." "Love's Arrows: Christ as Cupid in Late Medieval Art and Devotion," in *The Mind's Eye: Art and Theological Argument in the Middle Ages,* ed. Jeffrey F. Hamburger and Anne-Marie Bouché (Princeton: Department of Art and Archaeology, 2006), pp. 263–86 (263).

the power of courtly passion, and Chaucer's poem fashions secular love-lament into Christian theodicy. The "crossover" iconography of the picture is more than merely convenient in this setting, for the relation between text and image here reveals the ways in which classical narrative, in each medium, can be shaped by traditions of Christian complaint.

Bodleian MS Fairfax 16 is one of the so-called Oxford group of manuscript anthologies of fifteenth-century verse, which contain a variety of shorter Chaucerian poems, as well as courtly material by such authors as Sir John Clanvowe, Thomas Hoccleve, and John Lydgate.[7] The collection was most likely commissioned in the mid-fifteenth century by John Stanley (1400?–1469) from a commercial scriptorium or bookseller, perhaps in London. It has been designated "quasi-fascicular," for even though its sections were copied by the same scribe, they are separated by blank leaves and foliated by different hands; it seems to have been constructed from booklets chosen by the patron.[8] Booklet I, which begins with the *Complaint of Mars,* contains courtly poetry by Chaucer, Clanvowe, Lydgate, and Hoccleve, as well as two light, gaming verses, "The Rolles of Kyng Ragman," and "The Chaunces of the Dyce." Booklet II begins with an integrated grouping of some of Chaucer's minor lyrics, then concludes with a more miscellaneous selection of minor works by Hoccleve and Lydgate. Booklets III and IV contain whole poems: Lydgate's *Reason and Sensuality* and the anonymous *How a Lover Praiseth his Lady,* respectively. Booklet V includes two collections of love lyrics, the first entitled the *Venus Mass* or *A Lover's Mass,* and the second, untitled, perhaps attributable to Charles d'Orléans. Although the manuscript as a whole is miscellaneous, some patterns can be observed within its booklets, which evince a certain fixity of structure, and even between booklets that often traveled together.[9]

---

[7] For discussion of these manuscripts, including Fairfax 16, see Julia Boffey and John J. Thompson, "Anthologies and Miscellanies: Production and Choice of Texts," in *Book Production and Publishing in Britain, 1375–1475,* ed. Jeremy Griffiths and Derek Pearsall (Cambridge: Cambridge University Press, 1989), pp. 279–315, esp. 280–84.

[8] The designation comes from Boffey, *Manuscripts of English Courtly Love Lyrics,* p. 7. The facsimile gives a detailed discussion of the manuscript's construction; see Norton-Smith, *Bodleian Library MS Fairfax 16,* pp. vii–x.

[9] For a nuanced discussion of structural patterns in the Oxford group and related manuscripts, see A. S. G. Edwards, "Bodleian Library MS Arch. Selden B.24: A 'Transitional' Collection," in *The Whole Book: Cultural Perspectives on the Medieval Miscellany,* ed. Stephen G. Nichols and Siegfried Wenzel (Ann Arbor: University of Michigan Press, 1996), pp. 53–67, esp. 56–58

The frontispiece is an addition to Fairfax 16 as a whole, rather than a part of Booklet I, for it is painted on a singleton, and was probably contracted at the time the manuscript was commissioned. The image consists of three framed compartments, encompassing the figure of Mars on the left, Venus on the right, and Jupiter suspended above them both. Flower-and-spray border motifs surround the composition, with the Stanley of Hooton arms worked into the lower border.[10] J. J. G. Alexander decades ago identified the Fairfax artist as William Abell, "the most important native illuminator to have been working in the mid-fifteenth century."[11] More likely, the frontispiece is the work of an artist known as the Abingdon Missal Master, an associate of Abell, who collaborated with him on at least one manuscript.[12] Even if the artist cannot be named, the peculiarly English, rather than International, style of the hand suggests that Chaucer's poetry can be associated with visual materials nearer to home than continental manuscripts of the *Filostrato* or the *Roman de la Rose*.

The intended relation between the frontispiece and the textual contents of the manuscript is not easy to discern. The singleton was most likely added at the time the collection was constructed, but not necessarily with the *Complaint of Mars,* or even any particular text, in mind. As Boffey explains, "This seems to be a case in which a small amount of rich decoration was added to an already completed manuscript, and inserted in the most practically convenient position (the beginning) in an attempt to enhance the status of the collection as a whole."[13] The prominent inclusion of the Stanley of Hooton arms supports this argument, since the heraldry links the image more explicitly to the manuscript's patron and his chivalric interests than to any particular poem.[14] If it is

---

[10] See Norton-Smith, *Bodleian MS Fairfax 16,* for a discussion of the heraldry.

[11] The phrase quoted comes from Alexander's recent entry for Abell in the *Oxford Dictionary of National Biography* (Oxford: Oxford University Press, 2004). The identification was originally made in "William Abell, 'Lymnour,' and Fifteenth-Century English Illumination," in *Kunsthistorische Forschungen Otto Pächt zu seinem 70. Geburtstag,* ed. Artur Rosenauer and Gerold Weber (Salzburg: Residenz Verlag, 1972), pp. 166–72.

[12] For a revision of Alexander's list of manuscripts attributed to Abell, see Kathleen L. Scott, *A Survey of Manuscripts Illuminated in the British Isles: Later Gothic Manuscripts, 1390–1490* (London: Harvey Miller, 1996), pp. 264–65. For manuscripts attributed to the Abingdon Missal Master, see Scott, *Later Gothic Manuscripts,* pp. 265, 280–81. The collaborative work is Cambridge, St. John's MS H.5 (Scott, *Later Gothic Manuscripts,* no. 94).

[13] *Manuscripts of English Courtly Love Lyrics,* p. 42.

[14] See, for example, Norton-Smith, *Geoffrey Chaucer,* 26 n.12 (though he here thinks the owner is William Stanley). Sir John Stanley served the court of Henry VI as Sargeant

possible that the image was merely an expedient decoration unrelated to the literary contents of Fairfax 16, it is also possible that it should be connected to more than one poem in the manuscript. The *Complaint of Venus* follows the *Complaint of Mars* in this and most other manuscripts, and the rubric that heads them here reads jointly: "Complaynt of Mars and Venus."[15] Commentators who understand the two poems to be one have seen in the Fairfax image some support for their theories.[16] Even beyond the *Complaint of Venus,* there is more in the contents of Fairfax 16 to which the frontispiece might respond. Courtliness, complaint, and even the figure of Venus herself feature in such works as the anonymous *Venus Mass,* Lydgate's *Temple of Glass,* and Chaucer's *Parliament of Fowls.* In spite of the *ad hoc* combination of its fascicles, thematic unities in the manuscript's collection might be represented in its prefatory picture.[17]

Nonetheless, the physical conjunction of the image with the manuscript's first text argues for a special relation between them. The independent decision taken to add the picture to a manuscript after its construction might be seen to reinforce rather than diminish its importance; the frontispiece need not have been there, and yet someone found it important to include. And regardless of the intentions of the artist or the compiler or the patron, it seems likely that fifteenth-century readers encountered Chaucer's poem in the first instance with its pictorial preamble. Moreover, the structure of the image argues for the separation—or at least the separability—of the first two texts in the manuscript, for it depends upon the narrative of adultery told only in the *Complaint of Mars.*[18] The emblematic figure of the goddess herself

---

of the Armoury in the Tower of London (1431–60) and Usher of the Chamber (1440–55). He was also member of parliament and justice of the peace for Surrey.

[15] Bodleian MS Fairfax 16, fol. 15r. See also the contemporary table of contents on folio 2, which lists "[T]he complaynt of Mars and Venus," "[T]he complaynt of Mars by him self," and "[T]he complaynt of Venus by hir self."

[16] For an argument that the poems form two parts of a whole, see Rodney Merrill, "Chaucer's *Broche of Thebes*: The Unity of 'The Complaint of Mars' and 'The Complaint of Venus,'" *Literary Monographs* 5 (1973): 3–61. Merrill sees in the Fairfax image some support for his theory (12–14), and Julia Boffey also associates the frontispiece with both poems, for they are "amalgamated" in Fairfax 16 (*Manuscripts of English Courtly Love Lyrics,* p. 35).

[17] A recent reading of the manuscript as a whole around ideas of masculine community is offered by Teresa Tinkle, "The Imagined Chaucerian Community of Bodleian MS Fairfax 16," in *Chaucer and the Challenges of Medievalism: Studies in Honor of H. A. Kelly* (Frankfurt am Main: Peter Lang, 2003), pp. 157–74.

[18] Boffey concedes that the picture "functions effectively" only because of the more narrative parts of *Mars* (*Manuscripts of English Courtly Love Lyrics,* p. 36).

might reflect other mentions of her in the texts of Fairfax 16, but nowhere except in the manuscript's first poem is she connected with Mars and Jupiter.[19] The *Complaint of Venus* gives no hint of any figure apart from the speaker and the beloved, whereas the frontispiece is organized around the interaction among the three figures. And although Mars's lament is reflected in his declamatory posture, nowhere is the idea of Venus as complainant represented.[20]

In the *Complaint of Mars,* Chaucer grafts the eponymous lament onto the well-known story of Mars's adultery with Venus. The text comprises three sections: first, a proem in which a bird-narrator celebrates love and calls on lovers to choose their mates. Then follows the "story": the speaker's exemplary narration of Mars's love for Venus, their discovery, and their forcible separation. The movements of heavenly bodies—here the temporary conjunction of a slow planet and a faster-moving one—are made to symbolize the changing passions and jealousies of the Olympian gods. The opening establishes that Mars has won Venus's love, "As wel by hevenysh revolucioun / As by desert," that is, as much by simply traveling around in his orbit as by performing noble courtly feats.[21] After this elaborate astrological allegory, the poem concludes with Mars's complaint proper, in which he proclaims himself in courtly terms to be his lady's "truest servaunt and her knyght" (187), laments her departure, and poses philosophical questions about the fleeting na-

---

[19] For Chaucer's unusual combination of complaint with narrative in *Mars,* see W. A. Davenport, *Chaucer: Complaint and Narrative* (Cambridge: D. S. Brewer, 1988), esp. pp. 33–40. See also Carolynn Van Dyke, "'To Whom Shul We Compleyn?': The Poetics of Agency in Chaucer's Complaints," *Style* 31 (1997): 370–91.

[20] *Pace* Norton-Smith, *Bodleian MS Fairfax 16,* p. xii. Norton-Smith argues that the image represents the complaints of both Mars and Venus, based on his identification of a book carried under Venus's arm as a visual manifestation of her complaint. I am not convinced that we should read a book there, and at any rate I find the complaint of Mars more definitely represented in his oratorical gesture.

[21] Lines 30–31; *The Riverside Chaucer,* 3rd ed., gen. ed. Larry Benson (Boston: Houghton Mifflin, 1987). All subsequent quotations of Chaucer's works are from this edition. For discussions of the astrological details lying behind the poem, see J. C. Eade, "'We Ben to Lewed or to Slowe': Chaucer's Astronomy and Audience Participation," *SAC* 4 (1982): 53–85, esp. 69–76; Edgar S. Laird, "Astrology and Irony in Chaucer's *Complaint of Mars,*" *ChauR* 6 (1972): 229–31; Laird, "Chaucer's Complaint of Mars, Line 145: 'Venus valaunse,'" *PQ* 51 (1972): 486–89; J. M. Manly, "On the Date and Interpretation of Chaucer's *Complaint of Mars,*" *Harvard Studies and Notes in Philology and Literature* 5 (1896): 107–26; J. D. North, *Chaucer's Universe* (Oxford: Clarendon Press, 1988), pp. 304–25; Chauncey Wood, *Chaucer and the Country of the Stars: Poetic Uses of Astrological Imagery* (Princeton: Princeton University Press, 1970), pp. 115–20; and Johnstone Parr and Nancy Ann Holtz, "The Astronomy-Astrology in Chaucer's *The Complaint of Mars,*" *ChauR* 15 (1981): 255–66.

ture of earthly love. In addition to its formal amalgam of narrative and complaint, the *Complaint of Mars* is driven by a complex interplay of thematic conventions: astrological, mythological, courtly, Boethian— even the possibility of a reference to contemporary amorous scandals.[22] Criticism of the text has generally argued for the priority of one or another of its registers of meaning, and interpretations have been quite disparate, calling the poem variously moralizing, comic, occasional, or sagely philosophical.[23] But the poem's wit resides in its ability to imagine events equally in many different terms, and in the reader's knowledge that all of these contexts are always visible.[24] It seems clear that, as for the planetary Mars and Venus themselves, the conjunction is the point.

In bringing Mars and Venus together in such a wide variety of ways, Chaucer draws on a medieval mythographic tradition that is extensive, not to say unwieldy. Mythographic materials available to a late medieval author range from the sixth-century Fulgentius's *Mitologiae* to the fourteenth-century John Ridewall's *Fulgentius metaforalis,* and include the Third Vatican Mythographer's (Alberic of London's?) *De diis gentium et*

[22] One strand of the poem's criticism has tried to identify a contemporary illicit love affair to which it might refer. The matter turns upon the meaning of John Shirley's enigmatic rubrics in MS Trinity R.3.20, which might imply that the lovers in question are John Holland and Isabel of York or Elizabeth of Lancaster (both daughters of John of Gaunt). For further discussion of this issue, see G. H. Cowling, "Chaucer's *Complaintes of Mars and of Venus,*" *RES* 2 (1926): 405–10; Norton-Smith, *Bodleian Library MS Fairfax 16,* pp. 23–25; and Wood, *Chaucer and the Country of the Stars,* pp. 103–08. For the identification of the lovers as John of Gaunt and Katherine Swynford, see George Williams, "What Is the Meaning of Chaucer's *Complaint of Mars?" JEGP* 57 (1958): 167–76.

[23] For examples of occasional readings, see note 22. For moralizing readings, see Mark E. Amsler, "Mad Lovers and Other Hooked Fish: Chaucer's *Complaint of Mars,*" *Allegorica* 4 (1979): 301–14; James M. Dean, "Mars the Exegete in Chaucer's *Complaint of Mars,*" *CL* 41.2 (1989): 128–40; Neil C. Hultin, "Anti-Courtly Elements in Chaucer's *Complaint of Mars,*" *Annuale Medievale* 9 (1968): 58–75; and Wood, *Chaucer and the Country of the Stars,* pp. 130–41. For an account of the poem's comic realism, see Merrill, "Broche of Thebes," and for its "poetics of universal compassion," see Van Dyke, "To Whom Shul We Compleyn?" and "The Lyric Planet: Chaucer's Construction of Subjectivity in the *Complaint of Mars,*" *ChauR* 31 (1996): 164–72.

[24] The first appreciative study of the poem noted its "contradictions or enrichments of conventions"; see Gardiner Stillwell, "Convention and Individuality in Chaucer's *Complaint of Mars,*" *PQ* 35 (1956): 69–89 (69). More recently, Lee Patterson has observed that the poem "delineates a world in which the either/or of singularity is subverted by a dualistic both/and, in which oppositions are revealed to be counterparts." "Writing Amorous Wrongs: Chaucer and the Order of Complaint," in *The Idea of Medieval Literature: New Essays on Chaucer and Medieval Culture in Honor of Donald R. Howard,* ed. James M. Dean and Christian K. Zacher (Newark: University of Delaware Press, 1992), pp. 55–71 (66).

illorum allegoriis and the anonymous *De deorum imaginibus libellus* derived from it, as well as the works of contemporary poets such as Petrarch's *Africa,* Boccaccio's *De genealogiis deorum,* or Christine de Pisan's *Epistre d'Othea.*[25] These mythographic handbooks present the gods of the classical pantheon in a bewildering number of guises. Indeed, Theresa Tinkle has suggested in a book-length study of *Medieval Venuses and Cupids* that exuberant multiplicity of interpretation is the hallmark of mythographic writing. As Tinkle explains: "Venus may be historically a prostitute; naturally, a planet; allegorically, feminine vanity; morally, libido or licit and illicit loves; philosophically, celestial or earthly love. Mythographers typically develop more than one of these models, and Venus may signify all of these meanings within a single text."[26] Even though it remains impossible to trace with absolute certainty the particular handbooks upon which Chaucer drew, it is clear that he knew broadly of these mythographic traditions of imagining and understanding the Olympians, and that he used them creatively in the working of his poetic art.[27] Allusions to mythographic conventions surface in a number of

[25] For a useful introduction to medieval mythography generally, see Judson B. Allen, "Commentary as Criticism: The Text, Influence, and Literary Theory of the 'Fulgentius Metaphored' of John Ridewall," in *Acta Conventus Neo-Latini Amstelodamensis: Proceedings of the Second International Congress of Neo-Latin Studies, Amsterdam 19–24 August 1973,* ed. P. Tuynman, G. C. Kuiper, and E. Kessler, Humanistischa Bibliothek 1, Abhandlungen 26 (Munich: William Fink Verlag, 1979), pp. 25–47. See also Beryl Smalley, *English Friars and Antiquity in the Early Fourteenth Century* (New York: Barnes and Noble, 1960); Jane Chance, *Medieval Mythography,* 2 vols. (Gainesville: University Press of Florida, 1994–2000); Jane Chance, ed., *The Mythographic Art: Classical Fable and the Rise of the Vernacular in Early France and England* (Gainesville: University Press of Florida, 1990), esp. Chance, "The Medieval 'Apology for Poetry': Fabulous Narrative and Stories of the Gods," pp. 3–44.

[26] Tinkle, *Medieval Venuses and Cupids,* p. 49. Other specialized studies of the medieval Venus include George D. Economou, "The Two Venuses and Courtly Love," in *In Pursuit of Perfection: Courtly Love in Medieval Literature,* ed. Joan M. Ferrante and George D. Economou (Port Washington, N.Y.: Kennikat Press, 1975), pp. 17–50; John B. Friedman, "L'Iconographie de Venus et de son miroir à la fin du moyen age," in *L'Erotisme au Moyen Age,* ed. Bruno Roy (Montreal: Editions de l'Aurore, 1977), pp. 53–82; Robert Hollander, *Boccaccio's Two Venuses* (New York: Columbia University Press, 1977); John Mulryan, "Venus, Cupid, and the Italian Mythographers," *Humanistica Lovaniensia* 23 (1974): 31–41; D. W. Robertson, *A Preface to Chaucer: Studies in Medieval Perspectives* (Princeton: Princeton University Press, 1962), esp. pp. 370–74; and Earl G. Schreiber, "Venus in the Medieval Mythographic Tradition," *JEGP* 74 (1975): 519–35. Tinkle provides a useful challenge to the binary assumptions that characterize much of this scholarship; see *Medieval Venuses and Cupids,* esp. pp. 8–77.

[27] For speculations about Chaucer's mythographic reading, which derive mainly from his representation of Venus, see Ernest H. Wilkins, "Descriptions of Pagan Divinities from Petrarch to Chaucer," *Speculum* 32 (1957): 511–22 (arguing for the *Libellus*); John M. Steadman, "Venus's Citole in Chaucer's *Knight's Tale* and Berchorius," *Speculum* 34 (1959): 620–24 (arguing for Bersuire); and Betty Nye Quinn, "Venus, Chaucer, and

Chaucerian works, but the *Complaint of Mars,* with its complex mytho-logical-astrological allegory, represents the poet's most extended en-gagement with these materials.

Medieval mythography is, by and large, an ekphrastic genre; the Olympians are usually described (and sometimes moralized) in terms of their iconic attributes, their visual appearance. Even when no physical picture accompanies the text, the idea of artistic representation stands behind the verbal version of each figure: the crucial verb in Fulgentius and his fourteenth-century successors, for example, is usually *pingitur* ("Venus *is painted* nude, floating in the sea").[28] The textual tradition thus manifests itself as the imagined record of an artistic tradition; the verbal and the visual are mutually dependent in the construction of the mythographic figure. Appropriately, then, the actual images drawn from mythographic handbooks are as various in their form and their meaning as the texts they illustrate. Mythographic images of Venus *an-adyomene,* as we will see, often comprise picturesque Ovidian elements, such as doves, roses, Cupid, and Vulcan. But other images of the god-dess just as often imply moral interpretations, as in composite figures of Venus-Luxuria gazing in a mirror, or astrological forces, as in personifi-cations of the planet with those born under her sign. An early fifteenth-century Italian manuscript combines the personified planet Venus and her astrological "children" with revealing dress and a mirror, motifs of Luxury (fig. 2).[29]

It is undoubtedly by contrast with this complexity of signification that the Fairfax picture appears unnuanced. But the frontispiece, like

---

Peter Bersuire," *Speculum* 38 (1963): 479–80 (adding to the evidence for Bersuire). On Hyginus and Boccaccio as sources for the *Complaint of Mars,* see D. S. Brewer, "Chaucer's *Complaint of Mars,*" *N&Q* 199 (1954): 462–63. The most detailed study of Chaucer's Venus remains Meg Twycross, *The Medieval Anadyomene: A Study in Chaucer's Mythogra-phy* (Oxford: Blackwell for the Society for the Study of Medieval Languages and Litera-ture, 1972). For general studies of Chaucer's relation to the classics, see Jane Chance, *The Mythographic Chaucer: The Fabulation of Sexual Politics* (Minneapolis: University of Minnesota Press, 1995); John M. Fyler, *Chaucer and Ovid* (New Haven: Yale University Press, 1979); John P. McCall, *Chaucer Among the Gods: The Poetics of Classical Myth* (Uni-versity Park: Penn State University Press, 1979); and A. J. Minnis, *Chaucer and Pagan Antiquity* (Cambridge: D. S. Brewer, 1982).

[28] Smalley notes this tendency in her discussion of the purely verbal "pictures" of the classicizing friar John Ridevall; see *English Friars and Antiquity,* pp. 112–13. Twycross quotes Fulgentius as the origin of the idiom: "Hanc etiam nudam pingunt. . . . Hanc etiam in mari natantem pingunt. . . . Concha etiam marina pingitur portari" (*Medieval Anadyomene,* p. 18).

[29] "Prosdocimo de Beldomandi," Padua, 1435. Oxford, Bodleian MS Can. Misc. 554.

Fig. 2. Planetary Venus with Her Children. Oxford, Bodleian MS Canon. Misc. 554, fol. 172r. Bodleian Library, University of Oxford.

the *Complaint of Mars* itself, combines different layers of convention to create a picture that, if not explicitly witty, is nonetheless structured by complex and meaningful allusions. The portrait of Venus suggests the poem's double perspective in particularly striking terms, even though it is seemingly the most conventional of the three. She is Venus *anadyomene*, the goddess rising from the sea. At first glance, she seems a pure reflection of the most common traditions of Ovidian illustration, the visual embodiment of Chaucer's description in the *House of Fame*. In the dreamer's words:

> in portreyture
> I sawgh anoon-ryght hir figure
> Naked fletynge in a see,
> And also on hir hed, pardee,
> Hir rose garlond whit and red,
> And hir comb to kembe hir hed,
> Hir dowves, and daun Cupido
> Hir blynde sone, and Vulcano,
> That in his face was ful broun.
>
> (131–39)

The Fairfax frontispiece reflects all of these attributes associated with Venus *anadyomene* in medieval understanding: Vulcan at his forge, blind Cupid with his bow (his closed eyes here perhaps representing his blindness), a flower garland, a flock of doves. Damage to the manuscript page has obscured the object that this Venus holds, but it seems most likely to be a shell, metamorphosed by this time from the craft that carries the goddess (*concham portari*) into an attribute that she herself carries (*concham portare*).[30] A statue of a similar Venus figures prominently in the temple of *The Knight's Tale*.[31] As Meg Twycross and others have shown, many of these descriptive particulars derive from the late medieval mythographic handbooks with which Chaucer was demonstrably fa-

---

[30] Petrarch seems to have introduced this change, which may derive from an error in his copy of Fulgentius. See Twycross, *Medieval Anadyomene*, 21–22. For a more extreme (and more amusing) example of this kind of transformation, see Erwin Panofsky, *Renaissance and Renascences in Western Art* (New York: Harper and Row, 1972), pp. 86–87: Venus's *concam marinam* (seashell) turned into an *aucam marinam* (sea goose), with predictably nonsensical artistic results.

[31] *Knight's Tale*, I.1955–66. For a somewhat different vision of the goddess, cf. *Parliament of Fowls*, 260–73.

miliar, most likely Pierre Bersuire's *Ovidus moralizatus* or the anonymous *Libellus*.[32]

The Fairfax picture also includes as Venus's attendants the Three Graces, who take their characteristic medieval rather than their classical form. In ancient art, the Three Graces are usually depicted with their arms linked, the figure in the middle facing backward and the others forward, as in the well-known fresco from Pompeii (fig. 3). But in the

Fig. 3. Three Graces. Pompeii, House of Titus Dentatus Panthera, ca. A.D. 65–79. Museo Archaeologico Nazionale, Naples. (photo: Erich Lessing / Art Resource, N.Y.)

[32] For a summary of scholarship on which handbooks Chaucer might have known, see Twycross, *Medieval Anadyomene,* pp. 1–15.

Middle Ages, when verbal descriptions alone served to transmit these visual images, the traditional disposition of the figures was obscured, and the only stipulation on their representation became that two look forward and one looks back.[33] This detail, like so many in the mythographic tradition, took on a moral rather than an aesthetic meaning: "A benefit conferred is twice repaid."[34] The tradition was further transformed when Bersuire in his popular *Ovidius moralizatus* changed even the verbal description, calling instead for one of the Graces to be looking forward and the other two to be looking back. It is such a description, doubtless, that produced the Fairfax Graces, who bear almost no resemblance at all to their classical forebears.

The difference between images transmitted verbally and those transmitted visually is telling for the history of the medieval *anadyomene,* for it helps to account for the astonishing variety of her representations in art.[35] Even if the verbal traditions and the iconography they transmit are relatively similar, the artistic realizations of these descriptions can be surprisingly different; although the Fairfax Venus conforms neatly to the most common descriptions of the goddess rising from the sea, it does not finally *look* much like other pictures of her.[36] In one manuscript of John Ridewall's *Fulgentius metaforalis,* for example, she is shown with doves, a flower garland, and a conch shell or mirror, but she is swimming in the sea rather than standing in it (fig. 4).[37] And even when she

[33] For a brief history of the Graces, see Jean Seznec, *The Survival of the Pagan Gods: The Mythological Tradition and Its Place in Renaissance Humanism and Art,* trans. Barbara F. Sessions, Bollingen Series 38 (Princeton: Princeton University Press, 1953), pp. 208–9. See also Fritz Saxl and Erwin Panofsky, "Classical Mythology in Mediaeval Art," *Metropolitan Museum Studies* 4 (1933): 228–80 (257).

[34] The phrase is Seznec's, *Survival of the Pagan Gods,* p. 209.

[35] Because the Fairfax image draws so closely on traditions of depicting the *anadyomene,* it is less relevant to images of Venus in narrative contexts such as the *Romance of the Rose,* Boccaccio's *De claris mulieribus,* Christine de Pisan's *Epistre d'Othea,* and histories of the Trojan War that include the Judgment of Paris.

[36] For a survey of English medieval Venuses, see Fritz Saxl and Hans Meier, *Catalogue of Astrological and Mythological Illuminated Manuscripts of the Latin Middle Ages, Manuscripts in English Libraries (III),* ed. Harry Bober, 2 vols. (London: Warburg Institute, University of London, 1953). Bodleian MS Fairfax 16 itself is mentioned on pp. 382–83, Abb. 18.

[37] Rome, Vatican, Palat. lat. 1726 (reprinted in Seznec, fig. 31, p. 107). This change comes from confusion over "in mari natantem," which may mean either floating on or swimming in the sea. See Twycross, *Medieval Anadyomene,* 18 n. 31. See also Marion Lawrence, "The Birth of Venus in Roman Art," in *Essays in the History of Art Presented to Rudolf Wittkower,* ed. Douglas Fraser, Howard Hibbard, and Milton J. Levine (London: Phaidon, 1967), pp. 10–16; and Edgar Wind's Appendix 5, "Aphrodite's Shell," in *Pagan Mysteries in the Renaissance* (London: Faber, 1958), pp. 263–64, figs. 35, 36.

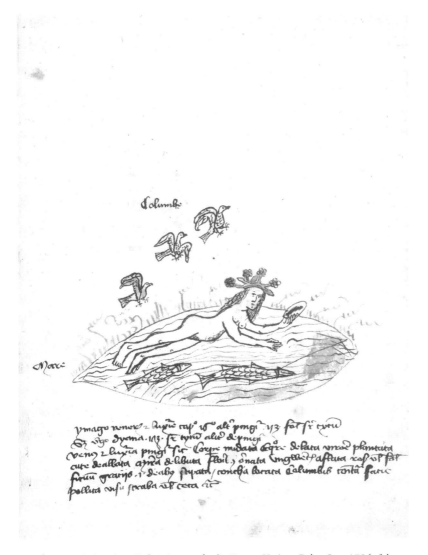

Fig. 4. Venus Swimming. *Fulgentius megaforalis,* Rome, Vatican Palat. Lat. 1726, fol. 43a. Biblioteca Apostolica Vaticana.

is standing in the sea, surrounded by all the attributes we have come to expect, the disposition of the figures does not necessarily recall the Fairfax Venus. There is no discernible iconographical difference between our Venus and an illustration from a fifteenth-century English manuscript of Ovid's *Metamorphoses,* but it is a very different picture (fig. 5).[38]

The Fairfax Venus is iconographically conventional, then, but parallels in form and sensibility must be sought elsewhere.[39] The image owes

Fig. 5. Venus *anadyomene.* Oxford, Bodleian MS Rawlinson B.214, fol. 198v. Bodleian Library, University of Oxford.

[38] Oxford, Bodleian MS Rawlinson B.214.

[39] For a connection between the physiognomy of this Venus and Hieronymus Bosch's Eve, see A. Boczkowska, "The Crab, the Sun, the Moon, and Venus: Studies in the Iconology of Hieronymus Bosch's Triptych, *The Garden of Earthly Delights,*" *Oud Holland* 91 (1977): 197–231 (215 and fig. 33).

a debt to medieval mythography, but it demonstrates, too, an important inheritance from a more surprising quarter: the Christian tradition of baptismal iconography that includes, for example, the image in *Les Très Riches Heures du Duc de Berry* of Christ's Baptism in the Jordan (fol. 109v; fig. 6).[40] Like Christ, the Fairfax Venus stands in a river rather than a sea; the surrounding landscape shows not only the promontories providing space for Vulcan and the Graces, but also the opposite bank. A tight circle of roses and doves surrounds the goddess's head in a striking visual reminiscence of a halo, an impression of divinity reinforced by golden rays. This "halo" is all the more interesting here because neither Mars nor Jupiter has one, though there is no clear rationale for the artist's distinction among the pagan gods. The frontal position of the leading dove could even be derived from representations of the descending Holy Spirit.[41] And even though Venus's raised hand is not absolutely unique—the Oxford manuscript, for example, includes this detail (see fig. 5)—her gesture here recalls Christ's benediction. Christ in his baptism is most often seen to be blessing in a gesture still more overt than the one depicted in the *Très Riches Heures;*[42] but even if the Fairfax artist's exemplar was more explicitly benedictional, the adjustment required by his classicizing secularization need not have been large.

The visual connection in the Fairfax frontispiece between Venus *anadyomene* and Christ in his baptism is less strange than may at first appear. Barbara Newman has recently traced widespread iconographies of secular love that became just as popular in late medieval Christian contexts: the bow and arrows, firebrand, flaming heart, and pierced heart that are associated both with Cupid and with Christ.[43] Conversely, the familiar languages of the late medieval "religion of love" appropriate a sacred vocabulary to transform *cupiditas* into *caritas*.[44] Representations of Venus

[40] For a facsimile, see *Les Très Riches Heures du Duc de Berry,* intro. Jean Longon and Raymond Cazelles, preface Millard Meiss, trans. Victoria Benedict (London: Thames and Hudson, 1969).

[41] Doves are of course a familiar Christian symbol as well as a Venerean one. For the white dove as the Christian soul, see W. S. Heckscher, "The *Anadyomene* in the Mediaeval Tradition (Pelagia-Cleopatra-Aphrodite), A Prelude to Botticelli's 'Birth of Venus.'" *Nederlands Kunsthistorisch Jaarboek* 7 (1956): 1–38 (21).

[42] For a useful survey of an enormous topic, see "The Baptism of Christ," in Gertrud Schiller, *Iconography of Christian Art,* trans. Janet Seligman, 2 vols. (Greenwich, Conn.: New York Graphic Society, 1971–72), pp. 127–43.

[43] Newman, "Love's Arrows."

[44] For a pertinent discussion of this familiar trope, see Alcuin Blamires, "The 'Religion of Love' in Chaucer's *Troilus and Criseyde* and Medieval Visual Art," in *Word and Visual Imagination: Studies in the Interaction of English Literature and the Visual Arts,* ed.

herself as the goddess of love can overlap with Christian iconography of the divine: she can be pictured with a crown, or with a nimbus, in a floating mandorla, or attended by kneeling worshipers. A divine Venus appears in a mandorla, for example, in the well-known Florentine *desco da parto,* probably a maternity gift from husband to wife, in which the goddess is adored by famous lovers kneeling below her.[45] She is deified in such an image, for in its structure it resembles the Assumption of the Virgin, in a way that dignifies the all-too-human adoration of Tristan, Paris, Lancelot, and the rest. This late medieval religion of love plays a role in the *Complaint of Mars,* for the god vows "perpetuall obeisaunce" to his lady, whom he calls "the verrey sours and welle / Of beaute, lust, fredom, and gentilnesse" (174–75). Other texts included in Fairfax 16 repeat the trope, confirming that the ennobling of secular love was one of its compiler's controlling interests.[46]

Comparing Venus with Christ might seem to evoke the medieval problem of the "two Venuses," in which one version of the goddess represents an ennobled kind of human *caritas,* conjugal and procreative, and the other represents a debased form of sexual *cupiditas* to be condemned.[47] But the comparison between the Fairfax Venus and Christ in baptism brings up issues far richer than that simple binary would allow. For in addition to drawing on images of an idealized Christian femininity, the goddess of love can in some ways resemble Christ himself. In his study of the ways in which early Christian iconography grew from depictions of the pagan gods, Thomas Mathews has explored the feminization of Christ in early depictions of him.[48] Mathews demonstrates that such transhistorically intractable attributes of Christ as his long hair borrow from pagan iconographies to assert both his potent divinity and his fruitfulness. Some images of Christ even display a decided ambiguity of body type along lines that have to do with fertility: full breasts and

---

Karl Josef Höltgen, Peter M. Daly, and Wolfgang Lottes (Erlangen: Univ.-Bibliothek Erlangen-Nürnberg, 1988), pp. 11–31.

[45] See Michael Camille, *The Medieval Art of Love: Objects and Subjects of Desire* (New York: Harry N. Abrams, 1998), fig. 23; and Blamires, "'Religion of Love,'" fig. 4. For Cupid in a mandorla, see Newman, "Love's Arrows," fig. 1.

[46] See Tinkle, "The Imagined Chaucerian Community," pp. 167–71.

[47] For a review of the problem of the "two Venuses," and for its inadequacy to the complexity of the medieval goddess, see Tinkle, *Medieval Venuses and Cupids,* pp. 9–41. See Patterson, "Writing Amorous Wrongs," 68–69 n. 18, for a review of the evidence that Chaucer's Venus could be beneficial.

[48] Thomas F. Mathews, *The Clash of Gods: A Reinterpretation of Early Christian Art* (Princeton: Princeton University Press, 1993), pp. 115–41.

Fig. 6. Limbourg Brothers, Baptism of Christ. *Les Très Riches Heures du Duc de Berry,* fol. 109v. Musée Condé, Chantilly, France. (photo: R. G. Ojeda, Réunion des Musées Nationaux / Art Resource, N.Y.)

hips at times distinguish Christ from his disciples. In a more theological vein, Christ's ambiguous gender seems to have enhanced the universal appeal of his image, in the context of both gnostic scriptures and also Paul's call to baptism in Galatians 3:28: "there is neither male nor female; for you are all one in Christ Jesus."[49] In fact, what Mathews calls "the most strikingly ambiguous image in Ravenna" is a baptismal mosaic in which the androgyny of the young Christ—genital specificity notwithstanding—is thrown into relief by the more clearly masculine (if less clearly male) figures of the Baptist and the personified River Jordan (fig. 7).[50]

If Christ can be seen, at least in these early images, to look a bit like Venus, then Venus *anadyomene* also functions upon occasion a bit like Christ.[51] Roman images of the *anadyomene* were notably different from the medieval ones—the classical goddess is generally shown wringing the water from her hair, swimming in the sea, floating in or even born from a shell, rather than carrying one. But these shell-borne Venuses were used in an environment that may prove instructive: they often appear in the context of burial—on sarcophagi, for example, such as this one now in the Louvre (fig. 8). The goddess on her shell represents a journey, a crossing, even new birth.[52] Venus is born from the sea, after all—the image of the *anadyomene,* as much as the Baptism of Christ, is a theogony. The shell that John uses to baptize Christ in the *Très Riches Heures,* and that still occasionally graces baptismal fonts, is a relic of this ancient and widespread connection between water and rebirth. Baptismal fonts were originally conch-shaped, and the word *concha* was used to describe them from the fourth century to the fourteenth.[53] Even Botticelli, in his version of the goddess rising from the sea on a shell,

[49] "Non est Iudaeus neque Graecus, non est servus neque liber, non est masculus neque femina, omnes enim vos unum estis in Christo Iesu" (Douai-Rheims Bible).

[50] Mathews, *The Clash of Gods,* p. 134.

[51] The cross-gendering worked both ways, for an eighth-century English sermon inveighs against a Venus mistakenly described as Mars's brother. See Ernst Robert Curtius, *European Literature and the Latin Middle Ages,* trans. Willard R. Trask (Princeton: Princeton University Press, 1990 [1953]), p. 406; and Wilhelm Levison, *England and the Continent in the Eighth Century* (Oxford: Clarendon Press, 1946), pp. 302–14.

[52] See Lawrence, "The Birth of Venus in Roman Art," pp. 10–16; and A. A. Barb, "Diva Matrix: A Faked Gnostic Intaglio in the Possession of P. P. Rubens and the Iconology of a Symbol," *Journal of the Warburg and Courtauld Institutes* 16 (1953): 193–238, esp. 204–07.

[53] Heckscher, "The *Anadyomene* in the Mediaeval Tradition," pp. 25–26.

Fig. 7. Baptism of Christ. Baptistry of the Arians, Ravenna. (photo: Scala / Art Resource, N.Y.)

Fig. 8. Venus *anadyomene*. Roman sarcophagus. Musée du Louvre, Paris. © Maurice and Pierre Chuzeville / Musée du Louvre.

profited from this kind of association, and some have observed that he patterned his famous picture on images of Christ's baptism.[54]

I have, at this point, strayed far from the Fairfax Venus itself—and even farther from Chaucer's *Complaint of Mars.* To return to my original question: How can we understand the baptismal imagery echoed here to enrich our reading of the poem? I am not claiming that this artist (or his audience) would have defended any fundamental similarity between the pagan goddess and their Savior. Undoubtedly the similarity of presentation here derives in part from pragmatic considerations: this artist used what imagery came to hand for his pictorial mythography. But to acknowledge this borrowing is not to say that his practice is without interpretive interest. The hybrid genealogy of the image indicates that the artist at work in Fairfax 16 engaged actively with, rather than thoughtlessly adopting, various artistic exemplars. And the result of his *bricolage* is meaningful in ways he may not have foreseen: as both medieval and modern readers of Fairfax 16 are in a position to see, the picture and the poem explore divinity in several different registers.

Again, the Fairfax artist's use of the Three Graces provides an important clue to interpretation of his picture, and to its relation to Chaucer's poem. Although the association of Venus with the Graces is common in the Ovidian mythographic tradition, it is not impossible to read at least one of these figures as supplicating, as well as attending, the goddess. The two who look away from the viewer look significantly toward their reigning deity, and one of these also lifts her hands in prayer. Although

[54] For the "rather unexpected" connection between Botticelli's Venus and the Baptism of Christ, see ibid., p. 6. Heckscher also connects the imagery of rebirth in Botticelli's painting to the vita of the fifth-century saint Pelagia of Antioch.

this visual detail does not illustrate, in a technical sense, any aspect of Chaucer's poem (in which the Three Graces play no role at all), it does accord with the reverential tone taken by Mars in that poem toward the power of his courtly mistress, who "hath take him in subjeccioun, / and as a maistresse taught him his lessoun" (32–33). The Graces, then, function surprisingly like the crowd on the banks of the Jordan in the *Trés Riches Heures;* they acclaim and worship the divine figure at the center. The evocation of imagery of Christ's baptism visually strengthens the impression of Venus as a courtly goddess.

The artist's exploration of divinity becomes clearer in the portraits of Mars and Jupiter, where the combination of Christian forms with classical subject matter may be less visually compelling, but is still more thematically suggestive. If the Fairfax Venus is conventional in surprising ways, the Fairfax Mars is surprisingly unconventional, and might be more closely related to the specifics of the text (see fig. 1).[55] The god's standard mythographical attributes are well represented by this image from the fifteenth-century Oxford manuscript from which we have already seen the portrait of Venus (fig. 9), and by the similar description in Chaucer's *Knight's Tale:*

> The statue of Mars upon a carte stood
> Armed, and looked grym as he were wood.
>
> .   .   .   .
>
> A wolf ther stood biforn hym at his feet
> With eyen rede, and of a man he eet.
>
> (2041–42; 2046–47)

By contrast, the Fairfax Mars does not claim the customary iconography of cart and whip. A wolf attends him, but a surprisingly unthreatening one, more heraldic than fearsome. Even more remarkable than the docility of the wolf is Mars's own peaceable expression. The *Complaint* describes him equally as a soldier "furious and wod" (123) and as a "woful" and disappointed lover (104), and in accordance with his amorous role the god here looks worried rather than traditionally irascible. A final oddity that may derive from the poem is Mars's peculiar *deshabille:* he is

---

[55] For studies of Mars in Chaucer, see Melvin Storm, "Chaucer's Poetic Treatment of the Figure of Mars" (Ph.D. dissertation, University of Illinois, Urbana-Champaign, 1973); "Troilus, Mars, and Late Medieval Chivalry," *Journal of Medieval and Renaissance Studies* 12 (1982) 45–65; and especially "The Mythological Tradition in Chaucer's *Complaint of Mars,*" *PQ* 57 (1978): 323–35.

Fig. 9. Mars. Oxford, Bodleian MS Rawlinson B.214, fol. 198v. Bodleian Library, University of Oxford.

armed, but incompletely, and his bare arm and leg are unattested else-where in mythographic and iconographic traditions. The most likely—though still inconclusive—explanation for this is that his bare limbs imply the Ovidian narrative by representing the situation of discovery: he is half-dressed because he is fleeing Venus's bed.[56] Indeed, Chaucer's poem makes a point of his need to arm himself: when Phebus arrives to put a halt to the lovers' dalliance, Venus moves on, making her escape, but Mars must pause to throw on his "helm of huge wyghte" (99) and other martial gear. Mars's heavy armor—that is, his slower planetary movement—impedes his flight and prevents him from joining his lady: "Ful hevy was he to walken over lond" (103).

The more meaningful links between picture and poem are to be found elsewhere—in echoes of Christian images similar to those we have already seen in the Fairfax Venus. In a telling detail, Mars is attended by what seem to be his astrological "children": three knights kneel be-hind him in an attenuated version of *Planetenkinder,* as, for example, in the Venus-Luxuria image we saw earlier. This tradition of the *Planeten-*

---

[56] This interpretation of the picture has provided the occasion for much of the moral-izing commentary on the poem. Christine de Pisan, however, in her *Epistre d'Othea,* explains that the moral of the episode is that a good knight (that is, Mars) should not be forgetful of time. She also explains that the myth can be read astrologically—a combination of registers that suggests perhaps she had Chaucer's poem in mind. For the wide variety in interpretations of the story of Mars and Venus in mythographic writings, see Tinkle, *Medieval Venuses and Cupids,* pp. 46–48.

kinder was familiar to Chaucer—the Wife of Bath names herself as both a child of Venus and of Mars[57]—and it has important implications for the Fairfax illustration. For although it is a traditional idea, these are not the usual wrathful children of Mars. They are soldiers, but they follow Chaucer's god in complaint, as he calls them to do, rather than in warfare. Most important, the complaint of these knights is represented in the image as a kind of prayer. More obviously even than the Graces, these figures resemble Christian supplicants, marked by their kneeling posture and the red crosses on their chests. These details transform Mars's knights from courtly complainants into devout petitioners—not disappointed lovers, but faithful followers of their god. At the end of his complaint, Mars beseeches the "hardy knyghtes of renoun" of his "devisioun"—astrological children ruled by his planetary influence—to join him in his lamentation. He also beseeches his "ladyes" to have pity on people in pain for the sake of their "emperise," Venus, who cannot attain her goal: "Now shulde your holy teres falle and reyne."[58] The combination of devotional and courtly language here in the detail of the "holy" tears shows the proximity between these supplicants and Christian petitioners at prayer.

The prayer of Mars's knights is important to the interpretation of poem and picture, for it mirrors the relation figured in both text and image between Mars himself and Jupiter. The most arresting feature of these two portraits, in fact, is not any iconographical attribute, but the gods' actions: in defiance of the clear frames surrounding each Olympian figure, Mars reaches up toward Jupiter, who responds with an answering gesture. This image has little to do with the conventional static representation of classical deities in mythographic catalogues, few of which depict any relation, even of a hierarchical kind, between Jupiter and the other gods.[59] The Oxford manuscript, for example, exhibits this characteristic fracturing of space, the complete dissociation of one figure from another (see fig. 5). Even in a more formal setting it is rare that a rela-

---

[57] "For certes, I am al Venerien / In feelynge, and myn herte is Marcien" (III.609–10).

[58] *Pace* Tinkle's claim that the manuscript's booklet 1 is concerned with creating "an imagined masculine community," Mars here addresses both knights and ladies. See Tinkle, "Imagined Chaucerian Community," p. 160.

[59] The interaction of the figures also argues against the link to *imagines deorum* derived from geomantic iconography proposed by Norton-Smith. *Bodleian MS Fairfax 16*, p. xiii.

tionship is figured between Jupiter and his pantheon.[60] Although the Jupiter of Mantegna's sixteenth-century Tarocchi, for instance, relates to a figure below him, that figure cannot be interpreted as a classical deity (fig. 10).[61] This Jupiter is hurling thunderbolts at humans, not counseling troubled Olympians.

Mars relates to Jupiter more as human than as Olympian in the Fairfax miniature, becoming a petitioning child of the planetary god, though not of course in a strict astrological sense. An image of Jupiter and his children from Christine de Pisan's *Epistre d'Othea* points up both similarities and crucial differences between the *Planetenkinder* tradition and the Fairfax picture (fig. 11). The disposition of the figures is the same—godly Jupiter above reaching down to supplicants with outstretched hands below—but in this case the pagan deity is said to be pouring a "sweet liquid" on his children. The allegory appended to the text likens the liquid to God's grace, and the picture, in fact, recalls images of the Descent of the Holy Spirit.[62] But the deity of the *Complaint of Mars* offers no sweet liquid of comfort—Mars is left at the end of the poem with no ready answers to his poignant questions. He asks:

> To what fyn made the God, that sit so hye,
> Benethen him love other companye
> And streyneth folk to love, malgre her hed?
> And then her joy, for oght I can espye,
> Ne lasteth not the twynkelyng of an ye,
> And somme han never joy til they be ded.
> What meneth this? What is this mystihed?
> Wherto contreyneth he his folk so faste
> Thing to desyre, but hit shulde laste?
>
> (218–26)

Mars finds God's role in human love especially mysterious, and especially blameworthy, wondering why "so juste a kyng / Doth such hardnesse to his creature" (231–32). He even accuses God of real cruelty,

---

[60] An example of a more formal but still-static arrangement is in an *Ovide moralisé* (Bibliotheque de Lyon, cod. 742), reprinted in Seznec, fig. 33.

[61] For the complete set, see *I Tarocchi detti del Mantegna,* preface Claudia Cieri Via (Pavia: Torchio de'Ricci, 1992).

[62] For discussion of the *Epistre d'Othea* and this illustration, see Millard Meiss, *French Painting in the Time of Jean, Duc de Berry: The Limbourgs and Their Contemporaries,* 2 vols. (New York: Braziller, 1974), 1:23–41 (23).

Fig. 10. Jupiter, from Mantegna's *Tarocchi*. National Gallery of Art, Ailsa Mellon Bruce Fund. Courtesy of the Board of Trustees, National Gallery of Art, Washington, D.C.

Fig. 11. Planetary Jupiter and His Children. Christine de Pisan, *Epitre d'Othea,* BN fr. 606, fol. 5v. Bibliothèque Nationale, Paris.

comparing him to a "fissher," who baits his "angle-hok" with romantic pleasures that leave lovers wounded, even if they eventually escape by breaking the line (237–38). This characterization of God as a cruel fisherman might mark Mars as a pagan, for although images of a deadly hook baited with sexual pleasure for example, are common, it can be answered in a Christian context by the salvific image of Christ's humanity as the bait that catches the devil on the hook of his divinity.[63] Mars even goes so far as to blame God for making Venus's irresistible beauty, comparing him to the jeweler responsible for creating the beautiful but deadly Brooch of Thebes (who, in a neat irony, turns out to have been the goddess's cuckolded husband, Vulcan).[64] Venus herself is not responsible for any tragedies of love, but rather the one who made her beauty—"In the worcher is the vyce," Mars claims, and, he adds belatedly, in the "covetour" who succumbs to his attraction (261–62). The stars cannot explain these difficult conundrums: in spite of his responsive gesture, the Fairfax Jupiter offers no clear astrological guidance for his petitioner, whose role in the poem more closely resembles the rather more complicated and uncertain position of human worshiper than that of pagan deity.

The unusual communication in the Fairfax frontispiece between Mars and Jupiter, across a pictorial frame that Venus respects (if Cupid does not),[65] suggests that we might also profitably think of their gestures in the context of Christian supplication on the one hand and divine intercession on the other. The iconography of prayer (as in Peter the Chanter's twelfth-century treatise on the subject) often involves the lifting of the hands over the head, as Mars does.[66] And certainly at times in medieval use of classical myth Jupiter was made analogous to the Chris-

---

[63] The idea of Christ as bait and fishhook comes up in Gregory of Nyssa's commentary on Job 41. For the contrasting metaphors of the hook baited with sexual pleasure and the Christian clergy as "fishers of men," see Amsler, "Mad Lovers and Other Hooked Fish"; and Hultin, "Anti-Courtly Elements," 70–73.

[64] For a reading of the Brooch of Thebes in the context of the *Complaint*, see Patterson, *Chaucer and the Subject of History*, pp. 76, 219.

[65] Chauncey Wood sees Mars and Venus as communicating gesturally, reading Mars's gesture closely against line 146 of the poem, in which he "salueth" his lady. Wood is eager to see the picture as a condemnation of lechery, but it seems clear from the direction of Mars's eyes that he instead means to communicate with the god above. Wood also reads Jupiter's gesture as "rebuke," but nothing in the picture necessitates such a reading. *Chaucer and the Country of the Stars*, p. 136.

[66] See Richard C. Trexler, *The Christian at Prayer: An Illustrated Prayer Manual Attributed to Peter the Chanter (d. 1197)*, Medieval and Renaissance Texts and Studies 44 (Binghamton, N.Y.: Center for Medieval and Early Renaissance Studies, 1987).

tian God; the Jupiter of the Tarocchi sits in a mandorla, looking strikingly like Christ in Majesty on a Gothic tympanum (see fig. 10), and there are suggestions of such an equivalence even in *The Knight's Tale* (I.2987–3074). The Fairfax Jupiter also brings to mind such analogies: he looks down as if from heaven upon the supplicant, and he appears in a radiant sunburst similar to the one that surrounds Mary in, for example, the Augustan *ara coeli* vision. Indeed, a similar architecture structures another of this artist's productions, which might have served as a formal model for the tripartite division of the Fairfax illustration: the tau-shaped cross in the Abingdon Missal crucifixion divides Mary from John, and Christ from God the Father, in just the same way as in the Fairfax frontispiece (fig. 12).[67] Here, too, God leans to the left to acknowledge the suffering figure, in this case Mary, below him.[68] He radiates divinity (just as Mary and John display their sanctity) through golden beams that descend upon the central figure of Christ on the cross. These divine rays recall versions of God as the *sol iustitiae,* such as this one from the fourteenth-century *Rothschild Canticles* (fig. 13).[69]

The connection of the Fairfax Jupiter to the sun is especially important, for it may help explain his presence in the frontispiece. I have suggested that the relationship of Mars and Jupiter is represented in both picture and poem, but in fact in the *Complaint of Mars* Jupiter is never named. In the astrological terms of Chaucer's poem, Mars appears to act most directly in relation to Phebus, the sun. The poem's bird-narrator bemoans the arrival of day, upbraiding the sun as the "candel of jelosye" (7) in an *aubade* that ironically anticipates the fate of the adulterous gods, who are eventually exposed by the "firy torches" of Phebus (27).[70] The Fairfax artist's titulus has therefore often been taken as a misidentification; and, indeed, the inclusion of Jupiter is at once probably the most mysterious feature of the frontispiece, and the most seemingly distant from Chaucer's poem. But the figure's association with the sun could easily imply a Christian paradigm, as well as a classical one; and Jupi-

---

[67] Norton-Smith notes the formal similarities; *Bodleian Library MS Fairfax 16,* p. xiii.

[68] Some understand God the Father here as leaning down to receive the dove of the Holy Spirit; see, for example, Richard Marks and Nigel Morgan, *The Golden Age of English Manuscript Painting, 1200–1500* (New York: Braziller, 1981), p. 119.

[69] See Jeffrey F. Hamburger, *The Rothschild Canticles: Art and Mysticism in Flanders and the Rhineland circa 1300* (New Haven: Yale University Press, 1990). Hamburger discusses the *sol iustitiae* primarily on pp. 64–66. The metaphor comes originally from Malachi 4.2.

[70] For a discussion of the *aubade* in the *Complaint of Mars,* see Paul Battles, "Chaucer and the Traditions of Dawn-Song," *ChauR* 31 (1997): 317–38, esp. 323–36.

Fig. 12. Crucifixion, Abingdon Missal. Oxford, Bodleian Library MS Digby 227, fol. 113v. Bodleian Library, University of Oxford.

Fig. 13. God as *Sol Justitiae, Rothschild Canticles*. New Haven, Beinecke Library MS 404, fol. 36r. Beinecke Library, Yale University.

ter—more than Phebus—represents Christian monotheism.[71] For even though the artist takes his primary inspiration from the poem's first section—the story of the astrological and human encounter among Venus, Mars, and Phebus—he also takes up the complaint proper: Mars's anguished cry protesting the injustices of "him that lordeth ech intelligence" (166), a nonspecific but monotheistic God, that "sit so hye" (218). Although Mars never directly answers his own question—"To

[71] Medieval tradition recognized that some pagans considered the entire Pantheon to be contained in the figure of Jove. See Augustine, *City of God*, bk. 4, chap. 11; and Vincent of Beauvais, *Speculum Doctrinale*, xix.18. Cited by Minnis, *Chaucer and Pagan Antiquity*, 50 n. 79.

whom shal I than pleyne of my distresse?" (191)—and he never addresses God directly, his existential torment is directed toward the one he sees as ultimately responsible. It is to this daring verbal picture that the Fairfax artist has responded with an idiosyncratic combination of pictorial conventions. To suggest iconographically that Jupiter is the "sun of justice," when Mars is so stridently casting doubt on God's goodness, is to pose forcefully the problem of Chaucer's *Complaint of Mars*.

In their exploration of divinity both sacred and secular, the poem and the picture draw on the conventions of a late medieval "religion of love," in which the lady is deified and the suitor humbled to the point of supplication. But this is more than the familiar adoption of religious language to describe a secular goddess. The crossover here does not simply imbue a human beloved with celestial qualities, but brings earthly love together with heavenly love to ask real, painful, and poignant questions about the relationships between the two. The interactions among the ancient gods in both picture and poem are finally more daring in their Christian parallels than the common courtly vocabulary would suggest, moving beyond adoration to complaint, beyond worship to radical existential doubt. The comparison works not to ennoble pagan worship or secular love, but to enable the expression of a Christian skepticism that otherwise could find few outlets.[72] This frontispiece is not merely an argument for a celestial vision of earthly love. Rather, it is an argument that the idealization of the lady that can lead to her identification with Christ is related to the anguish of the lover that can lead him to question God; the idealization of the lady and the anguish of the lover are two sides of the same problem. Venus's resemblance to Christ suggests that a beloved lady might be deified, but Mars's prayer—the most telling visual detail, and the one that corresponds more closely to the poem—suggests that God can be questioned. His supplication is not to the lady as to a goddess, but to God himself.

Although it is not a narrative image per se, the frontispiece depends upon the narrative that Chaucer tells at the opening of the *Complaint of Mars*. The characters pictured are the familiar gods of the classical pantheon, adorned with the iconographical symbols attributed to them by medieval commentary tradition. But the picture speaks most forcefully to the conclusion of Chaucer's poem, to Mars's complaint. Like the *Complaint of Mars* itself, the manuscript's prefatory picture represents both

---

[72] For one perspective on medieval atheism in connection to this sort of crossover, see V. A. Kolve, "God-Denying Fools and the Medieval 'Religion of Love,'" *SAC* 19 (1997): 3–59.

the story of the gods' interactions and their subjective responses to it. As Lee Patterson has described it, the poem asks "whether amorous wrongs can be righted by being written—whether, that is, the self can be repaired or justice can be done through poetry."[73] The Fairfax picture, as well as the poem, leaves that question open, and leaves the human petitioner without any concrete assurance that his complaint will be effective. If, as Newman has shown, Cupid is linked to Christ based on a likeness through suffering, Venus is linked to him through renewal and rebirth. Through imagery of baptism connected to Venus, the picture is about regeneration, but through imagery of prayer connected to Mars, it is also about anguish. By visual rather than textual means, the frontispiece combines narrative with complaint, Ovidian images with astrological ones, and amorous intrigues with serious theological problems.

The combination of classical, astrological, and Christian conventions is the central point of connection between picture and poem. Even from the second line of the text, Venus the Olympian goddess is also imagined as the morning star "rysen among yon rowes rede." A few lines later, the narrator in his "briddes wise" alludes to Saint John as Guarantor in an aside that, if not heavy with meaning, nonetheless marks the poem immediately with a Christian idiom (9). It is of course not unusual to find classical figures represented in Christian forms in medieval art and literature: from Amphiorax as a "bisshop" in *Troilus and Criseyde* to Mercury as an "ecclesiastical dignitary" in Western copies of Arabian astronomical manuscripts.[74] But to my knowledge no one has analyzed the similarities between Venus *anadyomene* and Christ in baptism, or the ways in which Christian prayer is figured among pagan deities. The presentation of theological questions in the context of pagan antiquity both mitigates and complicates their force—a characteristically Chaucerian move seen most richly of course in *Troilus and Criseyde* and *The Knight's Tale*. The Fairfax artist seems aware also of the philosophical richness of representing the classical past in imagery readily readable in Christian terms; he juxtaposes antique and Christian elements in such a way as to acknowledge, but gently, the serious implications of Mars's criticism. By manipulating these images just as Chaucer does, this artist engaged in a project more complicated than the simple adoption of iconographic convention, and here it appears that more is to be gained from investigating interpretive connections between the illustration and its text.

[73] Patterson, "Writing Amorous Wrongs," p. 57.
[74] For Amphiorax, see *Troilus and Criseyde* II.104–5; for Mercury, see Seznec, *Survival of the Pagan Gods,* pp. 156–60 (158).

Chaucer Appropriated:

The *Troilus* Frontispiece as Lancastrian Propaganda

Anita Helmbold
Taylor University College

F EW PORTRAITS SURVIVE to satisfy our historical and personal curiosity about the man who was Geoffrey Chaucer, and hence the portrait of him that prefaces Corpus Christi College Cambridge (CCCC) MS 61 has exercised continuing fascination over the minds of literary and historical scholars alike.[1] Unique among dedicatory miniatures, and borrowing, it may be, from a variety of pictorial traditions,[2] the frontispiece offers a dauntingly complex iconography that has made it difficult for scholars to come to agreement as to its proper context and meanings.

[1] Reproductions of the frontispiece have been published in a number of sources, although many of the published images are of poor quality. The manuscript facsimile, introduced by M. B. Parkes and Elizabeth Salter, in *Troilus and Criseyde: A Facsimile of Corpus Christi College MS 61* (Cambridge: Brewer, 1978), bears an excellent reproduction of the frontispiece, and Margaret Galway's article on the manuscript, "The *Troilus* Frontispiece," *MLR* 44 (1949): 161–77, offers a good-quality, full-color image facing page 161 of the text. See also Margaret Rickert, *Painting in Britain: The Middle Ages* (Baltimore: Penguin, 1954), plate 170, and O. Elfrida Saunders, *English Illumination* (1933; rpt. New York: Hacker, 1969), plate 129.

[2] Elizabeth Salter and Derek Pearsall provide a summary of eight different frontispiece models that would have been available as exemplars for the design of the *Troilus* frontispiece. Of these, five may have influenced the *Troilus* miniature: the first model, which portrays the author as a teacher, with the author lecturing from his text while a group of students, seated before him, follow the lecture by reading along in their own copies of the text; the third, "author as reader," with the author reading from an open book placed on a lectern before him; the fifth, which presents the author as a preacher, standing at a pulpit and addressing a listening audience; the seventh, in which the author is shown as the protégé of a patron, kneeling before his sponsor and presenting his work to him; and the eighth, in which the author could be represented in memorial fashion, portrayed in a famous scene from his life. See "Pictorial Illustration of Late Medieval Poetic Texts: The Role of the Frontispiece or Prefatory Picture," in *Medieval Iconography and Narrative: A Symposium* (Odense: Odense University Press, 1980), pp. 100–23, esp. pp. 115–16.

The origins and purpose of this intriguing portrait are shrouded in mystery, and scholars have taken the illustration as evidence to support a variety of contradictory positions. Its particular relation to the textual practices of Chaucer and his era remains a contentious issue, as does the question of the range of interpretations assignable to the performance that it depicts. Granted the referential importance of this unique illustration as demonstrative of key characteristics claimed for Chaucer and his literary milieu, the issues raised by this portrait continue to merit the scholar's attention.

The scarcity of records that might help researchers to draw a fuller picture of poetic activity during Chaucer's time is succinctly captured by Richard F. Green's observation that "amongst the nearly five hundred surviving Chaucer life-records edited by Crow and Olson, not a single one gives him the title of poet or links him with any kind of poetic activity, and the same would be true of almost all the documentary evidence collected on other household poets of the period."[3] In light of the paucity of available materials from which to cull evidence, it is hardly surprising that scholars have seized upon the *Troilus* frontispiece as a unique piece of documentation that can provide us with knowledge of an increasingly distant past. James McGregor, in a study of both the *Troilus* frontispiece and the Chaucer portrait accompanying Hoccleve's *De Regimine Principum,* points out that both illustrations "have long been objects of fascination. Each was created shortly after the death of the first great poet in English, and each promises to show us how he looked and how he presented his work to its first illustrious audience. . . . Not surprisingly, therefore, the use made of these pictures has always been documentary. . . . Yet the promise of these portraits has been uncertainly fulfilled."[4] This observation, now thirty years old, remains true today.

Interpreting the message of the frontispiece is complicated by the fact that the portrait is unique among miniatures depicting princes and poets, for it violates the well-established conventions for dedicatory miniatures.[5] Typical presentation pictures demonstrate a keen consciousness of role and status; they depict the poet, usually kneeling, before his prince, offering the prince his text. Emphasis falls upon the subservient

---

[3] Richard Firth Green, *Poets and Princepleasers: Literature and the English Court in the Late Middle Ages* (Toronto: University of Toronto Press, 1980), p. 6.

[4] James H. McGregor, "The Iconography of Chaucer in Hoccleve's *De Regimine Principum* and in the *Troilus* Frontispiece," *ChauR* 11 (1977): 338–50, quotation on 338.

[5] Ibid., p. 346.

role of the poet, and the dedicatory picture flatters and praises the prince for his scholarship, learning, or patronage. Seth Lerer summarizes the ways in which the *Troilus* frontispiece differs from other dedicatory pictures in its portrayal of the author: "Unlike his counterparts in the many presentation portraits that open medieval manuscripts, the poet is not kneeling before a king or patron but is elevated above his audience. He holds no book before him, and he is attired neither as a university clerk nor as an official servant, after the fashion of other author figures in vernacular texts."[6] For these reasons, the frontispiece has been resistant to any kind of critical consensus as to the meaning and proper interpretation of the scene depicted.

By its depiction of a richly dressed, fashionable, and presumably courtly audience, the frontispiece encourages us to consider its implications within a political, or perhaps rather, a politicized, context, so it is surprising that more scholars have not attempted to view the miniature from within a political framework. Margaret Galway has done so, but her view of a Ricardian provenance for the manuscript seems untenable in light of current estimates of the manuscript's age, which date it to the first quarter of the fifteenth century.[7] Both James McGregor and Seth Lerer situate the manuscript within a context of Chaucerian legacy construction during the reigns of the Lancastrian monarchs, and it is this context for the frontispiece that I wish to pursue further.

This essay will build on recent research to explore the possibility that this puzzling miniature may owe its iconography to a Henrician commission. While the name of Henry V has long been bandied about as a possible patron for the Corpus Christi *Troilus,* no serious study has yet considered the evidence that may serve to connect monarch and manuscript. While such an attribution remains, as it must, conjectural, current trends in scholarship lend credibility to the possibility that Henry originally bespoke the Corpus Christi *Troilus.* In contrast with theories

[6] Seth Lerer, *Chaucer and His Readers: Imagining the Author in Late Medieval England* (Princeton: Princeton University Press, 1993), p. 22.

[7] Like Galway, Aage Brusendorff claimed (*The Chaucer Tradition* [Oxford: Clarendon Press, 1925], p. 21) that we can "trace the history of the *Troilus* copy back to the reign of Richard II." Its composition can have been undertaken no earlier than 1385, the year in which Chaucer is thought to have completed *Troilus and Criseyde,* and it can have been completed no later than 1456, the year in which John Shirley, the first person who is definitely known to have handled the manuscript, died. On the basis of paleographical evidence, Parkes and Salter have proposed a date in the first quarter of the fifteenth century, and no evidence has arisen that would either refute their judgment or call it into question.

that have previously been put forth to account for the miniature's ico-nography, a Henrician commission best makes sense of the complexities embodied in the frontispiece illustration. If the manuscript originated in a Lancastrian commission, a compelling, coherent, and comprehensible narrative emerges that explains with striking clarity the function of the *Troilus* frontispiece: we discover that the miniature is most clearly expli-cable as a tool in the Lancastrian propaganda campaign for the promo-tion of English as the national language of England. In the discussion that follows, I will review briefly the various theories that have been posited to explain the frontispiece, identify the questions these theories have been unable to satisfactorily answer, and examine the reasons for believing that the manuscript may have originated in a royal commis-sion by Henry V.

Interpretations of the Frontispiece

Margaret Galway's study of the *Troilus* frontispiece, published in 1949, offers one of the earliest and most painstakingly detailed looks at the iconography of the prefatory illustration. She proposes that the illustra-tion should be read in a documentary sense, as a recollection of and as homage to a series of readings performed by Chaucer before the royal court. In Galway's view, Chaucer was most likely persuaded to under-take the writing of *Troilus and Criseyde* by Princess Joan, who intended the work as a wedding gift for Richard and Anne. Galway's study occu-pies an important position among analyses of the frontispiece, if only as an extreme against which other critics have reacted. Although she is not the only critic to have seen in the picture identifiable portraits of mem-bers of the court, James McGregor is not far from the mark when he comments that her identifications of the individuals pictured "have prompted universal skepticism."[8] On the other hand, however, most scholars agree that the man in the pulpit is most likely Chaucer (the rendering is not unlike other portraits of the poet) and that the finely dressed man who stands before him is Richard II.

Unlike Galway, for whom the historicity of the miniature is the key to unlocking its meaning, Laura Kendrick argues that it matters little whether the pictured performance ever took place; for Kendrick, the important issue is that such a performance could be conceived of as

[8] McGregor, "The Iconography of Chaucer," p. 346.

occurring. In her view, the illustration depicts a performance—not merely an oral reading or a recitation, but a dramatic enactment—of the story of Troilus and Criseyde before a fashionable audience.[9] She believes that the two standing figures placed near the pulpit in the frontispiece illustration are present not as spectators, but as actors in a drama. The elegant figure dressed in cloth of gold, whom others have identified as Richard II, is instead, in Kendrick's opinion, an actor miming the part of Troilus while the poet declaims the text from his pulpit.

Seth Lerer suggests a third view of the frontispiece, in which the position of the poet in the picture is central to an interpretation of the significance of the image's iconography. Lerer notes that the picture "shows the author not as subject {to his patron} but as center, elevated among his presumably royal audience. With his golden hair and rich brocade, Chaucer is himself an aureate figure, and the gold trimmings and bright colors of his audience" idealize the occasion as an event appropriate to a golden age of poetry.[10] Like Lerer, James McGregor sees the *Troilus* frontispiece as participating in the construction of a Chaucerian legacy; McGregor, however, describes this legacy not primarily as literary and poetic, but rather as political. He finds a similar principle at work in the Chaucer portrait that accompanies Hoccleve's *De Regimine Principum:* in his view, both elevate the poet, depicting him "as royal counselor, and {they} suggest that in this role the first poet of English plays his most important part."[11] McGregor reasons that although Chaucer did not make any direct contributions to the "advice to princes" genre, the impulse to honor and promote him by associating him with such a role is understandable.[12]

A fifth theory that has been advanced to explain the meaning of the *Troilus* frontispiece views the illustration as borrowing or adapting its iconography from "preaching" pictures. Intriguingly, scholars who have advanced such arguments have also typically cautioned against allowing the miniature evidentiary value as a depiction of Chaucer's audience and

[9] She sets forth this argument in *Chaucerian Play: Comedy and Control in the Canterbury Tales* (Berkeley and Los Angeles: University of California Press, 1988); see particularly pp. 163–70.

[10] Lerer, *Chaucer,* p. 54.

[11] McGregor, "Iconography," p. 349.

[12] Nevertheless, both *The Monk's Tale* and *Melibee* can be considered as narratives intended to provide "advice to princes." Green has argued that there is a "strong" likelihood that *Melibee* was written early in the reign of Richard II, specifically for the benefit of the young monarch (*Poets and Princepleasers,* p. 143).

of the mode of "publication" or delivery of his literary works.[13] Derek Pearsall expresses concern that the *Troilus* frontispiece may be misread as an indication that Chaucer functioned as a poet of the court. Although willing to grant that Chaucer may have been in the habit of sometimes reading his poetry aloud to a listening audience, Pearsall hastens to remind us that "there seems no reason to suppose that this listening audience was always or ever that of the *Troilus* frontispiece."[14] But in his haste to dissociate Chaucer from a courtly context, Pearsall dismisses the evidence too lightly: while the frontispiece cannot provide *proof* of the nature of Chaucer's audience, it does at least provide "reason to suppose" that his audience *may* have been akin to the one pictured.

The most recent theory concerning the manuscript's provenance comes from Kathleen Scott, who has suggested that Corpus Christi College Cambridge MS 61 may be traceable to the commission of a particular individual—in this case, Charles d'Orléans.[15] Scott suggests a motivation for the depiction of Chaucer with which the *Troilus* frontispiece presents us: Charles, as a poet himself and as a follower of Chaucer, may have found attractive the idea of picturing himself as being addressed by the poet or as standing at Chaucer's feet.[16] Scott's theory also

---

[13] Derek Brewer, for example, in *"Troilus and Criseyde,"* in *The Middle Ages,* ed. W. F. Bolton (London: Barrie and Jenkins, 1970), pp. 195–228, accounts for the illustration as "a product of the poem's power to create the sense of a listening group" (196). Similarly, V. J. Scattergood accounts for the choice of a preaching-picture exemplar on the basis that "a refashioned 'preaching' picture was the closest approximation the artist could find to communicate the myth of oral delivery, the sense of a listening group that Chaucer cultivates in the poem itself." See V. J. Scattergood and A. W. Sherbourne, *English Court Culture in the Later Middle Ages* (New York: St. Martin's Press, 1983), p. 31. Derek Pearsall argues that the picture is "fully explicable from within the poem. . . . [I]t represents as a reality the myth of delivery that Chaucer cultivates so assiduously in the poem, with his references to 'al this compaignye' of lovers 'in this place.' " See "The *Troilus* Frontispiece and Chaucer's Audience," *YES* 7 (1977): 68–74 (73).

[14] Ibid., p. 73. This consistent preference for "literary myth" over the possibility of the poem's being intended for oral performance would seem to contradict Pearsall's admission that Chaucer may have been in the habit of performing his poems orally before an audience. Although it was once fashionable to think of Chaucer, and especially of Caxton, as ushering in the era of silent reading, this view has increasingly been replaced by an understanding that stresses the endurance of oral presentation as a mode of experiencing texts in the late Middle Ages and beyond. See, for example, Joyce Coleman, *Public Reading and the Reading Public in Late Medieval England and France,* Cambridge Studies in Medieval Literature 26 (Cambridge: Cambridge University Press, 1996), and *Performing Medieval Narrative,* ed. Evelyn Birge Vitz, Nancy Freeman Regalado, and Marilyn Lawrence (Rochester, N.Y.: Brewer, 2005).

[15] See Kathleen Scott, "Limner-Power: A Book Artist in England *c.* 1420," in *Prestige, Authority, and Power in Late Medieval Manuscripts and Texts,* ed. Felicity Riddy (Rochester, N.Y.: York Medieval Press, 2000), pp. 55–75.

[16] Although the point is important to Scott's argument, the degree to which Charles deserves to be styled a "follower" of Chaucer remains debatable. Julia Boffey situates Charles's English poetry in connection with "courtly poets writing in English in a tradi-

allows her to account for the incomplete state of the manuscript on the basis of the change in Charles's fortunes in 1417, when English preparations for a further invasion of France caused Henry to place Charles under increased security at Pontefract Castle in Yorkshire.

The theories considered above, however, all leave unanswered one or more key questions about this intriguing miniature. First, this unusual frontispiece challenges us with the question, *Why* portray Chaucer (and, presumably, Richard II) in such a manner? While all of the theories discussed above grapple with this question in one way or another, the variety of conflicting interpretations that have been advanced reveal that none of these explanations has been sufficiently compelling in order to command a general critical consensus. More problematic perhaps is the question of why there is no book before a Chaucer who is presumably reading his text to a listening audience. Although Kendrick "solves" this problem by asserting that Chaucer simply declaims his text in accompaniment to a presumably mimed performance, the question of why he should declaim rather than read remains unanswered.

The final and perhaps most compelling unanswered question is the matter of whose purposes would best be served by a depiction elevating the poet over his monarch. Who would dare to commission a portrayal that so flagrantly violated the sanctioned and accepted notions of class and status? Who had a need to promote Chaucer's authority in so vigorous a fashion? And, finally, why and how should the figure usually thought to be Richard II, preserved in a deluxe and presumably treasured volume, have come to be defaced?[17] These questions can best be answered by locating the picture in its proper political context, a Lancastrian one. Doing so clarifies both its purposes and its early history and reveals that a coherent and comprehensible strategy underlies the anomalies that have served to make the *Troilus* frontispiece an object of pecu-

---

tion which was saturated with French precedents, but [which] was also, by the early to mid-fifteenth century, alive to Chaucer's example and to the possibilities of a vernacular literary tradition." See Julia Boffey, "Charles of Orleans Reading Chaucer's Dream Visions," in *Mediaevalitas: Reading the Middle Ages,* ed. Piero Boitani and Anna Torti, The J. A. W. Bennett Memorial Lectures, 9th ser. (Cambridge: Brewer, 1996), pp. 43–62 (43). Although Chaucerian echoes can be found in Charles's English poems, Boffey concedes that there are "difficulties in unraveling the nature of Charles's possible Chaucerian debt" (pp. 46–47); given the extensive borrowing, reworking, and influencing common among authors of this period, "Chaucerian" influences may have found their way into Charles's work through a variety of mediating sources. David Fein's study, *Charles d'Orléans* (Boston: Twayne, 1983), scarcely mentions Chaucer.

[17] Arguments that this is *not* Richard II must still account for the obvious importance of the figure depicted, who appears to be noble, and must confront the problem of Chaucer's elevation above him.

liar interest and fascination both to art historians and to literary scholars.

Qualifications of the Ideal Patron

As M. B. Parkes and Elizabeth Salter have explained, the early history of the manuscript containing the frontispiece is "obscure."[18] It is not surprising, therefore, that few scholars have attempted to argue a case for a particular individual as the probable commissioner of the manuscript; those who have discussed the *Troilus* frontispiece have accounted for the miniature as a product of the artist's interpretive response to the text. But as Sandra Hindman has shown,[19] programs of illustration were usually provided by an educated advisor, not planned by the limners themselves, whose roles were confined to a mastery of the skills of their craft. Almost certainly, then, the depiction of Chaucer in a public presentation before a royal audience is owed not to the manuscript's illustrator but to someone closer to its commissioner, with a clearer understanding of the reasons for which such a deluxe volume was sought and of the purposes to be served by the manuscript's illustration.

The uniqueness of the design of the frontispiece attests to particular purposes and intentions that might have revealed themselves more clearly and immediately had the original program of illustration planned for the manuscript been carried out to its completion.[20] Had the Corpus Christi *Troilus* been completed according to the illustration scheme suggested by the blanks for miniatures and in line with the quality embodied in the frontispiece illustration, it would, we can reasonably assume, have constituted one of the finest English manuscripts that the early fifteenth century could boast. "Unprecedented" is the word that best bespeaks its quality among Chaucer manuscripts; as Parkes and Salter observe:

No other Chaucer manuscript contains such an elaborate prefatory miniature; even the copy of *Troilus and Criseyde,* made for Henry V while still Prince of

---

[18] Parkes and Salter, *Troilus and Criseyde,* p. 11.

[19] Sandra L. Hindman, "The Roles of Author and Artist in the Procedure of Illustrating Late Medieval Texts," in *Text and Image,* ed. David W. Burchmore (Binghamton, N.Y.: Center for Medieval and Early Renaissance Studies, 1986), pp. 27–62.

[20] Scholars differ as to the precise number of miniatures envisioned for the manuscript, but a representative estimate is provided by Parkes and Salter (*Troilus and Criseyde,* p. 4), who set the number at ninety.

Wales, has nothing comparable. And the quality of the only extensive illustrative materials provided for the *Canterbury Tales* (in the Ellesmere and Cambridge University Library Gg.4.27 MSS, for instance) serves to throw into high relief the unique circumstance recorded by Corpus Christi MS.61: the introduction of a medieval English poem by an exceptional piece of international Gothic painting.[21]

Although we lack specific details that would identify for us the person who commissioned this unique work of art, the manuscript itself provides insight into some of the issues surrounding its origin. Parkes and Salter assert that we can be "reasonably confident, from the purity of its text and the unusually high standard of its prefatory picture[,] that the circumstances were informed by a proper understanding of what may have been due not only to the patron but also to the poem and, retrospectively, to its author."[22] The manuscript itself, by its remarkable quality, limits the range of patrons whom we may reasonably imagine to possess both the motivation and the means for acquiring it.

Elizabeth Salter and Derek Pearsall have attempted to provide a context that allows for both the quality of the manuscript and the nature of its frontispiece:

The richness of its specific recall of a whole range of courtly and aristocratic illustrated manuscripts, made in French workshops between 1380 and 1415 for a number of famous continental patrons, . . . suggests that it cannot be isolated from the lavish courtly circumstance to which it gives expression. If we believe that the *de luxe* quality of the Corpus Christi College copy of Chaucer's poem demands our acceptance of an original patronal situation of some importance, then it is also tempting to believe that the frontispiece commemorates an early fifteenth century sense of the poet's relationship to the courtly society of the preceding century, and the prestige enjoyed by his poetry. It need not, and no doubt, does not, record a special historical moment but, in the very care which was obviously taken with its ordering and design, it may still pay tribute to a historical reputation, fostered, as we know, "this side idolatry" throughout the fifteenth century. . . . [W]e may well look for a patron among those aristocratic families who would have had the strongest reasons for preserving traditions concerning the life, both literary and official, of Geoffrey Chaucer.[23]

[21] Parkes and Salter, *Troilus and Criseyde,* p. 15.
[22] Ibid., p. 22.
[23] Salter and Pearsall, "Pictorial Illustration," pp. 111–13.

The comments of Parkes, Salter, and Pearsall help to clarify and to define the patronal contexts among which one should look for the commissioner or possessor of the Corpus Christi *Troilus*. We must seek a patron of some importance, wealthy enough to afford the manuscript; someone interested in the story of Troilus and Criseyde; someone willing to exalt Chaucer's status, even though such exaltation comes at the expense of violating accepted social hierarchies; someone with a connection to and interest in bookmaking in the Continental, and particularly, in the French tradition; and someone with a strong reason for promoting the reputation of Geoffrey Chaucer.

Additional factors might help to strengthen the identification of a conjectural patron. The ideal commissioner would be someone who, in addition to meeting the above qualifications, could also provide a plausible reason for the incomplete state of the manuscript's illustrative program, someone who, during the period of the manuscript's production, had undergone a change in life circumstances sufficiently significant to require calling a halt to the work in progress on the manuscript. In addition, our ideal patron would help us account for the patterns of ownership once the manuscript had passed from his or her hands: we should seek a person from among those known to have connections with the people, or at least with the circles, to whom the manuscript later passed. Finally, the identification of an ideal patron requires that we posit a situation in which the scenario that the frontispiece depicts comes to be less valued than it was by its original owner. Indeed, so violent is the dislike on the part of some subsequent owner of the manuscript that it results in the defacement of the figure in cloth of gold.

The Case for a Henrician Commission

Henry V fits all of the criteria that we can construct for the ideal patron who commissioned the Corpus Christi College *Troilus*. We know that the expense of the manuscript would have been within the means of the royal coffers, and we know, too, that Henry V was familiar with and valued Chaucer's tale. In fact, Henry, as Prince of Wales, "owned one of the earliest and best copies of Chaucer's *Troilus and Criseyde* (Pierpont Morgan Library MS M.817)"; interestingly, it is "the only extant Chaucer manuscript for which we can prove royal ownership" during this period.[24] In style and elegance, it reveals some of the same features that

[24] Jeanne E. Krochalis, "The Books and Reading of Henry V and his Circle," *ChauR* 23 (1988–89): 50–77 (50).

214

characterize the Corpus Christi *Troilus:* the manuscript "is carefully and beautifully designed and written, with borders for every prologue and book, and a miniature on the opening leaf. The text is excellent."[25] Even so, it cannot compare to the fineness of the quality of the Corpus Christi *Troilus.* At about the time Henry acquired the Pierpont manuscript, he commissioned John Lydgate to write his *Troy Book.* These early commissions evidence his interest in Trojan history and in tales of heroic romance.

The Lancastrian kings differ from their predecessors on the English throne in terms of the languages represented in their collections of books. Richard II's library consisted largely of volumes in French and Latin; English was virtually unrepresented. Henry IV, however, appreciated literature in both French and English. Both Hoccleve and Chaucer addressed works to him—primarily complaints, however, rather than lengthier texts. Gower, disillusioned, it would seem, by Richard II, turned instead to Henry Bolingbroke, re-dedicating the *Confessio Amantis* to him in 1393, before Henry came to the throne, and addressing his Latin *Vox clamantis* to him in the same year as well.

In the absence of more definitive records one cannot say for certain, but Jeanne Krochalis points out that "Henry V is the first English king to suggest the possibility of a royal library." His will bequeathed a variety of holdings, including works on law, theology, sermons, and meditational literature, to institutions elsewhere, leaving to his infant son texts such as the "Bible, history, romances, prayerbooks . . . with many volumes in all fields in English." Like his father before him, Henry V demonstrates a bilingual interest in books: "Though he clearly read in French, and commissioned works from French authors, there is also a steady stream of works in English—mostly in verse—which he commissioned or read: Scogan, Duke Edward, Hoccleve, Chaucer, Lydgate, all attracted his patronage."[26] Unlike their predecessors, the Lancastrian kings demonstrate an interest in acquiring texts written in the vernacular.

The Incomplete Program of Illustration

Not only does Henry V evince an interest in acquiring and encouraging literature in the vernacular, but his life circumstances would also ac-

[25] Ibid., p. 63.
[26] Ibid., p. 69.

count for the incomplete state of CCCC MS 61's illustrative program. As A. S. G. Edwards and Derek Pearsall have pointed out, any number of factors could account for the absence of the planned miniatures;[27] for example, the commissioner of the manuscript may have run short of funds. Perhaps less plausibly, Edwards and Pearsall also suggest that the illustrative program may have called for resources beyond the reach of the atelier from which the work was commissioned: suitable exemplars for the proposed series of illustrations could not be found. While we cannot wholly dismiss such an explanation, we must recognize its improbability: any bookseller wishing to make a profit from such a luxurious venture as the volume in question is unlikely to have promised so extensive a pictorial program while undertaking the risk, indeed, the probability, of alienating his patron through failure to fulfill the work that had been contracted.[28]

Third, Edwards and Pearsall suggest that the patron may have been in no hurry to have the illustration of the manuscript completed; having obtained the highly satisfactory frontispiece, he or she may have reasoned that the missing pictures could be supplied at any time they were desired. Such an understanding of the reason for the manuscript's incompletion offers us a theory that is neither provable nor disprovable and that, if it is correct, offers us no assistance in identifying, or even in narrowing down, the potential field of candidates for the manuscript's unknown patron.

Finally, we may surmise that the manuscript owes its unfinished state neither to economic reversal, artistic incapacity, nor patronal lack of interest, but rather, to the death of the person who commissioned the work. For such a situation there is, at least, historical precedent.[29] In fact, when scholars have attempted to link Henry V with the Corpus Christi *Troilus,* it has usually been the date of his death, rather than any further consideration, that has led to the mention of his name: the year

[27] Anthony S. G. Edwards and Derek Pearsall, "The Manuscripts of the Major English Poetic Texts," in *Book Production and Publishing in Britain, 1375–1475,* ed. Jeremy Griffiths and Derek Pearsall (Cambridge: Cambridge University Press, 1989), pp. 257–78.

[28] On the other hand, if we accept this explanation for the absence of further illustration in the *Troilus* manuscript, we might be tempted to imagine that the publisher offered, in compensation for his inability to produce the lavish program of illustration that apparently had been planned, to preface the volume instead with a miniature of the finest quality.

[29] The most famous manuscript for which we know that work was abandoned upon the death of the patron is the *Très riches heures* of the Duc de Berry.

of Henry's death, 1422, fits well the current view that the manuscript and its illustration date to the first quarter of the fifteenth century. A. I. Doyle, for example, attempting to account for the manuscript's pictorial omissions, states that "Henry V's unexpected death might be an explanation, even though he may have had the Pierpont Morgan manuscript of the same poem."[30]

A Leaning Toward the French

In their discussion of possible owners or commissioners of the manuscript, Parkes and Salter remark that "the unique nature of the miniature in the context of early fifteenth-century English art suggests . . . that our search should concentrate upon families whose connections with France, during those years [1400–1425], were particularly close, and whose taste for French book-painting was particularly strong."[31] According to Salter, the artistic influences on the miniature are decidedly French: both the "immediate [and] the ultimate influences upon the stylistic modes of the miniature" are to be found "in that Parisian work of the late fourteenth and early fifteenth centuries to which so many brilliant Italian and Flemish artists contributed."[32]

Kathleen Scott concurs in finding the *Troilus* illuminator, whom she calls the "Corpus Master," to have received French training, and her recent research allows us to establish certain additional factors regarding his career. She suggests that this unidentified artist was most likely English, but trained by a French artist familiar with certain aspects of English book illustration, particularly border design.[33] Scott's research on the work of this unknown English artist leads her to conclude that he seems to have been able to command a particular type of patron— that is, to exercise some power over the scope of his craft. We can consider first the manuscripts in which his influence has been identified, and then what distinctions emerge in regard to the commissioners of these works.

[30] A. I. Doyle, "English Books In and Out of Court from Edward III to Henry VII," in *English Court Culture in the Later Middle Ages,* ed. V. J. Scattergood and A. W. Sherbourne (New York: St. Martin's Press, 1983), pp. 163–81 (175). Doyle's suggestion presupposes a Henrician commission, but Doyle neither draws out nor pursues this implication.

[31] Parkes and Salter, *Troilus and Criseyde,* p. 23.

[32] Ibid., pp. 19, 21.

[33] Scott, "Limner-Power," p. 56.

In addition to the frontispiece for the Corpus Christi College *Troilus,* the Corpus Master produced the illustration in a copy of John de Burgh's *Pupilla oculi,* preserved in Longleat House MS 24, as well as the illumination of British Library MS Royal 8.Giii, the *Compendium super Bibliam* of Petrus de Aureolis. Four other manuscripts also point to involvement by this illuminator: Scott argues that Bodleian Library MS Auct.f.inf.1.1 and British Library manuscripts Cotton Claudius D.i and Cotton Nero C.vi all reflect either "late work by the 'Corpus Master'" or "work together with an assistant trained under his direction."[34] Finally, Scott finds traces of his influence in Paris, Bibliothèque Nationale MS lat. 1196.

As regards patrons, what do these six manuscripts suggest? The first, Longleat House 24, appears to have been commissioned by three patrons, all of whom suggest associations with the Lancastrians and with France. Three coats of arms once appeared on the bottom of the introductory leaf of the manuscript,[35] but the most intriguing emblem is the one that is absent: the coat of arms that once occupied the central position on the opening leaf has been thoroughly erased. This missing coat of arms, occupying the position of greatest importance and prestige in the manuscript, has recently been identified by Kate Harris as belonging to Henry Scrope, third baron Scrope of Masham.[36] The implication of Scrope in the commission adds an unmistakably Lancastrian connection to the enterprise, not to mention a spicy dose of political intrigue.

Although Scrope, a Knight of the Garter, had enjoyed the confidence of both Henry IV and Henry V, serving for a time as treasurer and taking part in delicate diplomatic missions, he lost his life through his involvement with the Southampton Plot. On 5 August 1415, Scrope was executed for his complicity in the plan to depose Henry V and to

[34] Ibid., p. 67.

[35] On the left-hand are the arms of Robert FitzHugh, who served successively as canon at York, archdeacon of Northampton, and bishop of London. The coat of arms on the right belongs to Richard Holme, who served as canon both at Salisbury and York. Holme's insignia helps to establish a Lancastrian connection for the manuscript, since Holme served in a variety of capacities throughout the reign of Henry IV: as envoy to the French, in the years 1400–1402; as a member of the king's council, from 1408; and as envoy to the Duke of Burgundy, in the years 1412–13.

[36] See Kate Harris, "The Patronage and Dating of Longleat House MS 24," in *Prestige, Authority, and Power in Late Medieval Manuscripts and Texts,* ed. Felicity Riddy (Rochester, N.Y.: York Medieval Press, 2000), pp. 35–54. Kathleen Scott disputes Harris's identification of Henry Scrope. She offers an alternative bearer of the arms: Stephen Scrope, second baron Scrope of Masham and brother to Henry.

place on the throne in his stead Edmund Mortimer, fifth Earl of March.[37] Scrope's goods were confiscated by the crown; it is conceivable, though by no means certain, that the work of the Corpus Master could have come to the attention of the king as a result of the seizure of Scrope's valuables.[38]

The *Compendium super Bibliam* was commissioned by Philip Repingdon, "sometime supporter of John Wyclif, four times chancellor of Oxford, bishop of Lincoln and longtime friend and confessor to Henry IV."[39] Via Repingdon, the Corpus Master's work in this manuscript brings him into close connection with the Lancastrian throne, and Repingdon's Oxford connections also offer an important link to the circles of influence that seem to come closest to the *Troilus* manuscript as well.

The next three manuscripts, Bodleian Library MS Auct.f.inf.1.1 and British Library manuscripts Cotton Claudius D.i and Cotton Nero C.vi, share a single patron and cover a twenty-year period, 1420–40. All three were commissioned by John Whetehamstede, who served as abbot of St. Albans in the years to which these manuscripts date. Whetehamstede's connections with the Lancastrian regime are at a further remove from those of the commissioners of the other texts,[40] and yet the available evidence is suggestive. Whetehamstede had close connections to the abbey of Bury St. Edmunds and, in particular, to the poetry of John Lydgate, whom he engaged to write the *Lives of Saints Alban and Amphibal.* Whetehamstede was on good terms with the Lancastrian regime, and Lydgate, as it is generally agreed, was an important figure in Lancastrian politics and propaganda and a key player in efforts to elevate the status of Geoffrey Chaucer.[41]

[37] See T. B. Pugh, *Henry V and the Southampton Plot of 1415,* Southampton Record Series 30 (Southampton: Southampton University Press, 1988); for details of Scrope's involvement, see particularly pp. 109–21. These events are dramatized by Shakespeare in *Henry V,* 2.2.94–143.

[38] How closely Henry V, himself on the brink of departure for France, concerned himself with the disposal of the goods belonging to a former intimate remains uncertain, but the king did order their seizure and must have given some direction as to their redistribution as (unlike the case of fellow conspirators Cambridge and Grey), Scrope's goods were not permitted to remain within his family circle. See Christopher Allmand, *Henry V* (Berkeley and Los Angeles: University of California Press, 1992), p. 77.

[39] Scott, "Limner-Power," p. 63.

[40] Since these manuscripts date, on the whole, to the rule in minority of Henry VI, we should not expect the same degree of direct connection to the court as was possible during the reigns of the two preceding monarchs.

[41] See, for example, Paul Strohm's discussion in *England's Empty Throne: Usurpation and the Language of Legitimation, 1399–1422* (New Haven: Yale University Press, 1998), especially pp. 186–91, as well as his "Hoccleve, Lydgate, and the Lancastrian Court," in *The Cambridge History of Medieval English Literature,* ed. David Wallace (Cambridge:

I shall consider last, and out of its proper time sequence, the ownership and commissioning of Bibliothèque Nationale MS lat. 1196, since it serves as the basis for Scott's conjectures regarding the provenance of the *Troilus* frontispiece and thus is of particular interest to this study. This Book of Prayers was produced for Charles d'Orléans "probably in London, certainly after 1415 and probably before 1424, this is, after he had become a hostage at Agincourt and before he entered on a period of extreme hardship in captivity."[42]

However, the relationship of the Corpus Master to the artistry of Charles's Book of Prayers remains uncertain, at least more so than does the artist's association with the other manuscripts mentioned above, as Scott herself is careful to point out. Bibliothèque Nationale MS lat. 1196, Scott observes, "was illustrated by four artists, none of whom was the MS Corpus 61 Master, and was decorated by eleven border artists, one of whom was, I think, likely to be the Corpus Master."[43] Scott conjectures that Charles, in the early years of his captivity in England, may have imported to England from France illuminators of his own choice, including the Corpus Master, whom he employed, among others, in the decoration of his prayer book. He then retained the artist's services for work on the *Troilus* manuscript.[44]

Cambridge University Press, 1999), pp. 640–61, and Lee Patterson, "Making Identities in Fifteenth-Century England," in *New Historical Literary Study: Essays on Reproducing Texts, Representing History,* ed. Jeffrey N. Cox and Larry J. Reynolds (Princeton: Princeton University Press, 1993), pp. 69–107. For a challenge to the view of Lydgate as Lancastrian propagandist, see Scott-Morgan Straker in "Propaganda, Intentionality, and the Lancastrian Regime," in *John Lydgate: Poetry, Culture, and Lancastrian England,* ed. Larry Scanlon and James Simpson (Notre Dame: University of Notre Dame Press, 2006), pp. 98–128. For a survey of the contours of scholarship on this issue, see Nigel Mortimer, *John Lydgate's* Fall of Princes: *Narrative Tragedy in Its Literary and Political Contexts* (Oxford: Clarendon Press, 2005), pp. 51–52.

[42] Scott, "Limner-Power," p. 73. This increased hardship refers to the unusual decision reached by the king's council, in a meeting on 26 January 1424, to discontinue funding the upkeep in captivity of Charles and to require him to bear his own expenses for maintenance. (A similar constraint was laid at this time upon another French prisoner taken at the battle of Agincourt, John, Duke of Bourbon.) These expenses served only to complicate a financial picture that was already bleak: since the treaty of Buzançais, signed in November 1412, Charles had been under obligation to render to the English, whose assistance he had sought, a sum of 210,000 gold *écus.* As surety for this payment, Charles had been obliged to surrender up not merely valuables but a number of hostages, among them his younger brother, John of Angoulême, then twelve. Despite regular efforts to raise funds both prior to and during his captivity, Charles had not yet supplied sufficient payment to ransom his brother.

[43] Ibid., p. 73.

[44] Scott's theory presents certain difficulties. First, we know that work on the Book of Prayers continued during the years 1415–24, and Charles seems to have had ample access to limners at this time, since some fifteen different artists had a hand in the

Charles may indeed have brought artisans to England, but Scott's reconstruction of the Corpus Master's career requires that we accept the erased coat of arms on Longleat House MS 24 as having belonged to Stephen, rather than to Henry, Scrope. This identification is necessary if one is to accept the timeline that Scott proposes: Henry Scrope, executed prior to the battle of Agincourt, cannot have commissioned a manuscript containing artwork by a limner who was present in England only after the battle. But this identification does not help us to understand whose purposes would have been served by the removal of the central coat of arms from the Longleat manuscript; that mystery resolves itself much more satisfactorily if one accepts Harris's identification of Henry as the Scrope concerned.

A Lancastrian Agenda

The idea of Charles d'Orléans as the commissioner of the *Troilus* manuscript does provide us with a patron whose links with France are direct and unquestioned, but he is not the only candidate who fits such requirements. In this regard, Henry V is an equally plausible candidate: his interests in and connections to French culture are well known and well documented. His incursions into France were most likely those of a political opportunist, but they bespeak an emergent English nationalism as well. Henry's response to the political instability in France[45] re-

---

illustration of this text. Thus, the continuance of the prayer-book project does not seem to suggest that the illustration of the *Troilus* manuscript need have been abandoned in this same period. Second, if Charles commissioned the Corpus Christi *Troilus* for his own use while in captivity, why, we must wonder, did he request so deluxe a display copy of the text? Why not commission a work on a smaller scale, one that in style and size would be more suitable for everyday use? Finally, *Troilus and Criseyde* differs from the majority of the nearly one hundred texts that Charles had in possession while in captivity. The unifying feature of these works, Enid McLeod explains, is their seriousness; among them we find "no romances and no classical authors except for Seneca"; seven treatises on medicine; some works of the "advice to princes" genre; and, predominantly, works of a religious nature. The two texts that he is known to have commissioned in England are both religious works; in addition to the Book of Prayers, Charles commissioned Bibliothèque Nationale MS lat. 1201, a work comprised largely of extracts from Saint Bernard, Saint Augustine, Hugh of St. Victor, and John of Hovendene. See Enid McLeod, *Charles of Orleans: Prince and Poet* (New York: Viking Press, 1970).

[45] As V. J. Scattergood, in *Politics and Poetry in the Fifteenth Century* (London: Blandford, 1971), explains: "At the beginning of the [fifteenth] century the French political scene was one of extreme disorder. The central rule of Charles VI, who suffered from fits of insanity, was weak, and the princes of the royal family, his uncles, brothers and nephews, vied for authority in the court. . . . They differed on practically every aspect of policy, including their attitudes towards the English. . . . Matters came to a head in 1407, when John the Fearless had Louis [of Orleans] murdered in the streets of Paris by paid agents" (p. 47).

flects his shrewdness and his determination to achieve French influence: from the time he reached the throne, he "showed himself ready to negotiate with Charles VI and enter the French royal house by a marriage with the Princess Catherine; he was prepared to form an alliance with John the Fearless; and at the same time he made preparations for war."[46] He realized his ambitions militarily, gaining, by the Treaty of Troyes, not only the hand of Catherine in marriage, but the guarantee of the union of England and France under the English crown upon the death of Charles VI.

In light of Henry's aggressive stance toward obtaining a foothold in France, the *Troilus* frontispiece emerges as a visual and material statement of Henry's Continental ambitions. A. I. Doyle reflects that the manuscript, with its prefatory illustration, "is the clearest attempt to emulate the standard and style of early fifteenth-century books for the French court."[47] As such, the Corpus Christi *Troilus* offers a skillful blending of some of the highest literary and artistic achievements of both French and English culture, just as the king proposed to unite them under the English crown: the use of a French style of illumination with English content, a content that involves an English poet, speaking in English, to an English audience. Thus, the manuscript and its prefatory illustration blend two cultures, but, in keeping with Henry's emergent nationalism, it is English literature and English culture that are highlighted.

Few scholars have concerned themselves with the problem of why the miniature should choose to elevate, literally and therefore symbolically, the poet over his sovereign. Laura Kendrick, however, calls attention to this unusual status reversal. For Kendrick, the violation of established hierarchies that is implied in the elevation of Chaucer over the monarch virtually rules out the possibility that the richly attired figure could be the sovereign; for a society dominated by stringent conceptions of class, status, and role, the miniature's positioning of poet above prince constitutes a reversal of the typical positions of authority, which Kendrick finds "extremely daring—indeed, I think, too daring."[48] This conviction of the problem involved in the power relationships displayed leads her

---

[46] Ibid., p. 48.

[47] Doyle, "English Books," p. 175.

[48] Kendrick, *Chaucerian Play*, p. 163. This argument, if one grants its validity, would also tend to militate against the view that Charles d'Orléans would have chosen to depict himself as subservient to Chaucer, his social inferior.

to conclude that the figure over whom Chaucer towers cannot be Richard II: whereas the elevation of the poet over his peers might constitute an acceptable statement, the elevation of the poet over his prince would be unacceptable both on social and political grounds.

Henry V, however, had good reason to wish to elevate the status of Chaucer, and he also emerges as the one person who might most logically dare and desire to appropriate the image of Richard II and to subjugate him to his own particular purposes. Whatever Richard II's shortcomings as a monarch may have been, Henry Bolingbroke's seizure of the crown, however justified or justifiable, never constituted a universally popular act. Domestic discord and political uprisings periodically troubled the reign of Henry IV, and his son inherited this legacy from his father when he came to the throne in 1413. As his military maneuvers in France demonstrate, Henry V was a decisive ruler in terms of setting and acting on policy. A similar shrewdness and decisiveness manifests itself in his efforts to manage the legacy of Richard II's disenthronement and death in a manner that Henry IV could not credibly have managed, even had he sensed that such acts might prove politically expedient. Having Richard's body exhumed from King's Langley and reburied in greater honor in Westminster was most likely an act calculated to deflect criticism aimed at him by Ricardian supporters and to obtain greater public support and sympathy for the Lancastrian cause. By attempting to ease and smooth over tensions from the past, Henry V could hope to open up opportunities for his own brighter future.[49]

Henry's reburial of Richard's body suggests something of his attitude toward his former sovereign. Not content merely to let the legacy of the past stand as it had been left by his father, Henry calculated that a public act designed to bestow honor and dignity upon Richard need not have been wholly destabilizing to his own rule; instead, he must have imagined, it might help to bring stability and greater popularity to the Lancastrian regime. While others might have advised him to "let sleeping dogs lie," Henry risked the chance of a renewed outpouring of public sympathy for Richard's cause, a sympathy that could easily have

---

[49] Paul Strohm's *England's Empty Throne* provides an in-depth look at Lancastrian strategies for managing the legacy of Richard II, a spectral presence that continued to haunt and threaten Lancastrian claims to legitimacy. Within the ideological framework suggested by Strohm, the *Troilus* frontispiece could easily stand as one of "those officially sponsored symbolizations and enactments by which the Lancastrian monarchs sought to dominate their subjects' political imagination" (p. 2).

reopened the wounds felt by many upon Bolingbroke's seizure of the throne. The precise effect of Richard's reburial upon the Lancastrian grip on power remains conjectural, but it was accomplished without rioting in the streets and without instigating a mass uprising against the Lancastrians. Whether it gained additional respect for Henry V as the legitimate ruler of England remains unknown.[50]

What this incident does clearly demonstrate is that Henry V was not afraid to resurrect the legacy of Richard II and use his body to serve his own political purposes. Strictly speaking, it is difficult to imagine that someone who wished to honor Richard would commission the *Troilus* frontispiece with the sovereign placed elsewhere than in the dominant position of honor and authority. The miniature proclaims plainly enough that it was commissioned by someone to whose cause Chaucer was more important than Richard; this fact alone helps to narrow down the ring of persons whom one may reasonably suspect of having commissioned the work. Thus, that the miniature was requested by a political partisan of Richard seems highly implausible. We could, on the other hand, postulate its having been ordered by some especially enthusiastic and wealthy admirer of Chaucer, but we must ask whether even such fanatical devotion could account for the visual elevation of the poet above his sovereign in the miniature. Chaucer's status, pictorially speaking, could just as easily, and far more acceptably, have been signaled simply by granting him, within the context of the illustration, audience with the king. To place Chaucer below the monarch, or even at the king's own level, would just as effectively, and again, more acceptably, have signaled the poet's importance to the realm. When we ask who would have had both the audacity and the motive to position the main characters in the scene like so many pawns on a chess board, the Lancastrian circle immediately suggests itself as harboring the most likely perpetrators of such politically opportunistic manipulation. The positioning of an image of a living Richard in the static tableau of the *Troilus* frontispiece mimics, mirrors, and reenacts the statement made by Henry V's relocation of Richard's body to Westminster: the image and memory of the dead King Richard are thus exploited to further the art and purposes of Lancastrian self-promotion and national consolidation.

[50] Nigel Saul places the reburial in a favorable light, calling it "a useful symbolic way of healing the wounds that had been opened up by his father's usurpation." See *The Three Richards: Richard I, Richard II, and Richard III* (New York: Hambledon and London, 2005), p. 65.

The Uses of Chaucer

Scholars agree that the *Troilus* frontispiece accords Chaucer an exalted status; the illustration elevates the poet, both literally and symbolically, above the members of the crowd to whom he addresses his words. Seth Lerer sees the frontispiece as participating in a broad matrix of Chaucerian legacy-promotion; he opens *Chaucer and His Readers* with the important observation that "Chaucer—as author, as 'laureate,' and as 'father' of English poetry—is a construction of his later fifteenth-century scribes, readers, and poetic imitators."[51] I would add that Chaucer is also a construction of the Lancastrian regime. Lerer also points out that fifteenth-century poets define Chaucer as "the refiner of language and the English version of the classical *auctor* and the trecento *poeta*. The Chaucer who inhabits their verse is the kin of the performer at the center of the *Troilus* frontispiece: a laureate figure in an aureate world, a poet for a king whose glittering language befits his golden literary age."[52]

Why the need to heap such lavish praise upon the deceased Chaucer? If, as scholars currently believe, Chaucer was not in fact a court poet,[53] the question is well worth asking. The most plausible answer to this question would seem to be that, as others have asserted, Henry V may have placed Chaucer at the center of a campaign to promote the status of the English language. A number of scholars have called attention to the remarkable flourishing of the English language at just this period.[54] Although in the fourteenth century Middle English texts had begun to appear in increasing numbers in England, there seems to have been much less public demand for such written works before Henry IV's accession to the throne in 1399, by comparison with the proliferation of manuscripts in the years that followed. It seems that promoting Chaucer helped to promote the prestige and status of the English language and to create a growing demand for texts in the vernacular.

[51] Lerer, *Chaucer and His Readers,* p. 3.

[52] Ibid., p. 23.

[53] By this I mean that to the best of our knowledge, he was never commissioned to write poetry on behalf of court or crown nor paid for having done so. Paul Strohm, in his work *Social Chaucer* (Cambridge, Mass.: Harvard University Press, 1989), asserts that "current consensus regards Chaucer as writing mainly for social equals" and also contends that "th[is] shifting body of equals and near-equals I have indentified as his core audience continues to stand in *some* relation . . . to most of his major work" (p. 51; emphasis in original).

[54] Green highlights the growing demand for the translation of works into English in the period; *Poets and Princepleasers,* pp. 153–61; see also Scattergood, *Politics and Poetry,* particularly pp. 13–14.

John Fisher, who has developed the evidence for a deliberate promotion of English as the national language as a specifically Lancastrian policy, summarizes his argument in the introduction to *The Importance of Chaucer:*

The inference about the Lancastrian promotion of Chaucer's poetry rests in turn upon the inference that Henry V deliberately promoted the adoption of the vernacular. Most histories of the English language still seem to imply that standard English just happened, but I am sufficiently a disciple of Thomas Kuhn's *The Structure of Scientific Revolution{s}* to believe that most technical and cultural developments can be traced to innovation by one individual. . . . Henry's switch in 1417 to writing to his chancellor and the English cities in English was not precipitous, but the outgrowth of many years of thought and discussion. Part of this process of gestation could have been Henry's encouragement of his cousin (or uncle) Thomas Chaucer to assemble Thomas's father's (or stepfather's) foul papers and produce the fair copies of Chaucer's poems as models of cultivated English.[55]

John Bowers concurs in seeing a similar impetus and a circle of united forces at work: Geoffrey Chaucer, he argues, was "installed as the patriarch of English letters by Thomas Chaucer with the assistance of those Lancastrian supporters known to be connected with him, a father very much created by his own son, to fill the role" of a national poet.[56]

The promotion of English and the promotion of Chaucer as an exemplar of what could be achieved in the vernacular form two strands of a complex thread that seems to have woven itself throughout the period of Lancastrian rule as part of "a deliberate policy intended to engage the support of parliament and the English citizenry for a questionable usurpation of the throne. The publication of Chaucer's poems and his enshrinement as the perfecter of rhetoric in English were central to this

---

[55] Fisher, *The Importance of Chaucer* (Carbondale: Southern Illinois University Press, 1992), p. x. Fisher's arguments are presented here and also in "A Language Policy for Lancastrian England," *PMLA* 107 (1992): 1168–88. See also Lerer, *Chaucer and His Readers,* especially p. 48. Allmand makes similar claims for the king's intentional promotion of English as the national language; see *Henry V,* pp. 418–25, for a listing of further developments that helped to spur the adoption of English throughout a broader sector of society during his reign.

[56] John M. Bowers, "The House of Chaucer & Son: The Business of Lancastrian Canon-Formation," *MedPers* 6 (1991): 135–43 (141).

effort."[57] Denton Fox points out that "Chaucer, and often Gower and Lydgate, are praised repeatedly for being the first to bring into English the adornments of rhetoric."[58] Chaucer's improvement of the capacities of English forms a cornerstone of his praise. Although Norman Eliason insists that Chaucer's successors must have praised his versification, he admits that "their admiration of his versification is certainly less clear than that of his language, about which their comments are fairly lucid"; they extol his language by deeming it "ornate," in contrast with what they describe as the "rudeness" of the English language as employed by Chaucer's predecessors and contemporaries.[59]

As John Fisher has pointed out, the dedication to the *Troy Book* comes closer than any other surviving document to offering a statement of Lancastrian language policy. Lydgate, describing the impetus for the composition of his tale, explains that Henry

> comaunded the drery pitus fate
> Of hem of Troye in englysche to translate
>
> .   .   .   .
>
> By-cause he wolde to hyge and lowe
> The noble story openly wer knowe
> In oure tonge, aboute in every age,

[57] Fisher, "A Language Policy," p. 1170. The literary praise of Chaucer begins early. Lydgate's *The Floure of Curtesy,* which Walter Schirmer dates to the years 1400–1402, just after Henry IV's accession to the throne, offers some of the earliest literary homage to Chaucer. It describes him as having earned "a name / Of fayre makyng" as fair "as the laurer grene." Lydgate, *The Floure of Curtesy,* in *The Minor Poems of John Lydgate, Part II,* ed. Henry Noble MacCracken, EETS o.s. 192 (London: Oxford University Press, 1961), pp. 410–17, lines 236–38; Walter F. Schirmer, *John Lydgate: A Study in the Culture of the XVth Century,* trans. Ann E. Keep (London: Methuen, 1961). Fisher describes both this and another early Lydgatean work, *The Complaint of the Black Knight,* as "acts of homage to Chaucer" ("A Language Policy," p. 1176). Lydgate's *The Temple of Glas* is another work from this early period that also pays tribute to the late poet. Again and again, the praise that Chaucer's successors accord to him emphasizes his skill as a master, perfecter, and purifier of the English language and tongue.

[58] Denton Fox, "Chaucer's Influence on Fifteenth-Century Poetry," in *Companion to Chaucer Studies,* ed. Beryl Rowland (Oxford: Oxford University Press, 1968), pp. 385–402 (387).

[59] Norman E. Eliason, "Chaucer's Fifteenth-Century Successors," *Medieval and Renaissance Studies* 5 (1969): 103–21 (105). If we accept the thesis that the Lancastrians were busy about promoting English as the national language, we should also realize that their efforts would have involved not just the elevation of the prestige of English as a language capable of producing great literature; they would also need to have labored to produce, as the evidence shows that they did, a standardized dialect. The often-repeated references to the "rudeness" of other writers' English may also function as a stab at the provincial dialects in which many earlier manuscripts had been rendered.

And y-writen as wel in our langage
As in latyn or in frensche it is;
That of the story the trouthe we may nat mys
No more than doth eche other nacioun:
This was the fyn of his entencioun.[60]

Thus, even before his accession to the throne in 1413, Henry appears to have expressed concern for the rendering of a text into English style that would stand on a par with other versions in the prestige languages of Latin and French.

The frontispiece to CCCC MS 61 makes sense within the context of a program of Lancastrian literary promotion of the status of both Chaucer and English. In the picture, the presence or absence of a literary text in front of Chaucer makes little difference to the key element that it is designed to portray. Chaucer's preeminence as a user and perfecter of the English language—a reputation well established in fifteenth-century literature—rather than his skill as an author per se, is the concept or idea that the miniature promotes. The iconography of the frontispiece grants Chaucer a platform, literally and metaphorically, from which he can preach English to the still-too-linguistically-French court of Richard II. It is also noteworthy that despite the variety of attitudes and activities pictured for the various members of the audience, Richard himself is standing and apparently quite attentive to the words of Chaucer, hearing from Chaucer's own mouth the glories of the English language. The picture, commissioned by Henry V as part of a prestige manuscript, was designed to serve as Lancastrian propaganda, as a piece of historical fiction that would project backward in time the ascendancy and authority of Chaucer's decision to use and to improve English as the prestige language of the English people.

An Act of Vandalism

Granted that the Corpus Christi *Troilus* is a deluxe manuscript and that, as a prized possession, it has been so carefully preserved, it is perhaps all the more surprising that the face of one of the characters in the frontispiece illustration, the figure dressed in cloth of gold, has been rubbed out. This circumstance is difficult to account for unless we accept an

---

[60] John Lydgate, *Troy Book*, ed. Henry Bergen, EETS e.s. 97 (London: Paul, Trench, Trübner & Co., 1906), lines 105–6, 111–18.

explanation that was first advanced many years ago: Aage Brusendorff suggested "political reasons," on the theory that the manuscript passed into the hands of Lancastrian supporters.[61] We cannot establish definitively that the figure concerned was indeed meant as a representation of Richard II, but no other character would seem to provide an adequate explanation as to why the manuscript should have been defaced.

While Henry's successes in France may have encouraged him in the belief that he had consolidated support for his regime to a sufficient degree so as to render the *Troilus* frontispiece's depiction of Richard a calculated but acceptable risk, his early and unexpected death in 1422 may have given his political successors a different view of the matter. One can easily imagine the discomfort of Henry V's successors when faced with what, under such circumstances, they must have deemed an unnecessarily inflammatory portrait; presumably, the picture was defaced on orders from some powerful member of the ruling council before the manuscript was delivered into the hands of John Shirley, an important manuscript broker with Lancastrian connections, for further disposition.

Kinship and Connections: The Early Possessors of the Corpus Manuscript

Although there is no direct evidence in the Corpus Christi *Troilus* to link it with Henry V, something of the early connections of the manuscript can be deduced from the inscriptions in its margins. Connections among the earliest documentable owners of CCCC MS 61 consistently lead back to the circles of influence that are most closely connected with the monarchies of Henry V and Henry VI. That fifteenth-century owners and handlers of the manuscript should be important Lancastrian supporters is consistent with the view that the manuscript may have originated in a commission by Henry V and that, upon his death, the incomplete manuscript may have passed into the hands of Lancastrian supporters.

The first important marginal inscription reveals that the manuscript was at one time in the possession of John Shirley; the second important clue as to early ownership is the inscription of the name Anne Neville, written on folio 101v in a late fifteenth-century hand. Both names re-

---

[61] Brusendorff, *The Chaucer Tradition*, 22 n. 4.

connect the manuscript with the court of Henry V and with the social circles that centered on the Lancastrian throne. These later possessors of the manuscript reinforce the view that the Corpus Christi *Troilus* originated in a Lancastrian context.

John Shirley

The precise role of John Shirley in relation to fifteenth-century literary culture has been much debated, but certainly he was an avid handler and annotator of manuscripts. During the course of his ninety-year life-span, he worked as a "book dealer, publisher, prolific scribe and, not least, purveyor of much engaging information about the literary and aristocratic figures of his day."[62] Lydgate's prayer for king, queen, and people, inscribed by Shirley, identifies the Corpus Christi *Troilus* as having at some time been in Shirley's possession.[63] Shirley's name connects the manuscript not only with Lydgate, whom John Fisher identifies as the public relations mouthpiece for the Lancastrian campaign to promote the status of English as the national language, but also with the Beauchamps, whose relevance to the manuscript is considered below. Shirley's chief patron was Richard Beauchamp, to whom he acted as secretary; Shirley had been in France along with Beauchamp and with Henry V.

The Nevilles, Dukes of Westmorland

The next name associated with the manuscript, that of Neville, opens up an extensive network of relationships and possibilities. Although the inscription "'neuer Foryeteth' Anne neuill" identifies a particular individual, the name itself could belong to one of several people. One of the

---

[62] Parkes and Salter, *Troilus and Criseyde*, p. 23. Margaret Connolly, who has published the only book-length study to date on Shirley's life and career, *John Shirley: Book Production and the Noble Household in Fifteenth-Century England* (Brookfield, Vt.: Ashgate, 1998), argues for a more circumspect assessment of Shirley's role, one that recognizes the degree to which Shirley's activities would have been dictated by and responsive to his role as Beauchamp's secretary.

[63] Although the exact nature of Shirley's relationship to John Lydgate remains conjectural, the work of the two men is closely associated. See Connolly, *John Shirley*, p. 84; Derek Pearsall argues not only for Shirley's acquaintance with Lydgate, but suggests he was "at once his publisher and his literary agent." *John Lydgate* (Charlottesville: University Press of Virginia, 1970), pp. 74–75.

two identities most often suggested is Anne Neville (c. 1410–80),[64] daughter of Joan Beaufort and Ralph Neville. Joan Beaufort was the daughter of John of Gaunt and Katherine Swynford; she was therefore, as well, the niece of Chaucer's wife, Philippa de Roet. Thus she and her daughter Anne were related both to the family of Chaucer and to the Lancastrian monarchs. Her husband, Ralph Neville, is (in)famous for having helped John of Gaunt's son, Henry Bolingbroke, to depose Richard II in 1399.

The identification of the Anne concerned as the daughter of Joan Beaufort and Ralph Neville is potentially strengthened by the appearance of another inscription, in a similar hand, on folio 108r, which gives the name "Knyvett."[65] Anne's daughter, Joanna, married her second husband, Sir William Knyvett of Norfolk, in 1477: thus, the manuscript may have been passed from mother to daughter. However, since Anne herself married Humphrey Stafford in 1424, she is unlikely to have used the name "Neville" after this time; thus, she may well not be the person who inscribed the name "Anne Neville" in the manuscript in a late fifteenth-century hand. Nevertheless, as Parkes and Salter observe, "It is tempting to find [Anne (Beaufort) Neville's] ownership of the *Troilus* particularly convincing in the courtly contexts of the mid-fifteenth-century in England; she was, in company with ladies such as Jaquetta, Lady Rivers, and Alice de la Pole, Duchess of Suffolk (granddaughter of Chaucer) 'in frequent attendance' at the court of Henry VI

---

[64] The Beauchamps' involvement with the manuscript offers direct links to both Anne Neville and John Shirley. The second identity most often suggested for the Anne Neville who owned the *Troilus* manuscript is Anne Beauchamp, heiress of Richard. Anne, born in 1426, married Richard Neville (the "Kingmaker") in 1439 and died in 1492. Parkes and Salter suggest that "this identification [of Anne] might provide a clue as to where the manuscript was before it reached Shirley's hands." Parkes and Salter, *Troilus and Criseyde,* p. 12. In other words, if Anne Beauchamp-Neville is the woman concerned, the manuscript might conceivably have been commissioned by her father. Such a commission, however, as appealing it may be on other grounds, cannot account adequately for either the abandonment of the manuscript's illustrative program or for the defacing of the figure dressed in gold brocade.

[65] The two Anne Nevilles who are considered here, Anne (Beaufort) Neville and Anne Beauchamp Neville, are not the only Anne Nevilles of the late fifteenth and early sixteenth centuries. For a discussion of further possibilities, see A. I. Doyle in Appendix B to Christine de Pisan's *Epistle of Othea,* ed. Curt F. Bühler, trans. Stephen Scrope, EETS o.s. 264 (London: Oxford University Press, 1970). The name "Knyvett," however, involves us in an even more daunting array of potential identities. Parkes and Salter point out that "there are ten Knyvetts listed in the index of *Testamenta Vetusta* alone, any one of whom could have been responsible for the name inscribed on fol. 108ʳ. The name 'Knyvett' also appears in the Devonshire manuscript of the *Canterbury Tales* which contains Sir Edmund Knyvett's arms." *Troilus and Criseyde,* p. 12.

and Margaret of Anjou."[66] Anne's ownership of the manuscript would thus situate early ownership of the Corpus Christi *Troilus* in a context that is both distinctly Chaucerian and thoroughly Lancastrian.

Conclusion

I have argued that the strongest possible case can be made for the *Troilus* frontispiece's having originated in a commission from Henry V; his sponsorship of the manuscript provides the key that helps to unlock the mysteries that have so baffled scholars in regard to its interpretation. In life circumstances, Henry fits the picture of the manuscript's unnamed patron. He could afford the expenditure; the date of the manuscript accords with the years of his reign; and his death would account both for the abandonment of the illustrative plan as well as for the political uncertainty that may well have led to the defacing of the portrait of Richard II. We know, too, that close ties, not only social but also biological and political, connected the various persons involved both in supporting and promoting the Lancastrian monarchs and in exploring and disseminating the newly popularized literature in the English language; early known possessors of the manuscript were sympathizers with and close to the Lancastrian cause.

Henrician sponsorship of the manuscript provides an explanation for the status reversal of poet and monarch in the prefatory illustration: Henry V's reburial of Richard's bones in Westminster provides a documentable corollary that demonstrates his willingness to use Richard— and his belief that he could safely do so—to bolster his own popularity. In the case of the *Troilus* manuscript, the reversed positions of Chaucer and Richard II emphasize the status relations that the Lancastrians wish to promote: Chaucer lectures (or preaches to) the court of Richard II in the English language, and it is Chaucer, the famous purifier and beautifier of the English language, whom the portrait celebrates. In this sense, the miniature derives its iconography from that of the "preaching" or "teaching" picture: Chaucer expounds his ideas, to his flock or to his students, through the medium of the English language.

Furthermore, Henry's interest in the stories of Troy is manifest, since before he ever came to the throne he had commissioned both Lydgate's *Troy Book* and a copy (the Pierpont Morgan manuscript) of Chaucer's

[66] Parkes and Salter, *Troilus and Criseyde,* 23 n. 30.

Troilus and Criseyde. Both texts serve dynastic and nationalistic interests. Lydgate's *Troy Book* "provided Henry not just with a history . . . but with an authoritative version of the Trojan history that had, at least since the time of Henry II, served to support the legitimacy of insecure English kings. In representing Henry as the patron of what was taken to be the founding moment of English history, Lydgate was . . . affirming Henry's proprietorship over the national culture."[67] The Pierpont Morgan *Troilus* bespeaks Henry's interest in Chaucer's tale, and we can easily imagine it as a forerunner to the even more deluxe copy that survives as CCCC MS 61. It takes no stretch of the imagination, but rather, a logical extension of facts already known, to conceive of the Corpus Christi *Troilus* as having been envisioned by Henry V as a work to stand as a national treasure, proclaiming one of the great stories of Troy (to which England often traced its origins) in glorious English, the national language newly revived through the poetic efforts of Geoffrey Chaucer.

The artwork of the *Troilus* frontispiece, unprecedented in the history of English manuscript illustration, looks to France for its inspiration, and this fact, too, makes sense in the context of the king's commission of the manuscript. As a monarch with a no-nonsense plan for achieving ascendancy in France, Henry could conceivably have cultivated quite deliberately the miniature's blend of French style with English content. As Henry would seek political union, under English headship, between England and France, the *Troilus* frontispiece embodies, through its pictorial statement, an artistic union, a blending of some of the highest aesthetic achievements that both countries could offer: French bookpainting, combined with Chaucer's English poetry.

Finally, an association of Henry V with the Corpus Christi *Troilus* helps to explain one of the central mysteries that has made the picture such a puzzle to scholarship: why Chaucer should have no book before him as he addresses his royal audience. Given the Henrician commission, we will recognize that it is not preeminently as a poet but as a beautifier and promoter of the English language that the Chaucer of the *Troilus* frontispiece stands before us. We can name no other early fifteenth-century figure who seems to have had so consistent and so vested an interest as did Henry V in promoting the status of Chaucer as the finest poet in English, as the "first finder" of the language's capacities for

---

[67] Patterson, "Making Identities," p. 74.

exalted expression. Although the Lancastrian literary campaign to promote the status of English seems to have been well under way during Henry V's reign, this prefatory miniature seems to have been the first (or the first surviving) attempt to enshrine Chaucer's status in visual art, the pictorial counterpart to the verbal paeans that Chaucer's immediate successors so consistently accord him.

Women's Secrets:

Childbirth, Pollution, and Purification in Northern *Octavian*

Angela Florschuetz
Trinity University, San Antonio

T HE MOTIVATING CRISIS of the mid-fourteenth-century tail-rhyme romance *Octavian* is caused by the violent intrusion of the eponymous Emperor into his wife's birth-chamber, or lying-in room.[1] He intrudes at the instigation of his conniving mother, who has bribed a kitchen servant to join the delirious and exhausted new mother in her bed—nude. Upon his entrance, Octavian jumps to the obvious though erroneous conclusion that his wife is an adulteress. He deals with the situation with considerable dispatch, immediately beheading the terrified servant and tossing the severed head at his awakening wife. The

[1] The Middle English (Northern) *Octavian* romance is extant in two manuscripts, the Thornton manuscript (Lincoln, Dean and Chapter Library, MS 91), and the closely related Cambridge manuscript (Cambridge, University Library, MS Ff.2.38. A third version exists in a fragment of an early print by Wynkyn de Worde, Huntington (San Marino, Calif., Huntington Library 14615; *STC* 18779), containing less than half of the romance. Editions of all three can be found in Frances McSparran, ed. *Octavian,* EETS o.s. 289 (London: Oxford University Press, 1986). A related Middle English Octavian romance, commonly known as "Southern Octavian," also exists in a single manuscript, London, British Library, MS Cotton Caligula A.ii, available in Frances McSparran, ed. *Octovian Imperator* (Heidelberg: Carl Winter, 1979). The Southern version is less linear in its description of the abductions of the sons and their subsequent adventures, and also offers a much more elaborate account of Clement's adventures with the Sultan's flying horse. Internal evidence of the Thornton manuscript suggests that it was copied in the second quarter of the fifteenth century in the northeast Midlands, and the Cambridge manuscript later in that century, near Essex. McSparran suggests that both versions of the Northern *Octavian* were probably composed during the second half of the fourteenth century (*Octavian,* p. 42). The Thornton manuscript includes more details of Florent's narrative, including expanded episodes from the giant-slaying, Florent's knighting, and Clement's behavior at the feast celebrating the knighting. Unless otherwise marked by "C.," all citations refer to the Thornton text in McSparran's EETS edition.

slandered empress thus emerges from a premonitory nightmare only to enter a far more horrifying reality of violence, blood, and disgrace.

Octavian's violation and misrepresentation of the empress's lying-in room precipitate the central crisis of the plot: the scattering of the royal family and consequent endangering of the patrilineal line. His intrusion breaks the codes through which births, particularly aristocratic births, were culturally constructed and represented in medieval culture. Aristocratic births were configured within a matrix of gendered and political beliefs concerning the significance of the work performed within the lying-in room, work that could not be authorized or recognized if the crucial integrity of the space allotted for childbearing was broken. The poem does not allow this primal crisis to disappear; violent male intruders repeatedly disrupt this traditionally female zone at key moments throughout the romance. These repetitions reconstruct the violated area of the lying-in room and the ambivalent interpretations of the place of women in both religion and the state played out in this contested space, a space both endangering and endangered, which is adversely marked by discourses of contamination and sexual threat that ultimately threaten the integrity of the state. In its exploration of the legitimacy and consequences of ambivalent and ultimately self-contradictory sacred and secular discourses concerning the status of the lying-in room, *Octavian* explicates the complexities of identity available to the medieval aristocratic mother, as well as the resultant ambivalence of her political and spiritual status within her community. Ultimately, by staging an unjust violation of the lying-in room, which takes to extremes cultural suspicions centering on female sexuality in general and the reproductive body in particular, *Octavian* challenges both secular and sacred discursive and ritual practices that malign or undermine the validity of the lying-in room and the bodies that occupy and define it. The redramatizations of this first violent intrusion, which are enacted later in the romance, continue to interrogate aristocratic and ecclesiastic discourses that constructed the pregnant and postpartum body as the site of sexual, and thus, lineal contamination.

Octavian shares its concerns with the intersection of family, gender, and political stability through the production of heirs with a larger category of romances that focuses on women and children and often features the estrangement or separation of aristocratic families and the consequent problem of recognizing true heirs.[2] As such, this romance includes

---

[2] Middle English popular romances and related genres almost obsessively return to the problems and vicissitudes of producing and retaining viable heirs to continue valued

the common themes of the falsely accused aristocratic wife, the exile (through exposure to the sea or wilderness) of wife and or heirs, the unwitting reunion of father and heirs, and the eventual production of physical, magical, or divine proof of the heir's legitimacy—all elements that would be familiar to the audience of late medieval English romance. Geraldine Heng has suggested that this subgenre of romance be called "family romance," "to stretch and complicate" Freud's use of the same term.[3] Helen Cooper notes the fourteenth-century "flurry" of English-language romances and the overall "concern of the genre with true inheritance, the rightful passing on of land and power underwritten by Providence."[4] These romances, critics have suggested, often feature women more prominently than more chivalric and martial romances, foregrounding conventional female behavior and virtues rather than masculine endeavor.[5] David Salter has identified *Octavian* as a "represen-

---

bloodlines. *Sir Gowther* and Chaucer's *Clerk's Tale* also directly address the problems caused by the lack of an heir; *Melusine*, *Emaré*, and Chaucer's *Man of Law's Tale* feature claims of unsuitable, monstrous heirs, *Athelston* includes the violent slaying of the heir while still in his mother's body, and the *King of Tars* focuses on the racially hybrid production of a lump of flesh rather than a child and the subsequent transformation of the lump into a child, and in *Cheuelere Assigne* the seven children of the king are threatened by accusations of adulterous and bestial conception, attempted murder, and magical transformation into swans.

[3] Geraldine Heng, *Empire of Magic: Medieval Romance and the Politics of Cultural Fantasy* (New York: Columbia University Press, 2003), pp. 29, 185. Felicity Riddy also notes the centrality of families to fourteenth- and fifteenth-century popular English romance, but she avoids the term "family romance," preferring instead to associate the romances with the idea of the "domestic." "Middle English Romance: Family, Romance, Intimacy," in *The Cambridge Companion to Medieval Romance,* ed. Roberta L. Krueger (Cambridge: Cambridge University Press, 2000), pp. 235–52. In several of these romances, as in *Octavian,* the threat to dynastic stability comes as a result of the false accusation of the mother of sexual misconduct or monstrosity, leading to repudiation and/or exile. Nancy B. Black notes that the pattern of the falsely accused virtuous noblewoman, often referred to as the "calumniated wife" motif, was increasingly popular in Continental and English narratives from the early thirteenth through the fifteenth century. See Nancy Black, *Medieval Narratives of Accused Queens* (Gainesville: University Press of Florida, 2003), pp. 2–3. Black notes the prevalence of this theme in both romance and hagiography, in which women are frequently represented as suffering for choosing to be obedient to God or morality rather than men who desire them sexually (14–15). In addition to medieval narratives of female virtue under threat, Black links this motif to the biblical narrative of Susanna and the classical narrative of Lucretia (12, 18).

[4] Helen Cooper, *The English Romance in Time: Transforming Motifs from Geoffrey of Monmouth to the Death of Shakespeare* (Oxford: Oxford University Press, 2004), p. 324. Cooper links the rise of romance in Europe with the rise of primogeniture, suggesting that the genre and the legal practice each strive "to make the same point, that there will always be one claimant whose title can be proved rightful ahead of all rivals" (326).

[5] Heng, *Empire of Magic,* p. 185; David Salter, "'Born to Thraldom and Penance': Wives and Mothers in Middle English Romance," in *Writing Gender and Genre in Medieval Literature: Approaches to Old and Middle English Texts,* ed. Elaine Treharne (Cambridge:

tative" and "typical" example of Middle English popular romance, "particularly in its treatment of women within its highly conventional narrative form."[6] I do not disagree with this point, as the romance's rendition of familial crisis and resolution clearly seems to follow a recognizable pattern of convention that is well established. I would argue, however, that *Octavian*'s repeated attention to social rituals of reproduction and political legitimation takes these familiar concerns and tropes and focuses attention specifically on the tensions inherent in contemporary representations and treatments of childbirth and the rituals through which late medieval people and institutions, both secular and religious, experienced, constructed, and understood the significance of women's bodies and childbirth. These tensions in particular, the romance suggests, endanger the project of reproduction and thus political stability.

Octavian seems to offer a sort of catalogue of the potential difficulties and trials attendant on patrilineality as a system of aristocratic male reproduction. Infertility, infidelity, slander and deception, murder, misrecognition, abduction, abandonment, and, later, death in battle are each options that the poem offers as potential barriers to the smooth

---

D. S. Brewer, 2002), pp. 41–59 (44); Jennifer Fellows, "Mothers in Middle English Romance," in *Women and Literature in Britain, 1150–1550,* ed. Carol M. Meale (Cambridge: Cambridge University Press, 1993), pp. 40–60 (43–44).

[6] McSparran, *Octovian,* pp. 40–42. There were two French verse versions of the Octavian story, *Octavian* (FO) and *Florent et Octavian de Rome* (F&O), which later were rendered into prose versions. McSparran suggests that the French prose versions of the Octavian narrative were translated into Italian and German, and that the German version subsequently became the source for the Danish, Dutch, Icelandic, and Polish versions of the story. F&O is nearly three times as long as FO, and McSparran suggests that it is an expanded version of FO, though their exact relationship is unclear. The English versions of *Octavian* (both Northern and Southern) are closer to FO, typically following FO rather than F&O when the French versions diverge and the English redactions share the abduction by lioness and griffin and the island den scene, which is absent in F&O. Both English versions include the scene of Octavian throwing the kitchen servant's head at his wife, absent in FO. The empress's apparent barrenness is included in FO and Northern *Octavian* but is replaced in Southern *Octavian* with a long-single Octavian, who is eventually exhorted by his people to marry in a motif reminiscent of *The Clerk's Tale.* However, Northern *Octavian* shares some features with F&O absent in Southern *Octavian* and FO, notably the insinuation by the dowager empress that the empress's alleged infidelity is motivated by Octavian's sterility. In FO and Southern *Octavian,* the presence of twins alone is given as the initial proof of infidelity, as two children imply two fathers. Also, Northern *Octavian* elaborates on the empress's life in Jerusalem as an honored guest in the king's household, absent in FO. Both versions of Northern *Octavian* emphasize the long barrenness of Octavian's marriage. This essay focuses exclusively on Northern *Octavian,* as it seems to focus more consistently on the figure of the empress and the representation of maternity than either Southern *Octavian* or the French versions of the narrative.

transmission of patrilineage. The romance begins with the quandary of the eponymous emperor, whose wife has failed to conceive after several years of marriage. At his wife's suggestion, he erects an abbey and dedicates it to the Virgin Mary, with the desired result of a speedy pregnancy. However, Mary's apparent intercession on behalf of the empress does not ensure the smooth arrival and legitimation of the twin heirs. The birth is very difficult, leaving not only the exhausted mother, but also her companions, swooning and unconscious. This provides the opportunity for Octavian's mother to trick her son into believing her slanderous accusation of infidelity, which results in the murder of the servant and banishment of the empress and her twin sons. Both children are abducted by wild animals in the wilderness. Octavian, the elder son, is soon reunited with his mother, while Florent, the younger, is eventually adopted by Clement, a Parisian merchant, and predictably shows frequent signs of his inherently noble nature. After defeating a Saracen giant menacing Paris, Florent is brought to the attention of his father, Octavian, and they go to war against the Saracens together. Soon, however, both are captured, and from their safe haven in Jerusalem, the empress and the younger Octavian learn of the captivity of their long-estranged family members. With the lion that first abducted and then nurtured him, as well as Jerusalem's armies, Octavian's heir rides to his father and brother's rescue, bringing his calumniated mother in his retinue. Upon the emperor Octavian's release, his son reintroduces his parents, and the empress fortuitously recognizes in the mysterious young Florent her infant son carried away long ago by an ape. Reunited, the family travels to Rome to find along the way that the emperor's mother, learning that her deception was revealed, has cut her throat in shame. All enjoy a hearty laugh at this turn of events and the romance ends with the triumphant entrance of the reconstituted royal family into Rome.

The particular concern of Northern *Octavian* with the problems of perpetuating a continuous patrilineal line results in an unusual amount of representation and scrutiny of the domestic and public events and mechanics surrounding medieval aristocratic childbirth. The various stages of lying-in and birth, churching, or ritual purification, and thanksgiving a month after birth, and post-churching feasting and revelry are all noted and represented, generally as they go horribly awry, destabilizing the continuity and security that each is meant to enact within its communal context. In particular, the practices of lying-in and of churching feasts are represented as being subverted, which sabotages primogeniture, if not patrilineage itself. By presenting scenes of botched rituals of social legitimation following childbirth and the catastrophic results of their disruption, Northern *Octavian* emphasizes the crucial role these practices—some obscured from sight, others ostentatiously performed before the community—played in the communal production of political and social stability, as well as the anxieties about this stability that these practices both undermine and enact.

This essay will examine first the domestic and then the ecclesiastical practices through which medieval families and communities experienced and interpreted childbirth (lying-in, gossiping, churching, and feasting in particular) and will then juxtapose these normative rites with their disruption in Northern *Octavian*. In its rendering of a Roman dynastic crisis, *Octavian* not only repeats familiar conventions and tropes of the family romance and other genres but also draws attention to specific anxieties the particular treatment of these tropes illuminate in this romance: the ambivalent and sometimes contradictory political, scientific, and religious meanings of the pregnant and postpartum body as constructed by public and private rituals and representations of childbirth and its aftermath, the role of the birthing community in producing an heir, and the vulnerability to individuals, bloodlines, and social structures that these various medieval birthing practices often attempted to minimize, but that were paradoxically made evident by the insistence on the very need for those practices.

Secular Rituals of Aristocratic Childbirth

The emperor Octavian's intrusion into the lying-in chamber where his wife has just given birth is bloody and violent, marked by both horror and nightmare. The poem juxtaposes his entrance and subsequent decapitation of the servant with his unconscious wife's "dolefull swevenynge," delirious nightmares of her sons' abduction by a dragon, foreshadowing their eventual abductions by an ape, a lioness, and a griffin (line 161). Much emphasis is placed at this moment in the text on the blood that splashes from the servant and his severed head onto the bed and the sleeping empress. After the killing of the servant, "Alle was beblede with blode," a recasting of royal blood as contamination, staining everything within the area, literally and metaphorically (159). Soon thereafter, as the empress awakens, the first thing she sees is "þe clothes

240

all byblede," rather than her husband or the decapitated corpse of the servant (179). The repeated references to the bloodiness of the scene, particularly the blood on the sheets, emphasize not only the terror of childbed in general but also, and more importantly, the peculiar horror arising from the double contamination of the lying-in room by out-of-place men who transform the site from one of domestic and civil reproduction to one of violent and gruesome death and disorder. The transformation of "þe rechese þat scho [the empress] jn laye" into "the clothes all bybledde" signals a dramatic reverse from honor and poten-tial into a nightmare of disgrace, death, and catastrophe centered spe-cifically in the lying-in room (146, 179). The abject tableau of the prostrate body of the exhausted and now-suicidal empress with her en-raged husband standing over her, decapitated head of the kitchen boy in hand, is abruptly closed off with the announcement of the uneasy yet total silence that follows: "Wordis of this were spoken no mo" (184).

While the repeated attention to the bloody sheets of the birthing bed might suggest the trauma of childbirth, the excessiveness of the violence perpetrated there, as well as its source, points to the violation of a cul-turally imposed site of female privacy, through Octavian's deviant and violent entrance, an intrusion that seems to parallel the even more trans-gressive presence of the kitchen servant within the empress's bed. The very presence of these men in the lying-in room functions not only as a violation of propriety but also as the violation of the social codes forbid-ding both their presence and their acceptability as witnesses to what occurs within the lying-in room. The scene of derangement and dis-memberment that ensues represents the similar state of the space of the invaded lying-in room, culturally defined by the containment of the female child-bearing body in a space of enclosed and inviolate feminin-ity, a space doubly violated in *Octavian,* with disastrous results.

Late in her pregnancy, an aristocratic woman's bedchamber (also that of her husband) would be converted into the lying-in room, a space characterized by the ritualized separation of the pregnant woman from the outside world.[7] During the lying-in period, which consisted of the

---

[7] Gail McMurray Gibson, "Blessing from Sun and Moon: Churching as Women's Theatre," in *Bodies and Disciplines: Intersections of Literature and History in the Fifteenth Century,* ed. Barbara A. Hanawalt and David Wallace (Minneapolis: University of Min-nesota Press, 1996), pp. 139–54 (144); see also Adrian Wilson, "The Ceremony of Childbirth and Its Interpretation," in *Women as Mothers in Pre-Industrial England,* ed. Valerie Fildes (London: Routledge, 1990), pp. 68–107.

last four to six weeks of pregnancy and the period leading up to church-ing, men, including the woman's husband, were forbidden entry into the enclosed room.[8] The contained nature of the space was emphasized by its conversion and redefinition of boundaries through strategies of decoration and of gendered exclusion. Household expenditure records as well as letters and other documents reveal that often new furniture was purchased in the construction of the lying-in room and that the room was lavishly decorated in coordinated curtains, hangings, and rugs, which were used to cover the floors, walls, and even the ceiling.[9] The effect of these fabric boundaries was to fashion an enclosed and insulated space of reproduction located within the household, yet clearly consid-ered a special site of isolation from it, sealed off from the normal func-tions of both household and state. The importance of the enclosure of this space and its protection from outside intrusion was emphasized by the recommended measure of stuffing keyholes with fabric or other sub-stances to prevent violation of the lying-in room's integrity through peeping.[10] This practice clearly suggests not only the desire to keep the space inviolate and private but also the assumption that such a space will invite curiosity and the desire to witness what is being marked as secret and off-limits. Strategies to police and control this space, as well as the knowledge of the lying-in room and its practices, construct the chamber as a site of privileged knowledge that outsiders in general and men in particular are ineligible to share.

Secrecy is a practice that assumes and even demands speculation and curiosity about what is being concealed, particularly when that conceal-ment is lavishly and sometimes ostentatiously performed by those in-cluded in the secret. In these cases, knowledge becomes associated with a privileged few, and the rituals surrounding the enclosure of the preg-nant woman simultaneously close off and titillate, reminding those shut out that there is indeed something occurring in the forbidden space that

[8] Kay Staniland notes that "all of the late fifteenth-century accounts of court ceremo-nials simply use the formula 'when it plessithe the Queen to take to hir chambre', or a variation upon it, to describe the withdrawal of the heavily pregnant queen from the court. A sixteenth-century document [BL, Egerton MS 985, fol. 98] suggests that four to six weeks were normal." See Kay Staniland, "Royal Entry into the World," in *England in the Fifteenth Century: Proceedings of the 1986 Harlaxton Symposium,* ed. Daniel Williams (Woodbridge: Boydell Press, 1987), pp. 297–313 (301).

[9] Nicholas Orme, *From Childhood to Chivalry* (London: Methuen, 1984), pp. 8–9; see also Wilson, "The Ceremony of Childbirth," pp. 73–78.

[10] Orme, *From Childhood to Chivalry,* p. 8.

is both tempting and important to know, yet inaccessible. If, as Karma Lochrie argues, secrecy is a practice that works to exclude others from knowledge in order to construct those in the know as more powerful (within that venue) than those shut out, the separation of the lying-in room not only reiterates sexual difference in the hidden spectacle of childbirth but also works to redefine the meaning of that difference through access to that spectacle. These practices thus transform the meaning of the pregnant body from a representation of a husband's masculine dominance over the female body to a mysterious ritual that he must finance but is not permitted to observe.[11] This dynamic of male ignorance and blindness is shockingly reversed in one of the few significant deviations of the Cambridge manuscript of *Octavian,* when we are told: "The lady slept and wyste hyt noght: / Hur comfort was the mare" (C.179–80). Here ignorance and blindness are forced on the empress; she is completely (and apparently happily) ignorant of the actions within the lying-in space, but nevertheless subject to its consequences on her emergence from confinement. While she presumably awakens later to find a severed head in the bed and "the ryche clothys . . . all bybledd," this rude awakening is not represented in the Cambridge text and the empress's knowledge of events is left completely unexplained (C.176). Her ignorance, compounded by her innocence of the sexual crime imputed to her, seems monstrous and horrifying, highlighting the inversion of the "proper" state of the lying-in room as a site of validated feminine and maternal knowledge bracketed by masculine ignorance.

The space constructed within the boundaries of walls, hangings, and furniture was ritually and emphatically feminized. The conversion of a pregnant woman's bedchamber into a lying-in chamber was performed exclusively by women, typically her female friends, relatives, and servants.[12] During the time of her lying-in, the woman would traditionally be attended by many of these women, denominated her "gossips," as well as a female midwife. The exclusion of men was both mitigated and highlighted by the explicit substitution of female "officers" for each

---

[11] Karma Lochrie, *Covert Operations: The Medieval Uses of Secrecy* (Philadelphia: University of Pennsylvania Press, 1999), p. 93. For a reading of the pregnant body's representation of paternal and lordly dominance over a female body and feminized polity, see John Carmi Parsons, "The Pregnant Queen as Counselor and the Medieval Construction of Motherhood," in *Medieval Mothering,* ed. John Carmi Parsons and Bonnie Wheeler (New York: Garland, 1996), pp. 39–62 (46).

[12] Wilson, "The Ceremony of Childbirth," p. 73.

banished male servant and retainer.[13] The quotidian gendered division of household tasks, as Kim Phillips suggests, is made visible specifically through the carnivalesque exception provided by the exclusively feminized exception of the lying-in room.[14] These women functioned not only as attendants to the birth, but as witnesses as well, providing a sense that while mysteries were contained in the lying-in room, there was some sort of community surveillance of that space and evidence that the product of the lying-in room was legitimate. Serving as mediators between the lying-in room and the outside community and also as witnesses to the hidden event of childbirth, gossips and midwives were regarded as community representatives at the birth. The authority of those within the room was made most explicit in the case of the midwife, who was frequently involved in legal inquisitions regarding the probable legitimacy of children of questionable paternity.[15]

The bounded and inviolate space of the lying-in room figures its metonymy with the enclosed space of the womb, where interdicted male presences also must be completely excluded in order to preserve the patrilineal line. Thus, the enforced femininity of the lying-in room represents the inviolability of the pregnant woman's womb against the intrusion of an unauthorized male presence and resultant uncertainty as to the true paternity of the woman's child. In the case of the lying-in room, this interdiction extended even to the presence of the woman's husband.[16] The expulsion of males from this space contributed to the

---

[13] Staniland, "Royal Entry into the World," p. 302.

[14] Kim M. Phillips, *Medieval Maidens: Young Women and Gender in England, 1270–1540* (Manchester: Manchester University Press, 2003), pp. 116–17. Phillips cites a 1494 Royal Ordinance describing the enclosure of a pregnant queen after attending Mass: "Then all the ladies and gentlemen to go in with her; and after that no man to come into the chamber where 'she shall be delivered, save women; and they to be made all manner of officers, as butlers, panters, sewers, carvers, cupbearers; and all manner of officers shall bring to them all manner of things to the great chamber door and the women officers for to receive it in the chamber.'"

[15] Denise Ryan, "Playing the Midwife's Part in the English Nativity Plays," *RES* n.s 54 (2003): 435–48 (437). See Ryan for accounts of midwives used to interrogate women in labor as to the paternity of their newborns. Ryan also notes cases where midwives testified to courts corroborating claims of premature childbirth (rather than premarital or extramarital conception).

[16] Romances and gynecological texts both suggest that female shame or embarrassment prohibit men, including husbands, from seeing their wives during or immediately after childbirth. *Le Roman de Silence* suggests that it is only his great eagerness to learn the sex of his child that spurs the count to ignore both his shame (*vergoigne*) at approaching a woman in childbed and his wife's subsequent great shame or embarrassment (*moult grant vergoigne*). Heldris de Cornuälle, *Silence: A Thirteenth-Century French Romance,* ed. and trans. Sarah Roche-Mahdi (East Lansing: Michigan State University Press, 1992), lines 2004, 2007. The same desire to avoid slander or embarrassment at the hands of

association of the lying-in room with the secrets of the woman's reproductive body, to which men were equally not allowed access. Gibson notes that "neither the parts of the female childbearing body nor the domestic space in which an intimate community of women presided at the labour of childbirth and the ritual postpartum confinement or lying-in room was fit object for the male gaze."[17] While this statement surely captures the sense of men's interdiction from the lying-in room and the potential harm, gendered and lineal, that might come from transgression of this code, an underlying tension remains in the overall characterization of the room. For while there is a sense that the lying-in room is dangerous to men and masculinity, there is also a strong intimation of privilege associated with it, a privilege men are not invited or welcome to share.

The status of the lying-in room as a place of darkest mystery to men, as well as its position as a site of extreme liminality, suspended between the poles of life and death, marked both pregnancy and the lying-in room as sites of miraculous revelations and wonders. While the enclosure of the lying-in room marked it spatially as a site of extreme interiority, the juxtaposition of life and death that it contained produced the lying-in room's liminal status. According to John Carmi Parsons, the unborn child's position, "of this world, but not yet in it," lent even more of an aura of mystery to late pregnancy as the child might act as an intermediary between the world of its parents and other worlds, bringing otherworldly messages or information.[18] As a result, late pregnancy was often regarded as a time of miracles and prophetic revelations. Accordingly, *Octavian* emphatically constructs the empress's lying-in room as a place of mystery, even of miracles. This comes as a result of the empress's apparently miraculous impregnation, which occurs after her foundation of an abbey in honor of the Virgin Mary. The empress establishes the abbey as part of an explicit plan to seek Mary's intervention to help her conceive an heir. Thus, the pregnancy itself carries the weight of divine intervention. Further, the lying-in room is also the site

men who witness such a scene is evident in the fifteenth-century Middle English gynecological text, *The Knowing of Women's Kind in Childing,* ed. Alexandra Barratt (Turnhout: Brepols, 2001), pp. 40–42. The text suggests that its translation to the vernacular was completed in order to shield women from the embarrassment of male curiosity and slander by making it possible for women to treat other women.

[17] Gail McMurray Gibson, "Scene and Obscene: Seeing and Performing Late Medieval Childbirth," *JMEMSt* 29 (1999): 1–24 (8–9).
[18] Parsons, "The Pregnant Queen," p. 43.

of strange and prophetic dreams in which the empress accurately foretells both her own banishment and the subsequent abduction of her
children by wild creatures (161–71). However, the contamination of
this space through Octavian's intrusion and misreading masks these
signs of wonder associated with the birthing-room, transforming it instead into the patriarchal nightmare of diverted patrilineage.

The emphasis on the enclosed femininity of the space of birthing was
profound enough at times to inspire illicit curiosity about the proceedings behind the curtains, doors, or screens; fictitious representations of
violations of this space are not uncommon, occurring in romances such
as the *Roman de Silence* and the Middle English *Melusine* and suggested
in medieval mystery plays concerning the birth of Christ.[19] Literal invasions of the lying-in room were considered to be crimes against decency.
This is evidenced by the records of a fifteenth-century case against a
Belgian man, "One Henne Venden Damme, [who,] for having hid behind a staircase to eavesdrop upon his wife, she being in labour of childbirth, which thing doth not befit a man, for the said eavesdropping was
fined fifteen livres."[20] The necessary exclusion of men from gynecological knowledge or witnessing on the grounds of decency provided the
justification for female medical practitioners laid out in the 1322 legal
defense of the female physician Jacoba Felicie, which argued that "it is
better and more seemly that a wise woman learned in the art should
visit a sick woman and inquire into the secrets of her nature and her
hidden parts, than a man should do so, for whom it is not lawful to see
and seek out the aforesaid parts. . . . A man should ever avoid and flee
as much as he can the secrets of women and of her societies."[21] It is not
simply a man's physical presence in the lying-in room that is forbidden;
he is not supposed to know or witness what occurs within that space.
Transgression entails not only the violation of the space, but a reflection
on the man's status as a man, as suggested in the language used in both
legal arguments. At the same time, it is their privileged access to this
knowledge that constructs the women involved in a confinement as a
community, or "society."

---

[19] For a reading of this trope in mystery plays, see Gibson, "Scene and Obscene."

[20] Louis Théo Maes, "Les Délits de Moeurs dans les Droit Pénal Coutumier de Ma-
lines," *Revue du Nord* 30 (1948): 5–26 (11–12), quoted in Myriam Greilsammer, "The
Midwife, the Priest, and the Physician: The Subjugation of Midwives in the Low Countries at the End of the Middle Ages," *JMRS* 21 (1991): 285–329 (290).

[21] Renate Blumenfeld-Kosinski, *Not of Woman Born* (Ithaca: Cornell University Press,
1990), p. 94.

The notion that the space of the lying-in room enclosed an alternative female community, however, also gave rise to suspicions regarding the intent and behavior of that community and its consequences both inside and outside the lying-in room. In addition, while the official ceremonies that constructed and maintained the lying-in chamber focused on its dynastic purpose and the validation of its productive value for the realm, the isolation and imposed impermeability of this space inspired not only curiosity but also suspicion and even derision. The fifteenth-century satire *Les Quinze Joies de Mariage* identifies a wife's pregnancy and lying-in as the third of the dubious "joys" of marriage. The text opens its discussion of the husband's woes during his wife's pregnancy by archly suggesting that every pregnancy is fraught with the possibility of infidelity: "elle devient grousse, et a l'aventure ne sera pas de son mari, qui advient souvent."[22] After this sally, the text goes on to decry the extravagant expenditure of entertaining and maintaining the gossips and the demanding wife. The lying-in period is described as a time of female over-indulgence and husband-baiting, with devastating consequences for the rest of the husband's life. The gossips coach the wife in unchaste and self-indulgent behavior, and it is suggested that this behavior is maintained past the lying-in period.[23] The month or so of postpartum isolation is revealed to be nothing other than an expensive excuse for women to get together and drink copious amounts of good wine and eat hard-to-find and extravagant delicacies while assassinating the character of the pregnant woman's husband.[24] With this in mind, wife, gossips, and midwife are represented as colluding in order to deceive the husband as to the severity of his wife's condition so as to prolong the lying-in period and their expensive revelry. Both the threat of infidelity and illegitimacy and the description of the ruinous gluttony and subversive speech that characterize the lying-in room in this text suggest an anxiety that the lying-in room is a space where women gather to take advantage of and deceive men, the husband of the pregnant woman in particular. Secrecy is thus equated not only with power, but with deception and the shame

[22] "She becomes pregnant, and perhaps not by her husband, which often happens." *Les .XV. Joies de Mariage,* ed. Jean Rychner (Geneva: Librairie Droz, 1967), p. 18 (my translation).

[23] Ibid., pp. 19–26.

[24] The consistent association of women with both gluttony and sinful speech was a staple of medieval misogynistic material, as R. Howard Bloch has demonstrated. For an outline and analysis of this association, see his *Medieval Misogyny and the Invention of Western Romantic Love* (Chicago: University of Chicago Press, 1991), pp. 14–22, 65.

of the pregnant woman's husband and the patriarchal order he represents.

In *Octavian,* gossips are singled out as potential liabilities in the construction of the lying-in room through the deceptions of the dowager empress. The figure of the slanderous mother-in-law whose lies result in the expulsion of her grandchildren is a familiar character, from Chaucer's *Man of Law's Tale* and its analogues. As a privileged intimate, the mother-in-law stands in an excellent position to betray trust by undermining her daughter-in-law. In *Octavian,* the dowager empress's particular situation as a member of Octavian's household not only underscores her duplicitous treachery, but actually compounds it by a second related betrayal. As the mother-in-law of the empress and an apparent resident or guest of Octavian's household at the time of his wife's pregnancy, the dowager empress would certainly be recognized by the audience as one of the empress's childbed gossips. It is in fact her machinations and her ability as a gossip to travel between the lying-in room and the outside world that allow her to sabotage the apparent legitimacy of her grandsons. Instead of acting as a witness to the birth and hence legitimacy of Octavian's children, the dowager subverts this role in order to nullify the political and social value of the newborns, in direct violation of the codes that require her presence in the room in the first place. In her attempt to convince her son of his wife's infidelity, the dowager empress draws on the assumed partiality of the gossip for the pregnant woman who has summoned her to her bedside at this critical time. After the mass thanking God for the birth of his sons, Octavian encounters his mother, who expresses first her thanks for the safe delivery of the mother, but not the children. Then she informs her son that his wife's sons are not his:

> "Sone," scho said, "I am full blythe
> That þe empryse sal haf hyre lyfe,
> And lyffe with vs in lande;
> Bot mekyll sorowe dose it me
> That Rome sall wrange ayerde bee,
> And jn vncouthe hande."
> (103–8)

At this point, the dowager empress suggests that she has two contradictory allegiances, two communities whose interests diverge, an overriding anxiety of *Les Quinze Joies* in its treatment of gossips. The dowager skill-fully suggests that she has a sincere personal interest in the well-being of the empress and is happy for her safe delivery from childbirth. This interest evokes her role as gossip, whose foremost allegiance is to the pregnant woman, even at the expense of her husband. Her next state-ment, however, in which she bemoans the fate of Rome's inheritance by an illegitimate bastard, juxtaposes and contrasts her allegiance to the empress as a gossip and a woman with her allegiance to Rome. The dowager empress constructs a competition between the interests of the empress (and her sons) and of Rome, in direct contradiction of Octavi-an's rationale, earlier in the romance, for desiring his wife to conceive. Whereas earlier the delivery of the empress's child was linked to the security of Rome, the dowager empress insinuates that the interests of Octavian's wife and of his land are mutually exclusive and contradictory.

In doing this the dowager empress inverts the suspicions cast on gos-sips in *Les Quinze Joies;* whereas in the satire the solidarity of gossips, prolonging their own enjoyments at the husband's expense, lead to their deception of those outside the lying-in room, in *Octavian* deception is deployed not to protect or cosset the newly delivered woman and her reputation, but rather to defame and endanger her and her children. The tension represented in *Octavian* is not between the lying-in room and the community of women it represents and the masculine world of governance and inheritance, but rather between one gossip, the dowager empress, and both communities that are ideally protected by the lying-in room—that of the mother and her gossips, as well as of the father and primogeniture. The dowager's insistence that the interests of Rome and of the newly delivered mother are mutually exclusive serves only to highlight their interdependence: to believe the dowager's slander and to act on it virtually guarantees that "Rome sall wrange ayerde bee." The description of the violent scene in the lying-in room as "The grete treson that þere was wroght" also underscores the common interests of polity and the childbearing empress by conflating two betrayals into one.

The dowager empress has committed two separate acts of treason against communities of which she is a member. In betraying her com-munity of women, the dowager betrays the larger community of Rome, as well as her son, who represents Rome. By manipulating the lying-in room at its most vulnerable moment and then "exposing" it to male scrutiny and interpretation, the dowager empress conceals her own mas-sive act of treason behind an imaginary one, infidelity. The beleaguered empress's associations with Rome and later Jerusalem, both identified by medieval exegetes with "the Christian Church and soul," render this betrayal a reenactment of Judas' paradigmatic betrayal of Christ.[25] Late medieval identifications of Rome as the daughter of Sion and *synagoga* as the mother of Sion reinforce the status of the mother-in-law as a treacherous and perverse betrayer associated with the enemies not only of imperial Rome, but of Christianity itself.[26] The later triumph of the combined armies of Rome and Jerusalem over Eastern pagan enemies, followed by the reunion of Rome's imperial family and their return to Rome, links the domestic and political stability of Rome with its status as the seat of the Christian faith.

Within this context, it is not surprising that the knowledge that Octavian receives upon his intrusion into the birthing room is terribly distorted, with serious domestic and political consequences attached. Presumably, it is the threat to his masculine identity that induces Octavian to violate the lying-in room in the first place in order to discover its otherwise obscured truths. He approaches the room spurred by his mother's assertion that it is his own sexual deficiency in producing an heir that has compelled his wife to turn to other lovers to conceive and therefore secure her own threatened position in the household. Octavian's mother taunts her son, saying, "'sone myn . . . / For þou mAght no childir haue, / Scho has takyn thy kokes knaue'" (112–16). In this way, she links the lying-in space with the discourse of masculine powerlessness, but in a different formulation than do the practices of protective secrecy around the lying-in room.

The room is therefore linked with sexual shame and the supposed sexual inability of the emperor to provide his people with an heir. The intrusion of a father into this space results then in the realization of his greatest political fears—with the banishment of his sons, it becomes all too likely that "Rome sall wrange ayerde bee" (107). Octavian's mother offers a narrative that explicitly associates what happens in the lying-in room with her son's powerlessness, as well as with the "women's secret" of reproduction. The lying-in room, the dowager empress suggests, will make clear the consequences of her son's insufficient masculinity. Octavian's anxieties concerning sexual impotence drive him to reassert dominance over his wife's body and its secrets by entering the space defined

[25] Suzanne M. Yeager, "*The Siege of Jerusalem* and Biblical Exegesis: Writing About Romans in Fourteenth-Century England," *ChauR* 39 (2004): 70–102 (94, 89).

[26] Ibid., p. 84.

socially by his absence and ignorance. Octavian's mother thus deploys anxieties centering on the intersection of ignorance and secrecy surrounding the lying-in room and taunts her son into reorganizing the room's polarities—first through "discovering" the "secret" prepared for his view and then through his predictable assertion of patriarchal prerogative through violence. The isolation and silence that enshroud the lying-in room after this episode are reframed by Octavian's acquisition of his wife's "secrets" and the uneasy tension that results.

The third crucial aspect of the construction of the aristocratic woman's lying-in room, in addition to its enclosed and feminized status, was its purpose as the site of the reproduction of the state through birth. Childbirth itself was a mystery of state obscured from the sight of men, as "the late medieval woman's space of the birthing room enclosed women's bodies, women's discourse, and women's cultural performance, but also existed, first and foremost, to produce the male children that were the essential links in the chains of male order and control."[27] The political function of the royal lying-in room was often emphasized in the material construction of the space, and the room's enclosing hangings and rugs were to be made up predominantly of the royal colors of scarlet and gold, suitable to the purpose of the room and especially purchased and used to both frame and honor that specific occasion, the birth of the potential heir.[28] Gifts associated specifically with the room and its purpose, including the ritual *deschi* platter, were often decorated with images of the desired product of the birth, a young male child.[29]

In contemporary instructions for midwives, emphasis was placed on the comfort of the room, its consistency with the nobility of the woman's endeavor, its value to the family, and on the need to keep men out rather than on keeping the woman in. Midwives were especially enjoined to concentrate on the social construction of the lying-in room as a place where the woman's feelings and body must be dignified, rather than denigrated or repudiated.[30] This injunction underlines the prevalent ambivalence that characterized social interpretations of childbirth, as well as an authoritative attempt to limit or control that ambivalence, imposing a positive value on birth. Hence, the initial conversion of the lying-in room had the effect of a sort of dramatic staging for an aristo-

---

[27] Gibson, "Scene and Obscene," p. 11.
[28] Orme, *From Childhood to Chivalry,* p. 9.
[29] Gibson, "Scene and Obscene," pp. 11–13.
[30] Blumenfeld-Kosinski, *Not of Woman Born,* p. 16.

cratic or royal birth paradoxically meant to go unseen by the males of the household. The emphasis on the political status of the birthing and lying-in room is crucial to *Octavian,* which opens first with the explicit crisis of a long-childless emperor and his fears for his land's fate should he and his wife die without children "theire landis to rewle one ryghte," which creates his fear that the land will exist "in werre and in kare" should he fail to produce an heir (44–45, 68). This problem is further complicated by the possibility of his wife's alleged infidelity with a servant, a crisis also literally and explicitly located within the space of the lying-in room. The problematic nature of the lying-in room is emphasized by its simultaneous status as the focus of both political wish-fulfillment and of anxiety that the fulfillment of those desires might be illusory or unattainable. As such, it functions as the site of the reproduction of both order and chaos.

Octavian's intrusion into the lying-in room is characterized by violent imagery implicitly suggesting the destabilization of the state. Upon his entrance, he is struck dumb and "wode," maddened by the sight of another man lying in his wife's (and his own) bed (156). The presence of a kitchen servant in the king's bed, particularly on the occasion of the birth of the empire's heir, represents an unacceptable inversion of the proper order of the state, as does the presence, after Octavian's attack, of peasant blood on the emperor's sheets. The proper blood of the emperor and of his wife's labor is displaced by that of the poorest and most ignoble figure in the household, transforming the rich and glorious cloths of the royal bed into rags soaked with the blood of the mean. However, it is at just this moment of inversion that the text reminds us emphatically that, whatever Octavian's interpretation of the scene he finds in the room, his reading is incomplete and his actions unjust. The Thornton manuscript emphasizes the innocence of the "giltles knave" at the moment of his death by Octavian's hand, while the Cambridge text singles out the released "blode" as "gyltles," and later refers to "The grete treson that þere was wroght" (L.158, C.156, 178).

Ironically, this tableau works to refigure the typically stigmatized reading of blood revealed in childbed. In the Middle Ages, the blood of parturition was categorized as menstrual blood, as were forms of female genital bleeding.[31] As such, the blood of childbirth was generally repudi-

---

[31] Peggy McCracken, *The Curse of Eve, the Wound of the Hero* (Philadelphia: University of Pennsylvania Press, 2003), pp. ix, 3.

ated as a pollutant in the same way as menstrual blood. In *Octavian,* the decapitated servant's blood seems simultaneously to efface and double the blood of parturition, replacing and mingling with the mother's childbed blood, and destroying its political significance by appearing to manifest a literal alternative to the blood of the king and father. If, as Peggy McCracken suggests, the woman's blood signifies a sort of inherent sexual contamination specific to women, as well as the disruptive presence of the wife's alternative matrilineal genealogical narrative, *Octavian* takes this logic a step further.[32] Blood on the bedsheets, associated paradoxically with both virginity and the transmission of an illicit or underground matrilineal bloodline, becomes transformed into a completely alternate, and—within the logic of the narrative—fictive, genealogy, representing the patrilineage of the empress's supposed peasant lover. Finally, the image of the head toppling off the servant's body and into the emperor's bed implicitly suggests the fall of the royal head from the body politic, emphasized by Octavian's beastlike status as speechless and unreasoning: "wode."

The literal consequences of Octavian's "discovery" potentially mirror these details of the nightmarish tableau in that the true heirs to the empire are first threatened with execution and finally separated from the state through the banishment of both themselves and their mother. The literal decapitation of the kitchen servant becomes the likely foreshadowing of the realm's permanent state, with the expulsion of the infant heirs to Octavian's throne.

Childbirth and the Church

Within its political context, *Octavian* constructs the lying-in room as a positive space of state reproduction, although one that is nonetheless marked by anxieties concerning the unilaterally patrilineal character of that reproduction. However, the introduction of the discourse of sexual contamination into the lying-in room is further related to the medieval Christian church's frequent identification of this space as a site of particularly pernicious sexual contamination, a discourse that clearly resonated with aristocratic anxieties regarding the potential contamination of the patriline. In the case of church discourses regarding the woman's reproductive body and the rituals that were informed by them, however,

[32] Ibid., p. 58.

a woman's sexual contamination represented not merely potential, but inherent threats to both her husband and to the larger community of the faithful.

The status of the pregnant and recently delivered maternal body in the medieval church was highly ambiguous due to conflicting doctrinal opinions as to whether a pregnant woman was eligible to enter the church or to receive the sacraments. The close association of childbirth with sexuality and therefore with sin rendered the pregnant body particularly representative of sexual activity and man's fallen nature. McCracken notes that "while childbirth is not a sin in itself, it is associated with the pollution of sin, and the logic of churching reflects that association, even though the ritual is often characterized as one of thanksgiving"[33] At the same time, the association of childbearing with women's spiritual salvation problematized an outright condemnation of the gravid woman.[34] This potential contradiction had had a long history in the church, particularly in England. Many of Augustine's questions posed to Pope Gregory at the end of the sixth century related to the particular spiritual status of menstruating and pregnant women, as well as their eligibility to participate in Mass and the sacraments. Gregory's letter to Augustine, dated around 600, while considered moderate, highlights the contradictory nature of the church's response to pregnancy. According to Pope Gregory, churching was a ritual of thanksgiving rather than purification, and therefore a woman should be allowed to enter the church to give thanks immediately after birth, without sin.[35] In this message, Gregory also reminds Augustine that "the fruitfulness of the flesh is no sin in the eyes of Almighty God," and refers to pregnancy itself as God's "gift of grace."[36] For this reason, he explains, pregnant women are eligible to be baptized.

Clerical associations of women's bodies in general, and pregnant bodies in particular, with pollution became more prevalent and exaggerated in the later Middle Ages, and particularly during and after the "eleventh

[33] Ibid., p. 68.

[34] "Notwithstanding she shall be saved in childbearing, if they continue in faith and charity and holiness with sobriety" (I Timothy 2:14). In representations of childbirth and childbirth culture, Hellwarth sees a struggle with conflicting doctrines of fruitfulness and chastity. See Jennifer Wynne Hellwarth, *The Reproductive Unconscious in Medieval and Early Modern England* (New York: Routledge, 2002), p. 6.

[35] *Bede's Ecclesiastical History of the English People,* ed. Bertram Colgrave and R. A. B Mynors (Oxford: Clarendon Press, 1969), pp. i. 27, pp. 88, 89, 90, 91.

[36] Ibid., i. 27, pp. 89, 91.

and twelfth centuries amidst the turmoil and zeal of ecclesiastical reforms striving to make clerical celibacy the accepted norm and a reality
in the church."[37] The earliest liturgical evidence for formalized churching ceremonies appears to date from this time, according to Rieder, who
suggests that these rituals not only "cured" the contamination of the
pregnant body but also symbolically produced these bodies as polluted
in the first place through the call for the purification ceremony itself.
The definition of the pregnant body as a contaminated and potentially
contaminating object seems to have become increasingly recognized and
prevalent throughout the late Middle Ages, resulting in the widespread
practice by which women who had died in childbirth or before churching in the church itself were buried not in the church itself but in the
churchyard.[38]

In practice, the ritual of churching appears to have been widely
viewed by practitioners and by participants as an act of ritual purification, which coincided with thanksgiving. During the time of her confinement, a pregnant or postpartum woman was figuratively expelled
from the Christian community as a sexual contaminant, refused admit-
tance into sacred space, whether the church or (in some parishes) consecrated ground, and refused administration of holy rites. Still filled with
the "bodily fluids of lustful generation," the woman's womb became
doubly contaminated, by the presence of both the salacious liquids of
intercourse and the menstrual material forming the matter of the unborn child and staining the sheets at birth.[39] The humoral imbalances
and sexual contamination related to childbirth necessitated churching
and, in some cases, exorcism, as the pregnant woman was believed to
be particularly vulnerable to demonic possession.[40] For Taglia, the custom of refusing to bury either pregnant women or those who had died
in childbirth in holy ground due to the fear of spiritual contamination

---

[37] Paula M. Rieder, "Insecure Borders: Symbols of Clerical Privilege and Gender Am-
biguity in the Liturgy of Churching," in *The Material Culture of Sex, Procreation, and
Marriage in Premodern Europe,* ed. Anne L. McClanan and Karen Rosoff Encarnación
(New York: Palgrave, 2002), pp. 93–114 (99).

[38] Nicholas Orme, *Medieval Children* (New Haven: Yale University Press, 2001), p.
31.

[39] Gail McMurray Gibson, "Saint Anne and the Religion of Childbed: Some East
Anglian Texts and Talismans," in *Interpreting Cultural Symbols: Saint Anne in Late Medie-
val Society,* ed. Kathleen Ashley and Pamela Sheingorn (Atlanta: University of Georgia
Press, 1990), pp. 95–110 (96). See also Carolly Erickson, *The Medieval Vision: Essays in
History and Perception* (Oxford: Oxford University Press, 1976), p. 196.

[40] Rieder, "Insecure Borders," p. 99.

of the sacred through proximity to the woman's body and that of her potentially unbaptized child demonstrates that these compromised and contaminated bodies were "not and could never be part of the Christian community or the plan of salvation."[41] In some parishes, a woman was refused Christian burial in consecrated ground not only if she were still pregnant or just delivered at the time of her death, but also if the ritual purification of churching, typically performed thirty to forty days after birth, had yet to be carried out.[42] The belief that the contaminated and unpurified body of the recently pregnant woman would attract demons that could desecrate the entire churchyard constructed the pregnant woman specifically as a potential threat to the souls of the entire community.[43]

Christian rituals and ritualistic activity surrounding childbirth and the lying-in room structured that space as the site of a pregnant woman's profound and potentially permanent separation from the community of believers. When a woman neared childbirth, she was encouraged to go to confession, due to the physical and spiritual danger of her condition.[44] For noble and royal wives, this procedure was formalized in the ritual of houselling, in which the pregnant woman would walk from her home to a nearby chapel to confess her sins, then walk back home to her bedchamber, from which she would not emerge until thirty to forty days after she had given birth.[45] At this time, she would emerge with much pomp to attend her churching ceremony, which was modeled upon the Marian example, commemorating the presentation of Christ

[41] Kathryn Taglia, "The Cultural Construction of Childhood: Baptism, Communion, and Confirmation," in *Women, Marriage, and Family in Medieval Christendom: Essays in Memory of Michael M. Sheehan, C.S.B,* ed. Constance M. Rousseau and Joel T. Rosenthal (Kalamazoo: Western Michigan University Press, 1998), pp. 255–88 (259). For a discussion of the specific controversies concerning the appropriate burial site of a postpartum woman and/or her child who died during a Caesarean section, see Blumenfeld-Kosinski, *Not of Woman Born,* p. 26. See Erickson, *The Medieval Vision,* pp. 195–97, for a further discussion of church and folk beliefs concerning menstrual contamination, pregnancy, death, and burial.

[42] Orme, *From Childhood to Chivalry,* pp. 8–9; Blumenfeld-Kosinski, *Not of Woman Born,* p. 26; See also Gail McMurray Gibson, *Theatre of Devotion* (Chicago: University of Chicago Press, 1989), p. 61.

[43] Erickson, *The Medieval Vision,* p. 196.

[44] Orme, *From Childhood to Chivalry,* p. 9.

[45] The conversion of the woman's bedchamber into a lying-in room was completed at this time, and her return from the church marked the official change in status of the room. See Staniland, "Royal Entry into the World," p. 309.

to the temple forty days after she had given birth.[46] En route to the churching, the woman to be thus purified was accompanied by a number of the gossips who had attended her and wore a veil on the journey, maintaining the ritual containment of the contaminated woman, her isolation from the Christian community, to be lifted, with the veil, at the ceremony of purification.[47]

This ritual sequence of feminine separation, containment, and reintegration in many ways resembles the ritualistic domestic activity surrounding the domestic and dynastic lying-in room, yet it constructs the lying-in room as a space marked by an exile from community rather than the reproduction of it. Both Church and domestic rituals surrounding aristocratic childbirth center on the confinement and the creation of a ritualized space of childbirth that is nevertheless characterized by each discourse in radically different ways. Like the domestic ritual of childbearing, the dominant trope describing the condition of the lying-in room is of containment, but a containment signifying the figurative expulsion and absence of the pregnant woman from the community of the faithful through contamination, rather than the expulsion of men from the revelation of the mysteries of both the woman's body and the process of the reproduction of the state. Within sacred rituals concerned with childbirth, the dominant trope is that of the carnal and spiritual contamination of women in general, and of pregnant women in particular, and the character of the woman's confinement seems to figure her expulsion from the community of the righteous until the purification of that contamination.

While sacred and secular rituals and practices centered on the pregnant body seem to offer opposing constructions of the pregnant body

---

[46] Danièle Alexandre-Bidon and Didier Lett, *Children in the Middle Ages, Fifth Through Fifteenth Centuries* (Notre Dame: University of Notre Dame Press, 1999), p. 14. As Gibson notes, Mary's purification differed from that of other women as it was unnecessary due to the Virgin's sinless conception of Christ. Mary's submission to the ritual was seen as emblematic of her humility. See Gibson, "Blessing from Sun and Moon," p. 139. In his *Lyf of Oure Lady*, Lydgate lingers on Mary's exemption from Purification due to her unblemished purity, and hence her condescension and humility in suffering the ritual. Lydgate emphasizes the superfluity of the ritual twice in Book VI, lines 15–35 and 57–90. John Lydgate, *A Critical Edition of John Lydgate's Life of Our Lady*, ed. Joseph A. Lauritis, Ralph A. Klinefelter, and Vernon F. Gallagher, Duquesne Studies Philological Series 2 (Pittsburgh: Duquesne University Press, 1961).

[47] Gibson, "Blessing from Sun and Moon," p. 149; Wilson, "The Ceremony of Childbirth," p. 78.

and its societal significance, in everyday practice there was much inter-dependence between them. The resultant multiplicity of contradictory perspectives left the pregnant woman in a profoundly ambiguous posi-tion. For example, the interdiction against pregnant women leaving the birthing-room made their exclusion from the church somewhat redun-dant. In effect, a divergence developed in the church between doctrinal authorities, who seemed to validate the pregnant body, or at least not to discriminate strongly against it, and the logic of the sacred rituals surrounding that body, as well as the apparent interpretations of actual clergy, as evidenced by their practices within parishes that clearly identi-fied the pregnant and postpartum body as a dangerous contaminant. Local parish priests often seemed to gravitate toward the ritual interpre-tations of the pregnant body, rather than doctrinal assurances of the pregnant woman's position within the divine plan. These positions were taken despite documents discussing the position of the church, such as Gregory's response to Augustine, which seemed to mitigate the sense of contamination associated with the pregnant and postpartum body. Ultimately, even the most misogynistic interpretations of churching allowed for the ability of the polluted postpartum body to become reintegrated within the community, revalued through the ritual of puri-fication. Yet this was a status that could be granted only after a public ritual and after a certain amount of time had passed during which, pre-sumably, the malignant effects of the contaminated state would have faded. As a result, while the secular and sacred practices surrounding the pregnant woman seem to diverge greatly in their constructions of the value of what occurs within lived experience, these constructions seemed to intersect, resulting in a profound ambivalence, even confu-sion, regarding the status of the pregnant woman and the space and rituals associated with her pregnancy, delivery, and gradual reintegra-tion within the community.

The Postpartum Body and Community

While the actual ceremony of churching was constructed by church rit-ual and performed within the church space as a rite of purification carry-ing clear implications as to the degraded status of the pregnant female body, the journey to and return from the chapel was often attended by a festive atmosphere. The *Liber Regie Capelle* specifies that a delivered queen be dressed in particularly valuable (and usually new) robes and set up in an extravagant state bed as if she were still completely bed-bound.[48] Duchesses were to fold back the covers while a pair of dukes helped the queen from her bed. A procession including these figures as well as the gossips and midwife went to the church, where special prayers and blessings were performed before the queen could enter. Wealthy women often gave alms and donations at and near the church after the ceremony and arranged for minstrels or other entertainers to entertain the household during the post-churching celebrations, which in the case of very wealthy or noble mothers, could be lavish indeed, including feasts, jousts, and, eventually, the performance of masques.[49]

Purification or churching feasts and banquets appear to have become widespread in England during the thirteenth, fourteenth, and fifteenth centuries.[50] The post-churching celebration of a royal or aristocratic birth could be and often was an elaborately staged political spectacle signifying the power and wealth of the concerned family as well as the significance of the heir to the land. As this birth-centered celebration had the most available preparatory time and was conducted after most of the immediate perils of birth had passed for both mother and infant, it was generally the most extravagant opportunity for festivities following an aristocratic or royal birth.[51]

The post-churching celebration acted to refigure the significance of the churching ceremony, which strongly attributed negative implications to the politically expedient and anticipated birth of an heir, promoting a more positive interpretation of the ritual as an act of thanksgiving, a celebration of the woman's safe delivery, and a display of the affluence and rank of woman's family. The sumptuous celebration following a churching thus functioned as a juxtaposed response against the discourse of contamination associated by church ritual with child-bearing, offering a counterdiscourse that reconfigured the positive aristocratic interpretation of the lying-in room and its function within

[48] Staniland, "Royal Entry into the World," p. 308.

[49] See Gibson, "Blessing from Sun and Moon," p. 147; Staniland, "Royal Entry into the World," p. 308. For accounts of expenditures concerning churching and post-churching festivities, see also Jennifer Ward, *Women of the English Nobility and Gentry, 1066–1500* (Manchester: Manchester University Press, 1995), pp. 68–70.

[50] Becky Lee, "Men's Recollections of a Women's Rite: Medieval English Men's Recollections Regarding the Rite of Purification After Childbirth," *Gender & History* 14 (2002): 224–41 (230).

[51] See Staniland, "Royal Entry into the World," pp. 299–308, and Lee, "Men's Recollections," pp. 224–41, for more detailed descriptions of churching feasts in England in the fourteenth and fifteenth centuries.

society. In addition, it has been suggested that the very extravagance of the feasts and celebrations functioned not only as a declaration of a family's power and wealth but also served as a safeguard to smooth patrilineal transition at the death of the newborn's father. Becky Lee notes that in proof-of-age inquests, guests who had attended purification rituals were often used as witnesses to testify as to whether an heir was old enough to inherit his father's property in his own right.[52] To this end, purification feasts were intended to be as memorable as possible, so that the exact year of birth of a potential heir would be fixed in the memories of potential witnesses. In addition, gifts with the date inscribed on them were also distributed to prominent guests at the festivities in an attempt to fix the memory of the heir's date of birth and create a communally accepted fact or history of the heir's arrival and legitimacy, particularly in the memories of the more powerful guests. The event of birth itself as well as its communal significance therefore are given social reality and force through the churching feast and the opportunities it created to establish communal bonds between men and later to call on those men to testify on behalf of a deceased father's heir if need be, to safeguard his patrimony. This suggests that while the mother was the most visible celebrant and guest of honor at the festivities, patriarchal discourses and strategies were also overtly bound to the churching ritual. As both Lee and Parsons suggest, the churching ritual also underscored the sexual potency of the father, as the presence of his wife and child made obvious.[53] The coincident themes of inheritance and sexuality highlight the significance of the empress's purification feast as the moment that Octavian chooses to reveal his wife's "infidelity" and its consequences in *Octavian*.

The distortion of community interests constructed by the dowager empress earlier in the romance becomes fully realized at the purification feast of the empress, in a sort of parodic inversion of the forms of community bonding described by Lee as a chief product of purification feasts. Whereas Lee suggests that purification feasts often functioned as an opportunity for new fathers to forge, recognize, and advertise their bonds with other well-placed men in their community and acquain-

---

[52] Lee, "Men's Recollections," p. 224.

[53] See ibid, p. 236, and Parsons, "The Pregnant Queen," p. 49. Note that while Lee suggests that the purification festivities marked the return of the wife to the conjugal bed and therefore highlighted her active sexual status, Parsons suggests that the passive presence of the objectified mother acts to mask or de-emphasize her sexuality.

tance, *Octavian* suggests the potential for these communities to become destructive of the larger good if they follow the sort of competitive model against the female community of childbirth laid out by the dowager empress. At the feast, Octavian tells the story of his wife's "betrayal," omitting all names, to an ad hoc jury of men attending the feast, who are asked to judge the fate of the anonymous adulteress. The formation of a specifically masculine community of "All þe lordes" who "abowte hym stode" in order to make "juggement . . . Of hir what worthy were" suggests the implementation of the dowager empress's construction of mutually antagonistic camps of assumed adulterous and deceptive women and politically powerful men who represent the greater polity (212, 218–19). The condemnation of the empress for her "treson" recalls the "treson" within the lying-in room, as well as the essential ignorance, not only of the guests at the feast (and particularly the empress's father, who pronounces her sentence) but also of Octavian himself, who perpetuates his mother's counterproductive construction of society through his deliberate delineation of a gendered tension of which Rome is the biggest victim.

The struggle between secular aristocratic and sacred discourses surrounding the contained site of childbearing and represented in the juxtaposition between churching and post-churching festivities is dramatized by the entrapment and accusation of the empress, first by her mother-in-law, and again at her churching feast. At these moments in the romance, the sacred discourse of contamination problematically invades the aristocratic lying-in room, making it and the structures of lineal continuity, and hence the state's political status, unstable and unacceptably vulnerable. The invasion of men, and the breaking of the lying-in room's self-contained space of secrecy and of mystery, is made possible first by the imputation that the lying-in room is not in fact characterized by the positive interpretation granted by the aristocratic discourse, but rather as a space of sexual contamination, as suggested by the sacred discourses and representations concerning childbirth. The emperor's mother represents the lying-in room not as the site of simultaneous mystery and miraculous revelation, but rather as the place in which an unwelcome "truth," that of the "true" origin of the children, will be revealed. Ironically, it is this revelation that is false, engineered by the omnipresent figure of the evil mother-in-law. The dowager empress cannily represents the room and the mother as the site of sexual contamination, a discourse already allotted that space by the sacred interpretation of the pregnant body as a site of sexual pollution and of the lying-in room as a place of contamination and of death. The suggestion of sexual contamination is heightened by the class miscegenation implied by the presence of the kitchen lad in the empress's childbed, as well as by the direct association of the alleged adultery with the political consequences of such an act, the likelihood that the realm, so long heirless, is now in fact "wrange ayerde" and "in uncouthe hande" (107, 108). She asserts,

> ". . . sone myn,
> Wete þou wele þay [the children] are noghte thyne,
> And þat lykes me full ill.
> For þou myghte no childir haue,
> Scho hase takyn thy kokes knaue;
> I will it prove thurgh skyll."
>
> (112–17)

After bribing a reluctant and terrified kitchen servant to join the unconscious empress in her bed, Octavian's mother brings her son into the room, breaking taboo, supposedly revealing the truth concealed behind the walls and veils of the birthing room while in actuality rupturing that space and distorting the nature of the secrets created within. She uses the discourse of sexual contamination to make her claims appear more reasonable, playing on her son's own perceived inability either to know or participate in the mysteries confined in that space. With "skyll," the dowager joins the linked, though opposing, discourses of lineal reproduction and of sexual contamination already associated with the lying-in room, with disastrously effective and provocative results. While the secret of the lying-in room has changed in character, from the mysterious secrets of state regeneration to the revealed "truth" of sexual pollution, after its initial violation it is kept as tightly contained as if nothing untoward has happened, regaining the insularity granted it by both sacred and secular discourse.

With the entrance of Octavian and his mother into the lying-in room, the disruption of the room by the discourse of contamination produces an immediate and drastic effect on the space. It is transformed at once into a site resembling that described by the sacred interpretations of the status of the lying-in room, which indeed becomes the site of death, contamination by abjectified blood (that of the servant), and of the expulsion of the empress and her twin sons from the community and kingdom. Ironically, however, this transformation is easily interpreted as itself the product of a sort of contamination, perhaps not sexual in the manner suggested within sacred interpretations of the space, but surely gendered, the result of the breach of the inviolate space of birth, metonymic with the purity of the womb, by the intrusion of interdicted male presences. In effect, the presence of the sacred discourse of contamination emphasizes that contamination is taking place, transforming the practical identity of the problematic, yet politically necessary space by its mere presence, into its own object, its own constructed representation.

Ironically, it is at the feast marking the reintegration and purification of the empress that she is expelled yet again, significantly on the (false) accusation of sexual contamination. At the churching feast, the discourse of sexual contamination comes into direct conflict with the discourse of birth as state holiday and source of thanksgiving. Octavian's narrative reinvasion and disbanding of the contained and tabooed space of childbearing reverses the usual status of the post-churching celebration as the site of a secular rebuttal of church discourses of childbirth contamination, instead transforming that space of social reaffirmation of childbirth and its political and social value into a declaration that the church has essentially had it right after all. The banishment of the empress and her sons from her husband's lands functions as a dramatic reenactment of the figurative expulsion from and return to society represented within Christian rituals concerning childbirth. The acceptance of the sacred imputation of sexual shame within the lying-in room, however, has a high political cost—the loss of empress and heirs—and it is perhaps not surprising that the mass response of the aristocratic guests at the pronouncement of the Empress's sentence is not of vindication, but rather of intense grief, of "dole and grete peté" (232).

Despite the apparent ascendance of the sacred discourse of childbirth as a form of contamination within *Octavian,* this interpretation is thoroughly undermined within the romance itself. Most simply and directly, it is clear to the audience throughout that the empress herself is innocent of the sexual crime of which she is accused. Her innocence is merely emphasized by her literal unconsciousness of the man in bed next to her. Even this potential danger to her chastity is diffused by the servant's care to avoid even the possibility of touching her, as "euir he droghe hym ferre away / For þe rechese þat scho jn laye" (145–46). These strategies of narrative defense of the empress highlight the unwarranted nature of her expulsion and the accusation of sexual guilt leveled at her; from the secular point of view of the romance, in the space of the lying-in room, it is not the empress who is unclean; her expulsion is unjust and, politically, potentially disastrous. Aware of the falsity of the charges against the empress and cued by the romance's early emphasis on the emperor's dynastic woes, the audience's attention and sympathy is shifted away from the discourse of pollution and to the personal plight of the empress, which is linked to the political plight of Rome. Octavian's misreading of childbirth as adultery is undermined along with the legitimacy of any claim of sexual contamination attaching itself to the empress or to this birth. Further, the romance reimagines the generalized accusation of sexual contamination leveled at all women by the church and some secular discourses as a clearly spiteful and underhanded slander against a maligned and innocent woman who happens to be vital to the political future of Rome.

In addition to undermining her connection to any sort of discourse of sexual contamination, the romance reconstructs the empress's relationship to religion as a positive value, emphasizing her status as the romance's only overtly pious character. Her association with religion is made a part of her character's virtues and highlights her unique religious exemplarity in a romance that includes Saracen enemies and ostensibly holy wars, but no sustained emphasis on Christianity. In contrast, it is the empress who suggests the building of an abbey as a solution to her childlessness, she who begs that her children be christened before they die so that their souls might be spared, and she who, upon the loss of her children to the abducting animals, acknowledges her sorrows as just punishment for her sins and who vows to dedicate her life to holy works in Jerusalem (400–405). Significantly, this emphasis on the empress's piety is present only in the Middle English redactions of the romance; earlier versions lay pious remorse on the marginally more sympathetic Octavian.[54] The empress's piety and strong connections to Rome, then Jerusalem, and the later rescue of Christian forces against explicitly pagan enemies further validates the empress as a single site through which the imperial power of Rome's armies is fused in a Holy War with

[54] Harriet Hudson, "Introduction," in *Four Middle English Romances: Sir Isumbras, Octavian, Sir Eglamour of Artois, Sir Tryamour,* ed. Harriet Hudson (Kalamazoo: TEAMS/Medieval Institute Publications, 1996), pp. 47–48.

Jerusalem's armies, supported and embodied by the prowess of the younger Octavian and his leonine companion.[55]

The wrongful expulsion of the empress and her children causes a rupture in the political sphere of Rome. With the empress's banishment, the ruptured space of the lying-in room is repeatedly revisited in the wilderness, suggesting a need to restore the corrupted site of reproduction. Seeking solace at a fountain in a clearing, the empress's sons are, respectively, abducted by an ape and a lioness. Having abducted the heir to the throne, the lioness is herself attacked by a griffin, another heraldic beast, who carries her and the child to an isolated island, far from her own cubs (355–63). The child's safety, asserts the speaker, is due to his royal blood, "for it was a kynge sone iwysse, / The liones moghte do it no mys" (349–50). Instead, the lioness protects him and loves him and, significantly, legitimates him through his very immunity from her violence. Attacked by the male griffin within the isolated and enclosed space, the lioness returns the aggression and slays the griffin, rewriting the experience of the empress in such a way as to protect the integrity of the island's space from adult male intrusion, incorporating Octavian's own beastlike violence in the defense, rather than in the violation of the contained space of state reproduction.

The lioness then converts the island into a den, closely resembling the space of the lying-in room, for the sake of her new charge, whom she "lufe[s] . . . for hir whelpes sake," suckling him, playing with and kissing him (374, 376, 445–47). The lioness's policing of an isolated and contained space of mothering by a female mother figure is continued as she later slays two curious sailors who invade the island looking for water. The analogy of the island with the lying-in room is a function not only of its isolation, or of the violent repulsion of male intruders perpetrated by the lioness, but also by the fundamental inability of men confronted with the interdicted space to cope with what they see there. Like Octavian, the twelve soldiers who find the den are struck by "drede," rendered, in a phrase mirroring that used to describe Octavian,

---

[55] Suzanne Yeager notes the medieval identification of Rome as the New Jerusalem, an association that lent Rome a double status both "as city and as personification of the Church." The conflation of Rome and Jerusalem also allied imperial and religious ideologies while simultaneously encouraging ambivalent identifications with both Romans and defending Jews, she suggests. See Yeager, "*The Siege of Jerusalem* and Biblical Exegesis," pp. 71, 93–95.

"nere wode," by the sight of the lioness's home, as well as by the empress's safety within (447, 471). Like the lying-in room, the lioness's island den is the site of femininity, maternity, wonder, and brutal violence, this time appropriated from Octavian's misinformed rage and channeled toward the preservation of the crucial intact status of the lying-in room. Significantly, the lioness allows the empress to safely approach both herself and the child, reclaiming her son, and bringing him safely to the world outside. These repeated intrusions throughout seem to revisit the original site of intrusion, that of the lying-in room, as well as its catastrophic vulnerability, and, finally, of its restoration through the wondrous interference of a heraldic beast.

The fact that the abductor of the heir to Octavian's throne is not merely a heraldic beast, but a lioness, is crucial to her role in the reconstruction of the lying-in room and thus to the restoration of Octavian's ruptured state. The lioness's re-creation and restoration of the violated space of the lying-in room, as well as her implicit legitimation of the young heir to the Roman throne, allows the reconstruction of the lying-in room to take place without the potentially problematic presence of the empress's necessarily sexualized body. The lioness's parallels to the empress, her status as the mother of two lost offspring, her involuntary banishment from her home by an aggressive male intruder, and her association with royalty through her heraldic status make her a clear analogue to the beleaguered empress, but one better equipped to handle the vicissitudes of her predicament. Additionally, however, as a heraldic beast she seems to signify the secular and political significance of the child as a product of royalty, both legitimating him and repairing the tattered sense of wonder and mystery associated with the lying-in room without any association with the sexual process that brings the empress to the lying-in room in the first place. In addition, as a beast, the lioness is free of the bloody taint of contamination associated with human mothers through the blood of menstruation and parturition. Albert the Great explains the more advanced development of newborn animals as opposed to human babies due to the lack of menstruation in the animal world.[56] According to Albert, because female animals do not suffer the same humoral superfluities as do women, they do not menstruate and therefore retard the growth of their young by contact with that debased

[56] Clarissa Atkinson, *The Oldest Vocation: Christian Motherhood in the Middle Ages* (Ithaca: Cornell University Press, 1991), p. 41.

fluid, unlike human mothers. The lioness's status as a nonmenstruating stand-in for the empress further distances her from potential discourses of sexual impurity. Her creation of the den with her paws, and her early care of the child without the presence of his mother or of her gossips, displaces him from a site of containment characterized by individual women's femininity, putting him in a space represented by her own desexualized and totemic femininity. Thus, the lioness's restoration of the contained and inviolate space of state reproduction takes place through the displacement of the empress, who only reappears to carry her son to the aristocratic court of Jerusalem, where the wonder of the lioness's regal and mysterious presence serves as both the empress's vindication and her son's legitimation. The young Octavian becomes defined not as his mother's son, but as the legitimate son of a "kynge," of Octavian the elder, restoring lineal continuity by bypassing the potentially (though not actually) problematic empress altogether. Significantly, his mother only reappears at the end of the romance with the final reunion of the dispersed family.

Noble medieval childbirth was experienced by women and their communities largely as a staged performance rather than as a biological function through which maternal and lay female cultural identity is constructed through the placement of the gravid woman within a ritualized space. However, the conflicting discourses of secular and sacred authorities and customs made the exact status of that identity equivocal. As an expectant mother to an heir, an aristocratic woman could, depending on who was describing her, embody the stability and hopes of the realm, and her own centrality to the (re)production of the state, or she could, conversely, embody the wretched contamination and site of death that must be expelled from the community of the righteous for the protection of all. As in festive practices following the churching ritual for recently delivered women, *Octavian* marks and joins the competition between two related forms of discourse that attempt to bound and define the space of reproduction. The sacred discourse of female contamination is roundly displaced in *Octavian* by a counterdiscourse of male contamination and through the displacement of the female body as signifier of the ritualized space with the wondrous and heraldic figure of the lioness. In both the churching celebration and the romance, there is an emphasis on the political work performed within the lying-in room and its positive impact on societal stability, a theme emphasized within the physical construction of the lying-in space itself. Further, the very validity of the discourse of contamination concerning the lying-in room is revealed as catastrophically dangerous to the integrity of the state itself, and is thus not only undermined, but is repeatedly attacked through strategies of displacement and of refutation through the pious example of the empress. However, the romance ultimately does not function as a sort of proto-feminist vindication of the status of women in general but rather as a defense of the integrity of the state reproduced within the confines of the lying-in room against the corrosive associations of that space with sexual contamination, a threat absolutely inimical to the status of that space as a legitimate zone of state stability. Of course, the anxiety that the lying-in room was inherently marked by sexual contamination and the implicit threat of miscegenation suggests the resultant fear that any and every kingdom might indeed be "wrange ayerd," an untenable conclusion for aristocratic dynasties. The displacement of the empress by the lioness, however, demonstrates the lingering anxiety attached to the actual maternal body, and the desire for a less problematic and more incontrovertible vessel of legitimacy.

"Beginning and Beginning-Again":

Processions, Plays, and Civic Politics in York and Chester

Margaret Aziza Pappano and Nicole R. Rice
Queen's University and *St. John's University*

IN LATE MEDIEVAL ENGLAND, the expansion of Corpus Christi festivities to include long sermons, elaborate processions, and dramatic
performances suggests widespread enthusiasm for the new feast.[1] York
and Chester, unusually among English towns, developed processions
and biblical play cycles, both civic productions involving the craft
guilds, as linked forms of Corpus Christi performance.[2] This commonality, together with their abundance of records, invites a comparative analysis of procession and drama in these two towns.[3] In York and Chester,
the spilling over of the feast to different days bespeaks tension as well

We would like to thank the anonymous readers for *Studies in the Age of Chaucer* for
helpful suggestions on this essay. We are grateful for comments from participants in the
New Medievalisms conference at the University of Western Ontario in 2005, especially
Bruce Holsinger for insights on liturgy. Thanks are due members of the Yale University
Medieval and Renaissance Colloquium, particularly Marcia Colish and Scott Newstok,
for questions on the Chester material. We dedicate this article to Robert W. Hanning,
whose scholarship and teaching inspired our work.

[1] Corpus Christi was universally promulgated in 1317 and published in England in
1318. See Miri Rubin, *Corpus Christi: The Eucharist in Late Medieval Europe* (Cambridge:
Cambridge University Press, 1991), pp. 181, 199.

[2] Biblical cycle drama associated with Corpus Christi seems to have been the exception rather than the rule in later medieval England. Although liturgical processions for
Corpus Christi were relatively common, research into local dramatic traditions shows
that drama was not more widespread on Corpus Christi than on other occasions such as
Whitsuntide or Midsummer. See Alexandra Johnston, "The Feast of Corpus Christi in
the West Country," *Early Theatre* 6.1 (2003): 15–34.

[3] For a recent study that considers the York and Chester cycles comparatively, see
Christina M. Fitzgerald, *The Drama of Masculinity and Medieval English Guild Culture*
(New York: Palgrave, 2007). Fitzgerald's insight that these two cycles are both distinctly concerned with masculinity accords with our perspective, although we differ in
believing that the representations of masculinity must be further contextualized with
reference to artisanal politics and interests.

as celebration, as the feast day itself became unable to accommodate the diverse urban interests marking its observance. In both towns, processions and drama were separated from each other and performed on different days. Viewing this separation as more than simply a pragmatic decision to accommodate expanding play cycles, we explore a larger set of issues underlying the relation of procession to drama through a close analysis of each cycle's first pageant, an episode that interrogates civic ceremonial itself.[4] In doing so, we expand upon recent work that emphasizes the self-reflexivity of civic theater, offering a new explanatory paradigm for the treatment of the angelic fall in the York "Fall of the Angels" and the Chester "Fall of Lucifer" pageants.[5] Both are suffused with light imagery, and both stage the angels' fall in terms of a competition over brightness. The depiction of Lucifer as the chief angel who embodies and then loses God's light in the opening moments of creation was widespread in medieval commentary and drama. Yet the terms of contestation over light in these two urban pageants point to a specific historical form of light-bearing as a context for civic dramatic production. This contestation can be located within the struggle for craft guild precedence represented by the bearing of torches in the liturgical procession of Corpus Christi. In examining the urban contexts for this representation, we explore how the ceremonial practices of each city influenced the dramatic presentation of Lucifer's fall.

The legend of the angelic fall developed from biblical sources, including Genesis 1–3, the creation story, Genesis 6, the account of the "sons of God" who fell to earth in search of human wives, and Isaiah 14:12–15, in which the prophet refers to Lucifer, cast into hell for his attempt to rival God.[6] Meditating on the origins of evil, Augustine interpreted

[4] Following medieval usage, we employ the term "pageants" to refer to the short episodes that make up the larger cycles. "Pageant" (*pagina*) had a range of meanings in late medieval England: it could refer to a wagon used for performance or to the performance itself, whether a sort of mime show (tableau) or a fully scripted drama.

[5] Kathleen Ashley explores several of the York pageants as reflexive cultural productions commenting upon questions of status, work, and gender in late medieval York. She stresses the variety of forms reflexivity might take, from pageants that seem to celebrate a guild's participation in drama, to pageants that may offer "deliberate critique of the craft and its work through the visual and verbal signs." Kathleen Ashley, "Sponsorship, Reflexivity, and Resistance: Cultural Readings of the York Cycle Plays," in *The Performance of Middle English Culture: Essays on Chaucer and the Drama in Honor of Martin Stevens,* ed. James J. Paxson, Lawrence M. Clopper, and Sylvia Tomasch (Cambridge: D. S. Brewer, 1998), pp. 9–24, quotation on p. 18.

[6] For a full summary of patristic and early medieval commentary on the angelic fall, see Edward J. Montano, *The Sin of the Angels: Some Aspects of the Teaching of St. Thomas* (Washington, D.C.: Catholic University of America Press, 1955), pp. 1–78. The Isaiah verses, which describe Lucifer desiring in his heart to "exalt my throne above the stars of God . . . sit in the mount of the covenant . . . ascend above the height of the clouds

the angels' "turning away from him who supremely is, and their turning toward themselves" as the first-ever instance of pride.[7] While Augustine made little mention of the chief angel's physical appearance, the name Lucifer ("light-bearer"), the title of the morning star and a son of Jupiter in Roman tradition, bespeaks a connection with visible light. Saint Gregory described Lucifer as "clarior" [brighter] than all the other angels,[8] and in early medieval England the prolific abbot Ælfric imagined Lucifer admiring his own brightness.[9] Lucifer's traditional captivation by his own brightness as a precursor to his fall figures in several later medieval dramatizations of the angels' fall.[10] But while light becomes a central issue in the fifteenth-century French *Mistére du Viel Testament* and the Towneley *Creation* pageant, these dramas demonstrate an interest in brightness as it figures in Lucifer's competition with God, rather than portraying the conflict over brightness *among* angels, as in the York and Chester cycles.[11]

. . . like the most High," have dramatic potential "as the suggestion of a program of false impersonation of the Deity." R. W. Hanning, " 'You Have Begun a Parlous Pleye': The Nature and Limits of Dramatic Mimesis as a Theme in Four Middle English 'Fall of Lucifer' Cycle Plays," in *The Drama of the Middle Ages: Comparative and Critical Essays,* ed. Clifford Davidson, C. J. Gianakaris, and John H. Stroupe (New York: AMS Press, 1982), pp. 140–68, quotation on p. 143.

[7] The Latin reads, "ab illo, qui summe est, auersi ad se ipsos conuersi sunt." Augustine, *De Civitate Dei, Libri XI–XXII* (Turnhout: Brepols, 1955), p. 359. Translation from *The City of God,* trans. Henry Bettenson (New York: Penguin, 1972), p. 477. Augustine argued in *On the Literal Meaning of Genesis* and *City of God* that the creation and fall of the angels occurred virtually simultaneously, during the first day of creation. The York and Chester playwrights follow this chronology.

[8] Gregory the Great, *Moralia in Iob Libri XXIII–XXXV,* ed. Marc Adriaen (Turnhout: Brepols, 1985), p. 1666.

[9] Ælfric writes, "him wel gelicode his wurfulnisse þa: se hatte 'Lucifer,' þæt ys, 'Leohtberend', for ðære miclan beorhtnisse his mæran hiwes" (his magnificence pleased him very much: he was called 'Lucifer,' that is, 'Light-bearing,' on account of the great brightness of his glorious appearance). *The Old English Version of the Heptateuch, Ælfric's Treatise on the Old and New Testament, and His Preface to Genesis,* ed. S. J. Crawford, EETS o.s. 160 (London: Oxford University Press, 1922), p. 19 (text from BL MS Laud Misc. 509). Translation in Michael Fox, "Ælfric on the Creation and Fall of the Angels," *Anglo-Saxon England* 31 (2002): 175–200 (185).

[10] Augustine argued that good angels were separated from bad at the moment God separated light from dark, a tradition from which the York and Chester dramatists diverged. For discussion of this point, see Richard Beadle, "Poetry, Theology, and Drama in the York *Creation and Fall of Lucifer,*" in *Religion in the Poetry and Drama of the Late Middle Ages,* ed. Piero Boitani and Anna Torti (Cambridge: D. S. Brewer, 1990), pp. 213–27 (219–20).

[11] The auspices for these dramas are uncertain. The *Mistére* is a set of Old Testament episodes known to have been performed in Paris: see Barbara M. Craig, ed., *La Creacion, La Transgression,* and *L'Expulsion* of the *Mistére du Viel Testament,* University of Kansas Publications, Humanistic Studies 37 (Lawrence: University of Kansas Publications, 1968), pp. 1–2. The pageants in the Towneley manuscript, a dramatic anthology, were not associated with full-fledged craft production: see Barbara D. Palmer, " 'Towneley

The parallels that emerge between light as a source of strife among angels and light-bearing as a source of friction among guilds invite readers to consider how these first pageants in York and Chester accentuate the conditions of playing, guiding us to ask what was at stake, for city governments and guilds themselves, in the representational practices of civic devotional drama. York's and Chester's depictions of the angelic fall had differing associations with the liturgical Corpus Christi procession. York's "Fall of the Angels" was probably written during the first half of the fifteenth century to follow directly upon the Corpus Christi procession, which originally preceded the cycle on the same day. In Chester, the "Fall of Lucifer" pageant was added in the early sixteenth century, when the cycle was expanded and shifted from Corpus Christi to Whitsuntide (Pentecost), to be played on Whitsun Monday, about ten days before Corpus Christi.[12]

Both pageants, despite their differing dates and auspices, perform and recuperate the social disruption endemic to Corpus Christi, first calling into question the feast's ideology of civic wholeness and then endeavoring to remake it on terms more favorable to guild interests. After dramatizing Lucifer's sin of pride in terms of captivation by his physical light and staging battles for possession of light among good and bad angels, the York and Chester pageants end in strikingly similar ways, with God beginning again, resuming the first day of creation by separating darkness from light. While the struggles among angels over light and position onstage allude to the history of discord over processional order, these new beginnings articulate artisanal interests and diffuse the power associated with the top-down creation of arbitrary hierarchies of honor. In making such an assertion, we assume that although the dramatic texts were certainly not written by the guilds, they were composed in close collaboration with them so as to represent the guilds' distinctive features and particular interests.[13] In both pageants, these dramatic par-

---

Plays' or 'Wakefield Cycle' Revisited," *Comparative Drama* 21.4 (1987–88): 318–48 (341–42). The "Fall of Lucifer" episode from the N-Town manuscript, certainly not associated with urban craft-guild production, differs from the others in never mentioning Lucifer's role as light-bearer. See Stephen Spector, ed., *The N-Town Play*, 2 vols, EETS s.s. 11, 12 (Oxford: Oxford University Press, 1991), 1:23.77–78.

[12] A similar shift occurred in Exeter, where the mayor attempted to move the Skinners' play from Corpus Christi to Whitsuntide, in an apparent effort to augment his power over that of the ecclesiastical authorities, who controlled Corpus Christi festivities (Johnston, "The Feast of Corpus Christi," pp. 26–29).

[13] Guild relationships to the play texts varied between York and Chester: whereas in York, "ultimate control" over dramatic texts remained with the guilds producing them,

allels between God and the mayor suggest a local, artisanal version of a *speculum principis,* in which Tanners warn of the dangerous effects a mayor's arbitrary rule might have on the civic community.

Edward Said has argued that "a beginning is basically an idea that implies return and repetition rather than simple linear accomplishment."[14] Although he contends that "beginning and beginning-again are historical whereas origins are divine," our analysis shows that the "return and repetition" involved in beginning these dramatic cycles make the histories of civic performance visible in divine acts of creation.

Procession and Cycle Drama: Relations and Theories

Many towns in late medieval England, York and Chester among them, were ruled by urban oligarchies, small groups of men generally drawn from the merchant class, who succeeded in monopolizing government and controlling the economic structure—chiefly the artisanal or manufacturing body—for their own benefit. In the context of this centralized urban system, civic ceremonial often became the means by which the governing body sought to regulate or naturalize the prevailing social order, thereby "reproducing the political and economic relations that guaranteed oligarchic power," as Sheila Lindenbaum has argued about the London Midsummer Watch.[15] In similar fashion, Heather Swanson and Sarah Beckwith have studied how the powerful merchant oligarchy of York used the Corpus Christi cycle to impose its vision of corporate organization on the city.[16]

The inscription of local hierarchy was readily visible in the Corpus Christi processions of York and Chester, where proximity to the host conferred the greatest honor, so that whether the Eucharist was carried in the rear (as in York) or the front (as in Chester), clergy were closest,

---

in Chester the city held control over the texts. Alexandra F. Johnston, "The *York Cycle* and the *Chester Cycle:* What Do the Records Tell Us?" in *Editing Early English Drama: Special Problems and New Directions,* ed. A. F. Johnston (New York: AMS Press, 1987), pp. 121–43 (128).

[14] Edward Said, *Beginnings: Intention and Method* (New York: Basic Books, 1975), p. xiii.

[15] Sheila Lindenbaum, "Ceremony and Oligarchy: The London Midsummer Watch," in *City and Spectacle in Medieval Europe,* ed. Barbara A. Hanawalt and Kathryn L. Reyerson (Minneapolis: University of Minnesota Press, 1994), pp. 171–88 (178).

[16] Heather Swanson, *Medieval Artisans: An Urban Class in Late Medieval England* (Oxford: Basil Blackwell, 1989), esp. 107–26; Sarah Beckwith, *Signifying God: Social Relation and Symbolic Act in the York Corpus Christi Plays* (Chicago: University of Chicago Press, 2001), esp. pp. 23–55.

followed by town dignitaries, then craft guilds, in descending order of status as their distance from the host increased. Although ceremony might be controlled by these elite groups who placed themselves at the apex of the hierarchy, the control was never complete. Civic records from York and Chester, as well as other cities, including Beverley and Newcastle,[17] document intense friction and even physical violence over guild order in their Corpus Christi processions. As Miri Rubin observes, "The story of Corpus Christi processions is also one of *dis*order, of lawsuits generations long, of disputes over precedence and riots."[18] Drawing from the sociological theories of Pierre Bourdieu, Erik Paul Weissengruber argues that the participating guilds in York used the Corpus Christi festivities to "secure distinctions, distinctions that were to be sanctified by the presence of the sacrament."[19] Were such distinction compromised by placement in a low position, he suggests, the guilds were prepared to undermine the very symbols of civic authority by disrupting the festivities.

Such analyses, which point out how celebrations of Christ's body became occasions for contestation and disruption among competing interests, are indicative of the most recent scholarship that expresses skepticism over the tendency to see Corpus Christi ceremonies and other medieval rituals as achieving the unity they laid claim to. Many of these critics take explicit aim at Mervyn James's 1983 thesis about the formation of a "social body" in the late medieval town. While James had analyzed the "vertical structure of status and authority" characteristic of the Corpus Christi procession, he had suggested that the dramatic

---

[17] In Beverley in 1430, marching order for the Corpus Christi procession was officially recorded and accompanied by the threat of a forty-shilling fine, "[q]uedam discordia facta fuit inter Aldermannos et seneschallos arcium diversarum pro portacione cercorum sive tortorum suorum annuatim ante hec tempora in processione" ([d]issension having arisen between the aldermen and stewards of divers crafts as to the carrying of wax lights or torches yearly heretofore in the procession). Arthur F. Leach, ed., *Beverley Town Documents* (London: Bernard Quaritch, 1900), p. 35. See also J. J. Anderson, ed., *Records of Early English Drama: Newcastle Upon Tyne* (Toronto: University of Toronto Press, 1982), pp. 4, 6, 21.

[18] Rubin, *Corpus Christi,* p. 263.

[19] Erik Paul Weissengruber, "The Corpus Christi Procession in Medieval York: A Symbolic Struggle in Public Space," *Theatre Survey* 38.1 (1997): 117–38 (132). Bourdieu speaks of distinction in terms of the "symbolic transformations of *de facto* differences and more generally, the ranks, orders, grades and all the other symbolic hierarchies" incorporated from the structures themselves. See *Language and Symbolic Power,* ed. John B. Thompson, trans. Gino Raymond and Matthew Adamson (Cambridge: Polity Press, 1991), p. 238.

cycles, with their emphasis on "equality, change and social mobility," provided the "natural complement" to the hierarchical procession, allowing for a creative tension by which conflicts were transformed into a larger understanding of corporate membership (the "social body").[20] For our purposes, James is important for delineating a complex relation between procession and cycle. While some critics have tended to understand the relation as evolutionary—the cycles developing out of the procession[21]—others have dismissed the notion of any relation whatsoever.[22]

In this essay we argue that the guilds used cycle drama to comment upon and perhaps even reform the procession. While we do not see the two ceremonies as "complementary" in James's terms, we show that there was a dialogic rather than homeostatic relation between the two as we trace how, in the towns of Chester and York, the Corpus Christi festivities were gradually modified to separate the performances of procession and cycle to different days. Our contention is that the first pageants of these cycles, performed by the Tanners' guilds in both York and Chester,[23] dramatize the disputes of the torch-bearing procession, demonstrating the failure of hierarchy to ensure civic order. Hence, rather than view the processional "disruptions" as part of a symbolic struggle for individual distinction, as Weissengruber has argued via Bourdieu, we show that both pageants exhibit a critical relation to the hierarchical organization that fostered these disruptions and, as such, have political meaning and functions. Through these dramatizations, the guilds sought actively and eloquently to shape the celebration of Corpus Christi in their towns.

Corpus Christi Festivities in York

York supported both a Corpus Christi procession and play of some kind in the late fourteenth century, but only in 1415, with the creation of

---

[20] Mervyn James, "Ritual, Drama, and Social Body in the Late Medieval English Town," *Past and Present* 98 (1983): 3–29.

[21] Martin Stevens, "The York Cycle: From Procession to Play," *LeedsSE* n.s. 6 (1972): 37–61.

[22] Alexandra F. Johnston, "The Procession and Play of Corpus Christi in York after 1426," *LeedsSE* n.s. 7 (1974): 55–62.

[23] Different reasons have been proposed as to why the leather-making crafts were assigned this pageant. Richard Beadle suggests that the leather costumes typically required for devils may have prompted the affiliation ("Poetry, Theology, and Drama in the York *Creation and Fall of Lucifer*," 215). Anne Higgins observes that the fumes and

the *Ordo paginarum* (order of pageants), does a clearer picture emerge. At that time, the *Ordo,* a "checklist" delineating fifty-two pageants and their guild sponsors, was compiled and inserted into the back of the city's Memorandum Book.[24] Appended to the *Ordo* is a processional list in which ten guilds and the civic officeholders (the mayor, the twelve aldermen, and group of twenty-four), are listed as torchbearers.[25] A second list designates ten torches for the Corpus Christi guild.[26] Founded in 1408, this religious guild grew into an exceptionally large and powerful organization that included members from high ecclesiastical and temporal offices across England. While the Corpus Christi guild did succeed in gaining the most coveted ceremonial role of carrying the shrine housing the host and placing its priests and officers nearest the shrine, Alexandra Johnston has stressed that the procession continued to be a local civic affair, controlled by the mayor and city council of York, who most importantly decided the marching order of the participating crafts.[27]

The 1415 *Ordo* assigns the "Fall of the Angels" pageant to the guild of Tanners, yet this still leaves open the question of when exactly the text preserved in the Register was developed.[28] Many of the York pageants underwent considerable revision. Meg Twycross argues that "the second and third decades of the fifteenth century were a time of drastic change in the organization and contents of the Corpus Christi Play," proposing even that the 1415 *Ordo* may be reflective of something like "tableaux" rather than scripted pageants, which were developed subsequently.[29] Before the Register was compiled in the later fifteenth century—it is generally dated 1463–77—individual guilds maintained

---

boiling cauldrons of hell iconography suggest parallels with the tanning process. "Work and Plays: Guild Casting in the Corpus Christi Drama," *Medieval and Renaissance Drama in England* 7 (1995): 76–97 (81).

[24] Meg Twycross, "The *Ordo paginarum* Revisited, with a Digital Camera," in *"Bring furth the pagants": Essays in Early English Drama Presented to Alexandra F. Johnston,* ed. David N. Klausner and Karen Sawyer Marsalek (Toronto: Toronto University Press, 2007), pp. 105–31 (105).

[25] *Records of Early English Drama: York,* ed. Alexandra F. Johnston and Margaret Rogerson, 2 vols. (Toronto: Toronto University Press, 1979), 1:24. Hereafter cited as *REED:York* with reference to volume and page number.

[26] Ibid., 1:26.

[27] "The Guild of Corpus Christi and the Procession of Corpus Christi in York," *Mediaeval Studies* 38 (1976): 372–84 (384).

[28] The 1415 description reads, "Deus pater omnipotens creans & formans cellos Angelos & archangelos luciferum & angelos qui cum eo ceciderunt in infernum" (God the almighty Father, creating and forming the heavens, the angels and archangels, Lucifer and the angels who fell with him into hell) (*REED:York,* 1:17, 2:703).

[29] "The *Ordo paginarum* Revisited," 112.

their own "regynalls" of the pageants, probably altering the contents from time to time. Hence, although we know that the Tanners were responsible for a "Fall of the Angels" "pageant" as far back as 1415, the contents of the drama probably evolved in the decades following, a chronology that is important for understanding the pageant's relation to processional disputes.

At their inception, both Corpus Christi ceremonies were performed on the same day in processional fashion, but the dramatic cycle and procession held different meanings in York. On one hand, the cycle is almost entirely the product of the city's craft guilds. Although recent scholarship has suggested that the merchant oligarchy effectively used the cycle to enforce the specialized guild system upon the workers of the city,[30] these artisans, even with complaints and under duress, did stage the pageants and proudly claim ownership of them, as "mayntenez & sustenez par les Comunes & Artificers demesme la Citee en honour & reverence nostreseignour Iesu Crist & honour & profit de mesme la Citee" (maintained and supported by the commons and the craftsmen of the same city in honour and reverence of our Lord Jesus Christ and for the glory and benefit of the same city).[31] The artisans' time, labor, and expense are involved in the cycle's production. The procession, on the other hand, is of a more composite nature, made up of a large group of priests, the governing structure of the city, officials of the Corpus Christi guild, and representatives of some of the craft guilds. No one has yet satisfactorily explained why only a small portion of the city's numerous craft guilds participated in the torch procession.[32]

---

[30] See above, note 16.

[31] *REED:York,* 1:11, 2:696.

[32] There were perhaps ten guild participants for most of the fifteenth century, the Tanners' guild not among them. Based on a misreading of a record concerning the wearing of summer livery in the procession, Weissengruber does suggest that "only those guild members who could afford the garments of the city's 'honorable men'" could participate in the procession ("The Corpus Christi Procession," p. 119). In fact, the regulation appears to be referring to the proper clothing for the city officials' servants and is not directed at the guilds. With the exception of the Cobblers and the Porters, two small and poor crafts, the craft guilds listed as torchbearers in the procession are also responsible for pageants in the cycle, so it does not seem that a guild generally chose to participate in one ceremonial event rather than the other. James of course insisted that a guild needed to have a place in both play and procession "for the full expression of its place in the social body" ("Ritual, Drama, and Social Body," p. 16), although this clearly was not the case in York for most guilds. Possibly the governing council and Corpus Christi Guild did not want their presence in the procession overwhelmed by the crafts.

Although the rationale for participation in the procession remains unclear, one may say that, given the small number of guilds involved, it did not approach the representative and collective undertaking that characterized the cycle and, as such, had a much different meaning and function for the artisanal body. In Bourdieu's terms, York's Corpus Christi procession allowed the guilds to express distinction, for indeed the procession, organized hierarchically, offered perhaps more definitive modes of representing status and difference than the cycle. Not only were the guilds assigned particular places in the procession, but they were also assigned a specific number of torches, enabling rather precise means of exhibiting status to the town.

Guilds sometimes resorted to physical brawls to express their dissatisfaction over their placement in the procession, which served as a marker of a guild's relative importance or "honor" in the community. In 1419, members of the Skinners' guild reported that "diversi artifices carpentariorum et allutariorum civitatis . . . ipsorum torcheas accensas & ut portarentur in processione dicti festi . . . fregerunt & deorsum traxerunt cum fustibus suis & Carlelaxaes quos illuc portauerunt & alia enormia fecerunt in gravem perturbacionem pacis domini Regis & impedimentum ludi & processionis corporis christi" (various craftsmen of the carpenters and cordwainers . . . broke the burning torches as they were carried in the procession of the said feast . . . and then dragged them down with their staves and Carlisle axes which they brought there, and committed other enormities, to the grave disturbance of the king's peace and to the hindrance of the play and procession of Corpus Christi). The council proceeded to imprison two carpenters and a cordwainer; however, the carpenters quickly acknowledged their fault and, according to the record, "posuerunt se in misericordia gracia & ordinacione marioris & consilii" (placed themselves upon the mercy, grace, and regulation of the mayor and council).[33]

The civic document concentrates upon the ferocity of the attack, the consequences to devotional performance, and the swift enactment of justice, themes that we will see reiterated in the Tanners' "Fall of the Angels" pageant. The carpenters, making a quick confession and seeking "mercy, grace, and regulation" from the mayor and council, exalt their judicial power, positioning the civic authorities as the font of mercy and site of a restorative and rational order. Yet the document makes no

[33] REED:York, 1:32–33, 2:717–18.

mention of any similar propitiation from Thomas Durem, the cord-wainer involved in the disturbance. Some guilds were clearly less willing to accept the mayor's authority than others; indeed, several decades later the Cordwainers resisted their new placement in the processional order, carrying on a dispute with the mayor and city council that lasted about a dozen years and even involved the intervention of the king.[34]

From its earliest years until perhaps 1476, the procession preceded the cycle in York on the feast of Corpus Christi; hence a fracas in the procession, as in the assault on the Skinners, represented a serious disruption to the timing of the day's ceremonial events. In 1426, Friar William Melton offered some logistical advice on York's Corpus Christi festivities. Although he praised the play, Melton noted that the audience "non solum ipsi ludo in eodem festo verum eciam comessacionibus ebrietatibus clamoribus cantilenis & aliis insolenciis multum intendunt servicio divino officii ipsius diei minime intendentes" (attend not only to the play on the same feast, but also greatly to feastings, drunkenness, clamours, gossipings, and other wantonness, engaging the least in the divine service of the office of that day). Melton suggested that the play and procession should be held on different days so that the audience could attend church services. The city council records that they were persuaded by Melton and agreed that the cycle should be performed on Wednesday, the day before the Corpus Christi feast, and that "processio fiat semper modo solempni in die ipsius festi" (the procession should always be made solemnly on the day of the feast itself), so that the audience might also go to services and receive indulgences.[35] When pressed to differentiate the two ceremonies, the city, it seems, accepted Melton's distinction, aligning the procession with religious celebration in contradistinction to the cycle, which is associated with "wanton" behavior despite the history of violence endemic to the procession. At any rate, we see that procession and cycle were linked but opposed performances, each inscribed with particular meanings in the civic arena.

Melton's recommendation was not implemented until 1476, at which time the city council separated procession and cycle but awarded, it would appear, pride of place to the drama, which continued to be performed on the feast of Corpus Christi. The procession was slightly expanded and moved to the day after the official feast, as was the official

---

[34] Ibid., 1:162–63.
[35] Ibid., 1:42–44, 2:728–30.

Corpus Christi day sermon.[36] The 1476 record states that the guilds carrying torches should "pacifice eant in suis ordine forma et locis" (go peaceably in the order, manner, and places) set out by the clerk.[37] With this injunction, the record implies that the ordering of the procession continued to be a site of contestation.

A Turbulent Beginning

We can be fairly certain that the Tanners' pageant was developed while the procession and cycle were performed sequentially, the "Fall of the Angels" following closely upon the turbulent torch procession on the feast of Corpus Christi. As the first episode in the cycle, the "Fall of the Angels" records this fraught performance event, the difficulties, anxieties, and real disturbances associated with ordering the hierarchical procession that immediately preceded it. In particular, the pageant's emphasis on light, and the contest over who shines most brightly, reflects upon the guilds' struggles over torch-bearing precedence. Keeping with theological tradition, this episode first depicts God's creation of nine orders of angels, whom he dubs his "ministers." Among these, God singles out Lucifer as his special deputy, naming him "berar of lyghte" (36) and appointing him "moste nexte" (33) after himself.[38] God promises Lucifer that as long as he is "buxumly berande" (40), he will dwell in bliss and enjoy prosperity. Immediately, then, God establishes a hierarchical order, installing a leader whose chief job is to "bear" light to glorify him, echoing the very framework of the Corpus Christi procession, including the terminology of "berying" used for carrying torches.[39] Foreseeing potential strife, God warns the angels that those who are not "stabill in thoghte" (30) shall "be put to my presone at pyne" (32) (put in my prison to suffer), citing precisely those penalties experienced by the unruly Carpenters and Cordwainers imprisoned for attacking the Skinners in the 1419 procession.

[36] Processional marching orders from 1501 list sixteen crafts, representing about one-quarter of the city's craft guilds (ibid., 1:186). Determining the actual number of craft guilds in York is an impossible task, for some amalgamated and/or divided from year to year and some never registered ordinances.

[37] Ibid., 1:109, 2:777.

[38] All references to the York "Fall of the Angels" are from *The York Plays*, ed. Richard Beadle (London: Edward Arnold, 1982) and will be cited parenthetically by line number.

[39] *REED:York*, 1:58.

As soon as God exits, a division occurs among the angels. The good angels praise "þat lufly lorde of his lighte" (43) and express their hope that "never felyng of fylth may full us nor fade us" (60). In contrast, Lucifer and the rebellious angels are immediately mesmerized by their light-bearing capacities. Lucifer says.

> Þe bemes of my brighthode ar byrnande so bryghte,
> And I do semely in syghte myselfe now I se,
> For lyke a lorde am I lefte to lende in this lighte.
> More fayrere be far þan my feres,
>
> . . . .
>
> My powar es passande my peres.
>
> (50–56)

Lucifer's captivation by his own brightness leads him to compare himself with a lord and to vaunt himself as fairer and more powerful than the other angels. The brazen egotism he evinces in these lines proves corrupting, for another angel boasts of his brightness in nearly identical terms: "Þe bemes of my brighthede are bygged with þe beste. / My schewynge es schemerande and schynande" (68–69). When the other angel begins to imitate Lucifer, following him on his rebellious course, we see the dangers to a collective enterprise of individual striving. Not only does Lucifer disobey God, but he also fractures the community of angels. While the good angels understand their light to be the endowment of God, and hence a sign that unites them to him, Lucifer and the rebellious angels believe that their light is self-generated, existing independently of God and endowing them with individual powers. Such pursuit of individual honor quickly destabilizes the harmony of heaven.

Lucifer's misplaced equation of his light with power leads him to disobedience. He not only claims that his brightness places him above his peers to dwell "on heghte in þe hyeste of hewuen" (88), but he also compares himself to God:

> Ther sall I set myselfe full semely to seyghte,
> To ressayve my reverence thorowe righte o renowne;
> I sall be lyke unto hym that es hyeste on heghte.
>
> (89–91)

As the chief "bearer of light," Lucifer strives for a more exalted position, one close to God himself; this indeed was the subject of many guild quarrels, as each strove to be placed above their peers and closer to the body of Christ in the rear of the procession to receive greater "reverence" and "renowne" in the community. When the procession and cycle were viewed in succession, as they were for the first half-century, viewers would likely be reminded of the guilds' struggles over their assigned position in the marching order.⁴⁰ In the "Fall of the Angels," Lucifer's quest to be close to God anatomizes such struggles as vain strivings for illicit power—a demonic usurpation of a devotional enterprise.

Lucifer and the rebellious angels are soon struck down, transformed from shining angels to black devils in Hell. "Whare es my kynde become, so cumly and clere? / Nowe am I laytheste, allas, þat are was lighte. / My bryghtnes es blakkeste and blo nowe" (99–101), Lucifer laments. Lucifer has taken his "kynde" down with him, and the bad angel places the blame squarely on him for losing their light-bearing position: "Owte on þe Lucifer, lurdan, oure lyght has thou lorne. / . . . / to spill us þough was oure spedar, / For thow was oure lyghte and oure ledar" (108–11). A scuffle and fistfight ensue between the two devils, evoking the physical violence endemic to the disputes of the torch-bearing procession. When Lucifer complains that "ye smore me in smoke" (118), the memory of the smoldering torches, cast to the ground, might be evoked or might even be represented, if real torches were used to represent "light." In this scenario, the proper devotional attitude and reverence for the host are sacrificed to individual striving, as *fraternitas* quickly turns to chaos and loss of light, or distinction altogether.

As strife reigns in hell, the good angels praise God, emphasizing his righteousness and ability to judge each individual fairly according to his proper "work": "Thi rightewysnes to rewarde on rowe / Ilke warke eftyr is wroghte—/ thorowe grace of þi mercyfull myghte" (124–26). The angels that worship God will remain dwelling in heaven, rewarded for their obedience in recognizing that it was God who "us this lyghte lente" (121). The torches indeed were intended to signify, at least ostensibly, reverence for the host and the honor of the city rather than the power of the guild. To invest in the lights as signifying a guild's individual status rather than devotion to God is to rebel against the divinely sanctioned order, which is here framed in terms of guild members' dis-

---

⁴⁰Even after the procession and cycle were separated and performed on different days, the drama's commentary on processional disputes would have remained meaningful for the audience, for such public performances were sustained and layered in the cultural memory.

obedience to the mayor, the one who assigns places in the procession through his superior wisdom—and holds the power to punish and reward.

The Tanners and the Cordwainers: Rivals and Rebels

The analysis above suggests that the Tanners' pageant evolved in dialogue with the quarrels and disruptions of the torch procession on the feast of Corpus Christi. We find it especially significant that the Tanners reflect upon these disruptions, for in York processional disputes were more closely associated with their main rivals, the Cordwainers, than with any other guild. As already noted, craft participation in the York procession was somewhat arbitrary, with only ten guilds listed as participants in 1415. Among these, it is striking that the Cordwainers, although not placed particularly prominently, were assigned fourteen torches, far more than any other craft guild, and more even than the Guild of Corpus Christi.[41] The Cordwainers appear to have been particularly devoted to the procession, participating annually and upholding a large number of torches. However, despite or perhaps because of their devotion, the Cordwainers ran into more trouble than any other guild, fined and imprisoned on a number of occasions in the fifteenth century for violence or disruption to the procession.

The large and powerful crafts of Tanners and Cordwainers were involved in a protracted struggle throughout the fifteenth century, demanding numerous interventions by the civic authorities to maintain peace between the guilds. Historically, tanners, those who turned animal hide into leather, and cordwainers, makers of shoes, a major leather product in the Middle Ages, had constituted a single craft. But with the enforcement of the guild system and its attendant specializations in the fourteenth and fifteenth centuries, the two crafts were separated into makers of leather and makers of leather shoes. However, the potential for infringement on one another's work was so great that national legislation in 1389 prohibited cordwainers from tanning leather; this ban was lifted in 1402 but reinstated in 1423. When banned from tanning leather themselves, the cordwainers sought to increase control over their suppliers, the tanners, by demanding rights of search (inspection).[42]

---

[41] *REED:York,* 1:24.
[42] Swanson, *Medieval Artisans,* pp. 55–56.

There is evidence from the first few decades of the fifteenth century, when the Tanners' pageant was likely created, that they were already disputing with the Cordwainers, and we know that the Cordwainers had already disrupted the Corpus Christi procession. These events could well be the basis for the Tanners' interpretation of the "Fall of the Angels." Indeed, the earliest ordinances from the Tanners' guild in York, dated 1416, already speak of the "magna et diutina varietas lisque et discordia" (great and longlasting differences, quarrel and discord) between the two crafts.[43] These ordinances provide for a central inspection body consisting of two searchers from each of four crafts, the tanners, cordwainers, girdlers, and curriers. All tanned leather in York and its suburbs was to be inspected by this body before it could be sold. However, in 1430, the tanners, complaining that the system was overly burdensome, made a "rogatum magnum et peticionem humilem" (great request and humble petition) to the mayor and city council; they succeeded in having this provision repealed and were henceforth allowed to conduct their own searches within their craft.[44] By 1453, however, the Cordwainers appear to have regained the search of red leather.[45] The final set of ordinances available for the Tanners, dated 1476, makes no mention of their participation in a common search committee.[46] For the Tanners, seeking to preserve the integrity of their craft, the Cordwainers were troublemakers and interlopers, interfering with their work and causing them loss of profit.[47]

The Tanners were clearly interested in petitioning the governing council to keep the right to search leather for themselves. The "Fall of the Angels" pageant could provide an opportunity for the Tanners to dramatize their position by representing the Cordwainers as contentious and blind to communal interests. While seeking to appeal to the mayor as a wise individual who justly punishes wrongdoers, the Tanners might effectively undermine their troublesome rivals. In this way, the representational agenda of the pageant may be seen as a political strategy for the Tanners to curry favor. While such a particularized historical argu-

---

[43] *York Memorandum Book (1388–1493)*, ed. Maud Sellers, 2 vols. (Durham: Surtees Society, 1915), 2:162.

[44] Ibid., 2:165.

[45] *York City Chamberlains' Account Rolls, 1396–1500*, ed. R. B. Dobson (Durham: Surtees Society, 1978–79), p. 70.

[46] *York Memorandum Book*, 2:166–67.

[47] As the Chamberlains' accounts illustrate, the fines collected from searching red leather would devolve (at least partly) to the Cordwainers rather than to the Tanners.

ment is necessarily speculative, given the two hundred year performance history of the cycle, we must also note that the dispute between the Tanners and Cordwainers was virulent and endured perhaps as long, and that disruptions to the Corpus Christi procession were also ongoing and deeply entrenched affairs of civic life.[48]

From approximately 1482 to 1493 (and perhaps earlier), the Cordwainers engaged in a protracted struggle with the city council over their participation in the Corpus Christi procession.[49] While Weissengruber argues that the Cordwainers were protesting their new marching position next to the Weavers, which represented a demotion and "loss of distinction," we contend that something more was at stake. For more than a decade the Cordwainers refused to participate in the procession as the city council attempted to induce them to accept the marching position next to the Weavers. Only after pressure from Henry VII, a series of fines, imprisonments, and seizure of property did they finally agree. However, in agreeing to accept this new position, "going of the wevers left handes," they also demand in their ordinances the right "fromhenceforth for evermore . . . [to] have Serche of Rede and blak ledders."[50] While the Cordwainers may have felt disgruntled at being placed in a lower position in the procession, their quarrel may not have been so much with the Weavers as with the Tanners. In this document the Cordwainers cannily render their symbolic struggle over processional placement inseparable from their material struggle over the inspection of tanned leather.

How might townspeople have viewed the Tanners' pageant during this turbulent period? In 1490 the City Council conducted an inquiry into the Cordwainers' actions concerning the procession. Testimony from townspeople showed that the Cordwainers were attempting to gather support from other craftsmen to side against the mayoralty.[51]

---

[48] See Swanson, *Medieval Artisans*, pp. 138–39, on the longevity of strife between these guilds.

[49] A record dated June 21, 1476, shows the Cordwainers appealing to the city council to forgive them for the "riots, transgressions and offenses" they had committed. Although the circumstances are not mentioned, the petition occurs a week after Corpus Christi day of that year. See *The York House Books, 1461–1490*, ed. Lorraine Attreed, 2 vols. (Wolfboro Falls, N.H.: Alan Sutton, 1991), 1:40–41.

[50] *REED:York*, 1:172–73.

[51] William Cooke, a member of the Tailors' guild, which also marched in the procession, testified that John Smith, Cordwainer, "was at him showing that where the Mayor, Alderman and City council hath determined upon his craft they to pay ten pounds for non bearing of their torches, saying that if the Mayor, alderman and city council obtain against them in that than his craft to beware for they should be the next craft that should be in like trouble." While Smith's alleged demand to Cooke is enigmatic ("ye to

The proceedings disclose that the Cordwainers were attempting to organize some sort of large-scale rebellion against the council's authority. Witnesses reveal that the Cordwainers had tried to rally two, three, and even four hundred men to their cause: evidently they were prepared to turn their protest against processional order into a major public display of dissent. In such a context, the Tanners' pageant could have been played to promote that guild's own obedience and remind fellow citizens of the scheming Cordwainers, poised like Lucifer to take down his followers with him.

After the Fall: A New Beginning

Even if the Tanners effectively dramatized the dangers of following the rebellious Cordwainers in their pageant, ultimately the Cordwainers seem to have won, as they gained the right to search leather after agreeing to march in the procession in 1490, and also had these rights to search "forevermore" enshrined in their ordinances in 1493.[52] The evidence suggests that the Cordwainers succeeded in gaining these special rights by using their placement in the procession as a bargaining chip: they were clear that the price of their peaceful participation was the right to search red and black leather. To the Tanners, such a use of the procession to infringe upon their trade surely made them question the privileges the city council granted to processional participation—and by extension, the role of the procession in general. In this situation, the procession, a hierarchical and exclusive ceremony in which the mayor held the power of organization, enabled an arbitrary economic decision with negative consequences for their trade. Although the events described above took place after the Tanners' play was created, it is likely that given the widespread nature of protests over Corpus Christi processions, not only in York but also in many other English towns, similar conflicts had occurred before. Processions, like that of Chester discussed below, were frequently fraught occasions in which the mayor, seeking to exercise control, arbitrarily rewarded some guilds over others.

We believe that such arbitrary decision-making accounts for the Tan-

---

do for us as ye would we should do for you"), it implies an effort to gather support for the Cordwainers' demonstration. See *York Civic Records,* ed. Angelo Raine, 8 vols. (Wakefield: Yorkshire Archaeological Society Record Series, 1939), 2:57. The syntax of Raine's translation is somewhat unclear, and unfortunately the original document is not available in a modern edition.

[52] *York Civic Records,* 2:58.

ners' characterization of the torch procession in their drama as something of a failed beginning. For this reason, the "Fall of the Angels"
pageant ends not in the darkness of hell but with a new beginning that
casts the dispute of Lucifer and the rebellious angels as a prehistory, a
coming before. The drama thus constructs the procession and cycle as
"twyn[ned]" (153) or divided from each other, the former ceremony
split off from the remainder of the cycle. After the fall of the rebellious
angels, God calls the creation of day his "fyrst makyng" (145), although
he has already "made" the angels ("Of all the mightes I have made"
[33]) in the beginning of the episode. This is what he says:

> Ande in my fyrste makyng, to mustyr my mighte,
> Sen erthe es vayne and voyde and myrknes emel,
> I byd in my blyssing ȝhe aungels gyf lyghte
> To the erthe, for it faded when þe fendes fell.
> In hell sall never myrknes by myssande,
> Þe myrknes thus name I for nighte,
> The day, þat call I this lyghte—
>
> (145–51)

Hence, in the restarting of the action, God's second "first making," he
works in concert with the good angels, asking them to give light.[53] This
is an unusual depiction, as in Chester's "Fall of Lucifer," God makes the
day alone: "Lightnes and darkenes, I byde you twene: / The darke to
the nighte, the lighte to the day."[54] As a divinely-sanctioned but collaborative enterprise, light-bearing, now framed in craft terminology as a
"making,"[55] is shown as a harmonious working between God and the
angels, representative of the mayor and obedient craftsmen. God's order
to the angels to "give light" may function as an embedded stage direction, as the good angels step forward with torches to relight the pageant
and start the cycle anew.

[53] Scribe A, the scribe of the first three pageants recorded in the York Register, British
Library MS Additional 35290, has divided God's final speech in two with a red line,
contrary to his practice anywhere else. Elsewhere, lines occur to separate characters'
speeches from one another, never within the speech of a single character. The scribe's
rubrication makes the second part visually distinct from the first, implying that this
medieval reader also understood this part of the pageant as a new beginning.

[54] *The Chester Mystery Cycle,* ed. R. M. Lumiansky and David Mills, 2 vols., EETS s.s.
3, 9 (Oxford: Oxford University Press, 1974), 1:13.292–93. Hereafter this source will
be cited parenthetically with reference to line number.

[55] On the importance of "making" in the York Cycle, see Beckwith, *Signifying God,*
esp. pp. 42–71.

Through the use of light imagery, the Tanners' pageant performs creation not as a continuous act, but actually as a two-part process, the first part of which is cast off and separated from the rest. The darkness created by the rebellious angels' fall is figured as a stoppage in time, a return to the space before the torches are lit for the performance to begin. Because the "Fall of the Angels" immediately followed the torch procession, this scenario can be seen as a commentary on the tribulations of the procession that threatened to disrupt the smooth functioning of the Corpus Christi celebration. We propose that the Tanners' depiction of God beginning his creation anew with the cooperation of the angels speaks to their desire for a more inclusive and representative kind of ceremonial practice. When God summons the angels to "give light," he invites his own creatures to be part of the creation process. He does not name a new leader to replace Lucifer but simply calls upon the remaining angels, requiring their lights to continue with creation, which in essence becomes the cycle itself.

While the procession is figured more clearly as the work of the town oligarchy and the locus of much strife, the cycle is here seen as a joint enterprise, where power has been delegated and hierarchy is acceptably diffused into an imagined collaboration of "making." The dramatic strategy operates here to claim an absolute distinction between the procession, as a governmental tool, and the cycle itself, as an expression of a more representative body. The drama seeks to expunge hierarchy in the form of the procession from the cycle's etiology, rendering it a fall into darkness, blankness, or nothingness. When the angels step forward to "give light" at God's command, it is as if the cycle drama is just now beginning. Indeed, as the first pageant, performed at daybreak, the "Fall of the Angels" may be staking claims to creating or opening the "day" of the Corpus Christi feast.[56]

Chester: Civic Controversy and the Mayor's Power

Although early records documenting Corpus Christi celebrations are scarcer for Chester than for York, the Chester Mayor's Books reveal that the procession was marred several times by dissent among guilds during the period when procession and play were performed on the same day.

[56] Richard Beadle suggests that "the combining of the themes of creation and light with the physical setting of the dawn of the Corpus Christi day was a *coup de théâtre* in the grand manner" ("Poetry, Theology, and Drama," p. 227).

In 1399 a violent fracas took place in which the masters of the Weavers and Fullers allegedly attacked their journeymen and servants.[57] In 1474–75, the mayor personally adjudicated a dispute over marching order between the Bowyers and Fletchers on the one hand and the Coopers on the other. In its focus on light-bearing as a source of social disruption, the 1474–75 document signals concerns about hierarchy and distinction that will reappear in the Tanners' "Fall of Lucifer" episode, newly written for Chester's cycle when it was shifted to Whitsuntide.

The Fletchers (makers of arrows) and the Coopers (makers of barrels) marched together in the Corpus Christi procession, cooperating in the cost of torches and contributing to a pageant, the "Trial and Flagellation of Christ." Although it is unclear who made the decision that they should march together, both guilds seem to have resented the loss of status that their shared position implied, and both sued for a better rank in the procession. To resolve the dispute, the mayor imposed a new hierarchy by putting the Coopers first, in a more prestigious position with respect to the eucharistic host at the head of the procession, without offering any justification for his decision. The text of his order, preserved in the Mayor's Books, makes an initial reference to a disagreement over placement in the procession, then notes that the "seidez parties haue agreit thaym & ichon of thaym to abide perfourme & obeie such ordenaunce dome & awarde" as the mayor (John Southworth) should make.[58] The mayor, after hearing the two guilds' "greyvaunce & compleyntes," "hath ordenet demed & awerdet the saides parties to be gode ffrendes. . . . Also he hath ordenet & awardet that the saides cowpers & thaire Successors Cowpers of ye said Cety from hensforth shall bere thaire Lightes yerely iij lightez on that on side ye pauement and iij on that opposite . . . next before the lights of the saides ffletchers & bowers And the [said Bowyers and Fletchers] evenly to bere thaire lightes [next to] the saides Cowpers by the said Award."[59] The mayor's

---

[57] *Records of Early English Drama: Chester,* ed. Lawrence M. Clopper (Toronto: University of Toronto Press, 1979), pp. 5–6, for the Latin account, from the Mayor's Books, and 491–92 for a translation.

[58] *REED: Cheshire Including Chester,* ed. Elizabeth Baldwin, Lawrence M. Clopper, and David Mills, 2 vols. (Toronto: University of Toronto Press, 2007), 1:58. Hereafter *REED:Cheshire* with reference to volume and page number.

[59] Ibid., 1:58. Bracketed material from R. M. Lumiansky and David Mills, "Documents Providing External Evidence," in *The Chester Mystery Cycle: Essays and Documents* (Chapel Hill: University of North Carolina Press, 1983), pp. 203–310 (210).

command to obey his "ordenaunce dome & awarde" lends a solemn religious dimension to his authority. Even as he uses the phrase "gode frendes" to smooth over the new, apparently arbitrary distinction he has created between the crafts, the mayor acknowledges that imposition of hierarchy will always be linked to the danger of pride and the fear of losing status.

Chester's history of the Corpus Christi controversy and the mayor's role in managing processional disputes are critical to interpreting the social meanings of angelic discord and new beginnings in Chester's "Fall of Lucifer" pageant. In contrast to the York "Fall of the Angels," the Chester "Fall of Lucifer" was neither late medieval nor a Corpus Christi pageant. Although a Corpus Christi "play" is mentioned as early as 1422, the sparse fifteenth-century evidence suggests that the dramatic event originated, in Lawrence Clopper's words, as "more a Passion play than a cycle."[60] The Lucifer episode was added to Chester's civic play sequence around the time that the drama was shifted (by 1521) from Corpus Christi to a new liturgical occasion: the days following Whitsunday (Pentecost), the fiftieth day after Easter.[61] As of 1521, the expanded cycle was performed over a three-day period on Whitsun Monday, Tuesday, and Wednesday, with an ambulatory mode of staging that followed a different route from the Corpus Christi procession.[62]

Although no contemporary explanation survives for why the cycle was separated from the procession, moved to a new occasion, and expanded to include more pageants, many scholars view this separation as an assertion of civic control over festive performance: control that in

[60] Lawrence M. Clopper, "The History and Development of the Chester Cycle," MP 75 (1978): 219–46 (219). The 1422 record testifies to a dispute between Ironmongers and Carpenters over the recruitment of members of other guilds (Fletchers, Bowyers, Stringers, Coopers, and Turners) to help with the "Flagellation" and "Crucifixion" pageants.

[61] A documentary reference in 1521 to the "whitson playe & Corpus christi light" indicates that by then, the procession and cycle had been definitively separated (REED:Cheshire, 1:69). Peter W. Travis suggests that the "Fall of Lucifer" was added as part of the shift to Whitsunday: see Dramatic Design in the Chester Cycle (Chicago: University of Chicago Press, 1982), pp. 44–61. Clopper argues that the "Fall of Lucifer" was added after 1521 ("History and Development," p. 231).

[62] While the procession traveled from the church of St. Mary's (the traditional spiritual home of the Chester earls) to the church of St. John's, the bishop's seat, the Whitsun play traveled along a new route: starting at the Abbey gate and eventually fanning out into "every street" of the city. David Mills, "The Chester Mystery Plays: Truth and Tradition," in Courts, Counties, and the Capital in the Later Middle Ages, ed. Diana E. S. Dunn (Stroud: Sutton Publishing, 1996), pp. 1–26 (10, 22).

Chester was centered in the city council and with the mayor himself. Clopper suggests the change may have stemmed from the close relationship between the powerful guild merchant and the city council: "The guild mercatory was associated with the granting of important freedoms to the city; the production of the plays, therefore, celebrated the prestige of the city and the guild government and probably accounted for the insistence that the plays were devised by the supposed first mayor, John Arnewaye."[63] Focusing on the mayor himself, David Mills argues that "the shift at the turn of the fifteenth century from Corpus Christi to Whitsuntide correlates with the final appropriation of the plays as a celebration of mayoral office."[64] The mayor's power had increased steadily in the later medieval period: sharing power with the council, he presided over two of the city's three courts and controlled the Port of Chester as well as the Dee Estuary.[65] Under the terms of Chester's Great Charter of 1506, which granted the city palatine status and augmented its powers of self-government, mayors were afforded enhanced ceremonial dignity and frequent occasions for self-display.[66]

Just as a popular (though incorrect) legend held that an earlier mayor, John Arnewaye, had instituted the Corpus Christi drama in 1327–28, the Early Banns, originally composed for the Corpus Christi play and revised for the Whitsuntide performance, credit the mayor for moving the dramatic performance to Whitsun: "Our wurshipffull mair of this Citie / with all this Royall cominaltie / Solem pagens ordent hath he / At the fest of whitsonday tide."[67] After the descriptions of all the pageants, another stanza is devoted to the cycle, and then one to the procession. These two stanzas seem designed to justify their separation and to reassure listeners that the procession will still happen, now ten days later than the cycle. The first stanza promises "That played shalbe this godely play / In the whitson weeke / That is brefely forto sey / vppon monday tuysday and wennysday."[68] Subsequent lines remind listeners about the Corpus Christi procession: "Also maister Maire of this Citie / withall his

---

[63] Clopper, "History and Development," p. 245.

[64] Mills, "The Chester Mystery Plays," p. 18.

[65] See J. T. Driver, *Cheshire in the Later Middle Ages, 1399–1540* (Chester: Cheshire Community Council, 1971), pp. 29, 40.

[66] For example, the mayor was authorized to have his sword and mace carried before him and to process in ceremonial garb to worship every Sunday, attended by aldermen, sheriffs, and council (Mills, "The Chester Mystery Plays," p. 19).

[67] *REED:Cheshire,* 1:82.

[68] Ibid., 1:86; see Mills, "The Chester Mystery Plays," p. 18.

bretheryn accordingly / A Solempne procession ordent hath he / to be done to the best / Appon the day of corpus christi."[69] Thus, as Mills argues, "the plays are seen to be ordained and constructed by the individual mayor, not by custom or by the collective will of the citizens."[70]

The decision to change the cycle's occasion was in all likelihood made from the top down, and whatever the mayor's precise role in effecting the shift, he continued to control the organization and assignment of the pageants throughout the cycle's history.[71] But the Tanners' "Fall of Lucifer," the newly written first pageant of the expanded Whitsun cycle, may be read most profitably not only as a tool of mayoral self-promotion but also as a reflection of Chester's diverse artisanal interests and the city's own history of disruption in the Corpus Christi procession. The Tanners marched in Chester's Corpus Christi procession together with the Cordwainers, according to the guild list of about 1500.[72] Having battled the mayor throughout the late fourteenth century to be chartered as a distinct craft group, the Tanners had their own experience of controversy over hierarchy, amalgamation, and distinction.[73] Chester's "Fall of Lucifer" pageant, likely written, as noted earlier, in cooperation with guild members, and evidently approved by the mayor, exploits its primacy in the cycle to reflect critically upon the mayor's power to determine guild fortunes and upon the discord historically associated with Corpus Christi procession. In the pageant, while the angelic contest over light-bearing evokes Corpus Christi struggles, God's subsequent "beginning again" works to justify the shift to Whitsun, a new liturgical

[69] REED:Cheshire, 1:86.

[70] Mills, "The Chester Mystery Plays," p. 17.

[71] A note from 1539–40 asserts that "it is at the libertie and pleasure of the mair with the counsell of his bretheryn to Alter or Assigne any of the occupacons Aboue writen to any play or pagent as they think necessary or conuenyent" (REED:Cheshire, 1:81).

[72] See Clopper, "History and Development," p. 224. Clopper shows that this document, preserved among otherwise unrelated items in BL MS Harley 2104, does not list Corpus Christi pageants, as previous scholars had assumed, but rather indicates guild order in the procession. Although the order gives an idea of the episodes that each guild performed, it should be treated with care, as "other guilds in the list may have cooperated in a segment of the play but may have been listed separately for the procession" (p. 225).

[73] In 1362 the Tanners petitioned the mayor for a charter forbidding the Cordwainers from interfering with their craft. Although the charter was granted, it was revoked eight years later on the grounds that separating the trades was not conducive to the profit of the city, and the mayor granted the Skinners, Cordwainers, and Tanners a charter for practicing the three crafts jointly. See Rupert H. Morris, Chester in the Plantagenet and Tudor Reigns (Chester: G. R. Griffith, n.d.), p. 411.

season that might offer a new chance for a more expansive display of the crafts as a unified yet hierarchical body.

Chester's "Fall of Lucifer" and the Trouble with Corpus Christi

By giving Lucifer first rank within the larger hierarchy of the angels and associating his privileged position with light-bearing, the Chester "Fall of Lucifer" creates the conditions for social disruption, already associated with the tradition of light-bearing at Corpus Christi. In his opening speech, God refers to the perfection of his light and to the fact that he alone can hold distinction within unity: "I ame the tryall [triad] of the Trenitye / which never shall be twyninge, / pearles patron ymperiall, and Patris sapiencia. / My beames be all beawtitude; all blisse is in my buyldinge" (7–9). Although God's light is at once boundless and unified,[74] for the angels who have just been created, hierarchy becomes the central means for God to ensure his superior power. The terms of the angels' creation and separation call to mind the procession described in the Banns, of "marchaunts and craftys of the citie / by order passing in their degree." God declares, "Here have I you wrought with heavenly mighte, / of angells nine orders of greate beautye, / iech one with others, as it is righte, / to walke aboute the Trenitie" (64–67). Arraying the angels in "orders," God demands dignified, hierarchically organized movement.

God's subsequent warning to the angels implies anxiety that, like craft guilds disputing their position in the Corpus Christi procession, his creatures may attempt to violate the order he has ordained. God warns Lucifer and Lightbourne, Lucifer's second in command: "For crafte nor for cuninge, cast never comprehension; / exsalte you not to exelente into high exaltation. / Loke that you tende righte wisely, for hence I wilbe wendinge. / The worlde that is bouth voyde and vayne, I forme in the formacion, / with a dongion of darkenes which never shall have endinge" (70–74). As he prepares to form the terrestrial "worlde," God's language of "crafte and cuninge" admonishes participants not to transgress assigned positions. Being cast into darkness would represent banish-

---

[74] The image of God's light "diffusing itself in every direction and dimension, bringing eternity and infinity and time and space into existence" was a commonplace of Augustinian and Franciscan thought. See Norma Kroll, "Cosmic Characters and Human Form: Dramatic Interaction and Conflict in the Chester 'Fall of Lucifer,'" *Medieval & Renaissance Drama in England* 2 (1985): 33–50 (38).

ment from the ordered celestial realm, a loss of the stabilizing hierarchy necessary for the angels' articulation as a unified body.[75]

Even as God presides over the angelic hierarchies rather like the mayor managing the Corpus Christi procession, the pageant text suggests that the privilege of light-bearing coexists uneasily with the maintenance of a stable hierarchy. Whereas God earlier declared, "Here have I you wrought with heavenly mighte, / of angells nine orders of great beautye" (64–65), Lucifer impudently alters that formula: "Thou hast us marked with greate might and mayne, / in thy blesse evermore to byde and bee, / in lastinge life our life to leade. / And bearer of lighte thou has made me" (98–101). Imitating God, Lucifer emphasizes his singular power rather than his status as a "wrought" creature. Thus the "Fall of Lucifer," when read in parallel with the recorded guild controversy of 1474–75, recalls the way actual "bearers of light" fiercely defended their positions in the hierarchy, even in the knowledge that their positions, like many guild ascriptions themselves, were arbitrarily imposed. The early emphasis on God as "maker" of an unchanging hierarchy implicates God and, by extension, the mayor, in creating a structural contradiction between a stable hierarchy and a privileged position for Lucifer, a position that quickly engenders pride in its bearer.

Disorder and the Mockery of Christ's Body

As the first pageant in the new Whitsuntide cycle, the "Fall of Lucifer" suggests not only the Corpus Christi holiday's potential for destroying its own hierarchies but also its potential for making a mockery of Christ's body, the very entity the feast was created to revere. Lucifer's struggle for primacy over God involves a fight with other members of the angelic hierarchy, which one might read to figure other guilds. By making the focus of the conflict the possession of light and the co-opting of a central position onstage, the Tanners' pageant recalls discord between guilds over placement in the Corpus Christi procession. Lucifer's temporary usurpation of God's light and position, culminating in the preposterous demand to his fellow angels, "to your sovereigne kneele one your knee, / I ame your comforte, bouth lorde and head" (191–92), represents an unthinkable violation of order. No guild would ever at-

---

[75] Echoing Genesis 1:2 with the mention of a "dongeon of darkness," Chester's "Fall of Lucifer" episode is unique among the cycles in mentioning the creation of hell, which awaits any disobedient angels.

tempt to commandeer the head of the Corpus Christi procession, which belonged to Christ in the Eucharist.

Although the good angels, in refusing to follow Lucifer, express their desire to conserve God's hierarchy, the events of the pageant suggest that this structure cannot bind together the interests of all the competing parties. In response to Lucifer's demand that they assent to his proposition that "Of all heaven I beare the lighte" (128), the Virtues reply, "Wee will not assent unto your pride / nor in our hartes take such a thoughte; / but that our lorde shalbe our guyde, / and keepe that he to us hath wroughte" (134–37). Asserting faith in God as their "guyde" against Lucifer's sin of "pride," the obedient angels create a visual image that recalls the hierarchies onstage at the start of the drama, evoking an idealized Corpus Christi procession, in which guilds "kepe" order behind a designated "guyde": Christ in the Eucharist.

The gravity of Lucifer's attempt to exploit position and brightness to rival God is reflected in an insistent, disturbing focus on Lucifer's own body as the transmitter of light. Encouraged by Lightbourne, who claims, "The brightness of your bodie cleare / is brighter then God a thousandfolde" (164–65), Lucifer appropriates Christ-like language to display his own body, activating an even stronger association with the occasion of Corpus Christi. But Lucifer's rebellion against God evokes the challenge that individual pride presents to the wholeness of Christ's salvific body and to the idealized social body that it encompasses. Lucifer uses body, light, and physical positioning to challenge God outright: "Here will I sitt nowe in his steade, / to exsaulte myselfe in this same see. / Behoulde my bodye, handes and head—/ the mighte of God is marked in me" (186–89). This language strongly recalls Christ's familiar exhortation (in contemporary drama, lyrics, and sermons) to witness the bodily proof of his suffering in the Passion or triumph in the Resurrection.

The display of Christ's body is familiar from many of the other Chester pageants. In the "Last Judgment," the risen Christ will display his bleeding body to explain how he ransomed mankind from the devil: "Behould nowe, all men! Looke on mee / and see my blood fresche owt flee / that I bleede on roode-tree / for your salvatyon" (425–28). This passage, with its close parallels to Lucifer's speech, emphasizes the simultaneity of Christ's sacrifice and redemption of mankind, so that although the body presented onstage is broken and suffering, visually far removed from the white wholeness of the eucharistic wafer, it still redeems and unites "all men." Using parodically Christ-like language to show Lucifer "exalting" himself, the "Fall of Lucifer" exposes the ways in which efforts of individual guilds to exalt themselves above others may detract from the proper focus of Corpus Christi.

God's Anguish and the Renovation of Light

As God combines righteous anger with anguish at Lucifer's disobedience, the pageant comes full circle, using light to resume creation with a new focus on craft unity. This new beginning suggests that by moving the cycle to Pentecost, the mayor may escape from the social division and rancor that he himself fostered by instituting hierarchies of distinction among guilds. By depicting God's crisis over Lucifer's betrayal as a questioning of the original structure, the drama suggests doubt about the appropriateness of Corpus Christi as a day to celebrate God's glory with performance. Proceeding to resume Creation by dividing darkness from light, God's actions recall not only the Easter vigil, which they quote directly (Genesis 1), but by extension the Pentecost liturgy, whose hymns and sequences depict the Holy Spirit as a renovating force, a light that unifies rather than one that divides. Liturgical associations work subtly in this final section to justify and naturalize the shift from Corpus Christi to Pentecost.

As God steps in to banish Lucifer and Lightbourne to hell, he decries Lucifer's assault to the hierarchy but also poignantly asks why Lucifer disobeyed him.[76] He says,

> Lucifer, who set thee here when I was goe?
> What have I offended unto thee?
> I made thee my frende; thou arte my foe.
> Why haste thou trespassed thus to me?
> Above all angels there was no moe
> that sitt so nighe in my majestye.
> I charge you to fall til I byd 'Whoo,'
> Into the deepe pitt of hell ever to bee.
>
> (222–29)

---

[76] As Travis notes, at the end of the "Fall of Lucifer," "God descends from his august diction and displays a quite human sense of hurt and disappointment" (*Dramatic Design*, p. 73).

Even as he condemns Lucifer's attack on the hierarchy, God expresses a surprising anxiety that he has done something wrong. The echoes of Christ's "Improperia" speeches from the Good Friday liturgy, in which Christ accuses the Jews of betraying him, lend these lines a complex charge.[77] Although God appears almost pitiable here, audience members know that he, unlike Christ, has created the conditions for his own suffering. A few moments later God openly admits that he suffers along with the angels: "I maye well suffer: my wille is not soe / that they shoulde parte this from my blesse" (276–77). Given that God did little before his departure except install the angelic hierarchy, one might well conclude that his "offense" lay in the very order to Lucifer to combine the privilege of light-bearing with the directive to remain humble.

The notion that a problem existed in the original angelic hierarchy is reinforced by the fact that God, after dispatching the rebel angels to hell, resolves to start over in a more successful and profitable way. Unlike the new beginning of the York "Fall of the Angels," where God recruits the good angels to help shed light upon the earth, the Chester God does not interact further with the angels but instead draws attention to his cooperation with the other "two persons" of the Trinity. Although the essential content of God's last speech, in which he foretells the creation of humankind and divides light from dark, resembles that of the York pageant, this speech takes on a particular meaning in the context of Whitsuntide. God's references to the other members of the Trinity and to dividing light from darkness resonate with the Pentecost liturgy, which emphasizes the renovating power of the Holy Spirit and the unifying power of light. God says,

> And though they have broken my comaundement,
> me ruse yt sore full sufferently.
> Nevertheless, I will have myne intente—
> that I firste thought, yet soe will I.
> I and two persons be at one assente
> A sollempne matter for to trye.
> A full fayer image we have imente,

[77] The first three reproaches are: "Popule meus" (Micah 6:3), "Ego eduxi" (Jeremiah 2:21), and "Quid ultra" (Isaiah 5:2, 40). The Micah and Jeremiah texts echo most strongly in God's speech. Micah 6:3 reads: "O my people, what have I done to thee, or in what have I molested thee? answer thou me." Jeremiah 2:21 reads: "Yet, I planted thee a chosen vineyard, all true seed: how then art thou turned unto me into that which is good for nothing, O strange vineyard?"

that the same stydd shall multiplye.
In my blessinge here I begyne
The first that shalbe to my paye.
Lightenes and darkenes, I byde you twene:
The darke to the nighte, the lighte to the day.
Keepe your course for more or myne
and suffer not, to you I saye;
but save yourselfe, bouth out and in.
That is my will, and will allwaye.

(282–97)

Although one might hear a warning about Corpus Christi in this speech—"keeping your course" perhaps referring to maintaining processional order—certain aspects of the speech are distinct to this pageant and carry particular force in the context of the shift from Corpus Christi to Whitsuntide. God's references to the other "two persons" of the Trinity—Christ and the Holy Spirit—remind audiences that the Holy Spirit is the critical actor at Pentecost, which celebrates the Holy Spirit's descent upon the apostles. This visitation necessarily involved light, for the Holy Spirit was typically pictured as a flame infusing the apostles with fire.

The traditional sequence for the Mass of Pentecost, "Sancti spiritus adsit nobis gratia," sung on Whitsunday, the day before the play, speaks of the Holy Spirit as a renovating light drawing people away from darkness: "Spiritus alme, illustrator omnium, / Horridas nostrae mentis purga tenebras; / Amator sancte sensatorum semper cogitatuum, / Infunde unctionem Tuam clemens nostris sensibus" (Most gracious Spirit, light of all, / Our minds from darkness disenthrall; / O Thou, Who holy thoughts dost love, / Pour down Thine unction from above).[78] A later verse refers to the Holy Spirit's participation in the creation of heaven, earth, and sky, a creation that in the Chester "Fall of Lucifer" has already occurred in the first moments of the drama and continues as God returns to his "first intent," dividing dark from light in the next step of the creation story. Part of the sequence reads, "Quando machinam per Verbum suum fecit Deus caeli, terrae, marium, / Tu super aquas, foturus eas, numen Tuum expandisti, Spiritus" (When God did by the Word create / Heaven, earth and sky, that fabric great, / Thou brooding o'er

[78] Charles Buchanan Pearson, ed. and trans., *Sequences from the Sarum Missal* (London: Bell and Daldy, 1871), pp. 68–69.

the waters face / Didst shed abroad Thy mystic grace).[79] In the pageant, God's return to "my first intent" to finish the creation summarized in this Pentecost sequence, a process already put in motion but stalled by the fall of the angels, invites the audience to see this moment as the true beginning of the dramatic cycle, one that they should associate with the more liturgically significant occasion of Pentecost.

Moreover, if they had attended church at any point during the Whitsun octave, the audience of the "Fall of Lucifer" would have heard the following verses after the Alleluia: "Emitte Spiritum tuum et creabuntur: et renovabis faciem terrae" (Send forth thy Spirit, and they shall be created, and Thou shalt renew the face of the earth). This verse from Psalm 103.30, which also recalls God's imperative in Genesis 1:28 to replenish the earth after the Flood, would have been followed, on Whitsun Tuesday, by the following: "Veni, Sancte Spiritus, reple tuorum corda fidelium: et tui amoris in eis ignem accende" (Come holy Spirit, fill the hearts of thy faithful, and kindle in them the fire of thy love).[80] Together, these verses combine the image of light with the idea of renewal, a combination also present in God's speech. The cycle is thus made continuous with the liturgy of Pentecost, appropriate to this day, a time for renewal of obedience to God and recovery of apostolic fellowship.

Although the imagery of dividing light from darkness is not unique to the Chester pageant, this language, together with God's statement that this new creation "shall be to my paye" (that is, will produce social and material capital for the mayor himself), has a particular function in Chester. These discourses naturalize the move away from Corpus Christi and promote the cycle's new beginning on a day more profitable, perhaps not just for the mayor but also for the artisans involved in the dramatic production, notably those who, like the Tanners, did not have their own pageant before the Whitsun shift. Like the two stanzas in the Banns, which mention first the cycle and then the Corpus Christi procession, this Whitsun purification retains a disciplinary function with respect to Corpus Christi, preparing audiences and guild members themselves to arrive at Corpus Christi, ten days later, aware of the temptations that holiday's procession might present to their prideful tendencies. But even as the pageant, like the Whitsun Banns, credits the mayor

[79] Ibid., pp. 70–71.
[80] See Francis Henry Dickinson, ed., *Missale ad Usum Sarum* (London: Burntisland, 1861–83), pp. 429, 432.

for this new plan for spiritual renovation and social cohesion, the drama has also shown this venerable figure admitting his mistake and acknowledging its consequences for the unity of the artisanal body. Thus the guild-produced drama makes its own history and interests visible, staking a claim to the increased profit and social unity that may result from this new occasion for dramatic production.

Conclusion: Toward a Better Government

The concern of both "Fall of the Angels" pageants with the processional ceremonies from which they developed reveals something of the complexity of civic relations in York and Chester. Emphasizing the tension between merchant oligarchies and artisans in late medieval towns, recent scholarship has traced such tensions in the civic cycle drama as they unfold in the space between the guild players and merchant organizers of the Corpus Christi ceremonial. Since the merchant oligarchies were overseers of and prominent participants in the Corpus Christi procession, the vexed relation between procession and play also reveals some of these social tensions. The Tanners' pageant, a work that specifically engages with the procession, thus allows us to begin to trace an artisanal perspective on civic relations and understand how ceremonial language could be used to enunciate dissenting positions.

The York and Chester pageants we have considered were composed about a hundred years apart, and certainly urban relations changed during this time. However, the importance of the celebration of urban identity on and through the feast of Corpus Christi had a remarkably continuity until its final suppression. The unity, harmony, and inclusivity promised by Corpus Christi proved a resonant symbol for urban centers not only despite but also because of the strain of tense social relations. The symbol was an eminently useful one, open to manipulation by those in power: in a town context, frequently the merchant oligarchies. Our essay suggests that the artisans were cognizant of the symbolic manipulation of Corpus Christi and sought to respond through their own articulations of this ritual language. In York, the Tanners sought to prioritize the cycle drama, casting the procession as an unfair tool of mayoral privilege. Likewise, in Chester, the Tanners' pageant ultimately turns away from the town's troubled history of Corpus Christi celebration, seeking to focus on a new feast, Whitsuntide, with perhaps greater promise of democratic representation. Both of these plays reveal that the occasion of Corpus Christi, although a relatively recent feast, had accrued a reputation as a site of power struggle. Yet, while York's Tanners sought to appropriate the language of a corporate enterprise, the late date of the Chester pageant may indicate that the language of Corpus Christi had become too encumbered to recuperate.

Although the Tanners of Chester may advocate a new occasion altogether for civic celebration, neither drama turns away from hopeful civic relations. Both are engaged in a process of reform and renovation, seeking to find new modes of organization and expressions of ceremonial relations rather than to renounce them altogether. In this way, one can see that artisans like the Tanners were deeply invested in their local towns and sought ways within the mercantile-controlled political order to enunciate their own concerns with the organization of civic life, offering powerful mayors opportunities to reflect on their own conduct and its consequences for the civic body. Although tanning was a relatively lucrative occupation, tanners never attained social prominence, and very few ever became part of their town's governing body.[81] Their pageants in these cycles may be their major site for social commentary in which we can hear the murmurings of an artisanal voice.

[81] Tanners may have experienced a certain social marginalization because of the fumes and malodorous processes involved in leather making (Swanson, *Medieval Artisans*, p. 65). Notably, although among the largest crafts in York, Tanners were not included in either the thirteen major or fifteen minor crafts in the newly formed council when the city reorganized its governing structure in 1517 (ibid., p. 123).

"His guttys wer out shake":

Illness and Indigence in Lydgate's *Letter to Gloucester* and *Fabula duorum mercatorum*

Lisa H. Cooper

University of Wisconsin–Madison

The term poetry . . . can be considered synonymous with expenditure; it in fact signifies, in the most precise way, creation by means of loss.

—Georges Bataille, "The Notion of Expenditure"

Sometime after 1431, or so the generally accepted timeline has it, John Lydgate wrote to his patron Humphrey, Duke of Gloucester, and asked him for money. The monk and poet of Bury St. Edmunds had been, at Humphrey's request, hard at work writing the *Fall of Princes*—the poem that would by 1438 become a nine-book encyclopedia of noble tragedy—and he found himself short of funds.[1] It was, he

I presented an early version of this project at the 2006 ACMRS conference "Poverty and Prosperity" at Arizona State University, and thank Mark Cruse for his hospitality and intellectual generosity there. I also owe thanks to Andrea Denny-Brown for spending time and energy on my work at the expense of her own, and I am very grateful to the two anonymous readers for *SAC* for their many helpful comments and suggestions. The greatest debt I have incurred in writing this essay is to Lynn Festa; her gift to me of many a brilliant insight significantly enriched what would have otherwise been a much more impoverished study.

[1] My epigraph is from Georges Bataille, "The Notion of Expenditure," in *Visions of Excess: Selected Writings, 1927–1939*, ed. Allan Stoekl, trans. Allan Stoekl with Carl R. Lovitt and Donald M. Leslie Jr. (Minneapolis: University of Minnesota Press, 1985), pp. 116–29; rpt. in *The Bataille Reader*, ed. Fred Botting and Scott Wilson (Oxford: Blackwell, 1997), pp. 167–81, quotation on p. 171. For a review of Lydgate's career, see Derek Pearsall, *John Lydgate (1371–1449): A Bio-Bibliography*, English Literary Studies 71 (Victoria: University of Victoria, 1997); on the *Letter*, see p. 33. On the uncertain chronological relation of the *Letter* and *Fall*, see Eleanor Prescott Hammond, "Poet and Patron in the *Fall of Princes*: Lydgate and Humphrey of Gloucester," *Anglia* 38 (1914): 131–36; and *John Lydgate: Poems*, ed. John Norton-Smith (Oxford: Clarendon Press, 1966), pp. 114–16. For the important corrective that nothing in the *Letter* explicitly suggests that Lydgate is asking for payment for the *Fall*, see Richard Firth Green, *Poets and Princepleasers: Literature and the English Court in the Late Middle Ages* (Toronto: University of Toronto Press, 1980), p. 156. In this essay, I am concerned more with the *Letter* as a plea for payment per se rather than with its precise connection to the longer poem. On the more general "petitionary intention" of much fourteenth- and fifteenth-century autobiographical verse and the fictionalizing of that intention as a narrative

explained in the epistolary poem known as the *Letter to Gloucester,* a matter of life and death: without the duke's speedy attention and assistance, someone (or rather, as his poem suggested, *something*) would go the way of all flesh. "Riht myhty prynce, and it be your wille," he began,

> Condescende leiser for to take
> To seen the content of this litil bille,
> Which whan I wrot, myn hand I felte quake.
> Tokyn of mornyng, weryd clothys blake,
> Cause my purs was falle in gret rerage,
> Lynyng outward, his guttys wer out shake,
> Oonly for lak of plate and of coignage.[2]

The humor of this situation—a poet dressed in mourning weeds for his sick wallet—is countered to some extent by the rather graphic image on which it depends, that of a purse-turned-body displayed to least advantage. Not just "lyght" like the bag addressed in "The Complaint of Chaucer to His Purse" (c. 1399–1400), or "seeke" from loss of "stuf," like that owned by the speaker of Hoccleve's "La Male Regle" (c. 1405–6), Lydgate's mortally ill purse has been turned inside-out, its "guttys" violently deprived of all content.[3] The goal of this essay is likewise to

---

strategy, see J. A. Burrow, "The Poet as Petitioner," *SAC* 3 (1981): 61–75, quotation on p. 62.

[2] *The Minor Poems of John Lydgate, Part II: Secular Poems,* ed. Henry Noble MacCracken, EETS o.s. 192 (London: Oxford University Press, 1934), pp. 665–67, lines 1–8. All further quotations from the *Letter* will be from this edition, cited parenthetically by line number. The poem survives in seven manuscripts: London, British Library MS Harley 2255 (the basis for the EETS edition), MS Harley 2251, MS Additional 34360, MS Lansdowne 699; Leiden, University Library MS Vossius 9; Cambridge, Magdalene College MS Pepys 2011; and New York, Pierpont Morgan MS M.4.

[3] Geoffrey Chaucer, "The Complaint of Chaucer to His Purse," *The Riverside Chaucer,* gen. ed. Larry D. Benson, 3rd ed. (Boston: Houghton Mifflin, 1987), line 3; Thomas Hoccleve, "La Male Regle," in *Hoccleve's Works: The Minor Poems,* ed. Frederick J. Furnivall and I. Gollancz, 1892, rev. ed. Jerome Mitchell and A. I. Doyle, EETS e.s. 61 (London: Oxford University Press, 1972), lines 409, 349. All further quotations of these poets are from these editions. It is worth noting that Chaucer's "Purse" is unusual in his poetry for its personification of the object as a human being; in the *Canterbury Tales,* by contrast, bags and wallets never figure whole bodies, but only single body parts (see, for example, III.44b and VI.945). This is typical of Middle English generally, in whose anatomical lexicon "purse" most often refers to the scrotum (though Alison's "purs of lether" in *The Miller's Tale* [I.3250] and the "purs" of the wife in *The Shipman's Tale* [VII.248] are instead suggestive of the female genitalia). See *MED,* s.v. *purs(e,* 4a; and Juhanni Norri, *Names of Body Parts in English, 1400–1500* (Tuusula: Academia Scientiarum Fennica, 1998), pp. 179, 229, 245, and 387. Chaucer's "Purse" was almost certainly a model for Lydgate's *Letter,* and the two are found together in three manuscripts:

"out shake" the *Letter* for all that its central bodily metaphor is worth (though hopefully less violently and with less tragic result), and to do so by reading it alongside another poem that Lydgate is believed to have composed in the same period, the *Fabula duorum mercatorum* [The Story of the Two Merchants].[4] Before outlining my argument, it will be useful immediately to proffer a summary of both poems, acknowledging from the outset that at sixty-four lines arranged in eight stanzas, the *Letter* is much shorter than the *Fabula* (which runs to 910 lines in 130 stanzas), and that my description and subsequent analysis of the two works will by necessity be correspondingly weighted. But what may look in what follows like a focus on the details of the *Fabula* is not at all intended to imply the lesser significance of the *Letter;* instead, I hope the attention I pay the *Fabula* will allow us to see the details of the shorter poem afresh, and as participating in a discursive network that extends beyond the rather compact showcase in which they appear.

After its opening plea for attention, its reference to the writer's funereal attire, and its striking image of the gutted money-bag, in its second stanza the *Letter* relates the speaker's unsuccessful search for a doctor able to do something more with his treatment than further ravage the wallet. In the third through sixth stanzas, the financial crisis of poet and purse is elaborated by images of stalled ships that, lacking wind in their sails, cannot make land in the purse's empty harbor; of coins that never arrive from the mint; of weights or scales thrown out of balance; of the purse as a feverish patient; of eclipses and alchemical elements; and above all of the continued darkness and dryness plaguing the bag's inte-

---

British Library MS Harley 2251, MS Additional 34360, and Morgan MS M.4 (in which last codex they appear consecutively, with Lydgate's poem preceding Chaucer's [fols. 75v–77]). Yet Hoccleve's description of the parallel suffering of his body and purse in "La Male Regle" is in fact a closer analogue (see lines 337–38, 349–50, 409, 446–48). On Chaucer's petition, see especially Paul Strohm, "Saving the Appearances: Chaucer's 'Purse' and the Fabrications of the Lancastrian Claim," chapter 4 of his *Hochon's Arrow: The Social Imagination of Fourteenth-Century Texts* (Princeton: Princeton University Press, 1992), pp. 75–94; on Hoccleve's "La Male Regle," see Ethan Knapp, *The Bureaucratic Muse: Thomas Hoccleve and the Literature of Late Medieval England* (University Park: Pennsylvania State University Press, 2001), pp. 36–43.

[4] MacCracken, ed., *The Minor Poems of John Lydgate, Part II,* pp. 486–516. All further references are to this edition by line number. For a more recent but unpublished edition, see Pamela Farvolden, "A Critical Edition of John Lydgate's *Fabula Duorum Mercatorum*" (Ph.D. thesis, University of Alberta, 1993). The *Fabula* is found in six manuscripts, five of which also contain the *Letter:* these are British Library MS Harley 2255 (the basis for the EETS edition), MS Harley 2251, MS Additional 34360, and MS Lansdowne 699, as well as Leiden, University Library MS Vossius 9 (the sixth, not containing the *Letter,* is Oxford, Bodleian Library MS Rawlinson Poetry 32).

rior, which awaits the relief that only a bright influx of gold and silver can provide. The envoy of the last two stanzas briefly chastises the poem itself for its impertinence ("why art thu nat ashamyd, / So malapertly to shewe out thy constreynt?" [49–50]) but then relapses into lament, excusing its outspokenness on the metaphorical grounds of a poverty now figured as a drained barrel, a consumptive illness, a patch of barren soil, and finally as an empty sanctuary into which God is willed at the verses' end to send salvation in the form of the "cleer soun of plate and of coignage" (64).

The more extended narrative of the *Fabula* originates in a widespread tale that first appeared in Western Europe in Petrus Alphonsus's twelfth-century *Disciplina Clericalis* and remained popular through the early modern period. It is the story of two merchants, one from Egypt and the other from Baldac (in Syria), who, sight unseen, become close friends after each learns of the other's outstanding reputation for honest dealing.[5] Eventually, the Syrian merchant visits his friend in Egypt, where he falls desperately in love with his host's fiancée. Unwilling to betray their friendship, he takes no action regarding the girl and so falls into a life-threatening lovesickness, a melancholy from which he is saved only when the Egyptian learns what has caused the illness and then cures the Syrian by giving him his beloved to wed, along with her dowry. The Syrian and his new wife return home, where they begin to live happily ever after. The Egyptian, however, now has some bad luck in his business affairs. Losing all his wealth, he finds himself destitute, and so decides to travel to Baldac to ask his friend for help. Upon arriving in Syria, he takes overnight shelter in a temple. That same evening, a murder is committed near where the impoverished man sleeps, and so

---

[5] See *The Scholar's Guide: A Translation of the Twelfth-Century "Disciplina Clericalis" of Pedro Alfonso*, trans. Joseph Ramon Jones and John Esten Keller (Toronto: Pontifical Institute, 1969), pp. 38–41. As Robert Stretter observes, versions of the tale are also found in the *Alphabetum Narrationem* (#57), *Jacob's Well* (chap. 13) and the *Gesta Romanorum* (#171) as well as *Decameron* 10.8 and Thomas Elyot's *The Book Called the Governor* (II.12). See his "Rewriting Perfect Friendship in Chaucer's *Knight's Tale* and Lydgate's *Fabula Duorum Mercatorum*," *ChauR* 37 (2003): 234–52 (242). The two protagonists are merchants in the original narrative from the *Disciplina* as well as in the *Alphabetum*, *Jacob's Well*, and Lydgate's *Fabula*; in the others, they are either knights (the *Gesta*) or young noblemen (the *Decameron* and Elyot's *Book*). Of those starring merchants, Lydgate's is by far the most elaborate and the only version in verse; unless noted otherwise, the textual details I examine closely in what follows are entirely his. It is worth noting, however, that much of what I argue about the economic themes of the *Fabula* is in some sense latent in Petrus Alphonsus's brief narrative and ripe for development along precisely the lines Lydgate chose more than three centuries later.

eager is he to die in order to escape his misery that he confesses falsely to the crime and is condemned to death. Just as the sentence is pronounced, however, the Syrian merchant passes by and recognizes his friend; to save him, he claims to have committed the murder himself. This generous deed moves the real killer to confess the truth to the watching crowd, the king pardons all three men, and the Syrian merchant divides all his wealth with the Egyptian in order to restore him to prosperity.

As can already be observed from these two summaries alone, despite their differing genres and disparate lengths the *Letter* and *Fabula* are structured by a remarkably similar series of inversions and (in the case of the *Letter,* implied or desired rather than actualized) reversals: health is overturned by illness and is then recovered, wealth disintegrates into penury and is then restored. To take note of the shared form and content of both poems, as I will do in some detail below, is to do something more than remark yet again upon Lydgate's penchant for recycling words and images across his extensive oeuvre. It is rather to see one of the ways that the most prominent English poet of the age negotiated in his verse the anxieties attendant upon two different forms of socioeconomic exchange—that of patronage, on the one hand, and commerce, on the other.[6] My larger argument in what follows is that beyond their basic structural similarity, the verse petition and the longer romance operate as thematic or, better, as *economic* inversions of the other. By this I mean that in its attempt to manage the patron-client system of late medieval literary production in its speaker's best interest, the *Letter* affects a posture of commercialism: it implies by virtue of its predomi-

---

[6] The still-standard account of literary patronage in this period is Green, *Poets and Princepleasers;* see also Karl Julius Holzknecht, *Literary Patronage in the Middle Ages* (Philadelphia: Collegiate Press, 1923; rpt. New York: Octagon, 1966). On what he calls Lydgate's "fables of patronage"—the genre into which the *Letter* might be said to fit—see Seth Lerer, "Writing Like the Clerk: Laureate Poets and the Aureate World," chapter 1 of his *Chaucer and His Readers: Imagining the Author in Late-Medieval England* (Princeton: Princeton University Press, 1996), pp. 22–56; quotation on p. 61. For the caveat that "a poetic output so enormous and varied [as Lydgate's] cannot adequately be explained in terms of patronage," see Paul Strohm, "Hoccleve, Lydgate, and the Lancastrian Court," in *The Cambridge History of Medieval English Literature,* ed. David Wallace (Cambridge: Cambridge University Press, 1999), pp. 640–61 (652). On the impact of printing upon patronage and the literary market, see Alison V. Scott, "Marketing the Gift: Jonson, Multiple Patronage, and Strategic Exchange," *Parergon* 20.2 (2003): 135–59, and her full-length study, *Selfish Gifts: The Politics of Exchange and English Courtly Literature, 1580–1628* (Madison, N.J.: Fairleigh Dickinson University Press, 2006).

nantly mercantile metaphors that the poet is *not* a petitioner caught in the subservient role of literary beggar, but instead a kind of maker and merchant rightfully owed payment for the goods he has provided a customer.[7] By contrast, the *Fabula*—a tale starring two players skilled in just the sort of transactions toward which the *Letter* hopefully gestures— employs the language of courtly reciprocity to transform a commercial relationship into one reminiscent of patron and client (roles taken by each merchant in turn over the course of the tale's carefully balanced narrative).

In short, the two poems stand in chiastic relation to each other: the *Letter* playfully but not unpointedly tries to refigure a patronage relation into a more explicit business transaction between poet and duke, while the *Fabula* attempts to refashion the commercial relations joining the merchants of its title into a set of affective bonds. The fact that neither of these moves is entirely successful—the payment requested by the *Letter* still looks somewhat like a gift hoped for from a patron, and the gifts between friends in the *Fabula* like payments made between business associates—speaks to the degree to which the two types of exchange were in practice always more related modes than distinct systems.[8] By the later Middle Ages, aristocratic patronage had acquired something of a commercial veneer (including the phenomenon of contracted loyalty known as "bastard feudalism"),[9] while large-scale commercial ventures—which for England had yet to extend into the Mediterranean and remained largely continental—could still frequently

---

[7] As Lerer, *Chaucer and His Readers*, p. 38, observes, the *Letter* "sets us squarely in the everyday practicalities of making a living"; more generally, though still in terms of aristocratic patronage rather than the kind of merchant culture I reference here, he observes that "[i]n Lydgate's poetics, the business of writing becomes writing about business" (p. 39; see also p. 52 on "the business of the poem" transacted in so many of Lydgate's envoys).

[8] On the intertwining of gift and market economies in premodern Europe, see especially Natalie Zemon Davis, *The Gift in Sixteenth-Century France* (Madison: University of Wisconsin Press, 2000); and Valentin Groebner, *Liquid Assets, Dangerous Gifts: Presents and Politics at the End of the Middle Ages,* trans. Pamela E. Selwyn (Philadelphia: University of Pennsylvania Press, 2002). Davis, for example, notes that what she too calls the "gift mode" can exist alongside and overlap with "the mode of sales—of market buying-and-selling" (p. 9); see also pp. 37, 43–46, and 129. I thank Rick Keyser for pointing me to these sources.

[9] See Michael Hicks, *Bastard Feudalism* (New York: Longman, 1995), and his *English Political Culture in the Fifteenth Century* (London and New York: Routledge, 2002), pp. 141–63; see also R. H. Britnell, *The Commercialisation of English Society, 1000–1500* (Cambridge: Cambridge University Press, 1993), pp. 205–7.

depend on interpersonal ties.[10] I should emphasize at this point that I am not claiming that Lydgate himself actually felt much genuine anxiety about the form or functioning of either system. Although he did not spend the entirety of his career in residence at Bury St. Edmunds, as a monk the poet was shielded from the threat of financial insecurity in ways that Chaucer, Gower, and Hoccleve were not (and even these secular poets, as J. A. Burrow has observed, made use of the petitionary form in a semifictional fashion rather than in any strictly autobiographical sense).[11] It goes almost without saying that monasteries provided for the daily needs of their members, but it is worth remembering that Lydgate's home institution had long been one of the very richest establishments in England and so was even more certain of being able to do so than most, despite its abbot William Curteys's concerns over financial decline in the mid-1430s and his implementation of a budget designed to curtail expenses.[12] At the same time, in England by the fifteenth

[10] For an overview of the developments in European long-distance trade from the thirteenth through the fifteenth century, see Peter Spufford, *Power and Profit: The Merchant in Medieval Europe* (London: Thames and Hudson, 2002). On the entry of English merchants into the international marketplace on a large scale in the fourteenth century, see Christopher Dyer, *An Age of Transition? Economy and Society in England in the Later Middle Ages* (Oxford: Oxford University Press, 2001), p. 42. While the volume of English international trade declined in the fifteenth century, the general decrease in population in the wake of the plague meant that the volume per capita actually increased, and demand for consumer goods of all kinds rose to new levels. On these trends, see Dyer, *Making a Living in the Middle Ages: The People of Britain, 850–1520* (New Haven: Yale University Press, 2002), pp. 322–27, and Britnell, *Commercialisation,* pp. 155–64 and 169–71. On the fifteenth-century limitation of English trade to the Continent and the reliance of English merchants on informal agreements and bonds of trust, see Dyer, *Making a Living,* pp. 327–28; on those merchants' seeming preference for conducting international business in person even while others were relying increasingly on agents, see John Day, *The Medieval Market Economy* (Oxford: Basil Blackwell, 1987), p. 171. On the way one late medieval merchant handbook personalizes such international transactions, see my "Urban Utterances: Merchants, Artisans, and the Alphabet in Caxton's *Dialogues in French and English,*" NML 7 (2005): 127–61.
[11] See Burrow, "The Poet as Petitioner," esp. 67–75. On the conjunction of financial difficulty, the petition form, and the representation of selfhood in the early fifteenth century, see Knapp, *The Bureaucratic Muse,* pp. 20–29. For the argument that Lydgate, while not fixed there, would have most frequently been in residence at Bury, see Pearsall, *John Lydgate (1371–1449),* pp. 21–22.
[12] On the wealth of the abbey of Bury St. Edmunds, including during the fifteenth century, see A. Goodwin, *The Abbey of St. Edmundsbury* (Oxford: Basil Blackwell, 1931), esp. pp. 68–72, and Robert S. Gottfried, *Bury St. Edmunds and the Urban Crisis: 1290–1539* (Princeton: Princeton University Press, 1982), pp. 73–84; on Curteys's reforms, see Christopher Dyer, *Standards of Living in the Later Middle Ages: Social Change in England, c. 1200–1520* (Cambridge: Cambridge University Press, 1989), p. 98; on his abbacy, see Nigel Mortimer, *John Lydgate's "Fall of Princes": Narrative Tragedy in Its Literary and Political Contexts* (Oxford: Oxford University Press, 2005), pp. 139–48.

century an increasingly lax implementation of the Benedictine Rule's prohibition against individual property meant that monks were generally allowed to hold income-producing benefices and to acquire semiprivate funds in the form of allowances, bequests, and pensions, all of which were nominally gifts but which frequently look much more like direct payments for services rendered, both to the monastery and to layfolk beyond its walls.[13]

Thus we should not be surprised to find Lydgate appearing as an active participant within the late medieval economy rather than observing its complexities from the sidelines. The evidence for the monk's many and varied commissions comes largely from within his poems themselves or else from rubrics added by John Shirley to his copies of them, and what reward Lydgate actually received in return for most of his compositions will probably remain unknown.[14] Nevertheless, records of transactions that took place in the late 1430s testify directly to Lydgate's role as an economic player in and across monastic, courtly, and mercantile spheres. In 1438, he was paid by the abbot of St. Albans for the poem the *Life of St. Alban,* and in 1439 he was awarded a lifetime royal annuity from the customs at Ipswich (revised in 1440 to be drawn instead from the "Waytefee" in Norfolk and Suffolk). When problems arose with the initial payment of the annuity (perhaps, as Derek Pearsall suggests, because the original letters patent directed all the funds to Lydgate, causing some difficulty with Abbot Curteys over their impropriety vis-à-vis the Rule), Lydgate pursued the matter, writing Henry VI directly to ask him for a revised grant naming John Baret, a prominent citizen of Bury and the abbey's treasurer, as joint recipient. The king complied, and the poet then appears to have received payments without difficulty until his death in 1449.[15] At the same time, though no record of payment for them has survived, Lydgate's commissions to

[13] David Knowles, *The Religious Orders in England, Volume II: The End of the Middle Ages* (Cambridge: Cambridge University Press, 1955), pp. 170–74, 214, 240–44; as Knowles notes, records demonstrate that monks could also be paid wages directly by their superior for assorted tasks within the monastery (243). See also Barbara Harvey, *Living and Dying in England, 1100–1540: The Monastic Experience* (Oxford: Clarendon Press, 1993), pp. 1–2, 153, 211.

[14] On Shirley's career, see Margaret Connolly, *John Shirley: Book Production and the Noble Household in Fifteenth-Century England* (Aldershot: Ashgate, 1998).

[15] On these payments and Lydgate's struggle to claim his annuity, see Pearsall, *John Lydgate (1371–1449),* pp. 35–39, and Appendix, pp. 59–67, items #13–29.

produce mummings for the Mercers and Goldsmiths as well as other London poems like *The Legend of St. George* and *Bycorne and Chychevache* reveal his connections to and knowledge of urban merchant culture.[16] The diversity of socioeconomic situations to which Lydgate was exposed may help us to make some sense of the way in both *Letter* and *Fabula* a sick or endangered body is saved (or in the case of the *Letter,* left suspended in the hope of imminent salvation) by interventions that are actually somewhat more appropriate to the other's governing financial scenario; Lydgate's ability to imagine a solution to the problems of the one in terms of the other suggests the extent of his own direct experience of the benefits and pitfalls of both patronage and commerce.[17]

Richard Firth Green has noted of the payment to Lydgate for the *Life of St. Alban* that it is the first made to an English poet explicitly for his verse.[18] It is instructive to consider this fact in light of Georges Bataille's conception of poetry as a form of production that takes place at the expense of the poet, an idea toward which the epigraph to this essay has already gestured. In Bataille's romantic notion—and he himself admits

[16] Lydgate's connections to the Lancastrian court and to members of the aristocracy are well known. For a useful summary, see Pearsall, *John Lydgate (1371–1449)*; on the mummings and London poems, see pp. 29 and 31. On Lydgate's ties to merchant culture and his poems for the London bourgeoisie, see Claire Sponsler, "Alien Nation: London's Aliens and Lydgate's Mummings for the Mercers and Goldsmiths," in *The Postcolonial Middle Ages,* ed. Jeffrey Jerome Cohen (New York: St. Martin's Press, 2000), pp. 229–42; James Simpson, "The Energies of John Lydgate," in his *Reform and Cultural Revolution* (Oxford: Oxford University Press, 2002), pp. 34–67, esp. pp. 57–60; Maura Nolan, *John Lydgate and the Making of Public Culture* (Cambridge: Cambridge University Press, 2005), esp. pp. 5–8, 22–23, and 71–119; C. David Benson, "Civic Lydgate: The Poet and London," and Maura Nolan, "The Performance of the Literary: Lydgate's Mummings," both in *John Lydgate: Poetry, Culture, and Lancastrian England,* ed. Larry Scanlon and James Simpson (Notre Dame: University of Notre Dame Press, 2006), pp. 147–68 and 169–206. See also the essays collected in *Lydgate Matters: Poetry and Material Culture in the Fifteenth Century,* ed. Lisa H. Cooper and Andrea Denny-Brown (New York: Palgrave Macmillan, 2008), especially Claire Sponsler, "Lydgate and London's Public Culture" (pp. 13–33), Michelle R. Warren, "Lydgate, Lovelich, and London Letters" (pp. 113–38); Jennifer Floyd, "St. George and the 'Steyned Halle': Lydgate's Verse for the London Armourers" (pp. 139–64); and John M. Ganim, "Lydgate, London, and the Poetics of Exemption" (pp. 165–83). For a brief but insightful reading of the *Letter to Gloucester* along some of the same lines I pursue here, in the same volume see the afterword by D. Vance Smith, "Lydgate's Refrain: The Open When," pp. 185–95 (194–95).

[17] James Simpson makes a related point when he remarks on the "jurisdictional complexity of the institutions within which Lydgate worked" and the related "discursive variety" of his output ("The Energies of John Lydgate," p. 52).

[18] Green, *Poets and Princepleasers,* pp. 156–57.

that his is an ideal, that "the word 'poetry' can only be appropriately applied to an extremely rare residue of what it commonly signifies"— such "poetic expenditure" is not financial but emotional, even spiritual: "for the rare human beings who have this element at their disposal . . . the function of representation engages the very life of the one who assumes it. It condemns him to the most disappointing forms of activity, to misery, to despair, to the pursuit of inconsistent shadows that provide nothing but vertigo or rage."[19] I will return to this idea at the end of this essay. For now, and despite the anachronism of juxtaposing Bataille's image of literary poesis with the fifteenth-century situation of a poet who was (as far as we know) neither miserable nor despairing, let me remark that if in the *Fabula* we see Lydgate using the *trope* of misery and despair to literarily suggestive advantage, the *Letter* shows him using virtually the same mechanism in the hope of literal profit, or at least of fair recompense. It is, moreover, no accident that this poet— who, as Andrea Denny-Brown remarks, was a "tireless champion of measure in all things"[20]—centers both the *Letter* and the *Fabula* on fig-

[19] Bataille, "The Notion of Expenditure," p. 171. As Bruce Holsinger reminds us in "Para-Thomism: Bataille at Rheims," chapter 1 of his *The Premodern Condition: Medievalism and the Making of Theory* (Chicago: University of Chicago Press, 2005), pp. 26–56 (see also appendix 1, Bataille's own "Medieval French Literature, Chivalric Morals, and Poetry," trans. Laurence Petit, pp. 204–20), Bataille was trained as a medievalist and was deeply cognizant of French medieval poetry. It is therefore tempting to wonder what he made of the kind of verse that, like Lydgate's *Letter,* more or less overtly seeks economic reward. For Bataille, such begging-poems and passages (along with payments like those Lydgate received from his patrons and the institutions that they, and he, served) might easily have helped to confirm his view that most poetry, which "is hardly less debased than religion . . . has almost always been at the mercy of the great historical systems of appropriation." "The Use-Value of D. A. F. de Sade (An Open Letter to My Current Comrades)," *Visions of Excess,* pp. 99–102; rpt. in *The Bataille Reader,* pp. 147–64 (153). Holsinger, however, points out that in his *The Accursed Share,* Bataille characterizes the Middle Ages as a period of "limitless expenditure constantly in tension with the demands of religious ascesis and self-denial," whose profligate impulses can be contrasted to the productive emphasis of capitalism (*The Premodern Condition,* pp. 44–45).

[20] Andrea Denny-Brown, "Lydgate's Golden Cows: Appetite and Avarice in *Bycorne and Chychevache*" *Lydgate Matters,* pp. 35–56 (46). Denny-Brown's essay reveals the way Lydgate's frequent turn to images of lack and plenty in *Bycorne* and in other works speaks to a wider and widely shared set of concerns in this period about the intersection, and potential contradiction, of moral and material economies. Indeed, as Seth Lerer has suggested to me, the placement of the *Fabula*'s action in the Middle East, while in keeping with the tale's narrative tradition, is also suggestive regarding contemporary anxieties about the role played by profit-seeking English merchants in encouraging just the sort of consumer excess that Lydgate decries so explicitly elsewhere. The poem effectively converts the Eastern Other—so frequently represented in the medieval West as the epitome of the self-indulgent, accursed heathen—into a figure of Christian charity. It thus holds up these fictional foreign counterparts as moral exemplars, suggesting,

ures of plenitude, celebrated for their wholeness, and figures of lack, whose emptiness cries out to be filled. It is to exploring those images that I now turn.

The *Fabula* has always been read (that is, when it has been read at all) as a story about the triumph of male friendship over all obstacles. But the significance of this versified fable, like that of the *Letter,* springs less from its narrative of homosocial bonding than from its depiction of illness both physical and fiscal. It may at first seem like I am simply re-summarizing the *Fabula*'s plot when I insist on reviewing the way it portrays these ailments by way of a related nexus of images of scarcity and plenty; the poem is, after all, a tale of two merchants and their goods, and it is hard to imagine from where else its drama should come if not at least in part from the fact of their shared profession. Curiously, however, what limited scholarship exists on the fable has avoided the obvious in favor of tracing how Lydgate's story revisits and revises the love triangle of Chaucer's *Knight's Tale*.[21] This turn to the so-called father of English poetry to explain the work of one of his "sons" is an example in small of the critical phenomenon that has until very recently charac-terized Lydgate scholarship as a whole.[22] But it is only when we take

---

however obliquely, that English (and so Christian) merchants ought to be all the more able than the *Fabula*'s spiritually untaught protagonists—whose generous acts can be understood as all the more remarkable, given their pagan status—to act with similar selflessness. The *Fabula*'s final words point in this direction, for there the narrator prays that "God . . . His grace sende, / That euery freend to othir be as trewe, / As were thes marchauntis always iliche newe," and the poem's very last lines encourage its audience to join him in this socially and spiritually conscious appeal: "This is my desyr in al degrees of men: / That it so be, I pray you, seith 'Amen'" (906–10).

[21] See Pamela Farvolden, "'Love Can No Frenship': Erotic Triangles in Chaucer's 'Knight's Tale' and Lydgate's *Fabula duorum mercatorum,*" in *Sovereign Lady: Essays on Women in Middle English Literature,* ed. Muriel Whitaker (New York and London: Garland, 1995), pp. 21–44, and, more recently, Stretter, "Rewriting Perfect Friendship."

[22] On the fifteenth century's construction of Chaucer as a father-figure, see Lerer, *Chaucer and His Readers;* for a study of one example of Lydgate's self-positioning in this regard, see Daniel T. Kline, "Father Chaucer and the *Siege of Thebes:* Literary Paternity, Aggressive Difference, and the Prologue to Lydgate's Oedipal Canterbury Tale," *ChauR* 34 (1999): 217–35. For important examples of the current and ongoing revitalization of Lydgate studies, see the studies cited in note 16 above, as well as Mortimer, *John Lydgate's "Fall of Princes";* Robert J. Meyer-Lee, *Poets and Power from Chaucer to Wyatt* (Cambridge: Cambridge University Press, 2007), esp. pp. 49–87; Claire Sponsler, "'Eating Lessons: Lydgate's 'Dietary' and Consumer Conduct," in *Medieval Conduct,* ed. Kathleen Ashley and Robert L. A. Clark (Minneapolis: University of Minnesota Press, 2001), pp. 1–22; and Sponsler, "Text and Textile: Lydgate's Tapestry Poems," in *Medieval Fabrications: Dress, Textiles, Clothwork, and Other Cultural Imaginings,* ed. E. Jane Burns (New York: Palgrave Macmillan, 2004), pp. 19–34.

Lydgate on his own terms, removing him forcibly from the Chaucerian shade in which he himself often tried to stand, that the rich fullness—rather than barren emptiness—of his verse comes most clearly into view.

Take in this regard the *Fabula*'s neatly aligned opening description of both Egyptian merchant and Egyptian landscape, a longish passage in which human being and geographical territory mirror each other's bounty. The merchant is in fact said to be "bountevous" (3)—both virtuous and generous—while his homeland is annually made "plentevous," or abundantly fertile, by the "ouerflowyd" Nile (30, 25). The Egyptian is likewise someone in whom "alle vertues . . . wern aggregat" and who is "[o]f vices voyd" (5–6), while in Egypt "mercymony," goods, are "ful reedy and ful copious" (31–32).[23] Both person and place, in other words, are veritable treasuries, of *goodness* on the one hand and of *goods* on the other. To this moral and mercantile surfeit we can compare the third stanza of the *Letter to Gloucester,* in which the lack of a financial "flood" into the poet's purse has halted the passage of ships (that is, gold nobles, stamped with the image of a ship in this period) and so made the speaker's "custom skars" (19, 23).[24] Equally dry, remarks a later stanza of the *Letter,* is a "marbil stoon" from which it is "harde to likke hony . . . / For ther is nouthir licour nor moisture" (33–34).[25] In the *Fabula*'s opening, we learn that Egypt too is generally dry, "desolat / Of cloude and reynes," but with the crucial difference that its land is reliably "irrigat" each year by the mighty river (22–24). Not so the dry ground of the *Letter*-writer's purse, which without fiscal watering remains but "bareyn soyl" that is "sool and solitarye" (58).[26]

Although the Egyptian merchant of the *Fabula* is as ripe with goodness as his homeland from the poem's beginning, the promise of that

---

[23] In addition to the possible moral valence of the setting (see note 20 above), Egypt's plenty was a commonplace. See, for example, the late fourteenth-century encyclopedia *On the Properties of Things: John Trevisa's Translation of Bartolomaeus Anglicus De Proprietatibus Rerum,* gen. ed. M. C. Seymour, 3 vols. (Oxford: Clarendon Press, 1975–88), 2:756, XV.liii: "And oneliche Nilus moisteþ þat londe and renneþ þere aboute and makith it plenteuous with risynge and wexinge. And . . . [it] is so plenteuous of oþer marchaundises and chaffare, þat it filleþ nyȝe alle þe worlde with nedeful marchaundises."

[24] On the monetary allusion, see Hammond, "Poet and Patron," 127; Walter Schirmer, *John Lydgate: A Study in the Culture of the Fifteenth Century,* trans. Ann E. Keep (London: Methuen, 1964), p. 216; *John Lydgate: Poems,* ed. Norton-Smith, 116 n. 17.

[25] Compare the *Fabula,* which remarks that "to them, that han i-tastyd galle, / Mor aggreable is the hony soote" (127–28).

[26] This is a financial solitude that the Egyptian merchant will himself experience firsthand when the wheel of his fiscal fortunes has turned and he finds that "'I pleye sool'" (*Fabula,* 551).

ethical ripeness is only brought to fruition—a metaphor I use deliberately, for the concept of fruitfulness suffuses the tale[27]—when he and
the merchant from Baldac, though "disseueryd by absence" (87) become
so "ful . . . of oon accordement" that they are "[a]s oon in too and too
in oon for euere" (96–97).[28] This bond is further strengthened when the
two finally meet, and the Egyptian gives his friend free rein over his
goods with the words:

> "What so I haue, is platly in your myht.
> I feffe [*endow*] you fully in al my good and riht.
> Beth glad and wolcom: I can sey you no more.
> Haue her myn hand for now and evirmore."
>
> (179–82)

As Jonathan Gil Harris has shown, English mercantile writing of the
sixteenth century was to embrace the literary conventions of romance, a
form of narrative appropriation that, he argues, "lent a fairytale veneer
to the mercenary ambitions of mercantilism."[29] A similar move is being
made here in Lydgate's poem, as the forms and figures of courtship,
devotion, and promise step in to mask what in the fifteenth century
could easily have been imagined as a much more impersonal and largely
commercial relation.[30] In fact, it is worth noting that the poem, while
consistently emphasizing the fact of its protagonists' careers, never gives
them the chance to become business partners. They are from the outset
bound to each other "by report and by noon othir mene" (48), drawn
together by a mutual "affeccioun" (88) founded on their moral similarity; as the narrator explains, "[t]weyne of o kynde togidre drawe neere"
so that (in general as in this particular case) "[h]onour is weddyd vnto

---

[27] For example: "As for a norshyng, her frutys to fecunde, / With corn and greyn to
make the lond habounde" (27–28); and "But weel is hym, that may the frute atteyne, /
As whilom diden thes noble marchauntis tweyne" (132–33). That same fruit of prosperity, however, becomes later in the poem an example of the kind of wealth that can be
lost should it become excessive: "yiff a tre with frut be ovirlade. . . . / Both braunche
and bouh wol enclyne and fade. . . . / Right so it farith of fals felicite, / That yif his
weihte mesure do exceede, / Than of a fal gretly is to dreede" (610–16).

[28] For Stretter, these lines refer to the "proverbial one soul in two bodies" ("Rewriting
Perfect Friendship," 248).

[29] Jonathan Gil Harris, *Sick Economies: Drama, Mercantilism, and Disease in Shakespeare's
England* (Philadelphia: University of Pennsylvania Press, 2004), p. 12.

[30] In having the Egyptian "feffe" his friend (180), Lydgate does, however, allude to
the more formal financial arrangements of both land transfers and marriage contracts.
See *MED,* s.v. *feffen,* 1 and 3.

worthynesse" (73, 82). The imagery that here binds the merchants in loving friendship is not only proleptic of but in a sense also a prophylactic against the romantic love that will threaten to come between them. That is, the vocabulary of one-ness and likeness both anticipates the Syrian's attraction to and eventual union with the Egyptian's fiancée and simultaneously renders these events harmless by making the merchants' connection the primary one: the two men, after all, are here firmly "weddyd" to each other before they ever meet and well before the actual marriage takes place.[31] Furthermore, what might in another context have become a flourishing commercial exchange is here made to look instead like an ideal gift economy, in which neither surplus nor lack is experienced on either side.[32] The Egyptian and the Syrian apparently never exchange goods in a quest for profit, but rather share them out of a deeply equitable camaraderie:

> By lond or se the good her chapmen carye
> Was entircomownyd by her bothys assent:
> Yiff oon hadde ouht plesaunt or necessarye,
> Vnto the tothir anoon he hath it sent.
>
> (92–95)

Although the Syrian finally travels to Egypt not primarily to see his friend but rather "[f]or marchaundise, that was in that contre" (102), even the weather cooperates in the poem's program of subduing of the vagaries of commercial activity and allowing unobstructed courtship to blossom in its place. For in contrast to the "froward" [*unfavorable*] wind that in the *Letter* prevents golden ships from anchoring in the harbor of the speaker's purse (18), in the *Fabula* it is a "blisful wynd"—like many a helpful breeze in medieval romance—that "in-to [the Syrian's] seyl hath blowe / His ship to dryve" (104–5). And while a "skars" custom is the result of the contrary weather in the *Letter* (23), it is "no skarsete" but rather fullness of all kinds that greets the Syrian upon his arrival in Egypt, as we have already seen above in the Egyptian's welcoming of

---

[31] On the relationship of the protagonist's formal pledges to the conventions of noble courtesy, see Farvolden, " 'Love Can No Frenship,' " pp. 28–29 and 32–33.

[32] For a thorough overview of theories of both forms of exchange and the difficulty (in both theory and practice) of actually disentangling the two (something the contortions of the *Letter* and the *Fabula* make clear as well), see John Frow, "Gift and Commodity," in his *Time and Commodity Culture: Essays in Cultural Theory and Postmodernity* (Oxford: Oxford University Press, 1997), pp. 102–217.

his friend (179–82) and again as the visitor is shown to his room and then to dinner:

> Unto a chaumbre *ful* riche and weel arrayed
> Anoon he [the Egyptian] lad hym, which stood somwhat on heihte,
> And seide: "Freend, I am *ful* weel appayed,
> That I be grace of you have cauht a sihte;
> *For nothyng moore* myn herte myte lihte;
> Wherfore wolcom, also God me save,
> Vn-to your owne, and to *al* that I have."
>
> Of mete and drynk, deyntees and vitaille,
> Of divers wynes ther was *no skarsete,*
> Of straunge viaundys in sondry apparaille,
> That nevir aforn was seen such roialte:
> To moore and lasse it snowyd doun plente.
>
> (148–59; my emphasis)

In this passage the word "ful," most strictly an adverbial intensive meaning "very," contributes to the passage's overall impression of fullness both material and emotional; we are clearly to understand the Egyptian's home as a site not just of satisfactory completion but of repletion.[33]

And yet the Syrian guest's "weel arrayed" room soon becomes the setting for a somber scene reminiscent of the deathbed scenario described with dark humor by the speaker of the *Letter to Gloucester.* The begging-poem's fourth stanza relates how the purse becomes increasingly ill as its financial distress continues:

> Ther was no tokne sent doun from the Tour [*the Mint*],
> As any gossomer the countirpeys [*counterweight of a scale*] was liht;
> A ffretyng etyk [*wasting fever*] causyd his langour
> By a cotidian [*intermittent fever*] which heeld him day and nyght.
>
> (25–28)

Likewise struck by the "infirmyte" of a "brennyng feuere," the sick Syrian takes to "a bed [that] in haste was maad ful softely" for him (201–2,

---

[33] See *MED*, s.v. *ful* (adv.), 1 and 4. The passage's last line is clearly meant to evoke the largesse of Chaucer's Franklin, of whom the *General Prologue* relates that "[i]t snewed in his hous of mete and drynke" (I.345).

204), and there he languishes in terms that replicate the suffering of the purse in the begging-poem. For what next takes place, as the doctors are brought to the ailing man's room, is a scene of medical intervention that makes the body of the bed-ridden merchant look remarkably like the devastated pouch of the *Letter*. On that bag's behalf, Lydgate writes in the second stanza of the *Letter,* he "souhte leechys for a restoratiff" (9), but no doctor or apothecary could find a solution; indeed, ultimately the personified purse is even emptier than before, the "[b]otme of his stomak . . . tournyd vp-so-doun" by an overly effective "laxatif" that "[m]ade hym slendre by a consumpcioun" (13–15) even before the onset of the quotidian fever that begins ten lines later (25–28, quoted above).[34] Similarly, the doctors in the *Fabula* come prepared to turn the Syrian inside-out in order to discover the cause of his infirmity, bringing with them both "goode siropys to make dygestyues" and "[p]elotes {*pills*} expert for evacuatyues" (275–77). And because the doctors assume that the cause of the merchant's illness lies within, they look not just metaphorically but rather literally "[f]ul deepe" as they try "to serchen out the trouthe" (317): though they cannot actually open their patient up, they rely (as per standard medieval medical practice) on his body's excretions for their diagnosis, examining first his sweat and then his urine (270, 323–29).

The *Fabula* and *Letter* both reveal, to borrow another useful phrase from Harris's work on a later text (in this case, *The Merchant of Venice*), "the pathological underbelly of desire, whether romantic or commercial."[35] But unlike the distraught speaker of the *Letter,* who knows precisely what pathology has affected his purse, the Egyptian merchant and the "leechis many on" (267) whom he summons to his friend's sickbed are initially at a loss even to diagnose, let alone cure, the Syrian's illness. And in the poem's tracing of their frustrated search "to fynd out roote

---

[34] It is this kind of laxative that a thirteenth-century Latin verse satirically recommends: "O vos bursae turgidae, Romam veniatis; / Romae viget physica bursis constipatis" ["O you swollen purses, come to Rome! / [A]t Rome there is effective medicine for constipated purses"] ("Song Upon the Times," *Thomas Wright's Political Songs of England,* ed. Peter Coss [1839; Cambridge: Cambridge University Press, 1996], pp. 14–18, lines 59–60; my thanks to Andrea Denny-Brown for this reference. By contrast, Hoccleve claims in "La Male Regle" that the "coyn" for which he asks his sovereign will allow him to procure the "medecyne / As may myn hurtes alle, þat me greeue, / Exyle cleene / & voide me of pyne" (446–48); in fact, the passage is playfully ambiguous, suggesting that the coin itself may be the purgative. On these lines, see also Knapp, *The Bureaucratic Muse,* pp. 38–39.

[35] Harris, *Sick Economies,* p. 11.

and rynde / Of what humour was causyd his dissese" (271–72), we arrive at what is to my mind the most clever of Lydgate's verbal games in the *Fabula* in a passage—entirely of the English poet's devising—that mines medical treatises for what effectively become commercial puns. Reviewing humoral theory along with the attending doctors, the narrator describes all the ways in which the sick Syrian might have been suffering from some kind of "excesse" (290). The physicians discount "effymera," caused by too much food, or thought, or extreme temperature (288–94); "putrida," in which any humor "synneth in quantite" or whose "flowyng," unlike the Egyptian Nile, "is to plentevous" and "excedith mesoure" (295–98); and two types of "sinochus," diagnosed, respectively, as either the excessive "quantite" or "qualite" of a single humor (299–303).[36] But as we readers of the poem already know, the Syrian does not need to be emptied by the purgatives that the doctors have brought, since what ails him is not a surplus in need of voiding but a *lack* in need of filling.[37]

He has, in fact, what seems to be very much a merchant's disease, since what he requires is the " 'maiden' " whom, he notes to himself, his friend has " 'kept for his owne stoor' " (244). In other words, the Syrian, despite his joyful participation up to this point in the gift economy he has formed with his Egyptian friend, cannot help but consider the girl as a kind of commodity that was once freely available on the open market but is now, to his dismay, no longer in circulation.[38] To his still-

[36] For a reading of this passage in the context of other didactic literature, see my "The Poetics of Practicality," *Twenty-First Century Approaches to Literature: Middle English,* ed. Paul Strohm (Oxford: Oxford University Press), pp. 491–505 (500–501). On the centrality of the humors to medieval medical theory and of phlebotomy and uroscopy to medieval medical practice, see Nancy G. Siraisi, *Medieval and Early Renaissance Medicine: An Introduction to Knowledge and Practice* (Chicago: University of Chicago Press, 1990), pp. 101–106, 124–25, 137–41, and Carole Rawcliffe, *Medicine and Society in Later Medieval England* (Phoenix Mill, UK: Alan Sutton, 1995), pp. 33–36, 47, 59–68; on the English medical profession more broadly, see Faye Getz, *Medicine in the English Middle Ages* (Princeton: Princeton University Press, 1998).

[37] In Lydgate's *The Pilgrimage of the Life of Man,* by contrast, the "ryches and gret plente" that prevent wealthy men from entering heaven are compared to the "corruption of wyckyd humours & corrupt blood," a "suparfluyte" that must be drained for the sake of spiritual health (3 vols., ed. F. J. Furnivall and Katherine B. Locock, EETS e.s. 77, 83, 92 [London: Kegan Paul, Trench, Trübner, 1899–1904], lines 18304–13); see also lines 18355–59, in which poverty is described as the "medicyne and leche" that can lance the boil of "superfluyte". On the way Lydgate merges discourses of medicine and urban planning in his *Troy Book* to convey the importance of emptying both the city and the body politic of filth, see Paul Strohm, "Sovereignty and Sewage," *Lydgate Matters,* pp. 57–70.

[38] See *MED,* s.v. *stor(e,* (n. [1]), for the ways in which this term generally referred to movable goods.

mercantile mind, the girl is—like the goods the merchants exchanged earlier in the poem—a "necessarye" (94) for which he has nothing to recompense the Egyptian but his desire for her. And it is only once the physicians note this lack, signified by the "remys [*watery*], attenuat . . . ful thynne and wannyssh" quality of their patient's urine that they realize the Syrian has "falle[n]" into the "malencolye" of lovesickness (321–26).[39] Although this malady is physically manifested by "aquosite . . . / Without substaunce" and "voyde . . . of colour" (327–28), the problem, as the poem now indicates, is caused not by depletion but by inflation: lovesickness is a disease that leads the sufferer improperly to "trowe a wight for love mor fayr or pure, / Than evir hym ordeyned hath God or nature" (342–43). Despite the fact that its root lies in a kind of morally suspect overvaluation, a "corrupcioun . . . / of thilke vertu callid estimatiff" (337–38), the remedy for lovesickness (at least in this poem) is not to be found in a measured reestimation of the beloved's worth any more than it is in the "good siropys" and "precious poudrys" that the doctors come prepared to administer (275, 278). Rather, a cure lies only in attaining the unique object of desire that, as the poem is at pains to note, is one for which no substitute can be found. For though the Egyptian parades "alle the ladyes and maydenys of his hous" before his friend (372)—in a fashion that more closely resembles a display of wares from which the Syrian may choose a lover rather than an investigative lineup to discover the person he already loves—the sick man admits that he "'may nat chesyn'" any but the one he has already chosen: "'Ther is noon other, that I love can'" (410).

The commercial language that depicts the girl as accumulated property ("stoor," 244) and the medical discourse of melancholy that portrays her as something whose value can be assessed and even overestimated figures the Egyptian's fiancée more as commodity than person. By contrast (yet fully in line with the poem's program of refig-

---

[39] The examination of the patient's urine also occurs in the *Disciplina Clericalis, Alphabetum Narrationem,* and *Jacob's Well,* but without this level of detail. On lovesickness, see John Livingston Lowes, "The Loveres Maladye of Hereos," *MP* 11 (1914): 491–546; Mary Wack, *Lovesickness in the Middle Ages: The Viaticum and Its Commentaries* (Philadelphia: University of Pennsylvania Press, 1990); and Marion A. Wells, *The Secret Wound: Love-Melancholy and Early Modern Romance* (Stanford: Stanford University Press, 2007), esp. pp. 22–44. Urine's lack of color and its thinness was indeed taken to signify melancholy; as one medical text puts it, "If the uryn shewe white and thynne, it sygnifieth malencoly, ffor malencoly is colde and drye" (London, Wellcome Library, Western MS 537, fols. 16r–16v; qtd. in Rawcliffe, *Medicine and Society,* p. 48).

uring the impersonal international market as a familiar and affective domestic space), the language of love reinforces the kind of "private singularization" that, Igor Kopytoff notes, works to counter the impersonalizing force of commoditization.[40] The poem works hard to perform this kind of singularization, and it does so, somewhat paradoxically, by homing in on the girl's total possession of all desirable qualities. Capitalizing again on the double sense of "ful," it informs us that she is "[f]ul wys," "ful of honeste," "ful of affiaunce," and "ful war of governaunce" (379–80, 387, 389). But all this fullness never reaches the point of overflow since she is also "[i]n moral vertu mesuryd" (388) and is, in sum, a perfectly balanced entity: "In hir was nothyng, that nature myht amende" (392). Again, as conventional as this language may be, drawn as it is once more from the standard romance vocabulary of courtly love, what is remarkable is the way Lydgate's use of it plays so neatly against the trope of medical and mercantile emptiness that characterizes the lovelorn Syrian at this very same point in the poem. The girl, who is "hool of hir herte" (386), is what the merchant needs to become, as he himself will later say, " 'hool and sound' " (434).

For if his urine is "voyde . . . of color," so too by extension is the merchant's unfulfilled heart a void that he is at first left "al sool" to lament in a similarly "voyded" room (219). This is a psychosomatic emptiness that, like Lydgate's purse in the *Letter,* needs to be filled. But while the writer of the *Letter* needs an immediate cash payment in a patronage system dominated—and as the poem works to suggest, problematically so—by the largely arbitrary nature of the gift, the commercially adept Syrian merchant, who at this point imagines that he could never repay his friend for the girl, instead *needs* precisely the kind of offering that, in Georg Simmel's terms, "is not occasioned by any gratitude" but rather by "spontaneous devotion to the other."[41] The gift, as John Frow notes of Derrida's argument in *Given Time,* "is the opposite of and interrupts economy," and while for Derrida any return, even in the form of gratitude, cancels out the gift as such, the terms of the *Fabula* at this point in its narrative trajectory seem to suggest that this

---

[40] Igor Kopytoff, "The Cultural Biography of Things: Commoditization as Process," in *The Social Life of Things: Commodities in Cultural Perspective,* ed. Arjun Appadurai (Cambridge: Cambridge University Press, 1986), pp. 64–91 (80).

[41] Georg Simmel, "Faithfulness and Gratitude," in *The Sociology of Georg Simmel,* ed. Kurt H. Wolff (New York: Free Press, 1950), p. 393; qtd. in Frow, "Gift and Commodity," p. 107.

moment represents just such another interruption in the two men's already more-than-exclusively-economic connection to each other.[42] " 'To me,' " the generous Egyptian begs his sick friend, " 'vncloose the somme of your desyre,' " adding " 'mystrust to lokke it vp fro me' " (361, 363).[43]

The tenor (or, in metaphorical terms, the vehicle) of these encouraging words is yet another example of the way the *Fabula* tries to transfer the language of the market into the realm of the gift, for the mercantile vocabulary of containers, locks, and sums is deployed by the Egyptian (who earlier would "for no cost . . . spare / To haue restoored the sike to weelfare" [265–66]) with the exclusive aim of satisfying his friend's emotional needs. Opening under this friendly pressure his previously "closyd . . . wounde" and displaying the "bollyng" [*inflammation*] that "festrith" within (225, 227),[44] the Syrian in turn receives a double reward, or, more accurately, a double gift.[45] " 'I *gyf* hir the,' " the Egyptian says twice over of his decision to confer the girl upon his friend (420, 422; my emphasis). But just as important, or so it would seem given the stress the poem places on the matter, the Egyptian also volunteers to " 'bere thexpence fully and costage' " of the marriage ceremony (425). The double generosity of this gesture—the gift of money as well as of the girl—highlights the degree to which the poem is trying to leave the concerns of the market behind; the Egyptian, at least at this point, gives "ful and hool" without expectation of return (421).[46] Tellingly, at this point the poet too claims his own "wante [of] witt" to describe all the

[42] Frow, "Gift and Commodity," p. 107; his reference is to Jacques Derrida, *Given Time: I. Counterfeit Money,* trans. Peggy Kamuf (Chicago: University of Chicago Press, 1992), p. 12.

[43] This line both looks back to and yet reverses the terms of enclosure with which the men's mutual affection is at first described, when "Love," which "berith the keye and also the cliket" serves as a "trewe porteer" that "lok[e]s" them inside each other's hearts (61–63).

[44] On the hidden wound as an image of melancholic love, see Wells, *The Secret Wound,* pp. 70–74.

[45] Here again we can use a comparison with the *Fabula* to see more clearly how the *Letter* tries to invert patronage into commerce. For while in the romance it will be an unasked-for gift from a fellow merchant that heals the Syrian, the *Letter,* playing on the double meaning of the term for both a medical recipe and a sum of money, directly asks Gloucester ("my Lord") to doctor the sick purse with "a *receyt* of plate and coignage" (39–40; my emphasis). See *MED,* s.v. *receit(e,* 1 and 4.

[46] Later, however, the Egyptian will decide to "preeve his freend at neede" and travel to Syria "for to make assay" (642–43). The poem's struggle to maintain his first gift as a perfect one given without hope of reciprocation is demonstrated in the very next stanza, when, having arrived at his destination, the Egyptian decides he would rather be " 'ded . . . for shamfastnesse' " rather than " 'shewe a poynt to hym [the Syrian] of my distresse' " (650–51).

"passaunt costys" and "purveiance" of the wedding feast (438, 435–36); the surplus, almost excessive, nature of the gift in turn seems to exceed the limits of his language, or at least excuses his turn to *occupatio*. But what Lydgate still manages to make clear is that the Egyptian has not only played a better doctor than the doctors by opening "the tonne / Of friendly triacle" on his friend's behalf,[47] but has also more than made good any loss sustained by the Syrian during his illness: "nevir I radde yit," the narrator comments, "O freend to a-nothir that so weel hath hym quit" (446–48).

The language of "quitting," of payback, now also takes on a authori-ally self-reflexive cast, for here Lydgate interrupts the tale to inform its readers that his own narrative debt to them, as incurred up to this point, has been discharged in full:

> Off this mateer what shuld I write mor?
> I wil entrete this processe forth in pleyn:
> Hir and hir iowellys, hir richesse and hir stor
> He hath hym youen, the stoory seith certeyn,
> And hom with al repayred is ageyn
> And lad hir with him, as was his freendys wyl,
> Which cowde nat feyne his plesaunce to fulfyl.
>   (456–62)

Now that the Egyptian merchant has given ("youen") the girl and her goods ("hir richesse and . . . stor") to his friend—in another appearance of the verb "to give" that emphasizes the transaction as gift rather than commodity exchange—the poet can make claim to legitimate use of *occupatio,* implying in his "Off this mateer what shuld I write mor?" that there is nothing left to do but summarize the action so far "in pleyn."[48] At an earlier point the narrator, referring to the horror of any distance that separates "hem, that loven trewe," had cause to lament the "bitter

---

[47] In the *Letter,* by contrast, the "tonne" of the purse has been "attamyd" by poverty (51), which Hammond, "Poet and Patron," reads as a metaphor for piercing and ex-hausting (128). A vessel of metaphorical medicine appears later in the *Fabula* to repre-sent the kind Egyptian's subsequent loss of fortune. The poem notes that while "[w]ho that wil entren to tamen of the sweete, / He mvst as weel taken his aventure / To taste in bittir, or he the vessel leete" (701–3), the Egyptian has "i-dronken at the fulle" of both and especially of the latter (the bitter), so much so that it has "maad his hed to dulle, / That he ne lest but litil lawh or smyle" (708–11).

[48] On marriage as a prime site of premodern gift exchange, see Davis, *The Gift,* pp. 27–29.

bale hangyng in ballaunce" (120, 124)—a phrase that, like the "count-irpeys" [*counterweight*] of the *Letter* (26), practically begs us to picture a merchant's scales.[49] Here, just slightly past the midpoint of the *Fabula*, both the emotional and narrative budgets have been brought into balance; all has been, to pun slightly, but I think not inappropriately, on the language of the passage above, "repayred" and "fulfyl[ed]" (460, 462).[50] But in the second part of the poem the narrator, to his own proclaimed distress, must return to considering the ever-present threat of imbalance in the market economy to which its protagonists also belong, and in which that which easily comes may also easily go (even while in the *Fabula*'s final analysis this problem, too, will be solved by a generous gift rather than by the ebb and flow of the market).

This threat of financial upset is one lived out in the *Letter to Gloucester* and the *Fabula* alike. In the *Letter*, Lydgate notes that "[a]n ernest grote, whan it is dronke and goon, / Bargeyn of marchauntys, stant in aven-ture" (35–36).[51] Having spent freely in order to consume at will, the speaker now wryly joins his purse in the shared "adventure" of poverty: "My purs and I be callyd," he remarks, "to the lure / Off indigence, our stuff leyd in morgage" (37–38), a phrase recognizable as all the more fitting when we realize that in Middle English, *lure* can mean either an enticement *or* the open mouth of a bag.[52] A similar fiscal and physically figured disaster overtakes the generous Egyptian merchant in the *Fa-bula*, for when Fortune spins her wheel so that, like the "vp-so-doun" purse of the *Letter* (13), it too is "turned vp so doun," he "is ffallen and plonget in povert / Thoruh vanysshyng of his possessioun" (520–22).

---

[49] The concept of balance, present throughout the poem, appears explicitly at two other points within it: first, when the narrator reflects on the way friends share each other's pain, remarking that "[t]his is the ballaunce oonly of freendys riht" (216); and second, when the real killer steps forward and confesses to his crime in order to save the innocent Syrian, the justices are so amazed "[t]hat alle here wittis wer hangid in bal-launce" (833).

[50] While the line "And hom with al repayred is ageyn" (460) clearly means "And with all [of the gifts he] returned home again" (see *MED*, s.v. *repairen*), *repayred* can also serve as the past participle of the verb meaning to fix or to restore to health (see *MED*, s.v. *reparen* [v. (3)]).

[51] Harris notes that the word "adventure" is doubly freighted by the late sixteenth century, connoting both "romance quest and commercial venture" (*Sick Economies*, p. 10); Lydgate's use here seems to confirm that the commercial connotation was already in play by the early fifteenth century.

[52] It can also figure the open, voiding end of the human body's bag, its rectum. See *MED*, s.v. *lure*, and Jeremy J. Citrome, "Bodies that Splatter: Surgery, Chivalry, and the Body in the *Practica* of John Arderne," *Exemplaria* 13 (2001): 137–72 (146).

This "vanysshyng" of commercial capital effects a corresponding loss of social prestige: the merchant, a "new Iob, i-cast in indigence," is quite suddenly "valyd adoun from hih degre / Ful many a steihr in-to wrechydnesse" (526, 542–43). He has been, that is, *valley*-ed, or brought low, but also, and quite literally, *de-valued.*[53] And the experience of that devaluation is something that, as another potential pun on Lydgate's part may suggest, the merchant himself can only understand in the commercial terms he knows best: "Hym thouhte," the same passage notes, "it was to hym a newe emprise" (539).[54]

But while poverty may be a new business enterprise of sorts for the Egyptian, describing its somatic and psychic effects—the "languor" that results from the "infect of Fortune" (641, 672)[55]—is something of an exercise in duplication, if not repetition, for Lydgate, who has the newly impoverished merchant employ images of physical hardship, of past plenitude, and of painful lack, all familiar from the *Letter to Gloucester,* to bemoan his changed state:

> "Now hongir, thrust [*thirst*], vnkouth as vnto me,
> Vnwarly sweth my passyd habundaunce.
> Now cold, now nakyd in necessite
> I walke aboute for my sustenaunce.
> Whilom in plente and now al in grevaunce!
> Allas, my fulle [*full moon*] is derkyd in-to wane,
> With wynd forwhirlyd as is a mvant ffane [*weather vane*]."
>
> (568–72)

[53] "Value" in the sense of "the specific monetary value of a commodity" appears as a noun at least as early as 1303; as a verb meaning "to assess the monetary value of," it was in regular use—enough so as to appear in the *Rotuli Parliamentorum*—by 1439 (see *MED,* s.v. *valu(e,* 1a[c], and s.v. *valuen*).

[54] While the *MED,* s.v. *emprise,* does not indicate a possible commercial connotation of the term, whose primary meaning is "undertaking," the *OED,* s.v. *emprise,* notes two uses in the late fourteenth century (in Barbour's *The Bruce* and Gower's *Confessio Amantis*) that are inflected by a sense of value. Even if this kind of wordplay is not Lydgate's intention here, the fact that the Egyptian finds poverty to be a new "undertaking" implies that he is comparing it to his previously successful commercial activities.

[55] The concepts of commerce and infection are returned to near the poem's end, when the poet reflects on the difficulty a king has in preventing treason in his realm: "Ful hard it were taccomplisshen his desyr / Or in his rewme *such a bargeyn dryve: / The aeyer infect,* the weder is nat cleer / Ne never ne shal, whil tresoun is so ryve" (862–65, my emphasis). For an interesting playing out of the concept of infection and its relationship to language and the body in the work of another late medieval poet, see R. Allen Shoaf, *Chaucer's Body: The Anxiety of Circulation in the "Canterbury Tales"* (Gainesville: University Press of Florida, 2001).

The last two lines of this lament particularly recall the *Letter,* in which we have already seen a "froward" wind at work (18). Several lines later in that shorter work, playing on the alchemical terms for silver and gold, the poet comments upon the eclipse of "Sol and Luna" in his purse and its resultant "lynyng dirk" (29, 31), comparing the bag's shadowy interior with the brightness of the coins it lacks.[56] So too in the *Fabula,* in the passage just quoted above, that which was once "fulle" has not so much dissipated as darkened ("derkyd") into "wane." This is a darkness that contrasts both with the light of the tale's opening, where we learn that "no dirknesse of the nyht" can overcome the "beemys" of each merchant's virtue (66–67), and also with the "liht of presence" that the Syrian is said to experience with joy when he first arrives in his friend's homeland (119)—a light itself compared to the "blake nyht of sorwe" that characterizes absence (113).

The *Fabula*'s juxtaposition of darkness and light is but one of the several ways in which its poet reacts to the twinned tragedies of his tale. Thinking at the halfway point upon the mercantile ills he must describe in the "remenaunt" (518) of the fable (*remenaunt* being, of course, a term with its own financial connotations),[57] Lydgate comments of and *to* his own story that "It sitt the nat enlwmyned for to be / Of othir colour but oonly al of sable" (512–13).[58] Although the Egyptian merchant is anything but in the black, as we might say in our contemporary parlance, only black ink will do to tell his part of the story—if, that is, the poet can bear to keep moving his pen across the page. For like the lovestruck merchant unable to speak his pain in the first half of the narrative, so now does the poet here claim that he is practically struck dumb with grief, petrified by a Medusa-like Fortune:

> For verray dool I stond in iupartye:
> Al merthe of makyng my mateer mot refuse.
> Me in-to stoon transmwed hath Meduse

[56] On the connection of this passage to Lydgate's larger discourse of laureation (part of a brilliant reading of Lydgate's play with the terms "laureate" and "aureate"), see Lerer, *Chaucer and His Readers,* pp. 38–39. Chaucer too hopes once again to see his purse-lady's "colour lyk the sonne bryght / that of yelownesse hadde never pere" ("Purse," lines 10–11).

[57] See *MED,* s.v. *remenaunt,* 1c.

[58] On Lydgate's novel uses of the verb "enlumyne" in his poetry more generally, see Lois A. Ebin, *Illuminator, Makar, Vates: Visions of Poetry in the Fifteenth Century* (Lincoln: University of Nebraska Press, 1988), pp. 22–24.

For verray stonyng of Fortunys fikylnesse,
That for the merveyle no woord I can expresse.
(500–504)

While this is the most exaggerated of his emotional responses to the "makyng" of his "mateer," it is neither the first nor the last time that the narrator of the *Fabula* alludes to his own pain and suffering. "Allas, for dool myn herte I feele bleede," he remarks just before the Syrian merchant falls sick (199); and "[m]yn herte bleedith, whan I therof endite" he claims of the woeful parting of the two friends (465). Just as the Egyptian merchant, as the poet puts it, hid "[n]othyng" both "withyne and withoute" from his Syrian visitor (176–77), so too does Lydgate share with us the internal and external manifestations of his supposed emotional state, one whose symptoms, however clichéd, nevertheless also parallel those experienced by the characters in whom he invests his verbal energies (the generous Egyptian, for example, "[m]oornyng for absence . . . is lefft allone" when his friend and new wife depart [470]).[59]

The heartfelt sorrows, and particularly the financial woes of the Egyptian merchant that the poet of the *Fabula* makes his own, are the same grievances that the speaker of the *Letter to Gloucester* shares with his impoverished purse. In fact, the pecuniary pain suffered by the Egyptian in the *Fabula* and by the purse in the *Letter* produce exactly the same physical result in their stories' scribe, as this juxtaposition of passages, one of which we have already seen above, reveals:

Riht myhty prince, and it be your wille,
Condescende leiser for to take
To seen the content of this litil bille,
Which whan I wrot, *myn hand I felte quake.*
    (*Letter,* 1–4; my emphasis)

O seely marchaunt, *myn hand I feele quake*
To write thy woo in my translacioun;

---

[59] On Hoccleve's own use of the phrase "within and withoute" in "Thomas Hoccleve's Complaint" to describe both interior self and exterior condition (290–93), see Stephen Metcalf, "Inner and Outer," in *The Later Middle Ages,* ed. Stephen Metcalf (London: Methuen, 1981), pp. 108–71 (134–35). On Hoccleve's complaint poems as "occasions for . . . an incessant 'voiding,' 'vomiting,' and 'telling out' of the heart," see Jennifer E. Bryan, "Hoccleve, the Virgin, and the Politics of Complaint," *PMLA* 117 (2002): 1172–87 (1185).

> Ful offte I weepe also for thy sake,
> For to beholde the revolucioun
> Of thy degree and transmutacioun.
>
> (*Fabula,* 589–93; my emphasis)

For the poet of the *Letter,* economic and corporeal distress go virtually hand in hand; for the writer of the *Fabula,* the mere contemplation of a fictional character's poverty has a literal, deleterious effect on the hand that pens the tale.[60] The poet of the *Fabula* attempts to ease his suffering by explaining, almost as if to himself, that ill Fortune is in fact a kind of bitter but ultimately efficacious medicinal draught (701–4). Yet as the end of both *Letter* and *Fabula* make perfectly clear, it is not in Fortune but rather in *fortune* that a cure is to be found. Money—that liquidity to which the *Letter* refers in its pun on the historical remedy of "aurum potabile" [*drinkable gold*] (46), itself reminiscent of the "gold in physik" of which Chaucer's Physician is so fond (I.443)—is the potion that will save both the poet and the Egyptian merchant.[61]

The role that money plays in the resolution (or, in the case of the *Letter,* the imagined resolution) of these two poems reveals once more, and perhaps most clearly, how the two works function as economic inversions of each other. In the *Fabula,* money—in the form of capital—forms the second half of the Syrian merchant's gift to his friend: after rescuing him from death, he then "to richesse restor[es] [him] ageyn"

---

[60] The echo is briefly noted by Alessandra Petrina, *Cultural Politics in Fifteenth-Century England: The Case of Humphrey, Duke of Gloucester* (Leiden: Brill, 2004), p. 307. A similar image of pen in quaking hand appears in the Prologue to Book 3 of the *Fall of Princes,* just before the very lines about the writer's penury that have led scholars to connect the *Letter* to the *Fall.* The poet there claims that as he stood "[f]ul pale of cheer, astonyd in my look," and considered the onerous duty of translation, "[m]yn hand gan tremble; my penne I felte quake" (45–46). The recognizably Lydgatean quality of the image is suggested by Benedict Burgh's adoption of it in his continuation of Lydgate's unfinished version of the *Secretum secretorum,* where Burgh claims in his prologue that the difficulty of the task and his own ignorance of the material "myn hand make to quake" (*Lydgate and Burgh's Secrees of Old Philosoffres,* ed. Robert Steele, EETS e.s. 66 [London: Kegan Paul, Trench, Trübner, 1894], line 1555).

[61] Trevisa's *On the Properties of Things* explains that gold has "vertue to . . . clense superfluites ygedred in bodyes" (Seymour, gen. ed., *Trevisa's Translation of Bartolomaeus Anglicus De Proprietatibus Rerum,* 2:829, XVI.iv). On *aurum potabile* as a cure for various forms of lethargy (including lovesickness), see Lowes, "The Loveres Maladye," p. 520. For examples of what he calls "potable cash"—gilded and silver-plated drinking vessels full of coins—given by the cities of Basel and Augsburg as gifts to noble visitors in the late fifteenth century, see Groebner, *Liquid Assets,* pp. 28–30, 68, and 141; quotation on p. 28.

(882). The Syrian thus returns in kind the Egyptian's earlier double gift of life (in the form of the girl who healed his fatal lovesickness) and of money (the cost of his wedding and the girl's dowry). But unlike the Egyptian's initial gift to the Syrian, this second gift of the Syrian to the Egyptian does not so much displace commercial concerns as reembrace them, since in effect the "richesse" to which he is "restored" will enable the Egyptian to again enter the market economy from which his losses had temporarily exiled him. For all its attempts to create a realm of the gift untroubled by the concerns of the market, then, the conclusion of the *Fabula* would seem to suggest that an escape from those concerns is never fully possible, and perhaps not even entirely desirable.

The verbal alchemy of the *Letter* turns money into metaphor in order to present itself, at least on the surface, as a gift from poet to patron. In the process, however, the poem subtly suggests the ways in which the patronage system is little more than a market in disguise. Most importantly, the emphasis the *Letter* gives to commercial and financial terminology implies that the system might function more effectively if its participants were to acknowledge its true form. For while the poem implies that a gift of gold will ease the purse's "compleynt" of "nichil habet" (52),[62] the fact is that any gold turned over as a response to the "content of this litil bille" would almost automatically become less a gift than an explicit payment for services rendered—for, that is, the commodity that the poem, by virtue of its creative "bill[ing]" of its client, reveals itself to be.[63] Yet the poem's necessarily inconclusive ending, its very status as begging-poem whose author awaits a materially attentive response, suggests that—as for the merchants of the *Fabula,* for whom there is no real way out of the marketplace—so too for pa-

[62] See also Lerer, *Chaucer and His Readers,* pp. 38–39 and 205, and Smith, "Lydgate's Refrain," pp. 194–95. "Nichil habet," Norton-Smith notes, is a legal phrase referring to the "return made by the sheriff to the exchequer in cases where the party named in the writ had no goods upon which a levy could be made" (*John Lydgate: Poems,* 118 n. 52).

[63] While a "bille" could be any kind of formal document or petition, by the early fifteenth century it was already acquiring today's still-current sense of a record of debt or expense. See *MED,* s.v. *bille,* 5. In a sense, however, the *Letter* obliquely maintains one traditional form of literary patron-client exchange, in which verbal praise is proffered in hope of eventual reward. The poem's many word-games are a kind of covert flattery of Gloucester, since they imply that he will be as quick to understand them as the poet has been clever to use them. See Scott, "Marketing," p. 140, on the way early modern patronage poems could similarly "function as gifts while aiming to induce diversified and competitive rewards."

tron-dependent poets is there no self-evident way out of the equally uncertain system upon which they are forced to rely.

At the end of the *Fabula,* Lydgate tells his readers "platly" that a "thyng weel preevyd" needs no repetition (897–98). At the end of the *Letter,* however, it is apparent that the "cleer soun of plate" (64) is one he would be glad to hear again; in fact, as D. Vance Smith observes, the sound of money already suggestively reverberates throughout the poem, since the word "coignage" ends the last line of each stanza.[64] As I noted above, some scholars have argued—though we will probably never know if they are right—that Humphrey of Gloucester answered Lydgate's clever epistle with just such a sound, and that it was this gesture that earned the duke praise for largesse in the Prologue to Book 3 of the *Fall of Princes.* There, Lydgate claims to be looking back on an impoverished moment between his writing of the first two books of the poem and the next, a moment when his "purs [was] ay liht and void off coignage," and when it experienced not just "[a]n ebbe off plente" but also "scarsete atte fulle."[65] This oxymoronic but nonetheless painful condition, clearly reminiscent of the situation outlined in the *Letter,* lasted until Gloucester intervened "to make the wether fair," as the poet recalls:

> Mi lordis fredam and bounteuous largesse
> Into myn herte brouht in such gladnesse,
> That thoruh releuyng off his benygne grace,
> Fals Indigence list me no mor manace.
> (*Fall of Princes,* 73–77)

In the fiction of the *Fabula,* grief, Lydgate claims, has briefly "clubbyd" the ink in his "penne" so that it refuses to flow (510). In the less fictional world of fifteenth-century literary patronage, as Lydgate suggests here in the *Fall of Princes,* it is not grief but rather the "ebbe" of princely "plente" that can quite literally stop ink from flowing, and only princely generosity of a "bounteuous" nature that can likewise start it up again. As celebratory of his patron's "fredam and . . . largesse" as the passage

---

[64] Smith, "Lydgate's Refrain," p. 195. Chaucer's "Purse" likewise refers to his hope of hearing the "blisful soun" of his lady (line 9).

[65] John Lydgate, *The Fall of Princes,* ed. Henry Bergen, 4 vols., EETS e.s. 121, 122, 123, 124 (London: Oxford University Press, 1924), Book III, Prologue, line 69. All other references are to this edition.

may be, its metaphorical reference to the "wether" somewhat passive-aggressively hints at the problem with the patronage system of poetic production and reward in which the poet claims to find himself caught and which the *Letter* likewise subtly protests: namely, patronage's weatherlike arbitrariness and inconstancy, two faults that might be contrasted with the steadfast emotional and economic reciprocity that binds the two merchants of the *Fabula* from beginning to end of their story.

The "ebbe" and "scarsete" in this passage from the *Fall of Princes* should remind us, as well, of the cycles of drought and flood both monetary and meteorological in the *Letter* and the *Fabula,* even as they lead us to think further about the pecuniary cycles, however likewise performative, of Lydgate's own career. As the poet well knew, and as the Envoy to Book 9 of the *Fall of Princes* suggests—with its plea to be relieved once more of "cotidien" fever by "liberal largesse," of an "ebbe of froward skarsete" by a "spryng flood of gracious plente" and of "constreyned indigence" by "plentevous inffluence" (IX.3345–51)—the temporary reprieve of economic distress in a world governed by fickle Fortune (in all senses) or fickle friends is precisely that: temporary. What lasts, or so Lydgate suggests, is the *expression* of that distress, something that, as I have already argued above, the poet turns into a commodity in the *Letter* when he asks Gloucester to consider the "content of this litel bille" and—he implies—pay for its metaphorically full exploration of emptiness, its no-holds-barred exposure of the "lynyng" of the poet's "outward" purse (3, 7).

Returning now to Bataille's remark that "representation engages the very life of the one who assumes it," we might say that this is precisely what the *Letter* also argues when it uses an empty, mortally ill money-bag as a figure for the impoverished versifier.[66] But as many a medieval poet before and after Lydgate suggested to his (or her) patron, literary representation—*pace* Bataille—might also be said to *preserve* the life of those who support it, since such representation memorializes them for posterity. To this familiar *topos* Lydgate, as a monk in a position to pray as well as write for his patrons, could add a further enticement, something of which he takes full advantage in his 1441 petition to Henry VI requesting a revision to the terms of his annuity. Referring in that docu-

---

[66]Bataille, "The Notion of Expenditure," p. 171. Hoccleve's narrator in "La Male Regle" makes a similar move when he bemoans the fact that while his wallet is light from loss of stuffing ("my purs his stuf hath lore" [349]), his body, little more than a "Carkeis," is "repleet" with its own near-dead weight, its "heuynesse" (350).

ment to himself as "youre pouere and perpetuell oratour," the poet seems to play on the way the formulaic term *oratour,* used in many similar documents from this period to refer to the petitioner, can also refer to "an eloquent speaker" and to "one who prays."[67] Lydgate has already written eloquent speech—poetry—for Henry; in return for this new favor, as he promises the king, his "besecher" will "pray to God for you."[68] The value of Henry's return on this investment in the poet's "wele and profite," or so Lydgate's admittedly conventional but still-meaningful closing salutation suggests, is incalculable: in exchange for money paid, as the new royal patent puts it, "annuatim . . . durante vita sua" (annually during his lifetime), the poet will help the king secure eternity.[69]

Lydgate's *own* eternity, in a literary sense, is due in large measure not to Henry VI's interventions on his behalf, but rather to John Shirley, without whose efforts of copying and compiling a good deal of his corpus might not have survived. But Shirley's intercessions—at least as we can observe them in the kalendars, or versified tables of contents, that he appended to his compilations of the works in what are now British Library MS Additional 16165 and MS Additional 29729—were not limited to establishing the poet's afterlife in the canon of English literature. Probably composed in the mid-1430s, soon after Lydgate wrote both *Letter* and *Fabula,* the kalendars intervene in the here and now (or rather, the there and then) of the poet's economic existence; they refer directly, but in strikingly dissimilar ways, to Lydgate's active participation in systems of patronage and commerce, of getting gifts and spending money. In MS Additional 16165, Shirley apotheosizes "*Lydegate* þe Munk cloþed in blacke" by claiming that "[i]n his makyng þer is no lacke" (81–82).[70] He then proposes that the poet should receive fullness

---

[67] *MED,* s.v. *oratour.* On the monastic exchange of prayer in return for wealth, see Lester K. Little, *Religious Poverty and the Profit Economy in Medieval Europe* (Ithaca: Cornell University Press, 1978), pp. 66–67.

[68] Pearsall, *John Lydgate (1337–1449),* Appendix #19, p. 62.

[69] Pearsall, *John Lydgate (1337–1449),* Appendix #19, p. 62, and #20, p. 63.

[70] London, British Library MS Additional 16165, fols. 2–3, and MS Additional 29729, fols. 177v–179. My references to the kalendars are from Aage Brusendorff, *The Chaucer Tradition* (1925; London: Oxford University Press, 1967), pp. 453–60; another edition is "John Shirley: Two Versified Tables of Contents," in *English Verse between Chaucer and Surrey,* ed. Eleanor Prescott Hammond (1927; New York: Octagon, 1965), pp. 191–97. On Shirley's self-presentation in these verses, see Lerer, *Chaucer and His Readers,* pp. 123–24, 129–33. On MS Additional 16165, see Connolly, *John Shirley,* pp. 27–51.

of another sort in recompense for the absence of absence, the lasting plenitude, that characterizes his verse:

> And thankeþe daun Johan for his peyne
> Þat to plese gentyles is right feyne
> Boþe with his laboure and his goode
> God wolde of nobles he hade ful his hoode
>
> (83–86)

While reminiscent of the *Letter to Gloucester*'s plea on its writer's behalf, this passage, unlike that poem, more closely adheres to the basic formula of patron-client exchange. Shirley here represents Lydgate as a willing, eager servant of the aristocracy, who aims "to plese gentyles" with his "laboure and . . . goode" and to whom is owed gratitude—not payment—in exchange for such service; after all, while the copyist demands that his readers thank the monk, he leaves to God the responsibility for rewarding him with a hoodful of gold.

The explicit hope that the Lord will provide is of course an implicit suggestion as to what form the thanks of *lords* should take, and in the end Shirley's remark is no less disingenuous than is the *Letter*'s concluding wish that "God sende soone a . . . letuarye [*medicine*]" of "plate and coignage" (63–64).[71] Nevertheless, the relative conventionality of this first passage is one against which Shirley's comments in MS Additional 29729 (preserved in John Stow's mid-sixteenth-century hand) must stand in stark relief. In that second kalendar, we are given a rather different picture of the poet who "aught well be solempnysed" by "all oure engelishe nacion" (33, 32), but who has practically bankrupted himself in its service. "[F]or all his much konnynge," Shirley laments,

> wch were gret tresore to a kynge
> I meane this lidgate munke dame [*daun*] John
> his nobles bene spent I leue ychon
> and eke his shylinges nyghe by
> his thred bare coule [*cowl*] woll not ly

---

[71] See *MED*, s.v. *letuari(e*, on the way the word can refer to both a spiritual and a medical cure. Chaucer's Physician carries only the latter (I.426), but Lydgate is punning on the word's duality.

ellas ye lordes why nill ye se
and reward his pouerte

(37–44)[72]

Like the "lynyng outward" of the *Letter*'s purse, here the "thred bare coule" of "this lidgate" exposes not only the poet's supposed indigence but also the problems inherent to the systems of exchange in which he and his verse are implicated. These lines by Shirley construct the poet, in fact, much as this essay has argued that he used the *Letter* to construct himself: as someone caught between the rock of patronage and the hard place of the market (whose terrors we have seen him deflect in turn through the *Fabula*'s fiction of friendship). Having spent his "moche konnynge" on apparently unseeing "lordis" and his "nobles" and "shylinges" on himself, it is now Lydgate, rather than his purse, who for Shirley best figures the kind of "pouerte" that deserves "reward." Where the *Letter* uses the language of commercial transaction to reveal (if not fully to change) the fraught nature of patronage, and the *Fabula* employs the ideal of the gift in an (incomplete) attempt to transform its professional protagonists into mutual patrons, Shirley's two versions of Lydgate in the kalendars—as courtly servant in need of a gift, and as impoverished worker in need of payment—together celebrate the poet's *makyng,* writ large, in just the sort of contradictory terms the monk would have well understood. Moreover, in the kalendar to MS Additional 29729, it is Lydgate *himself* who becomes the prized commodity whose value we have only just begun to reestimate. "[S]uche as he is," Shirley declares, "haue we no mo" (36).

---

[72] Green cites lines 37–40 of this passage as evidence of Lydgate's (and other poets') need for "financial recognition" by their patrons (*Poets and Princepleasers,* p. 167). On Stow's copy, see Connolly, *John Shirley,* pp. 76–77; on this plea, which Connolly notes is unusual in having been made by Lydgate's scribe rather than by the poet himself, see pp. 84–85. As is evident from my argument, I understand the verses as far more meaningful than does Connolly, who sees them as a monastic and literary joke; this is not to say, however, that I take them to be true in any literal sense.

REVIEWS

JENNY ADAMS. *Power Play: The Literature and Politics of Chess in the Late Middle Ages*. Philadelphia: University of Pennsylvania Press, 2006. Pp. 252. $49.95.

The main thesis of Jenny Adams's book is brilliantly illustrated in her first chapter by reproductions on facing pages of two woodcuts from the first and second chapters of the 1483 edition of William Caxton's *The Game and Playe of the Chesse*. On the left we see a king's body being hacked into many pieces; on the right, we have a frontal view of a man seated at a game of chess holding up his king, with other chess pieces of different ranks on and off the board. The black-and-white squares of the chess board are a miniature of those of the floor of the room; the game replicates life, with the reader-viewer in the position of the second player. According to Adams, it is not only an individual king (Evilmero-dach) who is being dismembered and destroyed in the first woodcut, but it is also the older corporate model of the kingdom or state as the "body" of the king, an organic model whereby the body's different "members" had to accept their natural role of obeying the commands of and aiding or sustaining the head. Adams argues that the game of chess offered an alternative figure or metaphoric ground upon which to elaborate a theory of the proper functioning of the state (as well as of the individual).

In Caxton's second woodcut, the game's action occurs on the level playing field of the checkered board, where the opponent kings are the most important, but by no means the only chess pieces, and all must obey rules of movement defined by their status. Thus chess offers a different model of social order. As Adams puts it, "Rather than having their actions dictated by the 'head' of the state, who directed the actions of the body politic, members of a civic community are seen as beholden to a set of rules particularized to their own social station" (p. 11). The king's body has, in effect, been fragmented into a number of "indepen-dent bodies in the form of pieces bound to the state by rules rather than biology" (p. 20). The "state" in this figurative model is represented by the playing board itself, over which the viewer-player has a dominant perspective, even as he projects himself into the different social roles and capabilities and tries to make them work to best advantage together.

Borrowed from Arabic culture around the turn of the millennium, the pieces of the chess game and their moves were adapted to western European society: the counselor became a queen; the elephant, a bishop; the horse, a knight. For Adams, these changes indicate that "medieval culture wanted to see itself in the game" (p. 2). Lengthy allegorical explanation of the chess board and its pieces as a figure of the state did not appear, however, until the end of the thirteenth century with the Lombard Jacobus de Cessolis's *Liber de moribus hominum et officiis nobilium ac popularium super ludi scachorum* (The Book of the Morals of Men and the Duties of Nobles and Commoners, on the Game of Chess). Adams's first chapter studies the ideological innovation reflected in Jacobus de Cessolis's *Liber,* the importance of which is attested by more than three hundred surviving manuscripts and incunabula. The three following chapters treat the reception of this work—its rewriting, reframing, exegesis, and translation—in the fourteenth and fifteenth centuries in France and England.

Chapter 2 examines the very substantial remodeling of the *Liber*'s allegory to focus on the psychomachia of the lover (in imitation of the *Roman de la rose*) in the anonymous late fourteenth-century versified *Echecs amoureux* and its commentary of fifty years later by Evrart de Conty. This prose commentary explains the *Echecs amoureux* on three allegorical levels, correlating regulation of individual passions to civic and to cosmological order. Adams argues that these French works "reinscribe the *Liber*'s contractually based (i.e., nonorganic) society within the framework of organic order (lover's body as civic community) and natural structure (cosmos as chess game)" (p. 81).

The third chapter treats the symbolic uses of chess playing in Chaucerian fictions, especially the *Book of the Duchess* and the anonymous *Prologue* and *Tale of Beryn*. Whereas the *Liber* of Jacobus de Cessolis and the *Echecs amoureux* and its commentary focus on the benefits of chess as an art of governance, slight the risk of losing, and idealize a tied game, Chaucerian fictions focus on the danger of losing and treat chess as a form of imbalanced exchange or gambling.

In the fourth chapter, Adams first examines Thomas Hoccleve's recycling in his *Regement of Princes* of parts of Jacobus de Cessolis's *Liber*. Because Hoccleve, in giving advice to a king, adapts from the *Liber* so many exempla concerning the proper behavior of other estates (represented by chess pieces other than the king), Adams suggests that Hoccleve is implying "that the king might want to model himself on the virtues appropriate to other men" (p. 131). The second half of the fourth chapter treats differences between Caxton's two editions of *The Game and Playe of the Chesse* (his English translation of a French translation of Jacobus de Cessolis's *Liber*). Whereas the 1474 edition was addressed to the king's brother to teach him good governance, the 1483 edition was addressed to all people as containing "wholesome wisdom necessary for every estate and degree." Furthermore, Caxton illustrated the text of the new edition with a series of woodcuts that gloss the text in ways discussed above and also picture the different chess pieces ("such persons as longen to the playe"). Adams points out analogies between Caxton's second edition of *The Game and Playe of the Chesse* and his second edition of *The Canterbury Tales*, to which he added twenty-three woodcuts showing Chaucer, the individual pilgrims (representing different estates and professions), and also the pilgrim group seated at a table.

In a brief but evocative epilogue, Adams suggests that drama became the most powerful way to represent social order in the Renaissance, displacing political symbolism "from board to stage." *Power Play* makes an important contribution to our understanding of how late medieval thought is expressed in and elaborated around images.

LAURA KENDRICK
Université de Versailles

GAIL ASHTON and LOUISE SYLVESTER, eds. *Teaching Chaucer*. New York: Palgrave Macmillan, 2007. Pp. xi, 167. $27.95 paper.

As a volume dedicated to addressing Chaucer pedagogy in the age of new media, *Teaching Chaucer* is an uneven offering. Its essays range from those that engage closely and creatively with the demands of teaching particular Chaucerian texts to those where Chaucer is all but lost within the authors' fascination with pedagogic technology.

One of the volume's main strengths, beginning with Gail Ashton's introduction and continuing throughout the essays, lies in its diagnosis of the many challenges posed by students who are products of the "information age," and in the various essays' pragmatic acknowledgment that the problems created by undergraduate Web research are here to stay but can be negotiated by effective pedagogy and strategic use of Internet technology. Moira Fitzgibbons's essay is especially attentive to the need to guide the "point-and-click" generation into solid critical research, and to tackling the often flabby relativism that replaces analysis. Peggy Knapp also astutely diagnoses the key assumptions that an undergraduate student body is likely to have about Chaucer, and describes how she crafts classes that respond to and challenge these assumptions.

Taken together, these essays offer heartening evidence of how teachers of Chaucer are combining creativity and contemporaneity with historical sensitivity. Stephen Kruger's discussion of the linked assignment program he developed left me admiring how carefully he had devised the trajectory of his students' path toward familiarity with Chaucer and with research methods. Knapp's paper similarly focuses on the integrated suite of intellectual approaches (historicist, aesthetic, hermeneutic) she brings to teaching Chaucer. Louise Sylvester addresses the problems of teaching Chaucerian language in the context of literature classes by suggesting that integrating pragmatics and stylistics might offer a way forward. The emphasis of most essays, however, is on pedagogic technologies and methodologies. Lesley Coote argues, for instance, that since our culture is arguably the most visual since the Middle Ages, teaching through visual materials is historically apt, economical, and speaks to our students. Others, such as Fiona Tolhurst, advocate dramatic and performative methods for teaching Chaucerian voice. Simon Horobin's essay outlines his intelligent use of recent technological resources in Chaucer studies, such as the CD-Rom of *The Canterbury Tales Project* and electronic concordances, to construct problem-based classes in which students explore manuscript and dialect variation, as well as scribal, compilatorial, and modern editorial interventions, thus engaging with the complexities of manuscript work in a virtual environment.

Other essays, however, such as Coote's, become preoccupied with technical matters such as file sizes and software without explaining their specific significance for teaching Chaucer. Her immersion within electronic teaching culture is such that she does not offer sufficient explanation of the difference between Web sites and virtual learning environments, or of "gist" learning and its benefits. Ashton's contribution at times reads more like a paper on electronic learning than on

Chaucer teaching, and, apart from underdeveloped remarks about how certain techniques seem apposite for teaching medieval subjects, is more concerned with outlining her learning philosophies than with applying them expressly to teaching Chaucer. Philippa Semper's essay offers a more detailed and specific discussion of which e-resources are most useful, and is thoughtful on the subject of how to build a site that accommodates Web-surfing behavior but ensures quality control directed at medieval content. Knapp's essay is mercifully free of promotional claims about the "innovative" nature of her teaching. Indeed, her productive combination of Raymond Williams, Kant, and Gadamer gives the lie to the notion that "innovation," crudely construed, in teaching is always to be embraced, a notion that some contributors to this volume could have treated with greater skepticism given the widespread instrumentalization of "innovation" by university management to secure market share. Knapp's classroom is the model of a creative yet solidly intellectual reading and research environment, where skills are acquired organically, rather than in accordance with a "Best-Practice" manual.

The highly privileged classroom conditions described in many of the essays threaten at times to undermine the more universal nature of the volume's diagnosis of student culture. Other than Ashton's essay, there is little on offer for those who are compelled to face contemporary pedagogic dilemmas in the context of crowded classes. Fitzgibbons admits to, but does not elaborate on, the influence of her very privileged classroom conditions: she mentions that her assessment methods were less successful in a larger class, but does not reflect any further. Similarly, Tolhurst does not address the extent to which her extremely privileged teaching environment (seminars of approximately ten students, daily fifty-minute readings of Chaucer) makes her extensive assessment regimen possible in a way it would not be for many teaching Chaucer in less advantaged environments. Despite her avowal that the performance project she undertakes could be adapted for larger classes, she offers no guidance as to how this might work. Kruger's environment is less privileged, but since he does not specify how many students were subject to the very labor-intensive assessment process he describes, it is difficult to evaluate whether his methods might work in the context of large classes.

One disconcerting feature of some of the essays in this volume is their relatively unreflective use of currently fashionable para-pedagogic jargon, such as Ashton's "blended learning," "student-centredness," and the egregious "value-added lectures." Tolhurst's discourse similarly reflects her adherence to the ongoing current para-pedagogic assault on the shibboleth of the magisterial, "top-down" teacher. This seemingly untroubled acceptance of the consumerist ideology underlying much of the drive toward "student-centered" techniques represents one of this volume's missed opportunities. While there are numerous astute analyses of the pressures involved in communicating Chaucer to new-media-savvy undergraduates, there is a puzzling silence on the pressures of the institutional imperative to abandon challenging traditional pedagogic techniques in order to attract and retain students. Because of the many scholarly demands Chaucer studies places on information-age undergraduates, it offers a particularly fertile ground for exploring not just the technological opportunities but also the ideological stakes of transforming our teaching to accommodate our students. *Teaching Chaucer's* frequently admirable pragmatism would have been helpfully complicated by such an exploration.

LOUISE D'ARCENS
University of Wollongong

ANTHONY BALE. *The Jew in the Medieval Book: English Antisemitisms, 1350–1500.* Cambridge: Cambridge University Press, 2007. Pp. xiv, 266. £45.60; $85.00.

Meticulously researched and lucidly composed, Anthony Bale's *The Jew in the Medieval Book* combines rigorous historicist readings with excellent manuscript work. The book contributes to the vigorous conversation that has unfolded over the past decade on the relation of England's Jews to its literary culture. Scholars such as Sheila Delany, Denise Despres, Steven Kruger, Lisa Lampert, and Sylvia Tomasch (among literary critics); Ruth Mellinkoff and Debra Higgs Strickland (among art historians); and Jeremy Cohen, Kathleen Biddick, Robert Chazan, Gavin Langmuir, David Nirenberg, and Miri Rubin (among historians) have provided the foundation for Bale's project. The book's achievement is to have synthesized much of this work without offering a monolithic culmination or alternative. The analytical strength of *The Jew in the Medieval Book* derives from its rejection of the idea that the figure of the

Jew possesses a static role within some overarching hermeneutic. Bale employs an intertextual methodology to argue that the imagined Jew offers Christian writers a locus of discord and confusion where the past can be created, orthodoxy might be undercut, and the Other reveals "that which is inside" (p. 166).

As his starting date of 1350 indicates, Bale is interested in post-Expulsion depictions of Jews. Previous scholars have typically attempted to capture the Christian imagination of Judaism by deploying large conceptual frameworks: the virtual Jew (Tomasch), the spectral Jew (Kruger), the hermeneutic Jew (Cohen), the Protean Jew (Despres). Without directly engaging such capacious epistemologies, Bale implicitly follows Nirenberg (*Communities of Violence*) in arguing that anti-Semitism is better understood as *antisemitisms*: what he calls "massive, transhistorical narratives" (p. 9) must yield to dynamic local histories. Even if stereotypes invoked by a text might seem universal, such recurring slanders are given definitive shape through specific context, serving particular strategies. Bale therefore stresses the lack of agreement among Christian interpreters over the meaning of post-Incarnation Jews, observing that "even as established Christian interpretive models existed, writers rarely chose to subordinate their impressions of contemporary Judaism to such a model" (p. 25). Rather than invoke the Jew to confirm some preexisting doctrinal position, medieval writers employed Judaism to create a space in which theology could be questioned and destabilized. Jews as imagined by medieval English writers therefore functioned not as an assimilated component of Christian universal history, but as perturbing figures through whom authors were able to grapple with the discontents such a transhistorical model generated (p. 31).

Bale structures his book around four medieval narratives, each typifying a genre: the Jew of Tewkesbury, who tumbles into a latrine and dies in excrement because of his reverence for his Sabbath (History); the miracle of the boy who, after his murder at Jewish hands, continues to sing a Marian hymn (Miracle); the worship of the child martyr Robert of Bury St. Edmunds, supposedly killed by Jews in imitation of the torture of Jesus (Cult); and the *Arma Christi*, a display of the instruments of Christ's suffering that included a spitting Jew (Passion). Bale reads his texts within wide manuscript contexts. Thus the chapter on the caroling dead boy contains, as expected, a detailed examination of Chaucer's *Prioress's Tale*. Because the focus is on the "discontinuities and divergences," however, this supremely literary rendition finds itself jostled by versions of the same story from places both predictable (the Vernon manuscript) and surprising (an unattributed redaction of Chaucer's tale that was snuggled next to and finally intercut with Lydgate in BL Harley MS 2251).

The book is essential for any scholar studying late medieval piety, European literary culture, and social identity in its relation to alterity. The chapter examining Chaucerian materials will, however, be of special interest to the readers of this journal. Given that a series of original and highly influential articles have appeared over the past twenty years on *The Prioress's Tale* (especially the work of Aranye Fradenburg, Bruce Holsinger, and Lee Patterson), it may seem that little space remains for new readings. Chapter 3 ("Miracle: Shifting Definitions in 'The Miracle of the Boy Singer'") opens with an invocation of the Wandering Jew, *terra cognita* to be sure, but then surprises with a follow-up interrogatory of "What of the wandering Christian?" If Jew and Christian are "ambivalently interconnected," Bale reasons, shouldn't Chaucer's itinerant text—a framework narrative in which its structuring pilgrimage fails to reach its destination—offer a meditation on the multiple possibilities that straying into Jewish space offers? Bale tracks in *The Prioress's Tale* two warring elements, each with its own trajectory: an expansive land- and soundscape characterized by "extreme physicality and loss of control"; and a "lapidary vocabulary" that would immure such vagrancy within the gemlike martyr and his marble tomb. Chaucer's tale, Bale argues, resists the reduction into timelessness that other versions of the story embrace. The desire to limit and bound the narrative he ascribes to the Prioress, and the desire to keep alive its "bodily, historical and geographical disjunctions" he grants Chaucer. Bale's contextualization of the *litel clergeon* into the whole of Fragment VII (a series of narratives obsessed with male bodies, boys, chastity, violence) could be better. Yet he offers a compelling meditation on the space the tale opens to explore problems of genre, authority, and orthodoxy.

The Jew in the Medieval Book does not engage with actual Jews. Disallowing that a fantasy may engulf some portion of a historical reality and carry that reality far forward in time, the book is in a way as *Judenrein* as England post-1290. Bale writes in the introduction: "I do not aim to enfranchise those 'hidden from history,' a target implicit in much writing on historical Jewry" (p. 5; if the Jews are "hidden from history," they are hidden in plain sight). While such a recovery project is clearly not one every medievalist should undertake, the separation of Jewish reality from Christian imagining cannot so easily be assumed. Bale argues that "a contextualised, historically contingent antisemitism does not necessarily involve Jews but can stand alone in Christian culture" (p. 107). He is speaking about the events surrounding the cult of Robert of Bury St. Edmunds, a veneration that came into being as fifty-seven Jews lost their lives. The intimacy of its Jewish population to Bury's economic and cultural systems has been well documented. The violence exacted by Robert's cult was practiced against bodies onto which fantasies were projected, but these were also real bodies not nearly so passive as Bale's formulation implies. Medieval Jews were, as the events at York demonstrated, a people who could resist. Could they also survive their own eradication? Is it possible to hear something of a Jewish history resounding, even deep within a Christian fantasy—especially because, as Bale has so brilliantly emphasized, such Christian fantasies tend to be internally incoherent, heterogeneous, impossibly full?

Miri Rubin in her book *Gentile Tales* stages an astonishing sequence in the text's middle where the Jews answer back, giving them a voice that has much to say to the Christian fantasies she analyzes. Lee Patterson has done the same in his essay on *The Prioress's Tale* . . . as has Bale himself in two brilliant essays that laid the groundwork for this volume. Bale lacks such a moment here, but he has nonetheless authored a tremendous book. Because *The Jew in the Medieval Book* seamlessly combines the theoretical (Deleuze and Guattari, for example, make a catalytic appearance in the Chaucer chapter) with the archival and the historical, and because its ambit is so capacious and its findings so well argued, this volume will be required reading in medieval studies for years to come.

JEFFREY J. COHEN
George Washington University

JOHN M. BOWERS, *Chaucer and Langland: The Antagonistic Tradition.* Notre Dame, Ind.: University of Notre Dame Press, 2007. Pp. xii, 405. $45.00 paper.

The last two decades have witnessed a move out from what had been the strongholds of Middle English scholarship, Chaucer and Langland.

One strategy for reconnoitering new territories was to maintain logistical connection with the strongholds. Scholarly scouts did this by exploring the afterlives of both Chaucer and Langland in the fifteenth, and then, as scholarship became more adventurous, in the sixteenth centuries and beyond.

John Bowers was an innovative figure in that exploratory stage: already in 1985 he published an article in this journal, *"The Tale of Beryn and The Siege of Thebes* as Alternative Ideas of the *Canterbury Tales"* (*SAC* 7: 23–50). Then followed "The House of Chaucer and Son: The Business of Lancastrian Canon-Formation," *Medieval Perspectives* 6 (1991): 135–43; the far-reaching "Piers Plowman and the Police: Notes Toward a History of the Wycliffite Langland," *Yearbook of Langland Studies* 6 (1992): 1–50; the brilliant "Piers Plowman's William Langland: Editing the Text, Writing the Author's Life," *Yearbook of Langland Studies* 9 (1995): 65–102; and "Chaucer's Canterbury Tales Politically Corrected," in *Rewriting Chaucer: Culture, Authority, and the Idea of the Authentic Text*, ed. Thomas Prendergast and Barbara Kline (Columbus: Ohio State University Press, 1999).

The book under consideration here represents, as Bruce Holsinger says in his cover promotion, a "consolidation": pretty well each chapter of this book is dependent on work previously published by John Bowers. I'm not sure what rule publishers apply now for what proportion of a book can have already appeared, and I have certainly republished material myself. Whatever the rule, though, I suspect that Bowers has broken it here. For all that, it is welcome to have this material gathered in one place, all sustained by meticulous scholarly reference to the surrounding scholarship of what is by now a fully colonized field (100 pages of notes, and 57 pages of bibliography).

What has been gained, though, by presenting the material as a new argument, rather than as *Chaucer and Langland's Afterlives: Collected Essays by John Bowers*? In its current form, the book seeks to answer the question as to why Chaucer, not Langland, became, in Dryden's formulation, "the Father of English Poetry." The terms of Bowers's answer are strenuously political and, especially, theological (never aesthetic). The answer itself is as follows: that Langland's poem fell foul of censorship, whereas Chaucer himself adroitly performed a kind of "political correction" on the *Canterbury Tales* so as to survive the new conditions of censorship rising into menacing profile toward the end of his career. Despite a resurgence of Langland's fortunes in the mid-sixteenth century, the

Chaucer tradition was carefully managed by his son, well connected to Lancastrian power bases in such a way as to ensure Chaucer's position as the reliably conservative voice of a literary progenitor. Bowers treats the two traditions "in their mutual relationship, each necessary to con-figure the other" (p. 8). And that relationship is, he argues, antagonistic.

Thanks to the thorough presentation, always sensitive to cultural pol-itics, of the two *Nachleben*, Bowers unquestionably persuades us that the two traditions were significantly and interestingly different. Does he persuade that they were antagonistic?

The book is organized in a slightly odd way, with a very long Intro-duction (41 pages, 236 footnotes, called Chapter 1), in which the book's entire argument is not only outlined, but made, rendering its status uncertain (is it an introduction or the book's actual argument?). There follow six further chapters. Chapter 2 certainly argues for difference: 1360 for Langland was the Treaty of Bretigny, against whose terms Langland is savagely critical, while for Chaucer 1360 was when he was briefly in French captivity, generating Chaucer's hostility, so Bowers suggests, for all things French. Chapter 3 focuses on names, once again revealing difference: Chaucer's biographical, payable name is part of his oeuvre, and was used in the construction of a literary tradition, while Langland's name is discursive and/or hidden. This chapter rehearses Bowers' earlier work on the tendency of editors, up to Kane, to shape a poet's life in ways that turn out to have striking similarities to the edi-tor's own life. The Chaucer material is not symmetrical, since the discus-sion of how Chaucer's name is used does not extend beyond Lydgate. The fourth chapter introduces some antagonism, at least implicit or po-tential: *Piers Plowman* would have fallen foul of Arundelian censorship, while manuscripts of the *Canterbury Tales* were produced "under the di-rection of individuals with strong connections to the Lancastrian court" (p. 124). Still, potential antagonism must remain only potential unless it is explicit (and it's also true that *Piers* was bound with Chaucerian works, as in Huntington HM 114, from the second quarter of the fif-teenth century). This chapter also rehearses now-well-known arguments that, in the mid-sixteenth century, Bale enlisted Chaucer in the evangel-ical camp. (That implies that the "antagonism" isn't continuous; for some historical moments it served literary historians to set both Chaucer and Langland in harness.) In Chapter 5 the book's own prose and argu-ment comes alive: Bowers must argue a negative, that the contours and gaps in the *Canterbury Tales* derive from Chaucer adroitly adapting to new conditions of censorship. Even if this can never be conclusive, Bowers argues resourcefully. The penultimate chapter imagines that Chaucer's papers were kept at his Westminster tenement well beyond his death, before going on to argue how Hoccleve failed and Lydgate succeeded in joining the Chaucerian tradition. The final chapter takes the Langland tradition into the sixteenth century. Bowers argues that Langland's brief midcentury revival was short-lived because of little lasting value to shapers of a cultural tradition. In the course of this discussion, Bowers slightly misstates my own argument that the Langland tradition diminished (p. 218). I do not argue that, but rather that Langland's theology of works sat very uneasily with Protestant denigration of works, provoking not a diminution so much as an etiolation of the *Piers Plowman* tradition's real energy.

In short, this book consolidates previous *Nachleben* work; it is utterly persuasive in its account of a different tradition; it is less consistently persuasive in its account of an antagonistic tradition.

There is one significant error, and, to my mind, one lost opportunity. The error: Bowers asserts that Osbern Bokenham, by praising "Galfridus Anglicus" (*Legendys of Hooly Wummen,* lines 83–96), refers to Chaucer. Bokenham is unquestionably referring instead to Geoffrey of Vinsauf: the "newe poetrye" (line 88) can only be the *Poetria Nova.* The editor of the EETS edition, in the marginal glosses, makes the same mistake (p. 3). The lost opportunity is, in my view, the failure to situate Chaucer and Langland within London politics. In " 'After Craftes Conseil clotheth yow and fede': Langland and the City of London" (*England in the Fourteenth Century, Proceedings of the Harlaxton Conference, 1991,* ed. N. Rogers (Stamford, Conn.: Paul Watkins, 1993), pp. 111–29), I argued that Langland was aligned with the policies of John of Northampton. Northampton's enemy was Nicholas Brembre, with whom Chaucer had "extensive professional and factional dealings" (Paul Strohm, *Social Chaucer* [Cambridge, Mass.: Harvard University Press, 1989], p. 41). Langland and Chaucer were, then, most likely on opposed sides of London politics; that is a potential antagonism, which Bowers should have exploited.

JAMES SIMPSON
Harvard University

CHARLOTTE BREWER, *The Treasure-House of the Language: The Living OED*. New Haven: Yale University Press, 2007. Pp. xiv, 334. $35.00.

One thing many Chaucerians have in common, besides their interest in Chaucer, is departmental responsibility for a course on the history of English. The responsibility may reflect genuine interest and training, or the fact that the language backgrounds of medievalists make them well suited to work up such a course, or maybe a greater sense of collegiality and accommodation than that of their fussy modernist colleagues. And along with this responsibility comes recognition that few tools for historical analysis are more pervasive, limited, maddening, and, above all, essential than the celebrated *OED*. As welcome as a book on metrics or manuscripts might be to Chaucerians, then, just as welcome will be Charlotte Brewer's elegant, engrossing, and sophisticated account of this dictionary's life since its first appearance in 1928.

For some time now, social and political history has focused on the omnipresent if sometimes amorphous channeling of various kinds of social power. Presenting individuals as less agents than products, this is a historiography formed specifically in response to earlier kinds that concentrated on the great deeds of great men and women. And obviously, it can be a very effective historiography, as in John Willinsky's *Empire of Words: The Reign of the OED*. Brewer takes a different tack and shows that sometimes history really can happen because of the specific deeds of specific individuals (however great the individuals or their deeds turn out to be).

It's difficult to imagine the first *OED*, for example, without the indefatigable and purposeful efforts of James Murray. There may have been another qualified, dedicated individual who could have carried the project off—to completion, in a sense, thirteen years after he had died—but no obvious candidates present themselves. Skeat would have been too distracted by too many other projects; Furnivall was too distracted period; and Sweet would have been distracting to those around him. What Murray did was take the slimmest of ideas from the Philological Society and translate it into an objective, a method, a means to realize that method and objective, and, effectively, a professional enterprise. In the process, with very little to guide him, he did much to invent modern lexicography. He also, arguably, created a kind of white elephant for publishers, scholars, and his successors on the *OED*.

From the very beginning, Brewer shows, the enterprise has been torn between the conflicting needs to produce thorough and accurate material and to limit costs, particularly by limiting the time taken to do the work. And this conflict has been exacerbated by the fact that even the most well-intentioned lexicographers discovered that besides being a white elephant, the *OED* could be a bit of a cash cow: finish it, and they finished their jobs. Murray himself further exacerbated the efforts of his successors by his dictum that the history of every English word ought to be represented. Compounds, negatives, and nominal phrases all made realizing this injunction difficult enough, as did the limitation of any reading program that depends significantly, as the *OED* always has, on the kindness of readers. But once linguistic and social mores began to change in the last century, and the people and language habits of far-flung locales began to be accepted as making legitimate claims on the character of English, the notion that the lexicon could ever be circumscribed, much less recorded and defined, has evaporated. In a sense, far better than could any of his successors, wrestling as they have with new sociolects, regional dialects, and even World Englishes, Murray could know what English was, though even he, in the Preface, acknowledged a core and fringe vocabulary.

Many of the difficulties Brewer describes involve efforts to achieve, then, what may have only been just barely possible in Victorian England. And even before the last volume of the first edition had appeared, the failure of the *OED* to achieve this goal was apparent. But what to do? Should errors be corrected, additional quotations supplied, gaps filled? Should the focus of the dictionary lean more toward description, which Murray's methods embraced, or prescription, in the form of an avoidance of vulgarity and an emphasis on belletristic writing, which his methods also embraced? What proportion should there be between illustrative quotations and a word's currency? And even if the original had errors and omissions, how could the press, even as it marketed the dictionary as its flagship enterprise and a monument to learning, contemplate the investment of additional time and money to redo it?

The history Brewer traces suggests that these questions have never been satisfactorily answered. The 1933 Supplement sought only to fill in gaps, but even then the *OED* had to keep going in some sense, if only because it drove a number of lucrative spin-offs, such as the Shorter

OED and the Concise *OED*. In this vein, the press for a time contemplated a dictionary drawing only on literary examples, though it never came to fruition. And even as academics and word sleuths continued to collect examples of omissions, antedatings, and errors—not to mention pronunciations that reflected Murray's own idiosyncrasy of articulating initial *p* in words like *psychiatry*—the press quite understandably resisted any notion of wholesale revision. By the 1950s another supplement, this one focusing on modern words and filling in more gaps, though resisting the addition of quotations for any word cited as recently as the nineteenth century, was under way. Like everything else associated with the *OED*, it grew in the telling, and eventually appeared in four volumes from 1972 to 1986. In 1989, this supplement, melded into the first one and the original *OED*, was issued, perhaps a bit disingenuously, as a second edition. By this point, thanks to the advent of computer technology, a true revision could be contemplated, one that was infinitely expandable and need never appear in print, and this is *OED3*, currently in production and on-line, in part, since 2000. And through all these editorial crises, conflicts, and ministrations, it was again individual personality that not only shaped the enterprise but kept it alive: Onions and Craigie, the last connections to Murray and his aspirations; Sisam, a shadowy but ubiquitous figure who provided continuity for almost half a century; Wyllie, a tormented soul and tireless quotation collector; Burchfield, who brought production of the dictionary into the modern era; and now Simpson and Weiner, who have made possible the searchable glory that is *OED3*.

As the *OED* has grown and changed over the past century, a shift in emphasis has occurred that should both guide its editors and reassure its readers. Rather than the impossibility of providing a history of every word—for a language, like every natural language, whose lexicon changes daily—the value of realizing what is possible has become more prominent. The *OED* may be flawed, but for historical linguistics it is crucial and superior, I think, to any other dictionary in any language I know. Brewer's meticulously researched and clearly written book— telling the plot of a mystery in progress—shows that for all its claims to scientific accuracy and thoroughness, *OED* owes its successes (and failures) to the individuals who devoted their lives to it.

Tim William Machan
Marquette University

María Bullón-Fernández, ed. *England and Iberia in the Middle Ages, 12th–15th Century: Cultural, Literary, and Political Exchanges.* New York: Palgrave Macmillan, 2007. Pp. x, 250. $69.95.

When considering England's international relations during the late Middle Ages, both on a political and on a cultural level, scholars have traditionally focused most of their interest on two countries, France and Italy. The recent volume edited by Peter Brown, *A Companion to Medieval English Literature and Culture* (2007), clearly exemplifies this tendency, since its section "Encounters with Other Cultures" takes only these two countries into account in the context of contemporary Europe. The unsurprising absence of Iberia simply emphasizes, as stated by María Bullón-Fernández, that "[r]ecognition of . . . cultural and political traffic patterns, particularly regarding England and Iberia, has been slow to emerge among medievalists" (p. 2). The purpose of the collection of essays under review is to present arguments that should encourage full-scale scholarly attention to medieval Anglo-Iberian relations.

England and Iberia is concerned primarily with the contacts between England and the Christian kingdoms of Iberia, namely, Castile, the Catalano-Aragonese Crown, and Portugal. As Bullón-Fernández highlights in her introductory essay, the book explores cultural and political interactions not between geographical areas, but between national realities, and thus the Muslim presence in the Iberian Peninsula is excluded from consideration. Apropos the chronological boundaries, the choice of the twelfth century as a point of departure is a valid response to converging historical circumstances: while in England the Norman ruling class consolidated its power after the Conquest, the Iberian kingdoms began to take advantage of the debilitated Almoravide power around the 1130s. These conditions disposed the English and Iberian kingdoms to begin "more insistently to look outward to other countries in Europe" (p. 4). The fifteenth century, besides being the conventional closing point for discussions circumscribed to the medieval period, is also the natural temporal limit to this collection, since the Anglo-Iberian relations during the early modern period have been the object of numerous studies that have, however, paid little attention to their medieval background.

The three opening essays in the collection present general overviews of various aspects of the traffic between England and Iberia, while the rest discuss more specific cases. Jennifer Goodman Wollock examines the Anglo-Iberian chivalric interactions in their military, political, and literary dimensions, and suggests that "the crusade remains the central paradigm" (p. 17). That is, from an English perspective, the Iberian Peninsula represented the land where the Christian faith had to be defended against the Muslim infidel; in fact, the English involvement in Peninsular crusading activities is documented as early as 1112 and continued throughout the period covered by the book. But this crusading paradigm was reversed after the embracement of Protestantism in England, constructed then by the Spaniards as a modern bastion of infidelity.

The purpose of Lluís Cabré's essay is "to detect the existence of a British influence in Catalan writing" (p. 30) with special emphasis on texts that might have affected Joanot Martorell, author of *Tirant lo Blanc*. After tracing the presence of British texts and themes either in Latin, French, or in Catalan translation in the territories of the Crown of Aragon, Cabré revisits the issue of Martorell's knowledge of *Guy of Warwick*. He endorses the theory in favor of Martorell's acquaintance not with the English but with the French version of *Guy*, and he presents two new pieces of evidence, both of which seem, however, uncompelling. First, Cabré argues that the Catalan passage in chapter 115 of *Tirant*, "ciutats, viles i castells," is close to the French *Guy* "villes et forteresses" and removed from the English "Castell, *towre* nor cyte" (p. 39, my emphasis); but the fact that the meaning of *towre* may be "extended to include the whole fortress or stronghold of which a 'tower' was the original nucleus" (*OED* s.v. *tower*, n. 2) disproves this point. Second, the "soldà de Babilònia" (*Tirant*, chapter 135) matches with "le grand soudam de Babilonie" of the French *Guy*, while the English text reads "The ryche sowdan of Sysane"; but here Cabré fails to indicate that *Sysane* is most probably a corrupt reading, as Julius Zupitza, editor of the English *Guy*, suggests (EETS, e.s. 25 (1875): 78 n. 1), and thus cannot be used to exclude the possibility of the sultan of Babylon featuring in an English text encountered by Martorell.

The remaining essays expose the transversality and complexity of the Anglo-Iberian cultural contacts. Echevarría Arsuaga studies Jacobean pilgrimage from England and construes the shrine at Compostela as a mediator of the flux between England and Castile during a period of political uncertainty. Rose Walker associates the presence of "Iberian 'symptoms'" (p. 71) in English manuscripts and of English damp-fold illustration in Castilian codices with the royal marriages of Eleanor of Castile and Leonor of England, respectively. In her essay on Giles Despagne, Cynthia Chamberlain ably reconstructs the career of this body-guard at the service of Edward II, giving an account that illustrates the king's preference for, and confidence in, his Castilian retainers. The article by Jennifer Geouge sheds new light on the unbalanced and turbulent Anglo-Portuguese trade relations during the long reign of João I (1385–1433). Joyce Coleman focuses on the figure of João's wife, Philippa of Lancaster, and analyzes her role as promoter and purveyor of English culture, noticeable in her advocacy of the Use of Sarum, the sculptures made of Nottingham alabaster that adorn Portuguese churches, the Batalha Monastery, and most saliently the translations of Gower's *Confessio Amantis*. Coleman presents a strong case for identifying the Portuguese translator with the son of Philippa's treasurer, engaged by her to translate the work "as a present for her husband . . . she further had the work translated from Portuguese into Castilian as a gift for her half-sister, Catherine, and her brother-in-law, Enrique III of Castile" (p. 154). Amélia Hutchinson discusses the historicity of the episode known as "Os Doze de Inglaterra," determines the earliest extant version, and speculatively connects the narrative events with the Arthurian tradition. Finally, R. F. Yeager discusses Chaucer's exposure to what he calls the Matter of Spain, both during his travels in the Peninsula in 1366 and back in England through his likely contacts with the peninsular merchant community. Picking out the references to the Peninsula (to which *Almería* should be added; see Jeanne Krochalis, "'And riden in Belmarye': Chaucer's General Prologue, Line 57," *ANQ* 18.4 [2005], 3–8) in Chaucer's works, Yeager tentatively suggests the itinerary Chaucer followed in his visit to Spain, during which time it seems he acquired a rudimentary knowledge of Spanish and became partially acquainted with Castilian literary culture. Yeager cautiously concludes that while "Chaucer's involvement with Spanish literature . . . must remain speculative" (p. 201), if this did exist it certainly "prepared the ground for his Italian discoveries in the 1370s" (p. 202).

The issues covered by the nine essays included in *England and Iberia* are solid testimony to the intense and multifaceted exchanges between people from the two regions throughout the late Middle Ages. Significantly, this book reveals that the traffic between these nations was two-way, showing medieval England not only in her usual role as consumer of foreign fashions but also as exporter of cultural modes. This collection succeeds in properly illustrating the political and cultural implications of Anglo-Iberian relations and in highlighting the need for further scholarly consideration of this topic.

Jordi Sánchez-Martí
University of Alicante

Catherine A. M. Clarke. *Literary Landscapes and the Idea of England, 700–1400*. Cambridge: D. S. Brewer, 2006. Pp. xii, 160. £45.00; $80.00.

Near the end of this book, Catherine Clarke remarks that only her chronological focus has imposed limits on a "potentially enormous subject." In fact the corpus of materials revealed seems rather small for a seven-hundred-year span. Chapter 1, "The Edenic Island," relies heavily on Bede's well-known descriptions of Britain and Ireland. Clarke notes his debt to Gildas, brings in the very brief descriptions of the island of Farne in Bede's *Life of Cuthbert*, and adds Alcuin on York and the transformation of St Guthlac's island in the fen in Felix's *Life*. Chapter 2, on the *locus amoenus* tradition in Old English, covers sections of the poems *Phoenix*, *Genesis A*, *Guthlac A*, and a few lines of *The Seafarer*, with discussion of some Latin and one Irish sources and analogues. Chapter 3 considers landscape in the later monastic accounts of Glastonbury, Ely, and Ramsey, three island monasteries. The material here is less familiar, but once again Guthlac receives a certain prominence. Clarke notes that though he is strongly associated with Crowland, there was a cult of him at Glastonbury, which had a ninth-century abbot called Guthlac, and suggests that this could be part of a West Saxon strategy of appropriating Mercian and East Anglian saints. This allows Clarke to make a further argument for these island descriptions acting as "metonym or emblem for the island nation" of Britain. Her fourth chapter moves from islands to cities, and considers two twelfth-century texts on London and Chester, and three later ones including sections of Gower's *Vox Clamantis*, and a satirical poem that gives three lines to each of seven English cities, and pokes fun at their products—*verba vana* or "empty words" for London, "halfpenny pies (?)" for Norwich, *burges negones* or "niggardly citizens" for Bristol, and so on. A final chapter roves rather more widely in search of material, but at the expense of focus. Is Arthur's taunting speech in Layamon about the Avon being choked with dead warriors who look like steel fish an "ironic version" of the *locus amoenus* tradition, which "works to remind the audience that the idealized literary *locus amoenus* of England is constructed over the historical realities of conquest, invasion and conflict"? Not many readers of the poem over the last eight hundred years are likely to have thought so: the speech's sarcastic intention is overpoweringly strong.

The relative thinness of the material obliges the author to work hard at interpretation, and continuing threads in the argument are appropriation, resonance, polyphony, and commodification. Appropriation is necessary to connect the local or regional nature of so much of the material, essentially about islands and cities, with "the idea of England" announced in the title. Resonance serves much the same purpose. If the landscape of Glastonbury is "Edenic," and if Bede's account of Britain was similarly so, then the four-century gap between them becomes a continuity, at least in the mind of a well-read and well-instructed author or reader. The image of the monks of Ramsey severing themselves from "the barren olive-tree of the world" also "resonates with" the tree that represents Saint Dunstan in a vision recounted by William of Malmesbury, while a later version of the same vision, which mentions the many monks who will gather *in hac regione,* may be making a local tradition into a national one: but the connections seem forced. Polyphony is thoroughly congenial to the modern academic mind, but does not make much allowance for the exigencies and imperfections of composition. In 1392 the city of London was forced to pay King Richard II an enormous fine, and to stage a pageant of reconciliation, celebrated in Richard Maidstone's poem "Reconciliation." One stanza of this includes a catalogue of trees and of wild beasts, and one line of the latter includes the *cervus celer* among the tigers and panthers and predators. Richard's own emblem was the hart, and Clarke suggests that the "threatened and beleaguered" deer in "a hostile environment" may be the city's warning to Richard of his own vulnerability: a well-concealed warning, one has to say, and a motif more easily explained by the frequency of deer in wilderness descriptions. Commodification, finally, is seen as a feature of several accounts, which celebrate land as "a valuable possession," to be held, beheld, and fought over. But that, surely, is exactly what it was, and still is, though less apparently so now that there are many more obvious sources of wealth. There is a strong element of "appropriation" within this short work, as medieval works are brought into line with modern notions of the appropriate, and with the ongoing academic discussion of nationhood. The works and authors themselves, however, often seem obstinately committed to much narrower concerns and perspectives.

TOM SHIPPEY
Saint Louis University

LARA FARINA. *Erotic Discourse and Early English Religious Writing.* New York: Palgrave Macmillan, 2006. Pp. 179. $65.00.

Lara Farina's exploration of the erotic in early English religious writing is wide ranging—from the tenth-century hymn *Christ I* to the thirteenth-century *Love Ron* of the Franciscan Thomas de Hales. Farina also exhibits an acute awareness of the range of critical approaches available; feminist theory underlies her analysis, but she makes use of psychoanalytic and economic theories as she explores an important paradox in these texts: the coexistence of eroticism and asceticism, both occupying the "same representational ground" (p. 48), that is, the body.

It is the readers of these texts, and their assumed response to the erotic and affective writing, that is the focus of Farina's exegesis. The idea of the erotic is used to give a sense of connection between the works, although the chapters can stand on their own (and indeed the first chapter, that on *Christ I*, has appeared as a journal article). The inclusion of a chapter on a pre-1066 English text in a book dealing mainly with Middle English writing is useful for suggesting possible continuities between English literature before and after the Norman Conquest. Farina is concerned to stress the importance of bringing this early text into the discussion of erotic discourse; she acknowledges the "difficulty of discerning erotic elements in Old English literature" (p. 16), but believes this difficulty can itself be informative. Her most important contention is that "a practice of devotional reading both predates the organization of affective piety on the Continent and amends itself to fit contexts that were quite different than the reformist monasteries" (p. 3).

Farina is looking not for obvious sexual representation, but for an apprehension of interiority: "*Christ I*'s location of erotic interest in the half-visible interiority of the female body is thus perhaps its most lasting contribution to the history of sexual signification" (p. 33). The erotic is not limited to the blatantly sexual; it is located in the practice of reading as, variously, the discernment of sexualized meaning in text, sensual pleasure in reading, and the penetration of the text by the reader. The liturgical basis of *Christ I* requires a communal reading of the text and thus a social erotic. By "social erotic," Farina means the representation of desire as a social or collective phenomenon, arguing that "it is as a part of a community that the reader of *Christ I* learns how to desire, for desire becomes purposed, intelligible, in its social orchestration" (p. 32); here the social orchestration is the monastic liturgy. In contrast, Farina considers the reading of the thirteenth-century guide for female recluses, *Ancrene Wisse*, as a private and enclosed activity. Farina concentrates on the text's construction of the anchoress as physically enclosed in order to preserve her bodily integrity—the anchorhold acts as a metaphor for the enclosed body, as well as enclosing the body, allowing no penetration. In treating *Ancrene Wisse* solely as a text for anchoresses, however, Farina ignores the other readers inscribed within it. I would suggest that *Ancrene Wisse*, by being written with an awareness of other potential readers, men and women, lay and religious, also opens up the anchorhold to those in the world.

Farina shows how the text of *Ancrene Wisse* constructs the gendered space enclosing the sisters, protecting and defining them as anchoresses and as readers of the text. She argues that in constructing this space the author is creating a "source of worry," founded in the paradox of asceticism and eroticism: "the sealed space of the anchorhold is envisioned as promoting and protecting not chastity but the secret pleasures of a transgressive sexuality" (p. 57). Farina relies heavily on Ann Warren's account of anchoritism, an account which has, to some extent, been called into question; her account of *Ancrene Wisse* needs to be read alongside other recent work, in particular, the 2005 collection of essays *Anchorites, Wombs, and Tombs* edited by Liz Herbert McAvoy and Mari Hughes-Edwards, and *A Companion to Ancrene Wisse*, edited by Yoko Wada (D. S. Brewer, 2003). What is valuable about Farina's work is that she places this anchoritic text within the larger diachronic context of medieval religious writing, exploring common threads of eroticism as an aspect of *affectus*.

Farina also studies other texts associated with *Ancrene Wisse*; in particular, the works in the Wooing Group. Farina reads these works as expressions of "mystical desire" and starts her third chapter by stating, "My readers may find it odd that mysticism, that most obvious source of devotional eroticism in the Middle Ages, has been only tangentially discussed in chapters 1 and 2" (p. 63). Farina's twenty-first-century readers would undoubtedly understand eroticism as a valid expression of the mystical experience, but it was not ever thus. Cuthbert Butler, for example, was very coy about any erotic aspect of mysticism, writing of Bernard of Clairvaux's description of the spiritual marriage in the *Song of Songs*, "Let whoso will, see in this fine piece any note of sensuousness or of selfish enjoyment of spiritual delights" (in *Western Mysticism*, p. 172). For Farina, the sensuousness carries the meaning of Bernard's interpretation, and although his sermons are not within the scope of Farina's main analysis, his presence is felt throughout, with references to his "theology of love" (p. 89).

Farina stresses the social rather than individualistic approach to mysticism; that is, she believes it is important to understand the social context of mystical experience and writing rather than to think of mystics as exceptional individuals outside temporal and social influence. Farina exhibits a sensible caution here over psychological approaches to mysticism, and provides an interesting consideration of material structures and their articulation in the language of commerce; she examines in particular the role of the language of gifts both within texts and in textual production (pp. 82–83).

Farina is aware of the manuscript tradition of the Wooing Group and consequent issues of readership, an approach she extends to the final text considered, the *Love Ron* of Thomas de Hales. She argues persuasively for a reappraisal of the readership of the *Love Ron*, suggesting a readership more aristocratic and more sophisticated than has been assumed (p. 97). She acknowledges the importance of this lyric within an understanding of the development of vernacular spirituality aimed at lay readers: "A more accurate understanding of Thomas's audience is of importance for understanding the trajectory of religious literary eroticism in the thirteenth century and in the later medieval era" (p. 88). The trajectory of Farina's own work—from Anglo-Saxon monasticism via anchoritism to Franciscan spirituality aimed at a lay readership—is of great interest, although no conclusion is offered tracing this path. Farina is maybe too cautious to subscribe to any grand narrative but concentrates, rather, on the particular, and it is her analysis of particular texts—especially the *Christ I* and the *Love Ron*—that this reviewer especially appreciated.

CATE GUNN
Colne Engaine

JOHN M. FYLER. *Language and the Declining World in Chaucer, Dante, and Jean de Meun*. Cambridge: Cambridge University Press, 2007. Pp. xii, 306. £50.00; $101.00.

John Fyler's book is the product of wide reading and sustained reflection on the nature of medieval literary representation. Its roots lie in a project that sought to align the history of ideas with a critical interest in poetics and found important expression in studies like Marcia Colish's *The Mirror of Language* (1968), Brian Stock's *Myth and Science in the Twelfth Century* (1972), and Winthrop Wetherbee's *Platonism and Poetry in the Twelfth Century* (1972). This genealogy suggests the deep perspective informing Fyler's work, not its belatedness or isolation from contemporary literary studies. Fyler's understanding of the interpretive stakes of his topic clearly registers the influence of turns in recent decades to theory and history. As Fyler notes, his study shares some common territory with James M. Dean's *The World Grown Old in Later Medieval Literature* (1999), but his focus on medieval views of the origin and nature of language leads, I think, to a darker assessment than the pervasive trope of *senectus mundi*. For the imaginative and expressive possibilities that the question of language opened up for Dante, Jean de Meun and Chaucer are tied profoundly to loss, mourning, and the bitter freedom of disenchantment.

Fyler's opening chapter argues that medieval speculations about language are shaped decisively by Genesis 1 and the exegetical tradition established by Augustine and developed by other patristic and medieval commentators. Fyler identifies "three historical foci" in Genesis: the origin of language, the effects of the Fall, and the building of the Tower of Babel (p. 3). His analysis of the biblical text distinguishes God's (performative) language at the Creation from Adam's (denotative) naming of the birds and animals, the (mythological) language of his progeny after the Fall, and the (historical) languages generated after Babel by human confusion and depravity. The parentheses here are mine, and Fyler rightly reminds us that his delineation of these phases is analytical rather than purely descriptive; the commentary tradition does not distinguish this hierarchy of languages consistently. But his analytical point remains crucial because it situates language within a structure of impossible loss. As he goes on to show, alienation, difference, and division follow from recognizing an unrecoverable origin for language. Fyler's analytical step turns away from a diachronic account of biblical commentary, but it takes the book toward its critical topic, which is the poetic exploitation and not merely the application of ideas about language. Fyler is thus able, for example, to note that the Vetus Latina used by Augustine translated Eve's name as *vita*, "the name 'Life' being imposed at the moment when death entered the world" (p. 15) and that the iconography of Lamech, the first bigamist, depicts the arts of civilization as a continuing enactment of division (p. 31). He shows how the classical dispute between natural and conventional language unfolds in the Middle Ages with local and idiosyncratic uses of language theory alongside systematic treatments of signification. This working out of literary implications subsequently ranges across topics such as Pentecost, dream theory, and linguistic equivocation with valuable insights into a variety of didactic and poetic texts.

The chief arena in which Fyler examines the use of medieval language theory is high vernacular literature, notably in the links between Jean de Meun, Dante, and Chaucer. The chapter on Jean supplements the narrative in Genesis with Ovid's etiological myths from the *Metamorphoses* and elegiac poetry, and rightly connects language and love as analogues, particularly in the matter of deceptive speech. Jean is, for Fyler, a powerful advocate of the view that language is conventional, dependent on an arbitrary and socially ratified (hence historical) association between sign and referent. In the *Rose*, Fyler takes the repeated topos of the Golden Age, the seemingly authoritative figure of Reason, and the scandal of her saying "coilles" to the Lover as a matrix for examining how language can be said to signify properly. The problem, as Christine de Pisan and other medieval readers recognized, is that God's creation of things occurred without sin, but man's use of things, including the decorum of naming them, occurs in a fallen world in which even a figure like Reason connects words to things *ad placitum*. Fyler's argument is that in the *Rose* proper naming has thus moved from a rational possibility in an Adamic world to a symptom of "the deluded nostalgia for the Golden Age" (p. 95). If the argument elides the performative and denotative uses of language in Fyler's initial hierarchy, it nonetheless points to important conceptual shifts that inform meaning in poetic texts. The function of naming is to claim existence, while the uses we make of names (description, predication, analogy) are functions of intelligibility. As Fyler maps out Reason's conflicted position on words and things, he also demonstrates that intelligibility in a fallen, divided world becomes the abiding problem for medieval narrative poets.

Dante serves as the counterweight to Jean's skepticism over signification. Fyler generally views him as a poet who absorbs and redeploys the language doctrine of the commentary tradition. He reviews the passages in the *Commedia* where Dante employs the metaphor of language to describe his characters and his own art. Speech, Fyler says, "takes part in the degradation of the Fall, and the eternal reprobation of the damned in Hell," delineates the levels of Purgatory, and manifests in Paradise "the nobility of an effort pushed to the limits of human powers" (p. 119). His particular focus on Adam's language in *Paradiso* 26 interprets the imagined language of Eden as a necessary condition for fallenness, "a perfect language" whose loss furnishes a cause for mourning (p. 122). In other passages, differences in language reflect both alienation and human community, particularly in vernacular speech. Fyler ends the chapter by reading Chaucer's *House of Fame* as an informed, subversive engagement with the *Commedia* that "reveals his awareness of and response to Dante's concerns" with linguistic slippage (p. 145).

Fyler's extended treatment of Chaucer in the final chapter concentrates on *The Second Nun's Tale* and *The Canon's Yeoman's Tale*, Fragment VIII of the *Canterbury Tales*. As Joseph Grennen and others have shown, these two tales represent a consummate moment of Chaucerian poetic construction—a composite martyr's legend from Christian antiquity written before the *Legend of Good Women* (F426, G416) and then partnered with an alchemical "modern instance" that breaks into the frame of the Canterbury pilgrimage yet replicates the structural divisions of the earlier work. Fyler locates a concern with historical process in these tales and sets that concern against the nostalgia for a Golden Age that he finds in the Clerk, Merchant, Squire, and Franklin of Fragments IV and V. The end of the *Canterbury Tales* (Fragments VIII–X) thus stages both the decay of language and the world and an approach to the silence of spiritual truth and being out of which language originally appeared. Tracing this double movement allows Fyler to offer fine insights about Chaucer texts that have attracted considerable scholarly attention and to bring to the fore their resonance with Jean and Dante. His final section, on the maxim "wordes moote be cosyn to the dede" (I.742), reads the efforts to attain proper speech in the *Tales* against Dante's single volume bound with love (*Paradiso* 33.86), and it tracks the dispersal of language and writing into troping, counterfeit, and mere style.

Language and the Declining World presents a learned and elegant model for reading within an intertextual tradition of commentary and poetic influence. Tradition, as Fyler conceives it for Chaucer, is manifest in a "general dependence on a background of discussion and commentary" (p. 155); the same broad principle applies to Jean and Dante. Moreover, the links between the three poets mark a historical line of influence and transmission. One might object that Fyler's interpretive framework takes certain features of influence for granted. Speculation about language, particularly in the High and late Middle Ages, extended further than the question of origins. If learned commentary forms a background to vernacular poetry, we would like to see not just the major sources but also important intermediaries, such as Guyart Desmoulins's French translation of Peter Lombard's *Historia Scholastica*, which Fyler brings to bear on discussion of *The Canon's Yeoman's Tale*. Dante certainly operates within dominant forms of language doctrine, as Fyler shows, but the development of his views in earlier works as well as the *Commedia* is highly complex, and the *Paradiso* ends as much with the failure of language ("A l'alta fantasia qui mancò possa" [33.142]) as the alignment of desire, will, and divine love. Chaucer might seem in some ways too easy and obvious a destination for the book, but here Fyler shows the practical value of his approach and his careful attention to the absorption of ideas and poetic resonance. The trajectory he traces for language explains how Chaucer's famous evasions and indeterminacy are not just aesthetic effects but the consequence of a profound vision of a fallen world and failed language.

ROBERT R. EDWARDS
The Pennsylvania State University

ALEXANDRA GILLESPIE. *Print Culture and the Medieval Author: Chaucer, Lydgate, and Their Books, 1473–1557*. Oxford: Oxford University Press, 2006. Pp. xiv, 281. £53.00; $95.00.

Most books in the area of manuscript/early book studies make for dense reading. Marshaling codicological or transmission detail into a coherent and exciting literary history can be like herding cats. But when it works, it really works. Alexandra Gillespie's book is one that does.

Like all such studies, her thesis is complex, and justly so. She has chosen an especially difficult time span (1473–1557), which carries her across period boundaries that still—despite recent fascination with the long fifteenth century—remain semicharted territory. She covers the transition of Chaucer and Lydgate into print, beginning with a chapter on Caxton and coming up through the chapter "Assembling Chaucer's Texts in Print, 1517 to 1532" and "Court and Cloister: Editions of Lydgate, 1509 to 1534." The book ends with a broader discussion of sixteenth-century book-trade issues, "The Press, the Medieval Author, and the English Reformations, 1534 to 1557," intelligently invoking "reformations" in the plural.

Chaucer and Lydgate (whatever their unequal merits as poets) are the twin giants of secular book production in this period. Chapter 1 opens with Caxton's accolade of Lydgate as an important model for his own literary translations: "I . . . am not worthy to bere his penner and ynkhorne after hym, to medle me in that werke" (p. 27). But meddle he did, and Caxton's own authorship, or better, "translatorship," is the catalyst for Gillespie's multidisciplinary study of the political, oral, literary, and commercial factors in early print production. Using these issues to create a kind of bibliographic sociology, she sees early print as conducted in the "context of a set of social relations—a gift economy in which the writer is supplicant, 'bounde' or seeking bondage within a system of noble patronage and reward; networks of fellowship and fraternity in which the desire of 'gentilmen' is met by the printer who can then identify them as 'frendes'; a culture of Christian devotion . . . and finally a money economy" (p. 28). Gillespie keeps these various factors consistently in view and in tension throughout the book.

To hold all this together, she chose to focus on the idea of the author in late medieval/early modern culture. One of the delightful aspects of the book is that even though she begins by citing Foucault's now hoary "What is an author?" she very quickly moves beyond it. While she notes that medieval writers can and do name the *auctor* in ways that conform to Foucault, in medieval manuscripts the author's name and much else pertinent to reproduction history "regularly disappears." She also resists "the teleological drift of much work on early printing," and the current tendency to abandon the word "Renaissance" in favor of "Early Modern." By using both terms interchangeably in her book, she makes the point that "new ways of representing the medieval author in print are linked in this study to the Renaissance recuperation of classical traditions and to early modern social and religious change" (p. 9). Given its terminus in 1557, one hopes that her book will be edifying to early modern scholars: "one of the points I wish to make in this study is that the very accommodating idea of the author represented by classical tradition did not have to be reinvented by the Renaissance. . . . The author was a way of managing with the idea of the text in the world of the Middle Ages as well" (pp. 10–11). Amen, amen.

Even though early print is her topic, Gillespie's firm grasp of the recent exciting developments in Middle English manuscript studies allows her to see important continuities: the sudden rise of Middle English texts, the "paper revolution," the growth of "speculative trade in medieval manuscripts," the rapid reproduction of Gower's works, and the self-publishing habits of Hoccleve and Capgrave can all illuminate, in certain ways, the issues of the print period. Of this extrapolation, Gillespie writes: "Printing *accelerated* an existing traffic in texts, and changes we perceive as being in some way related to the newness of print—including the emergence of the author—cannot be detached from old ways of thinking about what it means for a text to be written, copied or read" (p. 16).

Gillespie typically tackles a problem by offering a succinct assessment of the previous scholarship, a moderate position on it, her own further evidence, and then a cross-grained example, just to remind us how complex all literary reception history is. The space available to me here does not allow for many examples, so I have chosen a few interesting ones having to do with Chaucerian transmission. In the third chapter, Gillespie discusses the gender issues of generations of "gentil" Chaucerian readers, up to the dangerous period of Henry VIII. Having traced the remarkable misogyny that dogs the reception of *Troilus and Criseyde* thus far, Gillespie closes the chapter with poignant and countervailing evidence from the Devonshire Manuscript, showing the *loyalty* men express about women under persecution in the social circle of Anne Boleyn (p. 143). The surprising, cross-grained, or sometimes counterintuitive reading is a hallmark of Gillespie's work; one can find it, for instance, in her evidence for Continental influence in the production of Chaucer's *Workes* of 1532, which is set against the evidence for its simultaneous assertion of English literary sovereignty (pp. 137–38). One sees it in her temperate analysis of the significance of John Shirley in relation to the rise of

"organized, commercial, and even speculative production of manuscripts in England before the arrival of the press." Downplaying Shirley's own role in this rise in favor of the Hammond-scribe's, she then
complicates the thesis by noting that even the Hammond-scribe's work
(1460–80) postdates the arrival of print (pp. 48–50). Finally, she argues
that just as Lydgate's *Troy Book* relies on Chaucerian authorship as a
springboard for authorial ambition, and Caxton's in turn on Lydgate, so
too do these *auctors* also "close in" upon the ambitions of the younger
writers (p. 42). Gillespie never settles for the easy or obvious answers.

Of course, some queries spring to mind. Given that the emphasis on
authorship throughout skews Gillespie's findings in favor of named authors and classical traditions, would there be a way to conceive of the
study so as to foreground, say, the 1550 editions of *Piers Plowman* as
much as, for instance, the 1532 Chaucer? Would more emphasis on the
printing of medieval mystical texts (as pioneered by Goldschmidt) reveal
a different kind of sociology of the book (one thinks of Kempe or the
Orcherd of Syon)? Undoubtedly it would. But these subjects, though mentioned, are not Gillespie's primary concern. Her primary concern—the
print tradition of Chaucer and Lydgate especially—is beautifully realized, and a great addition to our history of the book.

KATHRYN KERBY-FULTON
University of Notre Dame

FRANK GRADY. *Representing Righteous Heathens in Late Medieval England.*
New York: Palgrave Macmillan, 2005. Pp. 214. $65.00.

Representing Righteous Heathens is a sharply focused monograph that, in
spite of its concision, covers a great deal of ground. Frank Grady suggests that the trope of the "righteous heathen" must be understood not
only as a theological concept but as a literary "topos" (p. 70), and he
goes on to explore the various ways that this trope was deployed in the
cultural environment of late medieval England. The book is organized
into four main chapters, each centered on one facet of the rich literary
tradition of depicting righteous heathens in medieval England: "The
Trouble with Trajan," "Mandeville's 'Gret Meruaylle,'" "The Middle
English Alexander," and "The Rhetoric of the Righteous Heathen." A

concluding chapter, "Virtuous Pagans and Virtual Jews," productively moves the discourse of pagan alterity outside the simplistic framework of "heathen" nature (that is, the mere fact of exclusion from salvation by means of the mediation of the Church), exploring other forms of exclusion from the living body of Christ. Throughout *Representing Righteous Heathens*, Grady's apt, often witty, turns of phrase are much in evidence; his narration of contemporary analogues to the phenomenon of the righteous heathen, in the introduction (pp. 8–9) and conclusion (pp. 131–32), are well chosen and add to the historical resonance of the book's theme.

Beyond its fundamental premise, Grady's argument conveys broader implications concerning the role of temporality and the formal principles of literary allusion: first, he suggests that the attempt to recuperate ancient alterity, enacted in medieval narratives of the righteous heathen, provides a template for interpreting "the modern critical attempt to understand the Middle Ages" (p. 10). Second, concerning the "formal significance" (p. 6) of the trope of the righteous heathen, Grady shows that the device appears at critical narrative junctures in several of the works he surveys: in Chaucer's *Troilus*, as in the Alliterative *Morte Arthure*, "the virtuous pagan scene" serves as "an aesthetic resource" (p. 113) or, in Gower's *Confessio Amantis*, "as a formal resource for aesthetic organization" (p. 121). This latter insight is among the most striking features of *Representing Righteous Heathens*: too often, studies of alterity treat poetic depictions in isolation, as though literature had the same evidentiary status as philosophical or theological treatises, encyclopedias, or historical chronicles. This is not to suggest that such sources should be read naively; with regard to historiography, for example, scholars such as Gabrielle Spiegel and Nancy Partner have long since demonstrated conclusively that chronicles must be read both with attention to expectations arising from the genre and with a keen awareness of the text's moments of resistance. Grady, however, illustrates persuasively the extent to which formal principles specific to literary production dictate the nature of the portrayal of the righteous heathen, as well as determine the particular moments when the trope is demanded by the exigencies of the literary work.

In keeping with its specifically English focus, *Representing Righteous Heathens* is at its best when the literature under scrutiny is situated most explicitly in the local context: this is especially the case in the chapter on Alexander the Great, which includes detailed discussion of the wide range of Alexander texts current in late medieval English (written not only in Middle English but also in Latin and Anglo-French [pp. 79–80]), with particularly tantalizing notes concerning English ownership of manuscripts of relevant texts. Other chapters, especially that on Mandeville, are noticeably weaker in this respect; *Mandeville's Travels* is read as a specifically English example of the trope of the righteous heathen in spite of the fact that the book was composed in French, most likely on the Continent, and scholars such as M. C. Seymour have argued quite forcefully that the author's claim of English identity is itself merely a literary trope. Grady justifies his inclusion of Mandeville on the rather shaky grounds that "there are more English versions of the *Travels*" than are found in other vernaculars, "though there are more extant manuscripts in those languages" (p. 46). His choice of the Cotton version is similarly peculiar: he chooses it because "it is available in two relatively common critical editions" and "due to its relatively faithful and complete rendering of its French source" (147 n. 7). If fidelity to the source is desirable, it would have been preferable to use Christiane Deluz's excellent edition of the French text; if widespread circulation in medieval England were the most important criterion, it would have been best to use the Defective Version, which is by far most common among English manuscripts. I belabor this point not because the choice of texts is so important in itself, but because it illuminates an aspect of *Representing Righteous Heathens* that is both its greatest strength and its greatest weakness: that is, its limitation to the local context of late medieval England, so superbly defined in relation to the Alexander texts and in the chapter on Trajan (treating both *Piers Plowman* and *St. Erkenwald*), but less well grounded in the chapter on Mandeville.

If the strength of *Representing Righteous Heathens* lies in its close analysis of the texts and its illumination of the cultural contexts directing particular readings, its weakness lies in the larger framework of the argument, especially the concept of "heathen" nature. The term "heathen" does not occur in the late medieval English texts that Grady studies; instead, it is used rather indiscriminately to render a range of other terms, some of which differ significantly. For example, chapter 4 opens with a quotation from Lord Cobham that refers to the status "of heathen peoples" (p. 101). The original text in the notes shows that the term translated is "ethnicorum" (168 n. 2), sometimes translated "pagan" or "heathen," but a term that refers to ethnic or national origin in addition to religious deviation from the Christian norm. A few lines later, the term is glossed somewhat differently, as "infidels to the Christian faith" ("infideles . . . ad fidem Christianum" [p. 102]). If a "heathen" is one who is excluded from Christian salvation as mediated by the Church (which seems to be Grady's working definition), surely it is important to understand the nature of that exclusion. Does it arise from a deliberate disavowal of the Christian faith, as in the case of medieval Muslims or "Saracens"? Or does it arise from ignorance of Christian revelation, as in the case of the hypothetical virtuous pagan living on the banks of the Indus, described in Dante's *Commedia*? To what extent is ethnic or national difference understood as being coterminous with pagan or "heathen" identity?

These kinds of questions are not taken on directly in *Representing Righteous Heathens*, though they emerge obliquely in the spectrum of "righteous heathens" encountered in the chapter on Mandeville, ranging from the Muslim Sultan of Babylon to the Mongol Great Khan to the virtuous inhabitants of the Isle of Bragman. In the Introduction, Grady defines the problem of the righteous heathen as not singular, but rather made up "of different classes of heathens" (p. 5). A fuller definition of "heathen" nature, grounded in the terminology used to characterize these figures, would have been a useful foundation for the chapters that follow; in addition, it might have been wise to consider explicitly the consequences of choosing Trajan as the paradigmatic case of the virtuous heathen in medieval English literature. A study of the righteous heathen in medieval Italian literature, for example, might instead have focused on the hypothetical virtuous man, unaware of the Incarnation and consequent role of the Church in mediating salvation. While Dante shows up occasionally as a point of comparison in discussions of *Piers Plowman* (p. 17) and *Troilus and Criseyde* (172 n. 10), the reader lacks any sense of the wider framework of the trope of the righteous heathen—especially richly elaborated by Dante, as both Amilcare Iannucci and Marcia Colish have shown. In part, this is a limitation of the deliberately restricted, late medieval English focus of the volume; in part, however, it represents a somewhat undertheorized aspect of the very foundation of the book's argument.

The extremely flexible definition of "heathen" nature used in *Representing Righteous Heathens* leads occasionally to some blind spots, especially with regard to gender. In the Introduction, Grady notes offhandedly that the righteous heathen is always male (p. 7; cf. 173 n. 19: "the discourse of the virtuous pagan is a masculine one"). It is not clear why prominent female "local informants," such as Floripas in the Old French and Middle English *Fierabras* romance or Belacane in Wolfram von Eschenbach's *Parzival*, are excluded from the category of the righteous heathen, as they seem to provide witness to Christian truth from a pagan perspective no less than, for example, Mandeville's Sultan of Babylon. (Coincidentally, the romance of *Fierabras* is also related to a small error concerning the contents of an English manuscript said to contain both *Fierabras* and a vernacular romance of Alexander: "Un Volum del Romaunce . . . de Ferebras, de Alisaundre" (p. 78). This is much more likely to be a romance "of Fierabras of Alexandria," as many of the Old French versions are titled; if both romances were present, the entry would probably have read "de Ferebras e de Alisaundre.")

Representing Righteous Heathens is a valuable contribution to our understanding of non-Christian alterity as it was viewed in late medieval England, containing particularly fine close readings of *Piers Plowman*, *St. Erkenwald*, and *Alexander and Dindymus*. Grady has done much to illuminate the nature of the vernacular theology concerning salvation and redemption to be found in the diverse poetic production of late medieval England, as well as the nature of its "specifically insular audience" (p. 40). The book will certainly attract a wide readership and serve as a stimulus to further work in this rewarding field of study.

SUZANNE CONKLIN AKBARI
University of Toronto

NOAH D. GUYNN. *Allegory and Sexual Ethics in the High Middle Ages.* New York: Palgrave Macmillan, 2007. Pp. xii, 218. $65.00.

With this book, Noah Guynn makes a significant fresh contribution to literary scholarship and to the history of sexuality, deftly intertwining three distinctive balancing acts in interpretation. The first and most prominent is his attention to the contrasting forces at the heart of medieval allegory, the tension between "an overarching, formalized, and essentialist textual design and a more fluid, variable, or protean conception of textual meaning" (p. 3). Guynn provides a clear account of the importance of both tendencies, rather than the first alone, to ideological forces in the twelfth and thirteenth centuries. Guynn's conjoined consideration of secular and sacred figurations of desirable and deviant bodies also sets this book apart, since he manages to clarify the interrelation without obscuring differences. Guynn's investment in identifying the rhetorical figuration of sexual desire as a tool for consolidating social and political power has a dual nature as well; his commitment to understanding allegory's role in past cultural formations is matched by his commitment to recognizing the political stakes of reading allegory and ethics discourse today. Guynn argues that medieval allegory's ability to expose the contingent nature of meaning cannot be celebrated as a tool for political liberation; instead, "medieval allegories call for violent responses to symbolic or representational problems, for imposing consensus and conformity through physical brutality because it cannot be achieved through other means" (p. 173).

Guynn designates allegory as both the representation of a "symbolist mentality" (p. 17) and "the master trope of imaginative literature" (p. 18). Defining strict generic boundaries for allegory is not one of Guynn's aims. Guynn considers medieval romance as well as dream visions; patterns of textual structure and character introduction, homophonic resonances of words, personification, and simple metaphors are all grist for analysis. His broader understanding of allegory lays bare a commonality in the techniques of secular and ecclesiastical writings. As he demonstrates that "an implicit social hierarchy . . . precedes and predetermines the text's fascination with the slipperiness of its own meaning" (p. 9), the book moves rhythmically between the sacred and secular concerns of the hierarchy's upper margins. An opening chapter marks out the study's theoretical grounds with reference to patristic and ecclesiastical writers, including Augustine, Aquinas, and Alan of Lille, before the book turns to the secular and aristocratic interests of the *Roman d'Eneas* in the second chapter, then offers a fuller exploration of Alan's *Anticlaudianus* and *De Planctu Naturae* in chapter 3, and makes a return to the realm of lay readers and the secular clergy in the fourth and final chapter on the *Roman de la rose*. Each chapter connects the slipperiness in rhetorical representations of sexualized bodies to the justification of violence against actual bodies, protecting the challenged ideology of aristocratic sovereignty, the theocratic authority of the Church, or the masculinized prerogatives of the clergy.

In delineating the relationship of ideology and allegory, Guynn avoids the twin temptations of treating either the rhetorical strategies or their range of objectives reductively. As noted, Guynn insists upon allegory's polyvocality and interpretative ambiguity as he identifies these same qualities as a tool of polemic, rather than its antidote; he unmasks the enjoyable play of the self-deconstructing text as a calculated means of arousing the desire for stability and more aggressive policing of power. As Guynn acknowledges, it is not surprising that the *Roman d'Eneas*, *De Planctu Naturae*, and *Roman de la rose*, three seminal texts with powerful readerships, should rhetorically enforce privilege. Yet his nuanced analysis of the means by which these texts accomplished this feat is certain to provoke new thought as it challenges the assumption that medieval rulers, ecclesiastics, and clerics delighted in the rhetorical play of allegory due to some unspecified affinity with contemporary scholarly aesthetics.

The chapters of textual analysis all relate to the Augustinian-informed theoretical approach of the first chapter but are for the most part self-contained, perhaps a reflection of the fact that these portions of the project developed through the production of relevant articles. The crisp construction is admirable, although at times I found myself wishing for slightly messier textual interstices. More intrusion of the *Eneas* discussion into later chapters, for example, might have created space for reflecting on the concreteness in figuration found in the romance, in which even the god "Amors" takes the physical form of a human-constructed statue, in contrast to the analysis of more lively and abstract personifications from the *De Planctu* and the *Rose*. But each individual textual argument is of sufficient interest in itself, with the most important connections between chapters clearly rendered, resulting in a book equally useful as a whole or as separate chapters.

One claim of special interest found in chapter 2 follows a demonstration that females in *Eneas* name sodomy explicitly but explain its meaning not in denotative or anatomical discourse but rather in inventively rhetorical terms. Guynn claims that "not unlike an allegory, *sodomy* is both an abstract representation of moral failure . . . and a signifier pointing toward an ineffable meaning so outrageous it can only be spoken of 'otherwise,' through circumlocution" (p. 85, his emphasis). The observed parallel in operation marks a nice contrast with the equally rhetorical strategies of Alan of Lille discussed in chapter 3; sodomy is never directly named, nor is its cure, as the representation of bodies burrows more deeply into the play of interpretation. Language analysis is at its most fascinating in this chapter; Guynn's characterization of the gendered relationship between Nature and Genius is especially stimulating.

Chapter 4 reopens the debate on the sexual politics of the *Rose* by claiming that the unstable attribution of misogynistic and homophobic voices within allegory serves to privilege these voices, providing an interesting ideological reading of the signature practice on which so much ink has already been spilled. Discussion of Christine de Pisan's response to the *Rose* forms the conclusion of this chapter. Guynn champions Christine's allegorical staging of the recovery of female political power and voice, and condemnation of physical abuse in the *Cité des dames* as a "clearsighted" response to the *Rose*, presenting such work as preferable to the "rhetorical misstep" of suggesting the *Rose* be burned (p. 168)—but it might be more just not to discount entirely Christine's potential participation in the disturbing ideological violence Guynn discovers in male authors' figurations. Consideration of Sheila Delany's recent work on the political goals underlying Osbern Bokenham's advocacy for women might have been useful here.

Delany's earlier *Medieval Literary Politics* and the scholarship of Gordon Teskey and Larry Scanlon are important critical touchstones for this book, and Guynn productively integrates a range of post-Foucauldian scholarship on medieval sexuality, recognizing the work of Glenn Burger, William Burgwinkle, and Simon Gaunt, among others. The index lists critical perspectives under the modern authors' names but also itemizes them under the names of relevant medieval authors and texts, a reader-friendly feature. Guynn's sensitivity to the many signifying aspects of language extends from the argument proper into his apparatus for quotations: he modifies existing translations of non-English texts to take into account subsequent scholarship, such as Danuta Shanzer's work on Alan of Lille's Latin. Like the index and translations, the secondary bibliography is another useful tool. One single detail teases the reader impressed by the *tour de force* of attention to apparatus: an illumination from the *Pèlerinage de la vie humaine* appears on the book jacket, although discussion of this fourteenth-century allegory does not appear in the book. But I recognize my disappointed desire for Guynn's analysis of yet another text as just another indication of his book's high scholarly value.

STEPHANIE A. V. G. KAMATH
University of Massachusetts, Boston

AMANDA HOPKINS and CORY JAMES RUSHTON, eds. *The Erotic in the Literature of Medieval Britain*. Cambridge: D. S. Brewer, 2007. Pp. 182. £45.00; $80.00.

Building upon the very substantial—and, to take the long view of medieval scholarship, actually very recent—corpus of critical work by medievalists on constructions of gender and sexuality, the contributors to the collection *The Erotic in the Literature of Medieval Britain* engage with the notion of the erotic in order to read it on its own terms, whatever such may be. What *was* erotic, and what were its representations, in the Western European Middle Ages? As the editors ask in their introduction, "How can modern readers identify, analyse, appreciate the erotic in medieval literature? What response did medieval authors hope to provoke in their contemporary audience? . . . How is the modern reader to interpret the dynamic between the erotic and the transgressive?"

The result is a collection of essays that, while often uneven, is argued with a good deal of liveliness and, appropriately, delight. This collection has as its primary focus romances in English (the Alliterative *Morte Arthure*, *Sir Degarré*, *Sir Launfal*, and others, as well as the figure of Gawain as lover and the figure of the erotic enchantress), but also includes forays into *The Alphabet of Tales*, *Ancrene Wisse*, *The Wife of Bath's Prologue*, the Paston letters, *The Mabinogion*, and Latin lyric.

What constitutes the erotic is of course culturally specific, realized in local representational practices and personal expression. Thus to attempt to historicize the erotic and erotic experience is ambitious indeed, especially with respect to the Middle Ages. According to the *Oxford English Dictionary*, the word *erotic* ("of or pertaining to the passion of love; amatory" and "amatory poem") does not enter English until the mid-seventeenth century. (On the other hand, *lust* in the sense of "pleasure, delight" and even "desire, appetite" has been with us since the earliest English; *lust* in the sense of sinful "sensuous desire," as well as in the sense of "libidinous desire, degrading animal passion," followed soon after.) The *OED*'s entry on *erotica* is also brief, defining *erotica* as "matters of love; erotic literature or art (freq. as a heading in catalogues)." The seven entries on erotica range from 1854 to 1967, and I find the last, from George Steiner's "Night Words: High Pornography and Human Privacy," useful in discussing the essays at hand. Steiner writes: "Above the pulp line—but the exact boundaries are impossible to draw—lies the world of erotica, of sexual writing with literary pretensions or genuine claims. This world is much larger than is commonly realized." Steiner goes on to say: "What distinguishes the 'forbidden classic' from under-the-counter delights . . . is essentially, a matter of semantics, of the level of vocabulary and rhetorical device used to provoke erection" (pp. 70–71). In 1967, Steiner's essay offended. In 2008, one is simply annoyed at the assumption about the audience. Still, browsing the dictionary makes one wonder what a Middle English erotic "amatory poem" might be (January's morning cuckoo? Any number of Harley lyrics?), and what might be considered Middle English erotica (Chaucer's narratorial sleight in his description of Troilus and Criseyde's first union? The narrative of seductions in *Sir Gawain and the Green Knight*?)—*erotica* being something very different from the *erotic*.

Mindful of the difference, no contributor to *The Erotic in the Literature of Medieval Britain* offers a Steinerian taxonomy of erotic writing in medieval Britain. The first preposition in the title of the collection is crucial. More often than not, the erotic in the medieval texts under consideration is glimpsed through what Barthes calls "the hole in the discourse." Until recently, such "holes" have been roundly ignored, suppressed, forgotten, left unexplicated and untouched in literary scholarship. This collection asks us to start with the hole. In "A Fine and Private Place," for example, Jane Bliss focuses on what she sees as the author's anxious and occluded proscriptions against same-sex acts in the *Ancrene Wisse*.

Bliss's reading points to another kind of "hole in the discourse," and that is the hole in literary scholarship itself. In "Eros and Error: Gross Sexual Transgression in the *Fourth Branch* of the *Mabinogi*," Michael Cichon reads narratives of sexual transgression, including rape, as cautionary tales that nevertheless are erotically charged: the "hole" in this case is unavoidable, but how a reader treats it—jumps over it, goes around it, or confronts it head on—changes the way we read the, well, whole. For example, Thomas Howard Crofts, in "Perverse and Contrary Deeds: The Giant of Mont Saint Michel and the Alliterative *Morte Arthure*," pushes previous readings of the story-that-cannot-be-told to graphic extreme in the episode of the Giant and his rape of the duchess and her nurse.

In the context of this collection, in which the erotic is taken seriously in a designated safe space, as it were, I find it surprising that Simon Meecham-Jones, in "Sex in the Sight of God: Theology and the Erotic in Peter of Blois' 'Grates Ago Veneri,'" aestheticizes beyond recognition the rape at the center of the poem. He describes the rape as a "surrender," and the poem's main event as standing in for "the primacy of Faith over intellect," and does so without any reflection on the long history of troping rape in literary texts and the visual arts. Now, given his project here—reading a number of Latin lyrics that unequivocally describe sexual acts so that he may place the lyrics in their theological and philosophical context—to do so has validity. However, to ignore the "literal" narrative, not to allow for another reading, seems out of step with the purpose of this collection. This strikes me as a missed opportunity to raise some questions about the possible "erotics" of rape—which is, as many of the other essays in this collection suggest, bound up with the "erotics" of virginity. Only scare quotes will do.

While the essays in this collection offer many fine readings of texts, we are not that further along to defining what a medieval erotic *is* at the end of it. Still, given that scholars of medieval sexuality, sexual practices, and desire have had to contend with a shifting, oblique, or missing vocabulary, the contributors to *The Erotic in the Literature of Medieval Britain* address this problem in what is, perhaps, the only reasonable way to do so; that is, to read for the erotic in narratives of acts or instances of identity-formation, and to read for acts or instances of identity-formation in the erotic. The volume ends with an essay by Alex Davis, "Erotic Historiography: Writing the Self and History in Twelfth-Century Romance and the Renaissance," that not only serves as a way to contextualize the previous essays but also suggests why reading (for) the erotic is productive, for it "is not only an object of study, but also functions in terms of mapping the field of study; it has historiographic value."

Other essays include Sue Niebrzydowski, " 'So wel koude he me glose': The Wife of Bath and the Eroticism of Touch"; Cory Rushton, "The Lady's Man: Gawain as a Lover in Middle English Literature"; Corinne Saunders, "Erotic Magic: The Enchantress in Middle English Romance"; Amanda Hopkins, " 'wordy vnthur wede': Clothing, Nakedness, and the Erotic in Some Romances of Medieval Britain"; Robert Rouse, " 'Some Like it Hot': The Medieval Eroticism of Heat"; Margaret Robson, "How's Your Father? Sex and the Adolescent Girl in *Sir Degarré*"; Anthony Bale, "The Female 'Jewish' Libido in Medieval Culture"; Kristina Hildebrand, "Her Desire and His: Letters between Fifteenth-Century Lovers."

KATHLEEN COYNE KELLY
Northeastern University

SIMON HOROBIN. *Chaucer's Language*. Basingstoke and New York: Palgrave Macmillan, 2007. Pp. x, 198. $24.95; £14.99 paper.

There are several good books that offer a conspectus of Chaucer's language, but it has been some time since a dedicated handbook approachable by students has appeared (at least in English). In some respects, the likes of Ralph Elliott's *Chaucer's English* (1974) and David Burnley's *A Guide to Chaucer's Language* (1983), though both excellent, now appear too demanding for undergraduates who may be coming to the serious study of Middle English for the first time; and the emphases of teaching and scholarship have inevitably shifted somewhat in the meantime. Simon Horobin's admirable new book successfully meets the needs thus exposed: its adroit, patient exposition, which explicitly assumes no knowledge of Middle English or of "technical linguistic terminology" (p. ix), provides not only a practical guide to form and sense but also (as is to be expected from an author at the cutting edge of Middle English language scholarship) makes for a commendably lucid point of entry to the critical attitudes and theories that inform current research.

In the preliminary chapter ("Why Study Chaucer's Language?") Horobin argues with characteristic cogency and effectiveness for students' engagement with Middle English literature in its original form. He explores the fundamental similarities and the cautionary differences between Chaucer's language and the English of today at a practical level, with a demonstration of the tools available to the student in translating sample passages (glossaries, *MED*), and the sounding of *caveats* over some familiar "false friends." In tandem with this, he highlights the importance of context in determining the connotations of Chaucer's words and the significance of the variant forms manipulated by English authors before the solidification of a written Standard. The emphasis placed on both these aspects (context and variation) forms a key strength of the book as a whole.

Chapter 2 introduces the place of Middle English in the multilingual England of the period. Perhaps inevitably given the space at his disposal, Horobin's presentation of the history of Middle English literature is in some respects rather brief; as is often the case with student handbooks, he tends to downplay textual activity in English at the earlier end of the period (especially the twelfth century), though he effectively counters any impression that Chaucer "invented" literary English. His discussion of scholarly approaches to the rise of written English in the fourteenth and fifteenth centuries is, moreover, commendably careful and nuanced; he introduces a range of social and intellectual contexts, and makes a good case for utilitarianism (rather than nationalism per se) as a driving force. Chapter 3 brings us in earnest to the language itself, with quick guides to the Middle English dialects and the issue of standardization, including an up-to-date presentation of the stages in the development of London English. The characteristic features (and origins) of Middle English vocabulary, grammar, and spelling are then introduced, in sections that work as "tasters" for the fuller chapters to come dedicated to each topic (students needing a short survey of the basics can therefore turn here first). The evidence of the manuscripts themselves is also given due weight and is used to characterize Middle English scribal culture (as well as highlighting the sorts of interpretations made by subsequent editors) with a degree of detail and sensitivity unusual in a book for beginners.

Descriptive guides to each level of Chaucer's English begin with chapter 4, "Spelling and Pronunciation." After a patient introduction to phonemes and graphemes (and their possible relationships), and the rhyming and comparative evidence for Middle English phonology, the sounds and stress patterns themselves are set out. Due time is taken over the variants available to Chaucer and the apparent motivations for the occurrence of the less usual (especially rhyme). Chapter 5 moves us on to "Vocabulary." The elements derived from foreign sources are introduced in turn, primarily Latin, French, and Old Norse (though I did not understand why "neck" was presented as an instance of the latter [p. 69]). Their occurrence in Chaucer's lexicon next to words of native origin is then treated in more detail, with a particular focus on lexical field competition; a range of interesting examples illustrates the choice between synonyms in different contexts. Horobin's presentation here is subtle and penetrating, taking account not only of likely shades of connotation, but indicating the considerable interest to be had in examining Chaucer's sources (especially for the *Romaunt*), and identifying changes in diction across his career. Chapter 6, "Grammar," is largely descriptive, taking each part of speech in turn, but it presents a useful range of details (including the rarer/more marginal forms and how Chaucer exploits them); again, there is some helpful discussion of style and connotation, especially for *thou* vs. *ye*.

Chapter 7 ("Language and Style") begins the task of drawing together the material described in the foregoing chapters, to enable a more holistic discussion of Chaucer's linguistic tones and strategies. This chapter constitutes a fascinating introduction to "levels of style," including a knowledgeable and sensitive use of Chaucer's own comments on the subject, and a number of case studies of particular words and contexts. The primary focus is on poetry, but there is also a tremendously engaging section on Chaucer's prose, which introduces such issues as the "curial" style alongside some skillful source criticism. Chapter 8, finally, presents a very readable foray into "Discourse and Pragmatics" as applied to Chaucer. The topics covered include forms of address, politeness strategies (including the concept of "face"), discourse markers, and an entertaining section on swearing; there is then a final, synoptic discussion, which illustrates how Chaucer constructs a range of styles by manipulating these pragmatic conventions.

Middle English texts are presented cleanly and clearly throughout, with underlined words glossed in the right-hand margin. Annotation is kept light, constituted in the main by the short sections at the end of each chapter, which offer suggestions for further reading. There is also an Appendix of six annotated excerpts from Chaucer's texts; these provide further brief examples of the types of analysis taught in the book, and offer useful additional materials for the student to play with.

In sum, this is an excellent resource for those undertaking study of Chaucer's language for the first time. It contains a deceptively large amount of information for a slim volume, and presents it skillfully and with patient deference to the beginner. It has the air, in fact, of deriving ultimately from a very good introductory lecture course, and is none the worse for that. Its discursive, abundantly exemplified approach, indicative of an author impeccably well versed in the Chaucerian corpus, puts it very much in the same tradition as the books by Elliott and Burnley, appropriately and imaginatively updated for the modern student. Just occasionally I felt that more explanation could have been provided to meet the needs of absolute beginners, especially as regards grammar: I found no explanation of "case," for instance, even though it is referred to in passing as a concept, and case categories appear in the paradigms on pp. 97 and 100. In this connection, the Glossary of Linguistic Terms (pp. 192–93) strikes one as being too short realistically to aid the struggling novice (perhaps for fear of putting off nervous students by proffering too many technical terms in one place?). It also seems a pity that facsimiles of relevant manuscript folios could not have been introduced to accompany the discussion of scribal outputs and variant readings, adduced particularly at pp. 46–50. But these are quibbles. Attentive readers of this book will find themselves in command not just of the traditional "handbook" materials relevant to the study of Chaucerian English (grammar, phonology), but they should also come away with the linguistic tools required to analyze Chaucer's texts in close stylistic detail, and most importantly will find themselves stimulated by Horobin's canny examples to try their own hands at doing just this. The book will accordingly be a boon to undergraduates, particularly (but not only) those preparing for examinations that require detailed commentary on passages of Middle English. Issued with careful direction by teachers, its contents should also be of no little benefit and interest to high school students encountering medieval English for the first time.

RICHARD DANCE
St. Catharine's College, Cambridge

KATHRYN KERBY-FULTON. *Books Under Suspicion: Censorship and Tolerance of Revelatory Writing in Late Medieval England.* Notre Dame, Ind.: University of Notre Dame Press, 2006. Pp. lii, 562. $50.00.

Books Under Suspicion "explores censorship and tolerance of controversial revelatory theology in England from 1329 to 1437" (p. 2) and the "history of dissent *before* Wycliffism" (p. 30). Yet Wycliffism remains on the table throughout most of this book, beginning with the assertion that this particular heresy "represents a confluence of several different, indeed larger, kinds of struggle and dissent" (p. 4). Quite rightly, Kerby-Fulton states that "Wycliffism . . . would have looked [to medieval authorities] like part of a long-standing tradition of academic inquiry and interclerical controversy that periodically exploded into public struggle . . . with external authorities" (p. 5). She adds to the call for scholars of Wycliffism to broaden their insular view of heresy (see pp. 37, 100, 135); Pamela Gradon, Wendy Scase, and Rita Copeland have already made important strides in this respect, teaching us, as Kerby-Fulton plans to show here, that Wycliffism "was not unique (it was not even wholly original), and it was not alone in being suspect" (p. 3). For her, other modes of dissent "also deserve fair hearing" (p. 4). So *Books Under Suspicion* begins the hearing in its exploration of Hildegaardian, Joachite, Olivian, and Rupescissan radicalism in late medieval England.

Readers of *Books Under Suspicion* will find some useful summary of these radicalisms (pp. 38–62). They will also learn about the circulation in late medieval England of books (including derivatives and extracts) by Hildegaard of Bingen, Joachim of Fiore, Peter Olivi, and his student John of Rupescissa—mainly between pages 81–108. There are also provocative arguments later in this study, such as the suggestion that Guillaume Court, "one of FitzRalph's supporters" (p. 135), introduced the anti-Joachite Protocol of Anagni to England (and, specifically, to Richard Kilvington) as a means of bolstering their attacks against the friars with fresh facts. And there are especially stimulating paragraphs on the surge of Hildegaardian extracts in the late fourteenth and early fifteenth century (191 n. 12). It is in light of these particular and important contributions that much of *Books Under Suspicion* shows itself to be beholden to a judgment call not to write about those tantalizing books per se (p. 81; see p. 88), but rather to argue about the influence of their contents among fourteenth- and fifteenth-century vernacular writers: "This study, which has to be pioneering and cover so much ground at once, has only been able to gesture at much that still lies buried in manuscripts and archives. . . . Attempting to discuss both the intellectual issues and the manuscript evidence, throughout the study I have had to balance this history against the question of its impact on vernacular literary writers" (p. 396). Some of these readings are refreshing, such as the line-by-line comparison between Marguerite Porete's *Mirror*, its Middle English translation, and the articles of the Council of Vienne's *Ad Nostrum* (pp. 285–88); the questioning of the work of Walter Brut (pp. 305–8); and the parallels between Chaucer and Langland (pp. 343–44). Much of this book, however, pursues the additionally difficult and not entirely successful agenda of proving that "the major literary writers of the period show at least as much, if not more interest in kinds of radicalism other than Lollardy" (p. 12).

Kerby-Fulton finds Wycliffism to be inconsequential in the grand scheme of things because Wyclif and his followers, unlike "the major literary writers of the period," are claimed to be hostile to prophecy and visionary theology (pp. 70, 142, 230, 304). To my mind, the book itself disproves this point, once the arguments over some 500 pages are distilled. Wyclif did warm up to Hildegaardian prophecy (pp. 194–95); Wycliffites do engage in revelatory modes, such as Walter Brut (pp. 79, 305–8), William Ramsbury (pp. 266, 270–71), the author of *Opus Arduum* (pp. 99–100, 218), and the priest William Taylor (pp. 197–98); Wycliffite and prophetic texts travel together in mixed compilations (pp. 66–67 cite three manuscripts; see pp. 42, 466 n. 7); perceptions about Wycliffism and radical visionary theology are blended by chroniclers—in Henry Knighton's Amourian description of the Wycliffites preaching the "Eternal Evangel" (p. 161) and the accounts of Peter Patteshulle, the friar turned Wycliffite. Anyone who reads Wycliffite texts closely knows that what is said in this book of Amourian, Hildegaardian, and Joachite eschatology—all merged terms here—could be said of numerous Wycliffite materials: "a sense of the periodization of history that included waves of Antichristian forces, such as the Pharisees, the heretics of the early church, and the present pseudo-apostles" (p. 134); "the view that it was against scripture that ecclesiastics might have temporalities" (p. 138); "the wisdom of the nobility in taking church restoration in hand" (p. 180). None of this convinces me that the "Wycliffites were desperately trying to keep their agenda apart from the revelatory one" (p. 393), and scholars of Wycliffism who wish to build on the author's arguments will have to turn the other cheek during the assertion of hyperbolic claims *cum* epithets about their subject of study, such as "new-fangled Wycliffism" (p. 4), "just Johnny-come-latelys" (p. 5), authors of "romantic nonsense" (p. 175), "new-fangled reformers" (p. 232), the "fashion of our time" (p. 388), and figments of the modern scholarly imagination (see pp. 37, 120, 233, 295, 378).

To me, it seems that the author's own examples show that Wycliffism matters *more*, in collective terms, than the many single instances she cites and potentially oversells. I say this because there is the frequent tendency here to treat one particular event, text, manuscript book, or even passage from a large literary work as singularly representative of a state of affairs. A condemnation of a friar at Oxford indicates that the

"Continental Inquisition Comes Calling" (pp. 135, 139). One Amourian passage of fifteen lines in the *Romaunt* (7107–21) "packed a punch" and "made notorious among vernacular readers the sensational doctrine of the 'fals comparisoun'" (p. 148; see also p. 161)—yet surely the fact that the *Romaunt* survives in one manuscript copy and one fragment must mitigate this claim of notoriety and the intention of the "Middle English writer." One surviving manuscript book, Cambridge University Library MS Dd.i.17, indicates that "the York Austins . . . were at the forefront of the study and transmission of radical prophecy" (p. 125)—letting alone that the provenance of this manuscript is an unknown (see pp. 115, 439 n. 26). One reference in *Opus Arduum* to friars absconding with suspect books becomes, after many iterations (pp. xlv, 9, 11, 39–41, 74, 79, 95, 103, 105, 154, 159, 201, 210, 271, 332, 348), the "confiscation campaign c.1389" (p. 378)—an event uncorroborated by any other source, including metropolitan and episcopal registers. In an effort similar to the tendency to take the one for the many, any and all inspired events—be they the anti-Lancastrian Bridlington prophecies (pp. 17, 213, 245) or the miracles associated with the cult of Archbishop Scrope (pp. 16, 238–39)—are swept up into the category of special "revelation" and taken as evidence of the purported hyper-charged background of Joachite, Olivian, and Rupescissan controversy.

Readers will have to handle with care the book's effort to insist upon connections between insular and Continental works. Take the Wycliffite *Opus Arduum*, whose writer, so it is argued, was "once exposed . . . to apocalypticism like Rupescissa's" (p. 225). The proof that he was "reading John of Rupescissa" (p. 216), at least when it comes down to passages that cite or mirror his work, is in one exact phrase: the writer speaks of *Opus Arduum* as a product of divine inspiration and not "from his own head" (ex capite meo), and Rupescissa says, "those things I say concerning the future I do not say from my own head [de capite meo]" (p. 211). The expression "de capite meo," however, is not limited to Rupescissa and is rather a piece of scholastic phraseology used to describe unwarranted, fanciful philosophizing and theologizing. Why could not the expression come from, say, Bonaventure's much earlier ninth colloquy in *Collationes De Septem Donis Spiritus Sancti* ("Nunquid eas fabricabo de capite meo?"). To take another example, Julian of Norwich's description of the "chongyng of colour" of Jesus' face during the crucifixion—"this image . . . he portraied it"—is taken to mean that "*Christ himself {is} the artist*, creating his own self-portrait" (p. 320). By this reading, the author concludes that Julian's "scientific" approach to images "springs" from an "older tradition" in the likes of the twelfth-century "*De diuersis artibus* by Theophilus" (p. 319).

Then there is William Langland, who in this book is the first (see p. 4) and most frequently cited of Middle English authors. This poet, we are told, "went into battle against . . . the piracy of Wycliffism and its pernicious doctrine of predestination" (p. 378) by adopting Uthred of Bolton's inclusivist theologies of salvation. Kerby-Fulton's theses about the "radical predestinarian view" (p. 365) of Wycliffism, and its "draconian positions" (p. 391; see also pp. 222, 332, 360, 377–78), are, frankly, blanket statements and will appear to scholars as such once J. P. Hornbeck II's 2007 Oxford D.Phil. thesis, "The Development of Heresy: Doctrinal Variation in English 'Lollard' Dissent, 1381–1521," is consulted: it shows the breadth and variety of Wycliffite salvation theology. Had Kerby-Fulton included more Wycliffite texts in her analysis, she might have found what Hornbeck found. Meanwhile, I was not persuaded by any of the readings of Langland, because to me they seem like overreading. For instance, a passage in *Piers Plowman* (B.X.328–32), with the lines "And þanne shal þe Abbot of Abyngdoun and all his issue for euere / Have a knok of a kyng, and incurable þe wounde," is said to be "exactly" like "Olivi's exegesis of the beast's 'mortal wound' (plaga mortis) of Revelation 13:11," a wound "dealt by clerical poverty" (p. 144). This is not the only place where Middle English lines are supposedly "exactly" like statements in visionary revelation (see pp. 339, 345). Notwithstanding, as Langland has it, the "wound" is dealt by Constantine ("kyng"), not by "clerical poverty" (see also C.V.175; B.X.314–15; 326). It also matters that Langland, unlike Olivi, grounds his reflections in Isaiah 14:5–6, not Revelation. Other readings could use more work. The point that Langland "makes allusion to [the pseudo-Hildegaardian] 'Insurgent'" in C.XV.51*a* seems unlikely (see p. 191). So too does the suggestion that the line "Lawe wolde he ȝoue hym lyf *and he loked on hym* (C.XX.423–24)" is a "dramatic allusion to God's absolute power (*potentia absoluta*) in the Ockhamist sense" (p. 382), or the notion that John But's words in the A text of *Piers Plowman*—"þou shalt be lauȝth into lyȝth with loking of an eye"—is "an overlooked allusion to Uthred's condemned doctrine of *clara visio*" [p. 388]). Then there is the reading of the B text of *Piers Plowman* in Cambridge University Library MS Dd.i.17. The *Regnum spiritus sancti*, which is said to bear "a Joachite exegetical twist" (p. 117) in the way its material is extracted from its source, the *Belial*, also appears in Dd.i.17, along with many other items. And because *Piers Plowman* is compiled with *Regnum*, Langland's alliterative poem seems "nearly Joachite in exegetical complexity" (p. 119). Not only that: Langland's work could be *"mistaken* for Joachism" (p. 119; see pp. 156, 159, 338). I detect some problems with this analysis of *Piers Plowman* B, beginning with the curious citation of passages from a C-text edition of the poem ("CIII.436ff.," "C.XXI.219–24; BXIX.217 [*sic*]," "C.V168," "C.VIII.343ff," "C.XX.408–14" [pp. 118–20]) in the midst of a potentially important codicological reading of Dd.i.17. There is also no demonstration of how "C.XX.408–14" displays the "same combination of apocalyptic exegesis and salvational generosity [that] appears in various Joachite contexts" (p. 120); rather, we are told it is the same. Lastly, and as Kerby-Fulton acknowledges, Dd.i.17 exhibits "scribal highlighting" (p. 122) of choice prophetic passages in *Regnum*, but scholars might like to know that no such activity is on display in Dd.i.17's copy of Langland's poem, nothing in the relevant passages under discussion save a postmedieval note (according to Benson and Blanchfield) on the Abbot of Abingdon lines. I do not think it can be claimed, even as a hypothetical, that medieval readers could mistake the Dd.i.17 *Piers Plowman* for Joachism.

In view of the analyses mentioned above, it seems overconfident to my ears to claim with special emphasis that a particular kind of revelatory influence "was much more pervasive among all our writers than *concrete* evidence of Wycliffism" (p. 335; see also p. 12). The charges could be very easily reversed. It's one thing to grow weary of a critical paradigm that is much the sensation at conferences and goes by a funny name ("lollardy"), even if that paradigm is centered on massive amounts of textual and historical evidence. It's quite another to tire of that paradigm but endeavor to explain away its supporting evidence as just so much modern scholarly myopia, insularity, and pseudo-historiography. The latter is the impossible task pursued in *Books Under Suspicion*, which knows (but quickly forgets) that there was a copious secular, ecclesiastical, and authorial response to Wycliffism: "hundreds of pages of trial records, condemned articles, chronicle accounts, treatises, and antiheterodox legislation" (p. 12). If we are to believe that such cultural activity is suddenly outshone by the aforementioned, often one-word allusions to the *"more* dangerous" forms of "controversial thinking" (p. 14), then this book has set the bar too high for itself. To be clear, there is smart material here; readers especially will want to engage Kerby-

Fulton's analyses of the *Chastising of God's Children* and the Middle English translation of Porete's *Mirror*. Indeed, the author asks a lot of good questions, but my sense is that her considerable talents in codicology should have been brought more fully to bear in an evaluation of Hildegaardian and Joachite books in England without the repeated turn to Middle English texts by Langland, Chaucer, Julian, and Margery to prove the value or ubiquity of this or that radicalism, as if ubiquity is the sole criterion for importance. It is fair to say that the author understands perfectly well the difficulty of this project and the controversy and doubt it not only describes but is likely to produce: "How or whether these things impacted on Ricardian and early Lancastrian writers is very difficult to assess, and much of what I hope to do here is to simply open up new possibilities to allow others to explore and judge for themselves" (p. 37).

ANDREW COLE
University of Georgia

EMMA LIPTON. *Affections of the Mind: The Politics of Sacramental Marriage in Late Medieval English Literature*. Notre Dame, Ind.: University of Notre Dame Press, 2007. Pp. 246. $32.00 paper.

Emma Lipton looks at four very different texts from the late Middle Ages in England—Chaucer's *Franklin's Tale*, Gower's relatively ignored *Traitié pour Essampler les Amantz Marietz*, the plays dealing with Mary in the N-Town cycle, and *The Book of Margery Kempe*—for evidence that new views of marriage were developing with the increasing influence of the class she refers to as the "emergent lay middle strata of society." The nub of the argument has to do with the different concepts of marriage held by emerging new orders of society, as love became what she calls "a discourse of power" in the fourteenth century. This is obviously linked to other developments: the movement toward clerical celibacy from the twelfth century, and the growing emphasis in the late Middle Ages on the role of the marriage partners rather than the officiating cleric in the dispensation of the Sacrament. It is the emphasis that is new here, rather than the doctrine, and Lipton summarizes the argument succinctly: "The lay middle strata were specifically drawn to the sacramental model of marriage in contrast to the sexual model and the hierarchical model, embraced respectively by clergy and aristocracy" (p. 4).

Beginning from, and ending with, an interesting thought about how modern controversies about gay marriage show that marriage does not have as invariable a social operation as we might think, Lipton outlines the debates of the Sacrament in her period. The marked variety of genre and provenance in the texts considered leads to differences that are not quite articulated here, though they are obvious enough. Both the N-Town Mary plays and *Margery Kempe* are interestingly examined in relation to tensions between orthodoxy and heterodoxy in East Anglia, connected with controversies about Lollardy there; the centrally canonical *Franklin's Tale* clearly comes from a very different world. Gower's *Traitié*, written after the *Confessio Amantis* and appended to it in seven out of ten manuscripts, is a sententious series of short verse tales of classical heroes, written in Anglo-Norman French and Latin. Lipton shows revealingly that the *Traitié* is concerned with male behavior within marriage, rather than with kingship; it is interesting, for instance, that in the *Confessio Amantis,* Aristotle's advice to Alexander about the control of lust is expressly said to apply to him as king, whereas in the *Traitié* David's desire for Bathsheba is "the story of everyman." In the *Traitié,* Gower sets marriage above chastity, in language that Lipton shows to be secular-legal rather than ecclesiastical. The concern is with male behavior in marriage—a striking move away from what Coffman long ago called Gower's "most significant role": articulating the ideas and responsibilities of kingship.

The *Traitié* is the focus of the second chapter here, subtitled "Marriage and Masculinity in John Gower's *Traitié.*" The familiar *locus classicus* for the debate of husbandly responsibility in late Middle English literature is of course Chaucer's *Franklin's Tale*—and perhaps the preceding "Marriage Group," whatever terms we use to describe that nowadays. It is not surprising to hear in the opening chapter, "Married Friendship," that the *Franklin's Tale* "describes marriage as an equal and mutual relationship based in friendship"; but the discussion of how this works in the *Tale* is very enlightening, particularly on the old dilemma of the conclusion that removes Dorigen from the closing *démande,* "which was the mooste fre?"—the merchant-husband, the clerk or the philosopher, but not, it seems, the virtuous wife. Lipton's general argument provides a satisfactory answer, at least in the terms in which she scrutinizes the marriage texts of the period: the lay, bourgeois concern was with the responsibility of husbands, even if in this semihomiletic setting Dorigen has a degree of agency and choice far beyond that of the romance-heroine Emelye in *The Knight's Tale*. Lipton puts this—twice—in striking terms: "Whereas the opening of the tale is recounted in a compressed style that parodies the parataxis of romance, after the exchange of vows between Dorigen and Arveragus discourse-time extends well beyond story-time, and the narrative dilation seems to resemble the expansive form of sermons as the Franklin temporarily takes on the discursive style of a preacher," invoking what "thise clerkes seyn."

Interesting as these opening two chapters are, Lipton's theme becomes both clearer and more revealing in the last two, East Anglian chapters, which are the book's most valuable contribution, particularly because the political significance of the debates comes into clearer focus there. The N-Town plays examined (in the chapter "Performing Reform," which serves as an excellent introduction to the context of this fascinating compilation-cycle), are "Joachim and Anna," "The Marriage of Mary and Joseph," and "The Trial of Mary and Joseph." The general theme of the developing bourgeois view of marriage, relating to procreation, celibacy, and sexuality, is placed in the context of the line between orthodoxy and heterodoxy, recently shown by Anne Hudson, Sarah Beckwith, and Dyan Elliott (among others) to be a good deal more blurred than was previously assumed. Reading these plays in the context of contemporary East Anglian religious politics brings them to vivid life. In the first play Joachim, significantly, is a merchant: a figure of the lay bourgeoisie. Most effectively of all, the forensic exchanges with the Detractors in the Trial play are linked to the heresy trials in Norwich from 1428 to 1431, which show the accused attacking clerical authority by arguing that marriage was superior to celibacy.

This contextualizing is even more marked in the last chapter, "The Marriage of Love and Sex," about Margery Kempe's *Book*. To put it briefly, Lipton argues that Kempe's highly physical representation of her loving relations with Christ, while she resisted sexual commerce with her husband, was making a very strong statement of the necessity of sex in the most exalted marriage. Christ's mystical marriage with Margery is expressed in the terms of the marriage formula (where Lipton even draws on Austin's idea of the performative). The case against celibacy could not be put more forcefully. Like the N-Town chapter, this is an excellent introduction to the *Book*, setting it in the context of the newly popular bourgeois manuals of manners.

By the end, the term "Sacramental" in Lipton's title, accurate and justified as it is in Augustinian, doctrinal terms, seems slightly misleading. The emphasis has shifted decisively toward the secular bourgeois. The term "class" might have been adopted more generally than "strata" (especially as there is some uncertainty from the very start about whether to treat that noun as singular or plural). Lipton occasionally gives vent herself to a bourgeois, "middle strata" indignation: she says twice in so many words that in the *Traitié*, "Tristan and Ulysses are revealed to be domestic horrors" (they are certainly not a model of marital manners, it is true); *The Book of Margery Kempe* depicts "marital sex as horribly oppressive and unclean." But, even if the book does not exactly establish a genre of marriage-related literature from around 1400, it is a model of how texts can be read closely in their context to the benefit of both literary and historical understanding.

Bernard O'Donoghue
Wadham College, Oxford

Robert J. Meyer-Lee. *Poets and Power from Chaucer to Wyatt*. Cambridge: Cambridge University Press, 2007. Pp. xii, 297. £50.00; $90.00.

Robert Meyer-Lee's *Poets and Power from Chaucer to Wyatt* explores familiar territory from an unfamiliar perspective. In one sense this is yet another study of the evolution of premodern subjectivity, the development of a personal voice in reaction to, or in concert with, the exercise of institutionalized power. But rather than relying, like most new historicists, on an anachronistic Foucauldian paradigm, Meyer-Lee looks to sober literary history to provide him with a structure for his narrative. The results, while not likely to be uncontentious, are consistently perceptive and stimulating.

Down to the late fourteenth century, says Meyer-Lee, neither named authors (paradigmatically, writers of chronicles and histories) nor anonymous first-person lyricists were expected to project a sense of personal presence in their work. Self-expression was generic, not only in the literary sense (which it can hardly avoid being), but also in the sense that nonpatented drugs are generic—that is, nondiscrete, common to all. All

this changed with the arrival on the scene of the self-fashioning Petrarchan court poet, however. What Meyer-Lee calls "laureate poetics," by
forcing the writer to confront the source of his authority and the nature
of his relationship to political power, forced him into a new definition
of himself. In fifteenth-century England, he claims, this definition took
two principal forms, the sententious self-aggrandizement of John Lydgate and the self-conscious mendicancy of Thomas Hoccleve—the first
a court outsider drawn to look to the crown for poetic legitimation, the
second an insider forced to beg his very livelihood from the same source.
Meyer-Lee shows how the inevitable conflict between glorification and
subservience works itself out in the self-fashioning, not only of these
two poets, but in their successors, Benedict Burgh and George Ashby.
Of course, as he fully recognizes, nothing approaching a fully institutionalized laureateship existed in the English court before Henry VII
(and perhaps not even then), and one of the most fascinating sections of
the book is the disillusionment Meyer-Lee detects in the three early
Tudor writers, Stephen Hawes, Alexander Barclay, and John Skelton,
who had finally to come to terms with its unsatisfying actuality. Not
the least of this study's ironies is that laureate poetics seem only to
have functioned effectively as long as they were merely notional; the
appointment of an actual laureate was to signal their demise. In an
interesting coda, Meyer-Lee discusses the apparent turn from laureate
poetics exemplified by Sir Thomas Wyatt.

In many ways, *Poets and Power from Chaucer to Wyatt* rewrites standard
literary history, replacing Geoffrey Chaucer with John Lydgate at the
center of the late medieval English literary tradition. While this is not
necessarily wrong (later literary history may well diverge from contemporary perceptions—as New Criticism famously did in the case of the
metaphysicals, for example), it certainly seems counterintuitive. For
most readers, the Chaucerian persona looks far more highly-wrought
than its Lydgatean counterpart, despite the fact that Meyer-Lee leads us
to believe that Chaucer's laureate poetics were less evolved. What is
really at issue here, though, is not actual self-fashioning as such, but the
fashioning of a sense of individuality, and, as Meyer-Lee is quite ready
to concede, this is not something that interested Lydgate very much
(whether because of his personal inclinations, his monastic vocation, or
his laureate aspirations, is of course a moot point). Yet we might argue
that it is precisely his evocation of individuality that makes Geoffrey

Chaucer so attractive to later writers (and hence so central to the tradition). It is all very well for Meyer-Lee to conclude that Lydgate "permanently altered [literary] history's course by putting into place a relationship between poets and power that, even to this day, haunts English poetry's greatest claims to be something other than mere words" (p. 232), but the best illustration of that course he can come up with is a pompous and prosy sonnet in favor of capital punishment by a valetudinarian William Wordsworth—if this makes him "the most paradigmatic of English Romantics," give me a Browning monologue any day!

In view of the large claims made by *Poets and Power,* its somewhat selective use of evidence is rather worrying. Given Lydgate's enormous corpus, some omissions are inevitable (indeed merciful), but surely his *Testament* is particularly relevant here. After all, when he tackles self-fashioning head on, it is to Augustine, not Petrarch, that Lydgate turns. And what of Wyatt's clever little court satire "Myn owne Iohn Poynz"? And should we not learn more of what was happening on the Continent? The Burgundian court is mentioned, but François Villon (perhaps the most individual voice in all medieval literature) is not; nor are the *rhétoriqueurs* (perhaps the most stylistically self-conscious). What, indeed, was going on elsewhere in the English literary scene? Was self-fashioning not just as much a feature of the mystical tradition? It would be difficult to think of someone more remote from laureate poetics than Margery Kempe, yet for most readers the sense of a personal presence that she projects is as at least as strong as Thomas Hoccleve's. Finally, there is a certain reductiveness in all this: particularly in the case of John Skelton, it is somewhat galling to find that this brilliant, if flawed, poet is being judged by Lydgatean standards and found wanting.

I do not wish to end on a negative note. There is a great deal to admire in *Poets and Power*: it is clearly and forcefully written and offers a number of brilliant individual readings of poems by Lydgate and Hoccleve and their successors. Its central thesis is boldly presented, and while it is certainly bracing to be offered such an original taxonomy of late Middle English courtly poetics, readers must ultimately decide for themselves whether it is one that accounts for all the facts.

RICHARD FIRTH GREEN
The Ohio State University

SUSAN E. PHILLIPS. *Transforming Talk: The Problem with Gossip in Late Medieval England*. University Park: Pennsylvania State University Press, 2007. Pp. x, 238. $45.00.

Transforming Talk is a carefully researched book with a laudable objective ·to revise previous scholarship on gossip and its relation to authority. Sometimes Susan Phillips is successful in realizing her objective. Often, however, she falls short of her aim, failing to synthesize her observations into the sophisticated and ambitious readings that her perspicacity would lead us to expect. A major issue for much of the book is Phillips's puzzling reluctance to develop a more elaborate theory regarding the relationship between gender and gossip, even when both the texts and her own observations strongly suggest that ideas about gender play a crucial role in late medieval treatments of gossip.

The title tells us that *Transforming Talk* is about gossip in late medieval England, but Phillips's concerns are actually more specific than this, involving the relation between idle talk and the pastoral. The book investigates, in Phillips's words, "the intersection between unofficial speech, pastoral practice, and literary production in late medieval England" (p. 10). Thus, other gossip-related phenomena—like the increasing legal concern over defamation and scolding in late medieval and early modern England—are not extensively addressed in this work.

Phillips's engaging premise is that earlier studies have been mistaken in regarding gossip only as the resistant tool of marginalized groups. These studies—which focus on how medieval women used gossip to resist social oppression—fail to account for the influence of gossip on orthodox literary and religious practices. Phillips wishes to demonstrate that gossip in late medieval England was also a vehicle of canonical poets and ecclesiastical authorities, who used the discursive phenomenon of "idle talk" as a tool of literary and intellectual transformation. In the later Middle Ages, Phillips proposes, "transformation rather than transgression" (p. 5) best describes gossip's function.

The first chapter—which considers *Jacob's Well*, Robert Mannyng's *Handlyng Synne*, and Wrath's confession from Langland's *Piers Plowman* (B-text)—is the strongest of the book. Here Phillips examines how preachers and moralizing poets both decried idle talk as a grave sin and, ironically, exploited its discursive characteristics for their own rhetorical ends. The chapter begins with a refreshing critique of recent scholarship on late medieval religious culture, arguing that an intense focus on heresy has led scholars to ignore the importance of more workaday problems, like the idle talk of parishioners. Idle talk, Phillips argues, poses a fundamental challenge to ecclesiastical authority because "it is not just the pastime of unruly congregations, it is the strategy of the clerics who instruct them" (p. 15). Noting the clerical need to hold an audience's attention, as well as instruct them, Phillips outlines how, in their use of exempla, preachers and writers of penitential manuals often reproduced the idle talk they condemned. A section on Wrath's Confession in the *Piers Plowman* B-text examines Langland's consciousness that idle talk is embedded in confession "as it was both practiced and theorized by medieval authorities" (p. 42) and describes how authorities' exhortation to penitents to produce highly detailed accounts of sin encourages parishioners to gossip about the transgressions of others. These are all interesting points and it is too bad that Phillips's conclusion ventures only that exemplarity and confession are vulnerable to gossip because they both depend on storytelling.

Chapter 2—which aims to explore how Chaucer "uses idle talk not just as subject, but as method" (p. 66)—is praiseworthy for the fact that it broadens out from the *Canterbury Tales* to include one of the less-discussed dream visions (the *House of Fame*). And certainly there is much of value to say about gossip and its relation to Chaucer's writing. Unfortunately, Phillips does not say enough. To begin with, she considers too many Chaucerian passages to provide a satisfying reading of any single one. The *House of Fame, The Man of Law's Introduction*, the *Tales* of the Friar and Summoner, the Host's interjections, *The Canon's Yeoman's Tale*, and *The Wife of Bath's Prologue* and *Tale* are all considered in a mere fifty-two pages. Moreover, Phillips disappoints in her unwillingness to issue larger claims about the texts she considers. Over and over again, exciting observations about Chaucer's work devolve into very limited and modest conclusions. Her conclusion with regard to *The House of Fame*, for instance, is that Chaucer's authorial strategy in the piece is analogous to the idle talk he describes, "augmenting, conflating, concealing, and multiplying" (p. 80) his classical sources to make them new. This is quite a limited conclusion. I wish that Phillips had presented us with some analysis regarding why Chaucer would want to conflate his technique with idle talk when it is actually part of a long-standing medieval tradition of classical source alteration.

It is also in the Chaucer chapter that we see the first sign of Phillips's reluctance to formulate a more thorough reading out of the numerous, very insightful observations she makes regarding the role of gender in late medieval treatments of idle talk. An interesting section on the Host's commentaries notes the Host's habit of converting the tales he hears into exempla and using these exemplary readings as a vehicle for his gender politics. Phillips makes another fascinating observation when she notes that while Chaucer explicitly associates gossip with women in *The Wife of Bath's Prologue* and *Tale*, most of the gossips in the *Canterbury Tales* are men. In her discussion of *The Wife of Bath's Prologue*, Phillips proposes that "the Wife's mastery of gossip is less about women's inability to keep secrets than about idle talk's potential for narrative transformation" (p. 109). The gossiping men, the Host's obsession with gender, and the unruly woman who shows us how idle talk enables narrative transformation: all of this would seem to provide fertile ground for an analysis of Chaucer's take on the relation between gender and idle talk, and yet Phillips does not present us with anything but isolated observations.

Chapter 3—which considers Chaucer's *Shipman's Tale* and Dunbar's *Tretis of the Tua Mariit Wemen and the Wedo*—features the same strengths and weaknesses as Chapter 2. Phillips begins with an excellent examination of how pastoral practice and idle talk intertwine in the opening conversation of the monk and the wife of *The Shipman's Tale*, describing how the two use language to transform their relationship from confessor and penitent to gossiping lovers. Unfortunately, Phillips ends here and does not address how this conversation relates to the rest of the tale. Her analysis of Dunbar's poem describes the Wedo's appropriation of confessional practice. Noting that the poem merges a variety of different literary traditions, Phillips proposes that confessional gossip is not only Dunbar's subject but also his method, allowing him to conflate a variety of different literary traditions. Phillips's reading ends here, and we are left asking why Dunbar would choose women as his vehicles for undermining the pastoral and what this suggests about his views on the relationship of both women and the writer to idle talk.

After the first chapter, chapter 4 is the strongest of the book. It addresses two early sixteenth-century English translations of French works, the *Fyftene Joyes of Maryage* (1507, 1509) and the *Gospelles of Dystaues* (c. 1510), both published by Wynkyn de Worde. Asserting that previous work on female friends has focused too much on the tavern conviviality so often associated with "gossips," Phillips argues that these literary characters can only be understood through the lens of baptismal sponsorship. What follows is a highly edifying genealogy of gossips, tracing the different behaviors identified with literary gossips back to women's historical participation in the lying in and purification rituals of medieval childbirth.

Examining both the text and illustrations of the two translations, Phillips describes how both works raise the specter of women's pastoral instruction, and both foreclose on this possibility by making women's speech appear unproductive and ineffectual. Noting the emergence of unauthorized female textual communities in the later Middle Ages, Phillips proposes that the drunken gatherings of these "literary gossips" reveal deep cultural anxieties about the potential dangers posed by women's words. The strengths of this chapter also suggest problems with Phillips's original premise. By providing us with such a wonderfully thorough account of how "idle talk" could be mobilized to marginalize certain speakers and certain forms of speech, she returns us to the question of politics in a way that is not fully explained by her theory of gossip as transformation.

The responsibility for *Transforming Talk*'s failure to fulfill its promise should not be laid entirely at the author's doorstep. With a couple of notable exceptions (like Holly Crocker's *Chaucer's Visions of Manhood* and Tison Pugh's *Queering Medieval Genres*), books produced by the newest generation of scholars of Middle English have failed to expand upon the pioneering feminist and gender studies work of the 1990s. The widespread absence of new gender analysis in Middle English studies—compared with its continued flourishing in the study of other literary periods and even in other areas of medieval English studies, like history—suggests that this is less a problem with new scholars than it is with the leadership in the field: that is, those who guide dissertations and determine what gets published. Authority and marginalization, it appears, are salient issues not only for medieval authors but also for those who study them.

NICOLE NOLAN SIDHU
East Carolina University

MARTHA DANA RUST. *Imaginary Worlds in Medieval Books: Exploring the Manuscript Matrix*. New York: Palgrave Macmillan, 2007. Pp. 290. $69.95.

In *Imaginary Worlds in Medieval Books*, Martha Dana Rust offers readings of several fifteenth-century manuscripts and their texts in order to illuminate what she calls "the manuscript matrix." She expands the meaning of this term (borrowed from Stephen Nichols) through Heidegger, positing the medieval manuscript matrix as a "space that enables being and thinking," a virtual locale in which readers interact with books "as if they bounded a virtual, externalized imaginative faculty" (pp. 7, 5). This concept of a space that embraces both the physical volume and its reader's imagination is crucial to the book's primary objective: to bring together the material with the textual, and the codicological with the verbal, without giving primacy or priority to either one. This approach to medieval reading counterintuitively suggests that the literary concept of character can depend on such ephemeral details as rubrication and plot upon catchwords. As Rust explains, "The manuscript matrix is an imagined, virtual dimension in which physical form and linguistic content function in dialectical reciprocity: a space in which words and pages, 'colours' of rhetoric and colors of ink, fictional characters and alphabetical characters, covers of books and veils of allegory function together in one overarching, category-crossing metasystem of systems of signs" (p. 9).

Rust's unorthodox understanding of medieval reading relies on three of its best-known qualities: "involved" reading, or the kind of imaginative meditation presupposed by devotional texts such as Nicholas Love's *Mirror of the Blessed Life of Jesus Christ;* a widespread codicological consciousness that makes legible the material support of reading matter; and the close connections in the period between reading and seeing, through which books and words and letters themselves become visual as well as linguistic means of communication. Taking all these characteristics together, Rust brings us a series of "tales" from the manuscript matrix, beginning with an interpretation of *The Book of the Duchess.* From Chaucer, she derives four common features that structure these tales: an initiating situation involving a reader or writer and a material text; a trick, ruse, artifice, or experiment that serves as a catalyst; the representation of the main character in one of multiple semiotic systems; and finally the frequent definition of that character in codicological terms.

These features appear inconsistently throughout the three central chapters, which stand as independent case studies in the kinds of reading the manuscript matrix can produce. Chapter 1, "Into the Manuscript Matrix: Middle Letters for Readers of a Middle Sort," considers a number of Middle English abecedaria in their manuscript instantiations. Rust's interpretation turns on the words of an unidentified Italian preacher (perhaps Bernardino of Siena) describing a hierarchy of letters: pictures, written or alphabetic characters, spoken words, and mental letters ordained by God for contemplatives. It is the written characters he calls "middle letters," and Rust argues persuasively for the importance of these in a set of Middle English poems based on the alphabet. Chapter 2, " 'Straunge' Letters and Strange Loops in Bodleian Library MS Arch. Selden B.24," continues the connection between material books and immaterial texts, reading *Troilus and Criseyde* as it is preserved in one particular manuscript. Here Chaucer's heroine moves from the text into the book as she leaves Troy for the Greek camp, "slydyng" from the world of the poet into the world of the scribe and bringing romantic "variaunce" into contact with the textual kind. When Criseyde's signature—what should be "La vostre C"—looks instead very much like "Le vostre T," one can see lover, poet, and scribe all writing masculine will over feminine character. This chapter is the most successful in *Imaginary Worlds*, both for its persuasive argumentation and for the consequences of its imaginative reach. Chapter 3, "John's Page: A *Confessio amantis {librorum}* in Pierpont Morgan Library MS M.126," argues that Gower's *Confessio* as it is represented in one copiously illustrated manuscript stages connections between commentary and confession to show how several characters, and finally the author, exit the text and enter into the book. The three case studies conclude with an afterword about the scribe, "Ricardus Franciscus," who copied the Pierpont Morgan *Confessio*.

Rust gives ample warning that some of her readers may object to her enterprise in *Imaginary Worlds*: she acknowledges that her study may even seem "impressionistic," "subjective," "hypothetical," and "quixotic" (pp. 29–30). But she ultimately embraces these characterizations of her work, aiming to bring the forms of texts together with their meanings to "fulfill in a new and rigorous way" (p. 30) the promise of material philology. "Rigorous" is a surprise here in a catalogue of the author's goals, and it is not a word I would use to characterize this book. *Imaginary Worlds* is indeed imaginative, and its many strengths lie in Rust's ability to bring together her disparate materials in subjective and surprising ways. Its weaknesses likewise lie in its innovative methods, which are impressionistic and primarily analogical. Argument by analogy works to introduce a multitude of systems and terms without—for this reader—enough of an interpretative payoff for the work required to sort through them. If a set of stanzas function like a pair of prayer beads

(p. 61), or a manuscript opening is like the Theban history Criseyde leaves off reading (p. 111), or a commentary is like the process of empire-building (p. 129), or a pointing hand in a miniature is like a manicule in the margins (p. 146), the proof of the pudding is simply in how apt the local comparison seems.

Reading texts instead of manuscripts produces scholarly interpretations that have little to do with the ways in which medieval readers encountered their literature. Reading manuscripts instead of texts prioritizes histories of production over the verbal constructs at the center of the literary critical enterprise. *Imaginary Worlds in Medieval Books* seeks to bring literary criticism deeply into conversation with manuscript studies, and even though its conclusions are sometimes debatable, the project is important and worthy. Manuscripts give us more, Rust argues, than insight into the social and material conditions of medieval reading. They form a part of literary consciousness itself, and their physical features are never fully transparent to those—modern or medieval—who read texts in their original forms.

JESSICA BRANTLEY
Yale University

CATHERINE SANOK. *Her Life Historical: Exemplarity and Female Saints' Lives in Late Medieval England*. Philadelphia: University of Pennsylvania Press, 2007. Pp. xviii, 256. $55.00.

Her Life Historical is an extremely elegant book, well written and closely argued. Catherine Sanok uses the notion of exemplarity to understand the cultural position of the female saint's life in later medieval England. She concentrates on the fifteenth century and the "individual legend," a subgenre consisting of versions that "circulated independently of large legendaries" (pp. 39–41). In separate chapters she offers extended readings of Osbern Bokenham's midcentury *Legends of Holy Women*, which she takes as an attempt to construct a canon of the female saint's life, and of Henry Bradshaw's late-century *Life of St. Werburge*. She also offers a brilliant reading of Margery Kempe's use of both the Mary Magdalene and virgin martyr legends. These discussions are book-ended by two readings of Chaucer texts, *The Legend of Good Women* and *The Second Nun's Tale*.

Sanok treats exemplarity as a broadly based cultural and ideological reflex. She associates it with *imitatio* in the devotional, rather than specifically rhetorical sense. Exemplarity becomes a mode of imitating the past, or—perhaps to put the matter more precisely—a way of imagining continuity between past and present as if it were an imitation. Sanok's method is eclectic in the best sense. She draws on Michel de Certeau, Judith Butler, and Homi Bhabha. She also commandeers the phrase made famous by Benedict Anderson, "imagined community," and makes it one of the book's central tropes. In relation to the steadily growing conversation on exemplarity itself, Sanok belongs solidly among those stressing the mode's interest in continuity, as opposed to those who stress its unruliness. At the same time, this is a continuity enacted against a founding break. As she explains, "the central fiction of exemplarity is that ethics are transhistorical, independent of their particular historical moment and social context" (p. 7). Thus, "the mimesis implied in exemplarity . . . works like metaphor: it both affiliates two things and alienates or distances them from one another" (p. 14). A female reader embracing a saint as exemplar does so against the implicit recognition of the saint's sacral and historical distance.

Sanok's interest in *imitatio* leads her to characterize her book as a study of reception. Indeed, one of *Her Life Historical*'s many virtues is its lucid, careful deployment of current scholarship on later Middle English book ownership and patronage by women, and related textual matters, both in the second chapter, where she addresses these issues in general terms, and thereafter, as she focuses on individual works. However, the consistent central focus of Sanok's argument is narrower and more delimited. It is what she calls the "exemplary address" that female saints' lives characteristically make to an imagined female community. She concludes her survey of the external evidence with Chaucer's exploration of the "feminine audience created through hagiography's ethical address" in *The Legend of Good Women* (p. 42). She then argues in detail that Bokenham and Bradshaw use that address to envision an alternative form of community based on gender and defined by "devotional literature and practice" (p. 49). This is "a stable community . . . in contrast to the divided political community of the fifteenth century" (p. 83). In Bokenham's *Legends*, "the only English legendary organized by the category of sex" and the period's "best single witness to women's literary patronage" (p. 51), the main vehicle for this vision is the complex and often topical series of comparisons between his patrons and the saints whose legends he recounts.

Writing in the tense years just before the Wars of the Roses, Bokenham seeks stability in examples of contemporary female virtue. Bradshaw, writing after 1485, seeks stability by establishing a continuity with the distant past, exemplified in the life of the seventh-century Mercian princess and abbess St. Werburge. Her virginity intact throughout her life, in spite of various pressures to marry, and assaults by rapists miraculously turned back, Werburge's corpse remains incorruptible for two centuries, only to be allowed to decay in advance of the Danish invasions, "to protect it from contamination by pagan hands" (p. 101). As Sanok nicely observes, this delayed dissolution is an even greater miracle. In its decaying form, Werburge's corpse serves to protect Chester, and by extension England, from "innumerable barbarike nacions" (p. 102). Both *The Book of Margery Kempe* and *The Second Nun's Tale* provide a convincing counterpoint. Both use the "imitation of a traditional saint" to criticize the contemporary community "by comparing it to the social world depicted in traditional legends" (p. 116). Margery is like Mary Magdalene in receiving full remission for a life of sexual activity and self-regard, and, like her, even more strikingly in her weeping. She is thus able to approach the authority that enables Magdalene to preach, though she is careful never actually to claim it. Sanok reads Margery's reclamation of the state of a virgin as an *imitatio* of Cecilia, one that enables her, like Cecilia, to defy male judges. She then uses *The Second Nun's Tale* as a "vehicle for exploring saints' plays" (p. 166), especially virgin martyr pageants—now all lost. Noting their frequent affiliations with parish guilds, she suggests that they offered themselves as orthodox alternatives to clerical authority. Sanok reads the Second Nun as an "ethical imitation of the legend she tells" (p. 167). Like Cecilia, the Second Nun preaches to a public audience. In the world of the early Church, she recalls that women played an active role, contrasting unfavorably with the constraints placed on them in her own time.

As sometimes happens with tightly argued studies, this one is occasionally fuzzy around the edges. That this imagined female community is so thoroughly superintended by male writers strikes me as a problem, one that Sanok never really addresses, except for a brief acknowledgment at the end of David Aers's critique of similar arguments. I also found her view of fifteenth-century politics slightly formulaic—as if its disorder had the same paradigmatic valence for those who lived through it as it has come to acquire for modern historiography. She is surely wrong to claim that "the fantasy of a continuous political structure" was "impossible to sustain in fifteenth-century England" (p. 49). How else do we understand the motivation for the War of the Roses, except as competing versions of precisely that fantasy? The century's recurrent dynastic struggles should not blind us to the other models of national community that emerged or intensified, models of which Sanok herself has now happily offered us an additional, compelling instance.

LARRY SCANLON
Rutgers, N.J.

SUSAN SCHIBANOFF. *Chaucer's Queer Poetics: Rereading the Dream Trio*. Toronto: University of Toronto Press, 2006. Pp. x, 308. $75.00.

Chaucer's Queer Poetics takes its place alongside other important recent contributions to Chaucer criticism, like those by Glenn Burger and Carolyn Dinshaw, that explore queer sexualities, both as they are represented within individual texts and as they evoke models of reading that disturb comfortable "natural" responses to Chaucer's poetry. Susan Schibanoff's book goes further, however, in proposing a "queer poetics" (on analogy to Dinshaw's "sexual poetics," p. 13) that informs Chaucer's writing and extends back to his earliest poetry (most other Chaucer critics working within queer studies focus on the *Canterbury Tales*, especially on the Pardoner). In challenging the traditional division of Chaucer's career into French, Italian, and English periods, Schibanoff proposes a revisionist trajectory that has Chaucer experimenting with a queer narrator as early as his first major poem, *The Book of the Duchess*; then developing features of that narrator into a provisional, if inconclusive, poetic theory in *The House of Fame*; and finally confidently embodying aspects of a queer poetic in the allegorical figure of a "lesbian" Nature in the *Parliament of Fowls*. Schibanoff thus disrupts the traditional "escape narrative" of Chaucer's gradual liberation as an English poet of nature, subtly revealing the overlapping significances of terms like "English," "French," and "queer," at the same time introducing a rich and flexible new critical vocabulary for characterizing Chaucer's art.

Schibanoff constructs this vocabulary partly from close readings of Chaucer's three self-contained dream visions and partly from a learned investigation of Chaucer's sources and the intellectual traditions upon which he was drawing. This method gives her book an impressive scope and usefulness for both the uninitiated reader and the seasoned scholar. Readings of Chaucer's individual poems are interlaced with exciting new analyses of his source texts. In the Introduction and chapter 1, for example, Schibanoff quickly and clearly describes a heteronormative "hylomorphic" poetics, which imposed masculine form on feminine matter and which the Middle Ages derived from Aristotelian physics and biology. She follows this with a history of anti-French, "anti-courtly polemic" in contemporary critics and in their nineteenth-century and medieval forebears, placing next to each other such divergent figures as Orderic Vitalis (1075–1142) and Lee Patterson. The first chapter concludes with brief, acute readings of the twelfth-century *Roman d'Eneas*, and of Chaucer's *Miller's* and *Merchant's Tales*, texts that employ the character of the "queer foil," whose function she identifies as deflecting anxiety about male feminization in the courtly tradition.

Chapter 2 extends these themes and structures into *The Book of the Duchess*, where, Schibanoff argues, the narrator's passivity constitutes his "queerness" (in this case not to be taken over-literally) and "serves as the foil to enhance [the man in] Black's creative agency" (p. 89). The narrator's "unnatural" restraint implicitly challenges the hylomorphic poetics described earlier, which was transmitted by many of Chaucer's sources. The exchange between the dreaming narrator and the bereaved knight also substitutes a new Thomistic reciprocal pedagogy (pp. 83–86), which granted agency to both learner and teacher, for more conventional medieval models of "instruction" (p. 73), where knowledge was simply deposited by a master into the pupil's mind. While grounded in modern "queer theory," this reading of *The Book of the Duchess* is also historically informed and attuned to the poem's likely power dynamics, especially to the deference a young Chaucer would have owed to the subject and recipient of his poem, John of Gaunt.

In similar synthetic fashion, later chapters weave backgrounds and foregrounds together seamlessly. Schibanoff, for instance, follows up a thorough and critically current discussion of Dante's "hermaphrodite poetics" in the *Commedia* (chapter 3) with a discussion of the queer architectonics of Chaucer's *House of Fame* (chapter 4). Likewise, before the book moves on to "Nature's Queer Poetics" (the subtitle of chapter 6) in Chaucer's *Parliament of Fowls*, chapter 5 meticulously traces Nature's lineage back to the goddess Nature, and her sidekick Genius, in Jean de Meun and Alan of Lille and to the Aristotelian concept of *physis*, a locus of sexual equivocation due to its origins in the ambiguous Platonic World Soul (pp. 215–16). Schibanoff's reading of Alan's *Complaint of Nature* is particularly fertile and attentive to both the structure and detail of that difficult poem. This brief summary of the intricate alternation of source text, philosophical background, and Chaucerian countertext hardly does justice to the elegance, richness, and clarity of Schibanoff's treatment of the complex network of Chaucer's roots in a queer intellectual history to which her book makes a significant contribution.

Not all sections of the book are equally compelling. Over-reading and selective use of evidence occasionally mar the analysis, as, for example, when a single reference to Vulcan (line 138), another to Juno (lines 198–99), and a later allusion to Ganymede (line 589), form the basis of an elaborate argument that Book I of *The House of Fame* represents a failed attempt to "normalize" the Aeneas story (pp. 157–77). Such moments, however, are rare. More typical are the illuminating readings of the Ovidian mythographic tradition, of Jean Froissart and related French courtly writers, of Alan's *Anticlaudianus*, Dante's *Convivio*, and several other Chaucerian texts especially from the *Canterbury Tales* (on which *Chaucer's Queer Poetics* ends in its "Au revoir" chapter).

Its many virtues leave one all the more surprised that no sustained analysis of Chaucer's fourth and final dream vision appears in this excellent volume (why the "dream trio" and not the "dream quartet"?). The Prologue to *The Legend of Good Women*, cast as a dream, presents some of the clearest evidence in favor of the traditional "escape narrative" that Schibanoff vigorously debunks, as it arguably displays the effete (or queer) narrator in the process of being enslaved to a courtly poetic and devising, perhaps, a subversive mode of counterattack. What might Schibanoff have to say about the strained irony of the *Legend*? We never know, nor does it seem she ever intends to tell us, for even as she hints that the *Canterbury Tales* may be the subject of "another book" (p. 306), she is done with the *Legend* (beyond a handful of scattered references) before she begins.

It would be unfair to conclude, however, by criticizing Schibanoff for *not* writing about a text she does not set out to consider—especially when she herself as a writer is unfailingly generous and fair-minded with the work of her colleagues. *Chaucer's Queer Poetics* is a mature study that participates in the best traditions of scholarly discourse: collaborative, inquisitive, untiring, and refreshingly undoctrinaire.

KATHRYN L. LYNCH
Wellesley College

KARL TAMBURR. *The Harrowing of Hell in Medieval England*. Cambridge: D. S. Brewer, 2007. Pp. xii, 211. £50.00; $85.00.

The harrowing of hell is distinctive to the Middle Ages and in some ways helps to define medieval culture. Although medieval commentators were able to find only the most oblique references to it in the New Testament, its centrality to the life of Christ was seldom in dispute. In the *Legenda Aurea,* Jacobus de Voragine neatly sums up the medieval attitude to the harrowing in his chapter on the resurrection: "Concerning the seventh and last issue that needs to be considered here, namely how Christ led out the holy fathers who were in limbo and what he did there, the gospel has declared nothing openly. Nevertheless, Augustine in a certain one of his sermons and Nicodemus in his own gospel have revealed something of this."

The authorities are the pseudo-Augustine *Sermo 160 De Pascha* (*PL* 39:2059–61) and the *Gospel of Nicodemus*, which contains what in the Middle Ages was regarded as authentic testimony of the harrowing. Postmedieval theology, both Protestant and Catholic, based itself more strictly on the scriptural canon and so denied the authority of the apocryphal gospel. This characteristically medieval idea of the harrowing of hell has been explored a number of times in articles and within monographs and critical editions concerned with larger subjects. Karl Tamburr's book, however, is the first attempt to deal with the subject in its own right as it appeared in the culture of medieval England. The focus is mainly on textual traditions, including the liturgy, but there is as well a rich body of visual representations of the subject, and he uses this material here to provide points of reference in different periods and contexts.

This book has strengths and weaknesses. The strengths are its range of reference and the author's willingness to investigate a variety of texts and visual representations. It draws on material from the early Christian

402

period to the sixteenth century. Weaknesses emerge mainly in connection with specific issues, although there are flaws as well in the way Tamburr understands some of the functions of the harrowing of hell in medieval popular religion, or what has come to be known as vernacular theology. Tamburr describes the book as "a series of interrelated essays." This, he readily acknowledges, means that the study is not comprehensive; nevertheless, it would have been helpful for him to have made explicit the criteria for inclusion and exclusion of material. For example, why is there no mention of fifteenth-century Middle English prose translations of the *Gospel of Nicodemus* and their relationships to the literature of affective piety? The pseudo-Bonaventure *Meditationes Vitae Christi* makes much of Christ's descent into hell, but it receives no mention here. How does the harrowing of hell function in these contexts?

Some of the problems with the book stem from the way Tamburr struggles with the medieval theology of the redemption. In Christian writing, the harrowing of hell developed as a vehicle to dramatize ideas and arguments concerned with the redemption of human kind. Tamburr makes reference to formulations of aspects of the redemption but in places fails to recognize their theological implications or the contexts out of which they grew, as in the discussion of Ælfric's sermon for Palm Sunday (pp. 20–21). In the opening of chapter 4, Tamburr does not seem to grasp the dynamics and significances of Anselm's pivotal work, the *Cur Deus Homo*, and fails to take account of the range of research on the changes in attitudes to the redemption that emerged in the twelfth century, following Anselm. Tamburr's discussion of the harrowing of hell in *Piers Plowman* (B.XVIII/C.XX) refers to "the Devil's rights theory of the atonement" (p. 145). First, "atonement" is not medieval but sixteenth-century usage (meaning "at-one-ment"), where it translates *reconciliatio* in the Bible; the more appropriate term for medieval literature and theology is "redemption." Further, "the Devil's rights" is not a theory of the redemption but refers to only one aspect of the medieval doctrine. In its many forms, the harrowing of hell is a mirror of changing attitudes and doctrine concerning the redemption. This monograph would have had more coherence had the author developed a firmer grasp of this purpose for the subject of the harrowing of hell.

Most of the problems, however, concern specific issues of method and the use of secondary material, and these raise questions about how well informed the book is. I have given a few examples here. As one would expect in something so wide ranging, modern scholarship serves as the guide to primary sources, but in some instances the range of reference in secondary writing is narrow and incomplete. In 1933, J. A. MacCulloch published a classic monograph, the full title of which is *The Harrowing of Hell: A Comparative Study of an Early Christian Doctrine*. This book serves as Tamburr's main guide to the writings of the early church fathers where one would expect a synthesis based on more extensive and recent work on the secondary literature. Chapter 2 discusses the notion of Christ as the "warrior king" and makes much of the traditional theme of *Christus Victor*, but makes no use of or reference to Gustaf Aulén's classic book of the same title. Chapter 3 discusses the Seventh Blickling Homily and its Latin sources for the treatment of the harrowing of hell (pp. 72–73), but it fails to recognize that the third paragraph of the pseudo-Augustine *Sermo 160 De Pascha* has parallels in and very likely derives from chapters 22 and 23 of the Latin *Gospel of Nicodemus*, which explains why both texts contain the crucial statement of the devil's abuse of power. Tamburr's commentary on the homily (p. 73) is effectively a commentary on a portion of the *Gospel of Nicodemus*. For the York and Towneley plays of the harrowing, Tamburr seems not to be aware of the compiler's use of the Middle English *Stanzaic Gospel of Nicodemus* (pp. 121–22), and he does not recognize the significance for the play of the substitution of the debate between Jesus and Satan (lines 213–334) for the argument between Hell and Satan that originates in chapter 23 of the *Gospel of Nicodemus*: he discusses the form of this passage (pp. 125–28), but not what it indicates about how the compiler sought to adapt his raw material in response to contemporary ideas about the redemption. These points of reference are not obscure but are readily available in recent scholarship, and they should have been taken into account.

The bibliography needs to be brought up to date in certain areas. The most serious omission is James Cross's edition, *Two Old English Apocrypha and Their Manuscript Source: "The Gospel of Nichodemus" and "The Avenging of the Saviour"* (Cambridge University Press, 1996), which is based on an important discovery about the Latin textual tradition that lies behind the Old English translation and that for this and many other reasons replaces Hulme's printings of 1893 and 1903/4. The editions by Peter Clemoes and Malcolm Godden of Ælfric's homilies (EETS s.s. 5, 17, 18; 1979, 1997, 2000) have replaced Thorpe's edition of 1844–46. S. A. J. Bradley's volume of translations of Old English poetry (1982) has replaced R. K. Gordon's (1926) in the Everyman series.

This book is a worthwhile project with much of interest, and there is no doubting the author's enthusiasm for the subject. Unfortunately it contains a number of flaws that are distracting. A critical reading before publication could have detected and put right many of these problems.

WILLIAM MARX
University of Wales, Lampeter

ALFRED THOMAS. *A Blessed Shore: England and Bohemia from Chaucer to Shakespeare*. Ithaca: Cornell University Press, 2007. Pp. 256. $45.00.

"A quarrel in a far away country between people of whom we know nothing": with these words, Neville Chamberlain justified the Munich Agreement of 1938 to his English constituents, dismissing as irrelevant the struggles over the border regions of the young state of Czechoslovakia. The great chasm separating the British Isles from Bohemia—a kingdom roughly coextensive with today's Czech Republic—was not simply geographical, of course. India and its political interests seemed near enough to Chamberlain's still-imperial Britain. Nor, apparently, was this particular chasm a recent development. Shakespeare's attribution of a coastline to landlocked Bohemia in *The Winter's Tale* has frequently been cited as evidence of long-standing English ignorance of the most basic features of the small, central European kingdom. If subsequent events transformed Chamberlain's proud "appeasement" into one of foreign policy's dirtiest words, they did little to bring Bohemia's inhabitants further into the consciousness of Anglophones. With the Czechs sequestered on the far side of the Iron Curtain, it became easier than ever to forget that Bohemia had belonged to Latin Christendom and that Prague had once been a leading city of the Holy Roman Empire, even the capital city of emperors Charles IV (1346–78) and Rudolf II (1576–1612).

Alfred Thomas reminds us of Bohemia's premodern prominence with a welcome literary history that seeks to bridge two important—if partly imaginary—chasms: between Bohemia and England and between the Middle Ages and the Renaissance. To do so, Thomas spans the academic divisions that separate the study of Europe's past and its vernacular literatures according to the boundaries of its modern nation-states. That makes this book difficult to categorize. It also makes it a refreshing and important contribution to the study of European culture from the fourteenth through the seventeenth centuries.

Anne of Bohemia supplies the book's first connection between England and Bohemia. Daughter of Charles IV, king of Bohemia and Holy Roman Emperor, Anne was Richard II of England's queen from 1382 to 1394. We know frustratingly little about her activities. It is not even clear that she learned any English. But Thomas suggests in the first chapter that Anne, as a "cultural mediatrix," likely served Chaucer as an "imaginary" rather than a real patron, a symbol of the leading humanistic culture of her father's court. Here and in the second chapter, Thomas argues that members of Richard II's court would have recognized England as culturally marginal in comparison with the great imperial court of Charles IV at Prague. Richard's queen and his own later efforts to gain the imperial crown together provide Thomas the frames for discussing well-known works of medieval English literature—such as *The Legend of Good Women*, *The Parliament of Fowls*, *Sir Gawain and the Green Knight*, and the *Pearl*—in the context of far less familiar German and Czech vernacular works, including Smil Flaka's *The New Council* (1385), *The Plowman* (1401), *The Weaver* (c. 1406–7), and the fourteenth-century Czech verse *Life of Saint Catherine*. Similarities of genre, style, and symbolism may not uncover direct borrowing in either direction, but they certainly attest to a common literary culture.

Chapters 3 and 4 address the long-recognized influence of the ideas of John Wyclif (d. 1384) on Jan Hus (burned at the stake in 1415) and the Bohemian Hussites. Much of the third chapter is devoted to the vernacular works of Peter Chelcický, a second-generation follower of Hus, who rejected the militarism of both mainstream Hussites (Utraquists) and radical Taborites to champion pacifism and—Thomas argues—an American-style separation of church and state. In the same chapter, letters between Hus and a Lollard leader illustrate one of the book's central arguments—that writers from each land tended to idealize the other, constructing it as a utopian foil to their own land. Thus Hussites and Lollards each saw the other as an ideal home for pure religion communicated in vernacular language. Chapter 4 shifts to an exploration of women in fifteenth-century Bohemia, primarily through a close reading of an anti-Hussite Czech poem, "The Wycliffite Woman," a satirical dawn song that Thomas translates.

The final three chapters (5–7) draw heavily from accounts of and by travelers. Bohemian visitors to England included a Catholic ambassador from the fifteenth-century Hussite king and, in the seventeenth century, a Protestant baron, a noted engraver, and Comenius, the Protestant humanist and educator. Chapter 6 focuses on English travelers to Bohemia during the time of Shakespeare and Rudolf II, when recusants such as Elizabeth Jane Weston found Bohemia an oasis of toleration, a place where Protestants, Catholics, and Jews all flourished. The visits of John Dee, Edward Kelley, Sir Philip Sidney, and Edmund Campion S.J. further inform Thomas's attempt to characterize the Bohemia of Shakespeare's imagination. Thomas concludes that it was not geographical ignorance, but rather partial knowledge of Rudolf's court that inspired Shakespeare's account of the pagan land that provided a safe haven for Perdita in *The Winter's Tale*. For Thomas, Shakespeare's fictive Bohemia and his play's happy conclusion therefore offer "evidence of his ecumenical hopes for a world in which Catholics and Protestants might live together in peace and harmony" (p. 170).

Together, these chapters represent an impressive and important contribution. The book is fundamentally a literary history, and Thomas is strongest when he is analyzing texts, from medieval poems and mirrors for princes to early modern travel accounts. At times, the bridge he builds between the history and literature of England and Bohemia threatens to obscure the extent to which both kingdoms shared in a broader European culture. Late medieval ideals of female royal sanctity, for example, linked England not only to Bohemia but also to nearly every other ruling dynasty of Europe, as Gábor Klaniczay showed in *Holy Rulers and Blessed Princesses* (Cambridge, 2002). This book's broad and unconventional scope is its great strength, but the same scope will inevitably tempt specialists—like this reviewer, a historian of medieval Bohemia—to quibble over details and lament particular omissions. For instance, Thomas's extended analysis of the Wilton diptych's portrayal of Richard II with England's patron saints could be strengthened by comparison with the analogous depiction of Charles IV and Bohemia's patron saints on the well-studied altar panel commissioned by Prague's archbishop in the 1370s. Also, Milíč of Kroměříž, a Prague preacher and so-called Father of the Bohemian Reformation, was certainly never a Dominican, as Thomas asserts (p. 135). Indeed, the Dominicans, one of several influential religious orders in medieval Bohemia, stand out in this book for the surprising number of generalizations they attract.

Such details do not significantly mar the book's achievement. Perhaps most innovative is Thomas's focus on the Bohemia of English imagination and, to a lesser extent, the England of Bohemian imagination. This motif provides one of the book's stronger links between the otherwise relatively diverse chapters. In one sense, the chapter on the Czech anti-Hussite poem—"The Wycliffite Woman"—seems most out of place. Yet it too belongs here, as its detailed engagement with recent arguments about gender, literacy, and heresy in medieval England best exemplifies the book's consistent efforts to address scholars of medieval and Renaissance English literature. More than a few of them, I hope, will be inspired to explore further the Czech and German literature of medieval and early modern Bohemia. For this, they should begin by consulting Alfred Thomas's other publications.

DAVID MENGEL
Xavier University

MARION TURNER. *Chaucerian Conflict: Languages of Antagonism in Late Fourteenth-Century London*. Oxford: Clarendon Press, 2007. Pp. viii, 213. £53.00; $95.00.

We have come a long way from the "quiet hierarchies" that D. W. Robertson proposed for the intellectual and social formation of the medieval world. Now conflict, treason, heresy, and social rivalries are detected in every byway of fourteenth-century London. Book titles provide a synopsis of prevailing outlooks: Steven Justice's *Writing and Rebellion* (1994), Peggy Knapp's *Chaucer and the Social Contest* (2000), and my own *Chaucer and Langland: The Antagonistic Tradition* (2007). Marion Turner's book exposes a particularly deadly, depressing version of Greenblatt's arena of social contests. Chaucer was "concerned with depicting the inevitably destructive nature of human fellowship and society" (p. 2) and held out "no hope for social amelioration" (p. 5). So we have also come a long way from E. Talbot Donaldson's jolly, amicable author.

Chapter 1, "Discursive Turbulence," launches the now-normal historicist operation of reading between literary and nonliterary texts. Precise dating of the poet's output therefore becomes crucial, and *The House of*

Fame is repositioned to the mid-1380s on the basis of a long-standing view persuasively resurrected by Helen Cooper. Chaucer's dream-poem assumes new meaning in the context of Richard II's 1387 proclamation against slander as well as the parallel crackdown by Mayor Brembre that figured in the complaint of the *Mercers' Petition*. Chaucer personifies Slander as having the swiftness and destructive power of a cannonball (lines 1625–44), and his appeal for personal anonymity (lines 1876–82) fantasizes an evasion from this newly aggressive surveillance. As an enactment of caution, *The House of Fame* refuses to name the "man of gret auctorite" and breaks off without reporting what he said or he did.

Chapter 2, "Urban Treason," discusses how *Troilus* with its domestic betrayals, first by Calchas, then by his daughter Criseyde, and finally by Antenor—with the foreigner Sinon significantly omitted—gains meaning in context of the letters accusing London aldermen of aiding the 1381 rebels by opening the capital's gates. The manipulation of Deiphoebus dramatizes how appeals to "common profit" cloaked self-serving schemes that actually undercut prospects for peace. Perhaps the most lethal traitor is Pandarus, whose opportunistic, can-do optimism distracts from the tragic outcomes awaiting the principal players.

Chapter 3, "Troynovant in the Late Fourteenth Century," builds on the work of Sylvia Federico's *New Troy* to explore the civic fantasy "always already inhabited by potential division" (p. 56). Not gesturing to some past ideal, Chaucer becomes the realist whose Troy materializes as a palimpsest for London. His Troy/Troilus wordplay invokes the Freudian parallel between individual and national mythmaking. This nationalist mythology collapses in Chaucer's Trojan epic, just as it did in Gower's *Vox clamantis,* Maidstone's *Concordia,* and *St. Erkenwald*, because each text exposes divisive bids for dominance by royal power, juridical authority, and competing professional estates.

Chapter 4, "Ricardian Communities," focuses on the factionalist and early member of Chaucer's audience, Thomas Usk, who became a victim of these urban conflicts. His textual output neatly divides into the documentary *Appeal* and the literary *Testament of Love*. In his attempts to straddle the political divisions between royal court and civic communities—and extract from a misprision of *Troilus* a redemptive ideal of social coherence—Usk ended up abandoned by King Richard and scapegoated on behalf of urban interests by the Lords Appellant. As a royal servant, he clearly lacked the wiles of Pandarus (and Chaucer) to maneuver safely under the radar. Triangulating these two literary works with historical records of the 1380s, Turner offers perhaps the best intertextual reading to date of Usk's *Testament*.

Chapter 5, "The Canterbury Fellowship and Urban Associational Form," explores the reach of these urban antagonisms into the social harmony of the *Tales*, carefully policed by the Host and expressed in language reminiscent of the guild returns of 1388–89: "In compaigney we schal han no debaat" (*CT* III.1288). Pledges of fellowship prove illusory as mutual suspicion breeds the conflicts dramatized by the narrative *quitings*. Though cruelty marks the exchange between the London-based Cook and Manciple, the quarreling almost comes to blows between the Host of Southwark and the Pardoner of Charing Cross. Once insulted, Harry Bailey as "governour" cannot constrain his own violent outbursts.

Chapter 6, "Conflict Resolved?" investigates Sir John Clanvowe's *Two Ways* and Philippe de Mézières's *Letter to Richard II* to show how texts that purport to eulogize reconciliation actually advocate alternative violence. Writers advancing peace between England and France transferred the chivalric impulse for aggression into a call for armed crusade. Richard II's efforts at suspending war with France were interpreted as a betrayal of the realm, and his counselors deserved execution for their treasons. With documented links to so many courtiers allied with the peace movement, Chaucer's own pacifist sentiments run throughout his writings and seem most explicit in the *Melibee*—or maybe not. Turner's persuasive reading of this allegory reveals that Prudence, rather than preaching blanket forgiveness, advocates "profitable" pragmatics best understood in terms of the conflicting economic interests of landowning knights and city-dwelling merchants and tradesmen.

Most readers will find the claim that "Chaucer's texts frequently reflect the chaos of the London that he knew" (p. 5) contrary to their own encounters with his poems. What has bare-knuckle urban politics to do with Palamon and Arcite, Arveragus and Dorigen, or Custance and Saint Cecilia? David Wallace's "Absent City" reminds us of the extent to which the turbulent London of the fourteenth century is strangely *missing* from Chaucer's works when compared with Gower's *Vox* and Langland's *Piers Plowman*.

That said, Turner's contemporary critical methods become a welcome departure from the same-old. Who else has summoned Slavoj Žižek to discuss Thomas Usk and Philippe de Mézières? As thesis supervisor, Paul Strohm has bequeathed a "social Chaucer" embedded in the "textual environment" of London infighting and projecting those anxieties, in repressed form, upon narratives like *Troilus* explicitly remote in time and place. An astute reader of these poems as social documents, Marion Turner carries forward this historicist project with surprising insight and admirable, sustained scholarly rigor.

JOHN M. BOWERS
University of Nevada, Las Vegas

ALISON WIGGINS and ROSALIND FIELD, eds. *Guy of Warwick: Icon and Ancestor*. Cambridge: D. S. Brewer, 2007. Pp. xxii, 226. £50.00; $85.00.

Guy of Warwick is one of the most popular figures of medieval literature and culture, particularly in England, where he gained the status of national hero. The romance *Guy of Warwick* has enjoyed a recent resurgence in critical attention as scholars begin to question the unflattering assessments of its literary quality by nineteenth- and early twentieth-century antiquarians. Recognition by scholars such as Velma Bourgeois Richmond and Thorlac Turville-Petre of the extent to which Guy functioned as a touchstone for early English national identity has brought the romances of Guy of Warwick into a much-deserved critical spotlight that has broadened to include new work on Guy in other literary genres and in other artistic media.

As the first book-length scholarly volume (other than editions) on Guy to appear in over a decade, *Guy of Warwick: Icon and Ancestor* is a most welcome addition to current scholarship on the legendary hero and his place in the English imagination. The collection offers new interdisciplinary research on topics as diverse as the manuscript histories of the Anglo-Norman and English-language Guy romances; nontextual and illustrative representations of Guy in the Middle Ages and the early modern period; political uses of Guy and his legend; and representations of women in Guy texts. Moreover, the volume engages the most current and influential trends in literary studies: gender theory, East-West relations, literary political activism, and translation theory, to name just a few. For the reader who is less familiar with the Guy romances, the volume's appendix includes both a short and a more detailed summary based on the famous Auchinleck manuscript of ca. 1330: one will want to consult the more developed account if possible, as the abridged version is quite skeletal. It should be noted, too, that the articles are supplemented by a series of fifteen glossy black-and-white photographs of manuscript illustrations, woodcuts, and artifacts referred to in several of the pieces.

The brief "Editorial Introduction" that opens the volume serves primarily to highlight the four themes of the collection: "the 'popularity' of the tradition; Guy's 'Englishness'; the ancestral-baronial interest in the story; and the passage of the medieval legend into the Renaissance" (p. xvi). It is particularly interested in how notions of popularity intersect with definitions of "high" and "low" literature.

Judith Weiss's chapter, "*Gui de Warewic* at Home and Abroad: A Hero for Europe," suggests that *Gui* is unusual among Anglo-Norman romances because it depicts the Byzantine Empire remarkably favorably in contrast to the Holy Roman Empire. As Weiss demonstrates, this unique dichotomy is based on England's historically good relations with Constantinople, which became home to many English emigrants after the Norman Conquest of 1066. In support of her thesis, Weiss proposes that the romance may have been composed rather earlier than its traditional dating: she prefers a date closer to the first years of the thirteenth century than the middle. This chapter is undoubtedly a valuable asset to scholars of the Anglo-Norman *Gui* and opens room for further study both of medieval notions of place/space and of the relationships between this romance and its English adaptations.

The first two-thirds of Marianne Ailes's chapter, "*Gui de Warewic* in Its Manuscript Context," consist of a review of the manuscripts of the Anglo-Norman *Gui* romance, including physical descriptions, provenance (where indicated), and, in the case of the fragments, how they correspond to Alfred Ewert's published edition (1932–33). Ailes's primary goal is to look at the manuscript contexts of *Gui* in order to establish its insular interests and the importance of its "secular piety" as a major *raison d'être*. Ailes also suggests that scholars should reconsider the genre grouping of "ancestral romance," in which *Gui* has often been included, due to the inconsistency of ancestral themes among these romances and because medieval manuscripts do not support a strong generic categorization along these lines. The fewer than two pages devoted to an examination of genre and form may leave the reader hoping for a more thorough treatment of this topic in a future piece by the author.

Drawing on most of the extant manuscripts of the Anglo-Norman

Gui de Warewic and the Middle English *Guy of Warwick*, Ivanà Djordjevic ("*Guy of Warwick* as a Translation") argues convincingly for a fundamental reexamination of medieval translation theory. Respectfully distancing herself from scholars such as Susan Crane, who focus on the differences between the French and English versions of the texts they study in order to highlight emergent English identities, Djordjevic demonstrates that in at least some instances—*Gui*/*Guy* included—the linguistic similarities between Anglo-Norman and English are much closer than modern printed editions have led us to believe. Meticulously comparing lines and passages of *Gui* and *Guy*, Djordjevic shows that many characteristics of the Middle English romance—such as a "strident note of Christian self-righteousness" (p. 33)—that have been considered uniquely "English" are, in fact, translated directly or loosely from Anglo-Norman predecessors. As Djordjevic points out, this analysis leads one to suspect that many medieval translators/adapters remained as faithful to their originals as possible as much out of convenience as out of a particular sense of obligation or respect for their sources.

In "From *Gui* to *Guy*: The Fashioning of a Popular Romance," Rosalind Field (like Djordjevic in the previous chapter) strives to impart to the reader a strong sense of continuity between the Anglo-Norman and the Middle English Guy romances. Opening with a discussion of three different measures of popularity (number of surviving manuscripts; whether a narrative is "high" or "low" literature; and how broadly it appeals to a range of audiences), Field argues that, while critics concur that both *Gui* and *Guy* were successful in terms of number of manuscripts produced, many scholars have created a false dichotomy between *Gui* and *Guy* in terms of literary quality and audience appeal. Though the "discontinuities" that Field sees in the romance may not all be universally agreed upon, she successfully demonstrates that many of the so-called popular tendencies of the Middle English versions of *Guy* are already present in their Anglo-Norman predecessors. Both the Anglo-Norman and the Middle English romances develop a more broad appeal over time, for instance, in their focus on secular piety and the shift away from including "disturbing" incidents that are found in earlier versions of the poems.

Alison Wiggins's chapter, "The Manuscripts and Texts of the Middle English *Guy of Warwick*," includes careful analyses of their relationships to Anglo-Norman versions; how they adapt and revise Guy material in accordance with changing tastes; and the possible movements of the manuscripts themselves among families and regions. Of particular value are Wiggins's reappraisal of the likely production context of the Auchinleck manuscript—including the suggestion that manuscripts very like the Auchinleck were probably produced on a regular basis—and her lengthy commentary on the meticulous excisions of the Caius manuscript (1470s).

Moving away from the focus on romance established by this volume in its previous chapters, in "The *Speculum Guy de Warwick* and Lydgate's *Guy of Warwick*: The Non-Romance Middle English Tradition," A. S. G. Edwards reviews the surviving manuscripts of two didactic poems that apparently draw on the popularity of the figure of Guy to heighten the appeal of their religious instruction. Edwards discusses several of the manuscripts in terms of the contexts of their production, their wide geographical distributions, and their possible patrons. The strongest sections of the chapter trace instances in which these poems appear with other works, thus providing evidence for the various uses to which medieval (and, in Lydgate's case, Renaissance) audiences put them.

Robert Rouse's close reading of the Middle English *Guy* in "An Exemplary Life: Guy of Warwick as Medieval Culture-Hero" seeks to trace the development of Guy's character through a series of "multiple yet complementary identities" (p. 109): the pinnacle of secular chivalry, the penitent knight of Christ, the divinely appointed savior of England, and the saintly hermit. Rouse particularly concentrates on moments of transition—such as Guy's starlit epiphany after his marriage—teasing the key appeals of the romance out of these scenes of heightened symbolism. Among the most important reasons for its long and widespread popularity is the sense of English national identity that Guy embodies and which may be read as sanctioned by God. Rouse also demonstrates how the figure of Felice is designed to appeal to a female audience.

David Griffith's chapter, "The Visual History of Guy of Warwick," is a thorough exploration of the appearances and uses of the legend of Guy of Warwick in material culture, both in manuscripts and in other artifacts. Beginning his more-or-less chronological analysis with Peter Langtoft's early fourteenth-century *Chronique d'Angleterre*, Griffith moves on to include discussions of the Taymouth Hours, the Smithfield Decretals, the Auchinleck manuscript, misericords in Wells and Gloucester cathedrals, lost paintings and carvings at Winchester, and the tapestries, manuscripts, and silver-inlaid maple bowl associated with the Beauchamp Earls of Warwick and their families. Though one may

414

sometimes wish for further substantiation of claims made about these relics, the chapter is quite useful both in the range of texts and artifacts it considers and in its astute observations about the interdependence of political programs and material production.

Martha Driver's " 'In her owne persone semly and bewteus': Representing Women in Stories of Guy of Warwick" explores both literary and illustrative depictions of women in the *Guy of Warwick* romance, the Rous Rolls, the Beauchamp Pageants, and other nonromance texts. Driver's primary interest is to demonstrate ways in which the character of Felice is used to provide a model for, and later perhaps a comfort and complement to, the influential (and, like Felice, dynastically important) women of the Beauchamp family in late medieval England. Perhaps the most valuable contribution of this piece is Driver's identification of an editorial misrepresentation of a scene in the Cambridge University Library manuscript: as in certain other versions of the story, the scene under scrutiny includes the use of a half-ring as an identifier used by Guy and Felice. Because all other versions involving the half-ring have close ties to the Beauchamps, Driver suggests that a fresh look at the CUL romance may be in order.

Siân Echard's "Of Dragons and Saracens: Guy and Bevis in Early Print Illustration" offers a comparison of the programs of illustration, beginning in 1503, of the printed versions of two romances that early modern and recent critics alike have tended to conflate. Despite the superficial similarities, the Bevis illustrations tend to depict the hero in struggles against Saracens, while Guy is more often shown slaying monstrous beasts and giants. The fact that these two romances developed distinctive illustrative traditions indicates that printers anticipated and responded to their readers' tastes, choosing images based on market demands. Conversely, the choice of illustrated scenes seems in some cases to have influenced which episodes were highlighted in or dropped from the textual narratives when they were adapted for later audiences.

In "*Guy of Warwick* and *The Faerie Queene*, Book II: Chivalry Through the Ages," Andrew King argues that Spenser reinterprets medieval romance tales of high cultural value and gives them new life within a Protestant context. Drawing parallels between the quests of Guy of Warwick and Spenser's Guyon, King shows how both texts explore the meaning of chivalry as the achievement of temperance and restraint in the face of provocation. Tracing common tropes such as the loss/abandonment of the knight's horse—the defining symbol of chivalry—King

415

demonstrates the extent and richness of Spenser's use of Guy in his allegorical masterpiece.

In "Guy as Early Modern English Hero," Helen Cooper looks at Guy's literary and cultural history from about 1590 through the twentieth century. Unlike many medieval romances, which either disappeared from the English literary tradition or became material only for "lowly" chapbooks, Guy enjoyed the attention of playwrights and acclaimed poets who reworked the narrative for diverse Reformation audiences glad to lavish interest on a distinctly English hero. The success of Cooper's two primary texts, the play *A Tragical History of Guy of Warwick* (1661) and Samuel Rowlands's *Famous Historie of Guy of Warwick* (1609), demonstrates the ongoing adaptability and appeal of the legendary figure for political and religious environments far removed from his medieval origins.

Overall, this collection of articles is an enriching read that demonstrates a remarkable continuity among the individual pieces. The volume may be read as a more-or-less chronological account of the cultural history of Guy of Warwick; this sense of continuity is accentuated by the frequent references of the authors to one another's work. This intra-textuality, however, also leads to a certain amount of overlap and repetition from one chapter to the next. Taken individually, the selection of articles is a praiseworthy one, offering compelling reading not only for the Guy specialist but also for scholars of the medieval and early modern periods generally.

One of the volume's weaknesses is the fact that a number of the authors fail adequately to engage Richmond's *The Legend of Guy of Warwick* (1996), a seminal work on Guy that seems to have been overlooked in part because it has already established so much of what interests the authors under consideration here; this neglect, however, is by no means universal among the contributors. Some readers will be disappointed also by the lack of attention given to non-English and French versions of the Guy legend, but this makes sense given the volume's stated topic and interests, and should not be seen as inherently detracting from what is already a well-rounded book of outstanding scholarly significance.

REBECCA A. WILCOX
University of Texas at Austin

KAREN A. WINSTEAD. *John Capgrave's Fifteenth Century*. Philadelphia: University of Pennsylvania Press, 2007. Pp. xiii, 231. $55.00.

Karen A. Winstead reappraises John Capgrave, routinely either patronized or ignored by modern criticism, as a thoughtful writer with a consistent focus on the major issues of his day. Capgrave, an Augustinian friar from Lynn, was a prolific writer in Latin and English. Though his *Life of St. Katherine* and his *Solace of Pilgrims*, a guidebook to the sights of Rome, have attracted some attention in recent years, the canon of Capgrave studies is still very small, and his reputation lags behind those of his contemporaries Lydgate, Hoccleve, and Bokenham. M. C. Seymour's 1996 biography dismissed Capgrave as dull, conservative, and insufficiently attuned to the onward march of literary history. Winstead's analysis, reading Capgrave in close textual detail in order to outline his positions on four key points, shows this assessment to be inadequate not only to the author, but to the complexity of what constituted conservatism and orthodoxy in the fifteenth century.

Winstead reads Capgrave's *Lives* of Saint Augustine and Saint Katherine as negative and positive exempla of the responsibilities of scholarly Christians. In hagiography, apparently minor variations on the received narratives may be significant, and Capgrave's variations are not minor. His *Life* of Augustine, the (supposed) founder of Capgrave's order, is unique among English *Lives* of the saint in its praise of public activity. Capgrave's Augustine is a model of the mixed life who resists the temptation of reclusive contemplation in order to carry out his duties as preacher, bishop, and public intellectual. Conversely, Katherine withdraws into private study and thereby loses the confidence of her nobles, her realm, and her life. Though this narrative is common to all versions of her life, Winstead argues that Capgrave's emphases and alterations add up to an implicit criticism of the saint's neglect of her secular responsibilities. For Augustinian friars, just as for modern academics, a good life balanced scholarship, teaching, and pastoral care.

Winstead elucidates the gray areas of fifteenth-century ecclesiastical politics in order to make sense of Capgrave's nuanced position (similar to that of Reginald Pecock) on heresy and the Church's reaction to it. Capgrave, as might be expected of a long-serving member of a religious order, was orthodox in his beliefs and loyal to the institutional Church. However, he had some sympathy for certain positions that modern read-

417

ers might assume were the property of Lollards: he discussed theological issues in the vernacular and hinted that an intellectual crackdown on heresy might be counterproductive. His ideal was of a "rational, intellectualized faith grounded in the study of Scripture" (p. 78). Capgrave was not a Lollard sympathizer, but Winstead shows that in the mid-fifteenth century there was more to orthodoxy than Arundel's Constitutions—and that apparently bland genres such as hagiography might be vehicles for vernacular theological enquiry.

Oddly enough, Capgrave, the author of one of the longest virgin martyr legends in Middle English, seems not to have been very interested in virginity. The argument relies in part on the negative evidence of opportunities to expand on virginity that Capgrave neglected, and in part on evidence for his engagement with pious matrons. Winstead acknowledges that there is no specific record of Capgrave having contact with his contemporary and neighbor Margery Kempe (who found Lynn's Augustinian friars tolerant of her crying in sermons), but draws attention to similarities between her *Book* and Capgrave's representation of pious women. The analysis returns to the *Life of St. Katherine* (evidently Winstead's favorite of Capgrave's works) with a perceptive reading of Katherine's mother as a fifteenth-century noblewoman, managing family interests.

Finally, Capgrave is placed within the tradition that David Lawton describes as the "dullness" of the fifteenth century. Like contemporaries such as Lydgate and Hoccleve, Capgrave found conventionality a convenient vehicle for comment on unsettled times. Winstead compares the *St. Katherine* with Lydgate's *St. Edmund*, a text generally accepted to have offered instruction on kingship to the young Henry VI. Katherine again features as a negative example, a monarch whose reluctance to rule—expressed in terms very similar to hostile descriptions of Henry VI's ineffective rule—led to the invasion of her capital and her own death. In both instances, as Winstead acknowledges, the poets have to wrestle with the generic norms of hagiography in order to expand its remit, with the surprising result that Capgrave represents the pagan emperor Maxentius as, at least initially, a more competent ruler that the Christian queen Katherine.

Although these arguments produce a coherent account of Capgrave's thought and works, some details of the analysis may be questioned. It is possible that the emphasis on authorial intention and coherence understates the effects of patronage and genre, and Capgrave's political personality seems curiously static for a man who lived through seventy-one turbulent years. Winstead supports the claim that *St. Katherine* encoded anxieties over Henry VI's rule by referring to its limited circulation: its content, she implies, made it a risky text. However, none of Capgrave's works circulated widely: indeed, *St. Katherine*, with four extant manuscripts, was probably (then as now) the most popular. Capgrave's extant, but unedited biblical commentaries are barely mentioned: it would be interesting to know whether they bear out the identification of his "dissident orthodoxy," or whether he thought differently in Latin scholarship. However, these are minor quibbles. This book is a persuasive and subtle analysis of a neglected writer in his historical, political, and regional contexts, which enriches the fields of vernacular theology, East Anglian culture, and fifteenth-century literature.

SARAH SALIH
King's College London

Books Received

Allen, Valerie. *On Farting: Language and Laughter in the Middle Ages*. New York: Palgrave Macmillan, 2007. Pp. xiii, 239. $69.95.

Ashton, Gail. *Chaucer's The Canterbury Tales*. London and New York: Continuum, 2007. Pp. vi, 121. £50.00, $75.00 cloth; £10.99, $14.95 paper.

Baker, Peter S. *Introduction to Old English*. 2nd ed. Malden and Oxford: Blackwell, 2007. Pp. xv, 388. $39.95 paper.

Barney, Stephen A. *The Penn Commentary on Piers Plowman*. Vol. 5: *C Passus 20–22; B Passus 18–20*. Philadelphia: University of Pennsylvania Press, 2006. Pp. xvi, 309. $65.00.

Brantley, Jessica. *Reading in the Wilderness: Private Devotion and Public Performance in Late Medieval England*. Chicago: University of Chicago Press, 2007. Pp. xviii, 463. $45.00.

Bryan, Jennifer. *Looking Inward: Devotional Reading and the Private Self in Late Medieval England*. Philadelphia: University of Pennsylvania Press, 2007. Pp. x, 270. $49.95.

Carlson, David R., ed. *The Deposition of Richard II: "The Record and Process of the Renunciation and Deposition of Richard II" (1399) and Related Writings*. Toronto: Pontifical Institute of Mediaeval Studies, 2007. Pp. viii, 104. $12.95 paper.

Cawsey, Kathy, and Jason Harris, eds. *Transmission and Transformation in the Middle Ages: Texts and Contexts*. Dublin: Four Courts Press, 2007. Pp. 212. £65.00.

Classen, Albrecht. *The Medieval Chastity Belt: A Myth-Making Process*. New York: Palgrave Macmillan, 2007. Pp. x, 222. $69.95.

Davis, Isabel. *Writing Masculinity in the Later Middle Ages.* Cambridge and New York: Cambridge University Press, 2007. Pp. xiii, 222. £48.00; $85.00.

Dempsey, James, trans. *The Court Poetry of Chaucer: A Facing-Page Translation in Modern English.* Lewiston, N.Y.: Edwin Mellen Press, 2007. Pp. ii, 192. $109.95.

Drayson, Elizabeth. *The King and the Whore: King Roderick and La Cava.* New York: Palgrave Macmillan, 2007. Pp. xii, 263. $79.95.

Fulton, Rachel, and Bruce Holsinger, eds. *History in the Comic Mode: Medieval Communities and the Matter of Person.* New York: Columbia University Press, 2007. Pp. 408. $45.00.

Galloway, Andrew. *Medieval Literature and Culture.* New York: Continuum, 2006. Pp. 154. $90.00 cloth; $16.95 paper.

―――. *The Penn Commentary on* Piers Plowman. Vol. 1: *C Prologue-Passus 4; B Prologue-Passus 4; A Prologue-Passus 4.* Philadelphia: University of Pennsylvania Press, 2006. Pp. xiv, 491. $95.00.

Giancarlo, Matthew. *Parliament and Literature in Late Medieval England.* Cambridge and New York: Cambridge University Press, 2007. Pp. xiv, 289. £50.00; $95.00.

Glaser, Joseph, ed. and trans. *Middle English Poetry in Modern Verse.* Indianapolis: Hackett Publishing Company, 2007. Pp. xiii, 234. $39.95 cloth, $12.95 paper.

Hanna, Ralph, ed. *Richard Rolle: Uncollected Prose and Verse with Related Northern Texts.* EETS o.s. 329. Oxford and New York: Oxford University Press, 2007. Pp. lxxviii, 233. £65.00; $199.

Hunter, Michael. *Editing Early Modern Texts: An Introduction to Principles and Practice.* New York: Palgrave Macmillan, 2007. Pp. xii, 171. $69.95.

Kuskin, William. *Symbolic Caxton: Literary Culture and Print Capitalism*. Notre Dame: University of Notre Dame Press, 2008. Pp. xxvi, 390. $40.00 paper.

Larrington, Carolyne. *King Arthur's Enchantresses: Morgan and Her Sisters in Arthurian Tradition*. London and New York: I. B. Tauris, 2006. Pp. viii, 264. £20.00; $35.00.

Lightsey, Scott. *Manmade Marvels in Medieval Culture and Literature*. New York: Palgrave Macmillan, 2007. Pp. xvi, 212. $65.00.

Lindeboom, B. W. *Venus' Owne Clerk: Chaucer's Debt to the Confessio Amantis*. Amsterdam and New York: Rodopi, 2007. Pp. 477. €100; $135.00.

Machan, Tim William, ed. *Chaucer's "Boece": A Critical Edition Based on Cambridge University Library, MS Ii.3.21, ff. 9r–180v*. Heidelberg: Universitätsverlag Winter, 2008. Pp. xlii, 193. 58.00.

Muir, Lynette R. *Love and Conflict in Medieval Drama: The Plays and Their Legacy*. Cambridge and New York: Cambridge University Press, 2007. Pp. xvi, 294. £50.00; $90.00.

Normington, Katie. *Modern Mysteries: Contemporary Productions of Medieval English Cycle Dramas*. Cambridge: D. S. Brewer, 2007. Pp. xiv, 192. £30.00; $55.00.

Nuttall, Jenni. *The Creation of Lancastrian Kingship: Literature, Language, and Politics in Late Medieval England*. Cambridge and New York: Cambridge University Press, 2007. Pp. x, 187. £50.00; $90.00.

Pearcy, Roy J. *Logic and Humour in the Fabliaux: An Essay in Applied Narratology*. Cambridge: D. S. Brewer, 2007. Pp. viii, 251. £55.00; $90.00.

Sobecki, Sebastian I. *The Sea and Medieval English Literature*. Cambridge: D. S. Brewer, 2008. Pp. xii, 205. £45.00; $90.00.

Stanbury, Sarah. *The Visual Object of Desire in Late Medieval England*. Philadelphia: University of Pennsylvania Press, 2008. Pp. 291. $65.00.

Strohm, Paul, ed. *Oxford Twenty-First Century Approaches to Literature*, vol. 1: *Middle English*. Oxford and New York: Oxford University Press, 2007. Pp. xii, 521. £85.00; $160.00.

Wakelin, Daniel. *Humanism, Reading, and English Literature, 1430–1530*. Oxford and New York: Oxford University Press, 2007. Pp. 272. £50.00; $90.00.

Watt, Diane. *Medieval Women's Writing: Works by and for Women in England, 1100–1500*. Cambridge: Polity Press, 2007. Pp. viii, 208. £55.00 cloth; £16.99, $24.95 paper.

Wolfe, Heather, ed. *The Literary Legacy of Elizabeth Cary, 1613–1680*. New York: Palgrave Macmillan, 2007. Pp. xiii, 258. $69.95.

Yeager, R. F., ed. *On John Gower: Essays at the Millennium*. Kalamazoo: Medieval Institute Publications, 2007. Pp. x, 241. $40.00 cloth; $20.00 paper.

Zieman, Katherine. *Singing the New Song: Literacy and Liturgy in Late Medieval England*. Philadelphia: University of Pennsylvania Press, 2008. Pp. xvii, 294. $59.95.

An Annotated Chaucer Bibliography 2006

Compiled and edited by Mark Allen and Bege K. Bowers

Regular contributors:

Bruce W. Hozeski, *Ball State University* (Indiana)
George Nicholas, *Benedictine College* (Kansas)
Debra Best, *California State University at Dominguez Hills*
Gregory M. Sadlek, *Cleveland State University* (Ohio)
David Sprunger, *Concordia College* (Minnesota)
Winthrop Wetherbee, *Cornell University* (New York)
Elizabeth Dobbs, *Grinnell College* (Iowa)
Teresa P. Reed, *Jacksonville State University* (Alabama)
William Snell, *Keio University* (Japan)
Denise Stodola, *Kettering University* (Michigan)
Brian A. Shaw, *London, Ontario*
William Schipper, *Memorial University* (Newfoundland, Canada)
Martha Rust, *New York University*
Warren S. Moore, III, *Newberry College* (South Carolina)
Amy Goodwin, *Randolph-Macon College* (Virginia)
Cindy L. Vitto, *Rowan College of New Jersey*
Brother Anthony (Sonjae An), *Sogang University* (South Korea)
Anne Thornton, *Tufts University* (Massachusetts)
Martine Yvernault, *Université de Limoges*
Margaret Connolly, *University College, Cork* (Ireland)
R. D. Eaton, *Universiteit van Amsterdam* (The Netherlands)
Elaine Whitaker, *University of Alabama at Birmingham*
Stefania D'Agata D'Ottavi, *University of Macerata* (Italy)
Cynthia Ho, *University of North Carolina, Asheville*
Richard J. Utz, *University of Northern Iowa*
Rebecca Beal, *University of Scranton* (Pennsylvania)
Mark Allen and R. L. Smith, *University of Texas at San Antonio*
Joerg O. Fichte, *Universität Tübingen* (Tübingen, Germany)

John M. Crafton, *West Georgia College*
Robert Correale, *Wright State University* (Ohio)
Bege K. Bowers, *Youngstown State University* (Ohio)

Ad hoc contributions were made by Susan F. Priestley (University of Alabama at Birmingham), Nicole Provencher (University of Texas at San Antonio), and Jesús L. Serrano-Reyes (Córdoba). The bibliographers acknowledge with gratitude the MLA type simulation provided by the Center for Bibliographical Services of the Modern Language Association; postage from the University of Texas at San Antonio Department of English, Classics, and Philosophy; and assistance from the library staff, especially Susan McCray, at the University of Texas at San Antonio.

This bibliography continues the bibliographies published since 1975 in previous volumes of *Studies in the Age of Chaucer*. Bibliographic information up to 1975 can be found in Eleanor P. Hammond, *Chaucer: A Bibliographic Manual* (1908; reprint, New York: Peter Smith, 1933); D. D. Griffith, *Bibliography of Chaucer, 1908–1953* (Seattle: University of Washington Press, 1955); William R. Crawford, *Bibliography of Chaucer, 1954–63* (Seattle: University of Washington Press, 1967); and Lorrayne Y. Baird, *Bibliography of Chaucer, 1964–1973* (Boston: G. K. Hall, 1977). See also Lorrayne Y. Baird-Lange and Hildegard Schnuttgen, *Bibliography of Chaucer, 1974–1985* (Hamden, Conn.: Shoe String Press, 1988); and Bege K. Bowers and Mark Allen, eds., *Annotated Chaucer Bibliography, 1986–1996* (Notre Dame, Ind.: University of Notre Dame Press, 2002).

Additions and corrections to this bibliography should be sent to Mark Allen, Bibliographic Division, The New Chaucer Society, Department of English, Classics, and Philosophy, University of Texas at San Antonio 78249-0643 (Fax: 210-458-5366; e-mail: mark.allen@utsa.edu). An electronic version of this bibliography (1975–2006) is available via The New Chaucer Society Web page at <http://artsci.wustl.edu/~chaucer> or directly at <http://uchaucer.utsa.edu>. Authors are urged to send annotations for articles, reviews, and books that have been or might be overlooked.

Classifications

Abbreviations of Chaucer's Works

ABC	*An ABC*
Adam	*Adam Scriveyn*
Anel	*Anelida and Arcite*
Astr	*A Treatise on the Astrolabe*
Bal Compl	*A Balade of Complaint*
BD	*The Book of the Duchess*
Bo	*Boece*
Buk	*The Envoy to Bukton*
CkT, CkP, Rv–CkL	*The Cook's Tale, The Cook's Prologue, Reeve–Cook Link*
ClT, ClP, Cl–MerL	*The Clerk's Tale, The Clerk's Prologue, Clerk–Merchant Link*
Compl d'Am	*Complaynt d'Amours*
CT	*The Canterbury Tales*
CYT, CYP	*The Canon's Yeoman's Tale, The Canon's Yeoman's Prologue*
Equat	*The Equatorie of the Planetis*
For	*Fortune*
Form Age	*The Former Age*
FranT, FranP	*The Franklin's Tale, The Franklin's Prologue*
FrT, FrP, Fr–SumL	*The Friar's Tale, The Friar's Prologue, Friar–Summoner Link*
Gent	*Gentilesse*
GP	*The General Prologue*
HF	*The House of Fame*
KnT, Kn–MilL	*The Knight's Tale, Knight–Miller Link*
Lady	*A Complaint to His Lady*
LGW, LGWP	*The Legend of Good Women, The Legend of Good Women Prologue*
ManT, ManP	*The Manciple's Tale, The Manciple's Prologue*
Mars	*The Complaint of Mars*
Mel, Mel–MkL	*The Tale of Melibee, Melibee–Monk Link*
MercB	*Merciles Beaute*
MerT, MerE–SqH	*The Merchant's Tale, Merchant Endlink–Squire Headlink*

MilT, MilP, Mil–RvL	*The Miller's Tale, The Miller's Prologue, Miller–Reeve Link*
MkT, MkP, Mk–NPL	*The Monk's Tale, The Monk's Prologue, Monk–Nun's Priest Link*
MLT, MLH, MLP, MLE	*The Man of Law's Tale, Man of Law Headlink, The Man of Law's Prologue, Man of Law Endlink*
NPT, NPP, NPE	*The Nun's Priest's Tale, The Nun's Priest's Prologue, Nun's Priest's Endlink*
PardT, PardP	*The Pardoner's Tale, The Pardoner's Prologue*
ParsT, ParsP	*The Parson's Tale, The Parson's Prologue*
PF	*The Parliament of Fowls*
PhyT, Phy–PardL	*The Physician's Tale, Physician–Pardoner Link*
Pity	*The Complaint unto Pity*
Prov	*Proverbs*
PrT, PrP, Pr–ThL	*The Prioress's Tale, The Prioress's Prologue, Prioress–Thopas Link*
Purse	*The Complaint of Chaucer to His Purse*
Ret	*Chaucer's Retraction {Retractation}*
Rom	*The Romaunt of the Rose*
Ros	*To Rosemounde*
RvT, RvP	*The Reeve's Tale, The Reeve's Prologue*
Scog	*The Envoy to Scogan*
ShT, Sh–PrL	*The Shipman's Tale, Shipman–Prioress Link*
SNT, SNP, SN–CYL	*The Second Nun's Tale, The Second Nun's Prologue, Second Nun–Canon's Yeoman Link*
SqT, SqH, Sq–FranL	*The Squire's Tale, Squire Headlink, Squire–Franklin Link*
Sted	*Lak of Stedfastnesse*
SumT, SumP	*The Summoner's Tale, The Summoner's Prologue*
TC	*Troilus and Criseyde*
Th, Th–MelL	*The Tale of Sir Thopas, Sir Thopas–Melibee Link*
Truth	*Truth*
Ven	*The Complaint of Venus*

WBT, WBP, WB–FrL	*The Wife of Bath's Tale, The Wife of Bath's Prologue, Wife of Bath–Friar Link*
Wom Nob	*Womanly Noblesse*
Wom Unc	*Against Women Unconstant*

Periodical Abbreviations

AdI	*Annali d'Italianistica*
Anglia	*Anglia: Zeitschrift für Englische Philologie*
Anglistik	*Anglistik: Mitteilungen des Verbandes deutscher Anglisten*
AnLM	*Anuario de Letras Modernas*
ANQ	*ANQ: A Quarterly Journal of Short Articles, Notes, and Reviews*
Archiv	*Archiv für das Studium der Neueren Sprachen und Literaturen*
Atlantis	*Atlantis: Revista de la Asociacion Española de Estudios Anglo-Norteamericanos*
AUMLA	*AUMLA: Journal of the Australasian Universities Language and Literature Association*
BAM	*Bulletin des Anglicistes Médiévistes*
BJRL	*Bulletin of the John Rylands University Library of Manchester*
C&L	*Christianity and Literature*
CarmP	*Carmina Philosophiae: Journal of the International Boethius Society*
CE	*College English*
ChauR	*Chaucer Review*
CL	*Comparative Literature* (Eugene, Ore.)
Clio	*CLIO: A Journal of Literature, History, and the Philosophy of History*
CLS	*Comparative Literature Studies*
CML	*Classical and Modern Literature: A Quarterly* (Columbia, Mo.)
CollL	*College Literature*
Comitatus	*Comitatus: A Journal of Medieval and Renaissance Studies*
CRCL	*Canadian Review of Comparative Literature/Revue Canadienne de Littérature Comparée*
DAI	*Dissertation Abstracts International*
DR	*Dalhousie Review*
ÉA	*Études Anglaises: Grand-Bretagne, États-Unis*
EHR	*English Historical Review*
EIC	*Essays in Criticism: A Quarterly Journal of Literary Criticism*

ELH	*ELH: English Literary History*
ELN	*English Language Notes*
ELR	*English Literary Renaissance*
EMS	*English Manuscript Studies, 1100–1700*
Encomia	*Encomia: Bibliographical Bulletin of the International Courtly Literature Society*
English	*English: The Journal of the English Association*
Envoi	*Envoi: A Review Journal of Medieval Literature*
ES	*English Studies*
ESC	*English Studies in Canada*
Exemplaria	*Exemplaria: A Journal of Theory in Medieval and Renaissance Studies*
Expl	*Explicator*
Fabula	*Fabula: Zeitschrift für Erzählforschung/Journal of Folktale Studies*
FCS	*Fifteenth-Century Studies*
Florilegium	*Florilegium: Carleton University Papers on Late Antiquity and the Middle Ages*
FMLS	*Forum for Modern Language Studies*
Genre	*Genre: Forms of Discourse and Culture*
HLQ	*Huntington Library Quarterly: Studies in English and American History and Literature* (San Marino, Calif.)
Hortulus	*Hortulus: The Online Graduate Journal of Medieval Studies* <*http://www.hortulus.net/*>
IJES	*International Journal of English Studies*
JAIS	*Journal of Anglo-Italian Studies*
JEBS	*Journal of the Early Book Society*
JEGP	*Journal of English and Germanic Philology*
JELL	*Journal of English Language and Literature* (Korea)
JEngL	*Journal of English Linguistics*
JGN	*John Gower Newsletter*
JHiP	*Journal of Historical Pragmatics*
JMEMSt	*Journal of Medieval and Early Modern Studies*
JML	*Journal of Modern Literature*
JMRS	*Journal of Medieval and Renaissance Studies*
JNT	*Journal of Narrative Theory*
JRMMRA	*Quidditas: Journal of the Rocky Mountain Medieval and Renaissance Association*

L&LC	*Literary and Linguistic Computing: Journal of the Association for Literary and Linguistic Computing*
L&P	*Literature and Psychology*
L&T	*Literature and Theology: An International Journal of Religion, Theory, and Culture*
Lang&Lit	*Language and Literature: Journal of the Poetics and Linguistics Association*
Lang&S	*Language and Style: An International Journal*
LeedsSE	*Leeds Studies in English*
Library	*The Library: The Transactions of the Bibliographical Society*
MA	*Le Moyen Age: Revue d'Histoire et de Philologie* (Brussels, Belgium)
MÆ	*Medium Ævum*
M&H	*Medievalia et Humanistica: Studies in Medieval and Renaissance Culture*
Manuscripta	*Manuscripta* (St. Louis, Mo.)
Marginalia	*Marginalia: The Journal of the Medieval Reading Group at the University of Cambridge* <http://www.marginalia.co.uk/journal/>
Mediaevalia	*Mediaevalia: An Interdisciplinary Journal of Medieval Studies Worldwide*
MedievalF	*Medieval Forum* <http://www.sfsu.edu/~medieval/index.html>
MedPers	*Medieval Perspectives*
MES	*Medieval English Studies*
MFF	*Medieval Feminist Forum*
MichA	*Michigan Academician* (Ann Arbor, Mich.)
MLQ	*Modern Language Quarterly: A Journal of Literary History*
MLR	*The Modern Language Review*
MP	*Modern Philology: A Journal Devoted to Research in Medieval and Modern Literature*
N&Q	*Notes and Queries*
Neophil	*Neophilologus* (Dordrecht, Netherlands)
NLH	*New Literary History: A Journal of Theory and Interpretation*
NM	*Neuphilologische Mitteilungen: Bulletin of the Modern Language Society*

NML	*New Medieval Literatures*
NMS	*Nottingham Medieval Studies*
NOWELE	*NOWELE: North-Western European Language Evolution*
Parergon	*Parergon: Bulletin of the Australian and New Zealand Association for Medieval and Early Modern Studies*
PBA	*Proceedings of the British Academy*
PBSA	*Papers of the Bibliographical Society of America*
PLL	*Papers on Language and Literature: A Journal for Scholars and Critics of Language and Literature*
PMAM	*Publications of the Medieval Association of the Midwest*
PMLA	*Publications of the Modern Language Association of America*
PoeticaT	*Poetica: An International Journal of Linguistic Literary Studies*
PQ	*Philological Quarterly*
RCEI	*Revista Canaria de Estudios Ingleses*
RenD	*Renaissance Drama*
RenQ	*Renaissance Quarterly*
RES	*Review of English Studies*
RMRev	*Reading Medieval Reviews* <www.rdg.ac/uk/ AcaDepts/In/Medieval/rmr.htm>
SAC	*Studies in the Age of Chaucer*
SAP	*Studia Anglica Posnaniensia: An International Review of English*
SAQ	*South Atlantic Quarterly*
SB	*Studies in Bibliography: Papers of the Bibliographical Society of the University of Virginia*
SCJ	*The Sixteenth-Century Journal: Journal of Early Modern Studies* (Kirksville, Mo.)
SEL	*SEL: Studies in English Literature, 1500–1900*
SELIM	*SELIM: Journal of the Spanish Society for Medieval English Language and Literature*
ShakS	*Shakespeare Studies*
SIcon	*Studies in Iconography*
SiM	*Studies in Medievalism*
SIMELL	*Studies in Medieval English Language and Literature*
SMART	*Studies in Medieval and Renaissance Teaching*
SN	*Studia Neophilologica: A Journal of Germanic and Romance Languages and Literatures*

SoAR	*South Atlantic Review*
SP	*Studies in Philology*
Speculum	*Speculum: A Journal of Medieval Studies*
SSF	*Studies in Short Fiction*
SSt	*Spenser Studies: A Renaissance Poetry Annual*
TCBS	*Transactions of the Cambridge Bibliographical Society*
Text	*Text: Transactions of the Society for Textual Scholarship*
TLS	*Times Literary Supplement* (London, England)
TMR	*The Medieval Review* <http://www.hti.umich.edu/t/ tmr/>
Tr&Lit	*Translation and Literature*
TSLL	*Texas Studies in Literature and Language*
UTQ	*University of Toronto Quarterly: A Canadian Journal of the Humanities* (Toronto, Canada)
Viator	*Viator: Medieval and Renaissance Studies*
WS	*Women's Studies: An Interdisciplinary Journal*
YES	*Yearbook of English Studies*
YWES	*Year's Work in English Studies*
YLS	*The Yearbook of Langland Studies*

Bibliographical Citations and Annotations

Bibliographies, Reports, and Reference

1. Allen, Mark, and Bege K. Bowers. "An Annotated Chaucer Bibliography, 2004." *SAC* 28 (2006): 349–423. Continuation of *SAC* annual annotated bibliography (since 1975); based on contributions from an international bibliographic team, independent research, and *MLA Bibliography* listings. 218 items, plus listing of reviews for 74 books. Includes an author index.

2. Allen, Valerie, and Margaret Connolly. "Middle English: Chaucer." *YWES* 85 (2006): 236–63. A discursive bibliography of Chaucer studies for 2004, divided into four subcategories: general, *CT*, *TC*, and other works.

3. Andrew, Malcolm. *The Palgrave Literary Dictionary of Chaucer*. Palgrave Literary Dictionaries. New York: Palgrave Macmillan, 2006. xvi, 313 pp. Lists and describes Chaucer's works, major characters, sources, influences, themes, genres, and allusions; several manuscripts, editions, and scholars; and people and places in Chaucer's life. Alphabetical arrangement of some 720 entries, with a brief chronology of Chaucer's life and a short bibliography. See also no. 306.

4. Azuma, Yoshio. "A Concordance to *The General Prologue* in *The Canterbury Tales* Based on *The Riverside Chaucer* (6)." *Journal of Osaka Sangyo University, Humanities* 118 (2006): 83–113. Part six of a concordance to the *GP* in English. Introduction in Japanese.

5. Cooper, Helen. "Geoffrey Chaucer (ca. 1342–1400)." In Richard K. Emmerson and Sandra Clayton-Emmerson, eds. *Key Figures in Medieval Europe: An Encyclopedia*. New York: Routledge, 2006, pp. 131–35. An introduction to Chaucer and his works, with attention to his sources and influences. Includes a brief bibliography.

6. Staley, Lynn. "Geoffrey Chaucer." In David Scott Kastan, ed. *The Oxford Encyclopedia of British Literature*. 5 vols. Oxford: Oxford University Press, 2006, vol. 1, pp. 450–56. Treats Chaucer as a "means of entry" into the political and cultural world of late fourteenth-century England, surveying Chaucer's works (*CT* most extensively) and summarizing his life and reception. Includes a brief bibliography.

Recordings and Films

7. Blandeau, Agnès. "Images pasoliniennes en marge des *Canterbury Tales*." In Colette Stévanovitch, ed. *Marges/Seuils: Le liminal dans la littérature médiévale anglaise* (*SAC* 30 [2008], no. 148), pp. 317–29. Establishes the relationship between film pictures and manuscript margins as peripheral comments on the central object.

8. ———. *Pasolini, Chaucer and Boccaccio: Two Medieval Texts and Their Translation to Film*. Jefferson, N.C.: McFarland, 2006. viii, 210 pp. Blandeau studies Pasolini's cinematic trilogy of medieval tales: *The Decameron, CT,* and *One Thousand and One Nights*, focusing on the first two. Argues that Pasolini "puts two semiotic systems in translation with each other, not so much to transmit Boccaccio's and Chaucer's texts to a 20th-century audience as to offer the latter a refraction of the masterpieces, altered by the filter of his own fantasy." Parallels Pasolini's innovations with Chaucer's and offers a three-column comparison of Chaucer's tales, Pasolini's projected order of tales, and the order of elements in the completed film.

9. Brinkman, Baba. *The Rap "Canterbury Tales."* Canada: Spin Digital Media, 2004. 1 CD-ROM. Audio recording of hip-hop performance of adaptations of *GP* (cast as a bus trip), *KnT, MilPT, PardPT, WBPT*, and *Ret* (with additional tracks: "Rhyme Renaissance Prologue," "Rhyme Renaissance," and "Dead Poets"). Affiliated Web site at <http://www.babasword.com>. For print version, see no. 18.

10. Rogerson, Margaret. "Prime-time Drama: *Canterbury Tales* for the Small Screen." *SSEng* 32 (2006): 45–63. Surveys efforts to popularize *CT* through media (television, audio recordings, stage, and animation), commenting most extensively on the 2003 BBC television series.

See also nos. 77, 132, 168, 170.

Chaucer's Life

11. Cannon, Christopher. "The Lives of Geoffrey Chaucer." In Seth Lerer, ed. *The Yale Companion to Chaucer* (*SAC* 30 [2008], no. 131), pp. 31–54. Cannon observes parallels between the "forms of life Chaucer made in his poems" and "what can be reconstructed from his own life from the public record." Suggests that both the textual lives and Chau-

cer's biography derive "in part from social circumstances" that "made living unusually available to representation in texts."

12. Ormrod, W. M. "Who Was Alice Perrers?" *ChauR* 40 (2006): 219–29. Two documents in the National Archives (London) show that Alice Perrers was married to Janyn Perers, possibly an Italian, before becoming Edward III's mistress. These records hint that she was "a person of lower birth who made her fortune essentially through her own innate talent and ambition," thus disproving the hypothesis that she was an unmarried woman of genteel upbringing when she entered the household of Queen Philippa as a *domicella*.

13. Perry, Judy. "Katherine Roet's Swynfords: A Re-examination of Interfamily Relationships and Descent—Part 1 and Part 2." *Foundations: Newsletter of the Foundation for Medieval Genealogy* 1.2–3 (2003–4): 122–31 and 164–74. Perry documents the complex relationships among the Roets, Swynfords, Lancastrians, and Chaucer's family, rejecting speculation that Thomas Chaucer was the illegitimate son of John of Gaunt and commenting on the dowering of Elizabeth Chaucer at Barking Abbey. She examines various kinds of historical evidence, including heraldry.

14. Taggie, Benjamin F. "Chaucer in Spain: The Historical Context." In Benjamin F. Taggie, Richard W. Clement, and James E. Caraway, eds. *Spain and the Mediterranean.* Mediterranean Studies, no. 3. Kirksville, Mo.: Thomas Jefferson University Press, 1992, pp. 35–44. Same publication as *SAC* 29 (2007), no. 6, for which the bibliographical information was incomplete.

See also nos. 54, 247, 268.

Facsimiles, Editions, and Translations

15. Altmann, Barbara K., and R. Barton Palmer, trans. and eds. *An Anthology of Medieval Love Debate Poetry.* Gainesville: University Press of Florida, [2006]. xii, 397 pp. Translates into modern unrhymed pentameter the *LGWP*-F version and *LGW*, based on the *Riverside* edition, with a brief introduction and notes. Also translates works by Guillaume de Machaut (*Jugement dou roy de Behaigne* and *Jugement dou roy de Navarre*), Christine de Pizan (*Debat de deux amans*), and Alain Chartier (*Livre des quatre dames*).

16. Barney, Stephen A., ed. *Geoffrey Chaucer: "Troilus and Criseyde,"*

with Facing-Page "Il Filostrato": Authoritative Texts; "The Testament of Cresseid" by Robert Henryson, Criticism. Norton Critical Edition. New York: Norton, 2006. xxvii, 628 pp. Text of *TC* based on *Riverside* edition, with Boccaccio's *Il Filostrato* on facing pages, in the English translation of Robert P. apRoberts and Anna Bruni Benson. Includes Henryson's *Testament of Cresseid*, as edited by Robert L. Kindrick; ten reprinted interpretive essays; and a brief glossary and selective bibliography. Middle English texts include glosses in margins and notes at the bottom of the page.

17. Beidler, Peter G., ed. and trans. *The Canterbury Tales: Selected with Translations, Critical Introductions, and Notes.* New York: Bantam, 2006. xliii, 643 pp. Facing-page translation of selections from *CT*, based on the earlier version by A. Kent Hieatt and Constance Hieatt, augmented with expanded selections and apparatus. Selections include *GP*, *KnT*, *MilPT*, *RvPT*, *WBPT*, *MerPT*, *FranT*, *PardPT*, *ShT*, *PrPT*, and *NPT*. Apparatus includes a general introduction and a brief introduction (with selective notes) to the individual *Tales*.

18. Brinkman, Baba. *The Rap "Canterbury Tales."* Illustrations by Erik Brinkman. Vancouver: Talonbooks, 2006. 362 pp. Facing-page adaptations of *KnT* (abridged), *MilT*, *PardT*, and *WBT*, with Middle English and lyrics designed for rap performance. The Middle English text is glossed, and each *Tale* is accompanied by a brief introduction to the plot. Brinkman's introduction (pp. 9–52) compares features of Chaucer's poetry with features of rap and hip-hop culture ("competitive, descriptive, rhyming narrative verse"); assesses the roles of rhyme and rhythm in cultural history; and describes the development of his rap versions of *CT*. For audio version, see no. 9.

19. Choi, Yejung, and Ji-Soo Chang. " 'Diverse folk diversely they seyde': Korean Translations of *The Canterbury Tales.*" *Medieval and Early Modern English Studies* 12 (2004): 225–56 (in Korean, with English abstract). The authors critique several Korean translations of *CT* published since the early 1960s: those by J. Kim, B. Song, Dong-il Lee and Dong-choon Lee, and another attributed to J. Kim.

20. Cruz Cabanillas, Isabel de la. "The *Reeve's Tale*: Traducción e imposibles." *RAEL: Revista electrónica de lingüística aplicada* 3 (2004): 41–62. Explores difficulties of representing in Spanish translation the provincial Northern dialect of John and Aleyn of *RvT*.

21. Fisher, John H., and Mark Allen, eds. *The Complete Canterbury Tales of Geoffrey Chaucer.* Boston: Thomson Wadsworth, 2006. vii, 452

pp. 4 color plates. Revised edition of *CT*, based on Fisher's *Complete Poetry and Prose of Geoffrey Chaucer* (1977), with new on-page glosses and explanatory notes, plus bibliography (pp. 402–41). Includes lightly revised essays on Chaucer's life and language and a new introduction for each of the ten parts of the *Tales*. See also no. 331.

22. Galbraith, Steven K. "Spenser's First Folio: The Build-It-Yourself Edition." *SSt* 21 (2006): 21–49. Contrasts the absence of Spenser's portrait in the first folio edition of *The Faerie Queene* with sixteenth- and seventeenth-century Chaucer folios, which were printed throughout the sixteenth and seventeenth centuries.

23. Gillespie, Alexandra. *Print Culture and the Medieval Author: Chaucer, Lydgate, and Their Books, 1473–1557*. Oxford: Oxford University Press, 2006. xiii, 281 pp. Analyzing the impact of print on already-existing ideas of authorship, Gillespie argues that "the medieval author was a mechanism for ordering the new meanings of texts in print," even when the understanding of that author was a result, or "function," of interpretation of the author's texts. With its multiple narrators, *CT* exemplifies this function, for it illustrates how the concept of authority can both control and proliferate meaning. Chapter 3, "Assembling Chaucer's Texts in Print, 1517 to 1532," considers *TC* and *PF* along with 1526 and 1532 editions of Chaucer's works as examples of the "author function" within print culture. Also discusses *HF* and *Ret*.

24. Hagiwara, Fumiko, trans. "*The Parliament of Fowls* by Geoffrey Chaucer." *Hakuoh Women's Junior College Journal* 6.2 (1981): 19–41 (in Japanese). Translation of *PF*.

25. Kuskin, William, ed. *Caxton's Trace: Studies in the History of English Printing*. Notre Dame, Ind.: University of Notre Dame Press, 2006. xxvii, 394 pp. 28 b&w illus. Ten essays by various authors and an introduction by the editor, exploring the relationship of Caxton to early Continental printing and the influence of Caxton and his practice on English printing, ideas of authorship, editing, and language. Includes recurrent references to Chaucer, with sustained attention to editions of *CT*, *HF*, and *Gent*.

26. Reimer, Stephen R. "The Urry *Chaucer* and George Vertue." *ChauR* 41 (2006): 105–9. Proofs of George Vertue's prints held in the University of Southern California's Doheny Memorial Library provide firm evidence that Vertue executed all but one of the engravings in the 1721 edition of John Urry's *The Works of Geoffrey Chaucer* and that the engravings were based on Vertue's own drawings.

27. Robinson, Peter. *"The Canterbury Tales* and Other Medieval Texts." In Lou Burnard, Katherine O'Brien O'Keeffe, and John Unsworth, eds. *Electronic Textual Editing.* New York: MLA, 2006, pp. 74–91. Generates five general "propositions" about the nature and practice of electronic editing, explaining how the propositions developed from work of Robinson and others on *The Canterbury Tales Project* and indicating the applicability of the propositions to the construction of "e-texts" generally.

28. Seya, Yukio, trans. *The Romaunt of the Rose.* Tokyo: Nan'un-do, 2001 (in Japanese). 262 pp. Translation of *Rom.*

29. Shiomi, Tomoyuki. "Edward Burne-Jones and Geoffrey Chaucer." *The School of Human Studies, the School of Literature* (Taisho University) 85 (2000): 241–64 (in Japanese). Discusses Edward Burne-Jones's illustrations for the Kelmscott Chaucer.

30. Thomas, Paul, ed., with Bárbara Bordalejo and Orietta Da Rold and contributions by Daniel W. Mosser and Peter Robinson. *The Nun's Priest's Tale on CD-ROM. The Canterbury Tales Project.* Birmingham, UK: Scholarly Digital Editions, 2006. 1 CD-ROM. Includes interlinked images and transcriptions of all fifty-five pre-1500 versions of *NPT*, with complete collations (linked to variant maps), commentaries on family relationships of the versions, and stemmatic commentary on key readings. The search engine enables comparisons by spelling, word, line, witness, and complex combinations. Includes full descriptions of all witnesses and scribes (by Mosser), fully lemmatized databases of all spellings and words, and a bibliography. The editor's introduction comments on scribal variation and the utility of multispectral imaging for manuscript study.

See also nos. 9, 32, 121, 132, 253, 254, 266, 267, 273.

Manuscripts and Textual Studies

31. Blake, Norman, and Jacob Thaisen. "Spelling's Significance for Textual Studies." Special issue, *Nordic Journal of English Studies* 3.1 (2004): 93–107. Evaluating two *CT* manuscripts—Christ Church, Oxford, MS 152 (single exemplar) and British Library MS Harley 7334 (two exemplars)—the authors contend that analysis of spelling can be used to determine changes in exemplars in textual study. Because scribal

spelling habits are not uniform, evidence from spelling must be used in conjunction with other codicological evidence.

32. Boffey, Julia, and A. S. G. Edwards. "Manuscripts and Audience." In Corinne Saunders, ed. *A Concise Companion to Chaucer* (*SAC* 30 [2008], no. 143), pp. 34–50. The essay describes the "complex exercises in historical reconstruction" essential to bridge the distance between modern readers and Chaucer and his contemporary audience. Discusses Chaucer's literary production, his revisions, and scribal adaptations as evident in surviving manuscripts and references within the works themselves, contrasting modern presentations of Chaucer's works with the medieval perception of *CT* as unfinished and open-ended.

33. Livingston, Michael. "A Sixth Hand in Cambridge, Trinity College, MS R.3.19." *JEBS* 8 (2005): 229–37. Identifies characteristics of a sixth scribe (Scribe F) of MS R.3.19, copyist of the "whole of fol. 42, recto and verso."

34. Mooney, Linne R. "Chaucer's Scribe." *Speculum* 81 (2006): 97–138. Mooney surveys the manuscripts and life records of Adam Pinkhurst, identified as the scribe addressed in Chaucer's *Adam* and as the scribe of the Hengwrt and Ellesmere manuscripts, among others. Includes a chronology of manuscripts Pinkhurst is known to have copied, an outline of his career, and an appendix with detailed analysis of Pinkhurst's hand, including ten reproductions sampling his work.

35. Morrison, Stephen. "Scribes as Authors: Substantive Variation in Some Late Middle English Manuscripts." In Colette Stévanovitch, ed. *Marges/Seuils: Le liminal dans la littérature médiévale anglaise* (*SAC* 30 [2008], no. 148), pp. 61–80. Morrison examines textual transmission before print, referring to Chaucer as evidence of authors' concerns about deficient scribal copying.

36. ———. "What's in a Margin? Some Observations on the Function and Content of Margins in Medieval Literary Manuscripts." In Colette Stévanovitch, ed. *Marges/Seuils: Le liminal dans la littérature médiévale anglaise* (*SAC* 30 [2008], no. 148), pp. 97–106. Studies the contents, significance, and function of medieval manuscripts, commenting briefly on *WBP*.

37. Mosser, Daniel W. "The Scribe(s) of British Library MSS Egerton 2864 and Additional 5140: To 'Lump' or 'Split'?" *JEBS* 8 (2005): 215–28. A combination of linguistic and paleographical evidence suggests a single scribe for Egerton 2864, who differs from the scribes of Additional 5140. Mosser documents his article with illustrations.

38. Robertson, Mary. "The Name of the Scribe: Solving a Mystery Behind the Huntington's *Canterbury Tales*." *Huntington Frontiers* 2.1 (2006): 2–4. Announces Linne R. Mooney's identification of Adam Pinkhurst as the scribe of the Ellesmere manuscript of *CT*, held at the Huntington Library.

39. Scattergood, John. *Manuscripts and Ghosts: Essays on the Transmission of Medieval and Early Renaissance Literature*. Dublin: Four Courts Press, 2006. 320 pp. Reprints fifteen previously published essays by Scattergood, plus a sixteenth, original essay, "The Copying of Medieval and Early Renaissance Manuscripts" (pp. 21–82). The latter—which discusses the habits and status of medieval scribes, early printers, and attitudes among these conveyors of literature—comments on Chaucer and his transmission. Among the reprinted essays is Scattergood's "The Jongleur, the Copyist, and the Printer: The Tradition of Chaucer's *Wordes unto Adam, His Own Scriveyn*" (*SAC* 14 [1992], no. 274).

40. Timmerman, Anke. "New Perspectives on 'The Chaucer Ascription in Trinity College, Dublin MS D.2.8.'" *Ambix* 53 (2006): 161–65. Trinity College, Dublin, MS 389 (formerly D.2.8) includes three alchemical texts that are Chaucerian apocrypha. Timmerman corrects Gareth W. Dunleavy's 1965 discussion of this manuscript.

See also nos. 27, 30, 58, 92, 206, 248, 258, 266, 273.

Sources, Analogues, and Literary Relations

41. Beidler, Peter G. "New Terminology for Sources and Analogues: Or, Let's Forget the Lost French Source for *The Miller's Tale*." *SAC* 28 (2006): 225–30. Beidler proposes a refined taxonomy of terms to designate the relationships between a work and its sources (*hard source, soft source, hard analogue, soft analogue*, and *lost source*) and argues that—for lack of evidence—criticism should dispense with the notion of a lost French source for *MilT*.

42. Bradbury, Nancy Mason. "Proverb Tradition as a Soft Source for the *Canterbury Tales*." *SAC* 28 (2006): 237–42. Bradbury addresses Chaucer's uses of proverbs as a "crucial" form of "quoting behavior"—a form of "soft source" important to Chaucer's art and its reception in manuscripts and early editions. Draws examples from *KnT* and refers to uses of proverbs in other *Tales*.

43. Caie, Graham D. "Lay Literacy and the Medieval Bible." Special

issue, *Nordic Journal of English Studies* 3.1 (2004): 125–44. Caie describes how lay people gained access to the Bible in the late Middle Ages through sermons, compendia, and florilegia. Explores how Chaucer characterizes speakers through their uses of the Bible in *CT* (e.g., quotation, misquotation, selection, allusion), concentrating on the Wife of Bath and glosses to *WBP*.

44. Collette, Carolyn P. "Reading Chaucer Through Philippe de Mézières: Alchemy, the Individual, and the Good Society." In Christoph Huber and Henrike Lähnemann, eds. *Courtly Literature and Clerical Culture/Höfische Literatur und Klerikerkultur/Littérature courtoise et culture cléricale. Selected Papers from the Tenth Triennial Congress of the International Courtly Literature Society, Universität Tübingen, Deutschland, 28 Juli–3 August 2001.* Tübingen: Attempto, 2002, pp. 177–94. Collette reads the end of *CT* against Philippe de Mézières' *Songe du vieil pelerin*, indicating Chaucer's connections with contemporary Anglo-French literature and exploring the relations between politics and morality in four *Tales*: alchemy as a trope in *SNT* and *CYT*; speech in *ManT*; and critique of aristocratic excess in *ParsT*.

45. Diamond, Arlyn. "Colloquium: The Afterlife of Origins. Introduction." *SAC* 28 (2006): 217–20. Cites Chaucer's self-awareness in attention to his sources, comments on the role of "source study" in Chaucer criticism, and introduces eight brief essays first presented at the 2004 congress of The New Chaucer Society in Glasgow. See nos. 41, 42, 46, 50, 215, 216, 225, and 243.

46. Evans, Ruth. "The Afterword of Origins: A Response." *SAC* 28 (2006): 263–70. Considers the implications of source study and its revitalization in response to recent theory, raising questions about its (possibly irreconcilable) relationships with intertextuality, "genetic criticism," invention, translation, and electronic research. Responds to *SAC* 30 (2008), nos. 41, 42, 50, 215, 216, 225, and 243.

47. Gutierrez Arranz, José María. "'I wolde hyt here write': Mythologically Speaking About Chaucer." In Juan Camilo Conde Silvestre and Ma Nila Vázquez González, eds. *Medieval English Literary and Cultural Studies* (*SAC* 30 [2008], no. 110), pp. 71–80. Discusses the uses and functions of classical myth in Chaucer's works from a double perspective: Chaucer's knowledge of the different stories and his creative adaptations of this material.

48. Heffernan, Carol F. "Two 'English *Fabliaux*': Chaucer's 'Merchant's Tale' and 'Shipman's Tale' and Italian *Novelle*." *Neophil* 90

(2006): 333–49. Heffernan discusses the nature, origins, and development of Italian *novelle*; Boccaccio's innovations with the form; and the
likelihood that Chaucer had direct knowledge of *The Decameron*. Argues
that the influence of Italian *novelle* generally, and of *The Decameron* specifically, on *MerT* and *ShT* has been underestimated.

49. Mann, Jill. "'He Knew Nat Catoun': Medieval School-Texts and
Middle English Literature." In Jill Mann and Maura Nolan, eds. *The
Text in the Community: Essays on Medieval Works, Manuscripts, Authors, and
Readers*. Notre Dame, Ind.: University of Notre Dame Press, 2006, pp.
41–74. Mann describes the composition and influence of the *Liber Catonis*, a composite of six Latin texts that served as a school-text in medieval education, and considers it in light of other medieval school-texts.
Identifies places where works that constitute the *Liber Catonis* are echoed
in *CT* and in Langland's *Piers Plowman*.

50. McCormick, Betsy. "A Feel for the Game: Bourdieu, Source
Study, and the *Legend*." *SAC* 28 (2006): 257–61. Uses game theory
and Pierre Bourdieu's theory of "radical contextualization" to encourage
more deeply engaged source-in-context analysis of *LGW*.

51. Simpson, James. "Chaucer as a European Writer." In Seth Lerer,
ed. *The Yale Companion to Chaucer* (*SAC* 30 [2008], no. 131), pp. 55–86.
Simpson explores Chaucer's absorption of and reactions to Continental
influences (Latin, French, and Italian), emphasizing the recurrent influence of Ovid as a source and a model. *BD* is a poem of deference to
Gaunt and to French tradition; *HF* and *PF* are "manifesto" poems in
response to Dante. *TC* and *KnT* are darker versions of Boccaccio, more
attentive than Boccaccio to suffering. *LGW* is a work of pretended compliment to Cupid (and Richard II?); and in *CT* Chaucer makes himself
a "modern Ovid" by questioning literary and political structures.

52. Smith, D. Vance. "Chaucer as an English Writer." In Seth Lerer,
ed. *The Yale Companion to Chaucer* (*SAC* 30 [2008], no. 131), pp. 87–121.
Smith traces various threads of Chaucer's relationships with English poetic tradition: *GP* and Langland's *Piers Plowman*; *Th* and native romance; echoes of *Sir Orfeo*; alliterative verse in Chaucer; and the complex
concerns of native tradition, interrelations, incest, and mercantilism in
MLPT.

53. Sobecki, Sebastian. "'And to the herte she hireselven smot': The
Loveris Maladye and the Legitimate Suicides of Chaucer's and Gower's
Exemplary Lovers." *Mediaevalia* 25 (2003): 107–21. Victims of lovesick-
ness, lovers who commit suicide in Chaucer and Gower do so by stab-

bing themselves in the heart, an action not found in their sources. Nor is there medical precedent for regarding the heart as the central organ of the circulatory system. Love melancholy and love mania were regarded as serious medical conditions that helped to legitimate suicide within the courtly tradition. Sobecki draws examples from *HF*, *KnT*, *LGW*, and *Confessio Amantis*.

54. Yeager, R. F. "Books and Authority." In Corinne Saunders, ed. *A Concise Companion to Chaucer* (*SAC* 30 [2008], no. 143), pp. 51–67. Yeager summarizes Chaucer's education and career for the purpose of identifying the books, languages, and classical and vernacular literatures with which Chaucer was clearly acquainted. Discusses Chaucer's strategies for keeping literary authority at "stave's length" through a narrative persona and the dream vision and his techniques for "asserting a claim upon it" in his most mature works.

See also nos. 15, 60, 62, 121, 125, 149, 162, 166, 176, 183, 195, 199, 200, 202, 205, 206, 210, 215–18, 225, 230, 235, 243, 251, 252, 255, 256, 261, 265, 270, 274, 276, 278, 279, 284, 286, 291, 292, 300.

Chaucer's Influence and Later Allusion

55. Anderson, Judith H. "Allegory, Irony, Despair: Chaucer's *Pardoner's* and *Franklin's Tales* and Spenser's *Faerie Queene*, Books I and III." In Zachary Lesser and Benedict S. Robinson, eds. *Textual Conversations in the Renaissance: Ethics, Authors, Technologies*. Aldershot, Hampshire; and Burlington, Vt.: Ashgate, 2006, pp. 71–89. Explores intertextual relations between Spenser's *Faerie Queene* and Chaucer's *PardPT* and *FranT*. Archimago and Despair from Spenser's Book 1 gain dimension in light of the Pardoner and the Old Man of *PardT*; in Book 3, Spenser explores the "emotional plight" of Chaucer's Dorigen by dividing it into several parts.

56. Apstein, Barbara. "Chaucer, Virginia Woolf, and *Between the Acts*." *Woolf Studies Annual* 2 (1996): 117–33. Woolf deleted a description of Chaucer and one of the Pointz Hall library when revising materials for *Between the Acts*, reflecting her growing belief that books were no longer the center of culture in 1939–40. Traces references and allusions to Chaucer in Woolf's writings, published and unpublished.

57. Bawcutt, Priscilla. "Writing About Love in Late Medieval Scotland." In Helen Cooney, ed. *Writings on Love in the English Middle Ages*

(*SAC* 30 [2008], no. 111), pp. 179–96. Bawcutt surveys love poetry of medieval Scotland in various genres, emphasizing the variety of tones and exploring the importance of Chaucer's influence.

58. ———, and Janet Hadley Williams, eds. *A Companion to Medieval Scottish Poetry.* Woodbridge, Suffolk; and Rochester, N.Y.: D. S. Brewer, 2006. [x], 229 pp. Thirteen essays by various authors and an introduction by the editors. Topics include studies of individual poets and poems (Henryson, Dunbar, Douglas, Lyndsay, Richard Holland's *Buke of Howlat*, Gilbert Hay's *Buik of King Alexander the Conqueror*); the Selden manuscript (including works by Chaucer); historical writing; romance; and literary contexts. Includes a "Guide to Further Reading," an index of manuscript references, and a general index. References to Chaucer recur throughout, addressing his influence on individual works and on broader traditions.

59. Behrens, Katharina. "'Go Litel Boke'—To London: Bürgerliche Chaucer-Rezeption im 15. Jahrhundert." *Anglia* 124 (2006): 591–604. Behrens investigates the problems of authorship surrounding the dedicatory poem "Go litel boke, go litel tregedie" addressed to the four wardens of the mercer guild: John Olney, Geoffrey Feldyng, Geoffrey Boleyn, and John Burton. Alluding to *TC,* the poem concludes the version of the statute of 1442 governing the administration of a poorhouse endowed by Lord Mayor Richard Whittington in 1421. Considers a number of contemporary poets (e.g., Lydgate, Hoccleve) and scribes (e.g., Pinkhurst, Rumbold), providing no definitive solution.

60. Besserman, Lawrence. "Chaucer and Dickens Use Luke 23.34." *ChauR* 41 (2006): 99–104. Given his interest in Chaucer and his ownership of a copy of *TC*, Dickens's "comic literary use of the motif of 'Christ-forgives-his-killers'" may be an echo of Chaucer's use of the motif, which is based on Luke 23.34, in *TC* 3.1577.

61. Cooper, Helen. *Shakespeare and the Middle Ages: Inaugural Lecture Delivered at the University of Cambridge, 29 April 2005.* Cambridge: Cambridge University Press, 2006. 38 pp. Explores the continuities of the Middle Ages and Renaissance, emphasizing the inventiveness of the Middle Ages and the rootedness of the Renaissance in medieval traditions, focusing on drama and on Shakespeare in particular. Recurrent references to Chaucer, especially Shakespeare's dependence on him.

62. Dimmick, Jeremy. "Gower, Chaucer, and the Art of Repentance in Robert Greene's *Vision.*" *RES* 57 (2006): 456–73. Greene uses Chaucer and Gower to represent licentious comedy and moral literature, re-

spectively. In manipulating the debate between the medieval authors, Greene displays subtle awareness not only of his own literary persona but also of the authorial self-projections of Gower and Chaucer.

63. Faulkner, Peter. "The Story of Alcestis in William Morris and Ted Hughes." *Journal of William Morris Studies* 16.2–3 (2005): 56–79. Discussion of the Alcestis account in Morris's *Earthly Paradise* and in Ted Hughes's adaptation of Euripides's *Alcestis*, including comments on the influence of Chaucer's *LGWP* on Morris.

64. Kim, Myungsook. "Crossing the Boundaries Between Renaissance Literature and Linguistics: A Review of Chaucerism." *Medieval and Early Modern English Studies* 12 (2004): 67–84 (in Korean, with English abstract). Contrasts the "Chaucerism" of John Cheke and Edmund Spenser with the inkhorn habit of borrowing Latinate terms practiced by other Renaissance English writers.

65. Krier, Theresa. "Time Lords: Rhythm and Interval in Spenser's Stanzaic Narrative." *SSt* 21 (2006): 1–19. Krier notes the influence of early Chaucer works upon Spenser. Chaucer's early dream visions influenced Spenser and provide an example of linking plot to daily activity.

66. Lines, Candace. "The Erotic Politics of Grief in Surrey's 'So cruell prison.'" *SEL* 46 (2006): 1–26. Lines argues that the idealized chivalric homosocial bonding in Surrey's poem was influenced by *KnT*. Eulogizing the Duke of Richmond in this way critiques the debased version of political bonds in the court of Henry VIII.

67. Miralles Pérez, Antonio J. "Fading Knights and Thriving Men-at-Arms in Chaucer and Conan Doyle." In Juan Camilo Conde Silvestre and Ma Nila Vázquez González, eds. *Medieval English Literary and Cultural Studies* (*SAC* 30 [2008], no. 110), pp. 205–22. Conan Doyle's portrayals of knights from the Hundred Years' War in *The White Company* (1891) and *Sir Nigel* (1906) embody the same contradictions and ambiguities found in Chaucer's depiction of a fourteenth-century knight in *CT*.

68. Petrina, Alessandra. "'My Maisteris Dere': The Acknowledgement of Authority in *The Kingis Quair*." *Scottish Studies Review* 7 (2006): 9–23. Petrina considers the citation of Gower and Chaucer at the end of *The Kingis Quair* and the poem's context in Bodley MS Arch. Selden. B.24, a manuscript with a high number of misattributions to Chaucer; also speculates about intellectual exchange at the Lancastrian court among James I, Lydgate, and Hoccleve.

69. Phillips, Helen. "Chaucer and the Nineteenth-Century City." In

Ardis Butterfield, ed. *Chaucer and the City* (*SAC* 30 [2008], no. 108), pp. 193–210. The warm acclaim the Victorians gave to Chaucer reflects the nineteenth century's anxious and conflicted responses to rapid urbanization.

70. Reilly, Terry. "Reading 'The Lagoon' and Chaucer's 'The Knight's Tale' through Edward Said's *The World, the Text, and the Critic*." *Conradiana* 38.2 (2006): 175–82. The influence of *KnT* on Conrad's "The Lagoon" is evident in several details, in narrative method, and, more distantly, in the fact that each is written in English that is "unfixed and de-centered."

71. Scanlon, Larry, and James Simpson, eds. *John Lydgate: Poetry, Culture, and Lancastrian England*. Notre Dame, Ind.: University of Notre Dame Press, 2006. vi, 314 pp. An introduction by the editors and eleven essays by various authors seek to vitalize Lydgate studies, exploring the status of poet laureate, Lydgate's poetic style, his political poetry, and a number of literary poems and forms (e.g., mumming, translation) that have been considered marginal. Chaucer's influence is a recurrent topic, with particular attention to *ClT*, *HF*, and *PF*. See also no. 377.

72. Steinberg, Glenn. "Chaucer's Mutability in Spenser's *Mutabilitie Cantos*." *SEL* 46.1 (2006): 27–42. Steinberg examines differences between depictions of Nature in Spenser's *Mutabilitie Cantos* and in Chaucer's *PF*. For Spenser, disorder inheres in nature, while in Chaucer it results from human "pettiness and passion." Such differences remind us of changes between the fourteenth and sixteenth centuries, despite Spenser's insistence that he follows the work of his predecessor.

73. Trevisan, Sara. "Eliot's 'The Love Song of J. Alfred Prufrock.'" *Expl* 62.4 (2004): 221–23. Trevisan identifies in Eliot's "Prufrock" possible echoes of the Monk's description from *GP*. "Prufrock" may also have been influenced by Shakespeare's *Hamlet*.

74. Trigg, Stephanie. "Chaucer's Influence and Reception." In Seth Lerer, ed. *The Yale Companion to Chaucer* (*SAC* 30 [2008], no. 131), pp. 297–323. Trigg considers recurrent issues in the reception of Chaucer: responses to his self-shaped "poetic signature," admiration for his rhetoric and sentiment, and mourning for the loss of his genius by poets who seek to emulate him. Surveys rewritings and adaptations of *TC* and *CT* and raises questions about the reciprocity of canon formation and the institutions that produce such canons.

75. Williamson, Anne. "'Save his own soul he hath no star':

Thoughts Arising from *The Dream of Fair Women* (A Talk Given at the HWS Study Day, 16 February 2002)." *Henry Williamson Society Journal* 39 (2003): 30–60. Explores the possibility that Henry Williamson's novel *The Dream of Fair Women* was influenced by Tennyson's poem "A Dream of Fair Women" and, in turn, by Chaucer's *LGW*.

See also nos. 22, 84, 93, 112, 158, 175, 186, 211, 214, 230.

Style and Versification

76. Copeland, Rita. "Chaucer and Rhetoric." In Seth Lerer, ed. *The Yale Companion to Chaucer* (*SAC* 30 [2008], no. 131), pp. 122–43. Copeland outlines the classical-medieval tradition of rhetoric and its relationships with history, philosophy, and literary style. Considers the Pardoner as an embodiment of rhetoric and its potential for abuse; the Wife of Bath as rhetorical excess and rhetorical competence; *TC* as an exploration of narrative in relation to history; *Mel* as an application of rhetorical appropriateness (*kairos*); and *NPT* as an "essay in the theory of form" and a "rhetoric laboratory."

77. Fuller, David. "Reading Chaucer Aloud." In Corinne Saunders, ed. *A Concise Companion to Chaucer* (*SAC* 30 [2008], no. 143), pp. 263–84. Fuller insists that sound is "intrinsic to meaning" in reading Chaucer, commenting on the importance of metrical patterns and syntactic structures, appropriate intonation and pace, and pronunciation of final -*e*. Although it is difficult to approximate historical pronunciation of Chaucer's verse, reconstructive approaches and modern pronunciation are not mutually exclusive. The essay includes a list of audio and video recordings and evaluates a number of them.

78. Schaefer, Ursula. "Textualizing the Vernacular in Late Medieval England: Suggestions for Some Heuristic Reconsiderations." In Andrew James Johnston, Ferdinand von Mengden, and Stefan Thim, eds. *Language and Text: Current Perspectives on English and Germanic Historical Linguistics and Philology* (*SAC* 30 [2008], no. 124), pp. 269–90. Schaefer considers the process of vernacularization in late medieval English in comparison with other European languages, suggesting that quotations from the period about English are commonplaces rather than reflections of contemporary attitudes and calling for attention to the tradition of

ars dictandi. Also comments on *Mel* and *ParsT* as self-conscious examples of expository written prose.

See also nos. 52, 83, 97, 300.

Language and Word Studies

79. Caon, Luisella. "The Pronouns of Love and Sex: *Thou* and *Ye* Among Lovers in *The Canterbury Tales*." In C. C. Barfoot, ed. *"And Never Know the Joy": Sex and the Erotic in English Poetry*. Amsterdam and New York: Rodopi, 2006, pp. 33–47. Chaucer's uses of *thou* and *ye* pronouns "systematically" indicate the "degree of closeness or distance" between lovers in *CT*, indicating not only formality and informality but also intensity of emotion and shifts in attitudes. Caon surveys previous scholarship and draws examples from *WBT*, *MerT*, *MilT*, *RvT*, and *ShT*.

80. Diller, Hans-Jürgen. "Chaucer's Emotion Lexicon: *Passioun* and *Affeccioun*." In Nikolaus Ritt and Herbert Schendl, eds. *Rethinking Middle English: Linguistic and Literary Approaches* (*SAC* 30 [2008], no. 138), pp. 110–24. While six Middle English terms of emotion are in some measure coterminous—*onde, affect, mood, spirit, passioun,* and *affeccioun*—only the latter two closely approximate modern usage. *Passioun* connotes a state of being acted upon; *affeccioun* connotes action and, in Chaucer, is usually synonymous with *love*. Diller draws examples from *Bo, ParsT*, and *TC*.

81. Hall, Alaric. "Elves on the Brain: Chaucer, Old English, and *Elvish*." *Anglia* 124 (2006): 225–43. Reevaluation and continuation of the studies by John Burrow (*SAC* 19 [1997], no. 68) and Richard Firth Green (*SAC* 27 [2005], no. 71) on the meaning of the word *elvish* in *CT*. *Elvish* in *CYT* carries the meaning "delusory," whereas *elvish* in the prologue to *Th* means "abstracted."

82. Hughes, Geoffrey. *An Encyclopedia of Swearing: The Social History of Oaths, Profanity, Foul Language, and Ethnic Slurs in the English-Speaking World*. Armonk, N.Y.: M. E. Sharpe, 2006. xxv, 573 pp. Several hundred entries cover a wide range of historical and conceptual topics, individual words, important landmarks in the history of swearing, etc. Very few entries are given over to individual writers, although the entry on Chaucer is lengthy (pp. 67–73). It surveys the varieties of swearing, profanity, and obscenity in *CT* and cross-references related topics such as "Cherles Termes," "Saints' Names," and "Virago." The volume in-

cludes a brief bibliography for most entries, a brief chronology, and an index.

83. Jimura, Akiyuki. *Studies in Chaucer's Words and His Narratives*. Hiroshima: Keisuisha, 2005. vii, 263 pp. A study of Chaucer's works from a linguistic-stylistic approach, based on Jimura's doctoral dissertation (2002).

84. Johnston, Andrew James, and Claudia Lange. "The Beginnings of Standardization—An Epilogue." In Ursula Schaefer, ed. *The Beginnings of Standardization: Language and Culture in Fourteenth-Century England* (*SAC* 30 [2008], no. 144), pp. 183–200. The authors consider linguistic and cultural factors in English standardization of the fourteenth century, including the reciprocity of Chaucer's contributions to standardization and the role standardization played in " 'the making' of Chaucer."

85. Łozowski, Przemysław. "Polysemy in Context: *Meten* and *Dremen* in Chaucer." In Nikolaus Ritt and Herbert Schendl, eds. *Rethinking Middle English: Linguistic and Literary Approaches* (*SAC* 30 [2008], no. 138), pp. 125–46. Disputes the assumption that *meten* and *dremen* are synonyms in Chaucer and illustrates systematic differentiation in *WBT*, *NPT*, *BD*, *Rom*, *HF*, *Bo,* and *TC* (plus other, non-Chaucerian texts). In general, the late fourteenth century is a transitional period for dream vocabulary that invited more precise usage. The author correlates Chaucer's usage of *meten* and *dremen* and Macrobius's true and false dreams, respectively.

86. Maíz Arévalo, Carmen. "Are We So Different?: Towards a New Reading of the Wife of Bath and the Pardoner in Chaucer's *Canterbury Tales*." In Juan Camilo Conde Silvestre and Ma Nila Vázquez González, eds. *Medieval English Literary and Cultural Studies* (*SAC* 30 [2008], no. 110), pp. 81–94. Discusses linguistic pragmatics to disclose parallels between *WBPT* and *PardPT*, focusing on the relationship between the characters' uses of speech and the two works.

87. Miller, D. Gary. "The Morphological Legacy of French: Borrowed Suffixes on Native Bases in Middle English." *Diachronica* 14 (1997): 233–64. Miller tallies a number of "hybrid derivatives" from before 1500, focusing on top-frequency suffixes. Examples and conclusions involve Chaucerian usage, including Chaucer's tendency to develop "non-technical hybrids" and to use "non-prestige French affixes on native English bases" rather than to apply "abstract suffixes on bases of lower register."

88. Molencki, Rafał. "The Confusion Between *Thurven* and *Durren* in Middle English." In Nikolaus Ritt and Herbert Schendl, eds. *Rethinking Middle English: Linguistic and Literary Approaches* (*SAC* 30 [2008], no. 138), pp. 147–60. Molencki traces the phonetic and semantic conflation of *dare* and *tharf*, once distinct verbs, now obsolete. Scribal errors contributed to the obsolescence of *tharf* and its replacement with the more flexible OE *neden*. The essay draws examples from *WBP*, *SumT*, *Mel*, *ParsT*, and *TC*.

89. Nakao, Yoshiyuki. "The Interpretation of *Troilus and Criseyde* 3.587: '*syn I moste on yow triste.*'" In Michiko Ogura, ed. *Textual and Contextual Studies in Medieval English: Towards the Reunion of Linguistics and Philology* (*SAC* 30 [2008], no. 135), pp. 51–73. Nakao assesses Criseyde's comment on trusting Pandarus (*TC* 3.587) as ambiguous, considering "phonological, morphological, lexical/collocational, syntactic and pragmatic" aspects of Chaucer's use of *moste* as an auxiliary and an adverb.

90. Nevalainen, Terttu. "Negative Concord as an English 'Vernacular Universal': Social History and Linguistic Typology." *JEngL* 34 (2006): 257–78. Addresses historical sociolinguistic trends between 1400 and 1800, tracing the disappearance of multiple negative (negative concord) usage to the latter half of the eighteenth century. However, data also suggest that Late Middle English initiated the shift from negative concord to negative forms in conjunction with nonassertives (e.g., "not . . . anything"). Nevalainen draws data from *Bo*.

91. Ono, Hideshi. "Personal and Impersonal Uses of *Meten* and *Dremen* in Chaucer." *Hiroshima Studies in English Language and Literature* 43 (1988): 1–15. Ono examines Chaucer's personal and impersonal uses of the verbs *meten* and *dremen* to refer to dreams. The personal use emerged in the fourteenth century.

92. Pearsall, Derek. "Before-Chaucer Evidences of an English Literary Vernacular with a Standardizing Tendency." In Ursula Schaefer, ed. *The Beginnings of Standardization: Language and Culture in Fourteenth-Century England* (*SAC* 30 [2008], no. 144), pp. 27–41. Pearsall surveys traditional accounts of the rise of an English standard and comments on recent emphases and remaining issues. Considers the Auchinleck Manuscript as evidence of the London literary culture that precedes Chaucer.

93. Rissanen, Matti. "On the Development of Borrowed Connectives in Fourteenth-Century English: Evidence from Corpora." In Ursula Schaefer, ed. *The Beginnings of Standardization: Language and Culture in*

Fourteenth-Century England (*SAC* 30 [2008], no. 144), pp. 133–46. Rissanen analyzes the "grammaticalization" of several related conjunctions (*because, in case, save, except*) that suggest a complicated model of standardization. Popular texts such as Chaucer's *CT* may have had as much influence on standardization as administrative documents had.

94. Rothwell, W. "Anglo-French and English Society in Chaucer's 'The Reeve's Tale.'" *ES* 87 (2006): 511–38. Identifies in *RvT* lexical evidence of a culture permeated with French linguistic influence, evidence that could be reinforced by a more thorough linguistic study of *RvT* and the rest of Chaucer's corpus: "Far from being 'ephemeral and localized' or 'informal,' the contribution of Anglo-French to the lexis of English and to the evolution of English society was lasting and profound."

95. Stanley, Eric G. "Fear Chiefly in Old and Middle English." *PoeticaT* 66 (2006): 73–114. Etymological and semantic exploration of *fear* and related words that indicates nuances lost in translation between early English and modern editions and adaptations; discusses two uses of "no fere" in *TC* (3.583 and 1144) and an emendation of "thys fere" to "hys fere" in *HF* 174.

96. Watson, Nicholas. "Cultural Changes." In "*ELN* Forums. Cluster 1: 'Vernacular Theology' and Medieval Studies." *ELN* 44.1 (Spring 2006): 127–37. This final essay in the forum responds to preceding essays and argues that vernacular writing about religion is a political act subject to study as a "single area of discourse." Literary critics examining this area will find that "the logic that governs secular power and interest is subverted, inverted, or dissolved" in this discourse.

97. Windeatt, Barry. "Courtly Writing." In Corinne Saunders, ed. *A Concise Companion to Chaucer* (*SAC* 30 [2008], no. 143), pp. 90–109. Windeatt examines how the court and elements of courtly writing are represented and function in *BD, HF, PF,* and *LGWP*, with some attention to *SqT*. Comments on Machaut as Chaucer's model and how the dream vision gives Chaucer the liberty to examine both "the ethos and practice of courtly conduct" and "the checks and balances of power in courtly life." The act of courtly speech is crucial in all of the dream visions.

98. Yoshikawa, Fumiko. "Middle English Verbs with Both Impersonal Use and Reflexive Use." In Michiko Ogura, ed. *Textual and Contextual Studies in Medieval English: Towards the Reunion of Linguistics and Philology* (*SAC* 30 [2008], no. 135), pp. 205–16. Yoshikawa studies

Middle English verbs with both reflexive and impersonal uses in ten typical situations, considering Chaucer's uses of *menen* and *remembren* as examples where semantic value and the nature of the participants affect usage.

99. Zurcher, Andrew. "Spenser's Studied Archaism: The Case of 'Mote.'" *SSt* 21 (2006): 231–40. Zurcher studies usage of *mote* and *mought* and compares Spenser's and Chaucer's uses of modal auxiliaries.

See also nos. 20, 31, 64, 77, 124, 131, 138, 144, 161, 177, 183, 187, 205, 209, 212, 237, 242, 249, 250, 298.

Background and General Criticism

100. Adams, Jenny. *Power Play: The Literature and Politics of Chess in the Late Middle Ages*. The Middle Ages Series. Philadelphia: University of Pennsylvania Press, 2006. 252 pp. Studies the ways that chess represents types of political and social order, examining the *Liber de Moribus Hominum et Officiis Nobilium* of Jacobus de Cessolis, *Les echecs amoureux*, *BD*, the *Tale of Beryn*, Hoccleve's *Regement of Princes*, and the English translation of Jacobus's *Liber*, published by Caxton as *The Game and Play of Chess*. The discussions of *BD* and *Beryn* are revisions of previous publications: "Pawn Takes Knight's Queen: Playing with Chess in Chaucer's *Book of the Duchess*" (*SAC* 23 [2001], no. 225) and "Exchequers and Balances: Anxieties of Exchange in *The Tale of Beryn*" (*SAC* 28 [2006], no. 216).

101. Allen, Valerie. "Waxing Red: Shame and the Body, Shame and the Soul." In Lisa Perfetti, ed. *The Representation of Women's Emotions in Medieval and Early Modern Culture*. Gainesville: University Press of Florida, 2005, pp. 191–210. Uses examples from Chaucer, *Sir Gawain and the Green Knight*, and the *Ancrene Wisse* to explore how shame differs for men and women. For men, shame stems from a wide range of cultural experiences associated with chivalry, while women's shame is associated with "sexual honor." In addition, the rhetorical term *color* can connote shame. Comments on *BD, TC, LGW, PF, CYT, ClT, PhyT*, and *FranT*. See also no. 367.

102. Barnes, Geraldine. "Medieval Murder—Modern Crime Fiction." In Ruth Evans, Helen Fulton, and David Matthews, eds. *Medieval Cultural Studies: Essays in Honour of Stephen Knight* (*SAC* 30 [2008], no. 115), pp. 241–67. Barnes contrasts the absence of the city of London in

medieval fiction (*CkT*, *CYT*, and *Athelston*) with fictionalized descriptions of medieval London in murder mysteries written in the 1980s and 1990s by P. C. Doherty and Kate Sedley.

103. Bellamy, Elizabeth Jane. "Desires and Disavowals: Speculations on the Aftermath of Stephen Greenblatt's 'Psychoanalysis and Renaissance Culture.'" *Clio* 34.3 (2005): 297–315. Responding to Greenblatt's essay, Bellamy explores the status of psychoanalytic criticism in medieval studies, with particular focus on Chaucer studies.

104. Blackbourne, Matthew. "The Ricardian Revival of English Literature." *Medieval History Magazine* 6 (2004): 30–33. Brief summary of Ricardian literature and contemporary social and political events. Mentions Gower's works, *Piers Plowman*, *Sir Gawain and the Green Knight*, and Chaucer's works, especially *GP* and *WBPT*.

105. Blamires, Alcuin. *Chaucer, Ethics, and Gender*. Oxford: Oxford University Press, 2006. xii, 263 pp. Blamires elucidates ways in which *CT* and, to a lesser extent, *TC* engage moral and ethical discourse and shows this discourse at times to be gendered. Grounded in a range of Christian and classical sources, especially Stoic texts, Chaucer's "spectrum of nuances" makes various demands on his audience. Topics include friendship in *KnT* and *TC*; credulity and vision in *MilT*, *MerT*, and *WBT*; sexual pleasure and marital debt in *MerT*, *RvT*, *MilT*, and *PardPT*; sufficiency in *MLPT* and *ShT*; gendered varieties of liberality in *WBP* and *FranT*; patience and equanimity in *FranT*, *ClT*, and *NPT*; moral jurisdiction in *FrT*, *PhyT*, and *PardPT*; and speech and speechlessness in *SNT*, *CYPT*, *ManT*, and *ParsT*. Neither *ParsT* nor any allegorical standard establishes a single ethical norm for *CT*. See also no. 309.

106. Brewer, Derek. "Understanding Chivalry in Earlier English Literature." In Nikolaus Ritt and Herbert Schendl, eds. *Rethinking Middle English: Linguistic and Literary Approaches* (*SAC* 30 [2008], no. 138), pp. 1–16. Some scholars harbor a Golden-Age notion of chivalry not unlike that expressed in *ParsT*. Others, operating within a post-Freudian context, presume that the chivalric emphasis on ceremony must conceal inward anxiety or repression: hence, the prevalence of such catchwords as *crisis, revival,* and *nostalgia*. Citing *KnT*, *FranT*, and *TC*, Brewer urges readings that appreciate both "enriching differences" and "profound similarities" between modern and medieval cultural norms.

107. Butterfield, Ardis. "Chaucer and the Detritus of the City." In Ardis Butterfield, ed. *Chaucer and the City* (*SAC* 30 [2008], no. 108), pp.

3–24. Butterfield situates the study of Chaucer and London within a framework of theoretical approaches to the construction of urban space.

108. ———, ed. *Chaucer and the City*. Chaucer Studies, no. 37. Cambridge: D. S. Brewer, 2006. 231 pp. Twelve essays by various authors under the rubrics "Locations," "Communities," "Institutions," and "Afterlife." The introduction argues that any consideration of city life is an act of recovering the past. Chaucer allows the audience to hear and see medieval London. See nos. 69, 107, 114, 137, 157, 189, 229, 238, 242, 254, 289, and 301. See also no. 315.

109. Cawsey, Kathleen Eleanor. "Twentieth-Century Chaucer Studies and Theories of Audience." *DAI* A67.06 (2006): n.p. Cawsey examines the impact of assumptions about audience in the criticism of six twentieth-century Chaucer scholars (Kittredge, Lewis, Donaldson, Robertson, Dinshaw, and Patterson). These assumptions include whether the audience is diachronic or synchronic, the level of audience trust, and the audience's homogeneity.

110. Conde Silvestre, Juan Camilo; and Ma Nila Vázquez González, eds. *Medieval English Literary and Cultural Studies*. SELIM, no. 15. [Murcia: Universidad de Murcia], 2004. 251 pp. Includes five essays that pertain to Chaucer; see nos. 47, 67, 86, 142, and 169.

111. Cooney, Helen, ed. *Writings on Love in the English Middle Ages*. New York: Palgrave Macmillan, 2006. xiii, 204 pp. Eleven essays by various authors, an introduction by the editor, and an index. Topics include the theory of courtly love, love and social class, romance depictions of love, and readings of individual works. For seven essays that pertain to Chaucer, see nos. 57, 112, 141, 200, 206, 221, and 295.

112. Cooper, Helen. "Love Before Troilus." In Helen Cooney, ed. *Writings on Love in the English Middle Ages* (*SAC* 30 [2008], no. 111), pp. 25–43. Before *TC* and *KnT*, most romances in England were Anglo-Norman and largely uninfluenced by the conventions of courtly love and the Petrarchan tradition. The reputation of Chaucer's works overshadows that of these other works and their more practical ethos of love.

113. Eckhardt, Caroline D. "One Third of the Earth? Europe Seen and Unseen in the Middle English Chronicles of the Fourteenth Century." *CL* 58 (2006): 313–38. Traces conceptualizations of Europe available to fourteenth-century English chroniclers and then explores the use of these by the chroniclers, especially Robert Mannyng and John Trevisa. *TC* and *LGW* reflect a tradition that sees Europe as a territory whose

inhabitants traced their lineage to "Europa." *MLT* uses Europe as panegyric.

114. Evans, Ruth. "The Production of Space in Chaucer's London." In Ardis Butterfield, ed. *Chaucer and the City* (*SAC* 30 [2008], no. 108), pp. 41–56. Reads Chaucer's London in relationship to three topics: social space, Plato's order of the city, and the political tie between sovereign and subjects.

115. ———, Helen Fulton, and David Matthews, eds. *Medieval Cultural Studies: Essays in Honour of Stephen Knight*. Cardiff: University of Wales Press, 2006. xi, 286 pp. Seventeen essays by various authors on topics such as Robin Hood, Chaucer, medieval romance, medievalism, cultural studies, and modern crime fiction. Includes an introduction (pp. 1–6) and a bibliography of Knight's publications (pp. 269–77). For six essays that pertain to Chaucer, see nos. 102, 118, 132, 177, 210, and 227.

116. Fahey, Amy Elizabeth. "Heralds and Heraldry in English Literature." *DAI* A67.02 (2006): n.p. Explores relationships between heralds and poets as reflected in works by Chaucer (including *HF* and *KnT*), Malory, Skelton, and Spenser. These works "reveal complex concerns about literary and political authority, the public status of the poet, and the stability of both visual and written discourses of fame and reputation."

117. Farber, Lianna. *An Anatomy of Trade in Medieval Writing: Value, Consent, and Community*. Ithaca, N.Y.: Cornell University Press, 2006. x, 235 pp. Farber examines the "idea of trade . . . in medieval writing from the middle of the twelfth to the early fifteenth century," examining theoretical treatises and literary depictions of trade and its relations to valuation, marital exchanges, and ideals of community. Assesses "Precarious Value in Chaucer's *Shipman's Tale* and *Franklin's Tale*" (pp. 68–83)—a discussion of surplus and the impermanence of value in *ShT* and of the precariousness of value in *FranT*—and reprints "The Creation of Consent in Chaucer's *Physician's Tale*" (*SAC* 28 [2006], no. 146).

118. Fulton, Helen. "Cheapside in the Age of Chaucer." In Ruth Evans, Helen Fulton, and David Matthews, eds. *Medieval Cultural Studies: Essays in Honour of Stephen Knight* (*SAC* 30 [2008], no. 115), pp. 138–51. Processions and spectacles were attempts to contain rivalries between and within the official and unofficial hierarchies of late medieval London (city and crown, wards, crafts, and trades). Recurrently depicting a stable city, Chaucer also depicts urban tensions at times: in the

House of Rumor of *HF*, the description of the Guildsmen in *GP*, and *CkT*.

119. Gaylord, Alan T. "Reflections on D. W. Robertson, Jr., and 'Exegetical Criticism.'" *ChauR* 40 (2006): 311–33. A search of contemporary Chaucerian criticism for signs of whether D. W. Robertson's "exegetical criticism" continues to generate important work yields the conclusion "no, yes, and perhaps": "no," in the wake of the ascendance of historicist criticism; "yes," in the form of work that establishes new exegetical categories; and "perhaps," in work that corrects, "deconstructs," and provides "new syntheses" of Robertson's legacy.

120. Hamaguchi, Keiko. *Non-European Women in Chaucer: A Postcolonial Study*. Studies in English Medieval Language and Literature, 1436–1521, no. 14. Frankfurt am Main: Peter Lang, 2006. 194 pp. Applies postcolonial theory to explore how Chaucer represents non-European women as Other in both gender and culture and how Chaucer reflects his own position as a poet and his career in historical context. Treats *KnT*, *MLT*, *SqT*, *MkT*, *HF*, and *LGW*.

121. Higl, Andrew. "Printing Power: Selling Lydgate, Gower, and Chaucer." *Essays in Medieval Studies* 23 (2006): 57–77. Explores why Chaucer was more marketable than either Gower or Lydgate in sixteenth-century England: Chaucer's variety, flexibility, and malleability made him more adaptable to various publics and therefore more attractive to early printers than other writers were.

122. Horobin, David. *Falconry in Literature: The Symbolism of Falconry in English Literature from Chaucer to Marvell*. Blaine, Wash.: Hancock House, 2004. 223 pp. An illustrated guide to raptors in English literature (fourteenth century to seventeenth century), which explains their symbolic value in terms of historical training and hunting practices and rituals. Recurrent references to Chaucer's works, including *PF*, *SqT*, and *WBP*.

123. Johnson, Paul. *Creators: From Chaucer and Dürer to Picasso and Disney*. New York: HarperCollins, 2006. 310 pp. Appreciative discussion of the accomplishments of individual artists, designers, musicians, and authors, emphasizing their labors and the nature of their accomplishments. Chapter 2, "Chaucer: The Man in the Fourteenth-Century Street," discusses Chaucer's life, his linguistic innovation, and the social variety of his works, characterizing him as "probably the first man, and certainly the first writer, to see the English nation as a unity." See also no. 348.

124. Johnston, Andrew James, Ferdinand von Mengden, and Stefan Thim, eds. *Language and Text: Current Perspectives on English and Germanic Historical Linguistics and Philology.* Anglistische Forschungen, no. 359. Heidelberg: Winter, 2006. 426 pp. Twenty-four essays by various authors, presented as a festschrift for Klaus Dietz. Includes a wide variety of topics within German and English linguistics and medieval studies. Two essays pertain to Chaucer; see nos. 78 and 239.

125. Kerby-Fulton, Kathryn. *Books Under Suspicion: Censorship and Tolerance of Revelatory Writing in Late Medieval England.* Notre Dame, Ind.: University of Notre Dame Press, 2006. lii, 562 pp. 21 b&w illus.; 1 color illus. Studies the cultural, literary, and codicological contexts for English late medieval works of revealed writing—apocalyptic, visionary, mystical, prophetic, etc.—considering the reception of Continental works in England and works composed in English. Clarifies how works by Joachim of Fiore, William de St. Amour, Peter Olivi, William of Ockham, the *Opus arduum*, and others are related to and separate from Wycliffite writings, concentrating on their status as heretical texts and their influences on Middle English literature: Margery Kempe, Julian of Norwich, *Piers Plowman*, and several of Chaucer's works. Reads *Rom* (part C) in light of orthodoxy and the *Roman de la Rose*; *HF* as a "teasing satire of the revelatory" (especially Langland's *Piers*); *ClT* and *NPT* on free will and God's power; and *Ret* as a conservative withdrawal of humanist fiction. Contains a useful "Chronology" of non-Wycliffite cases of heresy and related events (xix–lii), plus three related appendices.

126. Knapp, Ethan. "Chaucer Criticism and Its Legacies." In Seth Lerer, ed. *The Yale Companion to Chaucer* (*SAC* 30 [2008], no. 131), pp. 324–56. Knapp surveys trends in academic critical approaches to Chaucer, focusing on interactions and tensions between philological study and interpretive criticism. Summarizes Chaucer's place in the rise of university curricula and explores landmark New Critical discussions of his realism, irony, and allegory. Closes with comments on the influences of New Historicism, feminism, queer theory, and psychoanalysis.

127. Kruger, Steven. "Dreaming." In Corinne Saunders, ed. *A Concise Companion to Chaucer* (*SAC* 30 [2008], no. 143), pp. 71–89. Kruger summarizes medieval dream theory and argues that Chaucer exploits "the complexities, ambiguities, and uncertainties of dreams, their causes, and their interpretation." Dreams pose interpretive problems in *NPT* and *TC*. As dream visions, *BD, HF, PF,* and *LGWP* take up psy-

chological or personal concerns and address philosophical and theological questions.

128. Krygier, Marcin, and Liliana Sikorska, eds. *Naked Wordes in Englissh.* Medieval English Mirror, no. 2. Frankfurt am Main: Peter Lang, 2005. 197 pp. Ten essays selected from the papers presented at the Third Medieval English Studies Symposium in Poznan, Poland, in November 2004, focusing on Old and Middle English language and literature. Two essays pertain to Chaucer; see nos. 155 and 224.

129. Lawton, Lesley. "Representing the Peasants' Revolt." In Jean-Paul Debax, ed. *Actes de l'atelier "Moyen Age" du XLVe congrès de la SAES (Société des Anglicistes de l'Enseignement Supérieur).* Paris: Publications de l'Association des Médiévistes Anglicistes de l'Enseignement Supérieur, 2006, pp. 31–46. Discusses John Gower's *Vox Clamantis,* with passing mention of Chaucer.

130. Lenz, Tanya S. "Chaucer's Oneiric Medicine: Dreams, Disease, Healing, and Literary Endeavor." *DAI* A67.06 (2006): n.p. Lenz considers the collision/juxtaposition of dreams and medical knowledge in *BD, HF, PF, TC,* and *NPT.* Argues that this confluence offers a previously neglected dimension of Chaucer's work.

131. Lerer, Seth, ed. *The Yale Companion to Chaucer.* New Haven and London: Yale University Press, 2006. ix, 420 pp. An introduction and ten essays by various authors, with several appendices (chronology, a guide to textual studies, order and pattern within *CT,* and maps), plus a bibliography and an index. Aimed at an American audience, the volume seeks to "combine interpretation with information." The introduction by Lerer (pp. 1–28) considers the "linguistic condition" and the nature of book production in Chaucer's time. For individual essays, see nos. 11, 51, 52, 74, 76, 126, 165, 252, 294, and 300.

132. Matthews, David. "What Was Medievalism? Medieval Studies, Medievalism, and Cultural Studies." In Ruth Evans, Helen Fulton, and David Matthews, eds. *Medieval Cultural Studies: Essays in Honour of Stephen Knight* (*SAC* 30 [2008], no. 115), pp. 9–22. Explores historical formulations of "medieval studies" and "medievalism," arguing that they are inseparable, and encouraging awareness of their interdependencies. Draws examples from Tyrwhitt's edition of *CT* and Helgeland's *A Knight's Tale,* among other works.

133. McSheffrey, Shannon. *Marriage, Sex, and Civic Culture in Late Medieval London.* Middle Ages Series. Philadelphia: University of Pennsylvania Press, 2006. viii, 291 pp. An introduction, seven chapters, and

a conclusion study marriage in London in the second half of the fifteenth century. The "fundamental argument is that bonds of marriage and sex were . . . intimate, deeply personal ties and matters of public concern, subject to intervention by everyone from a woman's or man's family, friends, and employers to the mayor of London himself." Chapter 5 mentions briefly that Walter weds Griselda in *ClT* by ambiguous words with only one witness in a suspect bedchamber contract. Chapter 6 mentions that, despite the depiction of the summoner in *FrT*, "there is little evidence of . . . church-police figures" in fifteenth-century London.

134. Minnis, Alastair, and Ian Johnson, eds. *The Cambridge History of Literary Criticism. Volume 2: The Middle Ages.* New York: Cambridge University Press, 2005. xvi, 865 pp. A capacious survey of critical theory and application in medieval letters, with twenty-seven essays by various authors, arranged in seven sections: the liberal arts and Latin textuality, the study of classical authors, textual psychologies, vernacular theory in the early Middle Ages, vernacular theory in the late Middle Ages, Latin and vernacular theory in Italian, and literary theory in Byzantium. Chaucer is referred to in passing (see the index), and discussed at some length in "Vernacular Literary Consciousness c. 1100–c. 1500: French, German and English Evidence" (pp. 422–71), by Kevin Brownlee, Tony Hunt, Ian Johnson, Alastair Minnis, and Nigel F. Palmer. See also no. 362.

135. Ogura, Michiko, ed. *Textual and Contextual Studies in Medieval English: Towards the Reunion of Linguistics and Philology.* Studies in English Medieval Language and Literature, no. 13. Frankfurt am Main: Peter Lang, 2006. Sixteen essays by various authors on linguistic topics in Old and Middle English, including a survey of the teaching of medieval English in Korea. The papers were presented at the first international conference of the Society of Historical English Language and Linguistics, Chiba University, Japan, September 1–3, 2005. For two papers that pertain to Chaucer, see nos. 89 and 98.

136. Patterson, Lee. *Temporal Circumstances: Form and History in the "Canterbury Tales."* The New Middle Ages. New York: Palgrave Macmillan, 2006. viii, 279 pp. Reprints seven of Patterson's essays, with a new introduction, "Historicism and Postmodernity" (pp. 1–18), that explains why he pursues the "micronarratives" of New Historicism rather than those of psychoanalytic criticism. Patterson affirms the functions of historical criticism despite postmodern challenges to certainty.

137. Pearsall, Derek. *"The Canterbury Tales* and London Club Cul-

ture." In Ardis Butterfield, ed. *Chaucer and the City* (*SAC* 30 [2008], no. 108), pp. 95–108. Argues that a substantial turn away from the topic of idealized love in Chaucer's writing after 1387 demonstrates a shift in his real and imagined audiences. In the second half of his career, Chaucer's audience may have been an almost exclusively male "Chaucer circle" whose tastes differed from earlier, court audiences.

138. Ritt, Nikolaus, and Herbert Schendl, eds. *Rethinking Middle English: Linguistic and Literary Approaches*. Studies in English Medieval Language and Literature, no. 10. New York and Frankfurt am Main: Peter Lang, 2005. xi, 339 pp. Includes four essays that pertain to Chaucer; see nos. 80, 85, 88, and 106.

139. Robertson, Elizabeth. "Introduction to *ELN* Forums. Cluster 1: 'Vernacular Theology' and Medieval Studies." *ELN* 44.1 (Spring 2006): 77–79. Robertson introduces a series of seven essays responding to Nicholas Watson's *Speculum* essay "Censorship and Cultural Change in Medieval England: Vernacular Theology, the Oxford Translation Debate, and Arundel's Constitutions of 1409" (*Speculum* 70 [1995]: 822–64). Robertson recounts the role of major Chaucerians in the examination of literary production through the lens of religion.

140. Salih, Sarah, ed. *A Companion to Middle English Hagiography*. Rochester, N.Y.; and Woodbridge, Suffolk: D. S. Brewer, 2006. x, 182 pp. Seven essays by various authors and an introduction by the editor. The book discusses late medieval English saints from a number of perspectives (readership, shrines and festivals, gender, historiography), with recurrent references to Chaucer, sustained discussion of *SNT*, references to *MLT*, and commentary on Chaucer's "manipulation of hagiographical commonplaces" in *LGW*.

141. Saunders, Corinne. "Love and Loyalty in Middle English Romance." In Helen Cooney, ed. *Writings on Love in the English Middle Ages* (*SAC* 30 [2008], no. 111), pp. 45–61. Apart from Chaucer's works, most romances in Middle English "rewrite" their French and Latin analogues, representing the virtuous aspects of love rather than the conventions of the courtly game. Chaucer's writing exemplifies the "extremes of *fin amour*."

142. ———. "Magic, Science, and Romance: Chaucer and the Supernatural." In Juan Camilo Conde Silvestre and Ma Nila Vázquez González, eds. *Medieval English Literary and Cultural Studies* (*SAC* 30 [2008], no. 110), pp. 121–43. Surveys medieval beliefs and learning about magic and explores the narrative function and resonance of magic and

the supernatural in Chaucer's writing. Also considers relations to natural philosophy or "science" and the shift from medieval to Renaissance notions of magic and the supernatural.

143. ———, ed. *A Concise Companion to Chaucer.* Blackwell Concise Companions to Literature and Culture. Malden, Mass.; Oxford; and Victoria: Blackwell, 2006. xii, 292 pp. Thirteen essays intended for the new and returning student of Chaucer. Following the editor's introduction (pp. 1–10) describing facets of Chaucer's art and life and the contents of the collection, the work is divided into parts: Chaucer in Context, Dream Visions, *Troilus and Criseyde, The Canterbury Tales,* and The Sound of Chaucer. For individual essays, see nos. 32, 54, 77, 97, 127, 150, 156, 160, 161, 163, 283, 284, and 292.

144. Schaefer, Ursula, ed. *The Beginnings of Standardization: Language and Culture in Fourteenth-Century England.* Studies in English Medieval Language and Literature, no. 15. Frankfurt am Main: Peter Lang, 2006. vi, 200 pp. Nine essays by various authors with an introduction and epilogue that discuss literary and linguistic aspects of early standardization in English. For five essays that consider Chaucer specifically, see nos. 84, 92, 93, 178, and 298.

145. Schibanoff, Susan. *Chaucer's Queer Poetics: Rereading the Dream Trio.* Toronto: University of Toronto Press, 2006. x, 365 pp. Schibanoff challenges the notion that Chaucer escaped from the decadent, "unmanly" influence of French verse to achieve his status as "father" of English poetry. In *BD,* Chaucer adopts the persona of "the weak, puerile, and loveless poet—the 'queer' poet"—to "inoculate" John of Gaunt against "contemporary moral censure." In *HF,* he adopts Dante's "hermaphroditic aesthetic"; the narrator of *HF* fails to achieve "the role of queer foil" but compels acknowledgment of "deviant poetics" and dismisses traditional authority. *PF* offers a queer view of Alan de Lille's *Plaint of Nature,* and Chaucer's Nature "is neither willing nor able to exclude sexual deviance from her realm." Traditional criticism of these poems is skewed by the "deep-rooted heterosexism of our most basic modern thinking about Chaucer's art" manifest in the "presumptively heterosexual organic metaphors" of literary criticism in general.

146. Schultz, James A. "Heterosexuality as a Threat to Medieval Studies." *Journal of the History of Sexuality* 15.1 (2006): 14–29. Schultz critiques uses of "heterosexual" as a term and as an ahistorical concept in queer studies of medieval literature. Chaucerian critics (and others) use the term in ways that "distort the very object" of their studies,

"thwart" history, and project modern sensibilities "backward" on the past. "Heterosexual" is as much a recent concept as is "homosexual."

147. Spellman, Mary Alice. "Rembrandt's Humor: Scatology, Satire, Burlesque, and Irony in Six Etchings." *DAI* A67.04 (2006): n.p. Spellman compares Rembrandt's *The Monk in the Cornfield* to Chaucerian satires of clergy.

148. Stévanovitch, Colette, ed. *Marges/Seuils: Le liminal dans la littérature médiévale anglaise.* Actes des journées d'étude de mai 2002, juin 2003, juin 2004. Publications de l'Association des Médiévistes Anglicistes de l'Enseignement Supérieur. Collection GRENDEL, no. 8. Nancy: AMAES, 2006. 404 pp. Includes seven essays that pertain to Chaucer; see nos. 7, 35, 36, 175, 176, 188, and 297.

149. Tambling, Jeremy. *Allegory and the Work of Melancholy: The Late Medieval and Shakespeare.* Internationale Forschungen zur Allgemeinen und Vergleichenden Literaturwissenschaft, no. 72. Amsterdam and New York: Rodopi, 2004. 233 pp. Tambling reads several late medieval and Renaissance texts in relation to Walter Benjamin's notions of melancholy and Freudian concepts of death, as well as allegory and history. Individual chapters treat *Piers Plowman*, Hoccleve's *Complaint and Dialogue*, Lydgate's *Fall of Princes*, Henryson's *Testament of Cresseid*, and Shakespeare's *Henry VI* and *Richard III*. A separate chapter—"The Knight Sets Forth: Chaucer, Chrétien, and Dürer" (pp. 64–93)— discusses "madness, complaint and violence" in *KnT*, focusing on exploration of the "reasons for destructiveness in people so committed to order." Tambling compares Arcite's melancholy to the love-madness in Chrétien's *Yvain*, reads the "modern instances" of *MkT* as a critique of *KnT*, and comments on relations between *KnT* and Albrecht Dürer's print *The Knight, Death, and the Devil.*

150. Turner, Marion. "Politics and London Life." In Corinne Saunders, ed. *A Concise Companion to Chaucer* (*SAC* 30 [2008], no. 143), pp. 13–33. Divided into three sections—"Politics and Discourse," "London Life and Chaucer's Poetry," and "Chaucer's Social Circle"—this essay surveys a variety of Chaucer's narratives and short poems, showing how they reflect urban and political elements in fourteenth-century London.

151. Utz, Richard J. "Past Perfect: 'Will It *Do* To Say Anything More About Chaucer?'" *North American Review* 291.6 (2006): 50. Comments on James Russell Lowell's essay "Chaucer," published in *North American Review* 111 (1870): 155–99.

152. Vander Elst, Stefan Erik Kristiaan. "Chaucer and the Crusades:

A Study in Late Medieval Literary and Political Thought." *DAI* A67.04 (2006): n.p. Reads the Knight and Squire (and their respective tales) as embodiments of differing philosophies toward the Crusades. The Knight is linked to the Crusades' earlier origins, while the Squire is seen as embodying a more romanticized approach to the conflicts.

153. Watts, William. "The Medieval Dream Vision as Survey of Medieval Literature." *SMART* 12.2 (2005): 67–95. Watts explains the pedagogy of teaching the dream vision at the undergraduate level, covering texts that include Macrobius, the *Dream of the Rood*, the *Roman de la Rose*, Dante, *Pearl*, *Piers Plowman*, Christine de Pizan's *Book of the City of Ladies*, and selections from Chaucer. Comments that *BD* and *HF* (like other works surveyed) allow students to explore the "processes of imitation, appropriation, and innovation" that characterize much medieval literature.

154. Wheeler, Bonnie, ed. *Mindful Spirit in Late Medieval Literature: Essays in Honor of Elizabeth D. Kirk*. New York: Palgrave Macmillan, 2006. viii, 266 pp. Seventeen essays by various authors on topics ranging from the Middle English St. Francis to the Passion plays, the York Cycle, John Wycliff, *Piers Plowman*, Gower, Margery Kempe, and other medieval writers and their literature. For two essays that pertain to Chaucer, see nos. 217 and 234.

155. Witalisz, Władysław. "On '. . . redoutynge of Mars and of his glorie'—Attitudes to War in Middle English Romance." In Marcin Krygier and Liliana Sikorska, eds. *Naked Wordes in Englissh* (*SAC* 30 [2008], no. 128), pp. 169–80. Witalisz explores ambivalent attitudes toward war in Middle English romances, particularly those concerned with Troy or King Arthur. Chaucer's attitude is "only implicit," and the antiwar stance attributed to him is based on "his deliberate silence on the subject."

The Canterbury Tales—General

156. Cartlidge, Neil. "Marriage, Sexuality, and the Family." In Corinne Saunders, ed. *A Concise Companion to Chaucer* (*SAC* 30 [2008], no. 143), pp. 218–40. Cartlidge examines the range of attitudes toward marriage, sexuality, and the family in *CT*—including questions of marriage as an ordering principle, sexuality as a threat to marriage, and sexuality as a form of aggression outside marriage. Also assesses notions of extended family, maternal grief, and paternal affection. Considers

MilT, RvT, MLT, WBPT, ClT, MerT, Sq-FranL, FranT, PhyT, PrT, and *ParsT.*

157. Cooper, Helen. "London and Southwark Poetic Companies: 'Si tost c'amis' and the *Canterbury Tales.*" In Ardis Butterfield, ed. *Chaucer and the City (SAC* 30 [2008], no. 108), pp. 109–28. Cooper discusses the poetic confraternities called *puys,* devoted to competitive writing of poetry. An edition and translation of Renaud de Hoiland's "Si tost c'amis" serves as an example of the kind of civil performance being rejected by the storytellers of *CT.*

158. Craig, Robert M. "Pilgrimage Route to Paradise: The Sacred and Profane Along the Dixie Highway." In Claudette Stager and Martha Carver, eds. *Looking Beyond the Highway: Dixie Roads and Culture.* Knoxville: University of Tennessee Press, 2006, pp. 267–87. Compares people and places of twentieth-century journeys on the Dixie Highway to several medieval pilgrimages, real and fictional, including *CT.*

159. Eyler, Joshua R. "Conditioning the Soul: Spiritual Athleticism in Medieval English Theology and Literature." *DAI* A67.05 (2006): n.p. Eyler considers the Pauline concept of "spiritual athleticism" (a means of struggling with temptation) in hagiographic literature and in canonical medieval English texts, including *CT.* Argues that the spiritual athlete moves from "trope in early medieval English texts to metaphorical construct in late medieval and early modern English literature."

160. Ferster, Judith. "Genre in and of the *Canterbury Tales.*" In Corinne Saunders, ed. *A Concise Companion to Chaucer (SAC* 30 [2008], no. 143), pp. 179–98. Ferster explores the importance of genre for understanding *CT,* a collection of different genres. Discusses how Chaucer stretches, plays with, and interrogates genre by combining features of genre and the expectations they create. Concentrates on the use of medieval estates satire and the representation of the narrator in *GP.* Also considers the dramatic approach to *CT* and the slipperiness of genre in the *Tales,* especially *MkT.*

161. Green, Richard Firth. "Morality and Immorality." In Corinne Saunders, ed. *A Concise Companion to Chaucer (SAC* 30 [2008], no. 143), pp. 199–217. Green confronts "the interpretive function of morality in medieval literature" and discusses why Chaucer's "moral horizons" in *CT* are elusive. Many of the *Tales* include competing morals; frameworks such as estates satire and the seven deadly sins were adapted to different ends and contested by different perspectives. Language itself accommo-

dates "disparate moral standards," evident in the changing meanings of *trouthe* in the late fourteenth century.

162. Hernández Pérez, Beatriz. *Voces prologales: Juan Ruiz y Geoffrey Chaucer.* Santa Cruz de Tenerife: La Página Ediciones, 2003. 272 pp. Compares varied uses of narrative voices in *CT* and Juan Ruiz's *Libro de buen amor* in light of the tradition of prologue writing. Chaucer and Ruiz employ satire and ambiguity to elicit a variety of questions from their audience—enough to arouse interest in their books.

163. Hirsh, John C. "Christianity and the Church." In Corinne Saunders, ed. *A Concise Companion to Chaucer* (*SAC* 30 [2008], no. 143), pp. 241–60. Hirsh summarizes how religious concepts, contexts, and developments in the politico-religious situation in Ricardian and Lancastrian England bear on our understanding of *CT*. Discusses the Great Schism, pilgrimage, mysticism, and the shared themes of travel, suffering, and reward in *MLT*, *ClT*, *PrT*, and *SNT*. Although changed since the time of Augustine, the notion of the common good informs the description of pilgrimage in *ParsP*.

164. Koldeweij, Jos. "'Shameless and Naked Images': Obscene Badges as Parodies of Popular Devotion." In Sarah Blick and Rita Tekippe, eds. *Art and Architecture of Late Medieval Pilgrimage in Northern Europe and the British Isles.* 2 vols. Studies in Medieval and Reformation Traditions, no. 104. Boston and Leiden: Brill, 2005, vol. 1, pp. 493–510. 26 b&w illus. Koldeweij comments on pilgrim badges and related materials mentioned in *CT* and illustrated in the Ellesmere manuscript. The commentary introduces a discussion of obscene badges (ca. 1350–ca. 1450) intended to mock pilgrimage.

165. Lerer, Seth. "*The Canterbury Tales.*" In Seth Lerer, ed. *The Yale Companion to Chaucer* (*SAC* 30 [2008], no. 131), pp. 243–94. Lerer reads *CT* as a "set of representative performances" that "question literary and social selves" and explore the functions of language, literature, and the imagination. Recurrent concern with clothing and representation, communication and monetary exchange, impersonation and competition, intention and effect. The structure of "quitting and response" in *CT* offers a model "for a future of literary history."

166. Mertens-Fonck, Paule. "Une référence envahissante aux *Débats du clerc et du chevalier* dans les *Contes de Canterbury.*" In Catherine Bel, Pascale Dumont, and Frank Willaert, eds. *Contez me tout: Mélanges de langue et de littérature médiévales offerts à Herman Braet.* Paris: Dudley, 2006, pp. 281–96. The structure of the Clerk-Knight debates, based on

the rivalry between a clerk and a knight, underlies most *Tales* in *CT* and can be used to reveal unsuspected meanings.

167. Pugh, Tison. "Queering Harry Bailly: Gendered Carnival, Social Ideologies, and Masculinity Under Duress in the *Canterbury Tales*." *ChauR* 41 (2006): 39–69. In his initial governance of the carnivalesque "play" of tale-telling, Harry Bailly augments his masculinity by "queering" his fellow pilgrims; by the end of *CT*, his own masculinity is "undermined" by his inability to control the carnival he set in motion and by the self-"queering" personal "revelations" the *Tales* provoke him to make.

168. Smith, Peter J., and Greg Walker. "Review of *The Canterbury Tales*, Adapted by Mike Poulton in Two Parts and Directed by Gregory Doran, Rebecca Catward, and Jonathan Munby for the Royal Shakespeare Company, The Swan Theatre, Stratford-upon-Avon, 19 and 21 December 2005, Centre Stalls." *Cahiers élisabéthains* 69 (2006): 53–57. Smith and Walker review the dramatic performance of *CT* (all but *CYT*), describing the staging and tracing the emotional swings of the adaptation. Includes one black-and-white and four color photographs of the production.

169. Sola Buil, Ricardo J. "Orality and Literacy in Chaucer: The Case of the Conquest and Destruction of Troy in *The Canterbury Tales*." In Juan Camilo Conde Silvestre and Ma Nila Vázquez González, eds. *Medieval English Literary and Cultural Studies* (*SAC* 30 [2008], no. 110), pp. 145–61. Evaluates the effects of the transition from orality to literacy in *CT*. Chaucer's oral mode of presentation conditions his manipulation of that tradition to the extent that it compels his audience to believe that he has read what, in fact, comes from a collective oral memory.

170. "Stratford, Swan. 8 December 2005–4 February 2006. *The Canterbury Tales*." *Theatre Record* 25.25 (2005): 1678–83; "[London], Gielgud. 13 July 2006. *The Canterbury Tales*." *Theatre Record* 26.14 (2006): 815–18. Reprints of Stratford and London newspaper and magazine reviews of Mike Poulton's two-part adaptation of *CT* for the stage, performed by the Royal Shakespeare Company. Includes cast list for each part.

See also nos. 7, 9, 17, 18, 21, 23, 25, 27, 31, 49, 51, 74, 82, 105, 136.

CT—The General Prologue

171. Lara Rallo, Carmen. " 'The hooly blisful martir for to seke': Una aproximación a los personajes eclesiásticos en el Prólogo General a los *Cuentos de Canterbury*." *Analecta Malacitana: Revista de la Sección de Filología de la Facultad de Filosofía y Letras* 27 (2004): 155–68. Assesses *GP* descriptions of the ecclesiastical pilgrims, showing that Chaucer's criticism of his church figures is ambiguous. Focuses on the Prioress but also comments on the Monk, the Friar, the Summoner, the Pardoner, and the idealized Parson.

172. Thompson, Kenneth J. "Chaucer's Warrior Bowman: The Roles and Equipment of the Knight's Yeoman." *ChauR* 40 (2006): 386–415. Although the Knight's Yeoman may be a "forster" (1.117) before all else, the skills he would possess in that role "would find ready application on military campaign," which helps to explain the Knight's choice of his Yeoman, rather than another servant, to accompany him (*GP* 1.101).

See also nos. 4, 52, 104, 118, 160, 162, 189, 245.

CT—The Knight and His Tale

173. Chung, Inju. "The Lord and the Poet: Theseus and the Knight in *The Knight's Tale*." *Medieval and Early Modern English Studies* 11 (2003): 299–316 (in Korean, with English abstract). The Knight's failure to provide narrative order and consistency in his characters is Chaucer's means to pose questions about the nature of human life in an unstable world.

174. Eyler, Joshua R., and John P. Sexton. "Once More to the Grove: A Note of Symbolic Space in the *Knight's Tale*." *ChauR* 40 (2006): 433–39. Following Arcite's death in *KnT*, Theseus designates for his funeral "that selve grove" (1. 2860) where Arcite and Palamon first fought privately, which technically would have been "destroyed" to erect the lists for the public tournament in which Arcite met his demise. This ostensible textual inconsistency "enforces . . . the chaotic conclusion of the tournament: nothing has truly been resolved."

175. Greenwood, Maria K. "Garlands of Derision: The Thematic Imagery of Garlands. Part II: The Garlands of Power: Chaucer's *The*

Knight's Tale and Shakespeare's *A Midsummer Night's Dream*." In Colette Stévanovitch, ed. *Marges/Seuils: Le liminal dans la littérature médiévale anglaise* (*SAC* 30 [2008], no. 148), pp. 271–89. As Greenwood has shown in a previous study, garlanding often implied criticism. In *KnT* and *A Midsummer's Night's Dream*, however, it is an acknowledgment of power.

176. ————. "Narrow Margins of Meaning and the Metamorphosis of the Power-holder: The Political Figure of Theseus in Chaucer and in Chaucer's Predecessors, Euripides, Statius, *Le Roman de Thèbes*, and Boccaccio's *Teseida*." In Colette Stévanovitch, ed. *Marges/Seuils: Le liminal dans la littérature médiévale anglaise* (*SAC* 30 [2008], no. 148), pp. 247–69. Focuses on Theseus in *KnT* as Chaucer's critique of power-holders in general.

177. Kelly, Henry Ansgar. "Chaucer's Knight and the Northern 'Crusades': The Example of Henry Bolingbroke." In Ruth Evans, Helen Fulton, and David Matthews, eds. *Medieval Cultural Studies: Essays in Honour of Stephen Knight* (*SAC* 30 [2008], no. 115), pp. 152–65. Kelly recounts military and political events in Lithuania around 1390–92 involving Roman Catholics, Greek Orthodox Christians, and recent converts. Focuses on the involvement of Henry Bolingbroke and on uses of the word *pagan*, as backdrop to Chaucer's *GP* description of the Knight.

178. Minnis, Alastair. "Standardizing Lay Culture: Secularity in French and English Literature of the Fourteenth Century." In Ursula Schaefer, ed. *The Beginnings of Standardization: Language and Culture in Fourteenth-Century England* (*SAC* 30 [2008], no. 144), pp. 43–60. Minnis discusses the impact of Aristotelian social and political theory on the rise of a growing lay culture in France and England. Considers similarities among several "discourses of secular power"—including Chaucer's *KnT* and Gower's advice to princes in *Confessio Amantis*—and suggests that they are rooted in Aristotle's *Ethics*, the pseudo-Aristotelian *Economics*, and related works.

179. Pearman, Tory Vandeventer. "Laying Siege to Female Power: Theseus the 'Conqueror' and Hippolita the 'Asseged' in Chaucer's 'The Knight's Tale.'" *Essays in Medieval Studies* 23 (2006): 31–40. The language used to describe Hippolyta in *KnT* undermines the praise of Theseus and exposes "the dramatic irony in the Knight's perception of Theseus's military exploits and subsequent exchange of ethnic women."

180. Rock, Catherine A. "Forsworn and Fordone: Arcite as Oath-Breaker in the *Knight's Tale*." *ChauR* 40 (2006): 416-32. Arcite breaks his oath of brotherhood with Palamon, the promise he made to Theseus

never to return to Athens, and the code of knighthood by doing menial labor disguised as a "povre laborer." The "ignoble, freakish manner of [his] death" thus suits the manner of his living.

181. Snyder, Martin. "The Role of Women in Chaucer's 'The Knight's Tale.'" *Journal of Liberal Arts* (Seijoh University) 2 (2006): 69–82. Snyder explores how, despite initial impressions to the contrary, women can be said to have a central function in *KnT*, even though no woman in the *Tale* serves as an agent of change.

See also nos. 51, 53, 66, 67, 70, 106, 112, 116, 120, 149, 152, 172, 184, 185, 269.

CT—The Miller and His Tale

182. Aloni, Gila. "Extimacy in the *Miller's Tale*." *ChauR* 41 (2006): 163–84. The relation between public and private in *MilT* may be understood as the condition of "extimacy": "the presence of the Other at the place thought to be most intimate." The "structure of extimacy" frustrates masculine attempts to control or acquire Alisoun as a private possession and affords her unusual freedom.

183. Biggs, Frederick M. "Seventeen Words of Middle Dutch Origin in the *Miller's Tale*?" *N&Q* 53 (2006): 407–9. In *Sources and Analogues of the "Canterbury Tales,"* Peter G. Beidler identifies *Heile van Beersele* as a likely source for *MilT*, supporting his argument with seventeen words he ascribes to Middle Dutch origin in *MilT*. Only one "or perhaps two" of those words prove to be "distinctively Dutch," however, thus providing little assistance in identifying Chaucer's source.

184. Bullón-Fernández, María. "Private Practices in Chaucer's *Miller's Tale*." *SAC* 28 (2006): 141–74. Explores links between privacy and urban spaces in Fragment 1 of *CT*, especially *MilT*, in which each of the major male characters fails to control his own *pryvetee*. The article follows Pierre Bourdieu in conceptualizing the practices of privacy as a developing *habitus*, exploring concerns with bodies, buildings, commerce, estate, and class competition among the characters and tellers of Part 1.

185. Cannon, Christopher. "The Boethianism of the 'Miller's Tale.'" In Mark Chinca, Timo Reuvekamp-Felber, and Christopher Young, eds. *Mittelalterliche Novellistik im Europäischen Kontext: Kulturwissenschaftliche Perspektiven*. Berlin: Erich Schmidt, 2006, pp. 326–46. Cannon explores the critique in *MilT* of the limited Boethianism of *KnT*. The double plot

of *MilT* and its emphasis on turning harm to joke are more genuinely Boethian than is the tragic emphasis of *KnT*.

186. Lyons, Mathew. *Impossible Journeys*. Cadogan Guides. London: Cadogan, 2005. 222 pp. Lyons describes twenty-four journeys derived from early travelogues, now known to be fictional or fanciful. Includes description of the likely spurious *Inventio Fortunata*, attributed to Nicholas of Lynn by Richard Hakluyt. Also speculates that Nicholas of *MilT* may be based on Nicholas of Lynn. Section titles imitate *CT* (e.g., "The Walker's Tale," "The Mapmaker's Tale").

187. Walter, Katie Louise. "The Middle English Term 'Froten': Absolon and Barber-Surgery." *N&Q* 53 (2006): 303–5. When Absolon "froteth" his lips upon realizing the real target of his kiss in *MilT*, he acts in accordance with his training as a barber-surgeon. More than a synonym for "to rub," the verb *froten* connotes a range of medical and surgical approaches to remedying oral suffering or, in Absolon's case, a literal and metaphorical "passion" of the mouth.

188. Yvernault, Martine. "Tel est vu qui croyait voir: Marges, brèches, et jeux optiques dans le *Conte du Meunier* de Chaucer." In Colette Stévanovitch, ed. *Marges/Seuils: Le liminal dans la littérature médiévale anglaise* (*SAC* 30 [2008], no. 148), pp. 209–24. Yvernault focuses on the narrative imbalance in *MilT* caused by the intrusions of the margin through description of holes and through open and broken architectural structures.

See also nos. 41, 79, 299.

CT—The Reeve and His Tale

See nos. 20, 79, 94, 184.

CT—The Cook and His Tale

189. Benson, C. David. "Literary Contests and London Records in the *Canterbury Tales*." In Ardis Butterfield, ed. *Chaucer and the City* (*SAC* 30 [2008], no. 108), pp. 129–44. Significantly, the setting of *GP* is located outside the limits of London proper, and most of the pilgrims are not Londoners. *CkT* offers a clear vision of fourteenth-century London and reflects what is both good and appalling about the city.

190. Casey, Jim. "Unfinished Business: The Termination of Chau-

cer's *Cook's Tale.*" *ChauR* 41 (2006): 185–96. In view of Chaucer's resistance to the "finality of closure," allusions to *CkT* in Fragment 9 suggest that *CkT* "may be complete for Chaucer, although not completed by the Cook." Perhaps the *Tale*'s "unfinished business" is an interruption by one of the other pilgrims, cutting short an increasingly vulgar piece.

See also nos. 102, 118, 184.

CT—The Man of Law and His Tale

191. Cooper, Christine F. "'But algates therby was she understonde': Translating Custance in Chaucer's *Man of Law's Tale.*" *YES* 36 (2006): 27–38. In *MLT*, Chaucer uses the case of Custance's Latin being understood by Northumbrians—an instance of xenoglossia, more characteristic of the saint's life genre—to focus on translation in various genres and to make Custance, "subtly active," an "apt figure of the translator him/herself."

192. Lavezzo, Kathy. "Beyond Rome: Mapping Gender and Justice in the *Man of Law's Tale.*" In Kathy Lavezzo. *Angels on the Edge of the World: Geography, Literature, and English Community, 1000–1534.* Ithaca, N.Y.: Cornell University Press, 2006, pp. 93–113. Revised version of an essay of the same title in *SAC* 24 (2002): 149–80. See *SAC* 26 (2004), no. 208.

193. Lim, Hyunyang Kim. "'Take Writing': News, Information, and Documentary Culture in Late Medieval England." *DAI* A67.06 (2006): n.p. In the context of an analysis of a news-hungry medieval culture, one chapter examines Chaucer's suspicion of written documents in *MLT*.

194. Wood, Marjorie Elizabeth. "The Sultaness, Donegild, and Fourteenth-Century Female Merchants: Intersecting Discourses of Gender, Economy, and Orientalism in Chaucer's *Man of Law's Tale.*" *Comitatus* 37 (2006): 65–85. Anxious about the threat of Eastern hegemony and the increasing authority of merchant women, the narrator of *MLT* crafts characters that subtly feminize the East, "Orientalize" the feminine, and discredit women's economic participation as a threat to patriarchal structure. The Wife of Bath destabilizes this subtext.

See also nos. 52, 113, 120, 140, 163, 224.

CT—The Wife of Bath and Her Tale

195. Baker, Michel van. "The Dame and the Knight: Marriage, Sovereignty, and Transformation." *Parabola* 29.1 (2004): 11–18. Commentary on *The Weddynge of Sir Gawen and Dame Ragnell* that emphasizes partnership in marriage. Occasional references to *WBT*.

196. Bardsley, Sandy. *Venomous Tongues: Speech and Gender in Late Medieval England.* Philadelphia: University of Pennsylvania Press, 2006. 214 pp. Includes brief discussion of the Wife of Bath's claim that verbal disorder is the special preserve of women; in this way, the Wife shares important parallels with the unruly wife of Noah in the Chester and York Flood plays.

197. Baumgardner, Rachel Ann. "I Alisoun, I Wife: Foucault's Three Egos and the *Wife of Bath's Prologue." MedievalF* 5 (2006): n.p. Read against Foucault's "What Is an Author?" the Wife of Bath of *WBP* fits the criteria for representation of a "third ego." Thereby, she can be seen as a character who "establishes her own personality." Chaucer serves as a "medium for her determined and unique personality."

198. Cawsey, Kathy. "Tutivillus and the 'Kyrkchaterars': Strategies of Control in the Middle Ages." *SP* 102 (2005): 434–51. Cawsey examines features of medieval tales of Tutivillus and explores how representations of female "discursive communities" and gossip in *WBPT* and plays about Noah illuminate these features through similar concerns with marginalized speech.

199. Desmond, Marilynn. *Ovid's Art and the Wife of Bath: The Ethics of Erotic Violence.* Ithaca, N.Y.: Cornell University Press, 2006. xiii, 206 pp. Desmond studies the discourse of erotic violence in medieval literature and iconography, surveying depictions of the "mounted Aristotle" and focusing on the adaptations of material from Ovid's *Ars Amatoria* found in the letters of Héloïse and Abélard, the *Roman de la Rose, WBP*, and Christine de Pizan's contributions to the *Querelle de la Rose*. The letters of Héloïse and Pizan "offer alternative perspectives" to the "canonical reworkings" of Ovid, while the *Roman* and *WBP* reflect the "erotic potential of intimate violence" that has connections with sadomasochism, as well as being rooted in the homoerotics of love in Ovid's imperial Rome. The popularity of the Wife of Bath today indicates that the "strategic relations" of love and violence in *WBP* continue to shape our contemporary attitudes.

200. Driver, Martha W. "Romancing the *Rose*: The Readings of

Chaucer and Christine." In Helen Cooney, ed. *Writings on Love in the English Middle Ages* (*SAC* 30 [2008], no. 111), pp. 147–62. Driver explores how the *Roman de la Rose* was "re-written" for late medieval audiences in various ways: Chaucer advocates contemporary views of the work in his adaptation of La Vieille in *WBP*, and Pizan criticizes such views in her *Book of the Three Virtues*. Also comments on Prudence's role in *Mel*.

201. Goodspeed-Chadwick, Julie Elaine. "Sexual Politics in 'The Wife of Bath's Prologue' and 'Tale': The Rhetorics of Domestic Violence and Rape." *Readerly/Writerly Texts* 11–12 (2004–5): 155–62. *WBPT* can be seen as Alison's "therapeutic" attempts to "educate the public at large" about domestic violence and rape. Although she succumbs at times to the rhetoric of "the woman as commodity" and misunderstands herself as "unrapeable," Alison vindicates women.

202. Guardia Massó, Pedro. "Marginación y opresión en *Los Cuentos de Canterbury* y en *Pedro el Labriego*." In Mercedes Brea, ed. *Marginales e marginados en la Época Medieval*. Cuadernos del CEMYR, no. 4. [La Laguna, Canary Islands]: Universidad de La Laguna, Centro de Estudios Medievales y Renacentistas, 1996, pp. 107–24. Guardia Massó examines ecclesiastical and sexual suppression in Lollardy, *Piers Plowman*, and *CT* (especially in *WBP*).

203. Kassell, Lauren. " 'All was this land full fill'd of faerie,' or Magic and the Past in Early Modern England." *Journal of the History of Ideas* 67.1 (2006): 107–22. Following a methodology outlined in Gabriel Naudé's seventeenth-century history of magic, the essay examines early modern historical accounts of magic to understand how magic came to be defined and debated. The title derives from *WBT*.

204. Mathur, Indira. "Prestucturing Reception Through Intertextuality in *The Wife of Bath's Prologue*." In Jean-Paul Debax, ed. *Actes de l'atelier "Moyen Age" du XLVe congrès de la SAES (Société des Anglicistes de l'Enseignement Supérieur)*. Paris: Publications de l'Association des Médiévistes Anglicistes de l'Enseignement Supérieur, 2006, pp. 101–10. Establishes a link between the "preamble" in *WBP* and the sermon genre.

205. Minnis, Alastair. "From *Coilles* to *Bel Chose*: Discourses of Obscenity in Jean de Meun and Chaucer." In Nicola McDonald, ed. *Medieval Obscenities*. York: York Medieval Press, 2006, pp. 156–78. Explores the "connection between dirty words and dirty things," focusing on the speech of "three outspoken female figures": Raison and La Vieille from the *Roman de la Rose* and Chaucer's Wife of Bath. While Raison attacks

"linguistic equivocation" and La Vieille speaks explicitly, the Wife's obscene euphemisms in *WBP* are "governed by the dictates of bourgeois respectability."

206. ———. "The Wisdom of Old Women: Alisoun of Bath as *Auctrice*." In Helen Cooney, ed. *Writings on Love in the English Middle Ages* (*SAC* 30 [2008], no. 111), pp. 99–114. In the Wife of Bath, Chaucer radically remakes La Vieille from the *Roman de la Rose*, granting her true wisdom and authority. The Wife of Bath successfully uses Latin tradition and academic techniques in *WBP*, and *WBT* reflects the profound wisdom of old women. Minnis considers the authenticity of the six disputed passages in *WBP* (44a–f, 575–84, 605–8, 609–12, 619–26, and 717–20).

207. Scheitzeneder, Franziska. "'For myn entente nys but for to pleye': On the Playground with the Wife of Bath, the Clerk of Oxford, and Jacques Derrida." *PhiN: Philologie im Netz* 36 (2006): 44–59. Reads the opposition between the Clerk and the Wife of Bath in light of Derrida's opposition between the structuralist desire to decipher signs and the poststructuralist impulse to play with the "instability of signs." The Wife is an "anachronistic allegory of Derrida's play of structure, whose only truth is that there is not a single truth." In his Envoy, the Clerk transgresses his own efforts to specify meaning.

208. Shimomura, Sachi. *Odd Bodies and Visible Ends in Medieval Literature*. The New Middle Ages. New York: Palgrave Macmillan, 2006. ix, 198 pp. Set against the eschatology of the Last Judgment, medieval narratives prompt their audiences to employ complex—often deferred—criteria for interpretation or evaluation. Shimomura considers how audience judgment is engaged and complicated in *Christ III*, several homilies and romances, *WBPT*, and *Sir Gawain and the Green Knight*, focusing on how eschatological tradition underlies and challenges the desire for closure and evaluation in medieval stories. Chapter 3 (pp. 85–125) assesses how the "discontinuous selves" represented in *WBP* anticipate the dynamics of transformation in *WBT*.

209. Thomas, Susanne Sara. "The Problem of Defining *Sovereynetee* in the *Wife of Bath's Tale*." *ChauR* 41 (2006): 87–97. While the knight of *WBT* returns from his quest with the word that saves his life—*sovereynetee*—he never understands its meaning: "independence and self-government." The wedding-night conversation between the knight and the "wyf" demonstrates her "sovereynetee" as well as her "power over" the knight; she controls his choices, ensuring that he will never attain

"sovereynetee" in relation to his "worldly appetit" for beauty and obedience.

See also nos. 36, 43, 76, 79, 86, 104, 122, 194, 214, 224.

CT—The Friar and His Tale

210. Phillips, Helen. "'A gay yeman, under a forest side': 'The Friar's Tale' and the Robin Hood Tradition." In Ruth Evans, Helen Fulton, and David Matthews, eds. *Medieval Cultural Studies: Essays in Honour of Stephen Knight* (*SAC* 30 [2008], no. 115), pp. 123–37. Phillips explores verbal, narrative, and thematic parallels between *FrT* and Robin Hood tales such as *Robin Hood and Guy of Gisburne*. Emphases on "grenewode," archery, disguise, commercialism, ecclesiastical corruption, oppression of the poor, and ultimate righteousness suggest that Chaucer had outlaw tales in mind when writing *FrT*.

See also no. 133.

CT—The Summoner and His Tale

211. Beechy, Tiffany. "Devil Take the Hindmost: Chaucer, John Gay, and the Pecuniary Anus." *ChauR* 41 (2006): 71–85. Studying *SumT* with John Gay's 1717 poem "An Answer to the Sompner's Prologue of Chaucer" reveals a continuum of greed in *SumT*, moving from goods of use value, to coins of exchange value, to excrement and insubstantial air, even as Chaucer satirizes social acceptance of such abstracted value in place of real goods.

212. Hayes, Mary. "Privy Speech: Sacred Silence, Dirty Secrets in the *Summoner's Tale*." *ChauR* 40 (2006): 263–88. Allusions in *SumT* to the silent canon—the clerical practice of offering the eucharistic consecration prayers silently—open a window on "lay-clerical relations," exposing the politics governing access to the secrets of the Eucharist. Through its critique of the silent canon, *SumT* "endorses lay private devotional speech," while questioning the capacity for any human discourse to "communicate with the divine or aptly articulate sacred mysteries."

CT—The Clerk and His Tale

213. Ashe, Laura. "Reading like a Clerk in the *Clerk's Tale*." *MLR* 101 (2006): 935–44. If reading is a transformative act, then Griselda's unwavering "reading" of Walter as a loving husband ultimately transforms him so that Walter's will conforms with hers. Thus, her association with the Clerk (especially as aligned against the Pardoner, who rejects the moral implications of his own tale) is apt. *ClT* demonstrates the moral power and importance of acts of interpretation, which can both find and plant good, even where no good was intended.

214. Denny-Brown, Andrea. "*Povre* Griselda and the All-Consuming *Archewyves*." *SAC* 28 (2006): 77–115. Denny-Brown assesses the vacillations between sartorial *richesse* and *rudenesse* in *ClT*, examining the gender and class implications of Griselda's dressing, undressing, and redressing and counterpointing Walter's attitudes toward clothing and material consumption with those of his people. The Clerk's own frugality disguises a "fascination" with "worldly, material aesthetics," and his *Envoy* engages his theme of *dispence* as well as it does the Wife of Bath. The essay also considers the reception of *ClT* in Lydgate's "A dyte of womenhis hornys" ("Horns Away").

215. Frese, Dolores Warwick. "The 'Buried Bodies' of Dante, Boccaccio, and, Petrarch: Chaucerian 'Sources' for the Critical Fiction of Obedient Wives." *SAC* 28 (2006): 249–56. Frese reads water, dressing, and "suckling" imagery in Boccaccio, Petrarch, and *ClT* as vestiges of Dante's concern in *De vulgari eloquentia* with using "vernacular" language for "literature of lasting value."

216. Goodwin, Amy W. "Chaucer's *Clerk's Tale*: Sources, Influences, and Allusions." *SAC* 28 (2006): 231–35. Goodwin explores the practical problems of source study—terminology and the constraints of publication—in relation to *ClT*. Comments on Boccaccio's and Philippe de Mézières's Griselda stories as "sources of invention" for Chaucer's version.

217. Patterson, Lee. "The Necessity of History: The Example of Chaucer's 'Clerk's Tale.'" In Bonnie Wheeler, ed. *Mindful Spirit in Late Medieval Literature: Essays in Honor of Elizabeth D. Kirk* (*SAC* 30 [2008], no. 154), pp. 187–210. Patterson reads *ClT* in light of negotiations over the marriage of Richard II and Isabelle of France in 1396 and of the texts surrounding those negotiations, especially those concerned with the ideology of sacral kingship. Chaucer knew of the marriage negotiations through John Pritwell, the royal sergeant-at-arms who obtained

safe conduct for diplomats and who worked with Chaucer when Chaucer was Clerk of the King's Works. Chaucer may have used *L'estoire de Griseldis* as well as Petrarch and the French translation as a reaction to the muting of political and literary issues.

218. Schöpflin, Karin. "Boccaccios Griselda und Hiob." *Romanistisches Jahrbuch* 42 (1991): 136–49. A detailed comparison of the Job story and Boccaccio's *Decameron* 10.10. Boccaccio's novella is seen as a variation of the biblical Job story that lacks the justification of God's divine attributes. Schöpflin argues that Boccaccio and subsequent authors such as Petrarch and Chaucer modeled their versions of the Griselda story on this interpretation of Job.

See also nos. 71, 125, 133, 163, 207, 224.

CT—The Merchant and His Tale

219. Palmer, James M. "Your Malady Is No 'Sodeyn Hap': Ophthalmology, Benvenutus Grassus, and January's Blindness." *ChauR* 41 (2006): 197–205. Considered in the light of writings by thirteenth-century ophthalmologist Benvenutus Grassus, January's blindness in *MerT* is no sudden infirmity. With his admitted habit of "overindulgence" in women, food, and drink, January has been working on becoming blind for quite some time.

See also nos. 48, 79, 299.

CT—The Squire and His Tale

220. Harwood, Britton J. "Chaucer and the Gift (If There Is Any)." *SP* 103 (2006): 26–46. Explores gift-giving in Part 5 of *CT*, from the magical gifts given to Ghengis Khan in *SqT* to the concern with generosity that ends *FranT*. Uses Derridean notions of gifts and exchange to argue that the sequence is Chaucer's means to "erase unproductive expenditure . . . by safely framing and containing it by economy and exchange."

See also nos. 97, 120, 122, 152.

CT—The Franklin and His Tale

221. Cartlidge, Neil. "'Nat that I chalange any thyng of right': Love, Loyalty, and Legality in the *Franklin's Tale*." In Helen Cooney, ed. *Writings on Love in the English Middle Ages* (*SAC* 30 [2008], no. 111), pp. 115–30. In *FranT*, Chaucer presents a "moral dilemma that might be described as scholastic in its contrived intractability." The *quaestio disputanda* posed at the end of *FranT* compels readers to confront the *Tale*'s irresolvable legal complexities of contract. Cartlidge shows parallels with other medieval texts that have legal implications.

222. Dobbs, Elizabeth A. "Re-Sounding Echo." *ChauR* 40 (2006): 289–310. Aurelius's comparison of himself to the nymph Echo early in *FranT* enables glimpses of Narcissus in Dorigen and emphasizes the importance of speech and interpretation in the *Tale*: in particular, Aurelius's Echo-like interpretations of Dorigen's speeches. Like Echo, Aurelius produces distorted versions of what he hears.

223. Nowlin, Steele. "Between Precedent and Possibility: Liminality, Historicity, and Narrative in Chaucer's *The Franklin's Tale*." *SP* 103 (2006): 47–67. Nowlin contends that *FranT* "offers an interpretation of the forces that shape the ability to imagine beyond exempla." Draws on Victor Turner's notions of liminality to discuss the concern with genre as frame in *FranT*, which shows how frames of reference give way to new ideas and possibilities.

224. Wicher, Andrzej. "Chaucer's 'Franklin's Tale' Seen in the Context of the Tales About Calumniated Women." In Marcin Krygier and Liliana Sikorska, eds. *Naked Wordes in Englissh* (*SAC* 30 [2008], no. 128), pp. 160–68. Wicher tallies a number of folktale motifs in *FranT* and argues that they are rationalized or obscured in ways that qualify the exemplary value of the *Tale*. Central is the motif of the "rash promise given to a supernatural suitor," with Arveragus, Aurelius, and the clerk functioning as "avatars" of the husband figure (and paralleling the three females in *WBT*). Wicher comments on other folktale elements in *WBT*, *ClT*, and *MLT*.

See also nos. 55, 106, 117, 220.

CT—The Physician and His Tale

225. Bleeth, Kenneth. "*The Physician's Tale* and Remembered Texts." *SAC* 28 (2006): 221–24. Argues that written texts are not the only valid

sources of *PhyT* and acknowledges the need to consider "remembered texts, semantic fields, and pictorial images"—"intertexts" theorized by Michael Riffaterre.

CT—The Pardoner and His Tale

226. Shaffern, Robert W. "The Pardoner's Promises: Preaching and Policing Indulgences in the Fourteenth-Century English Church." *Historian* 68.1 (2006): 49–65. Late medieval literary and historical attitudes toward pardoners suggest that the depictions in *Piers Plowman* and *PardPT* are exaggerated. Shaffern documents ecclesiastical efforts to control abuse of the office.

227. Trigg, Stephanie. "The Pardoner's 'lewed peple': Apes, Japes, and the Pre-history of Mass Culture." In Ruth Evans, Helen Fulton, and David Matthews, eds. *Medieval Cultural Studies: Essays in Honour of Stephen Knight* (*SAC* 30 [2008], no. 115), pp. 166–78. Trigg addresses relationships among the reading audience, the pilgrim audience, and the "lewed peple" of *PardPT*. Set against the *GP* description of the Parson and his flock, the Pardoner's description of his preaching to the people may indicate their resistance to him. This dynamic is a "proleptic glimpse" into some of the issues confronting modern cultural studies.

See also nos. 55, 76, 86, 213, 302.

CT—The Shipman and His Tale

228. Hume, Cathy. "Domestic Opportunities: The Social Comedy of the *Shipman's Tale*." *ChauR* 41 (2006): 138–62. Read in the light of late medieval letter collections and conduct manuals for women, the comedy of *ShT* springs from a recognition of the merchant's wife's "clever manipulation of her roles: as hostess, social networker, housekeeper, business assistant, and status symbol."

229. Kendall, Elliot. "The Great Household in the City: *The Shipman's Tale*." In Ardis Butterfield, ed. *Chaucer and the City* (*SAC* 30 [2008], no. 108), pp. 145–61. As reflected in *ShT*, medieval urban space allows the powerful to exert political influence by converting capital into noncommercial culture.

See also nos. 48, 79, 117.

CT—The Prioress and Her Tale

230. Bale, Anthony. *The Jew in the Medieval Book: English Antisemitisms, 1350–1500.* Cambridge Studies in Medieval Literature. Cambridge: Cambridge University Press, 2006. xiv, 266 pp. A study of the "reiteration, instability and changing valence of the Jewish image as inscribed in medieval English books," focusing on four generic narratives: the Jew of Tewkesbury, the Marian miracle of the boy singer, the cult of Robert of Bury St. Edmunds, and the "literary and decorative scheme" of the *Arma Christi.* Bale explores philosemitism as well as anti-Semitism to see how attitudes toward Jews constitute one of the defining myths or legends of the Middle Ages. Discusses *PrT* in light of analogous narratives, including fifteenth-century "reactions" to the *Tale* found in manuscript anthologies, which convey pious sentiment and diminish Chaucer's satire of the Prioress.

231. Bauer, Renate. "Opfer 'Christlicher' Gewalt: Juden im Texten des Englischen Mittelalters." In Manuel Braun and Cornelia Herberichs, eds. *Gewalt im Mittelalter: Realitäten—Imaginationen.* Munich: William Fink, 2005, pp. 181–201. Bauer assesses formulaic or stereotypic depictions of Jews in *Cursor Mundi,* Chaucer's *PrT,* Gower's *Confessio Amantis* (7.3207–3360), *Elene, The Siege of Jerusalem,* passion treatises, and *The Croxton Play of the Sacrament.*

232. Nakao, Yoshiyuki. "Death and Life in *The Prioress's Tale*: A Child Martyrdom and Its Expression Through Senses." In Mizuda Hidemi et al., eds. *Death and Life in Medieval Europe.* Hiroshima: Keisuisha, 2006, pp. 69–108 (in Japanese). Examines as ritual murder the death of the clergeon in *PrT.*

233. Quinn, William A. "The Shadow of Chaucer's Jews." *Exemplaria* 18 (2006): 299–326. *PrT* and *SNT* mirror each other but "with a telling difference." The two stand in relation to each other as Old Testament *figura* to New Testament fulfillment (the shadow and substance of the title). Ironically, in this figural scheme, *PrT* takes the place of the rejected term, the Jew.

234. Stanbury, Sarah. "Host Desecration, Chaucer's 'Prioress's Tale,' and Prague 1389." In Bonnie Wheeler, ed. *Mindful Spirit in Late Medieval Literature: Essays in Honor of Elizabeth D. Kirk* (*SAC* 30 [2008], no. 154), pp. 211–24. Accusations of eucharistic host desecration in Prague in 1389 may be read as a backdrop for *PrT.* Stanbury summarizes the events of mob violence that led to a massacre of Jews.

See also no. 163.

CT—The Tale of Sir Thopas

235. Børch, Marianne. "Writing Remembering Orality: Geoffrey Chaucer's *Sir Thopas*." *European Journal of English Studies* 10.2 (2006): 131–48. Børch discusses *Th* as an "oral romance," surveying its oral characteristics and exploring how these characteristics—when they are written—help to parody the "chivalric ethos" that underlies the genre of romance. *Th* also exposes for consideration the differences between written and oral modes of narration, which, in turn, reflect Chaucer's concern with the relations among his Continental and English models.

236. Liu, Yin. "Middle English Romance as Prototype Genre." *ChauR* 40 (2006): 335–53. A study of five Middle English lists of romances, including the list in Chaucer's *Th* (7.897–902). Liu uses the "prototype theory of categorization" from cognitive linguistics to provide the rationale for a flexible yet rigorous definition of the Middle English romance as a genre about which "there is plenty of fascinating work yet to be done."

237. Sayers, William. "Lexical and Literary Evidence for Medieval Trade in Precious Goods: Old French *Rohal*, *Roal*, and Middle English 'Walrus (and Narwhal?) Ivory.'" *NOWELE* 44 (2004): 101–19. Linguistic and economic background to uses of ivory in medieval decoration, including the saddle of Sir Thopas (*Th* 7.875–78).

See also nos. 52, 81.

CT—The Tale of Melibee

238. Turner, Marion. "Greater London." In Ardis Butterfield, ed. *Chaucer and the City* (*SAC* 30 [2008], no. 108), pp. 25–40. In *Mel*, Chaucer depicts space reflecting the split interests and antagonisms that dominated contemporary London.

See also nos. 76, 78, 200.

CT—The Monk and His Tale

See nos. 73, 120, 149, 160.

CT—The Nun's Priest and His Tale

239. Houwen, Luuk. "Every Picture Tells a Story: The Importance of Images in the Wider Dissemination and Reception of Texts." In An-

drew James Johnston, Ferdinand von Mengden, and Stefan Thim, eds. *Language and Text: Current Perspectives on English and Germanic Historical Linguistics and Philology* (*SAC* 30 [2008], no. 124), pp. 97–111. 13 b&w illus. Exemplifies text/image relationships by examining a number of misericords depicting scenes from the beast fable tradition of Reynard and other sly foxes. Considers the role of *NPT* in the development of this visual tradition.

See also nos. 30, 76, 125, 127, 129, 130.

CT—The Second Nun and Her Tale

240. Kaiser, Melanie L., and James M. Dean. "Chaucer and the Early Church." *MedievalF* 5 (2006): n.p. Depicting an idealized portrait of the early church, *SNT* is a means to critique the church of Chaucer's own time.

241. Little, Katherine C. "Images, Texts, and Exegetics in Chaucer's *Second Nun's Tale.*" *JMEMSt* 36 (2006): 103–34. Little reevaluates the Christian iconography in *SNT* in light of the Wycliffite debate over the use of images and their potential to become idolatry. Despite the importance of visual images, *SNT* shows a shift toward words and texts.

See also nos. 44, 140, 163, 233.

CT—The Canon's Yeoman and His Tale

242. Cannon, Christopher. "Chaucer and the Language of London." In Ardis Butterfield, ed. *Chaucer and the City* (*SAC* 30 [2008], no. 108), pp. 79–94. *CYT* is Chaucer's London tale *par excellence*; its "craft sounds" evoke both what the city is and what it is not.

243. Collette, Carolyn P. "The Alchemy of Imagination and the Labyrinth of Meaning: Some Caveats About the Afterlife of Sources." *SAC* 28 (2006): 243–48. Collette offers Umberto Eco's notion of a "rhizome labyrinth's indefinite structure" as a heuristic tool for describing the relationship of a text to its "cultural matrix" rather than to specific sources. Focuses on *CYT*.

See also nos. 44, 81, 102.

CT—The Manciple and His Tale

See no. 44.

CT—The Parson and His Tale

244. Huxtable, Michael J. "The Medieval Gaze at Grips with a Medieval World." In C. P. Biggam and C. J. Kay, eds. *Progress in Colour Studies: Volume I. Language and Culture*. Amsterdam and Philadelphia: Benjamins, 2006, pp. 199–217. Huxtable surveys medieval philosophical and religious understanding of sight and color as background to commentary on social concerns with color in sumptuary habits and heraldry. In *ParsT* 10.424–27, colorful clothing indicates a sinful nature.

245. Little, Katherine C. *Confession and Resistance: Defining the Self in Late Medieval England*. Notre Dame, Ind.: University of Notre Dame Press, 2006. vii, 196 pp. Centers on medieval *self-definition* rather than subjectivity and studies examples of Wycliffite lay instruction. The Lollards rejected auricular confession and emphasized personal contrition for sin. Lollard pastoral texts disrupted traditional discourses of self-definition by distinguishing discursive strands—narrative vs. pastoral language—that had been linked in earlier texts. The relationship between confession and creation of the medieval self is more complicated than is generally recognized (in the tradition of Foucault), and readers should resist prioritizing the confessing self, which causes "the perpetuation of . . . the 'antinomies' between self and other and individual and society." Chapter 3 discusses the Parson of *GP* and *ParsT*.

246. Smith, Nicole D. "The Parson's Predilection for Pleasure." *SAC* 28 (2006): 117–40. The indictment of fashionable male clothing in *ParsT* (10.422–30, "Superbia") is a "homoerotic moment" reflecting the Parson's own "scopophilic" pleasure, although the "turn to the fashionable female neutralizes any homoerotic tendency."

See also nos. 44, 78, 80, 106, 163, 227.

CT—Chaucer's Retraction

247. Vaughan, Míceál F. "Personal Politics and Thomas Gascoigne's Account of Chaucer's Death." *MÆ* 75 (2006): 103–22. Investigates the

anti-Lancastrian sentiments underlying Gascoigne's account of Chaucer's "deathbed repentance for his literary sins" in *Ret*.

See also nos. 23, 125, 260.

Anelida and Arcite

[No entries]

A Treatise on the Astrolabe

248. Eagleton, Catherine, and Matthew Spencer. "Copying and Conflation in Geoffrey Chaucer's *Treatise on the Astrolabe*: A Stemmatic Analysis Using Phylogenetic Software." *Studies in History and Philosophy of Science* 37 (2006): 237–68. Applies a technique from evolutionary biology—phylogenetic "neighborhood-joining"—to the witnesses to the text of *Astr* to produce a stemma, test the fragments and sections of longer versions against the stemma, and discuss the scribal conflation of various versions in their own productions. Concludes by commenting on scribes' concern with completeness of the text.

See also no. 186.

Boece

249. Ogura, Michiko. "Words of Emotion in Old and Middle English Translations of Boethius' *De Consolatione Philosophiae*." In Akio Oizumi, Jacek Fisiak, and John Scahill, eds. *Text and Language in Medieval English Prose: A Festschrift for Tadao Kubouchi*. Frankfurt am Main: Peter Lang, 2006, pp. 183–206. Ogura examines the lexicon of emotion (*anger, fear, joy, pleasure, sorrow, wonder*) in translations of Boethius by Jean de Meun, Chaucer, and Elizabeth I. Chaucer effectively uses three levels of word pairs: native, foreign, and combinations of native-foreign. He selects synonyms for translation in *Bo* by principles different from those reflected in his original texts.

See also nos. 80, 90, 293.

The Book of the Duchess

250. Jimura, Akiyuki. "Death and Life in Chaucer's *The Book of the Duchess*: With Special Reference to 'Herte.'" In Mizuda Hidemi et al., eds. *Death and Life in Medieval Europe*. Hiroshima: Keisuisha, 2006, pp. 109–40 (in Japanese). Examines Chaucer's varied and metaphorical use of *herte* in *BD*.

251. Kang, Ji-Soo. "Apocalyptic Imagination and Historical Text: A Study of *The Divine Comedy, The Book of the Duchess,* and *Pearl." Medieval and Early Modern English Studies* 11 (2003): 243–58 (in Korean, with English abstract). Considers relationships among apocalypse, history, and literary closure in Dante's *Paradiso*, Chaucer's *BD*, and *Pearl*. Dante brings apocalypse into history, while the other two poets use it to contrast human temporality.

252. Williams, Deanne. "The Dream Visions." In Seth Lerer, ed. *The Yale Companion to Chaucer* (*SAC* 30 [2008], no. 131), pp. 147–78. Williams summarizes the plots and themes of *BD*, *PF*, *HF*, and *LGW*, emphasizing Chaucer's layering of sources, his valorizing of English, and his concerns with interpretation and the truth value of literature.

See also nos. 51, 97, 100, 127, 130, 145, 153, 265.

The Equatorie of the Planetis

[No entries]

The House of Fame

253. Coletti, Theresa. "'Paths of Long Study': Reading Chaucer and Christine de Pizan in Tandem." *SAC* 28 (2006): 1–40. Coletti compares *HF* with Christine de Pizan's *Livre du chemin de long estude*, exploring their differing comments on and responses to their shared literary culture. Through parallel narrative gestures, the two poets consider textual authority, reader responsiveness, political roles of their art, vernacularity, and gender. The early Tudor association of the works is indicated by their inclusion in Richard Pynson's *Boke of Fame* (1526).

254. Davis, Paul. "After the Fire: Chaucer and Urban Poetics, 1666–1743." In Ardis Butterfield, ed. *Chaucer and the City* (*SAC* 30

[2008], no. 108), pp. 177–92. Davis discusses Alexander Pope's *The Temple of Fame*, a translation of *HF*.

255. Hwang, Joon Ho. "Vernacular Poetry, Text, and Fame in *The House of Fame*." *Medieval and Early Modern English Studies* 12 (2004): 371–92 (in Korean, with English abstract). *HF* reflects Chaucer's efforts to imitate Dante's innovation and use of the vernacular; the poem shows Chaucer's struggles with nonstandard forms of English and the lack of an English literary tradition.

See also nos. 23, 25, 51, 53, 71, 95, 97, 116, 118, 120, 125, 127, 130, 145, 153, 252.

The Legend of Good Women

256. Coleman, Joyce. "The Flower, the Leaf, and Philippa of Lancaster." In Carolyn P. Collette, ed. *The Legend of Good Women: Context and Reception* (*SAC* 30 [2008], no. 257), pp. 33–58. Coleman surveys the betrothals, marriage, and literary patronage of Philippa of Lancaster, suggesting that she may have given Chaucer a copy of Deschamps's "Ballade 765," which may have helped to inspire Chaucer's interest in flower and leaf debates that underlie *LGWP*. Includes a text and translation of Deschamps's ballade.

257. Collette, Carolyn P., ed. *The Legend of Good Women: Context and Reception*. Chaucer Studies, no. 36. Cambridge: D. S. Brewer, 2006. xviii, 203 pp. Eight essays by various authors, with an index and an introduction by the editor, who argues that Alceste's mediation is central to *LGW*, a poem about the "public dimension of ideal female behavior." The poem is best understood in the context of late medieval interest in reshaping narratives of exemplary women. For individual essays, see nos. 256, 259, 260, 262–64, 266, and 269.

258. Doyle, Kara A. "Thisbe Out of Context: Chaucer's Female Readers and the Findern Manuscript." *ChauR* 40 (2006): 231–61. Excerpted from Chaucer's *LGW* and thus lacking a narrative frame, the *Legend of Thisbe* in the Findern manuscript leaves room for the assumption that the manuscript's female readers saw Thisbe "as simply a victim." The excerpt's codicological context, however, suggests that its readers were well attuned to the commentaries on "the discourses of *fin' amors* and medieval misogyny" in which *LGW* participates.

259. Edwards, Robert R. "Ricardian Dreamwork: Chaucer, Cupid,

and Loyal Lovers." In Carolyn P. Collette, ed. *The Legend of Good Women: Context and Reception* (*SAC* 30 [2008], no. 257), pp. 59–82. Explores the "political erotics" of *LGWP*, especially the G version, assessing how Cupid's treatment of the narrator and Alceste's intercession reflect political conditions, concepts of tyranny, and notions of loyalty and fidelity.

260. Fumo, Jamie C. "The God of Love and Love of God: Palinodic Exchange in the Prologue of the *Legend of Good Women* and the 'Retraction.'" In Carolyn P. Collette, ed. *The Legend of Good Women: Context and Reception* (*SAC* 30 [2008], no. 257), pp. 157–75. Intertextual connections among *LGWP*, *Ret*, and the end of *TC* capitalize on the medieval scholastic literary theory of the co-authorship of books by human authors and God (*"duplex causa efficiens"*). All three works remind audiences of authorial responsibility and the need for accurate interpretation.

261. Gross, Karen Elizabeth. "Chaucer, Mary Magdalene, and the Consolation of Love." *ChauR* 41 (2006): 1–37. New facets of Chaucer's writing on love, consolation, and repentance are illuminated when we assume that Chaucer did translate Pseudo-Origen's *De Maria Magdalena*, as he claims to have done in *LGWP* G418 ("Orygenes upon the Maudeleyne").

262. McCormick, Betsy. "Remembering the Game: Debating the *Legend*'s Women." In Carolyn P. Collette, ed. *The Legend of Good Women: Context and Reception* (*SAC* 30 [2008], no. 257), pp. 105–31. McCormick outlines game theory and summarizes the medieval rhetorical tradition in which debate and dream vision were memorial and ethical media. She describes how exempla were used in the Querelle des Femmes, arguing that *LGW* engages the Querelle as a game and uses exempla in ways that evoke ethical responsibility from the reader.

263. McDonald, Nicola F. "Games Medieval Women Play." In Carolyn P. Collette, ed. *The Legend of Good Women: Context and Reception* (*SAC* 30 [2008], no. 257), pp. 176–97. McDonald describes the principles and operation of two late medieval ribald games of "amorous divination"—Ragman Roll and Chaunce of Dice—as a means to explore the female audience for such games and related literature, particularly *LGW*. *Demandes d'amour* and sexual riddles reveal that elite medieval women participated in ludic, sexually explicit discourse and double entendre.

264. Meecham-Jones, Simon. "Intention, Integrity, and 'Renoun': The Public Virtue of Chaucer's Good Women." In Carolyn P. Collette, ed. *The Legend of Good Women: Context and Reception* (*SAC* 30 [2008], no.

257), pp. 132–56. In *LGW*, Chaucer sets classical action in the context of Christian notions of moral intention; he poses a range of subtly differentiated portraits of difficulty in recording truth in human terms and human time. Knowability, the narrator's presence, exemplarity, heroic renown, privacy, humility, and suffering recur as concerns, posing and challenging classical ideas of virtue, patristic notions of merit, and other structures of certainty.

265. ———. " 'Myn Erthly God'—Paradigm and Parody in the Prologue to the *Legend of Good Women*." In Neil Thomas and Françoise Le Saux, eds. *Myth and Its Legacy in European Literature*. Durham Modern Languages Series. Durham: University of Durham, 1996, pp. 93–113. Meecham-Jones contrasts *LGWP* with *BD*, showing how the former exhibits the poet's confidence in adapting sources. Discusses the depiction of Alceste as a parody of figures such as Boethius's Philosophy, Dante's Beatrice, and the *Pearl*-maiden—assessing Alceste as a figure of insufficiency and exploring the "limited nature of any comprehension of truth."

266. Quinn, William A. "The *Legend of Good Women*: Performance, Performativity, and Presentation." In Carolyn P. Collette, ed. *The Legend of Good Women: Context and Reception* (*SAC* 30 [2008], no. 257), pp. 1–32. Quinn describes the "performance" features of each of the manuscripts and printed editions of *LGW*, exploring ideas of oral composition, performance theory, and performativity. Addresses how each witness to the text of *LGW* shapes the "protocols of 'reading' " the text, whether oral or silent.

267. Robertson, Kellie. *The Laborer's Two Bodies: Labor and the "Work" of the Text in Medieval Britain, 1350–1500*. New York: Palgrave Macmillan, 2006. ix, 276 pp. 7 b&w illus. Five chapters explore the "effects of labor laws" on vernacular writing in late medieval England: chronicles, anonymous dream visions, *LGW*, the Paston letters, and morality plays. Robertson focuses on interactions between theories of labor and textual production. Chapter 2 (pp. 51–77) is a revision of Robertson's previously published essay "Laboring in the God of Love's Garden: Chaucer's Prologue to *The Legend of Good Women*" (*SAC* 24 [2002]: 115–47), with an additional section on the role of William Morris's commentary on characterizing distinctions between Chaucer and Langland. See also no. 373. [*Note*: The title page of Robertson's book lists a different subtitle: *Literary and Legal Productions in Britain, 1350–1500*.]

268. Warburton, Rachel. "Reading Rape in Chaucer; *or* Are Cecily,

Lucretia, and Philomela *Good Women?*" In Mihoko Suzuki and Roseanna Dufault, eds. *Diversifying the Discourse: The Florence Howe Award for Outstanding Feminist Scholarship, 1990–2004.* New York: Modern Language Association of America, 2006, pp. 270–87. Warburton explores historical and literary connections between notions of female "goodness" and ability to be raped, examining the discourse of Cecily Chaumpaigne's accusation of rape and the tales of Lucretia and Philomela in *LGW*. The afterword, newly published here, emphasizes the way *LGW* renders impossible "female pleasures and intimacy between women." Originally published in *Henry Street* 10.1 (2003): 5–28.

269. Warren, Nancy Bradley. "'Olde Stories' and Amazons: The *Legend of Good Women*, the 'Knight's Tale,' and Fourteenth-Century Political Culture." In Carolyn P. Collette, ed. *The Legend of Good Women: Context and Reception* (*SAC* 30 [2008], no. 257), pp. 83–104. The "Amazonian" associations—legendary and figurative—of the women in *LGW* and *KnT* align the two narratives and suggest that the passive or intercessory roles of royal women in Chaucer's society entailed the "absent presence" of threat to that society.

270. Zissos, Andrew. "Reception of Valerius Flaccus' *Argonautica*." *International Journal of the Classical Tradition* 13.2 (2006): 165–85. Zissos surveys the reception of Valerius Flaccus's *Argonautica*, briefly discussing Chaucer's references to the author and the work in *LGW*, identified by E. F. Shannon in 1929. Chaucer was the first to refer to the poem after the postclassical period, although the poem was much more frequently cited after it was printed in 1474.

See also nos. 15, 50, 53, 63, 75, 97, 113, 120, 127, 140, 252.

The Parliament of Fowls

271. Klassen, Norman. "A Note on 'Hyre' in *Parliament of Fowls*, 284." *N&Q* 53 (2006): 154–57. The antecedent of *hyre* in *PF* 284 must be Venus rather than Diana. This reading reveals the logic of Chaucer's placement of Callisto and Atalanta at the head of his list of famous lovers and leads "inexorably to the conclusion that one wastes one's life in the service of Venus and that Chaucer has inverted the logic of male desire."

272. Wang, Denise Ming-yueh. "Order, Freedom, and 'Commune Profyt' in Chaucer's *Parlement of Foulys*." *Medieval and Early Modern En-*

glish Studies 11 (2003): 283–98. A construction of the dreamer, *PF* poses sociopolitical criticism through oppositions and explores the power of words.

See also nos. 23, 24, 51, 71, 97, 122, 127, 130, 145, 252.

The Romaunt of the Rose

273. Horobin, Simon. "A New Fragment of the *Romaunt of the Rose*." *SAC* 28 (2006): 205–15. Horobin describes and transcribes a single-leaf, forty-eight-line fragment of *Rom* (lines 2403–50), newly found among the Reverend Joass portion of the Sutherland collection of the National Library of Scotland. Also considers relationships among this fragment and the other early witnesses to *Rom*, i.e., Glasgow University Library Hunter 409 (V.3.7) and William Thynne's edition of 1532.

See also nos. 28, 125.

Troilus and Criseyde

274. An, Sonjae (Brother Anthony). "Echoes of Boethius and Dante in Chaucer's *Troilus and Criseyde*." *Medieval and Early Modern English Studies* 12 (2004): 393–418. Shows how allusions to Dante in *TC* combine with Boethian elements to offer an ironic commentary on Troilus's notion of happiness. Also comments on allusions to Statius.

275. Carruthers, Mary. "On Affliction and Reading, Weeping and Argument: Chaucer's Lachrymose Troilus in Context." *Representations* 93 (2006): 1–21. Carruthers reevaluates Troilus's weeping and lamentation in Book 4 of *TC* in the context of monastic tradition, including the works of Peter of Celle and Galen, that sees links "among perception, sensation, and rational process."

276. Clarke, K. P. "Eagles Mating with Doves: *Troilus and Criseyde*, II, 925–931, *Inferno* V and *Purgatorio* IX." *N&Q* 53 (2006): 297–99. The white eagle of Criseyde's dream of *TC* 2.925–931 is a "superimposition of the eagle of *Purgatorio* IX and the doves of *Inferno* V"; it links the love affair of *TC* with that of Dante's ruined Paolo and Francesca. The mating of doves and eagles in Criseyde's speech of 3.1492–98 is not the *impossibilium* it would appear to be, in keeping with the inevitability of Criseyde's betrayal of Troilus.

277. Currie, Joy M. "Rejecting Natural Law and Society's Dissolution in Chaucer's *Troilus*." *Mediaevalia* 24 (2003): 299–324. Currie explores the hypocrisy and factionalism that underlie the characters' ostensible concerns with natural law and the common good in *TC*, arguing that Chaucer exposes the negative consequences (individual and social) of breaches of natural law. Chaucer's Troy reflects the London of his day.

278. Edwards, Robert R. *The Flight from Desire: Augustine and Ovid to Chaucer*. The New Middle Ages. New York: Palgrave Macmillan, 2006. xi, 219 pp. Seven chapters on topics related to Ovid, Augustine, Héloïse and Abélard, Marie de France, Dante, *Roman de la Rose*, and Chaucer's relations with Boccaccio and Dante in *TC*. Grounded in Augustinian, Ovidian, and biblical models, *TC* (lines 5.540ff.) explores the impossibility of desire.

279. Gasse, Rosanne. "The Fierce Achilles in Chaucer, Gower, and the *Gawain* Poet." In E. L. Risden, ed. *"Sir Gawain" and the Classical Tradition: Essays on the Ancient Antecedents*. Jefferson, N.C.: McFarland, 2006, pp. 121–34. Gasse reads references to Achilles in *TC* as indications that the story of Achilles "is clearly the mirror of Troilus's narrative." References to Achilles in Gower's *Confessio Amantis* and in *Sir Gawain and the Green Knight* can help readers understand Chaucer's references.

280. Grady, Frank. *Representing Righteous Heathens in Late Medieval England*. The New Middle Ages. New York: Palgrave Macmillan, 2005. 214 pp. The virtuous pagan motif plays a minor thematic role but an important structural function in the scene of Troilus's ascent at the end of *TC*.

281. Hill, T. E. *"She, This in Blak": Vision, Truth, and Will in Geoffrey Chaucer's "Troilus and Criseyde."* Studies in Medieval History and Culture. New York: Routledge, 2006. ix, 147 pp. Argues that *TC* is largely concerned with "certitude and volition as they pertain to human perception and judgment" and as they relate to late medieval philosophical discussions of divine omnipotence and divine self-limitation. Troilus, Pandarus, and Criseyde represent "disparate accounts of the perceiving soul and differing philosophies of truth that exist in counterpoint"—Troilus as traditional perspectivism, Pandarus as self-interested valuation, and Criseyde as a kind of voluntarism that views knowledge as limited and intention as important. Hill introduces the poem with a summary of

fourteenth-century debates on epistemology, voluntarism, and the power of God.

282. Jimura, Akiyuki. "On Chaucer's Imagination: With Special Reference to Nature." *Hiroshima University Studies, Graduate School of Letters* 64 (2004): 63–76 (in Japanese). Discusses Chaucer's imagination, investigating the description of nature in *TC*.

283. Klassen, Norm. "Tragedy and Romance in Chaucer's 'Litel Bok' of *Troilus and Criseyde*." In Corinne Saunders, ed. *A Concise Companion to Chaucer* (*SAC* 30 [2008], no. 143), pp. 156–76. Klassen deconstructs concepts of genre and romance and medieval definitions of tragedy as they pertain to *TC*. Analyzes Troilus's "double sorwe," references to romance within *TC*, and the significance of Chaucer's phrase "litel bok." The poem illuminates the limitations of any one perspective.

284. Lynch, Andrew. "Love in Wartime: *Troilus and Criseyde* as Trojan History." In Corinne Saunders, ed. *A Concise Companion to Chaucer* (*SAC* 30 [2008], no. 143), pp. 113–33. Lynch explains the centrality of the legend of Troy to European narratives as a symbol of human instability and as a mirror of the present, especially in late medieval London. In comparison to its sources, *TC* keeps war on the periphery of the love story: Troilus is individualized as a lover, not as a warrior, but his changing motivations as a warrior lead to suicidal wrath.

285. Mieszkowski, Gretchen. *Medieval Go-Betweens and Chaucer's Pandarus*. The New Middle Ages. New York: Palgrave Macmillan, 2006. x, 218 pp. Western tradition bifurcates the go-between into two separate traditions: the first, working for idealized love; the second, working for lustful sexual conquest. Mieszkowski surveys go-between figures in medieval tradition and discusses how Pandarus belongs to both traditions at once. These functions collide most spectacularly in the consummation scene in Book 3 of *TC*.

286. Morgan, Gerald. *The Tragic Argument of "Troilus and Criseyde."* 2 vols. Lewiston, N.Y.: Mellen, 2005. xx, 691 pp. Morgan contends that *TC* is coherent; it has no sudden reversals, palinodes, or "unresolved dialectics." He discourages attention to Andreas Capellanus's theory of courtly love and encourages viewing *TC* in light of Dante's *Commedia*, demonstrating the latter's central importance in understanding key aspects of *TC*. Further, Morgan argues, the presence of Boccaccio's *Il Filostrato* is felt in every stanza, negating any need for critical concern with "medievalisation" in Chaucer's art. Above all, *TC* develops an argument that reflects medieval theological, philosophical, and ethical ideas.

287. Nair, Sashi. "'O brotel wele of mannes joie unstable!': Gender and Philosophy in *Troilus and Criseyde*." *Parergon* 23.2 (2006): 35–56. Explores Criseyde's "Boethian pragmatism" and her agency in *TC*, considering how they conflict with social gender-based social constraints and the constraints of the romance genre. The "incompatibility of Boethian philosophy and the romance genre result in Criseyde's exclusion from the poem's ending."

288. Nakao, Yoshiyuki. "The Structure of Chaucer's Ambiguity with a Focus on *Troilus and Criseyde* 5.1084." *SIMELL* 21 (2006): 55–63. Briefly sketches the methodology of Nakao's 2004 study, *The Structure of Chaucer's Ambiguity*, proposes a framework to describe how Chaucer's ambiguity may occur, and examines *TC* 5.1084 within that framework.

289. Nolan, Barbara. "Chaucer's Poetics of Dwelling in *Troilus and Criseyde*." In Ardis Butterfield, ed. *Chaucer and the City* (*SAC* 30 [2008], no. 108), pp. 57–75. Troy is insistently present in *TC* as a model of subjective city making.

290. Ransom, Daniel J. "Apollo's Holy Laurel: *Troilus and Criseyde* III, 542–43." *ChauR* 41 (2006): 206–12. Troilus's reference to Apollo speaking "out of a tree" (*TC* 3.543) is likely not a reflection of Chaucer's misunderstanding Ovid. Numerous authors Chaucer may have read, including Bartholomaeus Anglicus, provide grounds for the conclusion that the oracle of Apollo was expressed through a laurel tree.

291. Rossiter, W. T. "Casting Light on Clandestine Marriage in *Il Filostrato*." *Marginalia* 3 (2006): n.p. Argues that, despite critics' dismissal of the idea, a clandestine marriage is as likely in Boccaccio's *Il Filostrato* as in *TC*.

292. Saunders, Corinne. "Love and the Making of the Self: *Troilus and Criseyde*." In Corinne Saunders, ed. *A Concise Companion to Chaucer* (*SAC* 30 [2008], no. 143), pp. 134–55. Saunders traces elements of Chaucer's "rarefied treatment of love" to Marie de France, Chrétien de Troyes, *troubadours*, *trouvères*, and Ovid, arguing that Chaucer developed a notion of *fin' amors* to treat philosophical questions as well as the comic aspects of love. Criseyde is the "central enigma" of *TC*, but Troilus's experience as lover shapes the narrative, incapacitates him, and offers him a near-mystical experience. Criseyde's perspective is "more pragmatic and perhaps ultimately more tragic." Also considers Pandarus's disturbing role, the narrator's partiality for Criseyde, and Boethian philosophical ideas.

293. Sell, Jonathan P. A. "Cousin to Fortune: On Reading Chaucer's

Criseyde." *RCEI* 48 (2004): 193–204. Sell identifies "verbal parallels" and "ontological similarities" between Criseyde and Chaucer's version of Boethius's Fortune. Association with Fortune undermines "sentimental views of Criseyde" that Chaucer the narrator may share, though Chaucer himself may not.

294. Summit, Jennifer. *"Troilus and Criseyde."* In Seth Lerer, ed. *The Yale Companion to Chaucer* (*SAC* 30 [2008], no. 131), pp. 213–42. Book-by-book examination of *TC*, with consistent concern for the characters (especially Criseyde) and the construction of their subjectivities. Summit explores the poem's ongoing concern with how textuality and literary transmission are deeply related to issues of sexuality and the inner lives of people.

295. Windeatt, Barry. *"Troilus and Criseyde*: Love in a Manner of Speaking." In Helen Cooney, ed. *Writings on Love in the English Middle Ages* (*SAC* 30 [2008], no. 111), pp. 81–97. Windeatt assesses the uncertainties and experiences of love in *TC* and considers aspects of Chaucer's humanism and experimentalism. Rather than condemning worldly love, *TC* explores its many variations.

296. Yvernault, Martine. "Espaces réels, espaces imaginaires dans le *Troilus and Criseyde* de Chaucer." *Caietele Echinox* 10 (2006): 358–73. Analyzes the metaphors of space and architecture in relation to textual construction in *TC*.

297. ———. " 'Thus gan he make a mirour of his mynde' . . . Marges, marginalité, et jeux optiques dans le Livre I du *Troilus and Criseyde* de Chaucer." In Colette Stévanovitch, ed. *Marges/Seuils: Le liminal dans la littérature médiévale anglaise* (*SAC* 30 [2008], no. 148), pp. 197–208. Yvernault explores the relationships among marginal spaces, architectural frames, sense, and self-assertion.

See also nos. 16, 23, 51, 59, 60, 74, 76, 80, 89, 95, 105, 106, 112, 113, 127, 130, 260.

Lyrics and Short Poems

298. Boffey, Julia. "Forms of Standardization in Terms for Middle English Lyrics in the Fourteenth Century." In Ursula Schaefer, ed. *The Beginnings of Standardization: Language and Culture in Fourteenth-Century England* (*SAC* 30 [2008], no. 144), pp. 61–70. Analyzes the terms—

song, *dite*, *tretyse*, etc.—used for short poems in Middle English, including terms in Chaucer's works.

299. Hirsh, John C., ed. *Medieval Lyric: Middle English Lyrics, Ballads, and Carols*. Malden, Mass.: Blackwell, 2006. xiv, 220 pp. A classroom anthology with notes, marginal glosses, introductions, bibliographical citations, and occasional illustrations. Fifty poems arranged by topic into ten categories, with three appendices of additional poems, including one appendix titled "Some Lyrics of Geoffrey Chaucer." Includes *Truth*, *Purse*, *Ros*, *Sted*, *Adam*, and two lyrics embedded in narratives (*MLT* 2.841–54 and *MerT* 4.2138–48).

300. Holsinger, Bruce. "Lyrics and Short Poems." In Seth Lerer, ed. *The Yale Companion to Chaucer* (*SAC* 30 [2008], no. 131), pp. 179–212. Holsinger explores each of Chaucer's lyrics and short poems, explicating tensions of form and theme and explaining Chaucer's "cagey manipulation" of metrical and lyric conventions—English, French, and Italian. Rarely an inventor, Chaucer was a lyric innovator who experimented with relationships between emotion and form.

Adam Scriveyn

See nos. 34, 35, 39.

The Complaint of Chaucer to His Purse

301. Scattergood, John. "London and Money: Chaucer's *Complaint to His Purse*." In Ardis Butterfield, ed. *Chaucer and the City* (*SAC* 30 [2008], no. 108), pp. 162–73. Chaucer's begging poem reflects his anxieties about money within the complex moneyed economy of fourteenth-century London.

Gentilesse

See no. 25.

Chaucerian Apocrypha

302. Sturges, Robert S. "The Pardoner in Canterbury: Class, Gender, and Urban Space in the *Prologue to the Tale of Beryn*." *CollL* 33 (2006): 52–76. Sturges assesses the Pardoner and Kit from the *Prologue*

to Beryn as "comic critiques" of fifteenth-century urban concerns about class and gender. Three metaphors define urban space in the narrative: cathedral, walls, and tavern.

See also nos. 40, 68, 100.

Book Reviews

303. Akbari, Suzanne Conklin. *Seeing Through the Veil: Optical Theory and Medieval Allegory* (*SAC* 28 [2006], no. 59). Rev. John V. Fleming, *SAC* 28 (2006): 271–73; Andrew Taylor, *UTQ* 75.1 (2006): 233–34.

304. Allen, Elizabeth. *False Fables and Exemplary Truth in Later Middle English Literature* (*SAC* 29 [2007], no. 86). Rev. Edward Wheatley, *SAC* 28 (2006): 273–76.

305. Amodio, Mark C. *Oral Poetics in Middle English Poetry* (*SAC* 18 [1996], no. 71). Rev. Daniel Anlezark, *MÆ* 75 (2006): 144–45.

306. Andrew, Malcolm. *The Palgrave Literary Dictionary of Chaucer* (*SAC* 30 [2008], no. 3). Rev. Elliot Kendall, *TLS*, September 29, 2006, p. 33.

307. Benson, Robert G., and Susan J. Ridyard, eds. *New Readings of Chaucer's Poetry* (*SAC* 27 [2005], no. 90). Rev. Catherine A. M. Clarke, *MLR* 101 (2006): 513–14.

308. Black, Nancy B. *Medieval Narratives of Accused Queens* (*SAC* 27 [2005], no. 190). Rev. Stacy S. Klein, *TMR* 06.08.12, n.p.

309. Blamires, Alcuin. *Chaucer, Ethics, and Gender* (*SAC* 30 [2008], no. 105). Rev. K. P. Clarke, *RES* 57 (2006): 796–98.

310. Boitani, Piero, and Jill Mann, eds. *The Cambridge Companion to Chaucer*. 2nd ed. (*SAC* 27 [2005], no. 92). Rev. R. D. Eaton, *ES* 87 (2006): 112–13.

311. Børch, Marianne, ed. *Text and Voice: The Rhetoric of Authority in the Middle Ages* (*SAC* 28 [2006], no. 63). Rev. Michael Foster, *TMR* 06.05.05, n.p.

312. Borroff, Marie. *Traditions and Renewals: Chaucer, the "Gawain"-Poet, and Beyond* (*SAC* 27 [2005], no. 94). Rev. Lawrence M. Clopper, *JEGP* 105 (2006): 340.

313. Brown, Peter, ed. *A Companion to Chaucer* (*SAC* 24 [2002], no. 140). Rev. T. L. Burton, *AUMLA* 104 (2005): 151–53.

314. Brown, Sarah Annes. *The Metamorphosis of Ovid: From Chaucer to*

Ted Hughes (*SAC* 23 [2001], no. 230). Rev. Betty Rose Nagle, *CLS* 43 (2006): 210–13.

315. Butterfield, Ardis, ed. *Chaucer and the City* (*SAC* 30 [2008], no. 108). Rev. Catherine A. M. Clarke, *RES* 57 (2006): 798–99.

316. Cannon, Christopher. *The Grounds of English Literature* (*SAC* 29 [2007], no. 99). Rev. Ralph Hanna, *SAC* 28 (2006): 281–84; David Lawton, *Speculum* 81 (2006): 820–21.

317. Carlson, David R. *Chaucer's Jobs* (*SAC* 28 [2006], no. 8). Rev. Suzanne Akbari, *TMR* 06.02.25, n.p.; Kellie Robertson, *SAC* 28 (2006): 284–87.

318. Cheney, Patrick, and Frederick A. de Armas, eds. *European Literary Careers: The Author from Antiquity to the Renaissance* (*SAC* 27 [2005], no. 49). Rev. Barbara Simerka, *CLS* 43 (2006): 191–94.

319. Classen, Albrecht, ed. *Discourses on Love, Marriage, and Transgression in Medieval and Early Modern Literature* (*SAC* 29 [2007], no. 266). Rev. Susan Morrison, *TMR* 06.02.05, n.p.

320. Cooper, Helen. *The English Romance in Time: Transforming Motifs from Geoffrey of Monmouth to the Death of Shakespeare* (*SAC* 28 [2006], no. 65). Rev. Nancy Mason Bradbury, *Speculum* 81 (2006): 164–65; Meredith Reynolds, *SCJ* 37 (2006): 246–48.

321. Correale, Robert M., and Mary Hamel, eds. *Sources and Analogues of the "Canterbury Tales."* Vol. 2 (*SAC* 29 [2007], no. 46). Rev. Simon Horobin, *RES* 57 (2006): 411–12.

322. Cox, Catherine S. *The Judaic Other in Dante, the "Gawain" Poet, and Chaucer* (*SAC* 29 [2007], no. 231). Rev. Linda R. Bates, *Marginalia* 3 (2006): n.p.; Elisa Narin van Court, *TMR* 06.10.27, n.p.; Ruth Evans, *Bulletin of International Medieval Research* 12 (2006): 67–69; Andrew Galloway, *RES* 57 (2006): 401–2; James H. Morey, *Speculum* 81 (2006): 1174–76; Shirley Sharon-Zisser, *Arthuriana* 16.4 (2006): 82–83.

323. D'Arcy, Anne Marie, and Alan J. Fletcher, eds. *Studies in Late Medieval and Early Renaissance Texts in Honour of John Scattergood: "The key of all good remembrance"* (*SAC* 29 [2007], no. 103). Rev. Jenni Nuttall, *RES* 57 (2006): 575–78; Nicholas Perkins, *TLS*, March 24, 2006, p. 33.

324. Davenport, Tony. *Medieval Narrative: An Introduction* (*SAC* 28 [2006], no. 67). Rev. Siobhain Bly Calkin, *TMR* 06.02.03, n.p.

325. Delany, Sheila, ed. *Chaucer and the Jews: Sources, Contexts, Meanings* (*SAC* 26 [2004], no. 129). Rev. Ruth Nisse, *N&Q* 53 (2006): 98–99; Lawrence Warner, *Parergon* 23.1 (2006): 153–55.

326. Duncan, Thomas G., ed. *A Companion to the Middle English Lyric* (*SAC* 29 [2007], no. 105). Rev. Kathleen Palti, *N&Q* 53 (2006): 550–51.

327. Edwards, David L. *Poets and God: Chaucer, Shakespeare, Herbert, Milton, Wordsworth, Coleridge, Blake* (*SAC* 29 [2007], no. 107). Rev. Martin Haggerty, *New Blackfriars* 87 (2006): 323–24; David Jasper, *L&T* 20 (2006): 87–88.

328. Eisner, Sigmund, ed. *A Treatise on the Astrolabe*. Vol. 6, The Prose Treatises, pt. 1, of *A Variorum Edition of the Works of Geoffrey Chaucer* (*SAC* 26 [2004], no. 25). Rev. Catherine Eagleton, *British Journal for the History of Science* 38 (2005): 478; Jenna Mead, *Parergon* 23.1 (2006): 143–46.

329. Ellis, Steve, ed. *Chaucer: An Oxford Guide* (*SAC* 29 [2007], no. 108). Rev. Lisa Clark, *RMRev*, n.p.; P. Dean, *Use of English* 57.2 (2006): 148–50; Richard H. Osberg, *Arthuriana* 16.1 (2006): 73–75.

330. Federico, Sylvia. *New Troy: Fantasies of Empire in the Late Middle Ages* (*SAC* 27 [2005], no. 280). Rev. John M. Bowers, *Clio* 35.2 (2006): 263–70.

331. Fisher, John H., and Mark Allen, eds. *The Complete Canterbury Tales of Geoffrey Chaucer* (*SAC* 30 [2008], no. 21). Rev. *MedievalF* 5 (2006): n.p.

332. Forni, Kathleen, ed. *The Chaucerian Apocrypha: A Counterfeit Canon* (*SAC* 25 [2003], no. 292). Rev. Richard Osberg, *TMR* 06.06.16, n.p.

333. Fowler, Elizabeth. *Literary Character: The Human Figure in Early English Writing* (*SAC* 27 [2005], no. 230). Rev. William Askins, *Speculum* 81 (2006): 532–33.

334. Gadd, Ian, and Alexandra Gillespie, eds. *John Stow (1525–1605) and the Making of the English Past: Studies in Early Modern Culture and the History of the Book* (*SAC* 28 [2006], no. 17). Rev. Andrew Hadfield, *TLS*, April 14, 2006, p. 25; Rachel Ramsey, *SCJ* 37 (2006): 476–78.

335. Glaser, Joseph, trans. *Geoffrey Chaucer: "The Canterbury Tales" in Modern Verse* (*SAC* 29 [2007], no. 11). Rev. Tom Bishop, *TMR* 06.06.12, n.p.; Jennifer A. Smith, *Comitatus* 37 (2006): 229–30.

336. Green, Richard Firth, and Linne R. Mooney, eds. *Interstices: Studies in Late Middle English and Anglo-Latin Texts in Honour of A. G. Rigg* (*SAC* 28 [2006], no. 71). Rev. Michael Calabrese, *TMR* 06.01.17, n.p.; Fiona Somerset, *UTQ* 75.1 (2006): 235–36.

337. Hamaguchi, Keiko. *Chaucer and Women* (*SAC* 29 [2007], no. 114). Rev. Joanna Shearer, *MFF* 42 (2006): 111–13.

338. Hanna, Ralph. *London Literature, 1300–1380* (*SAC* 29 [2007], no. 116). Rev. Caroline M. Barron, *Journal of British Studies* 45 (2006): 876–78; Ardis Butterfield, *YLS* 19 (2005): 211–15; Elizabeth Edwards, *DR* 86 (2006): 475–77; Alexandra Gillespie, *HLQ* 69.2 (2006): 315; James Simpson, *SAC* 28 (2006): 292–95.

339. Harding, Wendy, ed. *Drama, Narrative and Poetry in the "Canterbury Tales"* (*SAC* 27 [2005], no. 114). Rev. Roger Dalrymple, *MLR* 101 (2006): 1081–82.

340. Heffernan, Carol F. *The Orient in Chaucer and Medieval Romance* (*SAC* 27 [2005], no. 115). Rev. Elizabeth Archibald, *MÆ* 75 (2006): 328–29; Arlyn Diamond, *Speculum* 81 (2006): 199–201.

341. Heng, Geraldine. *Empire of Magic: Medieval Romance and the Politics of Cultural Fantasy* (*SAC* 28 [2006], no. 127). Rev. Anne Laskaya, *MFF* 41 (2005): 111–14.

342. Hilmo, Maidie. *Medieval Images, Icons, and Illustrated English Literary Texts: From the Ruthwell Cross to the Ellesmere Chaucer* (*SAC* 28 [2006], no. 99). Rev. Karla Taylor, *SIcon* 27 (2006): 223–26.

343. Hirsh, John C. *Chaucer and the "Canterbury Tales": A Short Introduction* (*SAC* 27 [2005], no. 151). Rev. Christopher Stout, *RMRev*, n.p.

344. Hodges, Laura. *Chaucer and Clothing: Clerical and Academic Costume in the General Prologue to "The Canterbury Tales"* (*SAC* 29 [2007], no. 170). Rev. Andrea Denny-Brown, *SAC* 28 (2006): 300–303; Laura L. Howes, *Speculum* 81 (2006): 1209–11; S. H. Rigby, *EHR* 121 (2006): 594–95; Kathleen Tonry, *TMR* 06.08.11, n.p.

345. Horobin, Simon. *The Language of the Chaucer Tradition* (*SAC* 27 [2005], no. 74). Rev. Orietta Da Rold, *L&LC* 21 (2006): 127–28.

346. Jacobs, Kathryn Elisabeth. *Marriage Contracts from Chaucer to the Renaissance Stage* (*SAC* 25 [2003], no. 157). Rev. Allyson Foster, *CRCL* 29 (2002): 405–9.

347. Johnson, David F., and Elaine Treharne, eds. *Readings in Medieval Texts: Interpreting Old and Middle English Literature* (*SAC* 29 [2007], no. 120). Rev. Richard W. Dance, *TMR* 06.09.23, n.p.

348. Johnson, Paul. *Creators: From Chaucer and Dürer to Picasso and Disney* (*SAC* 30 [2008], no. 123). Rev. Roger Kimball, *National Review* 58.15 (2006): 40–41; William Packer, *Literary Review*, n.v. (August 2006): 44–45; Paul Walpole, *Virginia Quarterly Review* 82 (2006): 273.

349. Jones, Terry, Robert Yeager, Terry Dolan, Alan Fletcher, and

Juliette Dor. *Who Murdered Chaucer? A Medieval Mystery* (*SAC* 27 [2005], no. 14). Rev. Isamu Saito, *SIMELL* 21 (2006): 147–55.

350. Kabir, Ananya Jahanara, and Deanne Williams, eds. *Postcolonial Approaches to the European Middle Ages: Translating Cultures* (*SAC* 29 [2007], no. 52). Rev. Laurie Finke, *Arthuriana* 16.2 (2006): 105–7; Sharon Kinoshita, *TMR* 06.05.07, n.p.

351. Krueger, Roberta L., ed. *The Cambridge Companion to Medieval Romance* (*SAC* 24 [2002], no. 170). Rev. Kathy M. Krause, *Arthuriana* 16.4 (2006): 96–98.

352. Lampert, Lisa. *Gender and Jewish Difference from Paul to Shakespeare* (*SAC* 28 [2006], no. 157). Rev. Sheila Delany, *Speculum* 81 (2006): 551–53.

353. Lavezzo, Kathy, ed. *Imagining a Medieval English Nation* (*SAC* 28 [2006], no. 76). Rev. John M. Bowers, *Clio* 35.2 (2006): 263–70.

354. Lawton, David, Wendy Scase, and Rita Copeland, eds. *New Medieval Literatures* 6 (*SAC* 28 [2006], nos. 82, 140, 152, and 179). Rev. Jane Tolmie, *N&Q* 53 (2006): 125–27.

355. Machan, Tim William, ed., with the assistance of A. J. Minnis. *Sources of the Boece* (*SAC* 29 [2007], no. 271). Rev. Ian Johnson, *MÆ* 75 (2006): 329–30.

356. Matsuda, Takami, Richard A. Linenthal, and John Scahill, eds. *The Medieval Book Collector and a Modern Collector: Essays in Honour of Toshiyuki Takamiya* (*SAC* 28 [2006], no. 78). Rev. Simon Horobin, *JEBS* 9 (2006): 191–93.

357. McCarthy, Conor. *Marriage in Medieval England: Law, Literature, and Practice* (*SAC* 29 [2007], no. 127). Rev. M. Teresa Tavormina, *SAC* 28 (2006): 303–6.

358. McDonald, Nicola F., and W. M. Ormrod, eds. *Rites of Passage: Cultures of Transition in the Fourteenth Century* (*SAC* 28 [2006], no. 175). Rev. Charlotte Stanford, *TMR* 06.06.07, n.p.

359. McTurk, Rory. *Chaucer and the Norse and Celtic Worlds* (*SAC* 29 [2007], no. 48). Rev. Heather O'Donoghue, *RES* 57 (2006): 108–9.

360. Meyerson, Mark D., Daniel Thiery, and Oren Falk, eds. *"A Great Effusion of Blood"? Interpreting Medieval Violence* (*SAC* 28 [2006], no. 138). Rev. Christine M. Rose, *Arthuriana* 16.4 (2006): 104–7; Scott Waugh, *UTQ* 75.1 (2006): 232–33.

361. Miller, Mark. *Philosophical Chaucer: Love, Sex, and Agency in the "Canterbury Tales"* (*SAC* 29 [2007], no. 164). Rev. Suzanne Conklin

Akbari, *N&Q* 53 (2006): 551–53; Glenn Burger, *SAC* 28 (2006): 306–9; Andrew James Johnston, *Anglia* 124.2 (2006): 350–56.

362. Minnis, Alastair, and Ian Johnson, eds. *The Cambridge History of Literary Criticism. Volume 2: The Middle Ages* (*SAC* 30 [2008], no. 134). Rev. Leo Carruthers, *ÉA* 59 (2006): 218–19.

363. Mitchell, J. Allan. *Ethics and Exemplary Narratives in Chaucer and Gower* (*SAC* 28 [2006], no. 101). Rev. John C. Hirsh, *MÆ* 75 (2006): 151–52; Andrew James Johnston, *Anglia* 124 (2006): 350–56; Mark Miller, *Speculum* 81 (2006): 562–64.

364. Morse, Ruth. *Truth and Convention in the Middle Ages: Rhetoric, Representation, and Reality* (*SAC* 15 [1993], no. 121). Rev. James Wade, *Marginalia* 3 (2006): n.p.

365. Nolan, Maura. *John Lydgate and the Making of Public Culture.* Cambridge Studies in Medieval Literatuare, no. 58. Cambridge: Cambridge University Press, 2005. ix, 276 pp. Rev. Leo Carruthers, *ÉA* 59 (2006): 470–71; Nicholas Perkins, *N&Q* 53 (2006): 554–55; Emily Runde, *Comitatus* 37 (2006): 270–72.

366. Obermeier, Anita. *The History and Anatomy of Auctorial Self-Criticism in the European Middle Ages* (*SAC* 24 [2002], no. 179). Rev. Chauncey Wood, *CRCL* 29 (2002): 392–94.

367. Perfetti, Lisa, ed. *The Representation of Women's Emotions in Medieval and Early Modern Culture* (*SAC* 30 [2008], no. 101). Rev. Caroline Jewers, *Speculum* 81 (2006): 581–83; Elizabeth Robertson, *SAC* 28 (2006): 316–19.

368. Prendergast, Thomas A. *Chaucer's Dead Body: From Corpse to Corpus* (*SAC* 28 [2006], no. 46). Rev. Dosia Reichardt, *Parergon* 23.1 (2006): 192–94.

369. Pugh, Tison. *Queering Medieval Genres* (*SAC* 29 [2007], no. 132). Rev. Anna Klosowska, *SAC* 28 (2006): 319–22.

370. Raybin, David, and Linda Tarte Holley, eds. *Closure in "The Canterbury Tales": The Role of "The Parson's Tale"* (*SAC* 24 [2002], no. 337). Rev. Frances McCormack, *Bulletin of International Medieval Research* 12 (2006): 64–67.

371. Rhodes, Jim. *Poetry Does Theology: Chaucer, Grosseteste, and the "Pearl"-Poet* (*SAC* 25 [2003], no. 129). Rev. R. N. Swanson, *Heythrop Journal* 47 (2006): 639–40.

372. Richmond, Velma Bourgeois. *Chaucer as Children's Literature: Retellings from the Victorian and Edwardian Eras* (*SAC* 29 [2007], no. 137). Rev. Karen Youmans, *C&L* 55 (2006): 592–95.

373. Robertson, Kellie. *The Laborer's Two Bodies: Labor and the "Work" of the Text in Medieval Britain, 1350–1500* (*SAC* 30 [2008], no. 267). Rev. David Aers, *YLS* 19 (2005): 226–36.

374. Rosenthal, Joel T. *Telling Tales: Sources and Narration in Late Medieval England* (*SAC* 27 [2005], no. 15). Rev. Mark Amodio, *TMR* 06.02.09, n.p.

375. Sadlek, Gregory M. *Idleness Working: The Discourse of Love's Labor from Ovid Through Chaucer and Gower* (*SAC* 28 [2006], no. 84). Rev. John Ford, *TMR* 06.03.03, n.p.; Don A. Monson, *Encomia* 27 (2005): 66–69.

376. Saunders, Corinne, ed. *A Companion to Romance: From Classical to Contemporary* (*SAC* 29 [2007], no. 140). Rev. Joyce Boro, *N&Q* 53 (2006): 95.

377. Scanlon, Larry, and James Simpson, eds. *John Lydgate: Poetry, Culture, and Lancastrian England* (*SAC* 30 [2008], no. 71). Rev. Andrea Denny-Brown, *TMR* 06.11.07, n.p.

378. Schildgen, Brenda Deen. *Pagans, Tartars, Moslems, and Jews in Chaucer's "Canterbury Tales"* (*SAC* 25 [2003], no. 165). Rev. Denise Despres, *Religion and Literature* 36.4 (2006): 111.

379. Shepard, Alan, and Stephen D. Powell, eds. *Fantasies of Troy: Classical Tales and the Social Imaginary in Medieval and Early Modern Europe* (*SAC* 29 [2007], no. 286). Rev. J. Watkins, *Clio* 35.2 (2006): 270–74.

380. Shoaf, R. Allen. *Chaucer's Body: The Anxiety of Circulation in "The Canterbury Tales"* (*SAC* 25 [2003], no. 166). Rev. Frances McCormack, *Bulletin of International Medieval Research* 12 (2006): 62–64.

381. Smith, Warren S., ed. *Satiric Advice on Women and Marriage from Plautus to Chaucer* (*SAC* 29 [2007], no. 210). Rev. Susan Treggiari, *Classical Review* 56 (2006): 341–43.

382. Spearing, A. C. *Textual Subjectivity: The Encoding of Subjectivity in Medieval Narratives and Lyrics* (*SAC* 29 [2007], no. 143). Rev. Michael Foster, *Style* 39 (2005): 496–500.

383. Staley, Lynn. *Languages of Power in the Age of Richard II* (*SAC* 29 [2007], no. 144). Rev. Leo Carruthers, *ÉA* 59 (2006): 470–71; Andrew Galloway, *SAC* 28 (2006): 331–34; William McClellan, *Speculum* 81 (2006): 1259–61; Marion Turner, *MÆ* 75 (2006): 147–48.

384. Stein, Robert M., and Sandra Pierson Prior, eds. *Reading Medieval Culture: Essays in Honor of Robert W. Hanning* (*SAC* 29 [2007], no. 146). Rev. Laurie A. Finke, *Arthuriana* 16.1 (2006): 83–84; Sarah A. Kelen, *TMR* 06.09.17, n.p.; Lisa J. Kiser, *SAC* 28 (2006): 334–37.

385. Strohm, Paul. *Politique: Languages of Statecraft Between Chaucer*

and Shakespeare (*SAC* 29 [2007], no. 257). Rev. Charlotte C. Morse, *Speculum* 81 (2006): 1262–64.

386. Summers, Joanna. *Late-Medieval Prison Writing and the Politics of Autobiography* (*SAC* 29 [2007], no. 272). Rev. J. A. Burrow, *SAC* 28 (2006): 337–39; Isabel Davis, *TLS*, April 28, 2006, p. 35.

387. Van Dyke, Carolynn. *Chaucer's Agents: Cause and Representation in Chaucerian Narrative* (*SAC* 29 [2007], no. 151). Rev. Nicole Clifton, *Style* 40 (2006): 361–64.

388. Vitto, Cindy L., and Marcia Smith Marzec, eds. *New Perspectives on Criseyde* (*SAC* 28 [2006], no. 212). Rev. George Edmondson, *SAC* 28 (2006): 340–43.

389. Walker, Greg. *Writing Under Tyranny: English Literature and the Henrician Reform* (*SAC* 29 [2007], no. 33). Rev. Andrew Hadfield, *TLS*, April 28, 2006, p. 32; Roderick J. Lyall, *Cahiers élisabéthains* 70 (2006): 75–76.

390. Wallace, David. *Premodern Places: Calais to Surinam, Chaucer to Aphra Behn* (*SAC* 28 [2006], no. 92). Rev. Jenna Mead, *Parergon* 23.1 (2006): 230–34; K. Newman, *ShakS* 34 (2006): 251–56.

391. Waters, Claire M. *Angels and Earthly Creatures: Preaching, Performance, and Gender in the Later Middle Ages* (*SAC* 28 [2006], no. 93). Rev. Kerstin Pfeiffer, *L&T* 20 (2006): 215–17; Scott D. Troyan, *SMART* 13.2 (2006): 51–62.

392. Williams, Deanne. *The French Fetish from Chaucer to Shakespeare* (*SAC* 28 [2006], no. 94). Rev. Andrew James Johnston, *Anglia* 124.2 (2006): 350–56.

Author Index—Bibliography

INDEX

519